CCNA Security 210-260 Certification Guide

Build your knowledge of network security and pass your
CCNA Security exam (210-260)

Glen D. Singh
Michael Vinod
Vijay Anandh

BIRMINGHAM - MUMBAI

CCNA Security 210-260 Certification Guide

Commissioning Editor: Pratik Shah
Acquisition Editor: Rahul Nair
Content Development Editor: Sharon Raj
Technical Editor: Vishal Kamal Mewada
Copy Editor: Safis Editing
Project Coordinator: Virginia Dias
Proofreader: Safis Editing
Indexer: Mariammal Chettiyar
Graphics: Tom Scaria
Production Coordinator: Shraddha Falebhai

First published: June 2018

Production reference: 2140618

Published by Packt Publishing Ltd.
Livery Place
35 Livery Street
Birmingham
B3 2PB, UK.

ISBN 978-1-78712-887-3

www.packtpub.com

`mapt.io`

Mapt is an online digital library that gives you full access to over 5,000 books and videos, as well as industry leading tools to help you plan your personal development and advance your career. For more information, please visit our website.

Why subscribe?

- Spend less time learning and more time coding with practical eBooks and Videos from over 4,000 industry professionals

- Improve your learning with Skill Plans built especially for you

- Get a free eBook or video every month

- Mapt is fully searchable

- Copy and paste, print, and bookmark content

PacktPub.com

Did you know that Packt offers eBook versions of every book published, with PDF and ePub files available? You can upgrade to the eBook version at `www.PacktPub.com` and as a print book customer, you are entitled to a discount on the eBook copy. Get in touch with us at `service@packtpub.com` for more details.

At `www.PacktPub.com`, you can also read a collection of free technical articles, sign up for a range of free newsletters, and receive exclusive discounts and offers on Packt books and eBooks.

Contributors

About the authors

Glen D. Singh is a cybersecurity instructor and consultant for various institutions within the Republic of Trinidad and Tobago. He conducts multiple training exercises in offensive security, digital forensics, and network security annually. He also holds various information security certifications, such as the EC-Council's Certified Ethical Hacker (CEH), Computer Hacking Forensic Investigator (CHFI), Cisco's CCNA Security, CCNA Routing and Switching, and many others in the field of network security.

> *I would like to thank my parents for their unconditional support and motivation they've always given me to become a better person each day. Thanks to my family, friends, and students for their continued support, the people at Packt Publishing for providing this amazing opportunity, and everyone who reads and supports this amazing book.*

Michael Vinod is a freelance IT trainer and consultant specializing in Cisco routing, switching, and security technologies. He has expertise in the field of networking, with close to 3 years of field experience and 7 years of experience, as a Cisco training consultant. He has a passion for training individuals on Cisco technologies and has received accolades from various clients.

Vijay Anandh is an IT consultant and public speaker specializing in Cisco routing and switching, security, and F5 load balancer technologies. He has 9 years of combined experience as a training consultant and network architect.

About the reviewer

Gurmukh Singh helps companies scale complex infrastructure and optimize technology. He is an expert in Big Data implementations and architecting high throughput networks.

He has authored few books on Hadoop and heading few of the open source community meetups. He founded Netxillon technologies, providing consultancy and training in Big Data and security. He likes solving complex problems and loves coding.

Packt is searching for authors like you

If you're interested in becoming an author for Packt, please visit `authors.packtpub.com` and apply today. We have worked with thousands of developers and tech professionals, just like you, to help them share their insight with the global tech community. You can make a general application, apply for a specific hot topic that we are recruiting an author for, or submit your own idea.

Table of Contents

Preface

Cisco is one of the premier vendors for network equipment and certifications. With their line of security appliances and security intelligence, Cisco has become a one-stop-shop for all your needs, from routers and switches to network security appliance for threat prevention and mitigation. The CCNA Security (210-260) certification validates whether a network security professional is able to identify, prevent, and mitigate existing and newly emerging threats and vulnerabilities using Cisco's switches, routers, and security appliances on the network infrastructure.

This book teaches you the basic to advanced stages of security configurations of the Cisco switches, routers and the Adaptive Security Appliance (ASA), from understanding key concepts to the configuration and implementation of the devices on the network. The hands-on approach ensures that you get the experience you need to be a network security professional.

By the end of this book, you'll be able to understand the concepts of both offensive and defensive security, identify and mitigate threats and vulnerabilities, secure a network using Cisco switches and routers, and configure and deploy the Cisco **Adaptive Security Appliance (ASA)**.

Who this book is for

This book is for students, enthusiasts, network security engineers, cyber security professionals, and security professionals in general. The reader should have a valid CCENT or CCNA routing and switching certification before taking the CCNA security examination.

What this book covers

Chapter 1, *Exploring Security Threats*, provides an overview of the different types of attacks.

Chapter 2, *Delving into Security Toolkits*, provides insight into the different types of security devices.

Chapter 3, *Understanding Security Policies*, focuses on the concepts of security policies, assets, and other security design considerations.

Chapter 4, *Deep Diving into Cryptography*, covers different cryptographic algorithms and their uses.

Chapter 5, *Implementing the AAA Framework*, focuses on the need for authentication, authorization, and accounting (AAA) and their role in an organization.

Chapter 6, *Securing the Control and Management Planes*, covers the various security policies and concepts, using protocols and technologies to secure the control and management plane on a Cisco network.

Chapter 7, *Protecting Layer 2 Protocols*, helps you understand Layer 2 protocols on a switch network and how to protect it.

Chapter 8, *Protecting the Switch Infrastructure*, helps you understand and apply Layer 2 security on the network.

Chapter 9, *Exploring Firewall Technologies*, provides an insight into different firewall technologies and deployment models.

Chapter 10, *Cisco ASA*, gets you started with ASA and the basic configuration for deployment on a network.

Chapter 11, *Advanced ASA Configuration*, helps you dive further into advanced configurations such as routing, ACLs, Object Groups, and policies.

Chapter 12, *Configuring Zone-Based Firewalls*, enables configuring the Cisco IOS router to work as a firewall.

Chapter 13, *IPSec – The Protocol That Drives VPN*, explains the protocols and components, that combine to establish an IPSec VPN and their roles in securing traffic.

Chapter 14, *Configuring a Site-to-Site VPN*, helps you deploy a VPN between branch offices to secure traffic across an untrusted network.

Chapter 15, *Configuring a Remote-Access VPN*, helps you establish VPN connectivity between an client device and the corporate network for remote/teleworkers.

Chapter 16, *Working with IPS*, provides insight into configuring and deploying an IPS on the network to mitigate any threats.

Chapter 17, *Application and Endpoint Security*, explains the need for and benefits of applying endpoint security to ensure no threat is missed on the network.

To get the most out of this book

To get started, you'll need the following:

- Cisco IOS Router 3725 or another IOS router with the Zone-Based Policy Firewall and IPS capabilities
- Cisco IOS Switch 2960
- Cisco ASA 5505 or higher
- Cisco Configuration Professional (CCP) will provide a GUI during the configuration process on the IOS router
- Java Runtime Environment
- Any modern web browser, preferably Internet Explorer

If you're unable to get the physical hardware equipment, you can use a network simulator such as GNS3 (`https://www.gns3.com/`) and use the IOS images. Cisco Packet Tracer (`https://www.netacad.com/`) can also be used; however, the appliances in Cisco Packet Tracer does not support all the features and commands needed for CCNA security training.

Conventions

There are a number of text conventions used throughout this book.

`CodeInText`: Indicates code words in text, database table names, folder names, filenames, file extensions, pathnames, dummy URLs, user input, and Twitter handles. Here is an example: "On the victim's end, for every `SYN` packet received, it must reply with a `SYN/ACK` packet."

A block of code is set as follows:

```
vlan 200
  private-vlan primary
  private-vlan association 201
!
vlan 201
  private-vlan isolated
```

When we wish to draw your attention to a particular part of a code block, the relevant lines or items are set in bold:

```
vlan 200
  private-vlan primary
  private-vlan association 201
!
vlan 201
  private-vlan isolated
```

Any command-line input or output is written as follows:

```
Router1(config)#aaa accounting exec default start-stop group tacacs+
Router1(config)#aaa accounting commands 15 default start-stop group tacacs+
Router1(config)#aaa accounting network default start-stop group tacacs+
```

Bold: Indicates a new term, an important word, or words that you see onscreen. For example, words in menus or dialog boxes appear in the text like this. Here is an example: "Once again, navigate to **Configuration** | **Device Setup** | **Routing** | **Static Routes** on the ASDM. Click on **Add**."

Warnings or important notes appear like this.

Tips and tricks appear like this.

Get in touch

Feedback from our readers is always welcome.

General feedback: Email feedback@packtpub.com and mention the book title in the subject of your message. If you have questions about any aspect of this book, please email us at questions@packtpub.com.

Errata: Although we have taken every care to ensure the accuracy of our content, mistakes do happen. If you have found a mistake in this book, we would be grateful if you would report this to us. Please visit www.packtpub.com/submit-errata, selecting your book, clicking on the Errata Submission Form link, and entering the details.

Piracy: If you come across any illegal copies of our works in any form on the Internet, we would be grateful if you would provide us with the location address or website name. Please contact us at copyright@packtpub.com with a link to the material.

If you are interested in becoming an author: If there is a topic that you have expertise in and you are interested in either writing or contributing to a book, please visit authors.packtpub.com.

Reviews

Please leave a review. Once you have read and used this book, why not leave a review on the site that you purchased it from? Potential readers can then see and use your unbiased opinion to make purchase decisions, we at Packt can understand what you think about our products, and our authors can see your feedback on their book. Thank you!

For more information about Packt, please visit packtpub.com.

1

Exploring Security Threats

As networks grow and technology advances, so does the cyber threats landscape. Every hour a new threat emerges, and cybersecurity companies are battling to mitigate and prevent such malicious attacks from invading our computers and networks. This has been a challenge for all, from the evolution of a simple batch virus script to **Advanced Persistent Threats** (**APTs**). Cisco has created a certification that allows you to begin your career in network security, the **Cisco Certified Network Associate** (**CCNA**) security designation.

This certification focuses on understanding threats to secure your network using Cisco routers and switches and even configuring and setting up the Cisco **Adaptive Security Appliance** (**ASA**). After completion, you'll be able to function as a network security engineer and mitigate and prevent such threats from entering your network. This chapter covers the basic principles of implementing network security in an enterprise network.

Security is very important and if no proper security principles are followed, it will lead to financial risks, legal risks, and negative public relations implications. In some cases, the overall business may be placed at risk due to the noncompliance of security policies. The security of an enterprise network can be viewed from different perspectives. For a management team, the network is a tool that enables the business goals of the company. For end users, a network is just a tool for them to complete their job. Unfortunately, if an end user or a management team is not maintaining their data safely, it may lead to several vulnerabilities and security threats. If the hacker compromises and gains access to the data and applications, the security component of the network fails.

The following topics are the three basic concepts of network security:

- **Confidentiality**: The privacy of the data in the network. The data on the network should be protected from unauthorized users and they should not access the data by any means. The data can be protected by encrypting it.
- **Integrity**: The changes made to the data should only be made by the authorized users. If the data in transit is corrupted, it leads to a failure of integrity and a loss of revenue.
- **Availability**: A network, or data, should be available to its authorized users. The term availability refers to the provision of services that are dependent on networks, systems, and data. Any impact on the availability of the data leads to heavy loss of business and revenue.

The following diagram illustrates the working mechanism of the network security concept better known as the **CIA triad**:

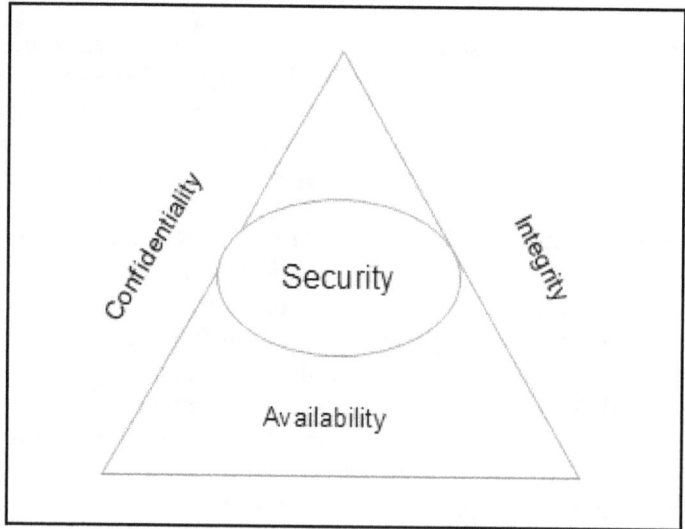

After completing this chapter, you will:

- Understand the basics of network security
- Understand the different security terminologies
- Understand different types of attack
- Understand the different types of security tools

Important terms in network security

Network security is a very broad concept; it starts with authenticating users and authorizing resources. It deals with security threats analysis and vulnerability checks.

Threats

A **threat** is the potential for an attacker to take advantage of a vulnerability on a system. An example of a threat can be a disgruntled employee who has been given a warning letter in an organization. This person may want to inflict harm to the company's network and has decided to research exploitation.

Some further examples of threats include malware, **Denial of Service (DoS)**, and phishing.

Let's now discuss risk and countermeasure:

- **Risk**: A risk is the likelihood of a threat actor taking advantage of a vulnerability that can attack a network system, which leads to damage to the network
- **Countermeasure**: A countermeasure can be a combination of a process and a device that can act together as a safeguard against potential attacks, thereby reducing security risks

> A firewall is configured with an **access control list**, and a server with **security policies**.

Vulnerability

Vulnerability is a weakness of the system, data, or any application, by which unauthorized persons can exploit it. Vulnerability on the network may occur due to various reasons:

- Result of a malicious attack
- Failure of a policy
- Weakness of the system or a policy
- Weakness of a protocol

Vulnerabilities are found in operating systems, routers, switches, firewalls, applications, antivirus software, and so on. An attacker uses these vulnerabilities to create a threat to the network. Generally, vulnerabilities arise due to high complexity or human error while developing an application and designing a network.

Analyzing vulnerability

Vulnerability analysis is the process of identifying security weaknesses on a computing platform or network. This aids the internal security team (blue team) in remediating any flaws that have been discovered. A security team is also responsible for conducting a vulnerability assessment to evaluate the cybersecurity risk and try to minimize/mitigate it as much as possible. Vulnerability assessments are usually conducted before and after applying any countermeasures within the organization. This helps with the evaluation process to determine whether the attack surfaces are reduced; it also ensures the proper practices are used and applied correctly.

The **blue team** is a group of individuals who's responsibilities are to perform security analysis on the information systems of an organization.

When an administrator dealing with security installs a patch on the endpoint security tool, there are chances of manual errors or misconfigurations in the tool that may open a door for a hacker to attack the node.

Periodic vulnerability testing/analysis is essential in such situations.

Vulnerability assessments have the following advantages:

- Help administrators to keep their data safe from hackers and attackers, which eliminates business risks.
- Vulnerability assessment tools help administrators to check for loopholes in the network architecture. These tools also examine whether there are any possible destructive actions that can cause damage to your application, software, or network.
- Vulnerability assessment tools detect attack pathways that may get missed in manual assessment, which increases the ROI.

Before performing a vulnerability assessment, the administrators should create a test plan, develop a threat model and verify the URLs, and access credentials.

There are two ways of conducting a vulnerability assessment. The first one is the **automated dynamic scanning** and the other is the manual **Vulnerability and Penetration Testing (VAPT)**.

In the automated method, a tool, such as *Burp Suite Pro, IBM Rational AppScan,* is used to scan the application and find security flaws. The manual testing is performed in the following steps:

1. Check SQL injection, XML injection, and LDAP injection flaws
2. Inspect poor authentication methods and cracked login processes
3. Inspect cookies and other session details
4. Inspect the default settings in the security configurations in the devices
5. Inspect broken encryption algorithms and other ciphers to secure the communications

Choose either automatic or manual testing methods to verify the scan results, collect evidence, and complete the reports.

Introduction to an attack

An attack is the process of attempting to steal data, destroy data, gain unauthorized access to a device, or even shut down/disable a system, preventing legitimate users from accessing the resources. An attack can be local, where a malicious user has physical access to the system and either executes a malicious payload or is attempting to gain access into the device. A remote attack requires the malicious user to send a payload over a network connection to the victim device in the hope that the attack would be successful and it would either gain control of the victim device or cause service interruptions (denial of service).

Attacks are mainly distinguished as either:

- Passive attacks
- Active attacks

Passive attacks

In a passive attack, the attacker is considered to be in a learning (monitoring) state to understand the details about the potential victim's device, how it performs and operates. This allows the attacker to have a better attack strategy. An example of a passive attack is where an attacker is sniffing the network traffic between a victim machine and its default gateway.

Types of passive attack:

- **Sniffing**: Capturing packets unknown to users on the network. The goal is to obtain any sensitive information sent across the network.
- **Port scanning**: Checking for open TCP and UDP ports. This will aid the attacker in determining the services running on the target/victim machine.

Active attacks

In an active attack, the attacker may have already done enough reconnaissance on the target device and is ready to execute its exploit against the victim. Sometimes, the attack can be a direct attack, meaning the exploit is sent from the attacker's machine to the target, or an indirect attack, where the attacker compromises another machine, making it a zombie, and using the zombie to pivot all the attacks through it. Therefore, the zombie would seem to be the attacker machine from the view of the victim.

Examples of active attacks include:

- **Denial of Service**: This attack focuses on exhausting the resources of a system, therefore legitimate users are not given access to the resource
- **Botnet**: The attacker sets up a **Command and Control** (**CnC**) server to control all its infected machines (zombies) to carry out malicious activities

Spoofing attacks

In a spoofing attack, the attacker uses false information to pretend to be a legitimate or authorized user/machine. When an attacker attempts to exploit a system or deliver a payload, they have to try to trick the user into falling victim to the attack. Sometimes, changing the source IP address and source MAC address of the packets originating from the attacking machine may trick the potential victim into thinking it's from a legitimate user and may disguise the attack's origins.

Internet protocol – the heart of internet communication

Internet Protocol (**IP**) is a connection protocol that exists at the Network layer (layer 3) of the **Open Systems Interconnection** (**OSI**) reference model. Internet protocol is used to assist routers or any layer 3 devices to forward packets to their corresponding destinations. One main characteristic of internet protocol is its nature of being a connectionless protocol, which means it provides delivery using best effort and is not guaranteed to be delivered to the recipient. Since IP is said to be connectionless, it depends on the upper layers to assist with the delivery of data. The layer above the Network layer is known as the **Transport layer**. There are two sub protocols, which are used primarily for delivery; these are known as the **User Datagram Protocol** (**UDP**) and the **Transmission Control Protocol** (**TCP**). An IP packet contains the following: source and destination IP addresses, version (IPv4 or IPv6), **Time to Live** (**TTL**) value, protocol (TCP, UDP, or ICMP), and flags.

It is through the forging of this source address that hackers are able to break into the network and mislead communication between the source and the destination. Almost all networks use routers as intermediate devices for the transmission of data. When the data is sent via routers, they identify the destination IP address from the header of the IP datagram to forward the packets to that destination. The source address is ignored by the routers. The source address is used only by the destination machine when a reply is sent back for the received packets.

How is an IP datagram spoofed?

In an IP packet/datagram, the header contains the addressing information, such as the sender's source and the destination's IP address. An IP packet is usually unencrypted, therefore if someone is sniffing the traffic between the sender and the receiver, the contents of the packet and its header information are captured. A malicious user or an attacker can modify the IP address on the IP packets originating from the attacker machine, making it seem to originate from somewhere else, which is known as IP spoofing. It tricks a potential victim into believing the IP packet came from a legitimate or trusted source, but is actually from a malicious user. The operating system has no way of determining whether the IP addresses actually belong to the legitimate machine or not. When the internet protocol was built, security was not a concern at the time, hence IP lacks security features.

There are different types of spoofing attacks:

- Address Resolution Protocol spoofing
- DNS spoofing

IP spoofing

Using the following scenario, an attacker sends a specially crafted packet to the web server (200.1.1.1). Within the IP header of the specially crafted packet, it has a source IP address of 203.155.182.1, which belongs to the potential victim machine and not the real IP address of the attacker. When the web server receives the packet and has to respond, it sees the sender's IP address is 203.155.182.1 and sends its response to the victim machine instead of the attacker:

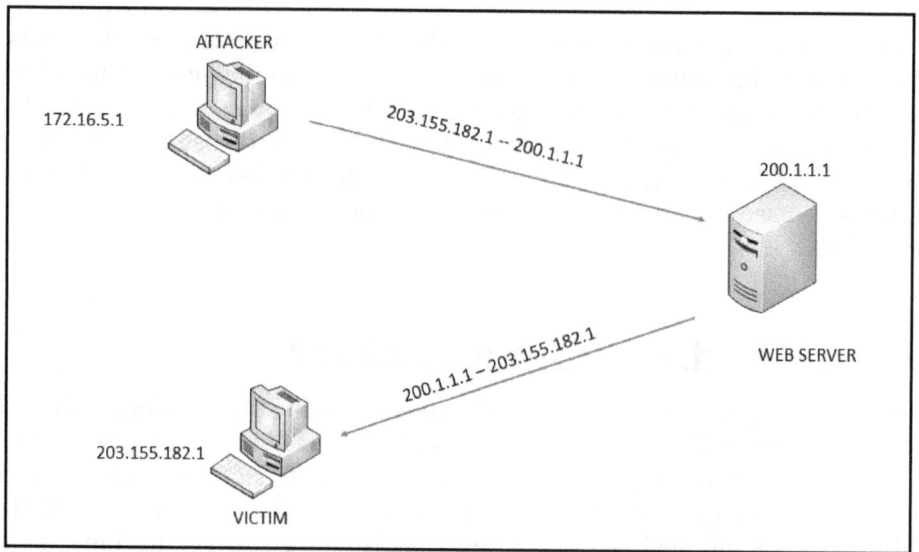

Attackers primarily use IP spoofing as a technique to bypass any filters, access lists, or even security appliances that act as countermeasures for spoofing attacks. The goal is to find a way into a network by tricking the system into believing it's a legit packet.

In this method, the attacker creates IP packets with a fake source IP address to hide the identity of the sender. Attackers use IP spoofing to overcome security measures, such as authentication-based IP networks. Attackers use randomly chosen IP address and spoof the original IP address to perform the DoS attack.

When two computers communicate, information about the IP address is placed on the source field of the packet. In an IP spoofing attack, the source IP address in the packet is not the original IP address of the source computer. By modifying the source IP address, the original sender can make the victim machine think the message originated from another source and therefore the sending machine or the attacker will be protected from being tracked.

Various options where IP spoofing can be used:

- Scanning
- Hijacking an online session
- Flooding

Scanning

Scanning is a process in which a malicious user sends probes to a victim machine to determine TCP/UDP open ports, the type of operating system and version, services running on the victim machine, and vulnerabilities:

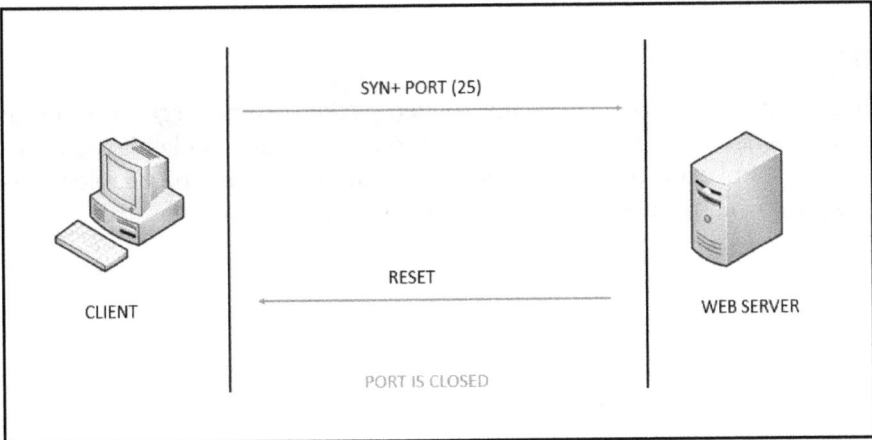

During the scanning phase, the attack may notice whether port 80 is open or not on the target device. If port 80 is open, we can determine there is a web server daemon running on the target device. The attacker can then use the Telnet protocol to perform banner-grabbing on the victim using port 80 as the destination port. This will determine the type and version of the web server, whether it's Microsoft IIS, Apache, or even nginx. Knowing this information will aid the attacker in fine-tuning their payload for the target device.

Hijacking an online session

In a session hijacking attack, an attacker can capture the cookie from a user who has logged on to a website and uses data found inside the cookie to also log on to the same website without having to enter a username and password combination. This would allow the attacker to gain access to the user (victim) account details.

The cookie can be captured using either sniffing or **man-in-the-middle** (**MITM**) attacks.

Flooding

In a flooding attack, the attacker sends unsolicited packets to the target continuously until the target is overwhelmed. The target will need to process each packet it receives, but due to the high influx of packets received, the target would eventually be unable to respond to a legitimate request from users or perform any further action.

ARP spoofing attacks

In an ARP spoofing attack, the attacker tries to map the MAC address with the IP address of a victim. The attacker can then intercept, steal, or delete the data. An ARP spoofing attack targets the nodes, layer **2** switches, and routers by disturbing the ARP caches of the connected systems:

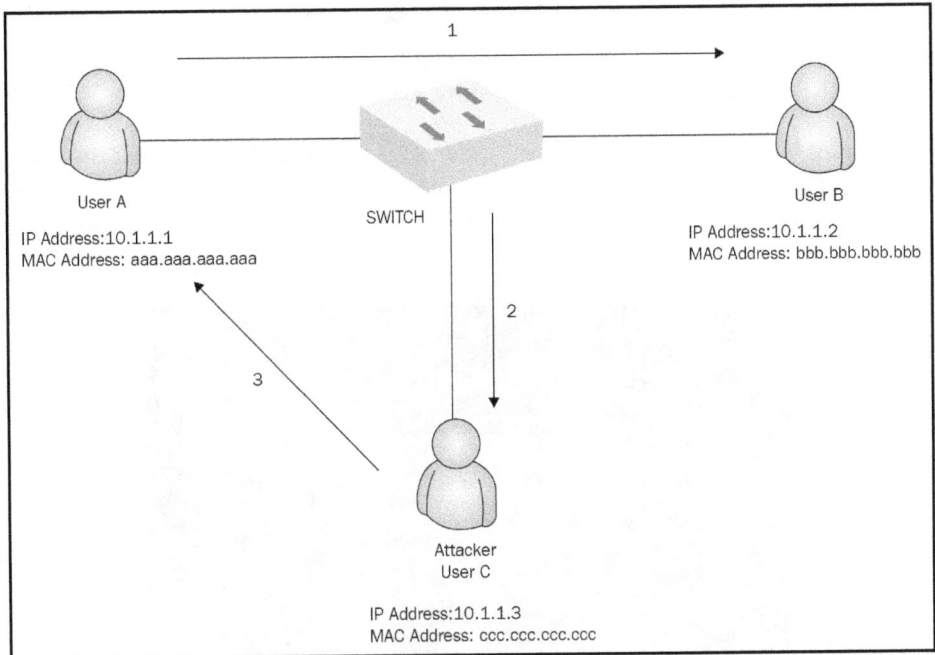

Hosts **A**, **B**, and **C** are connected to the switch. Host **A** broadcasts a request (ARP) asking for the MAC address of host **B**, after host **A** sends data to host **B**. The switch receives the broadcast and forwards the request, and when host **B** receives the ARP request, it fills the ARP cache with the ARP entry and the IP address of host **A** (10.1.1.1) and the MAC address of **A** (aaaa.aaaa.aaaa.aaaa). When host **B** replies, host **A** fills their ARP cache with the IP address of host **B** (10.1.1.2) and the MAC address of **B** (bbbb.bbbb.bbbb.bbbb). At the same time, host **C** tries to poison the ARP cache of hosts **A** and **B** by sending some fake ARP messages with the IP address of **B** and the MAC address of host **C** (cccc.cccc.cccc.cccc).

Now the ARP cache is poisoned and it uses the destination MAC address of host **C** (cccc.cccc.cccc.cccc) for the traffic intended for host **B**. The attacker on host **C** interrupts the traffic flow between host **A** and host **B**, as host **C** knows the MAC addresses of host **A** and host **B**.

Mitigating ARP spoofing attacks

ARP attacks cannot be mitigated straightforwardly; however, proactive measures can be taken against ARP-cache poisoning on your network.

Statically mapping the MAC addresses to the IP address is one approach against the unsolicited dynamic ARP requests sent by an attacker. You can see the ARP cache of a Windows system by simply opening a Command Prompt and typing the arp -a command, as shown:

```
C:\Users>arp -a

Interface: 10.123.75.150 --- 0x3
  Internet Address       Physical Address      Type
  10.123.75.1            00-1d-46-05-20-00     dynamic
  224.0.0.2             01-00-5e-00-00-02     static
  224.0.0.22            01-00-5e-00-00-16     static
  224.0.0.251           01-00-5e-00-00-fb     static
  224.0.0.252           01-00-5e-00-00-fc     static
  239.255.255.250       01-00-5e-7f-ff-fa     static
  255.255.255.255       ff-ff-ff-ff-ff-ff     static

Interface: 192.168.56.1 --- 0xc
  Internet Address       Physical Address      Type
  192.168.56.255        ff-ff-ff-ff-ff-ff     static
  224.0.0.2             01-00-5e-00-00-02     static
  224.0.0.22            01-00-5e-00-00-16     static
  224.0.0.251           01-00-5e-00-00-fb     static
  224.0.0.252           01-00-5e-00-00-fc     static
  239.255.255.250       01-00-5e-7f-ff-fa     static

Interface: 10.128.1.1 --- 0x12
  Internet Address       Physical Address      Type
  10.128.1.255          ff-ff-ff-ff-ff-ff     static
  224.0.0.2             01-00-5e-00-00-02     static
  224.0.0.22            01-00-5e-00-00-16     static
  224.0.0.251           01-00-5e-00-00-fb     static
  224.0.0.252           01-00-5e-00-00-fc     static
  239.255.255.250       01-00-5e-7f-ff-fa     static

Interface: 10.128.10.1 --- 0x33
  Internet Address       Physical Address      Type
  10.128.10.255         ff-ff-ff-ff-ff-ff     static
  224.0.0.2             01-00-5e-00-00-02     static
  224.0.0.22            01-00-5e-00-00-16     static
  224.0.0.251           01-00-5e-00-00-fb     static
  224.0.0.252           01-00-5e-00-00-fc     static
  239.255.255.250       01-00-5e-7f-ff-fa     static
```

In situations where network arrangements do not change often, static ARP entries can still be used. This will guarantee that devices will depend on their local ARP cache, as opposed to depending on ARP requests and responses:

- **Monitoring ARP traffic**: The other method of protecting against the ARP cache is monitoring the network traffic of hosts. This should be possible with a couple of interruption-based identification frameworks and utilities.
- **Dynamic ARP inspection**: This is one of the security features that verifies the ARP packet. Dynamic ARP inspection verifies, stores log information, and rejects all the invalid ARP bindings. Dynamic ARP inspection will be explained in more depth in the following chapters.

The DHCP process

Whenever a client connects to a network, it automatically searches for a **Dynamic Host Configuration Protocol** (**DHCP**) server. A DHCP server is used to primarily distribute an IP address, subnet mask, default gateway, and **Domain Name System (DNS)** server configurations to clients. When the client connects, it broadcasts a DHCPDISCOVER message with a destination MAC address of FFFF.FFFF.FFFF and a destination port of 67

The following is the DHCP four (4) way handshake:

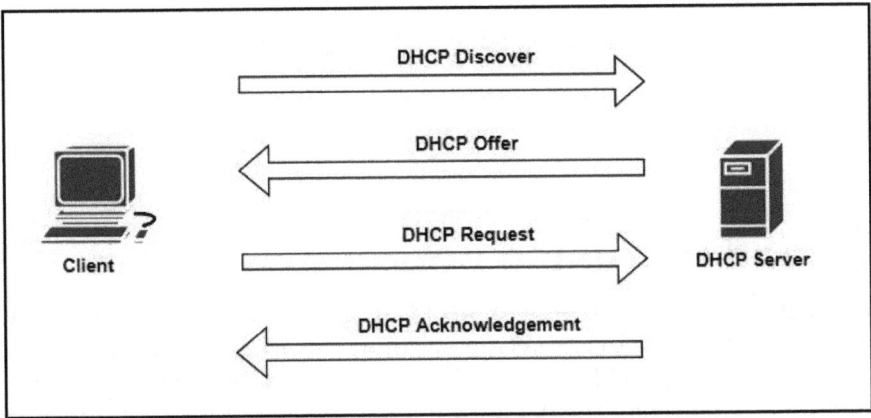

Port 67 is open on the DHCP server. A client uses 68 as the source port.

The DHCP server will respond, send a unicast `DHCP Offer` message back to the client with potentially usable IP configurations. The client will return a `DHCPREQUEST` back to the DHCP server, letting the server know it's going to accept the IP configurations from the previous message. They will send a `DHCP Acknowledgement` message to confirm the IP information the client is going to use for network communication.

A simple method to remember the DHCP process is to use an acronym. So **D** from **Discover**, **O** from **Offer**, **R** from **Request**, and **A** from **Acknowledgement**. Putting it all together, it spells **DORA**.

Why DHCP snooping?

DHCP snooping is a feature that exists on a switch. It creates two types of ports: **trusted** and **untrusted**. When DHCP snooping is enabled on a switch, all ports are labeled as untrusted, and this prevents any `DHCP Offer` and `DHCP ACK` messages from entering the switch. However, the port that is connected to the DHCP server should be configured manually as a trusted port. The trusted port allows the `DHCP Offer` and `DHCP ACK` messages to enter the switch.

The DHCP snooping feature is a countermeasure against any rogue DHCP server that may be attached to the network infrastructure.

DHCP snooping is enabled on the VLAN level on a switch.

Trusted and untrusted sources

At times, a malicious user may attempt to install a rogue DHCP server on the network in the hope that potential client devices become victims. We need to remember a few things about the DHCP server: it provides the IP address, subnet mask, default gateway, and DNS server configurations to clients. The default gateway is used to forward traffic destined for a network outside of the LAN, and the DNS server resolves hostnames and IP address. What if the clients are using another default gateway and/or a compromised DNS server with false DNS entries? The following table shows the switches and the classification of ports as trusted/untrusted:

Switches	Ports
F1/3 of switch	Trusted port
F1/1 of switch	Untrusted port
F1/2 of switch	Untrusted port

When the DHCP snooping features are configured on a Cisco switch, it immediately converts all ports to become **untrusted** ports. An untrusted port prevents any DHCP Offer and DHCP ACK messages from entering the switch port. However, the port that the DHCP server is connected to must be manually configured as a trusted port:

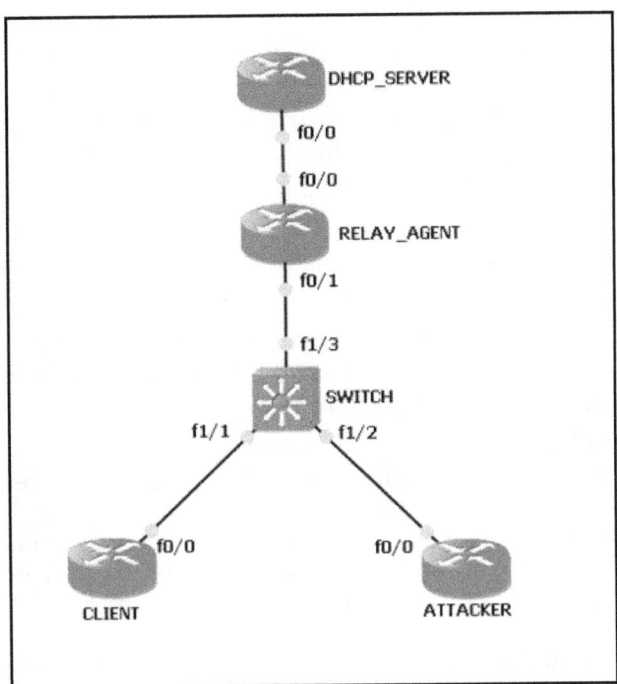

DHCP trust zone

The following describes how the DHCP snooping feature actually functions:

1. The DHCP snooping is enabled with the switch, the untrusted ports will forward only DHCPDISCOVER and DHCPREQUEST packets to the DHCP Server. The trusted port would only forward DHCP Offer and DHCP Ack packets back to the DHCP client.

 The DHCP server must be connected to a **trusted** port on the switch.

2. When the attacker sends multiple fake DHCPDISCOVER messages to the server, the CPU utilization of the DHCP server goes up, and at some point the server will be out of IP addresses for that particular network in its pool. To avoid this, the DHCP snooping feature rate limits the DHCP traffic from trusted and untrusted sources so that only one DHCPDISCOVER message can be sent by the client.

3. If any untrusted port exceeds the number of DHCPREQUEST messages, the port goes into an err-disabled state.

4. When DHCP snooping is enabled and configured, the switch maintains a DHCP snooping database that is used to keep track of untrusted sources, their leased IP address, and all the other TCP/IP settings.

5. DHCP snooping can also be enabled for a particular VLAN of the switch interface. By default, it is disabled on all the VLAN interfaces.

A DoS attack is a process by which an attacker tries to create a disturbance in the network by triggering unwanted traffic, and this disables the network. The objective of this attack is to not allow network services to be available to legitimate users.

DoS attacks look legitimate, but the size of the traffic might increase to a level that cannot be managed by the victim, for example:

- **Ping of Death** (**PoD**): Sending continuous ICMP messages that cause the victim to crash or be unable to respond to legitimate requests
- **TCP SYN flood**: Simply creating a half-open TCP session on the victim server, thereby halting the services offered by the victim

Ping of Death

The **Internet Control Message Protocol** (**ICMP**) can be used to check basic network connectivity between two devices. Attacks can manipulate the size of the ICMP message to be greater than the normal size. A simple utility that uses the ICMP is known as **ping**.

If an attacker sends a ping of 65,536 bytes or greater to another device on a network, it will cause the recipient machine (victim) to crash. This type of attack is known as **Ping of Death**.

Let's take a look at the following diagram to better understand what takes place:

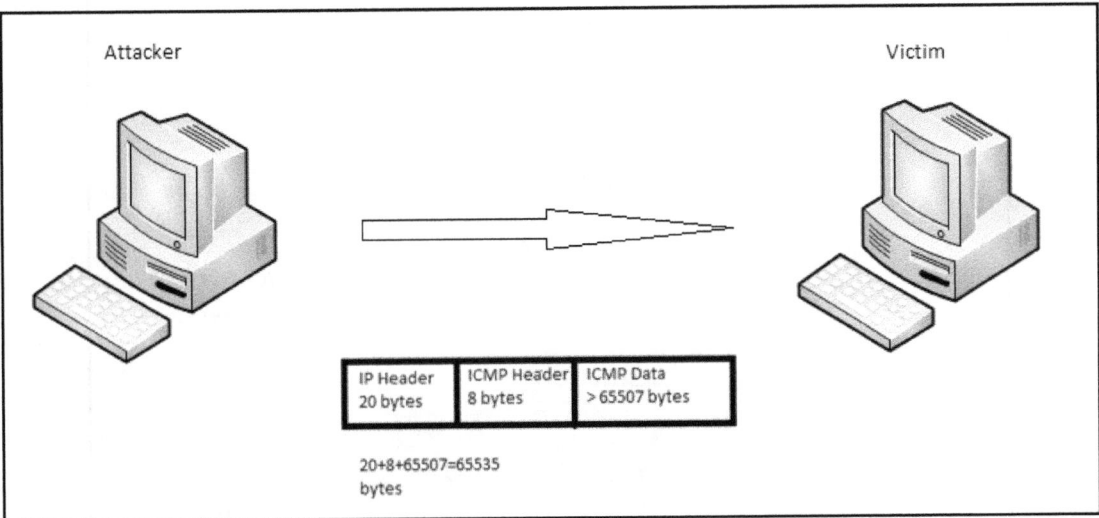

In this diagram, the victim that receives the fragmented packets will do the reassembly only to find that the final packet is greater than 65,536 bytes. Not knowing what to do with the packet, the system crashes or malfunctions, resulting in its inability to provide service to the legitimate users.

TCP SYN flood attacks

In most instances, whenever two devices want to communicate, they use the TCP protocol to ensure the message reaches both devices. The first process is known as the TCP three-way handshake. Once the handshake is completed, then data is allowed to flow between both devices. In a TCP SYN flood attack, the attacker sends a constant stream of **SYN** packets to the victim:

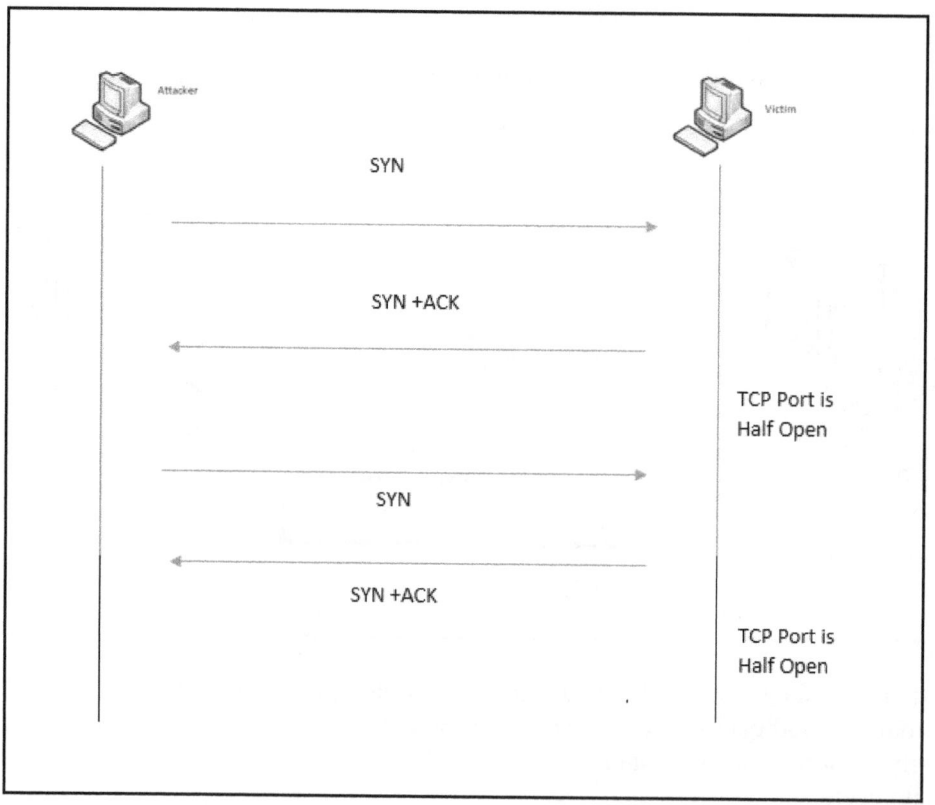

On the victim's end, for every SYN packet received, it must reply with an SYN/ACK packet. The attacker would receive this SYN/ACK packet but would not respond to it, therefore creating a lot of half-open connections on the victim machine. Remember, the attacker is continuously sending TCP SYN packets, which would eventually cause the victim's machine to exhaust its resources and not be able to create any future connections with other devices as long as the attack continues.

Password attacks

In a password attack, the attacker tries to obtain the password of a user account, an encrypted file, or even a network. The purpose can vary based on the attacker's intent. In doing so, there are a variety of different methods for attempting to gain the password of another person:

- **Brute force attack**: In a brute force attack, every possible combination of characters is attempted against the protected data until the correct combination is found. A brute force attack has the highest possibility of cracking the password; however, the downside is the length of time it may take before the password is found.
- **Dictionary attack**: This attack uses a password list to reference when attempting to crack the password. This attack may not always be a good choice since the success of the attack is only as good as the words that are in the actual wordlist of the password file.
- **Keylogger**: A keylogger can be either software- or hardware-based. The primary purpose of a keylogger is to capture keystrokes. This can be useful in capturing an unsuspecting user's password for a secure website, such as their online banking user account information.
- **Trojan Horse**: A Trojan Horse is a type of malware that disguises itself to look like a trusted program/software to trick its potential victims into installing it. Once installed, the actual malicious payload installs itself in the background and stays hidden from the victim. The payload can also be a software keylogger configured to send logs of data remotely back the attacker.

The main concept behind this attack is the weakness of the human mind in creating a strong password which contains alphanumeric characters, upper and lower cases with number(s) and a special character. This is sometimes an amateur way of obtaining critical information from users, such as bank account details, credit card PIN, or other confidential data. As a prerequisite, the attacker tries to look legitimate and provides information that looks real from a victim's perspective.

Different types of social engineering attacks can be seen:

- **Phishing**: This attack uses email as the mechanism through which an attacker disguised as a legitimate organization tries to get critical details, such as banking passwords.
- **Vishing**: This attack uses phones, through which the attacker tries to converse like a person from a legitimate organization and get critical details from the victim.
- **Spear phishing**: This attack is similar to phishing, but it focuses on a particular target from whom the attacker will steal information. It is important to note that the attacker gathers some information about the particular victim prior to launching this attack so that it looks like a particular email sent to the victim is legitimate, for example, targeting the CEO of an organization.
- **Pharming**: This is an attack where a rogue DNS server provides the wrong DNS IP for a particular URL, which leads the victim to a malicious site. Also, this can be done by injecting some incorrect DNS mappings into the *host* file on the Windows machine.
- **Smishing**: This attack uses SMS instead of email.

Buffer overflow attacks

In programming, a buffer is an area that is used to store data temporarily during program execution. The size of the buffer is usually fixed. Once the program closes, the contents of the buffer are also cleared. In a buffer overflow attack, the buffer is filled with more data than it can handle, causing the program to behave abnormally. Attackers use this attack to gain reverse shells into a victim machine by injecting shellcode as the payload.

Malware

Malware is any malicious software that can cause harm to any computing system or network. A piece of malware may have multiple functions, such as wiping data from a hard drive, capturing screenshots of the victim's monitor, or even creating a backdoor.

Some types of malware include:

- Viruses
- Crypto-malware, ransomware
- Worms
- Trojan Horse
- Rootkit
- Keylogger
- Adware/spyware
- Botnet

Network security tools

A tool is only as good as its wielder. There are many network security tool out there; some categories include tools for reconnaissance to help gather information on DNS, email addresses, and SNMP. At our fingertips, there's **Nmap** (**Network Mapper**), `https://nmap.org`, for exploitation development; the famous Metasploit from Rapid 7 (`https://www.rapid7.com/products/metasploit/`), for sniffing; Wireshark (`https://www.wireshark.org/`); and most importantly, one of the most advanced penetration platforms, Kali Linux (`https://www.kali.org/`) from Offensive Security.

We always need to remember hackers, network administrators, and cyber security professionals use network tools for different purposes. A white-hat hacker may use it to find vulnerabilities on a network before the black-hat hacker finds and exploits them. A penetration tester is trying to find and exploit any weakness in a network because it's their job.

Wireshark

Wireshark is referred to as the best protocol analyzer/sniffer. It has the ability to display all the **Protocol Data Units** (**PDUs**) for the four layers of the TCP/IP stack. Wireshark is a free tool for both Windows and Linux operating systems. It has the ability to see all the conversations/network traffic passing along a network segment:

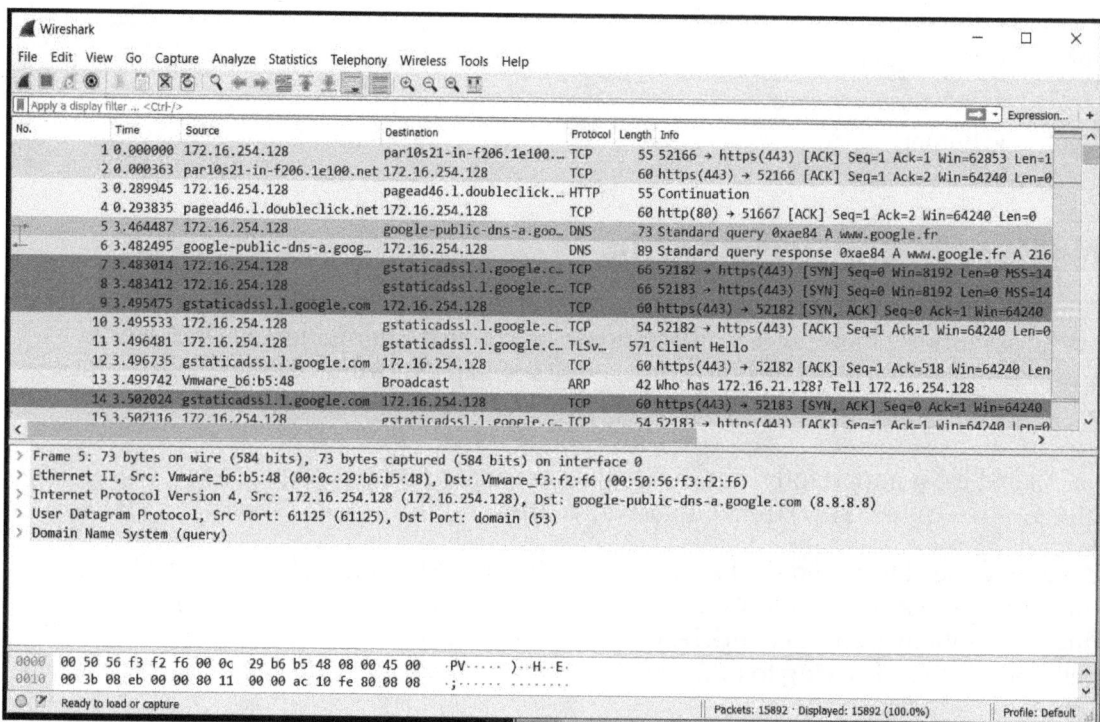

To start a capture on Wireshark, simply open it and click on **Capture** | **Options**, then select the interface you want to capture traffic on. Now, click on **Start**.

 Wireshark can be found at `https://www.wireshark.org/`.

Metasploit

Metasploit is an exploitation development framework. This is a free tool for students and people who want to learn hacking in an ethical manner. The tool can be used with both Windows and Linux:

This is the Command Prompt from which Metasploit can be used. The console is referred to as `msf`.

Kali Linux

Kali Linux is a penetration testing Linux distribution. It was created by Offensive Security as the successor to the famous BackTrack. Kali Linux is a single operating system with all the possible tools and utilities needed for conducting a penetration test and forensics.

The amazing benefit of this distro is that it can be installed on a virtual machine, on a hard drive, it can be live-booted via USB, and can be installed on mobile devices, such as the Google Nexus, OnePlus smartphones, and the Raspberry Pi computer.

There are many categories of tools, such as information-gathering, scanners, password-cracking, exploitation development, post-exploitation, and forensics. The possibilities with Kali Linux are endless.

Summary

In this chapter, we took a look at the CIA triad and its importance, network security terminologies, types of attacks, how IP works and its vulnerabilities to network attack, and some security tools.

In the next chapter, we will look at the uses of different types of firewall and the significance of IPS in network security.

2
Delving into Security Toolkits

The term *firewall* was derived from an automobile division. It actually means a segment that is extricated to release the engine screened-off area from the core of the automobile. But in the network world, it is used as a general term for how we isolate our internal network from outside attacks and threats. A firewall can be defined as any hardware or software that enables the filtering of packets or controls the flow of traffic. They are generally implemented at the perimeter of the network. They act as a border for trusted and untrusted zones.

For a company that secures the network and data, it will add complexity to the network administrator. The costs of maintaining and implementing such a high level of security, such as e-commerce, intranet, extranet, and email services, are always high, but when compared to the loss that is incurred due to the lack of high-level security, it is considered more important.

But if a company opts for a Cisco firewall, software, instead of hardware, would also have the same kind of security fulfillment. Cisco IOS provides full-featured firewall services when it is implemented properly on any Cisco router. It helps a network to break down into several small domains or sub networks, thereby helping to keep the possible security breach limited to one domain, if any, and preventing it from spreading across the entire network, which would result in a major loss.

There are two important parts of a firewall:

- A part to permit the traffic
- A part to block the traffic

Most firewalls permit traffic from a trusted zone to the untrusted zone without any special configuration. But the traffic flow from the untrusted zone to the trusted zone must be configured and must be explicitly permitted, so anything not configured or permitted from untrusted to trusted should be denied implicitly. A firewall is not limited to trusted and untrusted zones only; it also has a mid-zone called the **DMZ zone** (**Demilitarized zone** or **less-trusted zone**).

Basically, a firewall is a set of programs that can be enabled in a network gateway server and secures the resources of a private network from other external network users. The firewall operates based on the set of rules and policies defined by the administrator.

Firewalls come in two varieties:

- **Hardware firewall**: Examples are routers with built-in **Access Control List (ACL)**, **Adaptive Security Appliance (ASA)**, and **Personal Internet Exchange (PIX)**
- **Software firewall**: Operating systems with firewall software

All the messages entering inside and moving out from the internet to the intranet pass through the firewall. Thus, a firewall offers a preeminent security solution.

Firewalls are based on rules and policies. The rules configures on the firewall decide what type of connection should be allowed and how it should be allowed. The firewall also decides based on the direction of the packet flow:

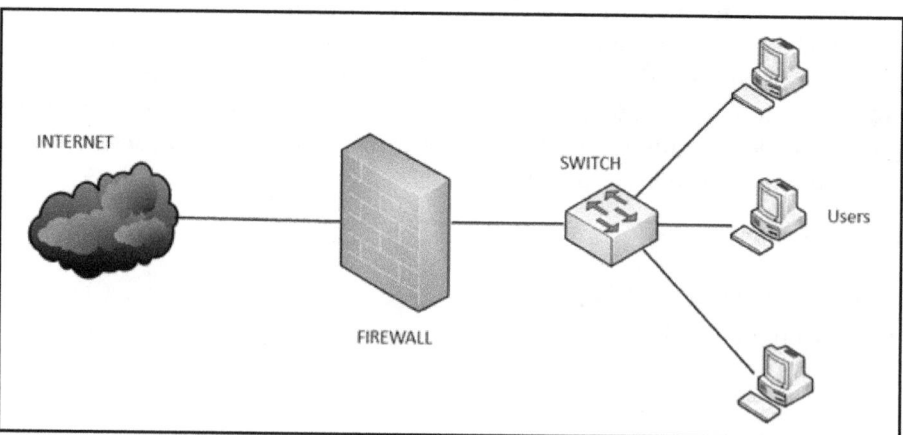

Apart from controlling unauthorized access to the network, firewalls also help to allow remote connection to a secure network using authentication mechanisms.

The rules that firewalls use are that nothing but security guidelines that can be configured by a user or a network administrator to permit/deny the traffic to file servers, web servers, FTP servers, and Telnet servers. Firewalls allow administrators to have immense control over the traffic flowing in and out of their systems/networks.

Upon completion of this chapter, you will understand:

- The uses of different types of firewall
- The significance of IPS in network security
- How VPNs can be used to securely access remote networks
- The benefits of ESA and WSA
- The different endpoint security tools

Firewall functions

Firewalls primarily have two functions:

- Packet filtering
- Network Address Translation

Most firewalls also perform two other important security services:

- Encrypted authentication
- Encrypted tunnels

Rules of a firewall

The rules of a firewall can be customized depending on our needs, requirements, and threat levels. There are different conditions on which firewall filters work. These are as follows:

- **IP address**: The first condition on which a firewall rule works is on IP address. The decision is based on the range of IP addresses and subnet masks.
- **Domain name**: The second condition on which a firewall works is on domain name. A firewall can be configured to permit or deny access to specified domain names of corporate websites or domain name extensions, such as `.org`, `.tv`, or `.biz`.
- **Protocols and ports**: The third condition a firewall works on is the protocols and its ports. A firewall can be configured to permit or deny some protocols and port numbers, such as SMTP, FTP, UDP, and SNMP. It can also be configured to inspect the traffic passing through the open ports of the server.
- **Keywords**: The fourth condition on which the firewall works is specific keywords. Firewalls can be configured to check some keywords or phrases to decide whether to permit offensive data to flow in the network or not.

The logic is based on a group of guidelines configured either statically or dynamically, based on the requests of information in the network. Most firewalls use the header information of the packet to determine whether it should be allowed or blocked.

Let's assume the following network topology to understand how a firewall uses the configured rules:

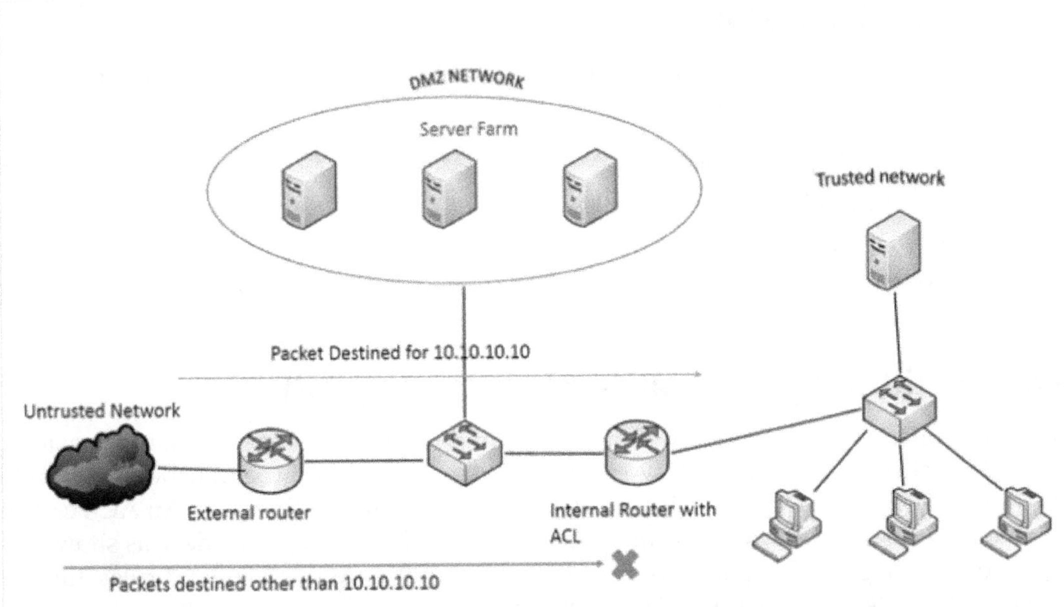

DMZ NETWORK

Server Farm

Trusted network

Packet Destined for 10.10.10.10

Untrusted Network

External router

Internal Router with ACL

Packets destined other than 10.10.10.10

Source Address	Source Port	Destination Address	Destination Port	Action
Any	Any	10.10.10.10	>1023	Allow
Any	Any	11.11.11.11	>1023	Deny

The rule in this diagram mentions that any incoming packet (**Source Address—Any** and **Source Port—Any**) that is intended for the internal network with a **Destination Address** of 10.10.10.10 and a **Destination Port** of more than 1023 is allowed to enter the network, and all other incoming packets with a destination other than 10.10.10.10 will be blocked.

You should be careful when configuring a rule, because it is very risky to allow any traffic through a firewall.

Types of firewall

Firewalls can be classified into the following types, based on their operation and the method used to inspect the packet:

- Packet-filtering firewalls
- Circuit-level gateway firewalls
- Application firewalls
- Zone-based firewalls

Packet-filtering firewall/stateless firewall

This type of firewall is nothing but routers that connect the internal network to the external network. Packet-filtering firewalls work on the network layer and the transport layer of the OSI model. Routers configured with an ACL are packet-filtering firewalls. An ACL can be defined based on the IP address, protocols, and packet attributes (IP header), as shown in the following diagram. If a packet does not meet the configured policies and rules, the packet is discarded and the routers will create a log:

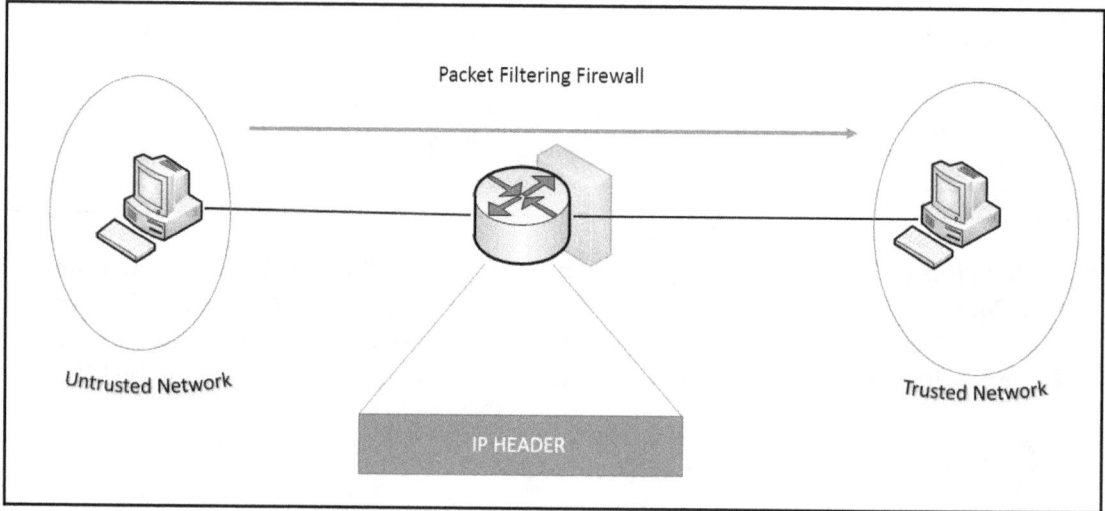

Circuit-level gateway firewall/stateful firewall

This is also known as a transparent proxy firewall. The word stateless indicates that the firewall checks the matching criteria and, if matched, forwards the traffic, but the return traffic will once again be inspected as a separate packet.

For example, assume web traffic is going from host **A** to server **B**. If this traffic was allowed by the firewall, the traffic would pass through. However, the return traffic, that is, from server **B** to host **A**, would once again be verified on the outbound interface of the firewall. If the firewall has a policy to block this traffic, then the return traffic gets dropped. This might not be proper policy enforcement on the firewall.

An example of a stateful firewall is **Cisco Adaptive Security Appliance (Cisco ASA)**:

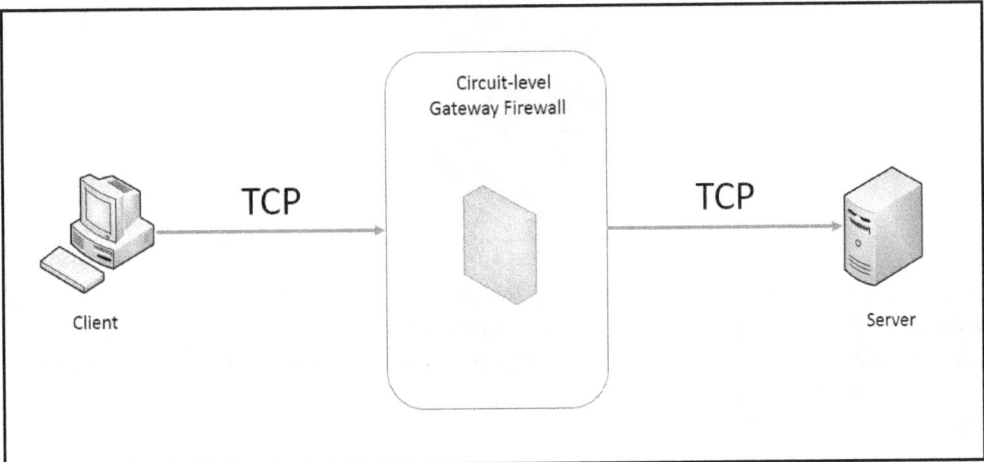

Application-layer firewall

It is a Layer-7 firewall that does a deep-packet inspection. The difference between an application-layer firewall and the firewalls mentioned earlier is that the application-layer firewall can check inside the content of the payload.

For example, this type of firewall does more than looking at just the port number, such as port 80 identifying HTTP. It can identify whether the structure of the HTTP payload looks like malicious code and can drop it.

Zone-based firewall

This is another layer-7 firewall that can perform deep-packet inspection. But, its added functionality is the capacity of this firewall to bundle some common interfaces under the zone and define a policy for a zone pair:

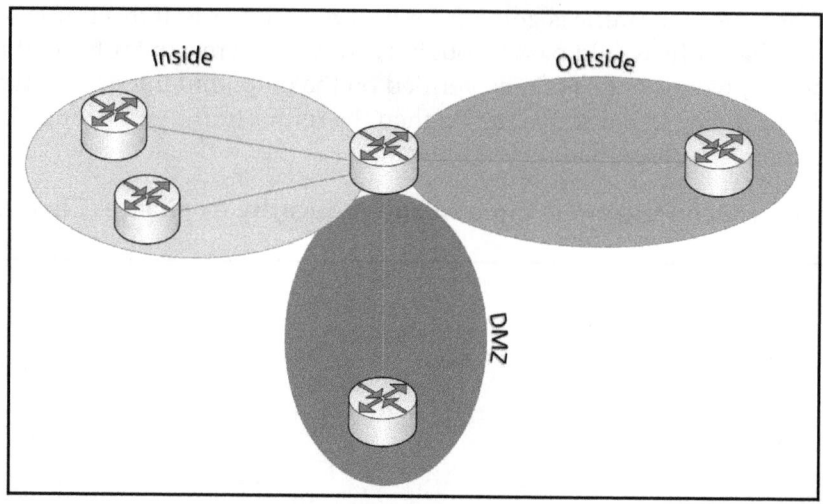

For example, if there are two LAN and one WAN connections, the firewall could bundle the two local interfaces under a zone called **inside zone** and map the WAN link to a zone called **outside zone**. The traffic can be classified using a class map. The policy is defined using a policy map. This policy will then be applied on the zone pair from the inside to outside zone or the outside to inside zone.

Here are the best practices for designing a sound firewall policy:

- **Trust no one**: It is always advisable to enable all the key services and deny the rest of the traffic. Analyze the privilege levels of the user and, based on the report, assign those services to them. You need to deploy the least-privilege principle, this concept gives a user access to only what is needed and nothing more.

- **Deny physical access to firewall**: It is always a good practice to keep any kind of physical access to a firewall controlled or deny it completely. For example, place the firewall inside a server farm/data center.

- **Allow only necessary protocols**: It's always good to have a prepared list of protocols, including those that should be allowed and those that need to be blocked.

- **Use logs and alerts**: A logging strategy must be followed to ensure the level and type of logging, and you need to be sure to monitor all those logs on a regular basis.

- **Segment security zone**: Create internal zones and explicitly define a policy for incoming traffic from the internet. Create a DMZ if public servers have to be placed.

- **Do not use a firewall as a server**: A firewall should never be used in server incorporation design. We should always uninstall or disable any unwanted software, as per the company requirement. Management tools are important ones that need to be removed.

- **Never use a firewall as a workstation**: In general, a user's system depends on a lot of client applications, such as Microsoft and Oracle, which can create vulnerability that viruses and worms may exploit.

- **Restrict access to firewalls**: Access to firewalls should be highly restricted. Only an administrator should be allowed to log in into strong password assigned to them. This can use OTP cards for better security.

- **Combine firewall technologies**: Packet filtering should not be done only for the line of defense. It can be incorporated with some inspections using protocols, stateful mechanisms, and applications.

- **Use a firewall as part of comprehensive security solutions**: A firewall should be positioned facing the internet directly for any incoming network traffic. A firewall should be used with other security appliances and applications to provide a defense in depth strategy.

- **Maintain the installation**: Software and patches should be kept updated. The updating of a firewall configuration, as per application and business requirements, might change.

Intrusion prevention system

An **intrusion prevention system** (**IPS**) is a proactive methodology to understand potential threats, stop attacks inline, and report them immediately. An IPS is a module or an individual device that can look into the payload of the traffic coming from the outside zone, thereby ensuring that any malicious traffic would be blocked inline:

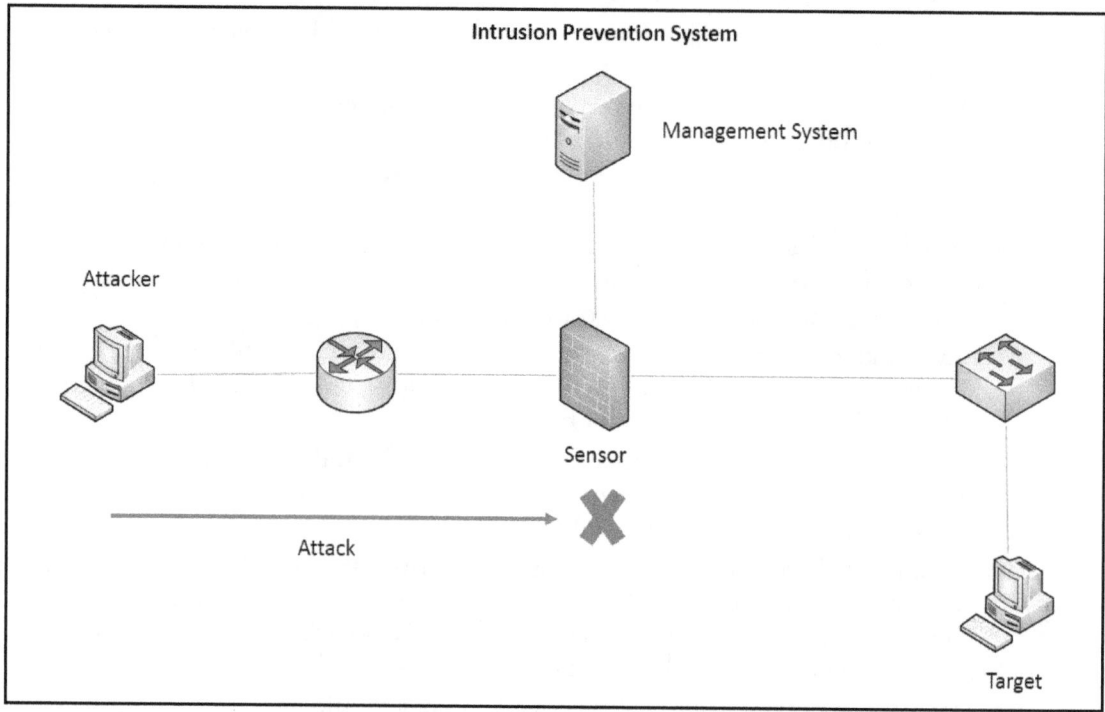

Intrusion detection system

An **intrusion detection system** (**IDS**) is a monitoring system that passively monitors incoming and outgoing network traffic for suspicious attacker activity. An IDS is a module that can alert network devices, but it cannot stop attacks from happening. Generally, an IDS is configured in promiscuous mode because it cannot block the attacks, but only send alerts:

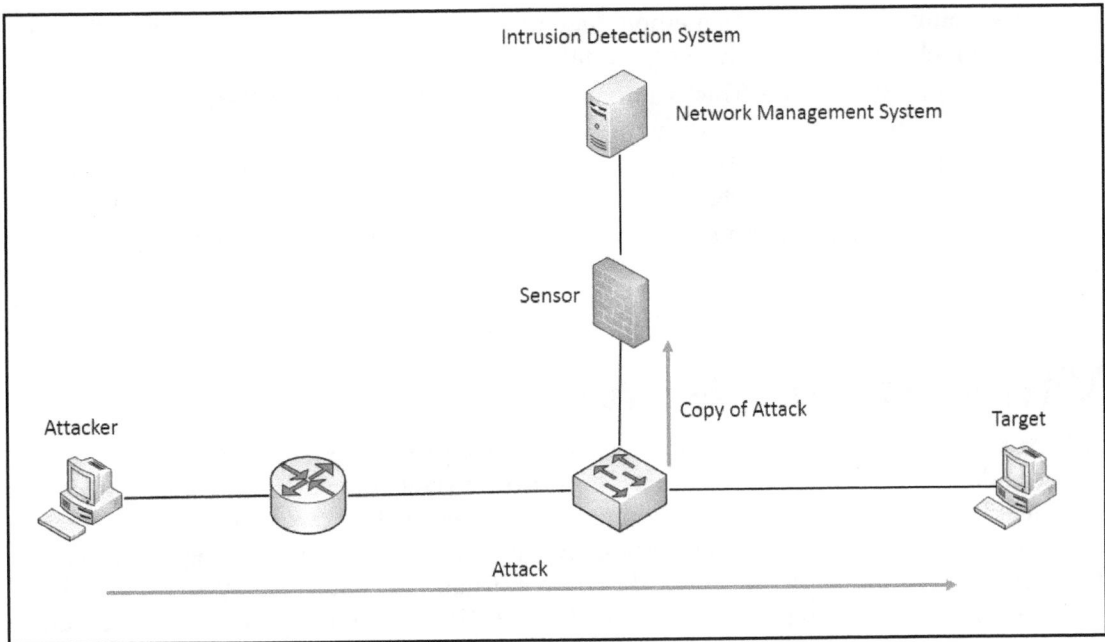

One major question you may have is how different is an IPS from a firewall that can also do deep-packet inspection? Well, the answer is that an IPS can identify traffic patterns that might match an attack, while a firewall can do an inspection on a per-packet basis, thereby they would not be intelligent enough to detect an attack. So, in any secure network, an IPS complements a firewall.

The different IPS and IDS identification methods are discussed here:

- **Signature-based**: The IPS verifies the traffic pattern against a database of well-known attacks referred to as signatures. If a particular traffic pattern matches the signature, it will trigger the signature.
- **Policy-based**: In this method, the IPS identifies any traffic outside the defined policy as malicious and blocks it.
- **Anomaly-based**: This method depends on a traffic baseline that is created based on observations made over a certain period of time.
- **Reputation-based**: This is a method that correlates all the different attacks across the globe and tries to verify the traffic pattern using that correlated database.
- **HIPS**: A host-based IPS is used on an individual machine instead of the entire network. This might be equivalent to an antivirus, but can analyze the attacks with a higher capability than an antivirus. This is of course operating system-dependent.

Virtual Private Network

A **Virtual Private Network** (**VPN**) is an extension of a private network into the public network domain. The public network would act as a private network and the user would be able to perform every function as if logged in to the private network. It also helps to allow a remote user to work with the same security and management policies defined by the administrator of the private network. This connection is established by a virtual point-to-point connection through a set of assigned connections and encryption, or a combination of both, depending on the business requirements.

VPNs allow employees to securely log in to their private network, even if they are not in their office premises. It is secure and cost-effective.

Any kind of network connection over an untrusted network, such as the internet, would benefit from implementing a VPN. Even inside an organization's premises, in order to implement a VPN, you need to create a secure private channel between network devices (**site-to-site VPN**), as well as between people and network devices (**remote-access VPN**):

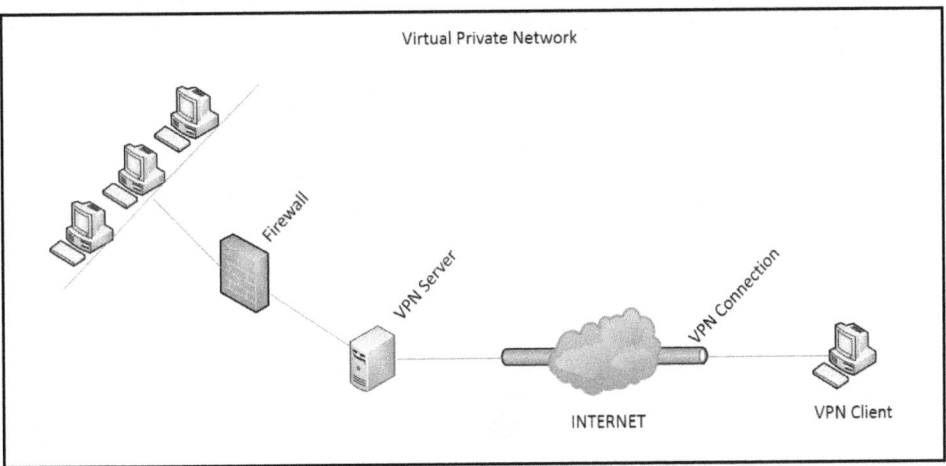

Benefits of VPN

A VPN can benefit the organization in the following ways:

- **Eliminating the need for long-distance leased lines**: Organizations need to rent network capacity, such as **T1/E1** lines, to achieve full, secured network connectivity between their office locations. A VPN would allow the user to log in to the private network using the public network, so there is no requirement for the company to procure a leased line. These connections can be tapped into the virtual network through much cheaper internet-connectivity options, such as broadband connections.

- **Reducing long-distance call charges**: A VPN would also enable the user to use VoIP services in a secured manner, thereby skipping logging in to the remote-access server by the business travelers who need to access the company's intranet. For example, with an internet VPN, clients need to connect to the nearest service provider's access point.

Site-to-site VPNs

A site-to-site VPN allows offices in multiple fixed location to establish a secure connection with each other over a public network, as shown in the following topology, with a lot of security measures bundled in. This enables the company's resources and data to be available to branch offices in other locations. For example, the server in the headquarters can be accessed securely by branch users:

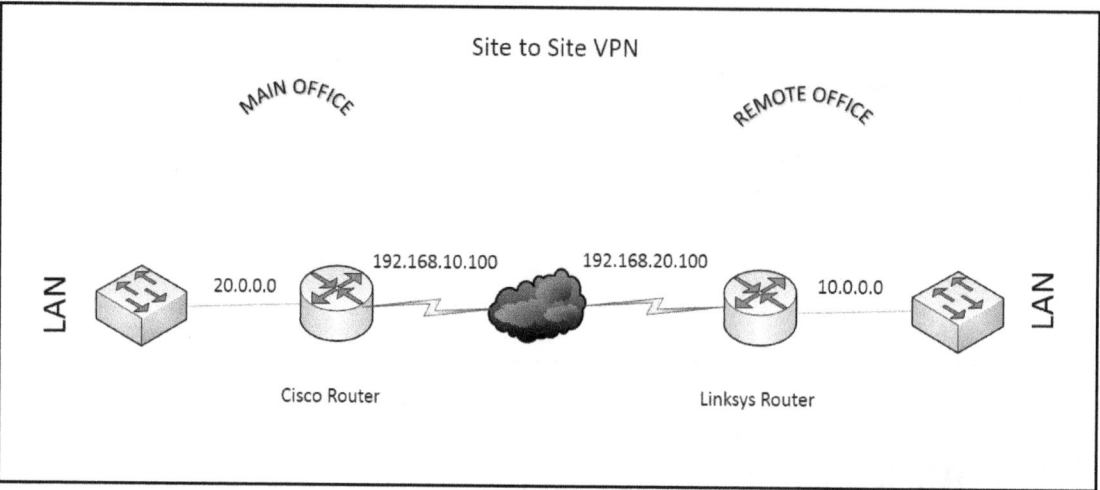

The two sites, using their VPN edge devices, set up the IPSEC VPN tunnel, which includes security parameters such as encryption algorithm, hashing algorithm, and authentication. Once the tunnel is established, the data from the LAN of the head office would be sent through the secured tunnel to the LAN of the branch office.

There are two types of site-to-site VPN:

- **Internet-based**: When a company has several branches located in different areas and they wish to join all of them as one private network, then they can connect each LAN to a single WAN.
- **Extranet-based**: When a company has to work very closely with their partners, vendors, or customers, then they can have an extranet VPN to build a connection that would require LAN connectivity. In this scenario, they can work in a secured manner by ensuring that all the data required is accessible and it also prevents access to their internal network.

Remote-access VPN

A Remote-access VPN is also called a **VPDN**, or **virtual private dial-up network**.

Similar to the site-to-site access evolution from WAN technologies, remote access has evolved from dial-up technology. The differentiating factors between these two types of VPN are:

- Remote-access VPN clients initiate the VPN on-demand
- The remote-access client requires the Cisco VPN client software to connect
- Remote-access uses a server client mechanism where the server authenticates first

This can be very flexible when implemented as a software solution on a remote user's PC. The teleworker can benefit from the same confidentiality, integrity, and authentication services of a site-to-site VPN.

It allows individual users to establish a secure connection with a remote computer network. They can access only the secured resources or data on that particular network, as if they were directly connected with the network. For example, a company where there are hundreds of sales personnel out in the field trying to access information from their sales servers can use a remote-access VPN:

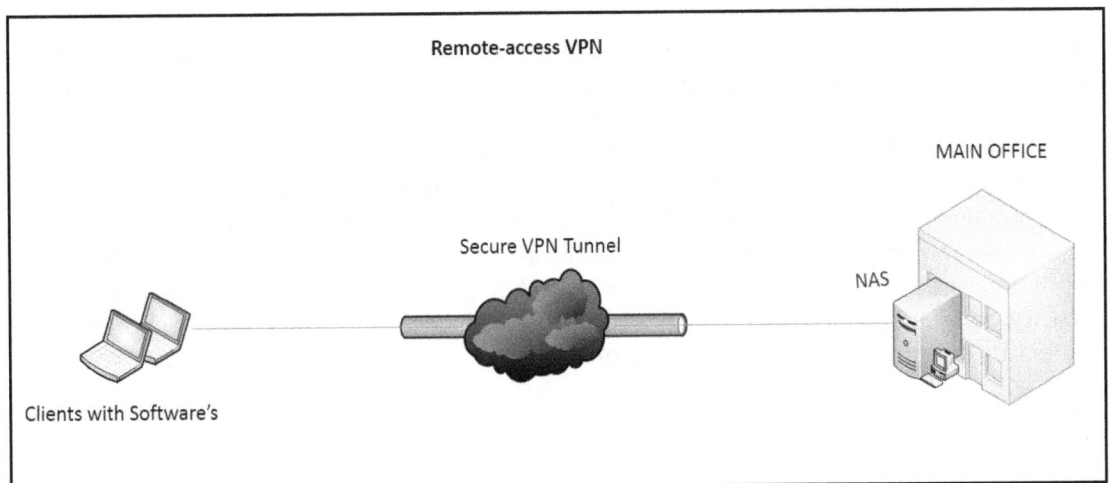

There are two components in a remote-access VPN:

- **Network access server (NAS)**: Also known as media gateway or remote-access server. NAS is a dedicated server that has multiple applications running in it. Users initially connect to the NAS server in order to get connected to the VPN. NAS also provides its own authentication services.
- **VPN client software**: This helps users to access their data via VPN. The client software establishes and maintains the connection with the NAS server. The modern operating system comes with a few built-in VPN applications; others must install third-party software specific to their organization's VPN configurations. The NAS, using a third-party **Certificate Authority** (**CA**), gets its digital certificate, which it will use to prove its identity to the client. Once successfully authenticated, the client software creates a tunnel connection to the NAS server, which is indicated by the user's IP address. The client software maintains the security level by using encryption standards, such as **Secure Socket Layer** (**SSL**).

Content security

Content security is a general term that talks about the confidentiality, legal concerns, and security of a company's intellectual property.

Attacks are not only launched by individuals outside of the company. Sometimes attacks are initiated by an individual inside your organization, who has legitimate access to the resources. These concerns increase daily, because organizations allow their employees to **bring your own devices** (**BYODs**) and allow employees to access their applications, data, and devices. There are vulnerabilities in the network/system, and there are chances of losing content, such as important data/files, while sending them via file sharing or emails. Companies should take the necessary steps to protect their content by defining some in-depth defensive policies. Content security cannot be achieved by implementing normal security policies, instead the company should take the necessary steps to protect their content by defining in-depth defensive policies.

Content Security Policy

The **Content Security Policy** (**CSP**) is a security policy to be implemented to protect networks from attacks that are initiated to steal the content and intellectual property of the company. The CSP provides a typical technique for website owners and companies to declare the rights and origins of the users of the content. Content security policies help security administrators to find and mitigate several types of threat, such as injection attacks and cross-site scripting attacks.

The CSP provides multi-layer security, so if one security layer fails, the other layers are still there to protect the network's applications, data, and devices.

There are different types of content security systems used by organizations:

- Policies that can be configured on the browser
- Hardware appliances
- Software/virtual appliances

Cisco Email Security Appliance

Email Security Appliance (**ESA**) provides comprehensive, simple, and fast-deploying security services for attacks initiated through email. Nowadays, spam and malware increase security complexity. ESA helps organizations to secure their email networks with low operating costs. ESA provides automated security policy settings, where the threat data is refreshed automatically every three to five minutes. It has a very flexible deployment choice and it also integrates with your organization's existing infrastructure.

Cisco ESA is a virtual appliance that allows network administrators to create multiple instances wherever required in the existing network infrastructure. This virtual appliance runs on VMware ESXI hypervisor and Cisco **Unified Computing System** (**UCS**) servers.

Some of the main capabilities of ESA are:

- **Threat intelligence**: Provides fast, comprehensive protection of email. ESA has 100 TB of security databases updated daily, which cover approximately 150 million endpoints.
- **Spam blocking**: ESA's multi-layer defensive solution stops spam messages by filtering based on the reputation of the sender and deep analysis of the message. More than 80% of spam messages are blocked even before hitting the network.

- **Graymail detection**: Graymail is mail from marketing websites, social networking sites, and so on. ESA monitors Graymail senders and allows the administrator to take appropriate action to unsubscribe links.

The following is a list of **Email Security Appliances** (**ESAs**) and their capacity respectively:

Model of ESA	Deployment size of Email Security Appliance
Cisco X1070	High performance for service providers and large enterprises
Cisco C680	High performance for service providers and large enterprises
Cisco C670	High performance for medium-sized enterprises
Cisco C380	High performance for medium-sized enterprises
Cisco C370	High performance for small-to-medium-sized enterprises
Cisco C170	For small businesses and branch offices

Cisco IronPort Web Security Appliance

As organizations increasingly allow their employees to use their own unregistered personal devices, attacks also increase. Hence, the company will need an effective solution for protecting web traffic. Cisco provides an effective solution called Cisco IronPort S670 **Web Security Appliance** (**WSA**). This has a combination of signature malware detection and inline file sharing.

 Cisco IronPort S670 has blocked more than 30 million malicious objects.

Cisco IronPort Web Security Appliance is a web proxy that checks and allows, or blocks, web traffic based on filters and inline file scanning. There are two capabilities of the WSA:

- **Web-Based Reputation Filters** (**WBRS**)
- Webroot and McAfee anti-malware scanning engines

When a user enters a URL in the web browser, this request is forwarded by the web cache communication protocol to the load-balanced pool of Cisco's WSA. The WSA checks whether to allow or block the website based on the score. The reputation score is stored in a cloud service called **Senderbase.org** (https://talosintelligence.com/).

Senderbase.org (`https://talosintelligence.com/`) allots reputation scores for each website, ranging from -10 to 10. Websites with a reputation score of -6 to -10 are blocked by the security appliance with scanning, and sites with a score of 6 to 10 are allowed without scanning.

Cisco WSA can be deployed in two methods:

- As an explicit proxy configuration
- As a transparent proxy

Cisco WSA will be dealt with in more detail in upcoming chapters.

Endpoint security

Endpoint security deals with securing end user's devices and the authentication of individual users. In an organization, before remote users access the network resources, the organization defines some policies that check for authentic and non-pirated software before allowing the user to access the network. In Cisco, this is executed by using NAS.

Three different types of device or software can be identified as portfolios for endpoint security:

- **Antivirus**: Antivirus is a software that can protect the end user from harmful attachments, such as viruses, and malicious code, such as worms, which can cause huge business impacts to the organizations. An example is: **Cisco Sophos antivirus technology** (`https://www.cisco.com/c/en/us/products/security/email-security/index.html`).

- **Personal firewall**: A personal firewall goes one step further than antivirus and has the capability to block applications that may cause harm to a particular user. As an extension, it also uses HIPS and HIDS, similar to the network-based intrusion prevention system. An example is: **Windows Firewall** (`https://www.microsoft.com/en-us/safety/pc-security/firewalls-whatis.aspx`), **Windows Defender** (`https://www.microsoft.com/en-us/safety/pc-security/windows-defender.aspx`).

- **Anti-spyware**: Generally, when a user clicks on an advertisement on a webpage, there is high chance that spyware might get installed on the user's machine. This leads to the exploitation of the machine's resources. Anti-spyware helps to mitigate this situation and block the unwanted spyware. An example is: **AVG Anti-Spyware** (`https://www.avg.com/en-ww/homepage#pc`).

Summary

In this chapter, we learned about firewall functions, their rules, and the types of firewalls, such as packet-filtering firewalls, stateful firewalls, application firewalls, and zone-based firewalls. We also looked at IPS, IDS, VPN, and content security in detail.

In the next chapter, we will discuss the concepts of security policies, assets, and other security design considerations.

Understanding Security Policies 3

A security policy for an organization can be defined as a set of rules, formed to secure a company's intellectual property. A security policy describes data flow limitations and restrictions to access by external sources, such as malicious programs, code files, and data. A security policy is used by the company's staff, IT users, and administrators, and so on. A security policy must be enforced on an organization's network so it helps them to protect the network from potential attack and threats.

The following should be considered before creating a security policy:

- A security policy can be formed to balance access and security, and to minimize risk
- A security policy created should not replace the thoughts of the user
- When a potential threat is identified, a security policy must be created in such a way that it can be changed

Also, the policies created should define the following:

- Aims of the policy
- Actions by the policy
- The device on which the policy is configured
- Consequences if there is a failure in the policy

Upon completing this chapter, you will:

- Understand the purpose of a security policy
- Understand the components of a security policy
- Understand risk and the purpose of implementing a risk-analysis mechanism
- Understand vulnerability and how it will affect the network and systems
- Understand threats and their different consequences
- Identify different asset levels of assets
- Understand the importance of countermeasures

- Identify the different types of security zones
- Understand the security mechanisms implemented on the data, management, and control planes
- Understand the different regulatory compliance mechanisms

Need for a security policy

A security policy plays a vital role in the deployment of a network topology. A security policy helps network administrators to prioritize their administration role. A proactive security policy protects the intellectual property of a company from several potential attacks/threats. This also helps the organization to introduce rules and regulations to the user, about how they should make use of their IT equipment.

A security policy helps baseline security terms to reduce the risk of losing an organization's artifacts. It provides an understanding for security administrators as to what steps they should take if there is a security violation, and what the consequences of the violation should be.

Five steps for a security policy

There are important steps to be followed to implement a security policy:

- **Identifying a risk**: Identifying an issue in the current environment involves understanding the use of resources by a legitimate or authorized user. The risk in the network can be identified by the use of good monitoring and reporting tools.
- **Conducting analysis**: A proper and efficient analysis should be conducted to understand the use of secure hardware and software used in the organization. Even *"too much is too bad,"* so administrators should take care to check that a high level of security does not disturb the smooth running of the business.
- **Drafting a language**: A rule or a language should be drafted and the administrator should make sure that the policies are read and agreed to by all the users inside the organization. In the case of enterprise companies, administrators can use a manual or automated tool to help the user sign the policy. There are some tools available on the internet to test the user's knowledge of the policy.
- **Performing a legal review**: A legal review can also be done to understand the perfect nature of the policy created, which will clearly explain the consequences if the user violates it.

- **Deploying an appropriate policy**: An appropriate policy is required to be deployed to explain the preceding factors.

Security policy components

A security policy consists of three important components:

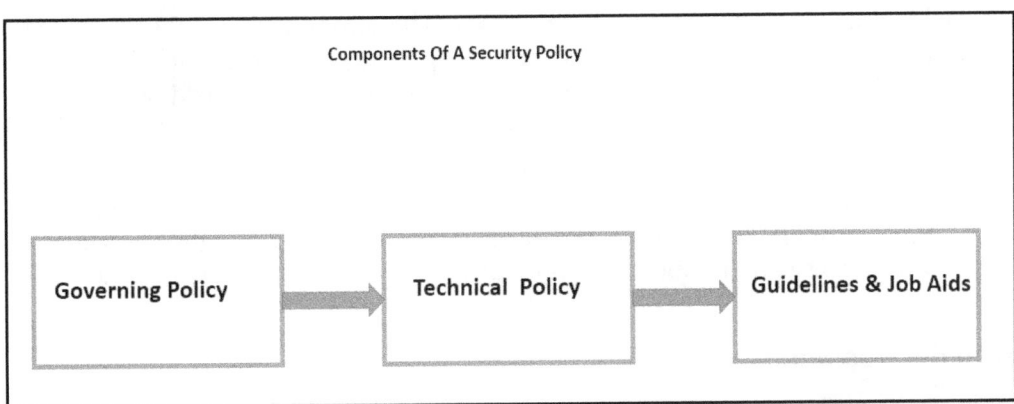

The following is an overview of each of the three components of a security policy:

- **Governing policy:** The governing policy talks about the concept and importance of the security information at a very high level and defines the stance of the organization on security policies. Governing policies are also created in alignment with other company policies, so they support most components of the security policy. The governing policy is mostly read and signed by the management users and it is also agreed to by the end users.
- **Technical policy:** These policies are used in most technical aspects of an IT environment and also cover some of the aspects and topics within the governing policy. Examples of technical policies are policies created for the use of an operating system, application, network, and handheld devices, such as mobiles, PDAs, and tablets.
- **Guidelines and job aids:** Guidelines and job aids are the documentation that offers a step-by-step outline to implement a specific security policy, depending on the analysis. Job aids act as a backup when a user or member of IT leaves the company and none of the intellectual properties are maintained safely. Thus guidelines and job aids help the organization maintain security. An example is a document that explains how to install a software application on an end user machine.

Best example for a security policy – a password policy

A password policy is created to provide the ability for the user to change their account password. To achieve this, a policy should be created that defines a secure password for the systems. The following are the steps to be followed to create a password policy:

- **Set password history**: Password history keeps track of old passwords to ensure they are not repeated.
- **Maximum and minimum password age**: The second factor in the password policy is deciding how long users can keep their passwords before they expire. The intention of this is to make the users change their password periodically.
- **Minimum password length**: This configures the minimum number of characters for a password. Best practice is to have at least 8 to 14 characters.
- **Complexity of the password**: The important factors in configuring complex passwords are that passwords should have a minimum of eight characters, which consist of numbers, symbols, and lowercase and uppercase letters.

How to develop a policy

Developing a policy is an art where multiple blocks are assembled together into a framework. This takes a lot time and several revisions. There are two different approaches used to deploy a policy. One approach is the *top-down* approach and the other is the *bottom-up* approach. Also, make sure that the new policy balances the current practices of the organization. Finally, the policy should be efficient and it should contain mechanisms to protect the organization against different types of potential attack.

Risk

Risk is the possibility of a vulnerability getting exploited. Risk can also be defined as a threat or attack that can cause damage to the business or the organization.

Risk analysis

It is used to forecast any possible risks that may arise within the organization in terms of assets usage, policy weakness, and so on. The impact would be in terms of financial loss, any critical data loss, and other concerns.

Benefits of risk analysis

The following are benefits of risk analysis:

- Business continuity can be smooth
- All stakeholders are well-informed about the risk and its consequences so that they try to take proactive steps in their respective roles against the risk
- From a network security perspective, it basically helps to manage assets and safeguard them from specific attacks

There are two ways in which risk analysis are implemented:

- Quantitative risk
- Qualitative risk

Quantitative risk

This method of analysis tries to put in some numbers so that there are some analytical values to identify the risks involved.

Let's discuss the terminologies involved in the risk calculation:

- **Asset Value (AV)**: The cost of an asset. For example, a router is an asset and the cost to purchase, install, and maintain it would be referred to as the asset value for the router.
- **Exposure Factor (EF)**: The amount the loss could have incurred on an asset. For example, the risk assessment team might check the EF due to a natural catastrophe affecting the server farm and at what percentage.
- **Single Loss Expectancy (SLE)**: The single instance of a threat on an asset and the loss incurred from it.

 Mathematically, SLE is equal to *AV*EF*.

- **Annualized Rate of Occurrence (ARO)**: The rate of the threat occurrence on a per-annum basis.
- **Annualized Loss Expectancy (ALE)**: The loss to the organization due to a threat occurring on a per-annum basis

 Mathematically ALE is equal to *ARO * SLE*.

Qualitative risk

This method of risk analysis is more useful in a scalable environment where assets keep growing. It may be difficult to use the quantitative method here because the calculations never end.

The good thing about qualitative risk analysis is that it can be implemented regardless of the size of the business or the assets that have to be protected. Further, this method has more descriptive scales of risk analysis, such as low, medium, or high, instead of analytical analysis. For these scales to be defined, a tool called the **risk assessment matrix** could be used. The analysis is also done based on the attributes and instincts of the organization's top management; that is, every organization base in their assets level and scaling factor can define the scale of the risk.

Vulnerability

A vulnerability can be defined as a flaw or weakness in the system that an attacker can use to attack the system/network. A vulnerability in the system/network can be caused as a result of a malicious attack, or it can be triggered accidentally because of the failure in the policy implementation. Vulnerabilities can also occur due to the installation of a new software update, due to the installation of unlicensed third-party tools, and so on.

There are two different terms to be remembered: bug and vulnerability. Both of these terms are similar, which explains the weakness in the programming. A bug may not be risky for the product, and the attackers may not use this to attack, but a vulnerability can create a way for the attackers to gain access to the system/network. Thus a vulnerability should be addressed and patched as soon as possible.

The following are some of examples of vulnerability exploits:

- An attacker installs malware to export sensitive data using a buffer overflow weakness. Using that malware, the attacker convinces the user and opens an email message.
- An employee of an organization copies an encrypted, hardened program to a USB drive and tries to crack it at his home.

Typically, network vulnerabilities are classified into three primary types:

- Technology weaknesses
- Configuration weaknesses
- Security policy weaknesses

Weakness in technology

Network technologies naturally have weaknesses that can be exploited by an attacker. Some of them are as follows:

- **TCP/IP protocol**: Protocols, such as HTTP and FTP, are generally not secure because they are not encrypted. Protocols, such as SMTP and SNMP, are insecure because SNMP queries are allowed to flow through a firewall and security systems as the scanners in the remote can acquire the filter rules.
- **Operating system**: Most operating systems have several known security problems.
- **Network equipment**: Weakness in password protection, authentication, and holes in firewalls are some examples of vulnerabilities in network devices.

Weakness in configuration

These are some common errors that network administrators make while configuring the network device:

- **Unfastened user accounts**: Attackers use several snooping tools to snoop the username and passwords exposed insecurely
- **Passwords and system accounts**: If administrators use easily guessed passwords without any special characters, hackers may also use this to exploit the network
- **Misconfiguration in internet services**: If JavaScript is turned on in web browsers, attackers can run an attack on the system
- **Misconfiguration in network equipment**: Configuration mistakes while configuring an access list, routing protocols, and firewall rules, and a lack of encryption can cause vulnerability

Weakness in a security policy

Mistakes in a security policy may increase the chance of vulnerabilities. Some policy weaknesses are as follows:

- **Lack of security policy**: If a particular issue has not been addressed during creation, a security policy can allow hackers to attack.
- **Policy weakness for hardware and software installation**: Installing unapproved or unlicensed third-party software and making unapproved changes in the network topology can allow an attacker to exploit the network.

Understanding vulnerabilities and taking the proper action to protect them are very important steps in mitigating threats to an organization. A vulnerability in the network may occur due to the following reasons:

- A weakness in the network/system
- Flaws in the policy
- Misconfigurations
- Weaknesses in the protocol
- Physical access to network resources
- Human mistakes
- Malicious software

There are some tools that help administrators perform an analysis:

- **Common Vulnerabilities and Exposures (CVE)**: This is a very famous database that provides some of the most common identifiers used to enable the exchange of data between different security products and also helps to evaluate the tools and services of an organization.
- **National Vulnerability Database (NVD)**: This US government database contains several standards of vulnerability management. The NVD also provides vulnerability management, security measurement, and compliance. This contains the checklist of security principles, a list of software weaknesses, and so on.

Threat

Threat is a way of creating a problem on the network by taking advantage of its vulnerability.

A threat can be worrisome for any network administrator in terms of protecting critical documents and assets that are of great importance to the organization. A threat can be initiated by a hacker (a criminal hacker) or accidentally (a natural disaster or a malfunction).

Threat consequence

Threat consequence is a scenario where the security parameters might be violated. This generally occurs due to the effect of a threat action. The different types of threat consequence are disclosure, deception, disruption, and usurpation.

Disclosure

An unauthorized user trying to access a network device in an illegitimate manner is referred to as disclosure.

Threat action – exposure

A threat action where the critical data is directly provided to an unauthorized user.

This includes the following:

- **Deliberate exposure**: Planned way of providing critical data to an unauthorized user
- **Scavenging**: Scanning through leftover data in a system to gain unauthorized access to sensitive data
- **Human error**: This involves human interaction that unintentionally results in a user gaining access to sensitive data
- **Hardware/software error**: An attacker creates the failure of a service or hardware component in the hope of gaining system access

Threat action – interception

A threat action where an unauthorized user directly accesses critical data flowing between authorized sources and destinations. This includes the following:

- **Theft**: Obtaining access to data by stealing media, such as HDD, CD/DVD Drives, and USB.

- **Wiretapping**: Monitoring and storing the data flowing between two endpoints in the communication system with the aim of stealing the information.
- **Man-in-the-Middle (MiTM)**: Intercepts traffic between the sender and the destination. Sensitive information can be obtained.

Threat action – inference

A threat action whereby an unauthorized entity indirectly accesses sensitive information by reasoning characteristics or byproducts of communications. This includes the following:

- **Traffic analysis**: Obtaining information about data by continuously observing the communication characteristics that carry the information
- **Signals analysis**: Monitoring and analyzing the signals emitted from an RF transmitter

Threat action – intrusion

This is a threat action where there is an attack on the computing system with the harmful intention of causing destruction. This includes the following:

- **Trespass**: Obtaining unauthorized access physically to sensitive information by overtaking the network/system's security
- **Penetration**: Obtaining unauthorized logical access to sensitive information by overtaking the network/system's security
- **Reverse-engineering**: Collecting sensitive information by stripping and analyzing the components of the system/network
- **Cryptanalysis**: The technique or process of deciphering an encrypted message without prior knowledge of the secret key

Deception

Deception is the art of falsifying an identity to trick another entity into believing its legitimacy.

Threat action – masquerade

In a masquerade attack, the attacker uses another identity to gain access to a system or network. This type of deception relies primarily on using a fake identity to be successful.

Threat action - falsification

A threat action where an attacker uses misleading or false information to trick an authorized system into believing its authenticity:

- **Substitution**: The replacement of valid data with false data to deceive an authorized entity
- **Insertion**: Introducing false data that serves to deceive an authorized object

Threat action – repudiation

This threat action denies the responsibility of an action.

Disruption

A circumstance or an event that disturbs or stops the ongoing operation of system services and functions.

Threat action – incapacitation

Incapacitation prevents or interrupts a system's operation by disabling a system component:

- **Malicious logic**: Any hardware, firmware, or software that is brought into the network/system with the intention of destroying its functions and resources
- **Physical destruction**: Intentional harm to a physical system causing the overall performance of the system to be affected
- **Human error**: An action that is caused by a human, whether intentional or unintentional, causing a service interruption
- **Hardware or software error**: A faulty component on a system or a faulty software bug causing an interruption in the system's service

Types of threat

There are various different types of threat:

- Physical damage, such as fire, water, and pollution
- Natural events, such as climatic conditions
- Loss of essential services, such as power, AC, and telecommunication

- Compromise of information, such as theft of media including HDD and CD drives
- Failure of technical equipment or software
- Abuse of rights and denial of actions

A threat agent is used to indicate an individual or group that can manifest a threat. It is essential to identify who would want to exploit the assets of a company, and how they might use them against the company.

Threat agents can take one or more of the following actions against an asset:

- **Access**: Simple unauthorized access
- **Misuse**: Unauthorized use of assets
- **Disclose**: The threat agent illicitly discloses sensitive information
- **Modify**: Unauthorized changes to an asset
- **Deny access**: Includes destruction, theft of non-data assets, and so on

The following are examples of the threat communities of the malicious threat landscape many companies face:

- **Internal**:
    - Employees
    - Vendors
    - Partners
- **External**:
    - Hackers
    - Spies
    - Nation-state intelligence services
    - Malware

Asset

An asset is items, property, information, or people that have a high value to the company and should be safeguarded/protected. Every company records all assets in all possible ways. Some companies use a balance sheet to record their assets. An asset can be a tangible asset; this includes physical assets such as buildings, or equipment such as network devices and phones. An asset can also be intangible such as domain names, patents, and software. Let's discuss the classification of assets.

Why classifying of assets is required

The main reason for classifying assets is so network administrators can take the appropriate action depending on the policy created.

For example, an employee of an organization wants to send internal training material to his colleague via email. Categorizing assets either as internal or confidential helps to protect that data.

The main steps that are required for the classification of an asset are as follows:

1. Identifying the asset
2. Asset accountability
3. Creating a plan for classifying the information
4. Implementing the plan created

Identifying the asset

Identification of an asset is essential for the business. After identification, multiple levels of security can be used for secure the assets.

Assets can be broadly classified into the following categories:

- **Information assets**: This is information/data about the organization. It can be in the form of databases, data files, procedures, and so on.
- **Software assets**: This can either be an application software that an organization creates by investing more time, or a system software such as an operating system, development tools, or utilities.
- **Physical assets**: These types of assets are hardware equipment such as workstations, servers, desktops, modems, fax machines, HDD, and power supplies.

Asset accountability

The next step is to create an accountability for the asset. Accountability for physical assets is maintained with the help of an asset register. Generally, every asset is assigned to an asset owner who will be responsible for that particular asset. The value of the asset will be calculated and it is known only to the asset owner. Calculating a true value for the asset is an important task that will help the organization to identify and implement strict measures to protect the asset from danger.

Creating a plan for asset classification

Classifying the asset into different levels helps the organization to protect the asset properly. Assets are classified based on factors such as confidentiality in distributing the asset, the value of the asset, how time-sensitive the asset is, access right provide to access the assets, and whether the asset can be destroyed if necessary.

Governmental classification of assets based on the preceding criteria is as follows:

- **Unclassified**: This is the lowest of the security classifications. This type of data is not too sensitive and it can be shared with anyone.
- **Confidential**: In this classification, the data can be sensitive, private, proprietary, or valuable. Disclosure of these files can cause serious problems for the organization's security.
- **Secret**: This classification is for information that is very restricted. These files are not to be disclosed, if they are, this can have a huge effect on the security.
- **Top Secret**: This is for information/files that need the highest level of protection. These files cannot be disclosed outside the organization.
- **Sensitive**: This classification defined who has access to it Whether is the general public, internet employees in an organization or just the senior management team. These files cannot be disclosed outside the organization.

Implementing the plan

The last step involves classifying the asset in a secure manner. Organizations and administrators should follow certain procedures while sharing asset information, inside or outside the organization. They can also use a classification label for each and every asset, and care should also be taken when using the classification label.

Countermeasures

They are policies and procedures that are used to safeguard the organization from attacks and potential threats. It is an action, steps, process, or a device that helps to mitigate threats or the effects of the threats. It does so by either reducing the weakness of the network or by reducing the threat. Countermeasures can be taken in the form of software or hardware. For example, a machine has been un-patched and the machine is highly vulnerable. If that machine is unplugged from the network and ceases to exchange data with any other device, you have successfully saved your network from vulnerabilities.

After identifying assets and considering the risks involved in securing the asset from threats and attacks, the organization should plan to implement countermeasures to protect any threats and minimize any risks of data loss or theft. These countermeasures can be classified the following types:

- **Administrative**: These are policies, procedures, guidelines, and standards. For example, an **Acceptable Use Policy** (**AUP**) is a policy that is agreed to by all the users in the network.
- **Physical**: Physical security controls prevent unauthorized users from accessing a secure location. For example, using a rack for the servers and wiring closets on the floor. Another example is using redundant power supplies for a system.
- **Logical**: This type of control includes passwords, firewalls, intrusion prevention systems, access lists, and VPNs. These are defined in software as opposed to the physical control, such as a physical lock on a door.

Zones

A zone is a logical area on the network, created by the administrator, in which devices with similar trust levels lie. It contains one or more services and independent information. Zones group all the services and independent information that requires similar security policies together. Each zone is associated to a security level or a policy. Once a zone is created, the interface of a zone is assigned to a particular zone. One device in the network can be part of one or more zones. One interface of a device cannot be part of multiple zones. Further division, of zones are also allowed as they can help to increase the level of security.

Dividing the network into zones increases the level of security inside the organization. For example, WAN-network technologies, such as **MPLS** short for, **Multiprotocol Label Switching** and VPNs, help us to isolate the traffic flow and provide extensions to different security zones. There is a logical zone called **self zone**. The traffic moving to and coming from the self zone is allowed by default, but administrators can configure policies to deny the traffic.

A zone should be created with the following properties:

- It must be created to resist attacks and threats
- The traffic sent over the network should flow across the zones so that they can audit the traffic and take the necessary steps
- Must have traffic-inspecting and traffic-filtering capabilities/policies

Networks can be divided into three zones, as follows:

- **Inside zone/private zone**: This is also referred to as a **trusted zone**. The interfaces are connected to the private network of the organization. It has a high level of trust. The devices in the private zone must be protected from people accessing from the other zones.
- **Outside zone/public zone:** This is referred to as an **untrusted zone**. The interfaces are connected to the internet or other public networks. It has the lowest level of trust. High levels of security policies should be configured to audit the traffic flowing from this zone.
- **Demilitarized zone:** This zone separates the internal, that is, the trusted zone, from the other untrusted zones. Generally, the servers that are facing the internet are located in this zone, as the servers are accessible from the untrusted (internet) zone but not from the trusted (internal) zone, thus providing an additional layer of security. Some special policies are required to allow selected traffic to access this zone.

The following diagram shows the zones in the organization:

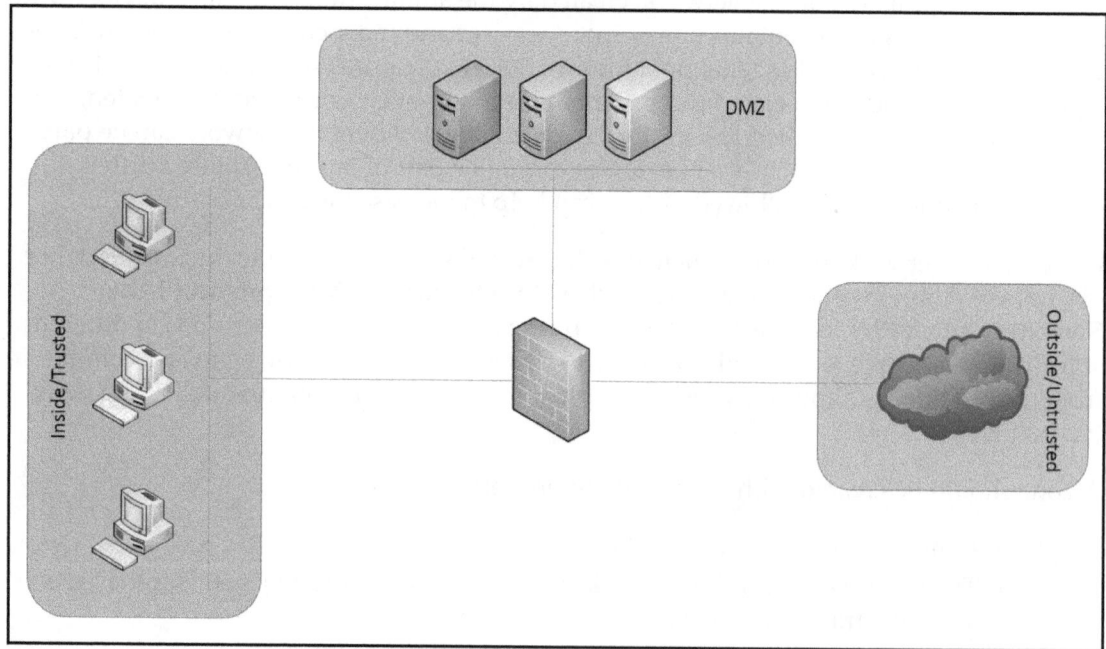

Planes

This is an area of operation that carries different types of traffic. This is a integral part of the network that helps process the traffic. The planes are implemented in the firmware of the network devices. An administrator can configure policies to prioritize the traffic flowing. There are three distinct planes:

- Data plane
- Control plane
- Management plane

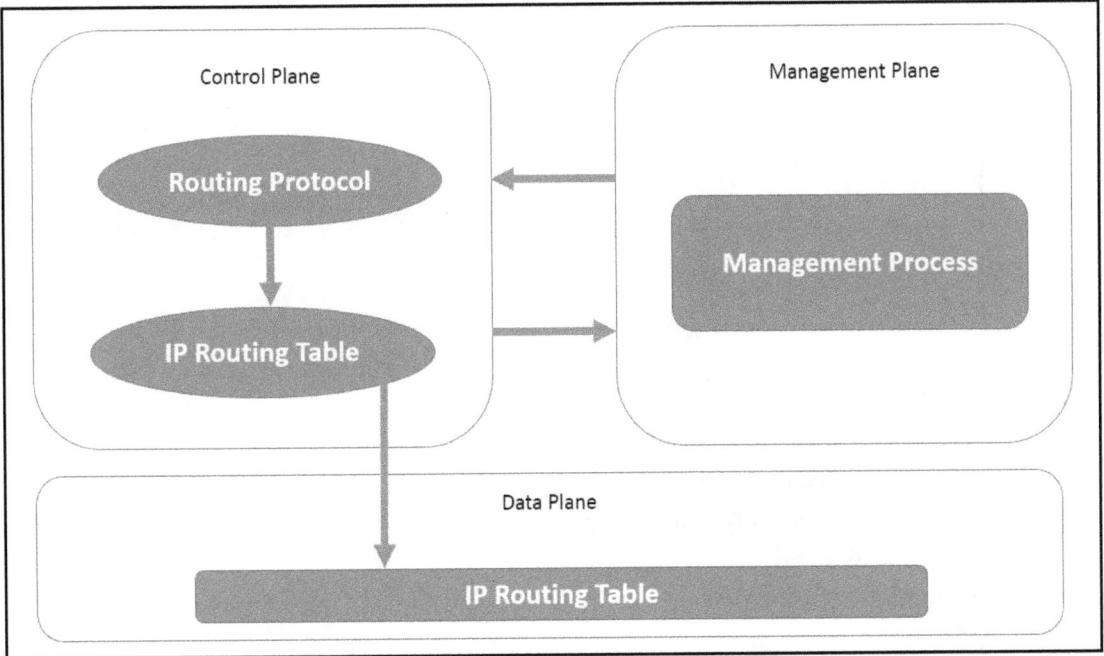

Data plane

This plane is referred to as the **user plane** or the forwarding plane. It is the part of the network through which the packets are sent and received. This takes care of packet flow. Policies created to affect user traffic are applied to this layer. The data plane is responsible for forwarding the traffic to the next hop using the information provided by the other planes:

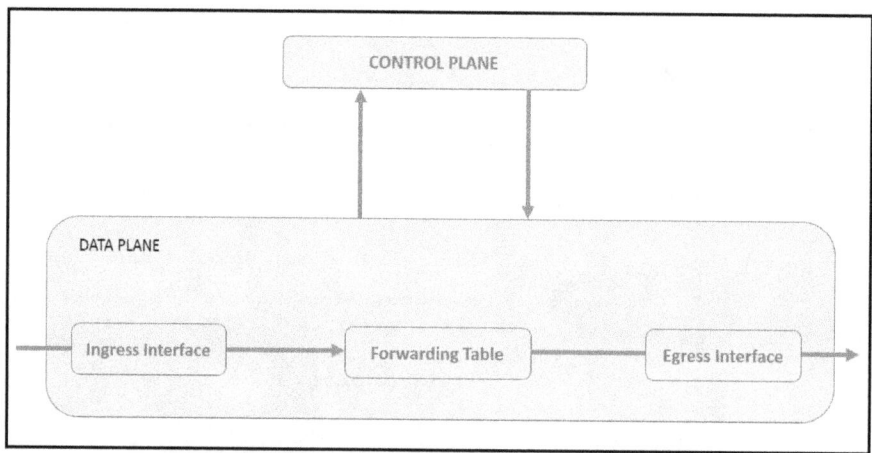

It also takes care of other activities such as:

- Creation and maintenance of NAT table
- Dynamic MAC address learning
- NetFlow data accountability
- Logging ACLs
- Error signaling (ICMP)

In case a data plane fails, traffic may not be forwarded to the correct destination.

Control plane

This is the part of the network that takes care of carrying the signaling traffic and routing operations in a router using control packets. The control packets begin from a router or are destined for a router. A routing table has the details of the destination address and the outgoing interfaces; the logic of the control plane defines how certain packets are to be discarded or offered with high-quality service.

Depending on the router implementation and configuration, the control plane creates a separate **forwarding information base** (**FIB**), but the data plane uses the FIB to look up and send the packets at a high speed. The following diagram shows the operation of the control plane:

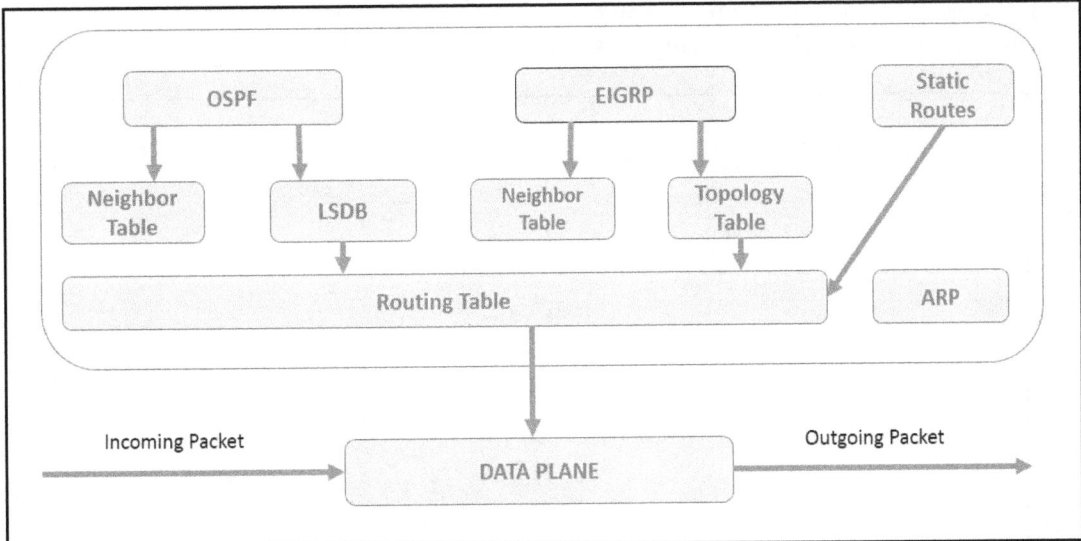

It also takes care of other activities such as:

- Interface state management (PPP, LACP)
- Connectivity management
- Device discovery—Neighbor (hello mechanisms)
- Device reachability information
- Provisioning services

In the event there is a failure in the control plane, the router will lose the ability to learn the routing information dynamically.

Management plane

This offers configuration, monitoring, and management services to all layers in the networking stack and other parts of the device. The difference, when compared to the control plane, is that the control plane is concerned with the FIB and routing table computation, and the management plane takes care of only the configuration of IP subnets and routing protocols. The following diagram shows the management plane:

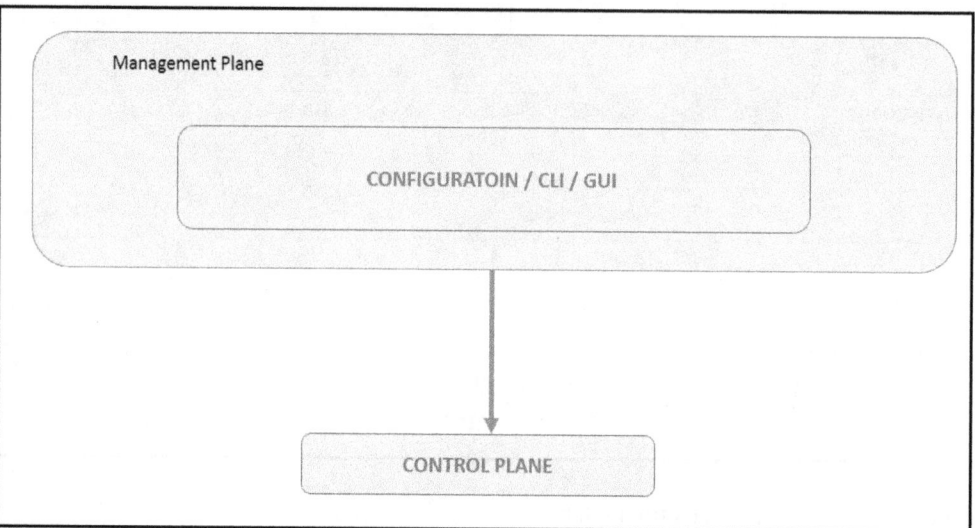

Regulatory compliance

This is the set of hierarchical systems whose job is to define best practices for any organization to comply with security policies and regulations; it also explains the consequences for those organizations that fail to comply with the standards.

We will go through some of the well-known regulatory compliance standards. These are used more in the United States than in other countries. In the rest of the world, similar standards may exist that cater to the needs of the organization's security regulations.

Payment Card Industry Data Security Standard (PCI DSS)

This standard is used along with global credit card organizations to reduce the amount of fraud in credit/debit card transactions. An audit is done annually to validate compliance in these organizations.

This body has a broadly-defined set of policies and procedures that can be used to optimize credit and debit card transactions in a secured manner and protect cardholders from unauthorized organizations or individuals who want to misuse their personal information.

This PCI follows a three-step process:

- **Assess**: In the first step, the assets and the business processes involving card payments are verified for any sort of weakness or vulnerabilities.
- **Remediate**: The second step involves covering up the weakness or vulnerabilities in the business processes.
- **Report**: This involve the complete analysis of the issues, after which they are submitted as a report to the organization, in the form of an audit report. Major cards, such as VISA and MasterCard, comply with these regulations to validate their systems and processes.

Health Insurance Portability and Accountability Act (HIPAA)

Any e-data with reference to patients' health details and other related information is managed and secured using the recommendations provided by this regulatory body.

This act includes five sections:

- **Title 1**: This section defines health insurance for people who have been removed from their jobs
- **Title 2**: This is used by the US Department of Health and Human Services to develop standards for healthcare transactions through e-commerce
- **Title 3**: This section manages tax-related details for healthcare
- **Title 4**: This section defines the health policy creation or changes for people who look for continued healthcare coverage
- **Title 5**: This defines guidelines for providing company insurance to US citizens who have lost their citizenship due to income tax issues

Sarbanes-Oxley Act (SOX)

This act was developed to support shareholders and the public in issues arising in accounting, and also to improve the efficiency of the organization's disclosures.

Federal Information Security Management Act (FISMA)

This act was implemented to protect government information, operations and assets against natural or man-made threats.

FISMA defines nine steps for ensuring compliance:

1. Define the information under a class that needs to be protected
2. Define the baseline controls
3. Define a risk-assessment procedure and use it to manipulate the controls if needed
4. Create a system security plan and define the controls for it
5. Implement the controls on the systems
6. Verify the efficiency of the security controls
7. Find the level of risk for business process
8. Author the systems
9. Monitor the controls on a periodic basis

GLBA

This stands for the **Gramm–Leach–Bliley Act (GLBA)**. This act was implemented to remove the fear from persons who have or is going to invest in smaller financial companies who are merging with larger organizations, and to explain their practices of information-sharing with customers and protecting critical data.

Most of the banking and insurance companies opted for this act, and the reason was that individuals invest more when an organization is doing well, but they invest into their savings accounts when the economy take a turn for the worse. With the help of this act, they were able to perform both savings and investments at the same financial institution, which would be able to do well in both good and poor economic situations.

Prior to this act, most of the organizations were already providing both savings and investment opportunities to their customers.

PIPED Act

This is a Canadian law that relates to data privacy. This is referred to as the **Personal Information Protection and Electronic Documentation Act** (**PIPEDA** or **PIPED Act**). This law provides regulations, for private companies, about the use and disclosure **Public Interest Immunity** (**PII**) in the course of business. This law also specifies how to use and handle electronic documents.

The law requires organizations:

- Should ask for consent before collecting information and they should also explain why they require this information and how it will be used.
- Should not use the collected personal information other than that for which users have consented. They are supposed to use the personal information reasonably and appropriately.
- Should state a responsible point of contact for protecting all the personal information.
- Should specify the security measures followed to protect the information.
- Should collect all personal information by lawful procedures.

The law gives individuals the right to:

- Understand the reasons why the organization collects their personal information
- Understand how the organization is collecting their personal Information

Data Protection Directive

The **Data Protection Directive** is a standard/law defined by the European Union, adopted in 1995, which regulates the collection, maintenance, and processing of personal information.

Digital Millennium Copyright Act (DMCA)

This act criminalizes the misuse and infringement of copyright to intellectual property on the internet.

Safe Harbor Act

This act handles the regulation of the export and handling of personal data in of European citizens' American companies.

Summary

In this chapter, we covered security policies that protect the assets and the objectives of the business, and the different components of a security policy, which are governing policy, technical policy, and guidelines and job aids. We then covered risks, vulnerabilities, threats, assets, countermeasures, zones, network equipment, and regulatory compliance.

In the next chapter, we will learn about cryptography and its types, services offered by cryptography, different types of ciphers, and different types of encryption algorithms.

Deep Diving into Cryptography

4

As technology advances to assist us in the modern world, so does the rise of new cyber threats. Some of these threats focus on stealing another person's **personal identifiable information** (**PII**) such as their identity, address, medical information, or even their credit card details as a user is conducting an online transaction on an e-commerce website. As security professionals, we try to ensure that our clients' data is not intercepted or leaked in any way. We use cryptographic methods to ensure the confidentiality of the data, whether it's data at rest, data in motion, or data in use.

In this chapter, we'll take a look at the following topics:

- An overview of cryptography
- Types of cipher
- Differences between symmetric and asymmetric algorithms
- Encryption algorithms
- Hashing algorithms
- Cryptographic systems
- Overview of the **Public Key Infrastructure** (**PKI**)

Let's begin!

What is cryptography?

The history of cryptography dates back to ancient times when messages were sent between two parties in a secure manner. In the modern age of technology, information security plays a vital role in everyday life, from entering your login information on a Facebook website to just chatting on the WhatsApp messenger platform.

Have you ever wondered whether, while chatting with someone on WhatsApp, the messages you send and receive could be intercepted and read by another person who is not authorized to view them? In the past, WhatsApp did not provide an end-to-end encryption service, which means that, if a malicious user were performing a **Man-in-the-Middle** (**MITM**) attack or even sniffing the traffic between the victim and the other person, they could see all the messages that were exchanged between the two parties in plain text. Some people think that they have *nothing* to hide when they send a message across an insecure platform, but what we have to remember is that time-sensitive information may be sent over, whether it's a password, telephone number, email address, residential address, or even something which is private to a user.

 WhatsApp now supports end-to-end encryption. Check `https://www.whatsapp.com/security/` for further details.

With cryptography, organizations are now able to protect their data and their customers' data securely using the appropriate algorithms and technologies. An example of cryptographic technology is the use of a **Virtual Private Network** (**VPN**) for connecting branch sites together over an unsecure network such as the internet, a remote access VPN for a teleworker employee, or even a field engineer who needs to access the corporate network while not in the office at the time.

Cryptography is the scrambling of data that is to be sent over an unsecure channel. Cryptography focuses on the confidentiality of data in different states: data at rest, data in motion, and data in use.

- **Data at rest**: Data at rest is data that's not in use and resides on a storage device such as a hard drive, CD/DVD ROM, flash/thumb drive, and so on. In this state, the data is dormant and encryption can be applied to ensure it's kept private. Even if it's stolen or lost, confidentiality is still maintained.
- **Data in motion**: Data in motion or data in transit is when the data is moving between devices. In this state, it's more vulnerable to cyberattacks such as MITM and sniffing. Technologies such as a VPN assist by ensuring a secure channel is used to transport the data over the untrusted or unsecure network connection. The use of **Secure Sockets Layer** (**SSL**)/**Transport Layer Security** (**TLS**) can secure data between a user's computer browser and a website.
- **Data in use**: Data is in its most vulnerable state as it is unencrypted and is currently being accessed by a user or multiple users at the same time. Because it's unencrypted, it's exposed to any type of cyber attack or threat.

Objectives of cryptography

In this section, we'll take a look at the four objectives of cryptography.

Confidentiality

It is also referred to as the privacy or secrecy of information. It maintains information and keeps it safe from unauthorized people. This can be attained through various means, such as by physical methods or through mathematical algorithms. Confidentiality in cryptography can be achieved by using scrambled text, cipher text, or encrypted text.

Data integrity

This helps to identify the alteration of data services. Data or information may get altered due to attacks by unauthorized people. This service should make sure that the information received by the receiver has not been altered or changed by any means while the information is in transit. Integrity in cryptography is achieved by using hashing.

Authentication

This helps to identify the source of the originator and other fields such as the date and time of creation of the information. This confirms that the receiver of the information is the one who is identified and verified by the sender. Authentication works based on credentials or keys. Only if the credentials match each other will the user who is accessing the file be authorized/allowed to access the information. Authentication can be enabled with the help of pre-shared private and public keys.

Non-repudiation

Non-repudiation is when you provide reassurance that an action has taken place. As a typical example, let's say it's lunchtime and you decide to head out of your office to buy lunch at a nearby restaurant. When you pay for your meal, the cashier issues you a receipt. The receipt usually contains the time, location, items purchased, the person who received the payment, and so on. The receipt/bill ensures and proves that the transaction took place.

Terminologies

During the course of this chapter, we will be using certain terms which you may be a bit unfamiliar with or even heard about. Here, we are going to provide a short list of terms and their meanings:

- **Message Digest 5 (MD5).**
- **Secure Hashing Algorithm (SHA).**
- **Advanced Encryption Standard (AES).**
- **Data Encryption Standard (DES).**
- **Triple Data Encryption Standard (3DES).**
- **Rivest Cipher 4 (RC4).**
- **Rivest, Shamir, and Adleman (RSA).** They are the creators of the RSA encryption technology.
- **Virtual Private Network (VPN).**
- **Secure Sockets Layer (SSL)** used to secure data over TCP connections.
- **Transport Layer Security (TLS)** is the successor to SSL and also secures TCP connections.
- **Hypertext Transfer Protocol Secure (HTTP).**
- **Internet Protocol Security (IPSec).**

Types of encryption

Here, we will discuss the main differences between symmetric and asymmetric encryption algorithms.

Symmetric encryption

Let's observe the following diagram. There are two devices wanting to exchange a message over an unsecure network such as the internet. Both **Bob** and **Alice** are worried that someone in between their machines may be monitoring their traffic and that their privacy is at risk:

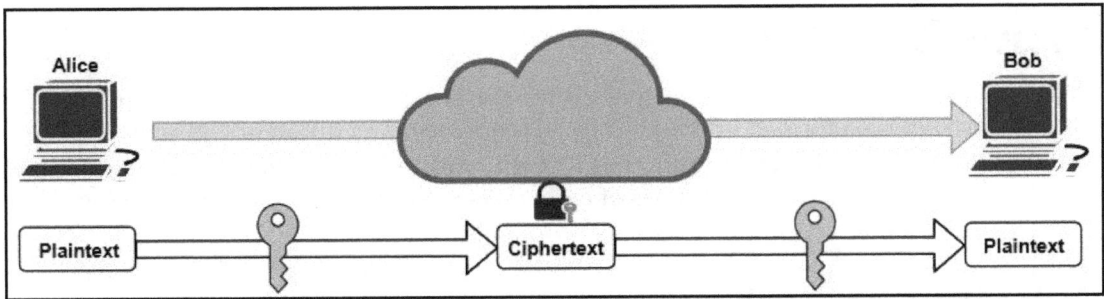

With symmetric encryption, **Alice** would use a secret key to encrypt or scramble her message for **Bob**. When **Bob** receives the **Ciphertext** (encrypted message), he would use the same secret key as **Alice** to decrypt the **Ciphertext** to obtain the actual message.

To describe symmetric encryption simply, this method uses the same key (secret) to encrypt and decrypt a message. If the key is lost or stolen, the message is vulnerable or compromised.

Asymmetric encryption

With asymmetric encryption, the main difference is that **Alice** would use a secret key to encrypt the message before sending it to **Bob**. When **Bob** receives the **Ciphertext**, he would use a different key to decrypt the message and read its contents:

In asymmetric encryption, two separate keys are used, one for the data encryption and another for the decryption. Therefore, if one of the keys is lost or stolen, the message is not compromised.

Types of cipher

What is a cipher? To put it simply, a cipher is the method in which data is converted from plaintext to ciphertext format. In cryptography, there are many different methods. Each method is known as a **cipher suite** and has its own advantages and disadvantages. In this section, we'll discuss the different types of ciphers used to encode and decode messages.

Substitution cipher

In a substitution cipher, also known as a **Caesar Cipher**, the secret key is the replacement of certain or all of the plaintext with another character, thus creating the ciphertext. For example, let's say you are writing the sentence, *"the quick brown fox jumps over the lazy dog."* We, as humans, will see it in its natural form, plaintext. If we were to use a key such as $A=Z$, $B=Y$, $C=X$ and so on, we would have the following:

Normal Sequence	A	B	C	D	E	F	G	H	I	J	K	L	M
Key	Z	Y	X	W	V	U	T	S	R	Q	P	O	N

Normal Sequence	N	O	P	Q	R	S	T	U	V	W	X	Y	Z
Key	M	L	K	J	I	H	G	F	E	D	C	B	A

If we encrypt the message: `the quick brown fox jumps over the lazy dog`, the ciphertext will result in: `gsv jfrxp yildm ulc qfnkh levi gsv ozab wlt`. Reversing the ciphertext using the preceding chart will result in the plaintext.

 The key is anything you choose. In the previous example, I decided the key would be the alphabet in reverse.

Transposition cipher

A transposition cipher simply manipulates the order or sequence of the message instead of trying to hide the message itself. There are many different transposition methods, one of which is known as **columnar transposition**. This variation uses the words of the message without spaces, where the width of the column itself is a fixed size and if there are any spaces remaining at the end of the last row, random characters are added to ensure the rows and columns are equal.

An example of columnar transposition while using the message `the quick brown fox jumps over the lazy dog` would result in the following:

```
thequi
ckbrow
nfoxju
mpsove
rthela
zydogz
```

Another version of a transposition cipher is the **rail fence cipher**. This version hides some of the characters of a message. Once again, we'll use the sentence `the quick brown fox jumps over the lazy dog` to demonstrate how the rail fence cipher works. The following is the result of the rail fence cipher:

```
t . . . u . . . b . . . n . . . j . . . s . . . r . . . l . . . d . .
```

Notice that there is a consistent thread where three characters are missing and there are no spaces between words. Each period (.) represents that a character is missing.

Block ciphers

Block ciphers encrypt a fixed size (block) of data at a time. If you're sending a message and your computer is using a block cipher encryption algorithm, it would create blocks of a fixed size such as 64-bits or even 128-bits and encrypt all the data inside each block. Some examples of block cipher algorithms are: Data Encryption Standard, Triple Data Encryption Standard, and Advanced Encryption Standard, to name just a few.

Stream ciphers

In a stream cipher, the algorithm encrypts each bit individually, therefore creating a continuous stream. An example of a stream cipher encryption algorithm is the **Rivest Cipher 4 (RC4)** cipher suite.

Key

A key, also referred to as the secret or even the secret key, is used to reorder the contents of a ciphertext back to its original form. A simple analogy we can use is a room with a single deadbolt lock. To secure the contents of the room, we would need to lock the door using a specific key. This would be considered to be the encryption aspect. Once the room is locked, only people with the appropriate key can unlock the room to view its contents. This would be considered decryption.

Encryption algorithms

Furthering our discussion, we will dive a little bit deeper into understanding the different algorithms and how they are used to provide confidentiality.

Data Encryption Standard

The **Data Encryption Standard** (**DES**) is a **symmetric** encryption algorithm which uses the same key to both encrypt and decrypt data. It does this by encrypting a **block of 64-bits** in size using a **56-bit key**. The size of the key makes a difference in the strength of the encryption itself; in this case, a 56-bit key is used per block. The smaller the key, the weaker and more vulnerable the encryption/algorithm is to being deciphered by a hacker.

Triple Data Encryption Standard (3DES)

The successor to the DES algorithm is the **Triple DES** (**3DES**), and this upgrade applies the DES three times to messages. The 3DES algorithm uses key sizes of *56-bits*, *112-bits*, and *168-bits*, respectively. However, the block size still remains the same, *56-bits*. To further explain how 3DES works, its uses a key to encrypt the plaintext, and the result will be ciphetext1, which is **round 1**. Next, it takes ciphertext1 and applies the algorithm again, resulting in ciphertext2; this is **round 2**. Once more, it runs the algorithm but on ciphertext2, giving the output as ciphertext3; this is the third round. The final output of the entire 3DES algorithm is ciphertext3.

Advanced Encryption Standard (AES)

The **Advanced Encryption Standard** (**AES**) has become the de facto for symmetric encryption standards due to its very strong encryption key sizes and its ability to encrypt large blocks of data at a time. AES uses various key sizes, and they are: *128-bits, 192-bits,* and *256-bits*, and the block size is *128-bits*.

Rivest Cipher 4

Rivest Cipher 4 (**RC4**) encrypts data using various key sizes ranging from *40-bits to 2,048-bits* in length. This is a stream cipher which encrypts each bit of data, unlike the block cipher method. Even though RC4 is capable of using large encryption keys to secure the data, the algorithm itself has vulnerabilities, making it insecure.

RSA (Rivest, Shamir, Adleman)

RSA was developed by Ron Rivest, Adi Shamir, and Leonard Adleman. Using the first letters of their last names, they derived RSA. This particular algorithm uses public key cryptography, which means that two different keys are used to encrypt and decrypt data. Two main characteristics of RSA are its ability to provide data confidentiality through the use of encryption techniques, and authentication across the internet. RSA uses variable key sizes ranging from *512-bits to 2,048-bits*, however a minimum key size of 1024-bits should be maintained. This algorithm falls under the Asymmetric encryption algorithm portfolio. Later in this chapter, we'll discuss a topic which will provide a real-world scenario for using RSA in a **Public Key Infrastructure** (**PKI**).

Hashing algorithms

As mentioned previously, in the computing world it a bit challenging for us humans to prove the integrity of a message. We use hashing algorithms to assist us in determining the integrity of a message. In this section, we're going to take a look at the two main hashing algorithms being used today, which are MD5 and SHA:

Why do we need to validate the integrity of a message? Let's assume that there are two people, **Bob** and **Alice**. They would both like to communicate over a network. **Alice** wants to send **Bob** a message, but **Bob** is also concerned that the message may be altered before it arrives at his end. To help **Bob** determine if the message was altered during transmission or not, **Alice** would need to create a cryptographic hash of the message and send both the message and the hash values to **Bob**:

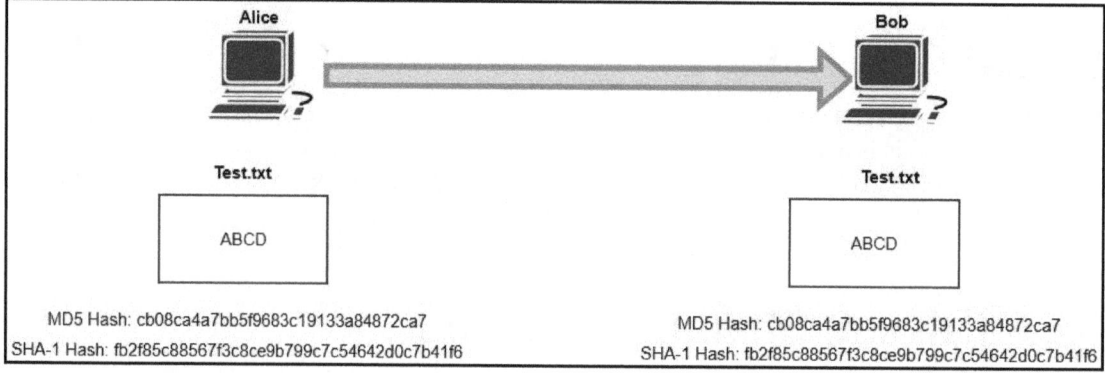

When **Bob** receives the message, **Bob** also creates a cryptographic hash of the message and compares it with the hash from **Alice**.

Message Digest 5 (MD5)

Message Digest 5 (MD5) creates a fixed size cryptographic string which represents the message. This output is known as digest. The resulting hash/digest is one-way and cannot be reversed. It takes the message, applies the MD5 algorithm, and outputs a 128-bit value. This digest is sent together with the message to its intended destination.

 MD5 contains collision vulnerabilities. A collision vulnerability/attack is where two or more entirely different files produce the same hash/digest. An MD5 collision occurred in 2008.

Secure Hashing Algorithm (SHA)

The **Secure Hashing Algorithm** (**SHA**) is another one-way hashing algorithm which was published by the National Institute of Standards and Technology as a U.S. Federal Information Processing Standard. Unlike MD5, SHA creates a 160-bit digest.

 In 2017, Google researchers demonstrated a SHA-1 collision.

Hashed Message Authentication Code (HMAC)

The **Hashed Message Authentication Code** (**HMAC**) is an additional layer of security which can be added during the hashing process. This actually increases the security and integrity of the hash/digest, making it much more difficult to compromise. By adding an HMAC key, the output of the hash/digest changes completely compared to using only either MD5 or the SHA.

Using a tool named *HashCalc* (`https://www.slavasoft.com/hashcalc`), we can compute the hashes of strings of data or even a file. HashCalc supports many hashing algorithms. If we generate the MD5 and SHA1 hashes for a string of text, the quick brown fox jumps over the lazy dog, we will get the following output:

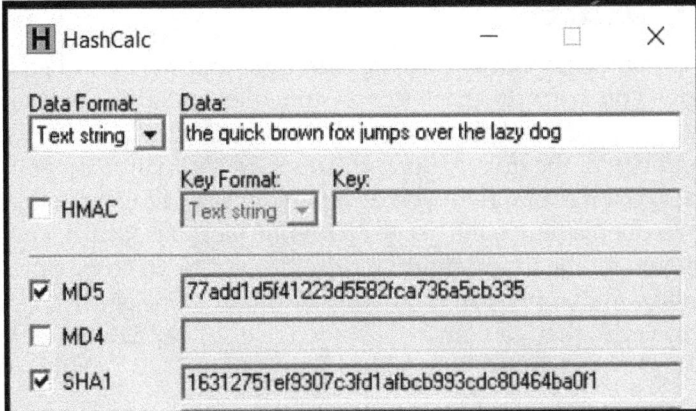

If we were to add an HMAC key, `ccnasecurity`, to the same string of text, the output would be as follows:

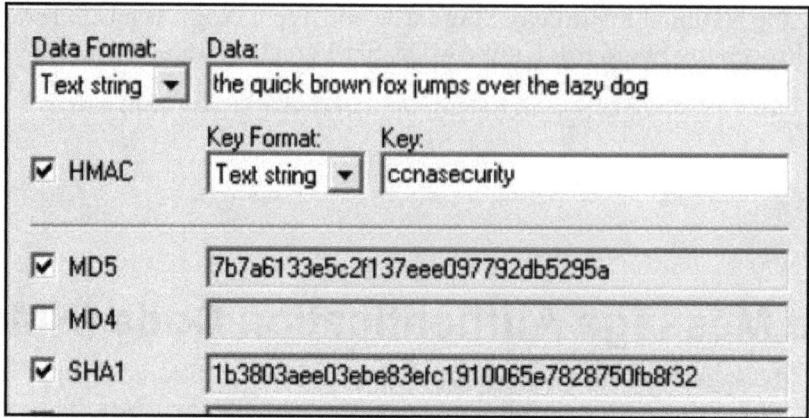

Cryptographic systems

In this section, we'll discuss the overview of the digital signature and its functionality with the **Secure Sockets Layer (SSL)** and the **Transport Layer Security (TLS)**.

Digital signature

You may be asking yourself, what is a digital signature and why do I need one? To get started, let's imagine you are writing a letter to someone, and at the end of the letter, you close it off with your regards and apply your signature. The purpose of your signature is to validate the authenticity of the document and to ensure it's written by you. The concept of a signature is the idea that it's unique to you as a person. We can use another analogy. Let's assume you want to open a new bank account at your local bank, and so you decide to visit the nearest branch, where the representative provides you with some documents that you are required to review and apply your signature to on each one accordingly. The purpose of your signature is to verify that you (and not someone else) validated the information on the documents.

This brings us to why we have or use a digital signature. As mentioned previously, integrity plays an important role in cryptography. When someone is sending a digital document or data across a network, we would like to give reassurance to the receiver of the document or data that it actually originated from us. One simple example is that Alice wants to send an email message to Bob. Alice can write the email and apply her digital signature to the message itself and send it to Bob. On the receiving end, Bob would be able to read the message, and Bob could also use the received signature to validate the actual sender and verify that the message was actually written by Alice.

The digital signature is combined with the PKI. PKI validates the integrity and authenticity of someone's identity on the internet. Later in this chapter, we will discuss the Public Key Infrastructure in further detail.

A digital signature can be used to prevent forgery.

Secure Sockets Layer (SSL)

The SSL is a security standard used to provide confidentiality by using encryption algorithms to create a secure link between a web server and a client web browser. The secure link will ensure all traffic between the web server and the browser remains private from prying eyes. With the advancement of the internet and e-commerce, it's much easier and convenient to purchase goods and shop online using a MasterCard or VISA card accordingly. However, can we tell for certain whether someone is sniffing the traffic between our computer and the web browser? What if when you enter your credit card number and CVV code on the checkout page of an e-commerce website, a malicious user captures it and decides to exceed your card's limit? Therefore, information security is quite important to ensure that e-commerce website owners provide a secure environment for us, the customers. They can install SSL digital certificates on their website to establish the encrypted channel for data transfer across the internet.

When a SSL digital certificate is generated, two keys are created, a public key and a private key. The public key is given to anyone who wants to communicate to the web server and the private key is kept on the web server.

There are three versions of SSL: SSL 1.0, 2.0, and 3.0. Each version was considered to be better than the last; however in 1996 a lot of vulnerabilities were discovered in SSL 3.0.

There are many vendors which provide SSL/TLS certificates:

- Symantec
- Comodo
- GoDaddy
- Entrust
- Let's Encrypt

Transport Layer Security

TLS is the successor to SSL. The use of the Secure Sockets Layer is not recommended according to the **Internet Engineering Task Force** (**IETF**). Since SSL 3.0 is known for its vulnerabilities, Transport Layer Security 1.0 was created back in 1999. Currently, there is TLS 1.0, 1.1, 1.2, and 1.3. The TLS protocols focus on providing confidentiality and integrity by applying both encryption and hashing techniques to the data being sent across the communication channel.

Pretty Good Privacy

The issue with digital privacy was a major concern for all, even back in the 1990s. A guy by the name of Phil Zimmermann created an encryption and authentication program called **Pretty Good Privacy** (**PGP**). This allows a user to encrypt, decrypt, and sign messages, whether a file or even an email message (text).

How does PGP ensure the confidentiality and integrity of a message? Earlier in the chapter, we used two fictional characters, Alice and Bob. Once again, we'll create another analogy to further explain and describe how PGP secures our message between one device to another.

Let's assume Alice wants to send a message to Bob using an email messaging system. However, there's sensitive/confidential data in part of the body of the email message. This is a major concern for both Alice and Bob. Let's start the process:

1. **Alice** writes the message, and she uses **Bob**'s public key to encrypt the message, creating ciphertext.
2. **Alice** send the ciphertext over to **Bob**:

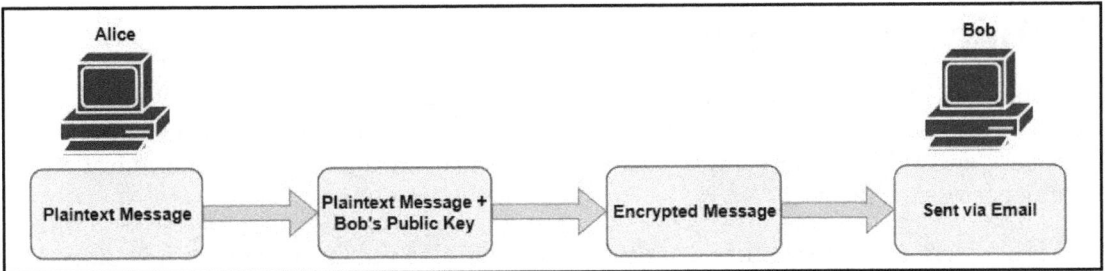

3. **Bob** receives the ciphertext and uses his private key to decrypt and read the message from **Alice**:

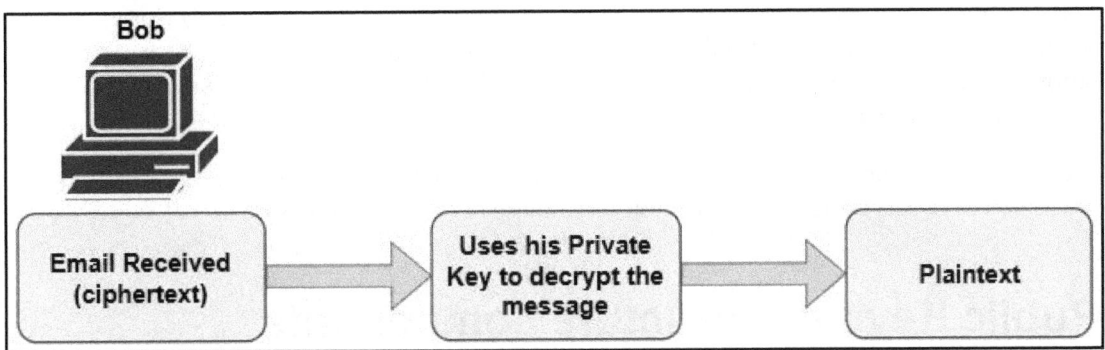

4. In return, if **Bob** wants to send **Alice** a message, **Bob** would use **Alice**'s public key to encrypt the message and send it.
5. Only **Alice**'s private key would be able to decrypt the message that **Bob** had sent.

In a public key system, two different keys are generated, a public key and private key. Only these key pairs can encrypt and decrypt messages between them. The public key is used to encrypt and the private key is used to decrypt.

Some uses of Pretty Good Privacy are as follows:

- Authentication of digital certificates
- Encryption and decryption of emails and files

 https://keybase.io/ provides PGP keys to anyone who would like to get started using PGP for digital signing and encryption.

Public Key Infrastructure

Sometimes, while doing research or even reading a document or book on cryptography, you'll notice that Public Key Infrastructure is mentioned. In this section, we'll be discussing the overview of PKI and its components to provide a secure and trusted communication channel across the internet.

PKI is a system of processes that work together to provide public key encryption and a digital signature over the internet. PKI manages and maintains the trustworthiness of a network. One main characteristic of PKI is its usage of public keys. If we recall from the previous section, if two devices want to communicate with each other, they must exchange their public keys with each other. In the previous example, we mentioned that Alice used Bob's public key to encrypt an email message before sending it to Bob. If Bob wants to securely communicate with Alice, he would use Alice's public key to encrypt the data before sending it. In return, both Alice and Bob will use their own private keys respectively to decrypt messages received on their end.

PKI makes very good use of both the public key (used for encrypting data) and the private key (used for decrypting data) and took advantage of the RSA algorithm.

Public Key Infrastructure components

In this section, we'll discuss the components of PKI. Let's begin.

Certificate Authority

The **Certificate Authority** (**CA**) is the device which issues and verifies digital certificates.

Some examples of certificate authorities are:

- GoDaddy
- Symantec
- Comodo
- Entrust
- Let's Encrypt

Certificate management system

The certificate management system generates, distributes, and stores the digital certificates.

Digital certificate

A digital certificate validates the ownership of a public key. In other words, it establishes the credentials of a person who is doing an online transaction between the client's web browser and the website. These certificates are formatted using the X.509 standard.

X.509

The X.509 standard is used to define a format for public key certificates. The following is the structure currently being used today:

- Certificate
  - Version Number
  - Serial Number
  - Signature Algorithm ID
  - Issuer Name
  - Validity period
    - Not Before
    - Not After
  - Subject name
  - Subject Public Key Info
    - Public Key Algorithm
    - Subject Public Key
  - Issuer Unique Identifier (optional)
  - Subject Unique Identifier (optional)
  - Extensions (optional)
    - ...
- Certificate Signature Algorithm
- Certificate Signature

The following is a digital certificate from the `https://www.cisco.com/` website:

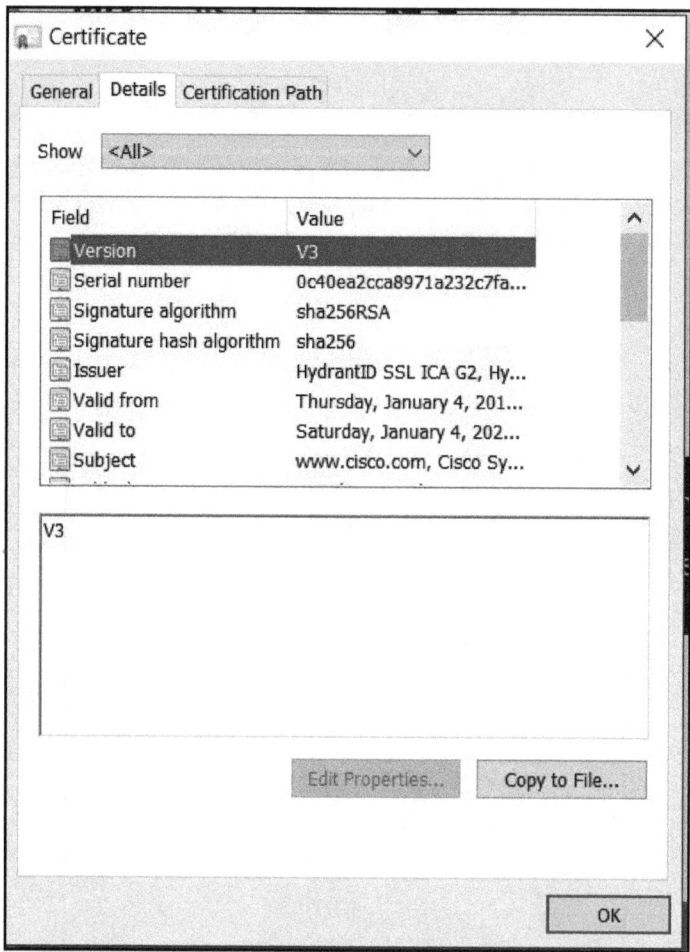

Registration Authority (RA)

The **Registration Authority** (**RA**) handles the verification of the person or device(s) who is requesting the digital certificate. The registration authority also has the ability to handle verification of the digital certificate if the actual CA is offline.

Putting the components of PKI together

Here, we will list the steps that take place when a user attempts to establish a secure channel to a website across the internet and verify the website's identity:

1. A user applies to the **Registration Authority** (**RA**) to issue a certificate.
2. The registration authority sends a request for issuing the certificate to the actual certificate authority. The registration authority's job, in this case, is to handle the verification of the applicant.
3. The certificate authority provides a public key certificate to the user.
4. The certificate authority sends an update to the **Validation Authority** (**VA**).
5. In the meantime, the user sends a message with the digital signature and a copy of the public key certificate.
6. The website owner who the user wants to communicate with sends their public key certificate of the user to the validation authority.
7. The validation authority determines the result.

Summary

In this chapter, we took a look at the importance of cryptography and its components, different types of cipher, and their characteristics, together with encryption algorithms, hashing algorithms, and cryptographic systems.

In the next chapter, we'll take a look at implementing the AAA framework.

5
Implementing the AAA Framework

The acronym AAA stands for authentication, authorization, and accounting. The AAA framework can be implemented on a Cisco IOS device to provide unified management of access privileges and logs:

- **Authentication**: This process ensures that when a user enters a username and password combination that it is validated if the user says who they are before access is granted on the system.
- **Authorization**: After the authentication phase is completed, the second step is to assign privileges to the user's account. The authorization aspects provides privileges for the user and determines what the user can or cannot do on the system.
- **Accounting**: This is about tracing and tracking the user once he/she logs into the system. Tracking is necessary for the administrator to understand the security measures taken and to perform investigation when a threat or an attack occurs.

The benefits of AAA are that it:

- Provides increased availability and scalability
- Increases control and flexibility
- Provides standard authentication methods

AAA is used to identify and verify the user on the management plane of the device. The use of AAA is that it creates a local database for usernames and passwords by means of running a configuration. If the administrators wants to allow multiple users to access the devices in the network, a centralized database which lists authorized users is created to authenticate the users. This is what an access control server also performs. A list of allowed and authorized usernames and passwords are configured on the ACS server and configure the devices that should refer to any of its decisions about authentication or authorization on the ACS server.

AAA allows a network device that a user is requesting to access management via **TACACS** (short for **Terminal Access Controller Access Control System**), **RADIUS** (**Remote Authentication Dial-In User Service**), **LDAP** (**Lightweight Directory Access Protocol**), or Microsoft Active Directory. Even though every method has multiple disadvantages, one common advantage is that you can log the user's request centrally with the help of a database. The other advantage is that it helps to have a single sign-on as the credentials are stored in the central database and used by the network device to authenticate a login request.

The problem with external authentication is that if the database fails, the reachability to the server gets affected. This issue can be solved by migrating the database to a local user database. Once the user is authenticated, the next step is about authorizing and controlling the users and what they can access. This might require some tools like **Cisco Access Control Server** (**Cisco ACS**) or the **Identity Services Engine** (**ISE**). After successful authorization that is permitting or denying a user from accessing certain resources, AAA also talks about archiving what users have accessed in their respective sessions. The Cisco IOS AAA client may reside on the router or on a **Network Access Server** (**NAS**) which performs the functions. This model does not scale for larger networks because there can be a large amount of stored data.

Components of AAA

Authentication, authorization, and accounting are the functional components, but they also contain certain core components. It's important to understand the core components of AAA and their functions, which are as follows:

- **Client**: A device that attempts to access the network by authenticating itself or acting as substitute to validate the user.
- **Policy Enforcement Point (PEP)**: It implements the requisites specified by client access. It is also referred to as the authenticator, VPN concentrator, **Wireless Access Point** (**WAP**), and so on.

- **Policy Information Point (PIP)**: It stores information and facilitates access decisions. A PIP could be a database containing device IDs, a user directory, or a one-time password, to name a few.
- **Policy Decision Point (PDP)**: It is responsible for collecting access requests from the PEP and also assigning the PIP to collect more information that would help in making an access decision. It is responsible for making the final decision about the network.
- **Accounting and Reporting System**: This feature tracks the use of the network and recognizes the identity, location, and the resources accessed by the user.

The following diagram explains the components and operation of AAA:

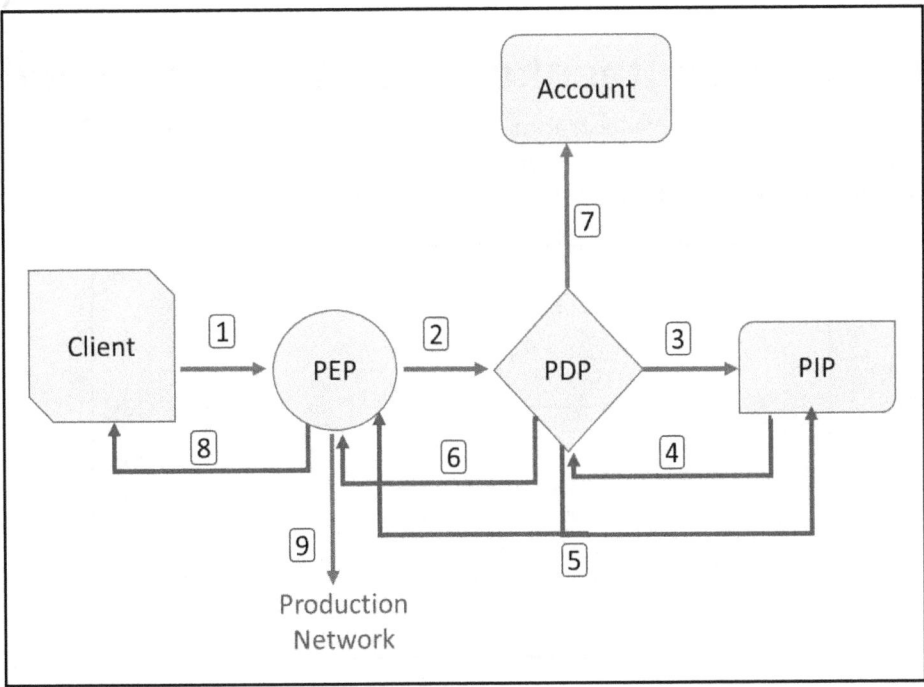

First, the client establishes connectivity with the network, and is then asked to provide identification before sending the message to PEP. Next, the information received by PEP is sent to PDP whereupon the PDP collects information from PIP about the client and authenticates the information. The PIP validates the user's credentials and send a success or failure message. It also sends additional information such as the role, location, and so on about the client to the PDP for evaluation.

PDP evaluates the client's information while also analyzing the role of PIP and PEP in dealing with the request. Upon deciding on the authorization, PDP also sends the authentication result to the PEP as well as the accounting system. PEP is responsible for sending the authorization message to the client. This, in turn, will access the network through the PEP.

Implementing Cisco AAA - authentication

AAA can be implemented in two forms: either locally on a device or with TACACS+ or RADIUS.

Implementing authentication using local services

In this section, we going to take look at implementing authentication on the Cisco IOS router. This feature will enable the router to act as an authentication server with all of the user accounts that are created and stored on the device itself:

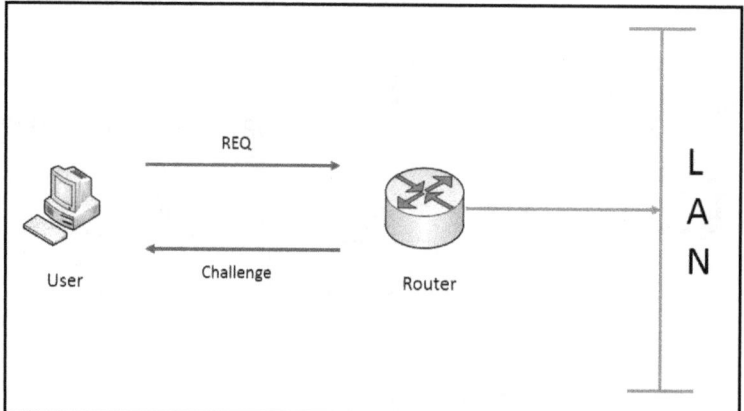

Whenever a user tries to log in, the router will query the local database to validate if the username and password combination exists and is accurate. If yes, this proves to the router that the user has validated their identity and is who they say they are.

The following are the steps to enable AAA using local services:

1. Enable AAA on the routers. On the CLI, use the following command. This command enables AAA and unlocks all other subcommands:

```
Router enable
Router # configure terminal
Router(config) # aaa new-model
```

2. Enable the username and password. The next step after you enable AAA is to create a username and password. The username and password can either be in the form of plain text or in encrypted form:

```
Router (config)# username ccnasecurity password cisco
```

3. The preceding command shows how to enable plain text. The following command shows how to create an encrypted password instead of plain text. This uses a MD5 hashing method for encryption:

```
Router (config)# username ccnasecurity secret cisco
```

3. Configure the device to use the local database:

```
Router (config) # aaa authentication login default local
```

4. This command creates a method list so that you can use the local authentication database. The preceding command can be explained as follows:
    • `aaa`: Enables the AAA feature on the router:

```
Router(config)# aaa ?
accounting Accounting configurations parameters.
authentication Authentication configurations parameters.
authorization Authorization configurations parameters.
!! Output Omitted !!
```

  • `authentication`: Specifies the set of configurations for authentication, authorization, or accounting:

```
Router(config)# aaa authentication ?
enable Set authentication list for enable.
login Set authentication lists for logins.
!! Output Omitted !!
```

  • `login`: Prompts the username and password while trying to log in via console, TTY, VTY, and auxiliary. This command is only used for administration access:

```
Router(config)# aaa authentication login ?
 WORD Named authentication list (max 31 characters, longer will
be rejected).
 default The default authentication list.
```

- default: To make the router use the default method list:

```
Router(config)# aaa authentication login default ?
 enable Use enable password for authentication.
 group Use Server-group
 line Use line password for authentication.
 local Use local username authentication.
 none NO authentication.
```

- local: This tells the router to use the local database as a reference:

```
Router(config)# aaa authentication login default local
```

Implementing authentication using external services

Due to the scaling of large networks, creating a user account on each router can be an inconvenience. If the account's details are adjusted on one device, the network engineer will need to replicate the changes to all other devices on the network individually. A convenient solution to adjust scaling and ensuring that all of the accounts and privileges are kept synchronized is to use a centralized AAA server such as a Cisco **Access Control Server** (**ACS**) or a Cisco **Identity Services Engine** (**ISE**):

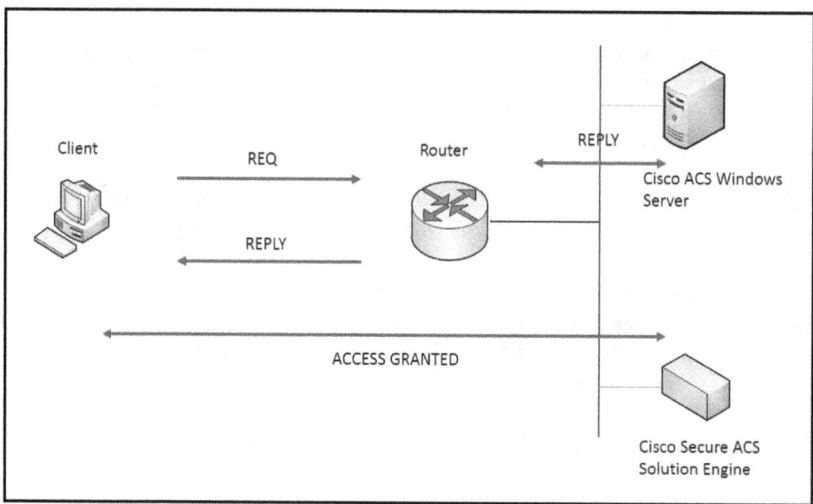

The user accounts are created on the ACS or ISE appliance. The routers and switches are configured to query the AAA server if they receive any login requests. The AAA server would also be responsible for providing privileges and getting logs of the activities of each user.

Examples of these security protocols are as follows:

- RADIUS
- TACACS+

TACACS+

This is a Cisco proprietary third-generation protocol that facilitates the use of AAA services. This protocol is derived from TACACS and XTACACS, and supports authentication, authorization, and accounting. Multiple servers can be used to handle different services. For example, one server can be used to handle authentication and another server can be used to handle authorization for a router.

TACACS+ provides additional layers of security by encrypting the messages between the client and the AAA server.

Here are the some of the special features of TACACS+:

- TACACS+ supports authorization commands with some advanced authentication mechanisms like Data Encryption Standard and **one-time password (OTP)** keys
- TACACS+ supports all 16 privilege levels (0-15)
- TACACS+ allows the blocking of specific port services such as a TTY or VTY
- The TACACS+ AAA server can contain an internal database size up to 5,000 users
- A TACACS+ server acts as a proxy server which authenticates, authorizes, and accounts access details

Configuring TACACS+

The following are the steps involved to configure external authentication using TACACS+.

1. Creating a username and password:

```
Router (config) # username ccnasecurity secret cisco
```

2. Enabling AAA on the device:

```
Router (config) # aaa new-model
```

3. Configuring the TACACS+ server. The next step is to configure the router to point to the TACACS+ server that has been created. This can be achieved by two methods. The first is to create a pointer on the router by specifying the IP address of the TACACS+ server and the shared key:

```
Router (config) # tacacs-server host 10.10.10.10 key secretkey
```

While the second is to create a group of TACACS+ servers and define the same:

```
Router (config) # aaa group server tacacs+ Authforlogin
Router (config-sg-tacacs+) #server 10.10.10.10
```

4. Defining a method list for AAA. The next step is to define a method list for AAA logins using the following parameters:

```
Router (config) # aaa authentication login default group tacacs+
local
```

Where:

- The keyword `aaa authentication login` specifies that this is only used for login authentication
- The keyword `default` is used in case of a custom name or when only one default list can be created for each function of AAA
- The keyword `group tacacs+` specifies the user who is going to use the configured TACACS+ servers
- The keyword `local` specifies the secondary authentication method in case the TACACS+ server is not reachable

5. Attaching the configured AAA authentication on the line modes:

```
Router (config) # line console 0
Router (config-line) # login authentication default
Router (config) # line vty 0 15
Router (config-line) # login authentication default
```

The keyword `default` here substitutes the default method list available.

Using AAA with TACACS+

Let's consider the example of a user connected to the router, and the TACACS+ server is requesting access to the router. The following are the steps involved in authenticating the user with TACACS+:

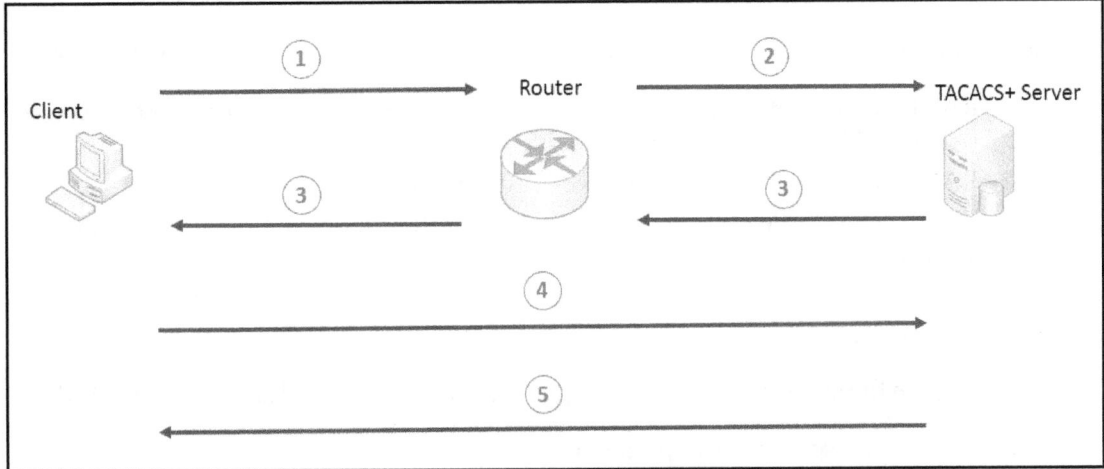

1. The **Client** sends a request message to the **Router**
2. The **Router** passes the request to the **TACACS+ Server** and requests for the login text
3. The **TACACS+ Server** prompts for the username and the password, and the **Router** passes the server request to the server
4. The **Client** sends the username and password to the router and the **Router** forwards the same to TACACS+
5. Then, the server replies with an ACCEPT or REJECT code

RADIUS

This is an open standard protocol that works in a client and server model. In the implementation of Cisco, the RADIUS client is configured on the Cisco routers and sends authentication or authorization requests to a RADIUS server which is located centrally.

RADIUS can be implemented in various network environments that are in need of high security levels. Some of the environments where RADIUS can be used are as follows:

1. It can be implemented in networks that are built with different vendor products. RADIUS can act as a single server-based database.
2. In networks environments where smart cards are used.
3. It can be used in environments where administrators need to do accounting independently.
4. It can be used in networks where administrators want to set up pre-authentication profiles. Pre-authentication mainly helps ISP's to manage ports and shared resources depending on the agreed upon service agreements.

On the other hand, RADIUS cannot be used for some situations, and they are as follows:

1. RADIUS does not support some of the protocols like **AppleTalk Remote Access** (**ARA**), X.25 PAD connections, and NetBIOS
2. RADIUS does not work on the two-way authentication model
3. RADIUS binds the user client to only one service model and does not support a variety of services

Configuring RADIUS

The following are the steps involved in configuring external authentication using RADIUS:

1. Creating a username and password:

```
Router (config) # username ccnasecurity secret cisco
```

2. Enabling AAA on the device:

```
Router (config) # aaa new-model
```

3. Configuring the RADIUS server. The next step is to configure the router to point to the RADIUS server that has been created. This can be achieved by creating a pointer on the router by specifying the IP address of the RADIUS server and the shared key:

```
Router (config) # radius-server host 10.10.10.10
Router (config) # radius-server key thesecretkey
```

4. Defining a method list for AAA. The next step is to define a method list for AAA logins using the following parameters:

```
Router (config) # aaa authentication login default group radius
local
```

5. Attaching the configured AAA authentication on the line modes:

```
Router (config) # line console 0
Router (config-line) # login authentication default
Router (config) # line vty 0 15
Router (config-line) # login authentication default
```

Using AAA with RADIUS

Let's consider that a user is attempting to log in to and authenticate an access server configured with RADIUS:

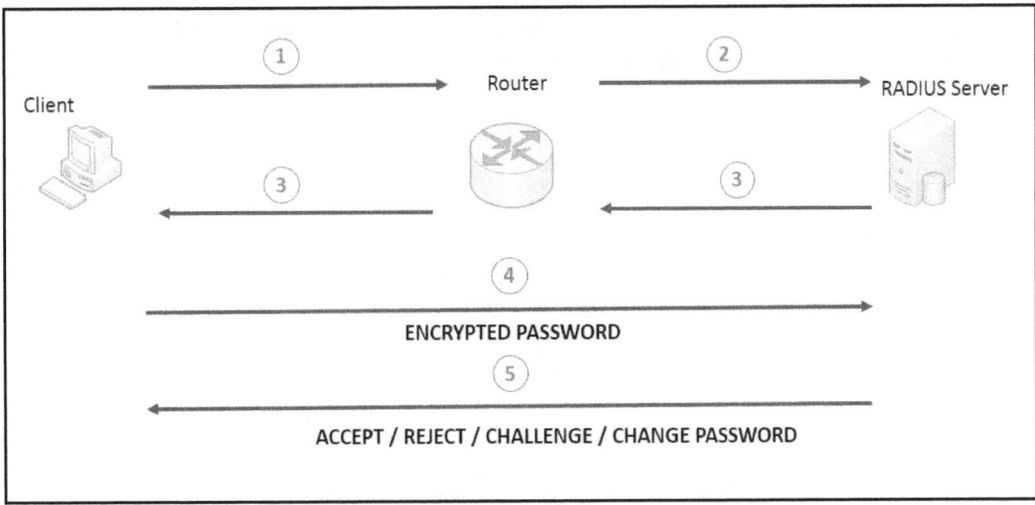

1. The **Client** sends a request message to the **Router**
2. The **Router** passes the request to the **RADIUS Server** and requests for the login text
3. The **RADIUS Server** prompts the user to enter their username and password
4. Once the user enters their credentials, their password is encrypted and is sent to the **RADIUS Server**

5. Then, the server replies with an **ACCEPT /REJECT / CHALLENGE / CHANGE PASSWORD** response code

1. The **ACCEPT** code specifies that the user is successfully authenticated
2. The **REJECT** code specifies that the user is not authenticated and is prompted to enter their password again
3. The **CHALLENGE** code specifies that the message has been sent to the users to collect some additional information
4. The **CHANGE PASSWORD** code specifies that the message sent to the user is to choose a new password

Example of AAA using local authentication

In the following example, let's understand the creation of AAA with the local database. AAA is implemented on **R1** and **R2** and is used to check the configured items:

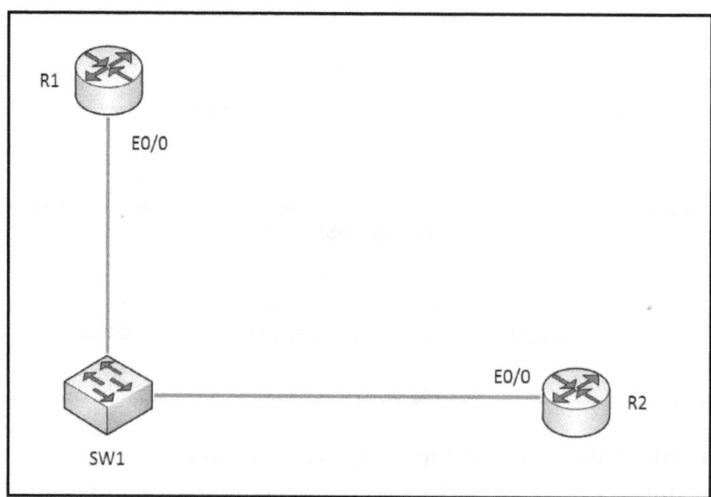

The configuration required on both routers is shown as follows:

- On the router **R1**:

```
R1#conf t
Enter configuration commands, one per line. End with CNTL/Z.
R1(config)#int e0/0
R1(config-if)#ip add
R1(config-if)#ip address 192.168.10.1 255.255.255.0
R1(config-if)#no shut
R1(config)#username ccnasecurity password cisco
R1(config)#aaa new-model
R1(config)#aaa authentication login default local none
R1(config)#aaa authentication login telnet_lines local
R1(config)#line vty 0 4
R1(config-line)#login authentication telnet_lines
```

- On the router **R2**:

```
R2#conf t
Enter configuration commands, one per line. End with CNTL/Z.
R2(config)#int e0/0
R2(config-if)#ip address 192.168.10.2 255.255.255.0
R2(config-if)#no shut
```

- To verify the configuration, open a Telnet session from **R1** to **R2**:

```
R2#telnet 192.168.10.1
Trying 192.168.10.1 ... Open

User Access Verification
Username: ccnasecurity
Password: cisco
R1
```

- The status can also be verified with the help of the debug commands:

```
R1#debug aaa authentication
AAA Authentication debugging is on
```

Choosing a protocol between the ACS server and the router

Generally, TACACS+ is used if authentication and authorization should be configured for CLI access. The reason why TACACS+ is preferred is because it has independently defined principles for authentication, authorization, and accounting. TACACS+ has a very granular level of control in terms of communicating, while on the other hand RADIUS does not have the same level of control.

The following table compares the two protocols:

Function	TACACS+	RADIUS
Functionality	Separates the elements of AAA	Combines the elements of AAA, but has different principles for accounting
Standard compliance	Cisco proprietary	Open standard
Transport layer feature	TCP	UDP
Confidentiality	All of the packets sent over are encrypted	Only the password is encrypted
Authorization	Command by command authorization	No explicit way for authorization
Accounting	Normal accounting support	More detailed accounting support

Example of AAA authentication using the TACACS+ server

In the following example, let's understand the creation of AAA using an external server.

The first step is to set up the TACACS+ server:

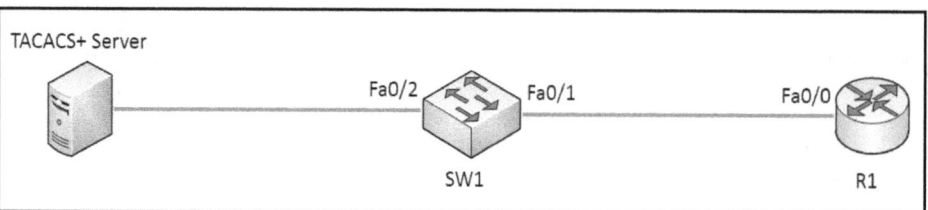

On the router **R1**:

```
R1(config)#int fa0/0
R1(config-if)#ip add
R1(config-if)#ip address 192.168.10.1 255.255.255.0
R1(config-if)#no shut
```

```
R1(config)#aaa new-model
R1(config)#tacacs-server host 192.168.10.2 key cisco
R1(config)#aaa authentication login CONSOLE_PORT group tacacs+
R1(config)#line console 0
R1(config-line)#login authentication CONSOLE_PORT
R1(config-line)#exit
```

Use the following code to verify the console to **R1**:

```
Press RETURN to get started!
User Access Verification

Username: ccnasecurity
Password:
R1
```

Command list

The following are the list of commands used in implementing authentication on a router:

Command	Description
service password-encryption	Encrypts all plaintext passwords
aaa new-model	Enables AAA on a Cisco device
aaa authentication	Defines the parameters of authentication
debug aaa authentication	Enables AAA authentication debugging
enable	Enters privileged EXEC mode
enable password password	Sets a local password to control access to various privilege levels
enable secret level level password	Sets a password for the privilege level
enable secret password	Configures an encrypted password
username username password password	Creates a local user account with a password
privilege level level	Configures a new privilege level for users and associates commands with that privilege level
show privilege	Displays the current level of privilege
enable secret password	Specifies an additional layer of security with the secret password

Issues with authentication

Consider the following example in which **Person A** needs to send a message to **Person B**, but there might be some issues in checking the authenticity of the sender:

- **Authenticity**: **Person B** should identify that the message is from **Person A**
- **Secrecy**: Others (**Person C**) should not sniff the message

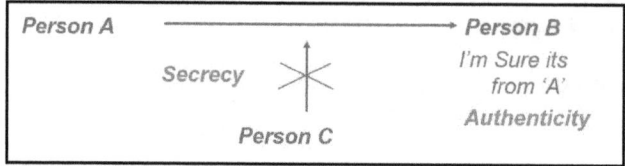

The solution to this problem is using the encryption algorithms.

Encryption

To ensure that data transfer is secure, the computer security systems adopt a mechanism known as **encryption**. Encryption is the process of converting a plaintext message into ciphertext, where only the person with the decryption key can read the ciphertext. Encryption enforces confidentiality on a computing system, and uses mathematical algorithms to scramble data. The scrambled data, after encryption, is known as **ciphertext**.

To read an encrypted file, use the decryption or secret key to open the message back into plaintext. This process is known as **decryption**. The efficiency of encryption depends on your choice of algorithm.

Encryption is vital as information is often sent from one computer to another via a network which can be unsafe if sensitive data is flowing from one device to another. It provides a degree of security, even if the information falls into the wrong hands.

There are two types of encryption:

- Symmetric encryption
- Asymmetric encryption

Symmetric encryption

Symmetric encryption is a traditional scheme of encryption where for both encryption and decryption, the *same secret key* is used. The same secret key is also shared by the sender and the receiver.

Advantages:

- The keys are very short
- Encryption and decryption is fast

Disadvantages:

- Requires secrecy for the secure transmission of keys
- Requires separate keys for every group of people who exchange information, otherwise secrecy across groups is not possible

Asymmetric encryption

Asymmetric encryption uses two different keys to encrypt and decrypt data: a **public key** and a **private key**. The public key can be distributed to all users, while the private key corresponds to the public key and is possessed only by the owner of the file. The public and private keys are related in that the public key is used to encrypt messages and decryption is done using the corresponding private key and vice versa.

Advantages:

- Increased security
- Ensures non-repudiation

Disadvantages:

- Encryption and decryption are very slow

Implementing Cisco AAA - authorization

This helps to limit the services available to a user. Once you enable authorization, the network servers use the information taken from the user's profile. The user's profile can be configured using a local database or external servers. Depending on the configuration of a user's profile, the user is allowed or denied access to a particular resource.

Prerequisites for authorization

The following are the steps to prepare the router for authorization:

1. Enable the AAA feature on the network access server
2. Complete the AAA authentication procedure since authorization is configured after authentication
3. Define the operational characteristics of RADIUS and TACACS+ if any of them are used for authorization
4. Finally, define the rights associated to the users with the help of their usernames

Configuring method lists for authorization

A method list is the way or a process that defines the sequence followed in authorization. It is a list of steps that is queried and executed. This also helps to enable multiple protocol services for authorization, thus enabling a backup scenario. Some of the methods listed are as follows:

- **Auth-proxy**: This is applied on a user basis. This is used to authenticate and authorize specific users who are blocked by the access-list with special permissions.
- **Commands**: This method is for all EXEC mode commands, including global configuration commands.
- **EXEC**: Applies to the attributes associated to the EXEC Terminal session.
- **Network**: This is used to authorize network connection-based protocols like PPP and so on.
- **Reverse Access**: This is used to reverse the telnet sessions.

Once a method list is defined, the list must be applied/associated with some of the specific lines or interfaces.

The default method list is applied automatically on all of the line modes and interfaces. Once another method list is assigned, the default method list is removed form that interface or line.

Different methods of authorization

There are 5 different authorization methods that AAA supports, and they are as follows:

- **None**: Authorization is not enabled or configured on the interface or line.
- **Local**: The access server checks references to its local database.
- **If-authenticated**: The user is permitted to access the resources, but only if the user is successfully authenticated.
- **TACACS+**: The database is stored on the TACACS+ security server and the rights for the user are defined by the TACACS+ security demon.
- **RADIUS**: The authorization database is stored in the RADIUS security server. It defines the permissions to the user who is associated with the attributes stored in the database.

Configuring the privilege level for AAA authorization

The levels which help to determine who should be permitted access to the device and what should be accessed on the device helps to control or enforce strict policies based on the job title of the administrator. For example, the senior network administrator and the senior security administrator get higher privilege level access and the junior network administrator and the junior network administrator get lower privilege level access. The Cisco IOS command-line interface has two levels of access privilege, and they are as follows:

- **Privilege level 1 (User EXEC mode)**: The lowest EXEC mode for user privileges. The user can only use user-level commands that are available in User Executable mode.
- **Privilege level 15 (Privileged mode)**: The highest level of user privileges. The user is able to use all enable-level commands in privileged mode.

Multiple privilege levels (customized) can be defined to different commands at each level. In total, there are 0 to 15 (16) privilege levels, where 0, 1, and 15 have predefined values. Commands and modes that are defined on the lower level are also available on the higher level. For example, a user with a privilege level of 5 can access commands allowed at levels 0 to 4. A user authorized to used privilege level 15 can use all of the IOS commands on the device.

The syntax to configure a custom privilege level is as follows:

```
Router (config)# privilege mode {level} {command}
```

Example of AAA authorization with privilege levels

On the router, we are going to execute the following commands which will secure access to the console port, the aux port and the VTY lines:

```
R1 (config)#line con 0
R1 (config-line)#exec-timeout 0 0
R1 (config-line)#password cisco
R1 (config-line)#logging synchronous
R1 (config-line)#enable password cisco
R1 (config-line)#line vty 0 4
R1(config-line)#login
R1(config-line)#password cisco
R1(config-line)#exec-timeout 0 0
R1(config-line)#line aux 0
R1(config-line)#exec-timeout 0 0
R1(config-line)#login
R1(config-line)#password cisco
```

Checking if the privilege level is configured on **R1**:

```
R1#show privilege
Current privilege level is 15
```

Configuring custom privilege levels by adding the following entries to the authentication database on **R1**:

```
R1(config)#username cisco0 privilege 0 password cisco0
R1(config)#username cisco15 privilege 15 password cisco15
R1(config)#username cisco7 privilege 7 password cisco7
R1(config)#aaa new-model
R1(config)#aaa authentication login default local
```

Implementing Cisco AAA - accounting

Accounting is one of the components of AAA. Accounting allows the security administrator to track the services that users are authorized for as well as the amount of network resources that have been used by the user. Each piece of accounting information has attribute-value pairs, which allow the user to monitor and manage activities like client billing and auditing.

Some of the different types of accounting methods are as follows:

- **Network**: This method involves verifying the sessions generated by network protocols like PPP, ARAP, and SLIP. This involves some statistical details like verifying the packet count and traffic utilization.
- **EXEC (Execution mode)**: This method verifies the session executed by the user at the user exec mode of the router.
- **Commands**: This method executes accounting for commands at a particular privilege level, ranging between 0 to 15.
- **Connection**: This method provides details and accounting on the outbound connections made to the network access server using protocols like Telnet, rlogin, and so on.
- **System**: This method accounts for all system-specific events, independent of users. An example of this would be reloads that occur on systems.
- **Resource**: Two options are available in regards to resources:
  - **Start-stop**: This subcommand allows the AAA client to send a message to initiate the server in order to start the accounting process. This message is sent in the background. The stop message is initiated to stop the accounting process.
  - **Stop-only**: This subcommand will make the server stop the accounting process at the end of the defined accounting process.

Configuring AAA - authorization and accounting

In this lab, we will learn how to configure AAA on a Cisco IOS Router and learn about its features.

Step 1

Configure the router's interface with an appropriate IP scheme, and on the host device, configure and set an IP address, subnet mask, and default gateway accordingly.

Step 2

The AAA feature can be used here to restrict a user's access rights and privileges on the device after they have been authenticated. By default, there are three privilege levels on the router, as follows:

Privilege level	Result
1	User level only (prompt is `router`), the default level for login
15	15 privileged level (prompt is `router#`), the level after going into enable mode
0	0 is not used often but includes five commands: `disable`, `enable`, `exit`, `help`, and `logout`

Levels 2 through 14 can be defined by using commands from one of the default privilege levels to the new level. configuring custom privilege levels can be used for different portfolios of network teams. For example, the security administrator can have a customized privilege level that can define only security-specific commands.

To verify the current privilege level, use the `show privilege` command in privilege mode, as follows:

```
Router1#show privilege
Current privilege level is 15
```

You can configure the custom privilege levels like so:

```
Router1(config)#username user1 privilege 0 password ccnasecurity0
Router1(config)#username user2 privilege 15 password ccnasecurity15
Router1(config)#username user3 privilege 7 password ccnasecurity7
Router1(config)#aaa new-model
Router1(config)#aaa authentication login default local
```

In the preceding example, when the user logs in as `user1`, the permitted user will only have permission to use the `disable`, `exit`, `help`, `enable`, and `logout` commands. The user logging in as `user2` will have permissions as a regular access to EXEC mode. The user with the username of `user3` will have access to the commands that are defined by the administrator.

 It is important to log in with a privilege level 15 user account in order to modify the default privilege level of IOS commands. Failure to do so will result in console session lockout when the `aaa authorization exec default local` command is entered.

Once logged in with `cisco15`, and entering privilege mode, enable AAA authorization and create a customer privilege level by using the following commands:

```
Router1(config)#aaa authorization exec default local
```

Next, specify which commands will be authorized on the privilege mode:

```
Router1(config)#aaa authorization commands 0 default local
Router1(config)#aaa authorization commands 15 default local
Router1(config)#aaa authorization commands 7 default local
```

As you can see from the preceding code, the user must be authorized to use commands defined in privilege levels 0, 7, and 15.

The following example demonstrates how to configure the router to query a TACACS+ server:

```
aaa authorization commands 0 default group tacacs+ local enable
```

The `group` keyword indicates a server group, while the `tacacs+` keyword indicates the type of AAA server (RADIUS or TACACS+). If configured with this command, the local database on `Router1` will only be used if the TACACS+ server is unavailable.

To specify which commands will be available in privilege level 7, On `Router1`, issue the following commands from the console:

```
Router1(config)#privilege configure level 7 snmp-server host
Router1(config)#privilege configure level 7 snmp-server enable
Router1(config)#privilege configure level 7 snmp-server
Router1(config)#privilege exec level 7 ping
Router1(config)#privilege exec level 7 configure terminal
Router1(config)#privilege exec level 7 configure
```

As per the previously mentioned commands, there are three commands that can be used in global configuration mode and three commands that can be used in privilege mode for a user who has logged in with the username `cisco7`.

Step 3

Here, we are going to Telnet from the **Host A** device to the router using the `cisco15` account on the router. Once you're logged in, you'll notice that you have immediately landed on privilege mode:

1. Let's run the `show privilege` command to verify what our privilege level is. When you're finished, log out of the Telnet session.
2. Log in into the router once again but instead use the `cisco0` account.
3. Execute the `show privileges` command to once again verify the privilege level and try to access privilege mode.
4. Enter ? to see the available commands that the user has available to them.
5. Log out of the Telnet session once more.

This time, Telnet into the router using the `cisco7` account. You'll notice that the `cisco7` account immediately landed on privilege mode, just like the `cisco15` account did.

Once again, enter the ? command to verify the available list of commands for this account on the router:

```
Router1#configure terminal
Router1(config)#?
Configure commands:
default Set a command to its defaults
end Exit from configure mode
exit Exit from configure mode
help Description of the interactive help system
no Negate a command or set its defaults
snmp-server Modify SNMP parameters
```

Step 4

In this step, we can configure accounting on `Router1` using AAA. Enter privilege EXEC mode either via console or Telnet as `cisco15`.

 If a TACACS+ server is not available, the results will not be stored but recording will occur.

Enter the following configurations on the router **R1**:

```
Router1(config)#aaa accounting exec default start-stop group tacacs+
Router1(config)#aaa accounting commands 15 default start-stop group tacacs+
Router1(config)#aaa accounting network default start-stop group tacacs+
Router1(config)#aaa accounting connection default start-stop group tacacs+
Router1(config)#aaa accounting system default start-stop group tacacs+
```

The following is a brief description of each of the command options:

Option	Result
aaa	Enables a AAA command
accounting	Enables accounting or tracking a feature of AAA
exec	Monitors EXEC commands on the device
commands 15	Monitors commands by privilege level 15 users, can be 0 to 15
network	Monitors network services like PPP, ARAP
connection	Monitors outbound Telnet, rlogin sessions
system	Monitors system events like reload, shutdown
start-stop	Includes both Start and Stop recordings
default	Uses the default list instead of a custom list
group	Uses a group of servers like primary and secondary
tacacs+	Uses the TACACS+ server

On `Router1`, enable debugging on the AAA accounting services on the router:

```
Router1#debug aaa accounting
AAA Accounting debugging is on
```

Using **Host A** once more, Telnet into the router using the `cisco15` account. Once connected, issue some basic commands like `show running-config`. Next, return to the console session and notice that the router displays in-depth details of the AAA accounting transactions taking place on the router itself. This is due to debugging the AAA accounting services on the router:

```
02:08:59: AAA/ACCT/CMD: User cisco15, Port tty2, Priv 15:"show running-
config cr"
02:08:59: AAA/ACCT/CMD: Found list "default"
02:08:59: AAA/ACCT: user cisco15, acct type 3 (3901449983):
```

```
Method=tacacs+ (tacacs+)
02:09:20: AAA/ACCT/CMD: User cisco15, Port tty2, Priv 15:"copy running-
config startup-config cr"
02:09:20: AAA/ACCT/CMD: Found list "default"
02:09:20: AAA/ACCT: user cisco15, acct type 3 (2545785330):
Method=tacacs+ (tacacs+)
```

Summary

In this chapter, we learned about Cisco, IOS, and AAA and how they can be implemented. We explored the components of AAA and implementing the Cisco AAA service on a IOS router.

In the next chapter, we will go into detail about securing the control and management plane.

6
Securing the Control and Management Planes

Network security refers to the various policies adopted by an organization or network administrator to monitor and prevent unauthorized access, this access can result in the misuse or tampering of data, or a disruption of the network. With the increase in the number of users preferring an on-the-go network, virtualized data centers, and services based on cloud computing, it is becoming challenging to manage a network. Therefore, a structured approach is required for the effective management of a network's security.

The ultimate objective of network security is to protect an organization's critical and sensitive data from unauthorized access and destruction while ensuring its availability and integrity. There are many options available, so organizations can choose the one that best suits their network and business requirements. One example is the **Cisco Security Manager**, which helps in managing the entire deployed network. However, before understanding the various other aspects of network management, it is important to know about security policies and their components.

In this chapter, we will cover the following topics:

- Security policy
- Technologies to implement secure management network
- Planning considerations for secure management
- Log messaging implementation for security

Introducing the security policy

Any organization depending on a network has a security policy in place. A security policy basically contains the following:

- The organization's objectives
- Rules and regulations for the network's users and administrators
- Requirements for the system and management that collectively ensure network security

A security policy also lays down the guidelines, standards, and procedures for the functioning of a network. The main components of a security policy are the governing policy, the end-user policy, and the technical policy:

- **Governing policy**: This policy contains the answers to the *"what needs a security policy"* question. It contains high-level categorization of the security elements that are important for the organization. People at the managerial or technical level are responsible for this policy.
- **End-user policy**: This policy contains the security requirements for the end users and also details the security policy questions of what elements need security, when it is required, and where it is required.
- **Technical policy**: These policies are more detailed compared to the governing policy ,and address only a specific issue, such as access control or physical security. This policy is used by members of the security staff.

IT governance, risk management, and compliance, referred to as IT GRC, are also significant components of a security policy. In organizations, the efforts in terms of IT governance, risk management, and compliance are often separated either by department or the type of regulation. This segregation—in order to achieve a secure IT environment that adheres to the regulatory compliance requirements—can create certain problems, such as incurring higher costs, the utilization of too many resources, and increased time and effort.

However, nowadays, organizations are working towards simplifying the process by converging the three components. This figure illustrates the convergence of the three components in an organization:

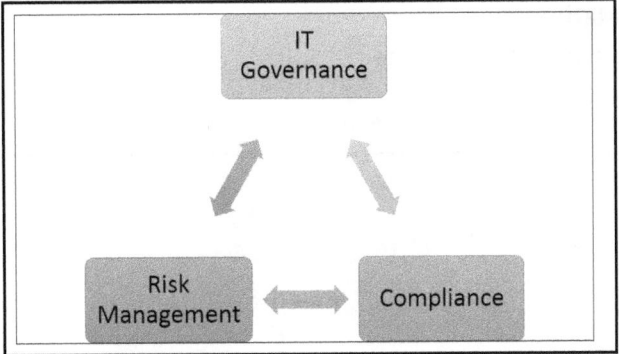

The result of this convergence, as illustrated, is an effective process to define risk based on an organization's rules and business objectives, and that comes within the framework of compliance regulations. While risk management identifies potential risks, how they occur, and determines their impact, IT governance, in addition to alleviating risks, creates rigorous prerequisites for the framework of information security.

The compliance component determines the levels of compliance and the impacts of non-compliance to the security policy. Apart from the security policy, secure network management depends on a structured approach, which is the life cycle approach. The convergence of the three components results in an ideal framework and context to create a life cycle approach to information security. It also results in reducing expenses and increasing effectiveness.

Phases of secure network life cycle

The life cycle approach to security management focuses on various elements of security, such as the assessment, testing, implementation, and monitoring phases of security. In an effort to provide a structured methodology for network security, it emphasizes and describes the roles of regulatory compliance, risks, and security policies in designing effective network frameworks.

As discussed, the components of IT governance, risk management, and compliance, forming the core of the security framework, ensure an economical and efficient process. Including the security component while in the **systems development life cycle** (**SDLC**) helps with less expensive and less effective security. The SDLC contains five phases. They are as follows:

- **Initiation**
- **Acquisition and Development**

- **Implementation**
- **Operations and Maintenance**
- **Disposition**

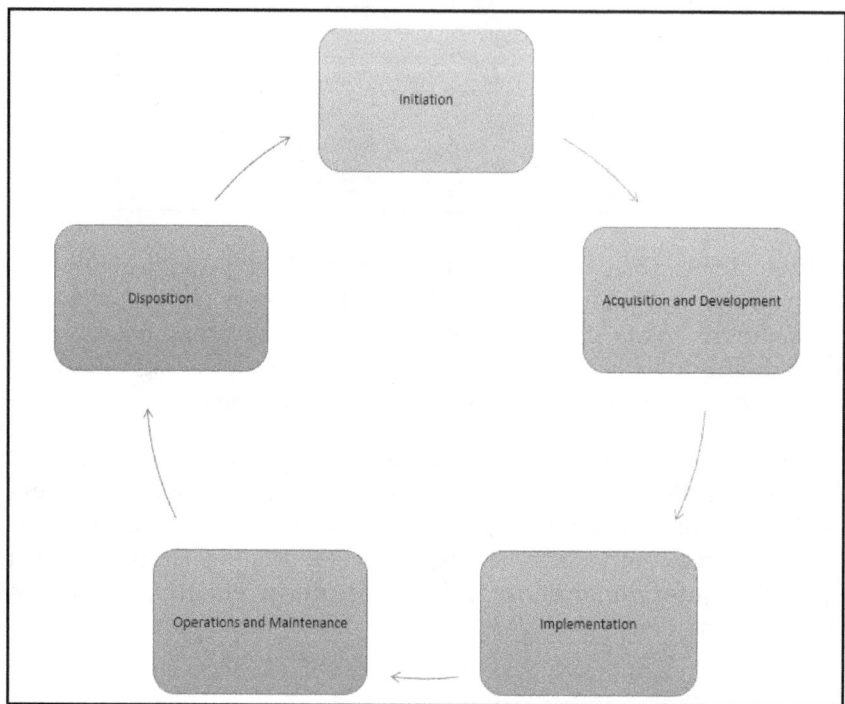

Each phase in the life cycle will be discussed in detail.

Initiation phase

During this phase, an organization states the need for systems and plans the systems' security by identifying the key security roles. Apart from evaluating the information that need to be stored, transmitted, or processed, the confidentiality, integrity, and availability of information should also be assessed. The initiation phase includes the two components.

Security categorization

Based on the potential impact of a security breach on individuals and organizations, this step identifies three levels of security—low, moderate, and high. Such categorization helps organizations to choose the best security methods when required.

Initial risk assessment

This step identifies the types of potential risks and based on that, describes the required security needs for the system.

Acquisition and development phase

In this phase, the system is designed, programmed, and developed. It has five key components.

Risk assessment

A risk assessment is conducted to identify the security requirements for the system. This analysis is based on the initial risk assessment, but is more detailed. Conducting a risk assessment enables an organization to identify the various potential risks to operations, assets, or even individuals arising from the storage or processing of information and operation of the information systems.

Requirements analysis of security functions

In this step, security plans are developed that determine security requirements for the information systems and contain the information pertaining to a selection of security controls, how these controls have to be implemented, and so on. Security controls are commonly of three types—administrative, logical, or technical and physical controls:

- Administrative controls are the policies, standards, or guidelines specifying and governing the security requirements of a program
- Technical controls are virtual controls, such as firewalls, anti-virus software, identification, and authentication mechanisms and passwords
- Physical controls may refer to a key that can give access to buildings or rooms, monitoring systems such as surveillance systems, gates, and even security personnel who monitor access to offices

Cost considerations and reporting

This step determines the cost involved in terms of hardware, software, training, personnel, and other assets in the process of developing information security.

Security control development

This step ensures the implementation of the security controls mentioned in the security plans. This step identifies whether any additional controls are required to support the existing ones.

Developmental security test and evaluation

This step ensures effective functioning of the security controls, especially the non-technical controls because they cannot be tested until the information system is installed. The testing of controls in the development phases ensures that the controls are functioning as desired before the implementation phase.

Implementation phase

In this phase, the security features are configured, their functionality tested, and they are installed. Finally, a formal certification or authorization is obtained to operate the system. The authorization ensures that the system is functioning as per the established techniques and procedures. It is also seen as an assurance that the required safety measures are in place to protect the organization's information.

Operations and maintenance phase

In this phase, the performance of the systems is constantly monitored and any additions or modifications to the existing systems are developed, tested, and components are replaced or added. It includes two components.

Configuration management and control

Configuration management and control activities involve the documentation of any potential or actual changes done to the security plan. This activity allows personnel to get an idea of the potential threats or impacts resulting from certain changes performed on an information system.

Since information systems are likely to undergo changes in terms of hardware or software, documenting the changes ensures monitoring and keeping track of the changes done to the system.

Continuous monitoring

This step ensures the effective functioning of the controls with constant monitoring and carrying out testing in periodic intervals of time.

Disposal phase

This phase involves planning for the disposal of the old hardware, software, and information to pave way for a new system. This could mean either storing the information on another system or deleting, erasing, or even overwriting the data as required.

However, the utmost care is required when choosing the disposal method, to avoid the unauthorized disclosure of sensitive data.

Technologies to implement secure management network

Once the design is in place, technologies are required to implement the network and ensure its security. There are certain technologies that are required to implement network security. Here, the discussion shall include a special focus on Cisco IOS devices. The technologies are as follows:

- Syslog protocol
- Network time protocol
- Simple Network Management Protocol

Syslog protocol

The syslog standard acts as a transport, facilitating a device to send notification messages through IP networks to syslog servers that receive the messages. Unlike the TCP protocol, in syslog, the receiver does not send an acknowledgement of the message received. This is basically because syslog uses the **User Datagram Protocol** (**UDP**) port 514. As UDP is a connectionless protocol, it does not provide any acknowledgements. Therefore, the sending device does not have an indication about the receipt of messages by the receiving syslog server and keeps generating messages.

Syslog messages can be sent to an external machine—that would act as a central syslog server—by configuring Cisco devices. The delivery of messages to the server, however, would depend on the connection strength between the Cisco device and the syslog server. For instance, if the connection is weak, the messages will not be delivered to the server.

Several Cisco devices such as routers, firewalls, and VPNs to create syslog messages for alerts and system information.

The packet size of syslog is 1,024 bytes with the following information:

- Facility
- Severity
- Hostname
- Timestamp
- Message

Facility

The syslog messages are classified into different types based on the sources of the message (from where they are generated). The categories are known as **facilities**. The facility messages are not reserved for or pre-assigned to the applications. The Cisco devices use one of these facilities.

Severity

This specifies the importance of the message. A severity is marked from **0** to **7**. Cisco devices use security levels to report the issues of software or hardware. The following are the values and descriptions of the severity levels:

Severity levels	Description
0	Emergency
1	Alert
2	Critical
3	Error
4	Warning
5	Notice
6	Information
7	Debug

The following table provides information about the use of severity levels in Cisco devices:

Severity level	Use
Emergency (1), Alert (2), Critical (3), Error (4), and Warning (5)	To report the issues related to hardware and software
Notice(5)	For system restart and interface status (up/down)
Information(6)	System reload
Debug(7)	Output of the debug command

Hostname

This field contains information about the IP address or the name of the host. If multiple IP address are used in multiple interfaces, it is the IP address of the interface from which the current message is transmitted.

Timestamp

This field contains the information about the local time of the device when the message gets created. The local time is displayed in the `MMM DD HH:MM:SS Timezone *` . format. The timestamp messages are prefixed with a asterisk (*) or colon (:).

It is always recommend to use network time protocol so that the time information will be accurate.

Message

This field contains the text information of the message. This information is about the process of the device. The message field begins with the percentage sign (%):

The following graphic displays the format of a **Syslog** message:

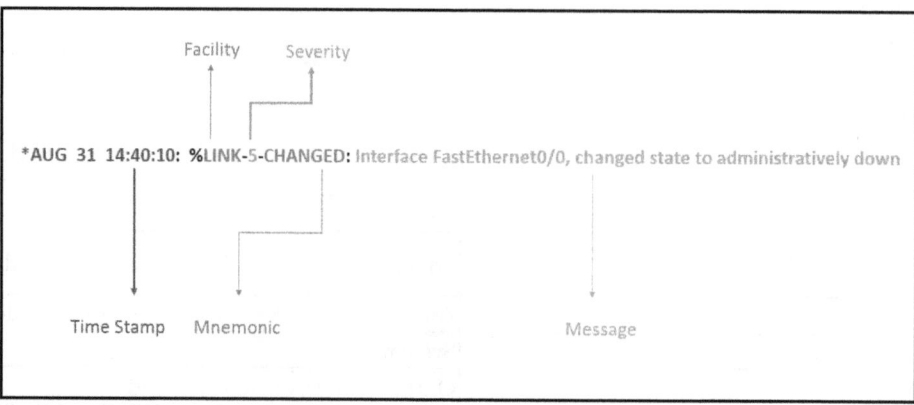

Configuring Cisco router for syslog server

The syslog protocol is used by many Cisco devices to manage system logs and alerts. However, these devices cannot store the logs as they do not have internal storage space. Therefore, to make up for this drawback, Cisco devices have the options of internal buffering and syslog. These terms are discussed in detail in later sections.

Before configuring a Cisco device to send syslog messages, ensure that the date, time, and time zone have been configured correctly. This is important because the wrong date and time can render the syslog data useless for troubleshooting.

All connected network devices should use a correct and synchronized system clock on all devices within the network. The built-in syslog client within the Cisco devices should be configured in order to enable syslog functionality in a Cisco network.

The following table shows the commands that should be executed to configure a Cisco-iOS-based router for sending syslog messages to an external syslog server:

Command	Description
`Router# configure terminal`	Enters the global configuration mode.
`Router(config)# service timestamps type datetime[msec] [localtime] [show-timezone]`	To instruct the system to timestamp syslog messages; the options for the type keyword are `debug` and `log`.
`Router(config)#logging host`	To specify the syslog server by IP address or hostname; multiple servers can be specified.
`Router(config)# logging trap level`	To specify the kind of messages, by severity level, to be sent to the syslog server. The default is informational and lower. The debug level should be used with caution because it can generate a large amount of syslog traffic in a busy network.
`Router(config)# logging facility facility-type`	To specify the facility level used by the syslog messages, the default is `local7`. Possible values are `local0`, `local1`, `local2`, `local3`, `local4`, `local5`, `local6`, and `local7`.
`Router(config)# End`	To return to privileged EXEC mode.
`Router# show logging`	To display logging configuration.

In the following example, we will configure **Router 1** as syslog client and the server as a syslog server. We will also control the different severity levels of the log messages that are collected on the **Syslog Server**:

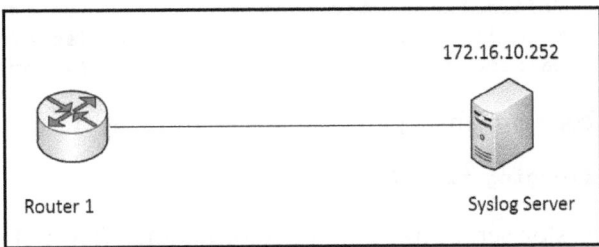

172.16.10.252

Router 1   Syslog Server

First, start a **Syslog Server** application on the server. Next, enable the timestamp service on **Router 1** for logging:

```
Router1#configure terminal
Enter configuration commands, one per line. End with CNTL/Z.
Router1(config)#service timestamps log datetime msec
Router1(config)#end
```

The next step is to configure the router (Router1) to send all the syslog messages to the configured syslog server:

```
Router1(config)#logging host 172.16.10.252

Mar 01, 02:43:18.4343: %SYS-5-CONFIG_I: Configured from console by console
*Mar 01, 02:43:18.4343: *Mar 01, 02:43:18.4343: %SYS-6-
LOGGINGHOST_STARTSTOP: Logging to host 127.168.10.252 port 514 started -
CLI initiated
*Mar 01, 02:43:18.4343: *Mar 01, 02:43:18.4343: %SYS-6-
LOGGINGHOST_STARTSTOP: Logging to host 172.16.10.252 port 514 started - CLI
initiated
```

Where 172.16.10.252 is the IP address of the syslog server. Then, configure the router to trap the syslog messages:

```
Router1(config)# logging trap ?

  <0-7>            Logging severity                   level
  alerts           Immediate action needed        (severity=1)
  critical         Critical conditions            (severity=2)
  debugging        Debugging messages             (severity=7)
  emergencies      System is unusable             (severity=0)
  errors           Error conditions               (severity=3)
  informational    Informational messages         (severity=6)
  notifications    Normal but significant conditions (severity=5)
  warnings         Warning conditions             (severity=4)
```

For example, we will configure the logging for level 6 by using the following command:

```
Router1(config)#logging trap 6
```

Once configured, the syslog server traps all the informational (level 6) items:

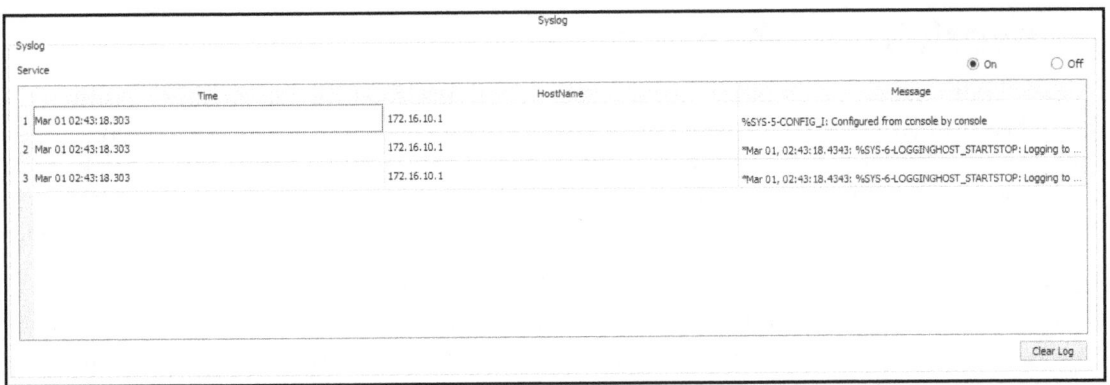

To verify the configured values of syslog, the show logging command can be used, and the output of show logging is as follows:

```
Router1#sh logging

Syslog logging: enabled (0 messages dropped, 0 messages rate-limited,
 0 flushes, 0 overruns, xml disabled, filtering disabled)No Active Message
Discriminator.
No Inactive Message Discriminator.
 Console logging: level debugging, 31 messages logged, xml disabled,
 filtering disabled
 Monitor logging: level debugging, 31 messages logged, xml disabled,
 filtering disabled
 Buffer logging: disabled, xml disabled,
 filtering disabledLogging Exception size (4096 bytes)
 Count and timestamp logging messages: disabled
 Persistent logging: disabled
No active filter modules.ESM: 0 messages dropped
 Trap logging: level informational, 31 message lines logged
 Logging to 127.168.10.252 (udp port 514, audit disabled,
 authentication disabled, encryption disabled, link up),
 24 message lines logged,
 0 message lines rate-limited,
 0 message lines dropped-by-MD,
 xml disabled, sequence number disabled
 filtering disabled
 Logging to 172.16.10.252 (udp port 514, audit disabled,
 authentication disabled, encryption disabled, link up),
 24 message lines logged,
 0 message lines rate-limited,
 0 message lines dropped-by-MD,
 xml disabled, sequence number disabled
 filtering disabled
```

Network Time Protocol

Time synchronization plays an important role in network security management. **Network Time Protocol** (**NTP**) is an internet protocol used to establish coordination between computer clock times across a network. It is important for systems across a network to have a network-wide accurate and common time. For instance, updates to a filesystem by multiple systems in the same location or different locations also require time coordination.

Using **Coordinated Universal Time** (**UTC**), NTP synchronizes computer clock time not only to minutes or seconds but to millisecond and even fractions of a millisecond. NTP acts as both protocol and server/client programs. A user can compile programs as NTP client, NTP server, or both.

In NTP, the devices are arranged in a hierarchical order, where the primary server is at the apex and the other follows it. The distance between the primary and secondary devices is defined by stratum levels.

Stratum-0 is the primary device with most accurate time settings, for example, atomic clocks.

Stratum-1 is the master servers, which are connected to the primary (**Stratum-0**) devices and take **Stratum-0** as a time source and **Stratum-2** as the secondary servers. In an NTP hierarchical system, devices on **Stratum-1** obtain their time from devices on **Stratum-0**; devices on **Stratum-2** receive their time information from servers on **Stratum-1**, and so on up to a maximum of 15 stratum levels:

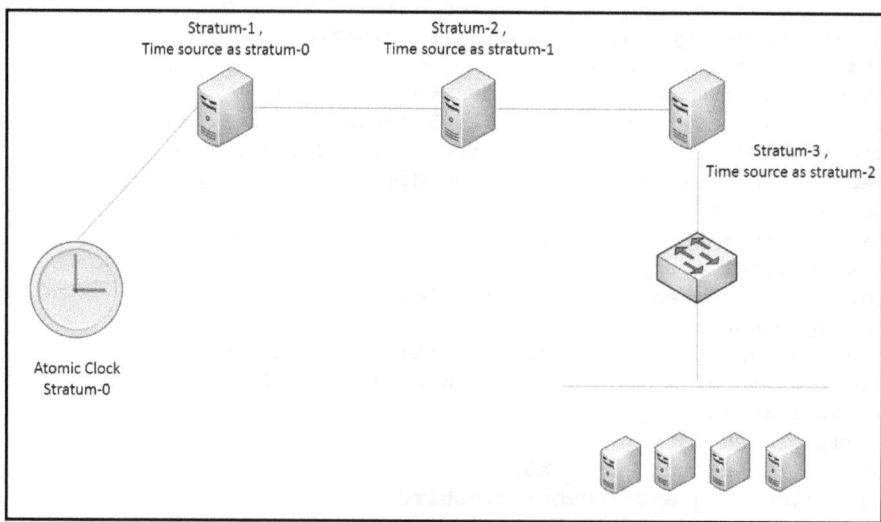

NTP supports up to stratum-15, that is, 16 devices in a hierarchical order. Stratum-16 is the device, for which the time is not synchronized.

There are four possible modes of NTP:

- **NTP client mode**: A network device in the client mode will let its clock synchronize from the other NTP server. These devices will not allow the other network devices to synchronize with their clocks.
- **NTP server mode**: This is a network device running NTP as a service, which allows the other device to synchronize only the time information. The NTP servers do not synchronize their time with other devices.
- **NTP peer mode**: In this mode, the device offers only the time to synchronize with the other peer devices.
- **Broadcast/multicast mode**: In this mode, the NTP servers send broadcast messages or multicast messages in order to synchronize the time information with the NTP clients in the network.

The process of setting up of the clock involves the following steps:

1. The NTP client contacts the time server and initiates a time request exchange.
2. This message exchange enables the client to calculate the link delay, and adjust its clock to match the clock of the server computer.
3. The initial setting of the clock requires a minimum of 6 message exchanges between the client and the server over a period of 5 to 10 minutes.
4. Once the clock is synchronized, the client keeps updating the clock every 10 minutes, requiring at least one message exchange.

A simpler and less secure version of NTP is **Simple Network Time Protocol (SNTP)**. A user can implement NTP on a network by using their own master clock or by using the NTP server that is available on the internet. If using one's own clock, the private network has to be synchronized with the UTC through a satellite or radio.

However, while implementing NAT, one needs to be careful. There is a chance of an attacker launching a DoS attack and sending bogus NTP data over the internet to the user's network. This is done with an aim to change the time on the system's clock, rendering the digital certificates invalid. Such attacks can be prevented by using NTP version 3, which supports the cryptographic authentication mechanism between NTP partners.

This mechanism can be used along with ACLs that identify the devices that are connected to other devices in the network:

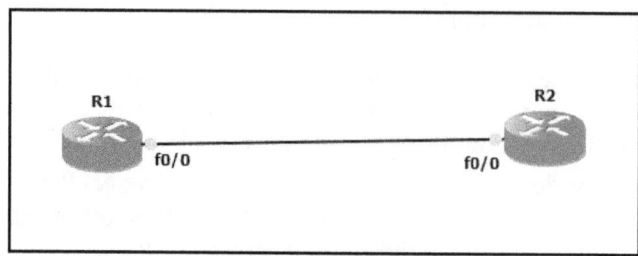

Let's see how to configure NTP from the preceding topology:

1. Configure the IP address on both routers:

   ```
   R1(config)#interface fa0/0
   R1(config-if)#ip address 10.1.1.1 255.255.255.252
   R2(config)#interface fa0/0
   R2(config-if)#ip address 10.1.1.2 255.255.255.252
   R2(config-if)#no shutdown
   ```

2. Configure the key string and key ID for the secure NTP transmission:

   ```
   R1(config)#ntp authentication-key 1 md5 cisco123
   R2(config)# ntp authentication-key 1 md5 cisco123
   ```

3. Configure the key ID to be identified as a trusted one:

   ```
   R1(config)#ntp trusted-key 1
   R2(config)#ntp trusted-key 1
   ```

4. Enable the NTP authentication process:

   ```
   R1(config)#ntp authenticate
   R2(config)#ntp authenticate
   ```

5. Configure R1 to be the NTP master:

   ```
   R1(config)#ntp master
   ```

6. Configure R2 to receive the time source from R1:

   ```
   R2(config)#ntp server 10.1.1.1
   ```

Secure Shell (SSH)

Network administrators use the Telnet protocol to connect to network devices remotely. Telnet provides the user with the flexibility to log in to the device with whatever privileges are configured. Even though Telnet provides more advantages, it is an insecure protocol that sends the information in plain text. **Secure Shell (SSH)** is an application and protocol that secures network sessions to remote network devices. SSH uses a connection-oriented mechanism over a port number of 22. Nowadays, network administrators use SSH instead of Telnet.

There are three main features of SSH:

- **Authentication**: To determine the identity of the user
- **Confidentiality via encryption**: To ensure that the information is only used by the authorized user in the network
- **Integrity**: To ensure that the information sent is modified by an unauthorized user in the network

There are two versions of SSH—version 1 and 2, and communication between the client and server is encrypted in both the servers. However, Cisco IOS software implements only version 1, and use of version 2 is suggested only when possible as it uses a more improved security-encryption algorithm:

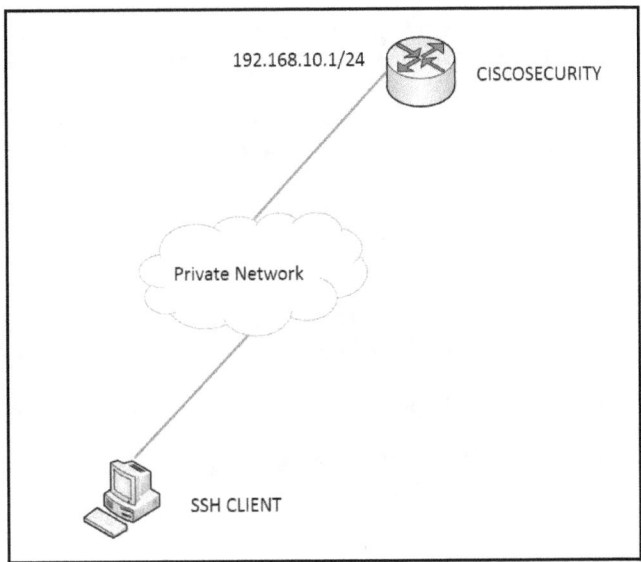

The first step is to configure a local database for user authentication. We will be using CCNASECURITY as the username and CCNASEC as the password. To achieve this, we are going to use the following commands:

```
CISCOSECURITY(config)#username CCNASECURITY password CCNASEC
CISCOSECURITY(config)#exit
```

Then, configure the router to allow users to securely access the CLI. Follow the steps to configure SSH on the router:

1. Configure the `hostname` command:

   ```
   Router(config)#hostname CISCOSECURITY
   ```

2. The next step is to configure a domain name. A domain name should be configured before generating RSA keys:

   ```
   CISCOSECURITY(config)#ip domain-name SECURITY.com
   ```

3. Generate the SSH key to be used:

   ```
   CISCOSECURITY(config)#crypto key generate rsa general-keys
   ```

4. Enable SSH transport support for the **Virtual Terminals** (**VTYs**). Use the following command to complete the preceding steps:

   ```
   CISCOSECURITY(config)#ip domain-name SECURITY.com
   CISCOSECURITY(config)#crypto key generate rsa general-keys

   The name for the keys will be: CISCOSECURITY.SECURITY.com
   Choose the size of the key modulus in the range of 360 to 2048 for
   your
    General Purpose Keys. Choosing a key modulus greater than 512 may
   take
    a few minutes.

   How many bits in the modulus [512]: 512
   % Generating 512 bit RSA keys, keys will be non-exportable...[OK]

   *Mar 1 01:13:53.619: RSA key size needs to be atleast 768 bits for
   ssh version 2
   *Mar 1 01:13:53.631: %SSH-5-ENABLED: SSH 1.5 has been enabled
   ```

5. The next step is to configure the device to use the local user database for authentication and enable SSH services:

```
CISCOSECURITY(config)#line vty 0 15
CISCOSECURITY(config-line)#login local
CISCOSECURITY(config-line)#transport input ssh
CISCOSECURITY(config-line)#exit
```

To recap, steps 1-5 demonstrated how configure a *hostname*, add a *domain name* on the router, generated encryption keys for using the SSH protocol and disabling the Telnet protocol, but ensuring the router will only accept incoming SSH sessions on the vty lines.

Now an SSH client tool can be used to verify the SSH configuration:

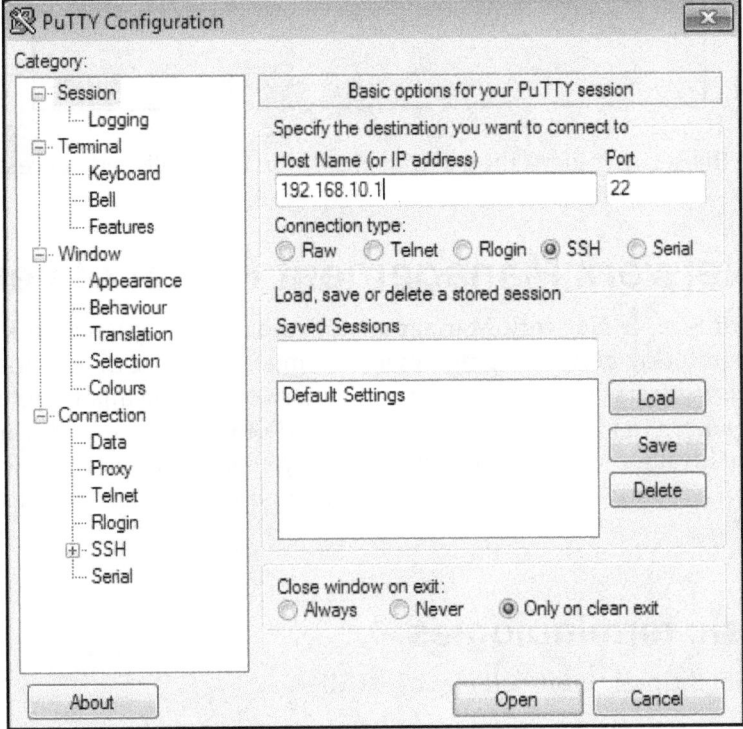

The tool shows a security alert to use the encryption algorithm created:

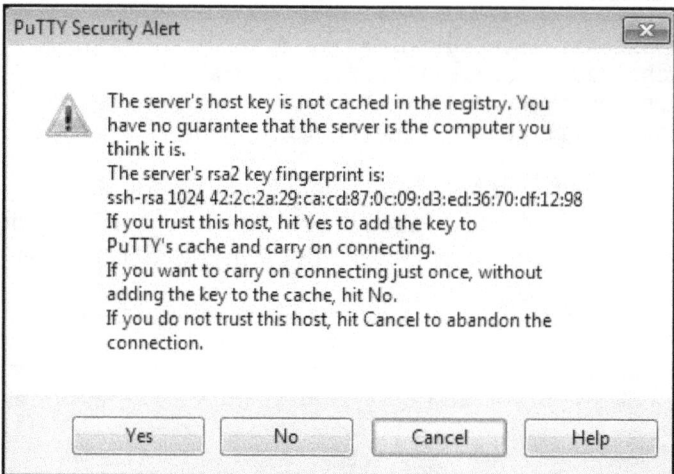

After accepting the security alert, the secure connection is established successfully.

Simple Network Management Protocol version 3

SNMP stands for **Simple Network Management Protocol**. This is a network application that involves monitoring and managing devices from a remote location. For example, if a network administrator has to manage a corporate network that spans 10 floors, it would be difficult for the admin to manage it without some sort of proactive monitoring. Hence SNMP would be ideal for scalable networks, ensuring that the different network parameters, such as bandwidth utilization, security, and availability are within the given threshold.

SNMP basic terminologies

The following are the basic terminologies of SNMP:

- **SNMP manager**: This is the server on which the SNMP program would be running. This device is responsible for collecting information from the clients to provide an overview and analysis of the network's status.

- **SNMP agent**: This is the SNMP client that is to be monitored and managed by the SNMP manager. This is a software that can be installed on any device connected on the network to enable SNMP client functionality. Examples of SNMP agent devices could be routers, switches, servers, desktops, or VoIP phones.
- **OID**: **Object Identifier** (**OID**) identifies the information on an SNMP client that needs to be managed and configured.
- **MIB**: **Managed Information Base** (**MIB**) refers to a common collection of OIDs.
- **Query**: An SNMP message that is sent from the SNMP manager to the agent device to get information about a particular OID.
- **Trap**: An SNMP message that is initiated in an unsolicited manner from the SNMP agent to the manager to provide information about some abnormal events that take place on the monitored device.

SNMP works using the UDP as the underlying layer 4 protocol. SNMP has evolved over three versions:

- SNMPv1
- SNMPv2
- SNMPv3

SNMPv1/v2c uses community strings as the basic security mechanism when forwarding critical SNMP traffic. There are two types of community strings: **Read Only** and **Read Write**. Read Only would be used for getting the SNMP OID information, while Read Write would be applicable for getting as well as setting the value of the OID. SNMPv3 is more secure compared to the previous versions. From a management plane security perspective, it is important to understand and implement SNMPv3.

SNMPv3 compared to its previous versions is more secure. Some of the security features that can be used in SNMPv3 include encryption, hashing, and authentication.

Apart from this, SNMPv3 has some new features when implementing it:

- SNMP view
- SNMP group
- SNMP user

SNMP view

This is basically to inform what OIDs a user is able to monitor and manage. To create an SNMP view:

```
Router(config)# snmp-server view <view name> <OID name> included
```

For example:

```
Router(config)#snmp-server view CISCO ifIndex included
```

Here, CISCO refers to the view name. ifIndex is the OID that provides Read Only information about the interface details such as interface description, interface type, and interface speed.

SNMP group

This is the group that is associated with an SNMP view that contains particular OID information. To create an SNMP group:

```
Router(config)#snmp-server group <Group name> v3 <noauth|auth|priv>
<read|write> <view name>
```

For example:

```
Router(config)#snmp-server group CISCO1 v3 priv read CISCO
```

Here, CISCO1 refers to the group name and the group is mapped to a view called **CISCO** and it is used to access the OID for a read-only purpose. Also, we can see that the security mechanism used here is priv, which basically allows both encryption and authentication.

SNMP user

This is the user that can be associated with a particular SNMP group. To create an SNMP user:

```
Router(config)#snmp-server user <username> <Group name> v3 auth <sha|md5>
<authentication password> priv <encryption algorithm> <encryption key>
```

For example:

```
Router(config)#snmp-server user MICHAEL CISCO1 v3 auth sha cisco123 priv
des56 secret123
```

Here, `MICHAEL` refers to the username and the user is mapped to a group called `CISCO1`. So basically, the user can access a view that is associated with this group. Also we can see that the password used here is `cisco123` and the encryption key is `secret123`.

SNMPv3 lab execution

In this section, we are going to configure Simple Network Management Protocol (SNMP) version 3 on a Cisco IOS router.

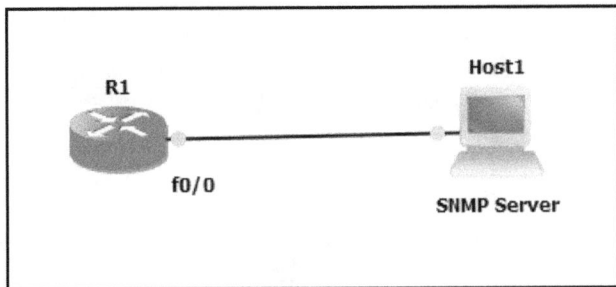

Let's Begin!

1. Configure the IP address on the router `R1 fa0/0` interface:

```
R1(config)#int fa0/0
R1(config-if)#ip address 192.168.56.3 255.255.255.0
R1(config-if)#no shutdown
```

2. Configure the SNMPv3 view, group and user:

```
R1(config)#snmp-server view INTF ifIndex included
R1(config)#snmp-server group CISCO v3 priv read INTF
R1(config)#snmp-server user MICHAEL CISCO v3 auth sha cisco123 priv
des56 secret123
```

3. Configure the SNMP server IP address:

```
R1(config)#snmp-server host 192.168.56.1 version 3 priv MICHAEL
```

The following a graphic displaying the login window for a tool, **OiDViEW** (http://www.oidview.com/):

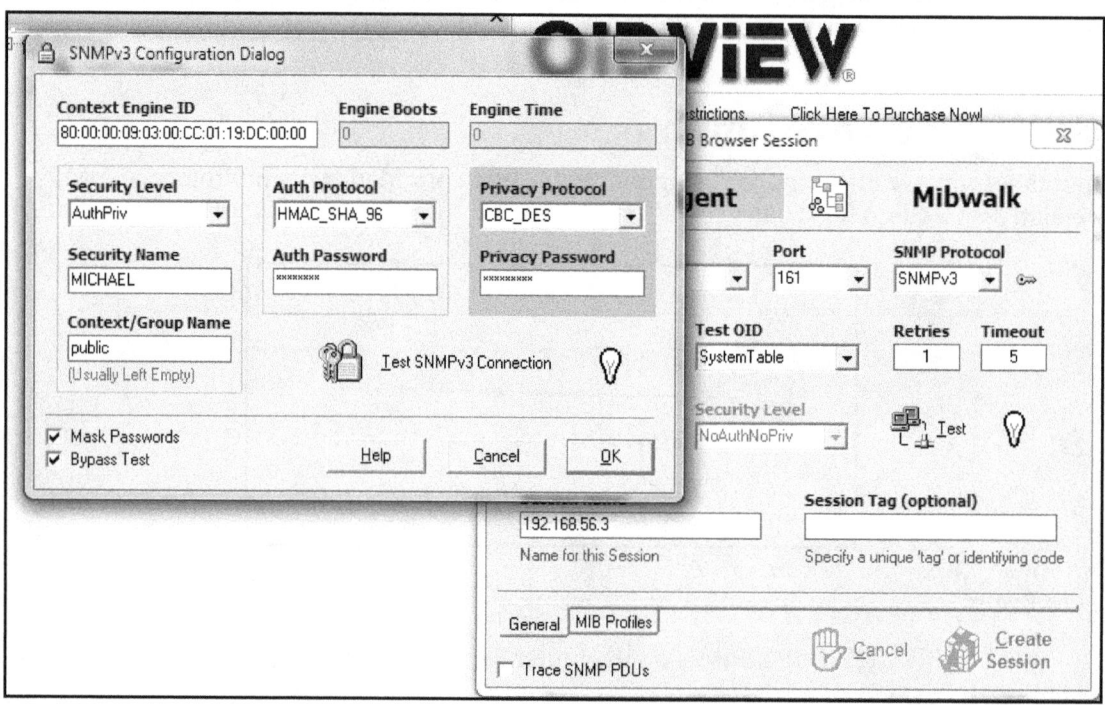

4. Verify the OID from an MIB browser on the SNMP server:

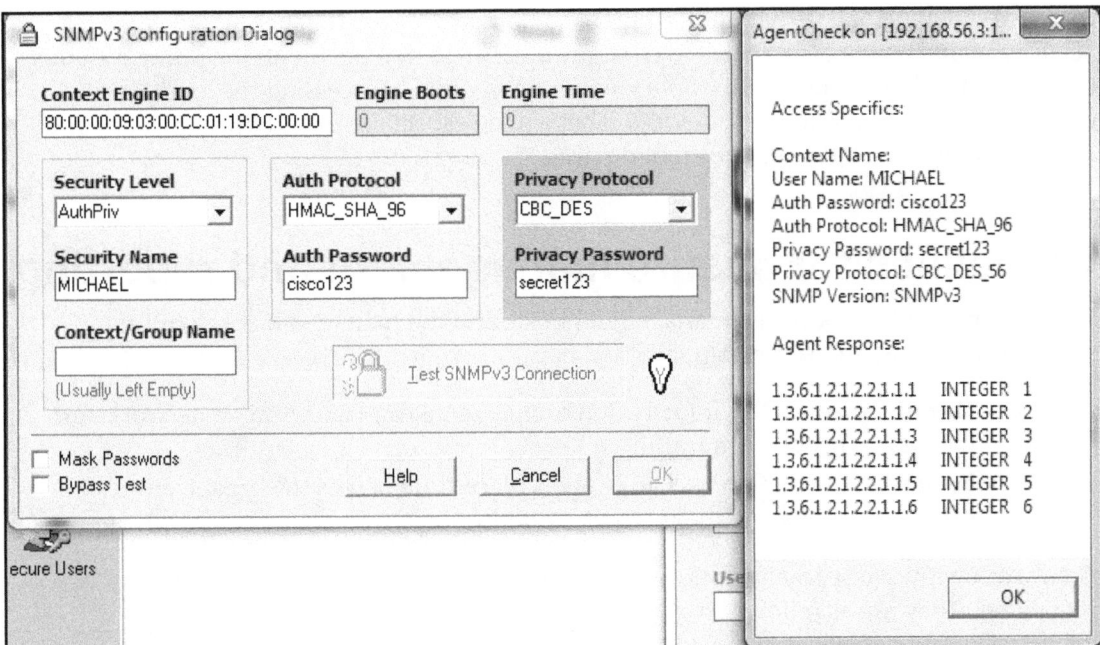

Planning considerations for secure management

When devices are being configured and implemented to ensure secure network management, it becomes important to consider a few other aspects as well. For a network containing only Cisco routers, configuring the devices will not be a complex task. On the contrary, logging and procuring information from multiple devices could be a complex and challenging task giving rise to a few concerns such as:

- Categorizing important logs/messages from regular ones
- Preventing the tampering of logs
- Ensuring time coordination
- Controlling the volume of messages
- Managing all devices

To address these concerns, it is important for an organization to seek input from the network and security teams to help identify its priorities in reporting and monitoring. A robust and detailed security policy would also help to address the mentioned concerns. Security management also relates to configuring change management. Including a change management plan in the security policy will help in quickly accessing the modifications made to the important network devices. This will be especially useful during a network attack to know the status of important devices.

Guidelines for secure management and reporting

The information flow between management hosts and the managed devices (routers, switches, firewalls, and so on) can take two paths:

- **Out-of-band (OOB)**: Information exchange takes place within a network and there is no production traffic
- **In-band**: Information exchange takes place from across the organization's production network, the Internet, or both

A network with two segments follows management, OOB, and in-band architecture guidelines. They are as follows:

- Keeping the clock synchronized across the host and network devices. Clock synchronization also ensures log messages synchronize with each other. In case of a network attack, accurate time helps to identify the sequence of events in which the attack occurred. Therefore, NTP plays an important role by ensuring accurate time on all devices.
- Recording system changes and archiving configurations.
- Ensuring high security while reducing the risk of insecure management protocols across the production network.
- Monitoring and managing devices using **Virtual Private Network (VPN)**, **Secure Shell (SSH)**, or **Secure Sockets Layer (SSL)**.

Log messaging implementation for security

An important part of a security policy is implementing the router logging facility. Cisco routers can contain logging information about any configuration changes, ACL violations, status change of the interface, and so on. Cisco routers also facilitate sending log messages to various locations. Configuring a router enables sending log messages to the following items:

- **Console logging**: Console logging is used to modify or test the router when it is connected to the console. Any messages sent by the console are not stored in the router. Therefore, it is not considered a major security event.
- **Buffered logging**: A router can be regulated to store the log messages in its memory. This is referred to as buffered logging. It is a useful security tool but whenever the router is rebooted, it clears the stored events, which is a major drawback.
- **SNMP traps**: The SNMP agent can process specific router events and then forward them as SNMP traps. SNMP traps is one of the message types used in SNMP protocol. It supports an agent to inform the management station about any significant events through an unsolicited SNMP message. SNMP traps that are addressed to the UDP `port162` facilitate security logging. However, they need to be configured and maintained like an SNMP system.
- **Syslog**: Configuring Cisco routers facilitates forwarding log messages to an external syslog service with a destination UDP port of `514`. Syslog has a central location to store all router messages and provides a long-term log storage facility. Hence, it is the most popular message-logging facility.

These components and devices aid in ensuring the effective management of network security in organizations. The next session will discuss implementing the data plane on Cisco Catalyst switches.

Control Plane Policing

Several security-related products, such as firewalls and an access-list in the router, help the administrator to protect moving through the router or the network. **Control Plane Policing (CoPP)** defines rules and policies to prevent attacks that are bound to the router. This is a Cisco—IOS feature that is specially designed for users to manage the flow of traffic that is handled by the **RP** (short for **route processor**). This helps to stop unnecessary traffic that was not processed by the route processor, thereby increasing security. CoPP sets policies to limit the attack caused directly to the router's interface using the IP address of the interface.

The primary responsibility of the Cisco IOS router is to forward IP packets to their destinations, it is also responsible for processing the traffic of the control and management planes. CoPP policies help administrators protect the control and management planes, and provide a stable routing table and packet delivery. If the attacker is trying to increase the amount of traffic on the management traffic, such as **SSL/HTTPS**, that can be limited and completely stopped with the help of CoPP policies.

The following are the benefits of CoPP policies:

- Helps to protect against the DoS attacks
- Offers an efficient quality of service
- Offers a mechanism for dropping non-processed TCP/UDP packets
- Offers a dedicated control plane interface for traffic processing
- Provides protection for the CPU to provide more resources for important jobs, such as routing

In CoPP, the traffic is first grouped into several class maps and then policies are applied to the traffic groups. The first rule in setting up the policy is to group the traffic types into appropriate class maps. For example, if all the SSH/SSL/HTTP/HTTPS management traffic can be put into one single class, then there might be issues in handling excess amounts of one type of traffic. Also, it would be very complex to place each type of traffic in its own class.

The best procedure for grouping is to configure the class maps to all traffic to be sent in the policy maps. Then, monitor the traffic to have a clear picture of different traffic types and add it into the appropriate class maps. The following are the different groups and class maps that can be created:

- The fragmented or non-fragmented packets of known malicious programs
- A class for all the routing protocols
- A class for SSH and Telnet and other management protocols such as SNMP, FTP, and TFTP
- A class for all the IP traffic
- Network application traffic such as HSRP, IGMP, and DHCP

Implementing class-map

In **Modular Quality of Service** (**MQC**), the statement class-map defines the name of the classes. It consists of one or more match statements that includes the classification of the packets. The keyword match supports the following items:

- Can contain access-control lists
- Can contain the IP type of service packets
- Can contain ARP protocol packets

The following steps show the configuration of CoPP:

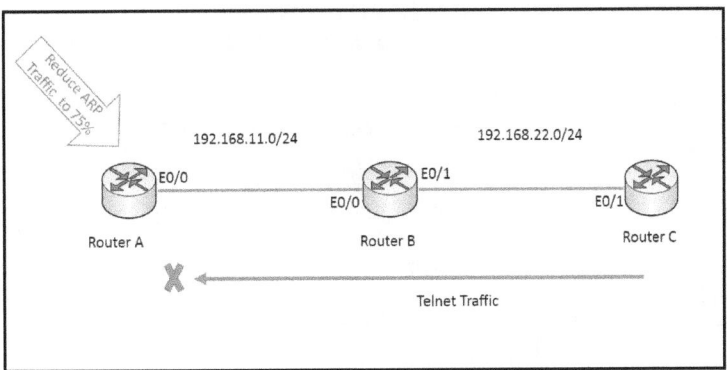

The following commands show how to configure a control-plane policing to reduce the ARP traffic sent to **Router A** to **75%** and to drop the Telnet traffic from **Router C** to **Router A**.

The first step is create a class-map for the ARP traffic and Telnet, then create a policy map and apply the policy map to the control plane:

```
RouterA(config)#class-map ARP
RouterA(config-cmap)#match protocol arp
```

After the creation of class-map that matches the ARP protocol, create a policy map to reduce the packets to 75% per second:

```
RouterA(config)#policy-map POLICY
RouterA(config-pmap)#class ARP
RouterA(config-pmap-c)#police rate ?
 <1-2000000000> Rate value in the range 8000-2,000,000,000 bps or
1-2,000,000
 pps
 percent % of interface bandwidth for rate
RouterA(config-pmap-c)#police rate 75 pps
RouterA(config-pmap-c-police)#exit
```

Now the ARP protocol on RouterA is reduced to 75% packets per second.

The next step is to create an access-list to group the Telnet packets:

```
RouterA(config)#ip access-list extended TELNET
RouterA(config-ext-nacl)#permit tcp host 192.168.22.2 any eq telnet
RouterA(config-ext-nacl)#exit
RouterA(config)#class-map TELNET
RouterA(config-cmap)#match access-group name TELNET
RouterA(config-cmap)#exit
```

Then, configure policing for the TELNET class map you created:

```
RouterA(config-pmap)#class TELNET
RouterA(config-pmap-c)#?
QoS policy-map class configuration commands:
  bandwidth          Bandwidth
  compression        Activate Compression
  drop               Drop all packets
  exit               Exit from QoS class action configuration mode
  netflow-sampler    NetFlow action
RouterA(config-pmap-c)#drop
RouterA(config-pmap-c)#exit
RouterA(config-pmap)#exit
RouterA(config)#control-plane
RouterA(config-cp)#?
Control Plane configuration commands:
  exit                     Exit from control-plane configuration mode
  no                       Negate or set default values of a command
  service-policy           Configure QOS Service Policy
RouterA(config-cp)#service-policy input POLICY
RouterA(config-cp)#exit
```

Summary

In this chapter, we learned about securing the network management plane, components of a security policy, convergence of the IT GRC components, the five phases of the SDLC, syslog protocol, Network Time Protocol and **Simple Network Management Protocol Version 3** (**SNMPv3**), and Network Time Protocol.

In the next chapter, we will discuss protecting Layer 2 protocols in detail.

7
Protecting Layer 2 Protocols

This chapter deals with the concept of protecting the resources/IT infrastructure from internal threats. Internal threats refer to people who are recruited by the organization as employees who are provided access to the internal resources. Mostly organizations focus on securing the network from external threats but fail to address the internal vulnerabilities.

Traditionally, internal users have been able to connect a PC to a switched network and gain immediate access to enterprise resources. As networks grow and resources become available, it is important to limit the access that internal users receive. More technically, a user from the HR department should have a connection to the port that terminates on their respective desk. Access to switches is a convenient entrypoint for internal attackers whose intent is to unlawfully gain access to an enterprise network from outside the organization's premises. An attacker can set up rogue access points and protocol analyzers to launch all types of attacks.

Switches have various methodologies that secure the access of attackers. Users can be authenticated as they connect and also can be authorized to perform certain configurations on a switch. In addition, Cisco switches can detect and prevent certain types of attacks. Several features can be used to validate information passing through a switch.

Layer 2 attack mitigation

All layers of TCP/IP have their own security threats and vulnerabilities. Unfortunately, if the lower layer is hacked, communications are compromised without the other layers being aware of the problem. Everything at Layer 3 and higher is encapsulated into some type of Layer 2 frame. If an attacker can interrupt, copy, redirect, or confuse the Layer 2 forwarding, they can also disrupt the functions of the upper-layer protocols:

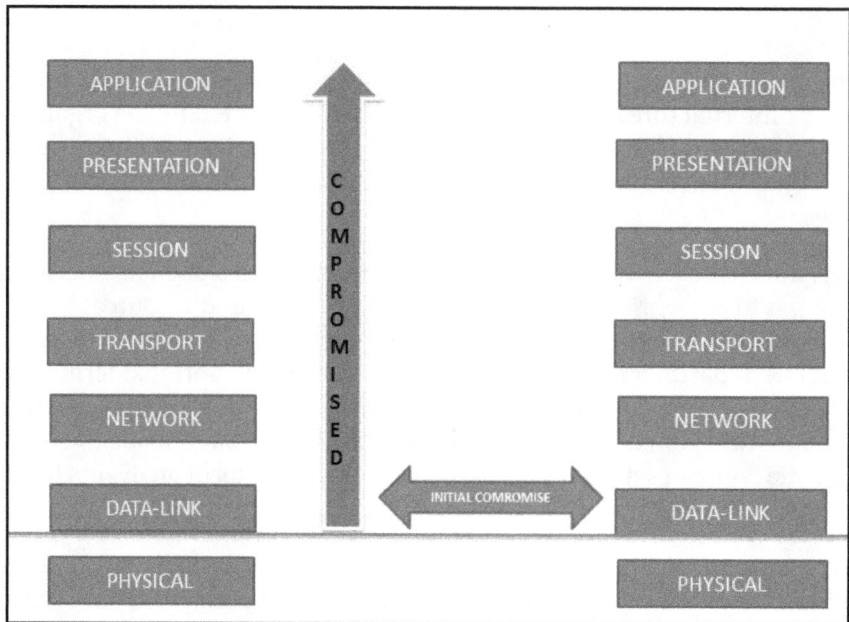

For example, an internal attacker who is connected to the network using some port-scanning tools to scan the open ports can gain access to the switch through which they can start accessing the upper-layer devices.

Port scanning is a reconnaissance mechanism that attackers use to scan the ports that are active.

Features of the Virtual Local Area Network

Virtual Local Area Networks (**VLANs**) are defined as separate broadcast domains, which are local to the switch and controls broadcast, multicast, unicast, and unknown unicast frames. They are defined in an internal database (VLAN.dat) of the switch. The desired ports of a switch can be assigned to the VLANs as per the requirements. VLANs are assigned numbers for identification within a switch or among other switches in the topology. They have a variety of parameters that can be configured to identify them from each other, such as type, name, and state. There are some VLANs that are reserved for special purposes.

The following figure illustrates the hierarchical network diagram of Cisco's hierarchical architecture, where VLANs are generally implemented in the access layer where end users are connected. The network with IP addresses ranging from 10.1.1.0/24—10.1.4.0/24 is assigned to the VLAN named **IT** and **Human Resources**, 10.2.1.0/24 to 10.2.4.0/24 is assigned to **Sales** and **Marketing**, and 10.3.1.0/24 to 10.3.4.0/24 is assigned to **Finance** and **Accounting**:

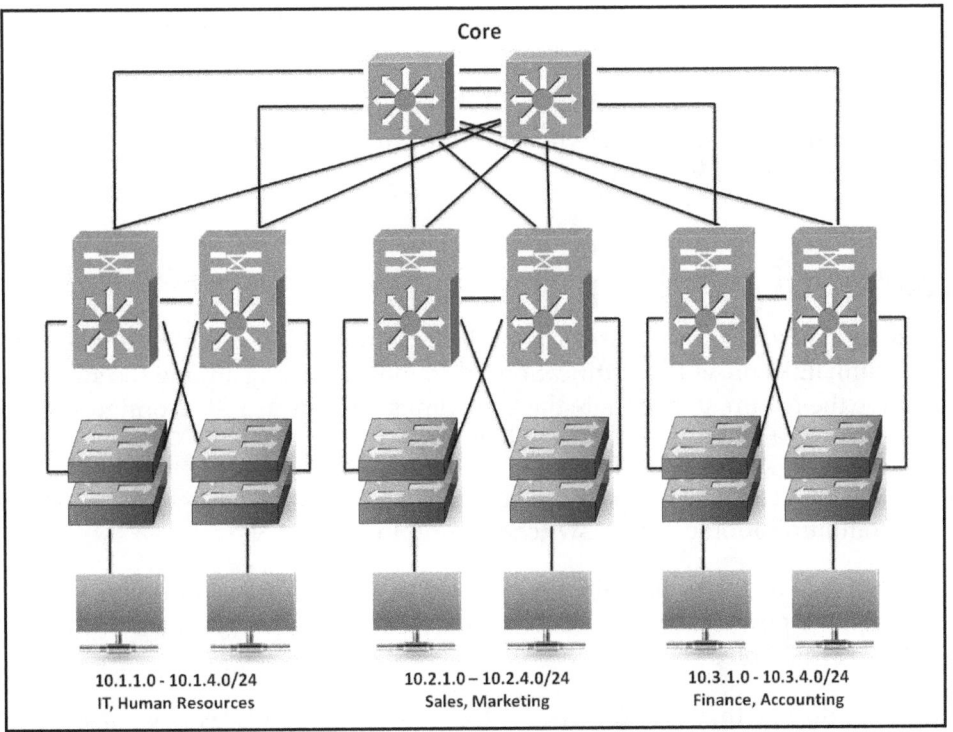

VLAN tagging

When there is a single switch in a VLAN segment, no tagging is required, since the switch is aware of the ports connected based on the CAM table. Things become a little complicated as we introduce more switches in the existing topology and the packets needs to commute over one or more aggregated ports, known as **trunks**:

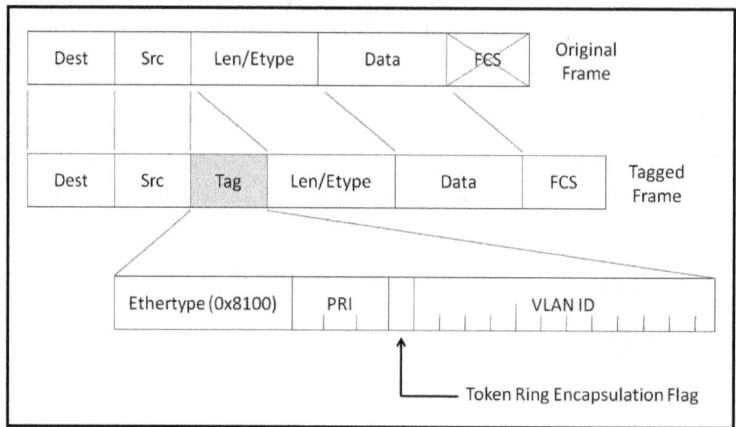

A tag is a 16-bit field that is inserted into an Ethernet frame. When a switchport is encapsulated with an ISL or tagged with a 802.1Q protocol, the mechanism adds the **VLAN identification number** or **VLAN ID**.

Features of trunking

VLANs are local to each other's databases and their information is not passed between switches. Trunk links provide identification for frames travelling among the switches. Some switches have the feature to negotiate the trunk links. Trunks must be configured on both the ends of the link, that is, on both the switchports.

As discussed, trunks are used to pass information between VLANs among the switches. This helps communication between switches for multiple VLANs.

An access port is allowed to share the traffic of a single VLAN. For example, in switch A, if a FastEthernet 0/2 port has been assigned to VLAN 600 then that port would carry the traffic of VLAN 600 only.

A trunk port is the one that would carry the traffic of multiple VLANs over a single link, irrespective of the ports.

For example, in switch **B**, if a FastEthernet 0 / 4 port has been configured to carry the traffic of VLANs from 3-8, then they would allow any frame with that respective VLAN tagging:

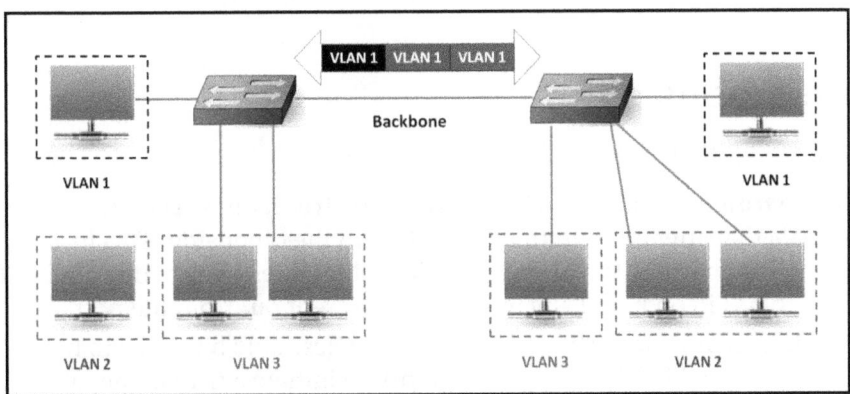

In order to identify the traffic, VLAN tagging is done on the frame so that these trunk ports can mobile the frames accordingly.

There is also an automatic trunking mechanism known as **DTP**, the **dynamic trunking protocol**. This allows the trunk to be dynamically configured between two switches. All Cisco switches can use this protocol to form a trunk link. If one side of the link is the trunk, then it will send DTP signals to the other side of the link. If the signals are accepted/matched then they tend to form a trunk link.

Points to remember:

- Switches should have same trunking mechanism configured on their ends of the trunk link.
- Some iOS do not support DTP, in such cases the command—switchport mode trunk can be used to switch on trunking on that port.
- DTP does not offer any benefit when the user is trying to trunk with a non-Cisco switch.
- It is advisable to use the negotiate option when DTP is not supported and also for hardcoding the port as either access or trunk.
- Cisco 2950 and 3500XL switches do not support DTP and would always be used for configuring manual trunking.
- The 2950 and some 4000 switches support only 802.1Q trunking and provide no options for changing the trunk type.

- **Cisco Discovery Protocol** (CDP) version 2 passes native VLAN information between Cisco switches. If there is a native VLAN mismatch, a CDP error message would be displayed on the console output.

Trunking modes

The following are different types of trunking modes:

- **Mode trunk**: Trunking is ON for the mode trunk links. They will also send DTP signals that attempt to initiate a trunk with the other side. This forms a trunk with other ports in the on, auto, or desirable states, which are running DTP. A port that is in on mode always tags frames sent out from the port.
- **Mode dynamic desirable**: Mode dynamic desirable links like to become trunk links and send DTP signals that attempt to initiate a trunk. They will only become trunk links if the other side responds to the DTP signal. This forms a trunk with other ports in the on, auto, or desirable states that is running DTP.
- **Mode dynamic auto**: These links will only become trunk links if they receive a DTP signal from a link that is already trunking or desires to trunk. This will only form a trunk with other ports in the on or desirable states. This is the default mode for CatOS switches.
- **Mode nonegotiate**: Sets trunking on and disables DTP. These will only become trunks with ports in on or nonegotiate mode.
- No switchport mode trunk: This option sets trunking and DTP capabilities off. This is the recommended setting for any access port because it will prevent any dynamic establishments of trunk links.

The following graphic displays the possible outcome of a shared link between switches if either **Switch-A** or **Switch-B** has their port/interface configured in a particular state/trunking mode:

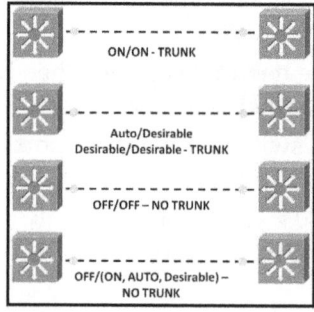

The following is an example with configurations to understand this concept better:

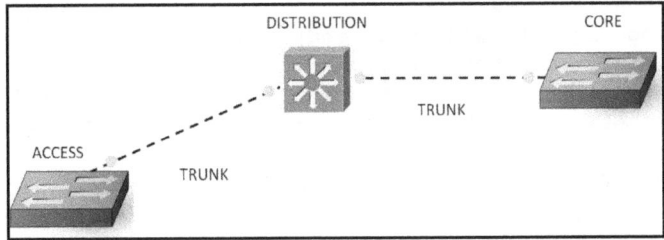

Overview of the configurations which will be apply to the above topology:

- 802.1Q is configured between the access and distribution switches
- ISL is configured between the distribution and core switches
- The core switch is configured for auto-trunking mode and negotiates the encapsulation on the link
- The trunk between the access switch is configured for VLAN 8, 9, and 10
- The trunk between the core and distribution is configured for VLAN 1 and 10

On the core switch, we going to execute the following command:

```
Core(config)#interface gigabitethernet 1/1
Core(config-if)#switchport encapsulation negotiate
Core(config-if)#switchport mode dynamic auto
Core(config-if)#switchport trunk allowed vlan remove 2-1001
Core(config-if)#switchport trunk allowed vlan add 10
Core(config-if)#end
Core#copy running-configstartup-config
```

On the access switch:

```
Access(config)#interface gigabitethernet 0/1
Access(config-if)#switchport mode trunk
Access(config-if)#switchport trunk encapsulation dot1q
Access(config-if)#switchport trunk allowed vlan remove 2-1001
Access(config-if)#switchport trunk allowed vlan add 5,8,10
Access(config-if)#end
Access#copy running-configstartup-config
```

On the distribution switch:

```
Distribution(config)#interface gigabitethernet 0/1
Distribution(config-if)#switchport mode trunk
Distribution(config)#switchport trunk encapsulation ISL
Distribution(config)#switchport trunk allowed vlan remove 2-1001
Distribution(config)#switchport trunk allowed vlan add 1,10
Distribution(config)#end
Distribution#copy running-configstartup-config
```

VLAN Trunking Protocol

VLAN Trunking Protocol (VTP) is used to sync name settings and to prune VLANs from the trunk links that are destined for Layer 2 devices that do not have any ports active in that respective VLAN. The user can also specify a VTP domain name for identifying it easily. It requires you to enable trunking, through which the VTP domain name would get popularized, even to the switch on which the domain name is not configured. VTPs with the different domain name will not exchange any information.

Some features of VTP are as follows:

- VTP sends information to maintain VLANs on trunked switches to accelerate the trunking
- It is a Cisco proprietary protocol for managing VLANs and runs on any type of trunk mechanism
- VTP is functioned in common VTP domain between switches
- VTP passwords can be set to control the exchange of information
- VLAN 2 to VLAN 1002 are managed by VTP
- VTP allows switches to exchange their updates based on the revision number
- There are three different modes of VTP to operate
- VTP can prune unwanted VLANs from trunk links

By default, no VTP passwords are set, so any switch with trunk enabled port can join the domain or any switch with the same VTP domain name can join it and capture the traffic, so to secure this VTP password is set. And the information is exchanged after the successful authorization:

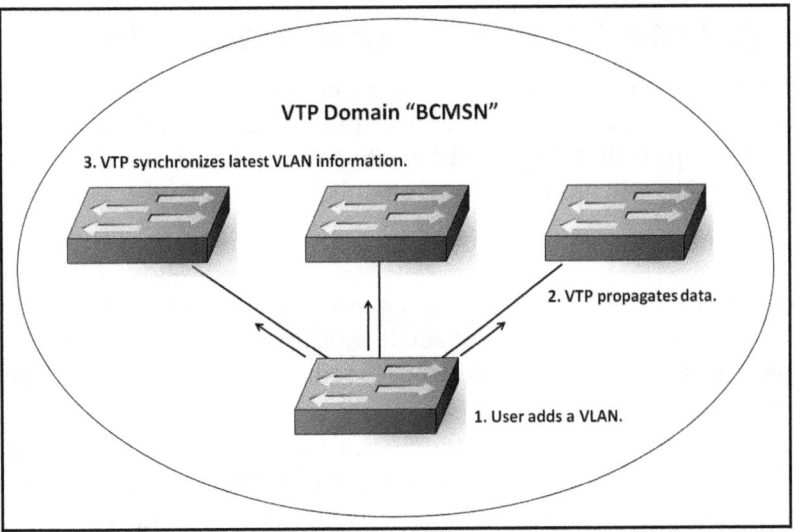

Three different modes are assigned to VTP-enabled switches. They are server (default mode), client, and transparent, respectively. Hence the switch can be configured in any of these VTP modes to function:

- **Server**: This is the default mode of VTP. In VTP server mode, we can create, modify, and delete VLANs. We can also configure other parameters such VTP password, version, or pruning for the entire domain. These servers share their VLAN information and sync with other switch's databases based on the updates received on their trunk links.

- **Transparent**: These switches do not participate in the domain. They neither update their database nor do they advertise any information with the other switches. The only function that they perform in the case of VTPv2, is to pass on the update received on their port to the next switch in the domain.

- **Client**: They also operate in a similar manner with that of the server, but the only difference is that they cannot create, modify, or delete any VLANs like the server VTPs can do.

 VTP pruning is a feature of VTP that does not allow the unnecessary traffic to pass the trunk.

Spanning Tree Protocol fundamentals

The switched network is a very crucial part of the networking, since they are prone to loops when redundant links exists. It becomes very important to manage the loop prevention. The problem with loops is that they would create a storm, which would consume the entire bandwidth causing the switches to perform unwell.

Solutions to loop:

- The primary solution would be to have a single link connecting the switches, and this might be helpful in case of small enterprises with a small team size. But when we talk about bigger enterprises redundancy is the most required element of the network.
- Another solution is to deploy the **Spanning Tree Protocol** (**STP**). The main living task of STP is to prevent loops by temporarily blocking the redundant link.
- The topology of redundant connections between three switches, where Switch A has the MAC address of aaa, switch **B** has the MAC address of bbb, and switch **C** has the MAC address of ccc:

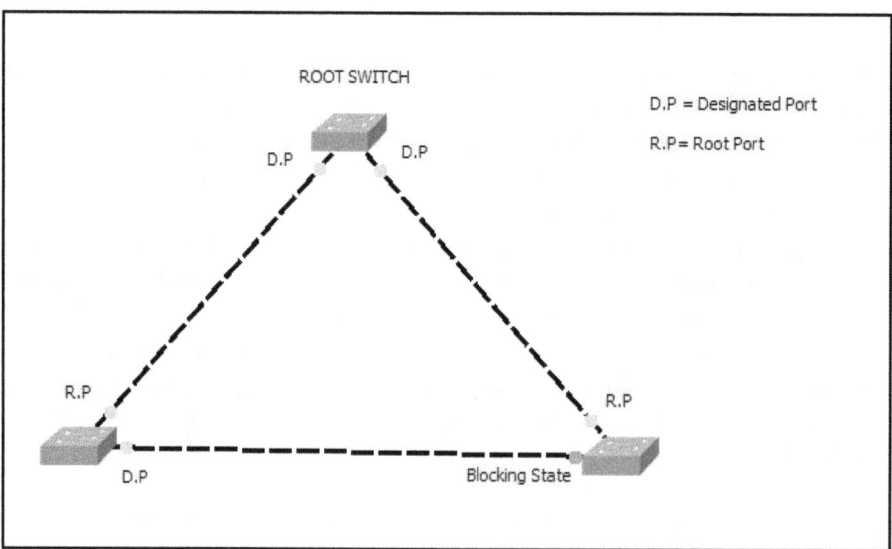

After the election and selection root bridge in STP, the connected ports on the switch would immediately pick up the roles based on their position and their functionality in the topology:

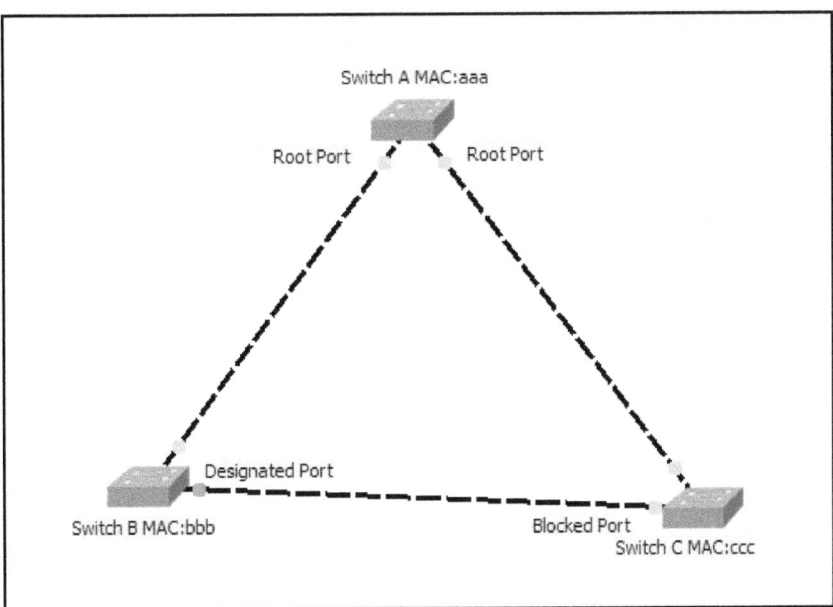

The ports are:

- **Root port**: It is the best selected path to the root bridge
- **Designated port**: It is the best selected path given to a specific switched segment, the port connected to a root port is the designated port
- **Alternate port**: It is the backup of the root port, if by any case the roots link goes faulty, then this port would immediately take the role of the root port
- **Backup port**: It is the port that is the backup of the designated port

The STP blocks the alternate and the backup port to prevent loops in the topology. This is how STP functions.

Port states

The STP-enabled ports have different states, as follows:

- **Blocking state**: This is the initial state of each port when the switch is powered on. Ports that are in the blocking state will not forward any traffic. They only listen to the traffic and continue to be in the blocking state. If they receive any topology change notification frames, then they would convert into the listening state till the change gets stabilized and these port would be ready to take a new state, if required.
- **Listening state**: Ports in this state do not forward any traffic. They only listen to the traffic. This is the next immediate state of the blocking state. This is also the first step of start-frame forwarding. The time it takes for the transition is 15 seconds by default.
- **Learning state**: Ports in this state start learning the addresses while listening to the traffic of the connected device in that segment. The default time is 15 seconds.
- **Forwarding state**: In this state, the ports would forward and will continue listening to the traffic, that is, learning the addresses.
- **Disabled ports**: These ports neither listen nor forward any traffic.

Steps in implementing STP

The steps followed by STP to complete its cycle are as follows:

- Root bridge election
- Root port election
- Designated port election
- Alternative/blocking port election

Root bridge election

The bridge with the lowest bridge ID is elected as the root bridge. The bridge ID consists of the following:

- Priority number
- MAC address of bridge

Example: `32768.00:00:00:00:00:01 / [Priority number].[MAC Address]`

During the root bridge election process the Priority number is compared first. If the priority number is equal, then the MAC address is used as a tie-breaker.

Root port election

Each port that has the lowest path cost to the root bridge is assigned the role of the root port. The path cost is calculated by the cumulative cost of all paths to the root bridge:

- Root ports are only assigned to non-root bridges
- Each non-root bridge only has one root port

Designated port election

Each port with the lowest accumulative path cost to the root bridge is assigned the role of designated port:

- Each segment (path) has one designated port
- Designated ports are assigned to all bridges (non-root and root)

In the event of two ports containing the same path cost, the neighboring switches bridge ID is used. Again the lowest bridge ID wins.

Alternative port election

All remaining ports are set to alternative and the state transitioned to blocking.

A useful command in STP:

```
Enabling STP
```

Cisco Discovery Protocol

CDP stands for **Cisco Discovery Protocol**. This is a Cisco proprietary mechanism that can be used for verifying the Cisco devices connected directly to the host.

CDP sends the host details to its Cisco neighbor every 60 seconds by default and places a hold time of 180 seconds. If a CDP message does not reach the neighbor within 180 seconds, it will consider the neighbor dead and remove it from the CDP table.

To enable CDP globally:

```
Sw(config)#cdp run
```

This command enables CDP on all the interfaces. This may pose a security threat as an interface that is connected to the internet may leave its information open to some unknown user which might be exploited. Hence its better to turn on CDP on the required interfaces alone.

To enable CDP on the interfaces:

```
Sw(config-if)#cdp enable
```

To disable CDP on a particular interface, use the `no cdp enable` command on the corresponding interface mode.

To verify the information that a neighbor sends through CDP:

```
Sw#show cdp neighbors
```

This output gives the neighbor's hostname, interface connected to the neighbor, model of the Cisco neighbor, and so on.

To get detailed information, such as the IP address of the neighbor:

```
Sw#show cdp neighbor detail
```

For example:

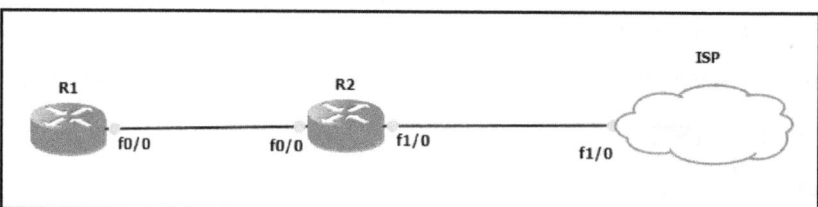

In this example, we have two routers connected to the external internet. The R2 router is connected to the public cloud on the `f1/0` interface. We can realize a vulnerability if CDP is turned on in this interface. Hence we can disable CDP on the `f1/0` interface:

```
R2(config)#interface FastEthernet 1/0
R2(config-if)#no cdp enable
```

As a result, we can see the output shown on R2:

```
R2#sh cdp neighbors
Capability Codes: R - Router, T - Trans Bridge, B - Source Route Bridge
 S - Switch, H - Host, I - IGMP, r - Repeater
Device ID   Local Intrface   Holdtme    Capability   Platform     Port ID
R1          Fas 0/0          166        R S I        3640         Fas 0/0
```

Thus we can enable CDP in a more secured manner.

Layer 2 protection toolkit

Let's see how we can prevent VLAN hopping.

VLAN hopping is a practice where the traffic is moved from one VLAN to another VLAN without being routed, so an attacker can jack in anytime and gain the information. You can launch an attack on VLAN hopping by *switch-spoofing* and *double-tagging*.

Let's understand them one by one.

In a Cisco switch, by default a trunk port carries traffic of all the VLANs configured in the respective switch. So if an attacker can make the switch to transform into a trunk port, then they have access to all the information of all the VLANs. To break this attack, we can disable trunking on all ports that need not run the functionality of the trunk. Also disable DTP on the ports, since they are by default in auto mode which means they became trunk ports as and when they receive DTP frames.

The following exhibits how to disable a trunk on Cisco switch **A**:

```
SwitchA(config)#int fa0/1
SwitchA(config-if)#switchport mode access
SwitchA(config-if)#exit
```

The following exhibits how to prevent the use of DTP in Cisco switch **A**:

```
SwitchA(config)#int fa0/1
SwitchA(config-if)#switchport trunk encapsulation dot1q
SwitchA(config-if)#switchport mode trunk
SwitchA(config-if)#switchport nonegotiate
```

Double tagging: as per 802.1Q, a VLAN is termed as native VLAN, which means that no tagging is required for those frames as they travel from one switch to another. If an attacker has an address of native VLAN, then he can use this particular feature of native VLAN to send traffic that has two 802.1Q tags. The switch won't examine the frame because of its outer tagging and the target VLAN to which the attacker wants to send the traffic.

How to set a native VLAN in a Cisco switch:

```
SwitchA(config)#int fa0/1
SwitchA(config-if)#switchport trunk native vlan 100
```

Protecting with a BPDU guard

This feature is enabled on ports that have the Cisco **portfast** feature enabled in it. This feature is enabled on those ports that are connected to the hosts and end devices. Since portfast is connected to end devices, they would skip some states of STP, and save the convergence time and indicates to the switch that no BPDU frames are expected to be received on the local interface which has the portfast configuration. Therefore if any port that has the BPDU guard enabled in it receives any BPDU, the port is disabled thereby shutting the attacker down.

Configuring a BPDU guard in a Cisco switch **A**:

```
SwitchA(config)#int fa0/1
SwitchA(config-if)#spanning-tree portfast bpduguard
```

Protecting with root guard

This feature is one of the spanning tree enhancements given by Cisco. Root guard is required when the administrator needs to place the root bridge in a network topology. The root guard feature can be enabled on all the Cisco switches. When enabled in a port, the port turns into a designated port, unless two or more ports of the root bridge are connected together. When a bridge receives superior **BPDUs** (short for, **Bridge Protocol Data Units**) on a port enabled with root guard, root guard puts the port into a state that is equal to a listening state (root- inconsistent state). Traffic will not be forwarded through this port.

The root bridge priority can be set to 0 manually to ensure the root bridge position, but you don't have a guarantee of a bridge with a priority of 0 and a lower MAC Address.

Switch A has the lowest bridge ID and it becomes the **Root Bridge**. Now **Switch D** begins to participate in STP and it has the lowest priority or the lowest bridge ID value, so **Switch D** will be elected as the new root bridge:

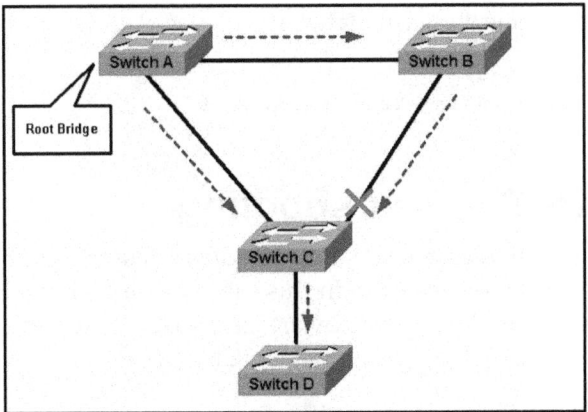

If the link between the **Switch A** and **B** is a one Gigabit link and the link between **Switch A** and **C**, **Switch B** and **C** is 100 Mbps link, the new root puts the link between **Switch A** and **B** in the blocking state. This alters the data flow in the topology and may cause connectivity outage:

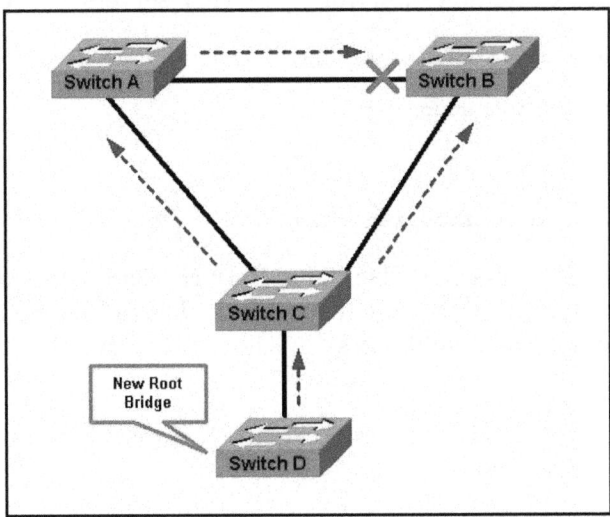

Enabling the root guard feature on a port basis defends against such issues

If root guard is enabled on the port of **Switch C** connected to **Switch D**, when it receives a superior BPDU, the root guard puts the port into an STP inconsistent state so no traffic will pass. The inconsistent state is automatically recovered when **Switch D** stops to send superior BPDUs.

The configuration of root guard on a switchport:

```
SwitchA(config)#int fa0/2
SwitchA(config-if)#spanning-tree guard root
```

Combating DHCP server spoofing

Most clients, in today's scenarios, receive their IP address using DHCP, not statistically configured for their information security. In this case, if an attacker injects his fake DHCP server then he gains access to the systems by assigning the IP address from his server, if only his server responds faster than the actual DHCP server.

In the this case, the fake DHCP assigns the IP address, and the information is routed to the attacker's desired gateway, which can be also the attacker's IP address. This can go undetected for a very long time, since everything is functioning properly for the client.

The DHCP snooping feature is used to mitigate this attack. This feature enables us to configure the switch ports either in the trusted or untrusted state. If a port is trusted, then it is allowed to receive the communication from the DHCP servers or else they are disabled.

The command used to enable DHCP snooping:

```
SwitchA(config)#ip dhcp snooping
```

To enable in VLANs:

```
SwitchA(config)#ip dhcp snooping vlan 1-100
```

A different kind of DHCP attack is the **Denial of Service** (**DoS**) attack against the DHCP Server, where the attacker can repeatedly request IP address assignments from the DHCP server, thus depleting the pool of addresses. This is achieved by using different MAC addresses.

This can be mitigated by the DHCP snooping feature by limiting the number of DHCP messages per second per interface.

The command to limit the DHCP messages:

```
SwitchA(config)#int fa0/4
SwitchA(config-if)#ip dhcp snooping limit rate 4
```

Mitigating CAM-table overflow attacks

A switch uses the **CAM** (short for, **Content Addressable Memory**) table to store the MAC addresses learned by it during the transaction phase of traffic, this helps in taking the decision to forward/filter the data from the source to the destination in a single, connected LAN segment. The switch is a Layer 2 device, and they operate using MAC addresses. The MAC address table has a size limit:

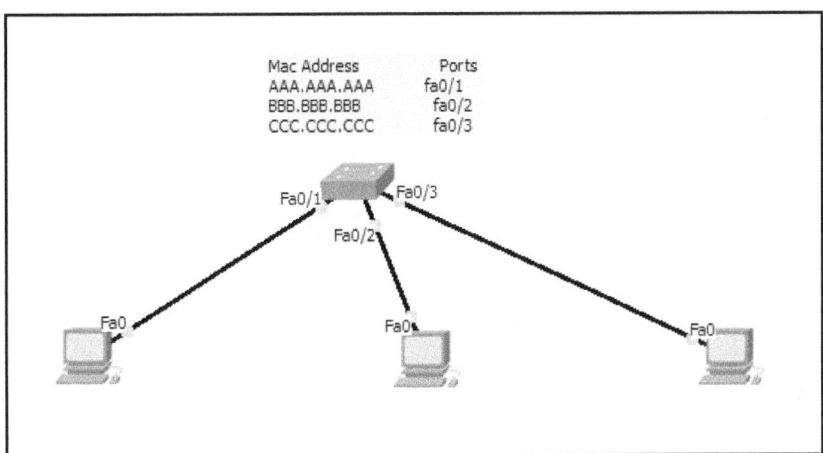

When the CAM table is filled and saturated, it is unable to learn new MAC addresses. As a result, it floods out the frames to all the interfaces except to the one from where the frame has been received.

If an attacker PC is connected to a switch, and it makes the CAM table overflow, then the traffic from the other hosts would be flooded to their system, where they can capture the data. The *macof* utility is used to overflow the CAM table. The size of the CAM table varies from switch to switch, which can be set to a limit by the administrators. The behavior of flooding the frames with an unlearned destination MAC address is known as the **fail-open mode**.

MAC spoofing attack

MAC address spoofing is another type of attack on the switch's CAM table where the attacker creates false MAC address and inserts them into a switch. Switches have the habit of learning all the MAC address of the connected ports. When an attacker inserts a false MAC address, switches relearn the MAC address. So this changes the logical flow of data and it may also cause flooding.

Port security configuration

Port security is one of the interface-level features that helps the administrator to decide the number of users that can be allowed to a switchport. Port security can be configured even before you introduce the switch to the network. When a MAC address is assigned to a secure port, the switch doesn't forward the frames with the source address outside the well-defined group of addresses. With the help of this feature, the size of the MAC address table can be defined. A violation of switchport security has some consequences too.

There are three types of methods to validate port security:

- Protect
- Restrict
- Shutdown

Protect

When you configure a port with switchport security, the port will check whether the incoming frame is from a known MAC or an unknown MAC. If it is from a known or assigned MAC address, then it would allow the traffic, otherwise it would drop the frame.

Restrict

It would operate in a similar manner as that of protect, but in this case it would send an SNMP trap to the server. It would increment the count of violation as well.

Shutdown

Shutting down the interface is the most secured and strictest approach of all. It not only shut downs but also generates notifications.

Port security is not the result of the saturated CAM table but also when a different MAC address is trying to share frames using a secured port. We will understand those scenarios in the following explanations. There are three types of secured MAC address ports.

Using a single-line command, an administrator can ensure that a device has its MAC address statically configured for a set port, and can only access the port on a switch.

For example, if a host with the `1111.2222.3333.4444` MAC address has been statically configured to access the FastEthernet `0/3` port, and if a device with the `3333.5555.6bc4.3456` MAC address tries to access the FastEthernet `0/3` port, then one of the preceding responses would take place.

The command to secure the MAC address statically:

```
SwitchA(config)#int fa0/3
SwitchA(config-if)# switchport port-security mac-address 0000.0000.0003
```

Sticky secure MAC address: In a sticky secure MAC address environment, a switchport learns the MAC address, which should be allowed to access the port, via a sticky command. When a device is connected to a port where this feature enabled, the port will immediately store that MAC address and allow only that device to access the port. It also depends on how many MAC addresses can be learned by the port. This is configured by the administration as per his requirement.

The command to sticky-secure MAC addresses:

```
SwitchA(config)#int fa0/2
SwitchA(config-if)# switchport port-security mac-address sticky
```

Dynamically secure MAC addresses: These MAC addresses are stored in a CAM table and not in the switch's running config. They learn MAC addresses in a very similar manner to a sticky-secure MAC address, in a dynamic fashion but they don't save the MAC address for the next access authorization. They would erase it after some time from the CAM table.

The command to dynamically store MAC address:

```
SwitchA(config)#int interface-id
SwitchA(config-if)# switchport mode {access | trunk}
SwitchA(config-if)#switchport port-security
SwitchA(config-if)# switchport port-security maximum value
SwitchA(config-if)#switchport port-security violation {protect | restrict |
shutdown [vlan]}
```

A quick glance at the port security configuration on an interface:

Switch Commands	Objective
Switch(config)# interface interface_id	enters the physical interface to configure
Switch(config-if)# switchport mode access	Sets the interface mode as access;
Switch(config-if)# switchport port-security	Enables port security on the interface
Switch(config-if)# switchport port-security maximum value	Sets the maximum number of secure MAC addresses for the interface. The range is 1 to 3072; the default is 1
Switch(config-if)# switchport port-security violation {restrict | shutdown}	Sets the violation mode, the action to be taken when a security violation is detected
Switch(config-if)# switchport port-security limit rate invalid-source-mac	Sets the rate limit for bad packets.
Switch(config-if)# switchport port-security mac-address mac_address	Enters a secure MAC address for the interface.
Switch(config-if)# switchport port-security mac-address sticky	Enable sticky learning on the interface.
Switch# show port-security address interface interface_id Switch# show port-security address	Verifies your entries.

Let's have a look at few more handy facts about port security configuration.

Here are the default settings in a switch with respect to switchport security:

- Port security is disabled on a port by default. You need to enable it with the command.
- Maximum number of secure MAC addresses in a port is **1**.
- Default violation mode is shutdown.
- Sticky is disabled.
- Static aging is disabled.
- Aging type is disabled.

Limitations of port security configuration:

- A secure port cannot be a trunk port
- A secure port cannot be a destination port for **Switch Port Analyzer** (**SPAN**)
- A secure port cannot belong to an EtherChannel port-channel interface
- A secure port and static MAC address configuration are mutually exclusive

LAB: securing Layer 2 switches

Objectives to secure Layer 2 switches:

- Assign the central switch as the root bridge
- Secure spanning-tree parameters to prevent STP manipulation attacks
- Enable storm control to prevent broadcast storms

We'll be using the following topology for our lab configuration:

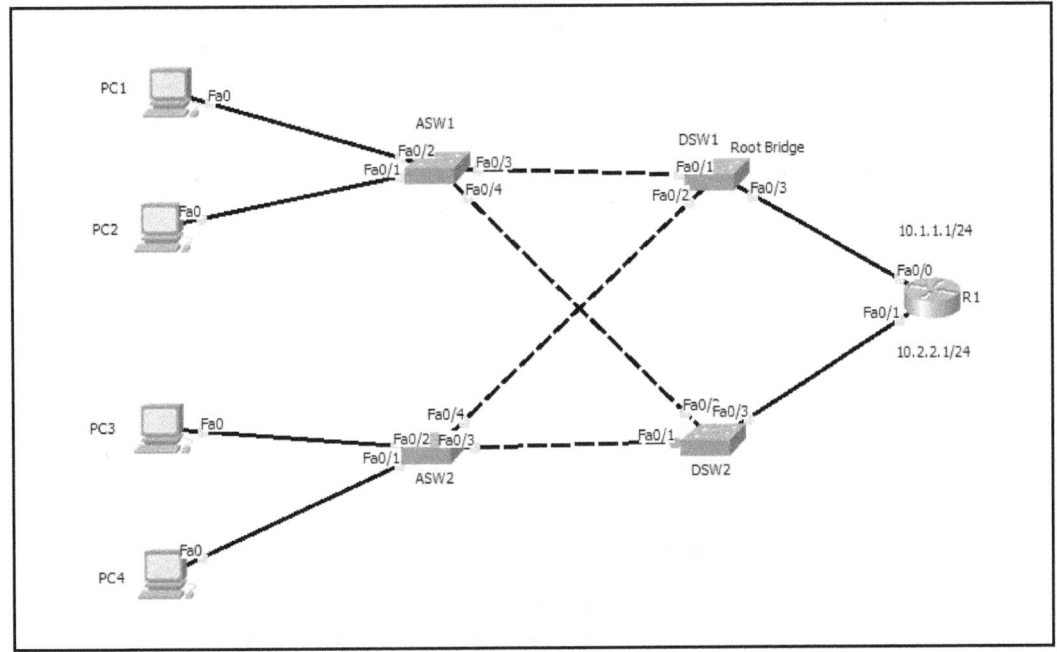

Configuring and securing **Spanning-Tree Protocol** (STP):

1. Determine the current root bridge. Issue the `show spanning-tree` command on all switches to determine the root bridge and to see the ports in use and their status.

    - DSW1:

```
DSW1#sh spanning-tree
VLAN0001
 Spanning tree enabled protocol ieee
 Root ID Priority 32769
 Address 0005.5E66.2637
 This bridge is the root
 Hello Time 2 sec Max Age 20 sec Forward Delay 15 sec

Bridge ID Priority 32769 (priority 32768 sys-id-ext 1)
 Address 0005.5E66.2637
 Hello Time 2 sec Max Age 20 sec Forward Delay 15 sec
 Aging Time 20
```

Interface Type	Role	Sts	Cost	Prio.Nbr
Fa0/3 P2p	Desg	FWD	19	128.3
Fa0/1 P2p	Desg	FWD	19	128.1
Fa0/2 P2p	Desg	FWD	19	128.2

    - DSW2:

```
DSW2#sh spanning-tree
VLAN0001
 Spanning tree enabled protocol ieee
 Root ID Priority 32769

 Address 0005.5E66.2637
 Cost 38
 Port 2(FastEthernet0/2)
 Hello Time 2 sec Max Age 20 sec Forward Delay 15 sec

Bridge ID Priority 32769 (priority 32768 sys-id-ext 1)
 Address 00E0.F9E6.BCAB
 Hello Time 2 sec Max Age 20 sec Forward Delay 15 sec
```

```
Aging Time 20

Interface          Role Sts    Cost      Prio.Nbr
Type
----------------   ---- ---  ---------- -------- ----------------
------------------
Fa0/1              Altn BLK     19        128.1
P2p
Fa0/2              Root FWD     19        128.2
P2p
Fa0/3              Desg FWD     19        128.3
P2p
```

Which switch is the current root-bridge? Based on the current root-bridge, what is the resulting spanning-tree?

2. Assign DSW1 as the primary root bridge:

   DSW1(config)#spanning-tree vlan 1 root primary

3. Assign DSW2 as a secondary root bridge:

   DSW2(config)#spanning-tree vlan 1 root secondary

4. Verify the spanning-tree configuration. Issue the show spanning-tree command to verify that DSW1 switch is the root bridge.

```
DSW1#sh spanning-tree
VLAN0001
  Spanning tree enabled protocol ieee
  Root ID Priority 24577
  Address 0005.5E66.2637
  This bridge is the root
  Hello Time 2 sec Max Age 20 sec Forward Delay 15 sec

Bridge ID Priority 24577 (priority 24576 sys-id-ext 1)
  Address 0005.5E66.2637
  Hello Time 2 sec Max Age 20 sec Forward Delay 15 sec
  Aging Time 20
Interface          Role Sts    Cost      Prio.Nbr        Type
----------------   ---- ---  ---------- -------- ----------------------
----------
Fa0/2              Desg FWD     19        128.2           P2p
Fa0/3              Desg FWD     19        128.3           P2p
Fa0/1              Desg FWD     19        128.1           P2p
```

 Which switch is the current root-bridge?

To protect against STP attacks:

1. Enable portfast on all access ports. On the connected access ports of the ASW1 and ASW2 switches, use the `spanning-tree portfast` command, for example:

```
ASW1(config-if)#int fa0/2
ASW1(config-if)#spanning-tree portfast
%Warning: portfast should only be enabled on ports connected to a
single host. Connecting hubs, concentrators, switches, bridges,
etc... to this interface when portfast is enabled, can cause
temporary bridging loops.

Use with CAUTION

%Portfast has been configured on FastEthernet0/2 but will only have
effect when the interface is in a non-trunking mode.
```

2. On ASW2, on the connected ports, use the `spanning-tree portfast` command:

```
ASW2 (config)#int fa0/1
ASW2 (config-if)#spanning-tree portfast

%Warning: portfast should only be enabled on ports connected to a
single host. Connecting hubs, concentrators, switches, bridges,
etc... To this interface when portfast is enabled, can cause
temporary bridging loops.

Use with CAUTION

%Portfast has been configured on FastEthernet0/1 but will only have
effect when the interface is in a non-trunking mode.
```

3. Enable the BPDU guard on ASW1 and ASW2 access ports:

```
ASW1 (config) #int fa0/1
ASW1 (config-if) #spanning-tree bpduguard enable.
```

4. Verify the configuration by issuing the **show running-config** command on both the switches. The output is shown here:

```
ASW1#sh running-config
Building configuration...
```

```
Current configuration : 1091 bytes
version 12.2
no service timestamps log datetime msec
no service timestamps debug datetime msec
no service password-encryption
!
hostname ASW1
!
!
spanning-tree mode pvst
!
interface FastEthernet0/1
 spanning-tree bpduguard enable
!
interface FastEthernet0/2
 spanning-tree portfast

<<Output Omitted>>
```

5. Enable the root guard on the non-root ports. Use the `show spanning-tree` command to determine the location of the root port on each switch:

```
ASW1#sh spanning-tree
VLAN0001
  Spanning tree enabled protocol ieee
  Root ID Priority 24577
  Address 0005.5E66.2637
  Cost 19
  Port 3(FastEthernet0/3)
  Hello Time 2 sec Max Age 20 sec Forward Delay 15 sec
  Bridge ID Priority 32769 (priority 32768 sys-id-ext 1)
  Address 0006.2A8E.A067
  Hello Time 2 sec Max Age 20 sec Forward Delay 15 sec
  Aging Time 20
Interface         Role  Sts  Cost       Prio.Nbr           Type
----------------- ----  ---  ---------  --------  -----------------------
----------
Fa0/1             Desg  FWD  19         128.1              P2p
Fa0/2             Desg  FWD  19         128.2              P2p
Fa0/3             Root  FWD  19         128.3              P2p
Fa0/4             Desg  FWD  19         128.4              P2p
```

6. You can notice Fa0/3 on ASW1 is a root port. Enable the root guard on non-root ports:

```
ASW1 (config) #int fa0/1
ASW1 (config-if)#spanning-tree guard root
```

7. Enable storm control for broadcasts on all ports connecting the switches (trunk ports). Set a 50% rising suppression level using the storm-control broadcast command. Enable storm-control on interfaces connecting DSW1, ASW1, and ASW2:

```
ASW1 (config) #int fa0/1
ASW1 (config-if) #storm-control broadcast level 10
```

8. Verify the storm control configuration. Verify your configuration with the show storm-control broadcast command and the show run command:

```
ASW1#sh storm-control broadcast
Interface      Filter State      Upper      Lower      Current
----------   --------------   ------------   ------------   -----------
   Fa0/3        Link Up        10.00%     10.00%         0.00%
ASW1#sh run
Building configuration...
Current configuration : 1174 bytes
!
version 12.2
no service timestamps log datetime msec
no service timestamps debug datetime msec
no service password-encryption
!
hostname ASW1
!
!
!
!
spanning-tree mode pvst
!
interface FastEthernet0/1
 spanning-tree guard root
 spanning-tree bpduguard enable
!
interface FastEthernet0/2
 spanning-tree portfast
!
interface FastEthernet0/3
 switchport mode trunk
 storm-control broadcast level 10
!
interface FastEthernet0/4
!
interface FastEthernet0/5
!
interface FastEthernet0/6 interface GigabitEthernet1/2
```

```
!
interface Vlan1
 no ip address
 shutdown
!
!
line con 0
!
line vty 0 4
 login
line vty 5 15
 login
!
!
end
```

Lab-port security

As per the diagram, the topology consists of three users connected to the FastEthernet 0/12 switchport via a hub. So logically, three MAC addresses are connected to the switchport.

The lab objective is to allow only PC0, that is, MAC address 00E0.B04D.2789:

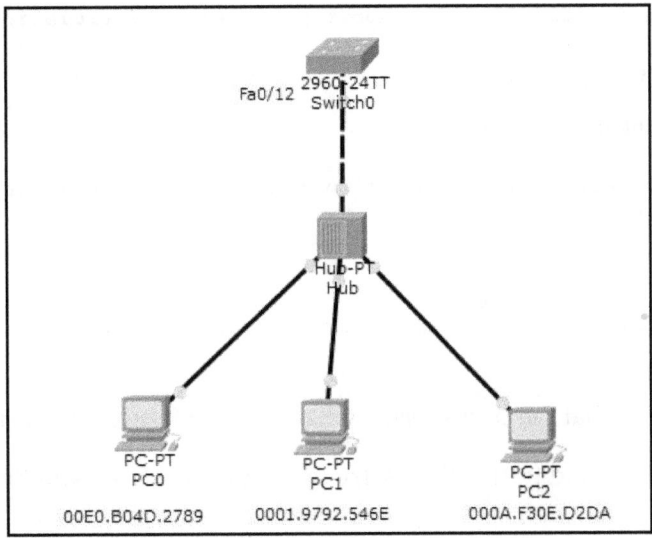

Configuring port security:

1. Enable port security on the FastEthernet 0/12 interface:

```
Switch(config)#interface FastEthernet 0/12
Switch(config-if)#switchport mode access
Switch(config-if)#switchport port-security
```

2. Enable the number of users allowed. Since we want to allow only one user, we can define the value as 1:

```
Switch(config-if)#switchport port-security maximum 1
```

3. Enable the user's specific MAC address, if required. By default, the switchport will use a method called sticky that associates any random MAC to be the trusted user. But here we want to associate a specific user. Hence we explicitly specify the MAC address:

```
Switch(config-if)#switchport port-security mac-address
00E0.B04D.2789
```

4. Provide the violation method, which defines how the switch will react when it receives an unauthorized MAC address on its port:

```
Switch(config-if)#switchport port-security violation shutdown
```

5. Verify the port's security:

```
Switch#show port-security

Secure Port MaxSecureAddr CurrentAddr SecurityViolation Security
Action
--------------------------------------------------------------------
-
Fa0/12          1              1                0              Shutdown
--------------------------------------------------------------------
---
```

This verifies that the port's security has been configured on FastEthernet 0/12.

6. Initiate some bad traffic, that is, try to use the port from another MAC address:

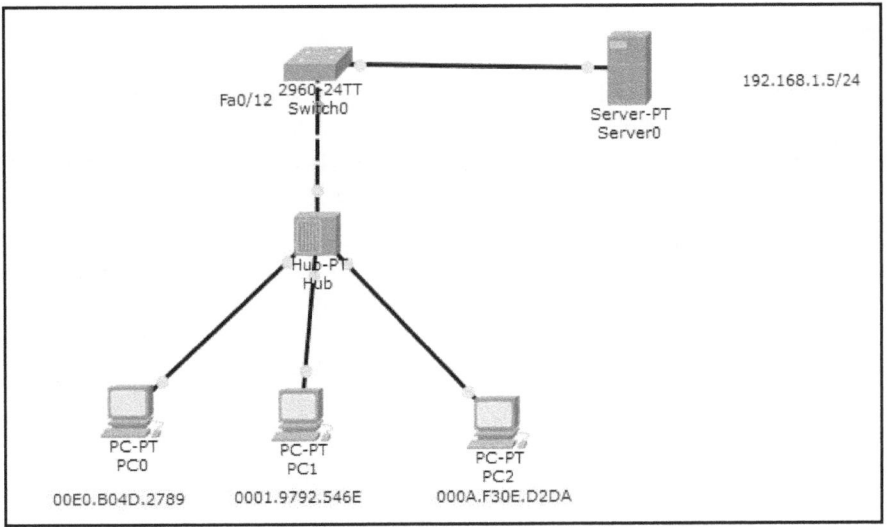

We will initiate an ICMP echo request to the server from `PC1`, which is now the unauthorized user:

```
C:\>ping 192.168.1.5

Pinging 192.168.1.5 with 32 bytes of data:

Request timed out.
Request timed out.
Request timed out.
Request timed out.

Ping statistics for 192.168.1.5:
    Packets: Sent = 4, Received = 0, Lost = 4 (100% loss),
```

The packets have been dropped. Let's confirm whether the port's security initiated this action:

```
Switch#show port-security
Secure Port MaxSecureAddr CurrentAddr SecurityViolation Security Action
-------------------------------------------------------------------------
Fa0/12          1            1             1            Shutdown
```

From the output, we can realize that the security violation count has incremented to 1 from 0, which confirms that the port's security initiated the packet to be dropped and to error-disable the port.

Summary

In this chapter, we learned how Layer 2 can be compromised if left unattended, and how VLAN and trunking work. We also saw the different modes of trunking. We then covered the VLAN trunking protocol and how it operates. We also covered Cisco Discovery Protocol and how it can be used in a secure manner.

In the next chapter, we will learn about the security implementation of Layer 2 infrastructure.

8
Protecting the Switch Infrastructure

Private VLANs VACL trunking vulnerabilities port security

VLANs generally refer to single logical broadcast domains that segregate two switch ports and does not allow them to communicate at the Layer-2 level. In a basic VLAN configuration, it is mandatory to associate each VLAN with a different subnet so that the VLANs can be associated with unique subnets for performing inter-VLAN communication. Let's consider a scenario where we need to create a huge number of VLANs. If we do not have enough subnets to accommodate the VLANs, we won't be able to create the VLANs. Hence, from a scalability perspective, we need to create VLANs that can still be part of the same subnet. This can be fulfilled by using the concept of private VLANs.

In this chapter we will learn:

- What is a private VLAN?
- Access Control List.
- VLAN hopping.

What is a private VLAN?

Private VLAN is a security concept that is used primarily in data centers or server farms where multiple servers from different organizations are connected together.

There may be a situation where **Team A** may be placing two servers, **Team B** would be placing another two servers, and **Team C** has one server, all in the same physical data center space. Obviously, **Team A** would to isolate their network traffic from the other teams and vice verse. This would improve their security and privacy.

We may realize at this point that to fulfill this requirement, we can create three VLANs on the switch connected to the three teams' devices. And for communication purposes, each VLAN has to be associated with a subnet. But if instead of three, there a hundred VLAN requirements, we may need to accommodate a hundred subnets, which in most cases can cause a scalability issue.

Hence to fulfill the requirement, we can go for private VLANs where we associate all the users connected to a group of switches under a single VLAN. So basically the isolation happens within a single VLAN that addresses the scalability factor of using multiple subnets.

Private VLANs can be sub-categorized into two VLANs:

- Primary VLAN
- Secondary VLAN

In private VLANs, we also come across three port types:

- Promiscuous
- Community
- Isolated

Generally, the primary VLAN is associated with the promiscuous port and the secondary VLAN can be used for community and isolated ports. Let's break it down.

The primary VLAN is the single VLAN that maps a group of ports under one single, private VLAN domain. Multiple secondary VLANs can be associated with the primary VLAN. The point to be noted is that the primary VLAN only would be transparent to the external world operations, such as inter-VLAN routing.

Secondary VLANs can be created for community ports and isolated ports. So what are the functionalities of these ports? Community ports are the ports that can talk to their community ports as well as the promiscuous port but not with isolated ports. Isolated ports can only communicate with the promiscuous port. Promiscuous ports are the ports that can communicate with all ports.

Let's explain that with an illustration:

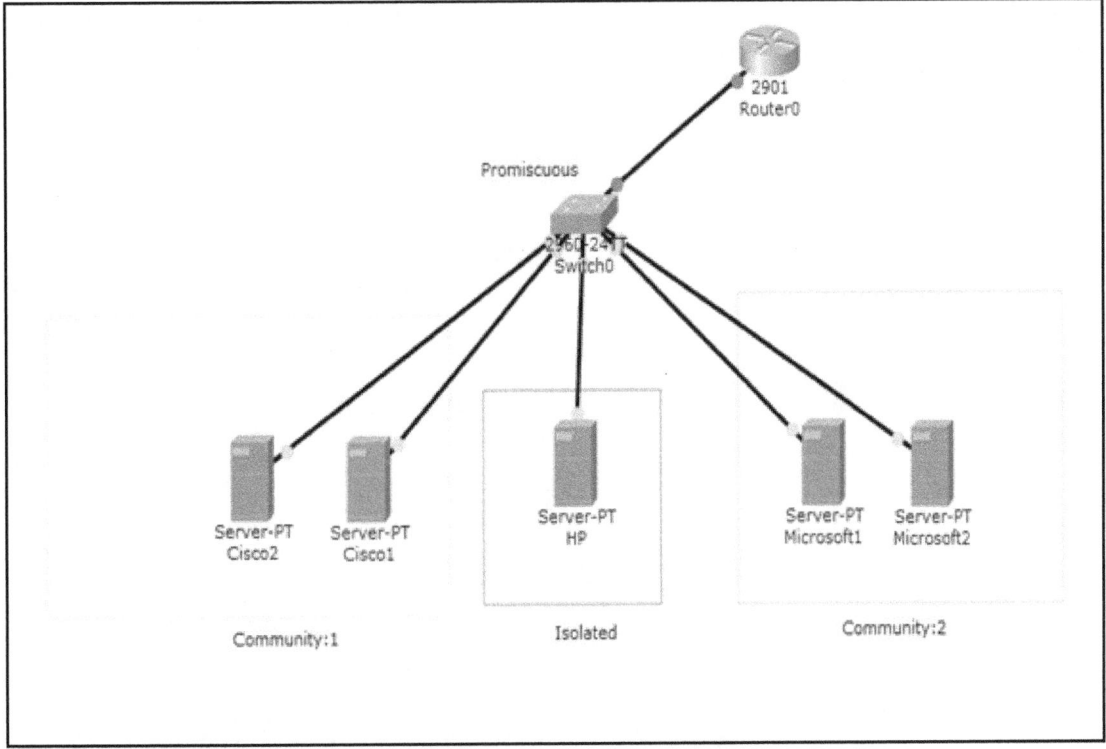

In this example, we can see that the data center switch is connecting three different organizations servers, namely Cisco, HP, and Microsoft.

Since Cisco and Microsoft have two servers each, they would like to create two community VLANs so that the Cisco servers can talk to each other and avoid communication with other servers. We can expect a similar requirement for the Microsoft servers.

Since HP has a single server, there is no need for the server to talk to other servers. Hence HP can be associated with an isolated VLAN so that it can only communicate with the promiscuous port.

As all the users need to talk to the external world, which is through the default gateway, the switch port connected to the router should be configured as a member of the primary VLAN, which is the promiscuous port.

Private VLAN lab

In this lab, an isolated private VLAN would be created to allow two servers owned by two different organizations within the same IP range to communicate with their default gateway, but not with each other:

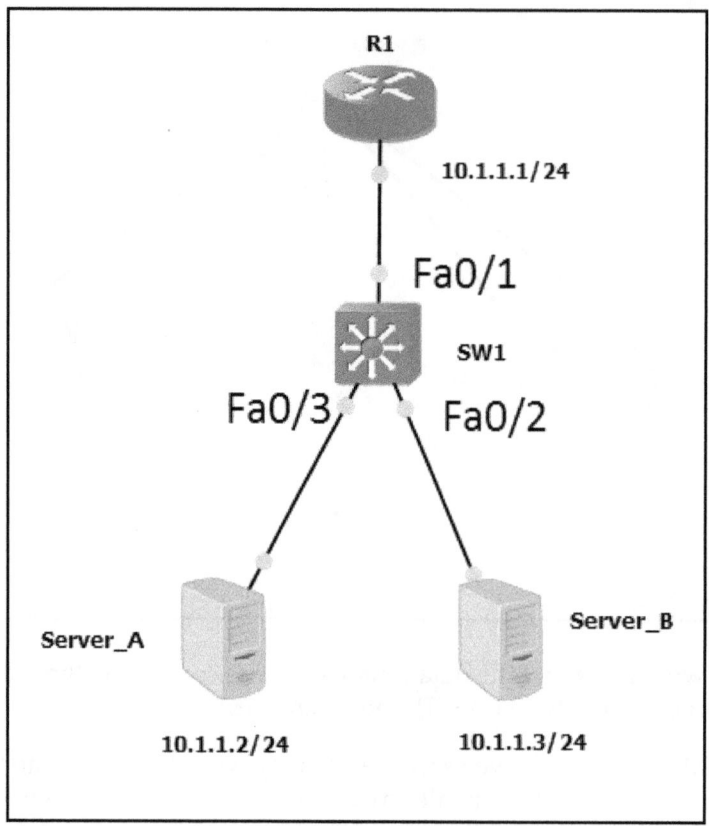

Before starting the private VLAN configuration, it is mandatory to configure the VTP mode as transparent. Recall that VTP is a protocol that is used to synchronize the VLAN databases on all switches. But since private VLANs are not carried by VTP, it is better to configure the mode as transparent as that would be used for local VLANs:

```
SW1(config)# vtp mode transparent
```

Private VLANs have to be created before associating to a port, just like normal VLANs. Upon creating the VLANs, the type (isolated, community, or primary) should be provided. We are creating an isolated VLAN, 201, and mapping it to the primary VLAN, 200:

```
SW1(config)# vlan 201
SW1(config-vlan)# private-vlan isolated
SW1(config-vlan)# vlan 200
SW1(config-vlan)# private-vlan primary
SW1(config-vlan)# private-vlan association 201
```

Our completed VLAN configuration looks like this:

```
vlan 200
  private-vlan primary
  private-vlan association 201
!
vlan 201
  private-vlan isolated
```

Next, we configure the respective interfaces to be associated with the primary and isolated VLANs. The uplink port to the router would be set to the promiscuous mode, with the primary VLAN mapped to the secondary VLAN:

```
SW1(config)# interface f0/1
SW1(config-if)# switchport mode private-vlan promiscuous
SW1(config-if)# switchport private-vlan mapping 200 201
```

The two server ports will be configured in host mode wherein they would be identified as isolated VLAN ports with the 201 VLAN 201 defined:

```
SW1(config)# interface f0/3
SW1(config-if)# switchport mode private-vlan host
SW1(config-if)# switchport private-vlan host-association 200 201
SW1(config-if)# interface f0/2
SW1(config-if)# switchport mode private-vlan host
SW1(config-if)# switchport private-vlan host-association 200 201
```

At this point, our private VLAN configuration is complete. We can verify private VLAN interface assignments with the show vlan private-vlan command:

```
SW1# show vlan private-vlan

Primary Secondary Type             Ports
------- --------- ---------------- -----------------------------------------
---
200     201       isolated         Fa0/1, Fa0/3, Fa0/2
SW1# show interface status
```

```
Port        Name                  Status       Vlan        Duplex   Speed
Type
Fa0/1                             connected    200            a-full     a-100
10/100BaseTX
Fa0/2                             connected    200,201     a-full    a-100
10/100BaseTX
Fa0/3                             connected    200,201     a-full    a-100
10/100BaseTX
Fa0/4                             notconnect   1                      auto
auto        10/100BaseTX
```

The `show interface switchport` command is used for verifying private VLAN details per interface.

Finally, we can check whether the router can communicate with both servers, which should be successful but the servers should not communicate directly with one another:

```
R1# ping 10.1.1.2
Type escape sequence to abort.
Sending 5, 100-byte ICMP Echos to 10.1.1.2, timeout is 2 seconds:
!!!!!
Success rate is 100 percent (5/5), round-trip min/avg/max = 1/2/4 ms
R1# ping 10.1.1.3

Type escape sequence to abort.
Sending 5, 100-byte ICMP Echos to 10.1.1.3, timeout is 2 seconds:
!!!!!
Success rate is 100 percent (5/5), round-trip min/avg/max = 1/1/4 ms

Server_A# ping 10.1.1.3

Type escape sequence to abort.
Sending 5, 100-byte ICMP Echos to 10.1.1.3, timeout is 2 seconds:
.....
Success rate is 0 percent (0/5)
```

Access Control List

An Access Control List (ACL) is used to filter incoming or outgoing network traffic of an interface, whether it's on a Cisco Router or Adaptive Security Appliance (ASA). Without Access Control List (ACL) any type of network traffic will be allowed to flow freely between networks/interfaces and this can be a security flaw.

Access Control List is a hierarchical set of statements that have matching criteria and an action that is triggered once the matching criteria are fulfilled. If the packet's detail does not match the first line, it moves to the second line, and so on until it gets a match. If none of the lines matches the packet's detail, the packet gets dropped. This is because of the inherent characteristic of an ACL, which is called **implicit deny**.

Ideally, an Access Control List would be configured on Layer 3 devices and would be applied on Layer 3 interfaces for inspection to happen when the packet moves from one network to another. When there is a requirement for an access list to work within the same VLAN, that is where we can use the concept of the VLAN access list.

VLAN ACLs (VACLs)

VLAN ACLs (VACLs) can be used for intra-VLAN traffic filtering. For example, if within VLAN 2, a PC is not supposed to ping a server that is also on the same VLAN, but the rest of the users in VLAN 2 can be allowed, then a VACL can be implemented for VLAN 2 alone.

Steps for configuring VACL:

The following are the steps to configure VACL:

1. Create a normal access list on the switch that matches your source IP and destination IP. As usual, this can be fulfilled using a standard Access Control List or an extended access list:

   ```
   Switch(config)# access-list <acl no> <permit| deny> <protocol>
   <source ip><source wildcard mask><operator> <source port
   number><destination ip><destination wildcard
   mask><operator><destination port number>
   ```

2. Create a VLAN access map. This is basically having two statements: match and action. Match is to match the ACL, and action is to either permit or deny the traffic that matches the ACL:

   ```
   Switch(config)#vlan access-map <VACL Name> <Sequence No>
   Switch(config-access-map)#match ip address <ACL number>
   Switch(config-access-map)#action <permit|drop>
   ```

3. Associate this VLAN access list with the VLAN so that this would be used for inspection only on that VLAN:

```
Switch(config)#vlan filter <VACL Name> vlan-list <vlan id>
```

One important point to note is that the access list used in step 1 is used only for matching the IP address. It is only in step 2 that the VACL filters the traffic based on the match. The permit in the ACL is identifying the IP addresses to be matched. If there is a deny statement in the ACL, then the corresponding IP address would not be matched by the VACL:

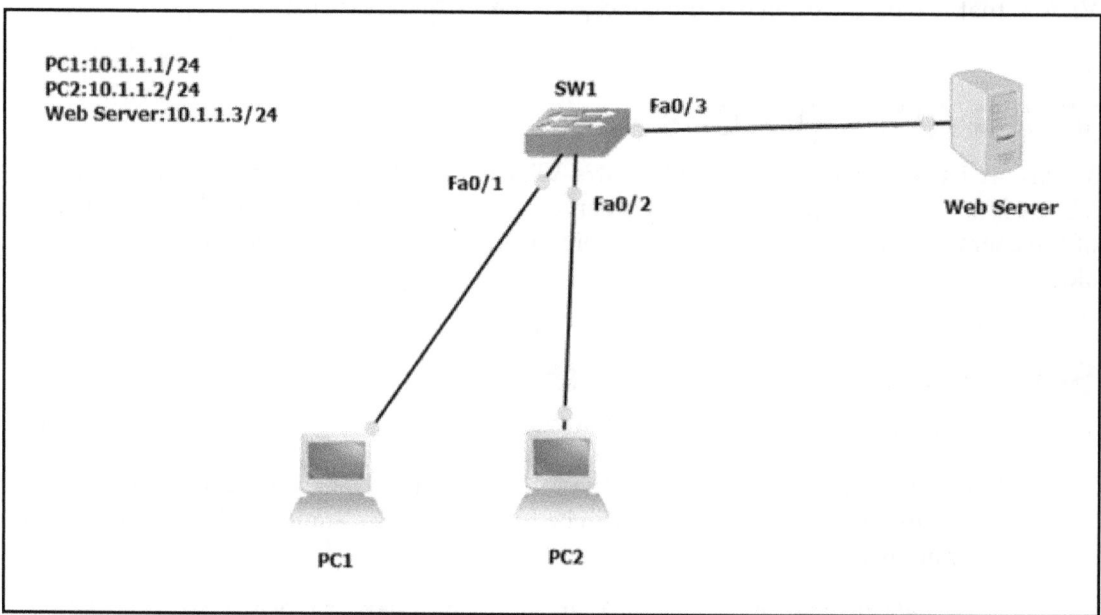

PC1:10.1.1.1/24
PC2:10.1.1.2/24
Web Server:10.1.1.3/24

The objective of this lab is to allow us block **PC1** from accessing the web server and allowing **PC2** to access the Server. All the hosts are in VLAN 15:

```
Sw1(config)#access-list 100 permit ip host 10.1.1.1 host 10.1.1.3
```

Access list `100` is created to match the traffic from PC1 to the web server:

```
Sw1(config)#vlan access-map BLOCKPC1 10
Sw1(config-access-map)#match ip address 100
Sw1(config-access-map)#action drop
Sw1(config)#vlan access-map BLOCKPC1 20
Sw1(config-access-map)#action permit
```

A VACL named `BLOCKPC1` is created. The first line matches the `100` ACL and the matched traffic would be dropped. Hence, if the switch receives a packet with a source address of `10.1.1.1` and a destination address of `10.1.1.3`, the packet would be dropped. The second line of the VACL is an implicit permit that allows all other traffic that is not matched by ACL `100` to be forwarded. Ultimately, the PC2 traffic to the server would be allowed by the second line of the VACL:

```
Sw1(config)# vlan filter BLOCKPC1 vlan-list 15
```

In the step 3, the VACL named `BLOCKPC1` is applied to a VLAN filter so that the traffic inspection can happen for only the VLAN `15` subnet.

As a final verification, PC1, when trying to reach the web server for any traffic, would not be allowed and PC2 would be allowed to access the server.

Thus, by implementing VACL, we are able to apply an inspection policy on a per-VLAN basis.

Trunking-related attacks

DTP is a common Layer 2 protocol that is used to negotiate a switch port to take a role as an access or a trunk link. There are two modes that are used in DTP for the negotiation process:

- **Dynamic desirable**: This mode negotiates the other side of the port to form a trunk link by sending out DTP frames. If the other side is manually configured as the access mode, then the port negotiates to form an access link. On all other combinations, this mode should be able to form a trunk link.
- **Dynamic auto**: This mode negotiates the other side of the port to form an access link ideally. But when it connects with dynamic desirable on the other side of the port, it would form a trunk as dynamic desirable is more powerful than dynamic auto.

Now, most of the Cisco switches have the factory default switch port mode settings as either dynamic desirable or dynamic auto. If an administrator leaves the switch port default settings then there is a vulnerability, that is, if an unauthorized user connects to one of the unused ports and generates an unsolicited DTP frame, the user might end up becoming a trunk. Ideally, the attacker would like to do this to identify the different VLAN traffic running on the production as well as to launch further attacks on the production network.

VLAN hopping

This is one of the VLAN-related attacks that can be executed. The objective behind this attack is that the attacker wants to move from the given VLAN to a new VLAN where the intended victim is placed. This can be evoked by using a concept called **double-tagging**.

Double-tagging

Double-tagging is a method by which the attacker tries to reach a different VLAN using the vulnerabilities in the trunk port configuration.

This is achieved by first making note of the native VLAN configured on the trunk link connected to the switch ports. The attacker creates a trunk port between their PC and the switch by using the DTP negotiation methods. Then the attacker creates a double tag with the intended VLAN as the inside tag, and the native VLAN as the outside tag. When the switch receives the frame, it sees the outer tag as native VLAN and therefore discards the outer tag. Hence it would look as if the frame is intended to get the VLAN on which the victim is placed. This is done to ensure that the attacker can hop from one VLAN to another:

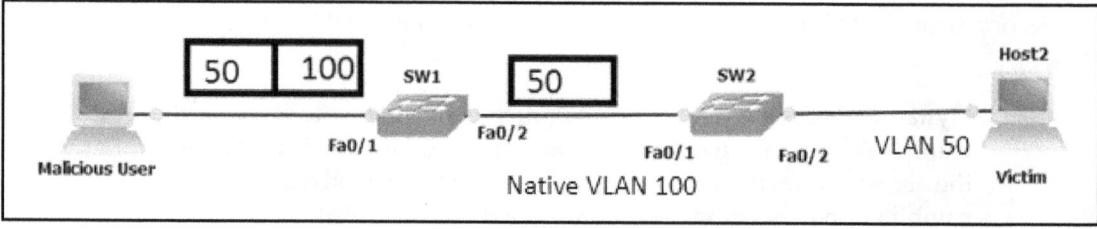

As per the diagram, the **Malicious User** is trying to reach **VLAN 50**, where the victim is placed. The **Malicious User** tries to first form a trunk link between their PC and **SW1**. This is basically done by exploiting the vulnerability on the switchport. That is since the default switchport settings on **SW1** might be either dynamic desirable or dynamic auto, the attacker can craft some DTP frames to negotiate the **SW1** port to become a trunk link.

Once the attacker forms the trunk link, it will try to generate a dot1q frame with an inner tag and an outer tag. The inner tag would be the victim's VLAN ID and the outer tag would be the native VLAN ID that is used between **SW1** and **SW2**. Here, the native VLAN ID is **100**. This information might have been obtained through some promiscuous learning.

Once SW1 receives this double-tag frame and checks that the outer tag belongs to the native VLAN, it would remove the outer tag. Hence the frame would be sent with the inner tag that would be forwarded to **SW2**.

SW2 receives this frame and notices that the tag is for **VLAN 100**. Hence it will untag the frame and send it out on the **Fa0/2** port, which is an access port in **VLAN 100**. This frame hits the victim, which is the objective of the hacker.

Why did this occur?

- Native VLAN should never be configured as a production VLAN. Rather, it can be an unused VLAN.
- All ports that are connected to end devices should be configured as access ports and disable DTP on those ports. This will avoid any malicious user from negotiating it as a trunk link with DTP.

Summary

In this chapter, we learned how private VLANs can be used in server farms, the different port roles in private VLAN, the basic configuration of private VLANs, and the difference between ACL and VACL. We also learned the steps involved in building a VACL, and how VACL can be used to filter traffic on a specific VLAN.

In the next chapter, we will learn about firewall technologies.

Exploring Firewall Technologies

9

The term firewall is derived from an automobile division. The firewall exists in the zone between the car's engine and the passenger's cabin of an automobile, and is used to prevent any heat/combustion from the engine reaching the people in the passengers cabin; in other words, it's a protective barrier. But in a network world, it is being used as a metaphorical term for how we separate our internal network from outside danger. Firewalls can be defined as any hardware or software that enables the filtering of the packets or controls the flow of traffic. They are generally implemented in a network perimeter. They act as a border for trusted and untrusted zones:

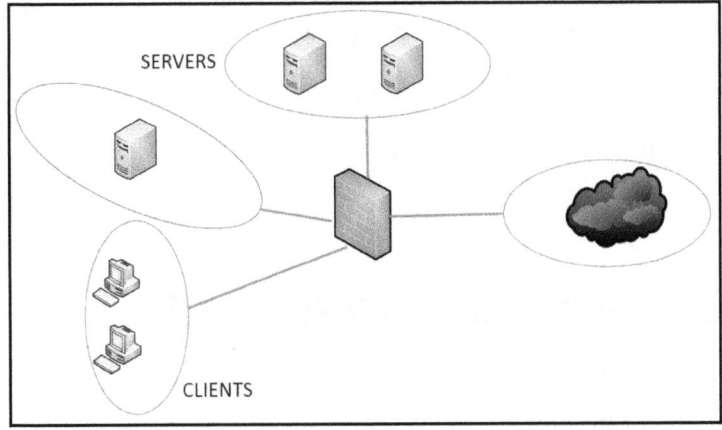

For a company, securing the network and data adds complexity. The costs of maintaining and implementing such high-level security for securing things such as e-commerce, intranet, extranet, or email services are always high, but when compared to the loss that incurred due to a lack of high-level security, it is something that is considered more important.

But if a company opts for Cisco IOS Firewall, software, instead of hardware, would also have the same kind of security satisfaction. Cisco IOS provides full-featured firewall services when it is implanted properly on any Cisco router. It helps a network to break down into several small domains or sub-networks, thereby helping by keeping the possible security breach limited to one domain, if any, and not allowing it to spread to the entire network—that would result in a major loss.

Two crucial apparatuses are used to carry out the functions of the firewall:

- An apparatus to block the traffic
- An apparatus to permit the traffic

Most firewalls would permit traffic from a trusted zone to an untrusted zone without any special configuration. But the reverse has to be configured and must be explicitly permitted, hence anything not configured/explicitly permitted from an untrusted zone to a trusted zone should be implicitly denied. A firewall is not limited to trusted and untrusted zones; there are mid-zones, generally known as **DMZs** (**Demilitarized Zones**, or **less trusted zones**).

Basically, a firewall is a set of programs that can be enabled in a network gateway server that secure the resources of a private network from other external network users.

The following topics will be covered:

- What is a Firewall
- Types of Firewalls

Services offered by the firewall

Services offered by the firewall are:

- Static-packet filtering
- Circuit-level firewalls
- Proxy server
- Application server
- NAT
- Stateful packet inspection

Static-packet filtering

It is a firewall and the routing ability of a device that can filter packets based on fields of the packet and the rules configured by the administrator. The administrator can define rules (ACLs) to manage allowed ports and IP addresses at Layer 3 and Layer 4:

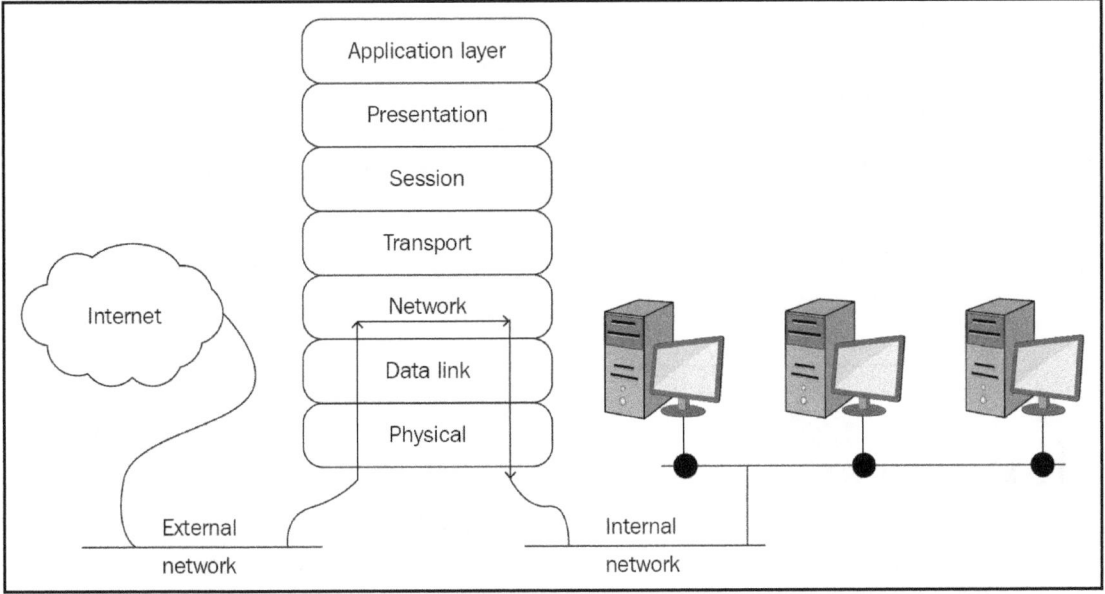

Circuit-level firewalls

It is also known as a **transparent proxy firewall**. This firewall cannot change the request or response beyond the authentication and authorization required by the proxy:

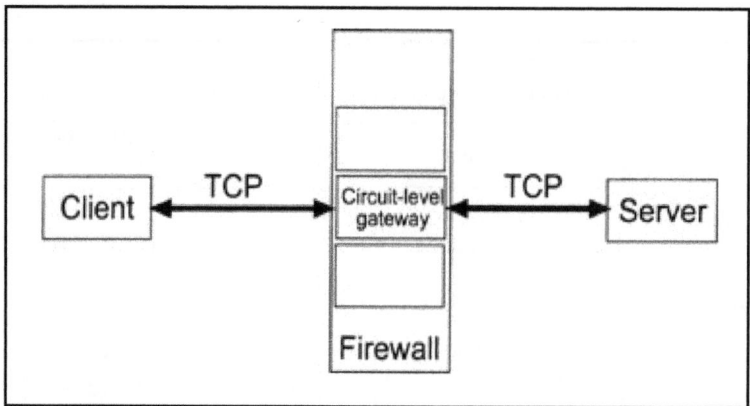

Proxy server

It is a server or a computer that provides indirect access (network connections) to the other network services. When a client requires a connection with the network, the client sends a request and the proxy server serves the requirement form the cache.

There are four different types of proxy servers:

- Transparent proxy
- Anonymous proxy
- Distorting proxy
- High-anonymity proxy

The following graphic displays the appropriate placement of the proxy server:

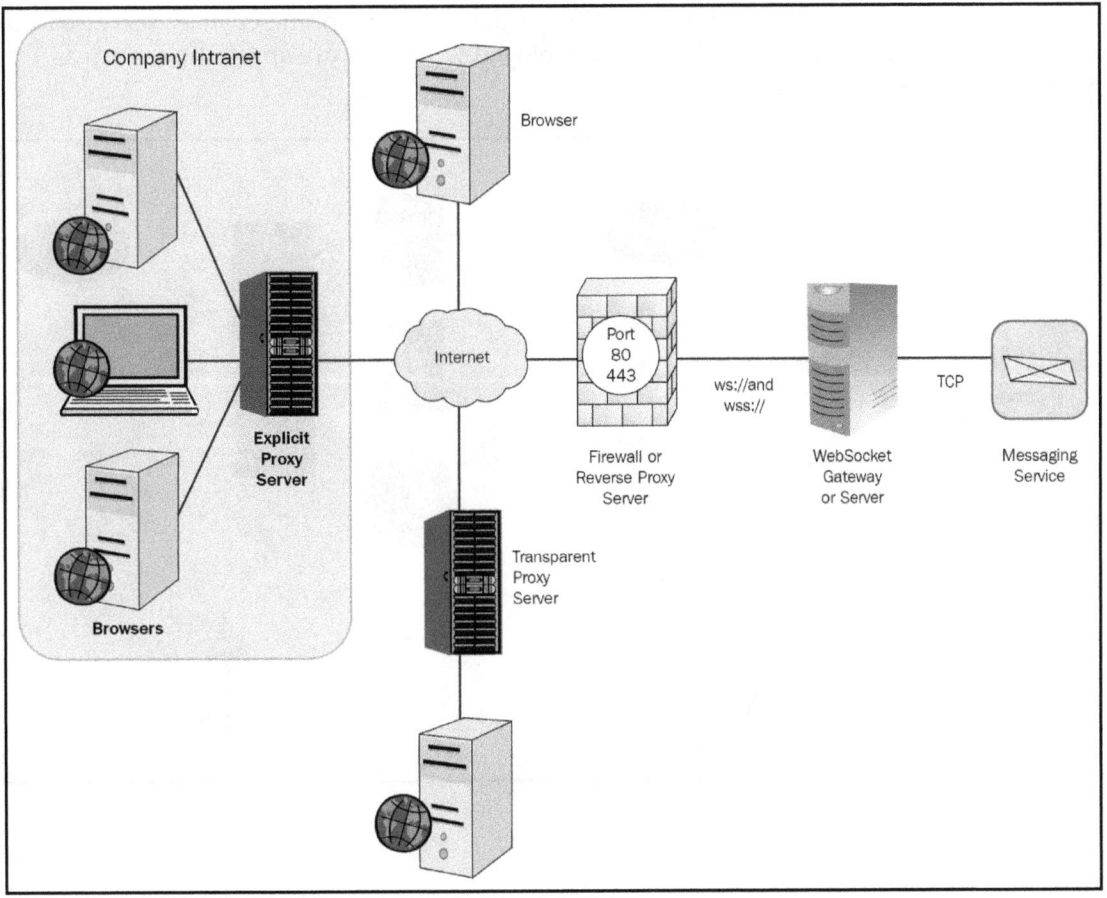

Application server

It is a server that provides an environment for arranging and running custom, server-based business applications that can be built and deployed with software applications such as Microsoft .NET Framework 3.0:

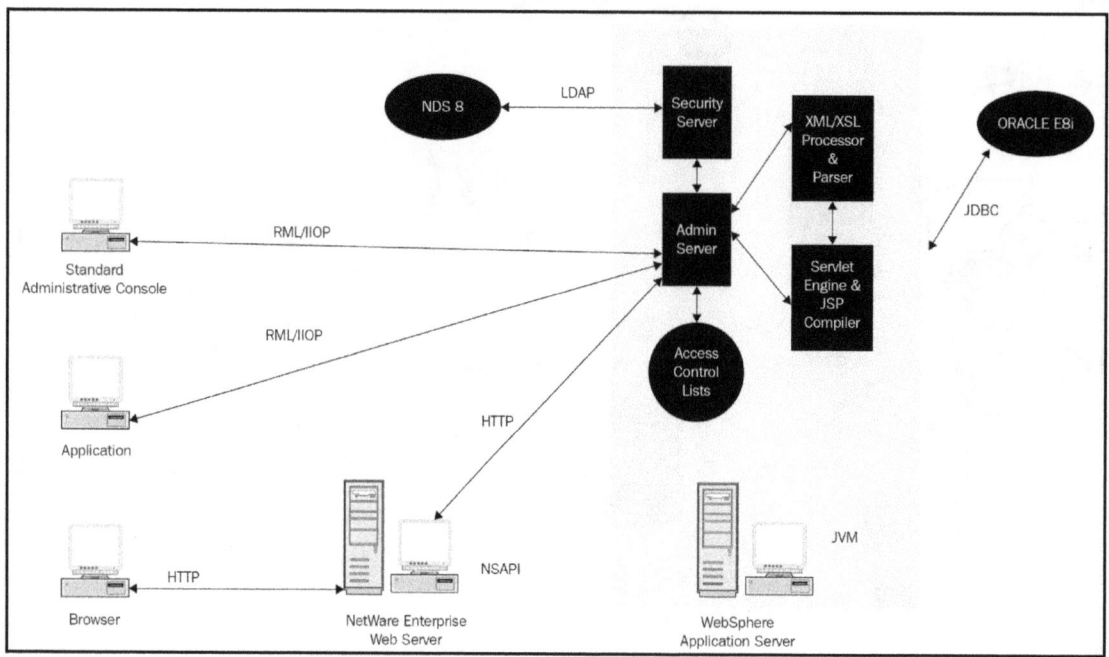

Network Address Translation

It is a translation method used inside a network with a dissimilar IP address known within another network. **Network Address Translation** (**NAT**) can be performed on a router and it is often called a **corporate firewall**. The Cisco version of NAT enables an administrator to create tables:

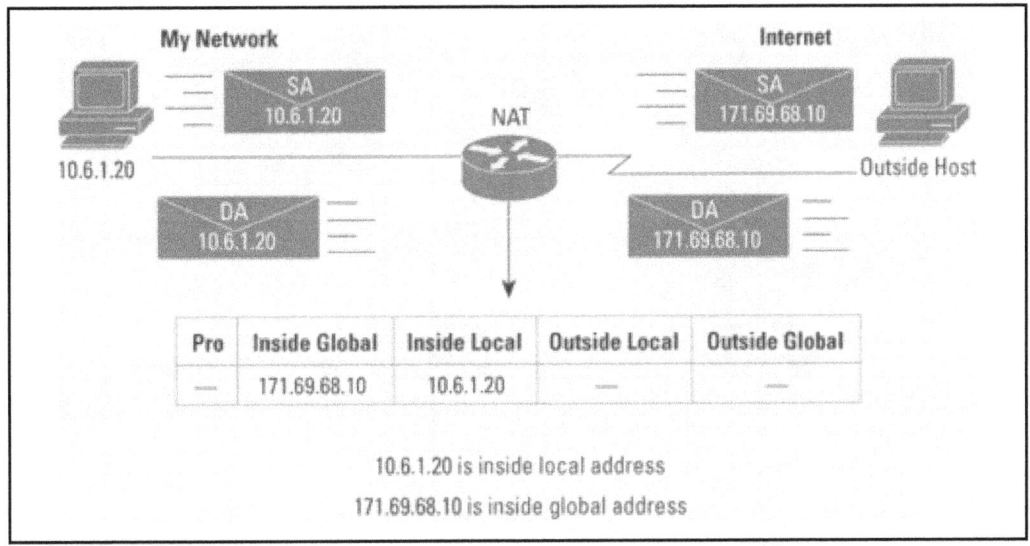

Pro	Inside Global	Inside Local	Outside Local	Outside Global
—	171.69.68.10	10.6.1.20	—	—

10.6.1.20 is inside local address

171.69.68.10 is inside global address

Stateful inspection

It is also known as **dynamic packet filtering**. It screens the status of active connections and uses this information to regulate which network packets to permit through the firewall:

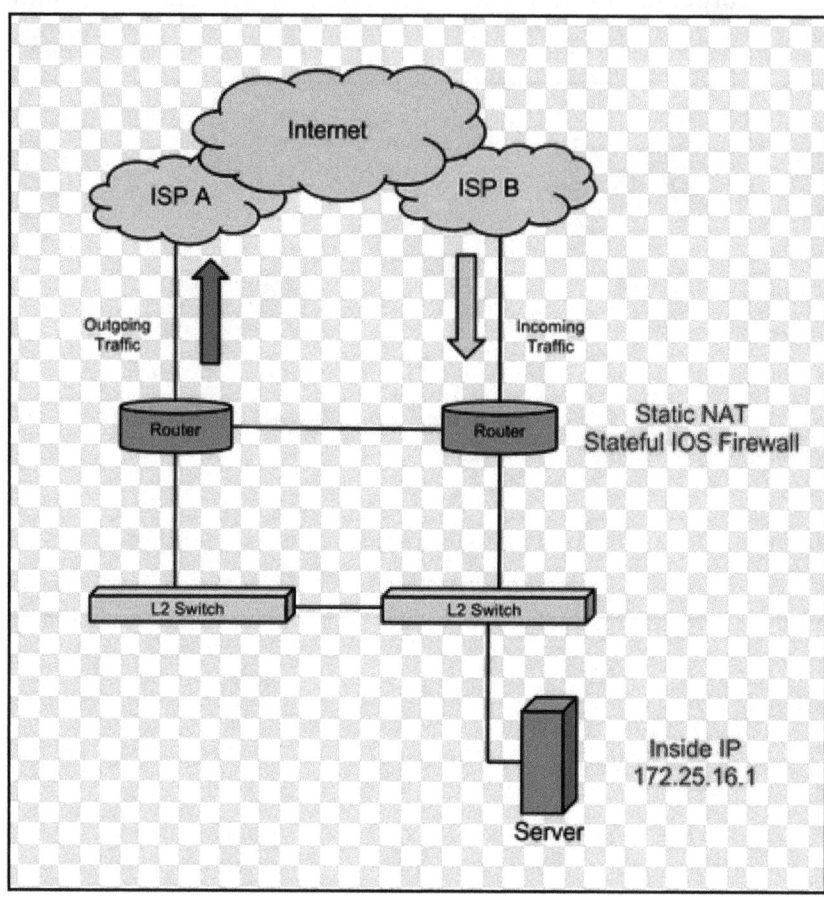

Firewalls in a layered defense strategy

In a layered defense strategy, firewalls provide perimeter security for the entire network and for internal network segments in the core. They can be used on separate VLAN segments. They can be used to separate the internal networks, separating one segment from the rest of the segments:

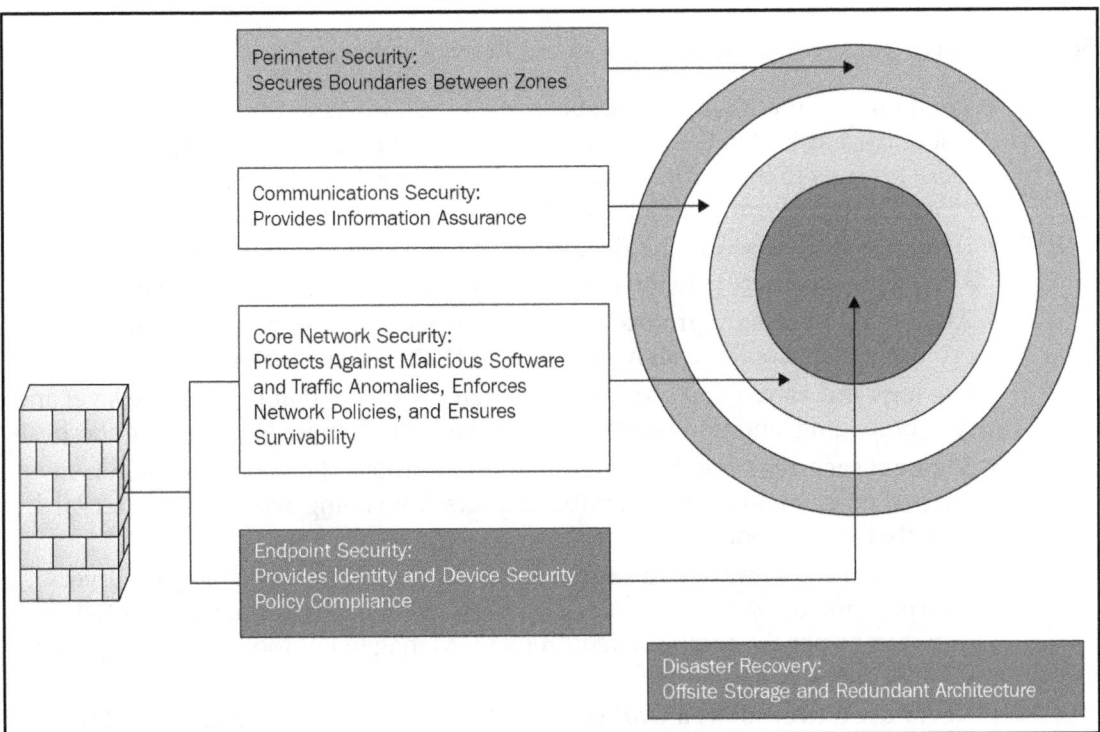

Several firewalls are used with several layers incorporated in them. Let's understand this process.

When the traffic flows in from an untrusted network, it encounters packet filter on the external router. In the next phase, the traffic steps into either a screened host firewall or a bastion host system. Then this system checks whether there are any suspicious packets, if yes, then it would get discarded. If the packet is not rejected then it would go to the interior screening router. After crossing all these checks, the packet travels to the final destination. This multilayer approach is called **DMZ** or a **screened-subnet configuration**.

To build a complete defense in depth:

- Firewalls don't protect from a large number of intrusions that get injected via the hosts in the network
- Firewalls can't trace the rogue modems in the setup
- Firewalls don't have any planned disaster-recovery mechanisms and they are deployed because of the high CPU utilization and hardware failure

Best practices to guide you in designing a sound firewall policy:

- **Trust no one**: It is always advisable to enable all the key services and deny the rest of the traffic. Analyze the uses of the user and, based on the report, assign those services to them. You need to deploy the least-privilege principle to deny all access to perform one's job smoothly.
- **Deny physical access to the firewall**: It is always a good practice to keep any kind of physical access to the firewall controlled or to deny it completely.
- **Allow only necessary protocols**: It's always good to have a prepared list of protocols that should be allowed and ones that need to be blocked.
- **Use logs and alerts**: You must have a logging strategy that projects the level and type of logging, and you need be sure to monitor all those logs on a regular basis.
- **Segment security zone**: Firewalls are used to protect the internal system from internal misuse and to protect public servers from being accessed by external security threats from the internet.
- **Do not use the firewall as a server**: Firewalls should never be used in server-incorporation design. We should always uninstall or disable any unwanted software, as per the company requirement. Management tools are the important ones that need to be removed.
- **Never use a firewall as a workstation**: In general, users' systems depend on a lot of client applications, such as Microsoft and Oracle, that can open a gate to viruses, worms, and so on.
- **Set connection limits**: Enforcing connection limits on the Cisco security appliance firewalls can mitigate worms and the like. Default connection limits can be changed in the global settings.
- **Restrict access to firewalls**: Access to firewalls should be highly restricted. Only an administrator should be allowed to log in with strong passwords assigned to them. You can also use OTP cards for better security.

- **Combine firewall technology**: Packet filtering should not be done only for the line of defense. It can be incorporated with some inspections, such as protocol, stateful, or application.
- **Use firewalls as part of a comprehensive security solution**: Firewalls should be used in juxtaposition with other devices to build a full security solution. They should be integrated with other technologies.
- **Maintain the installation**: Software and patches should be kept updated. Update firewall configurations as application requirements change.

Transparent firewall

As an additional security measure, we have the transparent firewall. In a traditional configuration of networks, a firewall acts as a router or default gateway for the hosts that connect to its filtered subnet. We have a Layer 2 firewall, known as a **transparent firewall**, which acts like a covertness firewall. These types of firewalls are used only when a gateway of web proxy or anti-spam is needed, and they should have features such as Proxy ARP and disabling NAT.

Proxy ARP is a technique where a device answers an ARP request intended for another device:

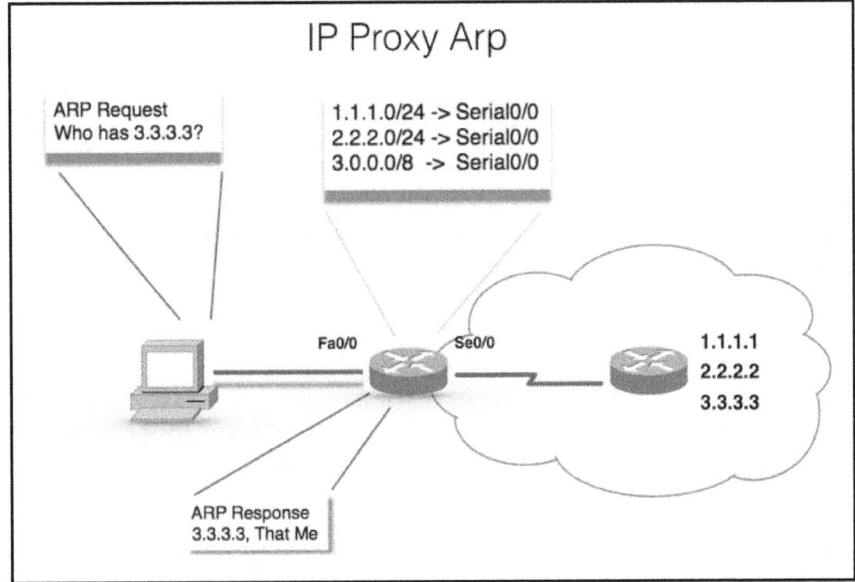

The characteristics of a transparent firewall:

- The transparent firewall mode supports inside and outside interfaces
- It can be run on a single as well as multiple context modes
- Packets are bridged by the security appliance from one VLAN to the other, instead of being routed
- MAC lookups are performed rather than routing table lookups

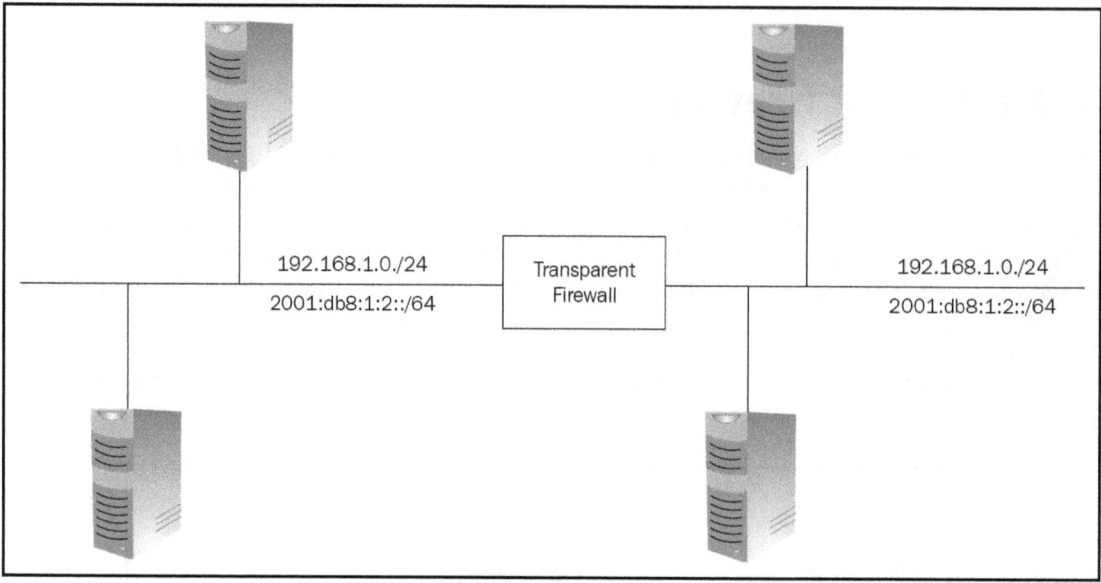

A transparent firewall can be introduced very easily into an existing network, since it's not a routed hop and it doesn't require an IP address. There are no routing patterns or NAT configurations, and very little troubleshooting. The transparent mode acts as a bridge but still, it doesn't allow Layer 3 traffic to pass through security appliance from a lower security level interface to a higher security level interface.

We can control the passage of traffic with ACL, either extended or EtherType ACL. If no ACL is configured, then it would only ARP traffic, which can be controlled by ARP inspection. It also doesn't allow CDP packets or any other invalid EtherType packets greater than or equal to 0x600. For example, the IS-IS packet is not allowed but will allow BPDUs.

One should consider the fact that as an L2 device, the security appliance must be on a different VLAN to keep it secured from any accidental access.

Application-layer firewalls

The application-layer firewalls are also known as **proxy firewalls** or **application gateways**. They allow the greatest level of control and work across all seven layers of OSI. The filtering effect takes place at layers 3, 4, 5, and 7.

Many application-layer firewalls include some specialized application software and proxy servers. Specific traffic, such as FTP or HTTP, is managed by the proxy server. These servers are specific to their original design for the protocols. They help in report generation for auditing purposes by providing enhanced access control and validating every piece of data:

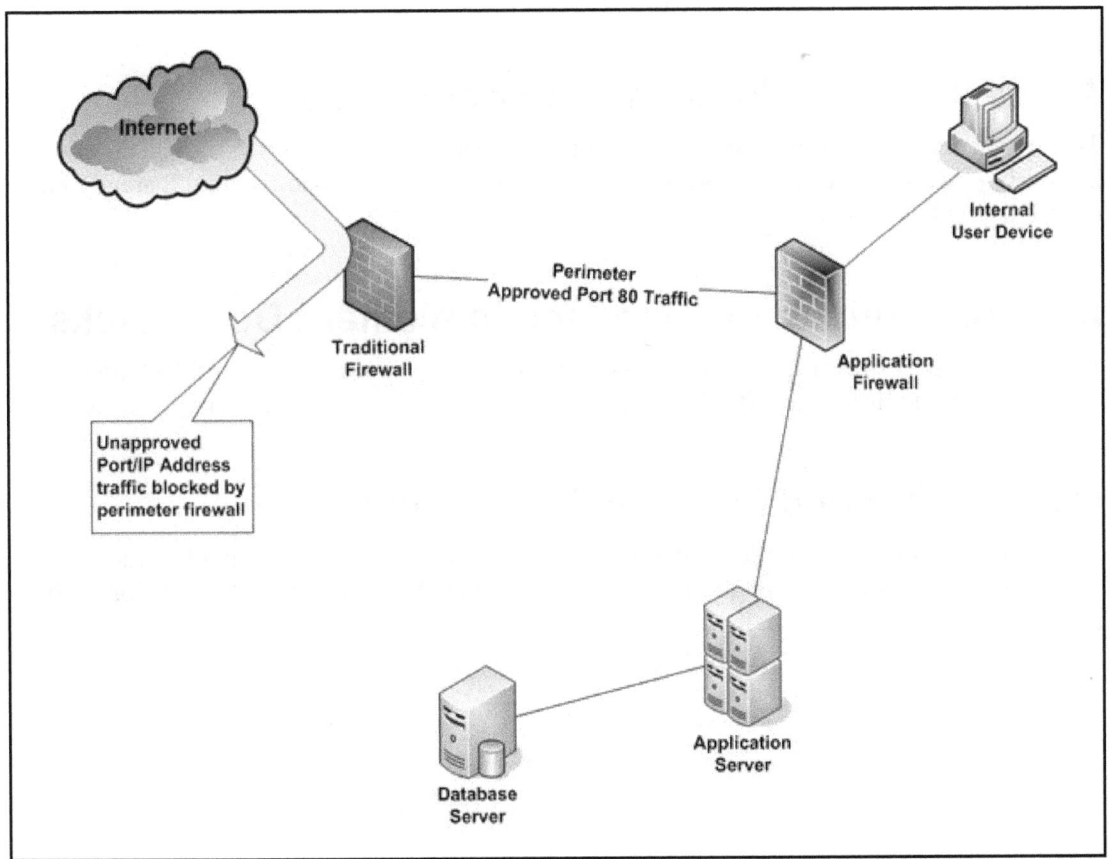

Proxy firewalls serve as an intermediary between networks, such as the internet and the company's internal network. In a proxy firewall environment, there isn't any direct connection. The proxy servers provide the only visible IP address on the internet. The client connects to the proxy server to submit their request pertaining to Layer 7, which includes destination as well as data. Based on the configuration on the proxy server, it can analyze, filter, or change the data itself before processing. It can make a copy of all the incoming packets and change the source address, in order to hide the internal address from the outside internet world, before it is sent out to the destination. And when it receives a response from the destination, it becomes its responsibility to ensure the delivery of that response to the right client.

The following are some benefits of application-layer firewalls.

Authenticates individuals and not devices

This implies connection requests are authenticated before traffic is allowed to cross an internal or external resource. This ensures authenticating the user/individual instead of a device trying to connect.

It's more difficult to spoof and implement DoS attacks

Application-layer firewalls help in preventing most of the spoof attacks, and DoS attacks are limited to the firewall itself. This helps in reducing the burden on internal resources.

Can monitor and filter application data

Application-layer firewalls allow an administrator to control what commands and functionality rights/access are given based on their role, the required authentication, and the information pertaining to it.

Logging information in more detail

Logs are generated with such detail that you can monitor the actual data an individual is trafficking it across. This also helps in tracking various new ways of attacks, since we can monitor how a hacker is trying to crack into the system. Logging would also prove more useful to trace the amount of bandwidth being used by an individual resource, the sites that are being accessed, and which resource is being utilized most often.

Working with the application-layer firewall

Application-level proxy firewalls control how internal users are accessing the outside internet. They do it by running a protocol stack for each type of service that they want to provide. In some network environments, we can see that the proxy servers are used to block all incoming traffics and allow only the internal resource to access the internet.

Application-level proxy server

The proxy server is a computer or a router that interrupts the communication between customer and provider and acts as a relay. They generally prevent the attacker from entering into a private network.

The application-level proxy server is a form of proxy server that is specific to a particular application and protocol. They have complete information about the content of the packets.

SOCKS is an IP-based circuit-level proxy server software that supports TCP and UDP applications:

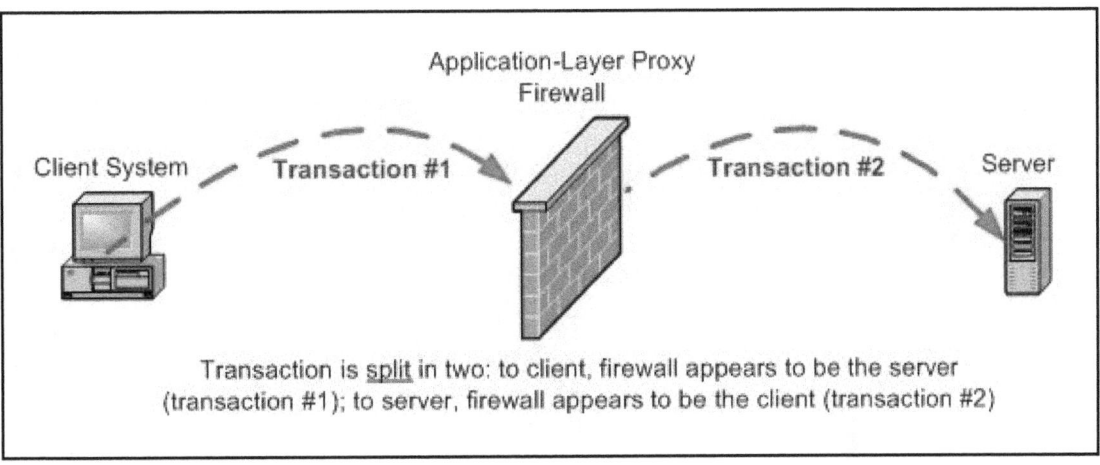

Typical proxy server deployment

The following figure shows how a proxy server can be deployed in an environment. One interface of the router is connected to the internet and the other to the client. When the client requests a connection to the internet, the proxy server receives the requests, checks the request, and repacks the request. As an application-level firewall has information about the packet, they are processor sensitive. These firewalls are also protocol-specific so they use more memory to process a request:

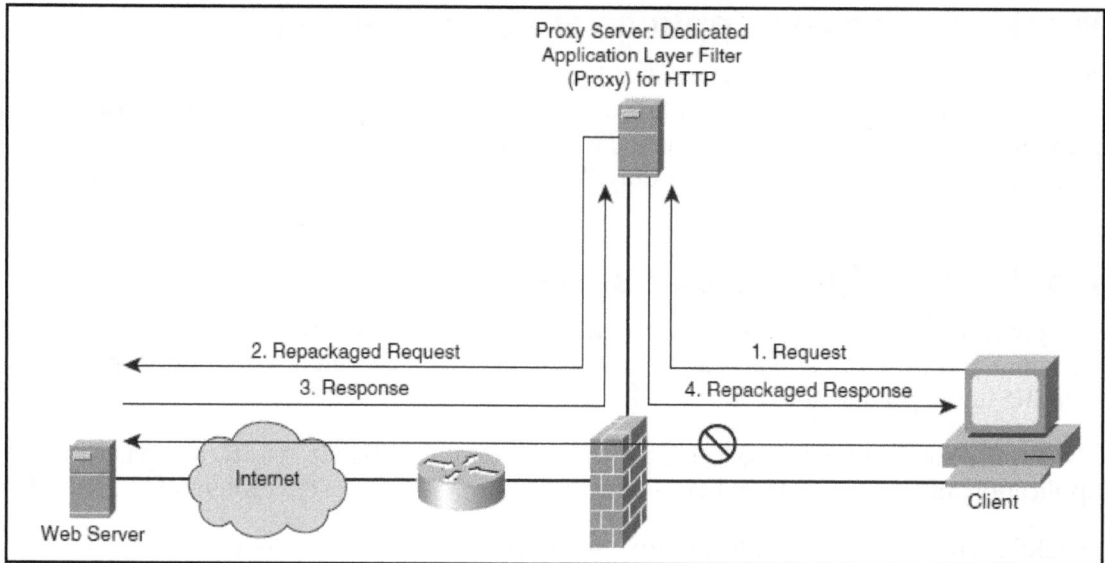

Let's understand how the process works:

1. The proxy server receives a request from the sender/clients
2. The server performs user authentication according to the norms/configurations made into it
3. It forwards Layer 3 and Layer 4 packets to check the rules of the firewall and tries to access the requested website using the internet
4. The proxy server returns the request of the client; the proxy server forwards only Layer 5 and Layer 7 messages and the information allowed by the server

The main reason behind the architecture of application-layer firewalls is solely to provide the highest level of filtering for a specific protocol. Despite everything, the proxy server lowers the speed of network performance since it needs to evaluate the most significant amount of information embedded in packets.

Areas of opportunity

Application-layer firewalls are very processor-intensive; they require a lot of memory and CPU cycles to process every packet that needs to undergo scrutiny. The detailed logging is quite beneficial, but still, that consumes a lot of resources within the device. Two solutions have been designed:

- Using **CXTP** (short for, **Context Transfer Protocol**) to authenticate and authorize, instead of monitoring the data on a connection
- Ensuring that layer firewalls would monitor the imperative applications, as per the company requirement only

Additionally, there are some other limitations, such as they don't support all applications, since the monitoring has a limited number of connection types—Telnet, FTP, or web services. Another limitation is that they require vendor-specific software, which limits the scalability and may create management issues.

Packet filtering and the OSI model

Static packet-filtering firewalls act as L3 devices. Filtering and ACL rules are applied to determine the acceptance/rejection of a packet from a particular source, destination, IP address, port number, or packet type. The strategy is to check whether any packet is trying to enter the internal network from the external claiming to be an internal packet.

As we are already aware, each service has a port number assigned to it. So packet-filtering can be done based on port numbers. A simple way is to block the port number to block a particular service. For example, if a Telnet service needs to be blocked, then you can simply block port number 23 and restrict the access of the Telnet service.

Static packet-filtering firewalls are similar to packet-filtering routers, but there is a slight difference. The filtering firewalls are very scalable and application-independent in nature, hence they have high performance standards.

Summary

In this chapter, we introduced firewalls and the services they offer. We also saw how firewalls work in a defense strategy by providing perimeter security for the entire network. We then saw how a transparent firewall and an application-layer firewall work as a means for providing additional security.

In the next chapter, we will learn about the ASA functionality and the basic configuration of Cisco ASA.

10
Cisco ASA

In this chapter, are going to take a look at securing our network using the Cisco **Adaptive Security Appliance** (**ASA**). We will begin by understanding the Adaptive Security Appliance and its features. Next, we will dive into basic configurations of the ASA, such as getting the device up and running efficiently on your perimeter network. Further, we will introduce the **Adaptive Security Device Manager** (**ASDM**) to assist us in our configurations and administration of the ASA.

The following topics will be covered in the chapter:

- Cisco ASA portfolio
- Adaptive Security Appliance features
- Basic ASA configuration

Cisco ASA portfolio

The purpose of a firewall is to filter incoming and outgoing traffic between networks. The ASA is a family of next-generation firewalls from Cisco systems. The ASA is a standalone appliance that provides stateful and packet filtering, **Network Address Translation** (**NAT**), routing, **Dynamic Host Configuration Protocol** (**DHCP**), **Virtual Private Network** (**VPN**) capabilities, botnet filtering, **Advanced Malware Protection** (**AMP**), and deep packet inspection. Those are only a few of the features and services it offers. In the next section, we will dive a bit deeper into discussing the features of the ASA and its abilities to prevent threats from entering a network/organization.

The following is a picture of Cisco ASA 5505:

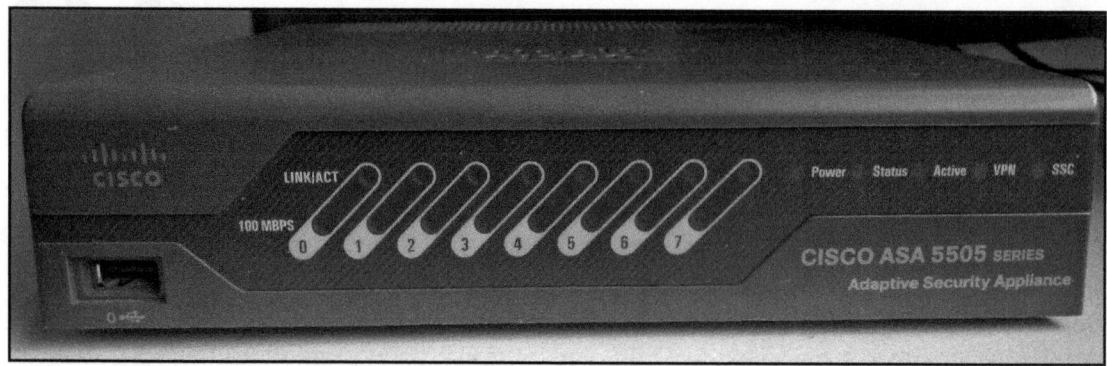

The ASA comes in many different shapes and sizes to fit business needs. Some models include: 5505, 5510, 5520, 5540, 5550, 5506-X, 5506W-H, 5506H-X, 5508-X, 5516-X, 5525-X, 5545-X, and 5555-X. You may ask yourself, what's the main difference between the Cisco ASA 5500 series appliance and the newer Cisco ASA 5500-X series? To answer that question, Cisco has developed a new technology called **FirePOWER**, which is supported on the 5500-X appliances.

You may have noticed each ASA has a different model number. The model number defines the capacity for the number of nodes and bandwidth it can support in an organization/network. Therefore, each ASA is designed for a particular network size, ranging from small office, branch office, medium-to-large networks, to internet edge and datacenter networks.

ASA features

In the previous section, we mentioned some of the features and services of the ASA. Here, we are going to discuss the key features and services in the ASA and how they can assist your organization and fit business needs. Whether you are a student, a network security engineer, a cyber security professional, or simply an enthusiast, understanding the functionality of the ASA will be helpful in the journey ahead.

Let's begin!

First, let's discuss a few things about the ASA and how it determines (by default) whether traffic is allowed to flow from one interface to another. Each interface on the ASA is assigned to a network ,or what is better known as a **zone**. A zone is simply an area on the network. There are typically three zones: the **INSIDE** zone, the **OUTSIDE** zone, and the Demilitarized zone. Each zone has a security level defined by a number ranging from 0 to 100. The number determines the trust level of a zone and if traffic is allowed to flow between zones, whether unidirectional or bidirectional.

How exactly does the security level play a role in each zone? Let's break this down a bit further: a zone with a 100 security level is a fully trusted zone, such as your private **Local Area Network (LAN)**. An untrusted zone, such as the internet, typically has a security level of 0. The DMZ is the semi-trusted area in your network. Within the DMZ, you'll find your public servers. In a typical DMZ, your organization may have several servers that require a direct internet connection, in other words, they are public-facing. The purpose of the DMZ is to allow partial access from the internet to the DMZ only, and not access from the internet to the private LAN. The DMZ usually has a security level ranging from 1 to 99.

> Two or more zones can have the same security-level value. In a case like this, bidirectional traffic is NOT allowed between those zones by default. These options can be modified.

Stateful filtering

Stateful filtering is a feature that monitors traffic originating from one zone and moving to another. It keeps track of this information and would allow only the returning traffic through the ASA.

Traffic originating from a zone with a higher security level, such as the **INSIDE zone** (**100**), is allowed to go to a zone with a lower security level, such as the **OUTSIDE** (**0**) and **DMZ** (**50**), and the return traffic is allowed because the ASA keeps track of the flows of traffic in a state table (stateful filtering):

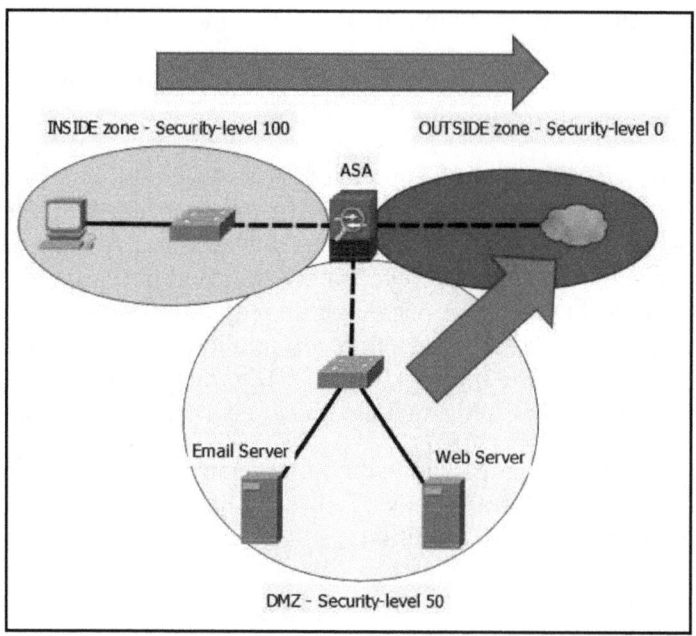

However, traffic originating from the **OUTSIDE** (**0**) zone is not allowed to reach the **INSIDE** (**100**) zone or the DMZ (50) by default, nor is traffic originating from the **DMZ** (**50**) allowed to access the **INSIDE** (**100**) zone.

Packet filtering

Packet filtering enables an ASA to either permit or deny traffic based on a packet's source, and/or destination IP address, and/or source, and destination Port number. The ASA can achieve this by using an **Access Control List** (**ACL**).

For example, let say you want to restrict users from the 192.168.1.0/24 network from visiting the Cisco website. We know a web server typically uses port 80 (this would be our destination port) and the IP address for https://www.cisco.com/ is 23.37.75.188 (our destination IP address). Therefore, we would create an ACL to achieve this function on the ASA. Assuming our internal network is 192.168.1.0/24, our ACL would typically be access-list 100 deny tcp 192.168.1.0 0.0.0.255 23.37.75.188 255.255.255.255 eq 80. Don't worry, we'll discuss ACLs in the later chapters.

Network Address Translation

Network Address Translation (**NAT**) allows private IP addresses (RFC 1918) to be translated into another IP address. An example would be devices, such as computers, that are sitting on the private LAN trying to access https://www.cisco.com/ on the internet. Because their private IP addresses are non-routable on the internet, each device would require a public IP address. Using NAT on the Cisco router or ASA, the appliance allows devices with private IP addresses to be translated to the public IP address (which is on the internet-facing port). NAT allows a network to be hidden behind a single IP address for security purposes. It is also used to conserve the public IPv4 address space.

Routing

The ASA has routing capabilities like a router. It has the ability to exchange routing information for **Routing Information Protocol (RIP)**, **Enhanced Interior Gateway Routing Protocol (EIGRP)**, and **Open Shortest Path First (OSPF)**. The ASA supports static routing.

Dynamic Host Configuration Protocol

The ASA can function as both a **Dynamic Host Configuration Protocol (DHCP)** server and a DHCP client for receiving an IP address on its interface(s). The DHCP server enables the ASA to automatically assign dynamic IP addresses, subnet mask, default-gateway, DNS server, and so on to clients or any device that is requesting an IP address on the network. The DHCP server can be useful for small companies and branch offices.

Virtual Private Network

A **Virtual Private Network** (**VPN**) allows a secure connection between two devices/networks over an untrusted network. The ASA can support both an **IPSec** (short for, **Internet Protocol Security**) and **SSL** (short for, **Secure Sockets Layer**). It has the ability to establish site-to-site and remote access VPNs.

Botnet filtering

A bot (robot) is a small piece of malicious code that infects a device, making it a zombie machine. The bot listens for instruction from a **Command and Control** (**CnC**) server. A group of zombies makes up a botnet (bot network) and they can all be controlled from a single CnC server to perform malicious activities.

The botnet filtering on the ASA is a license-based service from Cisco that allows the firewall to monitor, detect, and prevent such threats.

Advanced Malware Protection

With the evolution of **Advanced Persistent Threats** (**APTs**), the Cisco **Advanced Malware Protection** (**AMP**) provides malware protection before, during, and after an attack. AMO is a feature that provides next-generation abilities in the ASAs (5500-X models).

Authentication, authorization, and accounting

The Cisco ASA support **authentication**, **authorization**, and **accounting** (**AAA**). This feature allows the ASA to act as a local AAA server or can query a remote AAA appliance, such as a **Remote Authentication Dial-In User Service** (**RADIUS**) or a **Terminal Access Controller Access-Control System Plus** (**TACACS+**) server.

Class map and policy map

The ASA uses class map to identify traffic, IP addresses, Layer 4 protocols, or application protocols. A policy map is used to perform an action (permit, deny, and so on). A service policy is a used to apply a policy on either all interfaces or a single interface on the ASA. To give an example, let's say we want to block all outgoing HTTP traffic, first we would create a class map to identify the HTTP traffic, then a policy map to deny/drop the outgoing traffic, and finally use a service policy to apply the policy on the interface of our choosing.

Basic ASA configuration

The following are the components needed to begin the configurations on the **Adaptive Security Appliance (ASA)** :

- Cisco ASA
- Console cable
- USB-to-serial converter (optional)
- Ethernet cables (optional)
- Terminal emulation program: PuTTY, SecureCRT, or TeraTerm
- Laptop/PC

Before we get started, there are several methods for setting up and managing the ASA. The common method, which you may already know, is via the CLI using a Terminal-emulation program. However there is another, using the **Adaptive Security Device Manager (ASDM)**, which provides a Graphical User Interface for the ASA. There is also the **Cisco Security Manager (CSM)**, which is a commercial tool created by Cisco for enterprise management of their routers, switches, and security devices.

For the remainder of this book, we'll be using both the CLI and the ASDM to administer and manage the ASA.

With the purchase of an ASA, in the contents of the box you'll receive a console cable (light blue color). This cable is used to initially access and configure the ASA. The cable has two different ends, an RS-232 (DB-9) connector and an RJ-45 connector. Modern laptops/PCs no longer ship with an RS-232 port, therefore you will need a USB-to-serial adapter for bridging the cables together.

The following is an picture of the console cable:

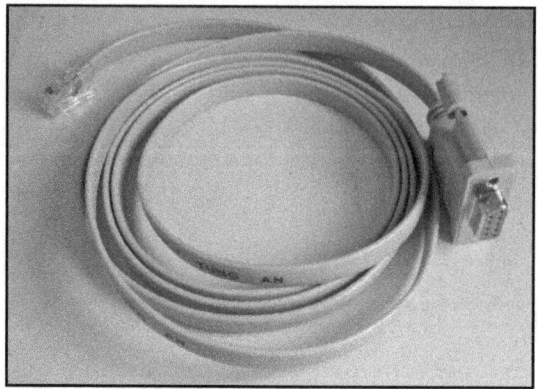

The following is a picture of USB to Serial converter cable:

Take the RJ-45 end of the console cable and plug it into the console port of the ASA (located at the back of the device). Now take the other end and plug it into your laptop/PC. Ensure the power supply is connected properly on the ASA and power on the device. The following picture shows the console port of a Cisco ASA 5505:

Download PuTTY from `https://www.putty.org/` and open it. The **Connection type** should be set to **Serial** and **Speed** `9600`. Then click **Open**:

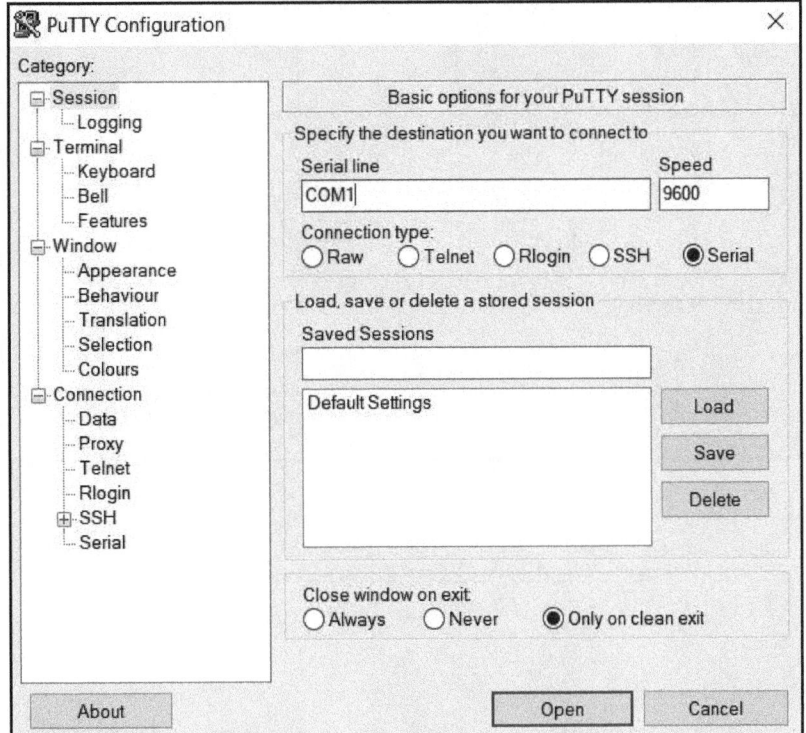

If you are using SecureCRT (`https://www.vandyke.com/`), use the following settings (be sure to adjust the COM port accordingly):

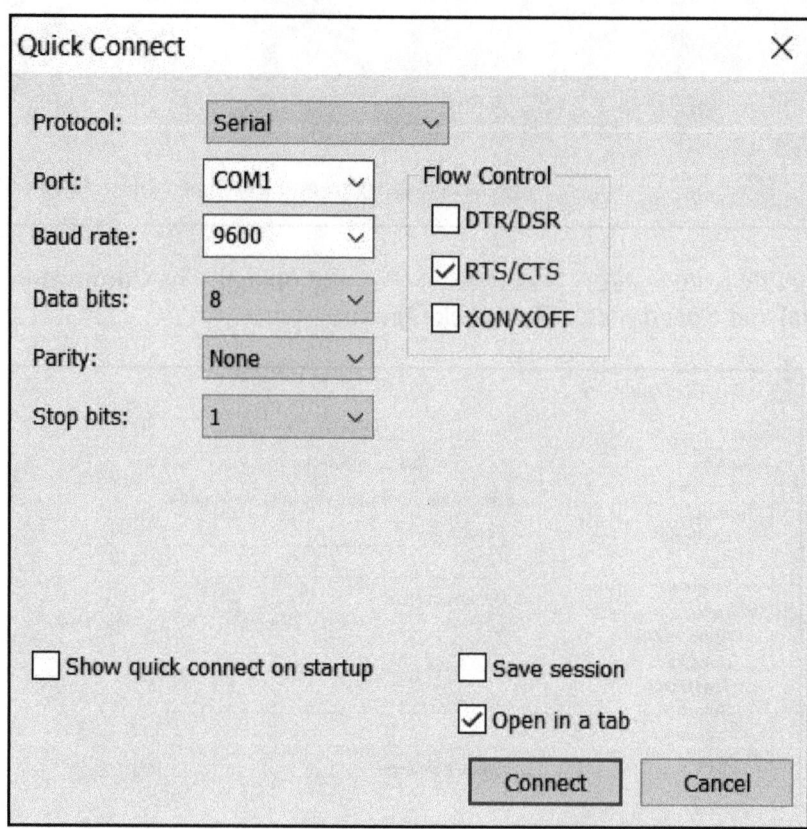

When the ASA boots for the first time, you'll receive a system message asking whether you want to use the interactive wizard to assist in getting your ASA up and ready. If you type yes and hit *Enter*, the following options will be provided:

```
Pre-configure Firewall now through interactive prompts [yes]? yes
Firewall Mode [Routed]:
Enable password [<use current password>]: cisco123
Allow password recovery [yes]?
Clock (UTC):
  Year [2018]:
  Month [Mar]:
  Day [1]:
  Time [19:52:02]:
Inside IP address: 192.168.1.1
Inside network mask: 255.255.255.0
Host name: ASA-1
Domain name: ccnasec.local
IP address of host running Device Manager: 192.168.1.254

The following configuration will be used:
Enable password: cisco123
Allow password recovery: yes
Clock (UTC): 19:52:02 Mar 1 2018
Firewall Mode: Routed
Inside IP address: 192.168.1.1
Inside network mask: 255.255.255.0
Host name: ASA-1
Domain name: ccnasec.local
IP address of host running Device Manager: 192.168.1.254

Use this configuration and write to flash? yes
INFO: Security level for "inside" set to 100 by default.
WARNING: http server is not yet enabled to allow ASDM access.
Cryptochecksum: 13fc03ab a8c834b2 5e77683f da4d9e8f

2224 bytes copied in 1.780 secs (2224 bytes/sec)


Type help or '?' for a list of available commands.
ASA-1>
```

Please note that by hitting the *Enter* key, the default values in the square brackets [] will be applied for each line. In the preceding capture, the date and time were left as the default values on the ASA.

If we had entered no, the ASA goes into a default state and uses ciscoasa as the default hostname. This brings us to the user EXEC mode, indicated with a > symbol:

```
ciscoasa>
```

The following is a screenshot of the CLI:

```
Pre-configure Firewall now through interactive prompts [yes]? no



Type help or '?' for a list of available commands.
ciscoasa> _
```

 If you want to invoke the interactive wizard at a later time, you can use the setup command.

Next, we are going to type enable to access the privilege EXEC mode. You will be prompted for a password; because this the initial boot without any prior configuration, the password is *blank*, simply hit *Enter* again and you will notice the prompt has changed. The privilege EXEC mode is indicated using a # symbol:

```
ciscoasa> enable
Password:
ciscoasa#
```

```
ciscoasa> enable
Password:
ciscoasa# _
```

Let's look at various information about the ASA device using the show version command. The show version will provide us with the device uptime, ASDM version, operating system version, model, serial, available features, processor type, amount of RAM, interfaces, and licenses:

```
ciscoasa# show version
```

```
ciscoasa# show version

Cisco Adaptive Security Appliance Software Version 8.2(5)59
Device Manager Version 7.6(2)150

Compiled on Fri 12-Feb-16 11:35 by builders
System image file is "disk0:/asa825-59-k8.bin"
Config file at boot was "startup-config"

ciscoasa up 23 mins 30 secs
```

As we can see in the preceding screenshot, the system version is 8.2, the ASDM version
7.6, the location of the system image and the device up time:

```
Hardware:   ASA5505, 512 MB RAM, CPU Geode 500 MHz
Internal ATA Compact Flash, 128MB
BIOS Flash Firmware Hub @ 0xffe00000, 1024KB

Encryption hardware device : Cisco ASA-5505 on-board accelerator (revision 0x0)
                             Boot microcode   : CN1000-MC-BOOT-2.00
                             SSL/IKE microcode: CNLite-MC-SSLm-PLUS-2.03
                             IPSec microcode  : CNlite-MC-IPSECm-MAIN-2.05

 0: Int: Internal-Data0/0   : address is 2c54.2d91.5c2e, irq 11
 1: Ext: Ethernet0/0        : address is 2c54.2d91.5c26, irq 255
 2: Ext: Ethernet0/1        : address is 2c54.2d91.5c27, irq 255
 3: Ext: Ethernet0/2        : address is 2c54.2d91.5c28, irq 255
 4: Ext: Ethernet0/3        : address is 2c54.2d91.5c29, irq 255
 5: Ext: Ethernet0/4        : address is 2c54.2d91.5c2a, irq 255
 6: Ext: Ethernet0/5        : address is 2c54.2d91.5c2b, irq 255
 7: Ext: Ethernet0/6        : address is 2c54.2d91.5c2c, irq 255
 8: Ext: Ethernet0/7        : address is 2c54.2d91.5c2d, irq 255
 9: Int: Internal-Data0/1   : address is 0000.0003.0002, irq 255
10: Int: Not used           : irq 255
11: Int: Not used           : irq 255

Licensed features for this platform:
Maximum Physical Interfaces    : 8
VLANs                          : 20, DMZ Unrestricted
Inside Hosts                   : Unlimited
Failover                       : Active/Standby
VPN-DES                        : Enabled
VPN-3DES-AES                   : Enabled
SSL VPN Peers                  : 2
Total VPN Peers                : 25
Dual ISPs                      : Enabled
VLAN Trunk Ports               : 8
Shared License                 : Disabled
AnyConnect for Mobile          : Disabled
AnyConnect for Cisco VPN Phone : Disabled
AnyConnect Essentials          : Disabled
Advanced Endpoint Assessment   : Disabled
UC Phone Proxy Sessions        : 2
Total UC Proxy Sessions        : 2
Botnet Traffic Filter          : Disabled

This platform has an ASA 5505 Security Plus license.

Serial Number: JMX1616420U
Running Activation Key: 0x1830ed41 0xd871093b 0xf4b3958c 0xb2d8281c 0xc0110db2
Configuration register is 0x1
Configuration last modified by enable_15 at 11:47:29.019 UTC Fri Mar 2 2018
```

 If you are using **Cisco Packet Tracer** (https://www.netacad.com/courses/packet-tracer), there's an ASA 5505, however only CLI access is available.

The following is a show version output from an ASA 5505 from the Cisco Packet Tracer program:

```
ciscoasa#show version

Cisco Adaptive Security Appliance Software Version 8.4(2)
Device Manager Version 6.4(5)

Compiled on Wed 15-Jun-11 18:17 by mnguyen
System image file is "disk0:/asa842-k8.bin"
Config file at boot was "startup-config"

ciscoasa up 27 seconds

Hardware:   ASA5505, 512 MB RAM, CPU Geode 500 MHz
Internal ATA Compact Flash, 128MB
BIOS Flash M50FW016 @ 0xfff00000, 2048KB

Encryption hardware device : Cisco ASA-5505 on-board accelerator (revision
0x0)
Boot microcode : CN1000-MC-BOOT-2.00
SSL/IKE microcode : CNLite-MC-SSLm-PLUS-2.03
IPSec microcode : CNlite-MC-IPSECm-MAIN-2.06
Number of accelerators: 1

0: Int: Internal-Data0/0 : address is 44d3.caef.1e22, irq 11
1: Ext: Ethernet0/0 : address is 0001.9692.AE01, irq 255
2: Ext: Ethernet0/1 : address is 0001.9692.AE02, irq 255
3: Ext: Ethernet0/2 : address is 0001.9692.AE03, irq 255
4: Ext: Ethernet0/3 : address is 0001.9692.AE04, irq 255
5: Ext: Ethernet0/4 : address is 0001.9692.AE05, irq 255
6: Ext: Ethernet0/5 : address is 0001.9692.AE06, irq 255
7: Ext: Ethernet0/6 : address is 0001.9692.AE07, irq 255
8: Ext: Ethernet0/7 : address is 0001.9692.AE08, irq 255
9: Int: Internal-Data0/1 : address is 0000.0003.0002, irq 255
10: Int: Not used : irq 255
11: Int: Not used : irq 255

Licensed features for this platform:
Maximum Physical Interfaces : 8 perpetual
VLANs : 3 DMZ Restricted
Dual ISPs : Disabled perpetual
```

```
VLAN Trunk Ports : 0 perpetual
Inside Hosts : 10 perpetual
Failover : Disabled perpetual
VPN-DES : Enabled perpetual
VPN-3DES-AES : Enabled perpetual
AnyConnect Premium Peers : 2 perpetual
AnyConnect Essentials : Disabled perpetual
Other VPN Peers : 10 perpetual
Total VPN Peers : 25 perpetual
Shared License : Disabled perpetual
AnyConnect for Mobile : Disabled perpetual
AnyConnect for Cisco VPN Phone : Disabled perpetual
Advanced Endpoint Assessment : Disabled perpetual
UC Phone Proxy Sessions : 2 perpetual
Total UC Proxy Sessions : 2 perpetual
Botnet Traffic Filter : Disabled perpetual
Intercompany Media Engine : Disabled perpetual

This platform has a Base license.

Serial Number: JMX15361AKD
Running Permanent Activation Key: 0x77E8213D 0x81D8D4DA 0x7CDDD6CE
0x5C6827E3 0x6AB8A1E4
Configuration register is 0x1
Configuration has not been modified since last system restart.
```

Viewing the filesystem

We can display the filesystem of the ASA using the show file system command. We can even view the contents of the flash using show flash:, and so on for the other locations available:

```
ciscoasa# show file system
```

```
ciscoasa# show file system

File Systems:

      Size(b)        Free(b)        Type      Flags   Prefixes
* 536535040       535822336        disk       rw       disk0: flash:
            -              -        network    rw       tftp:
            -              -        opaque     rw       system:
            -              -        network    ro       http:
            -              -        network    ro       https:
            -              -        network    rw       scp:
            -              -        network    rw       ftp:
            -              -        network    wo       cluster:
            -              -        stub       ro       cluster_trace:
            -              -        network    rw       smb:
```

 The commands used on the Cisco ASA are very similar to what is used on the Cisco switches and routers.

Setting a hostname

Whenever we remotely access a device across a network via the CLI, the quickest way to determine whether we have logged on to the correct device is by its hostname. Each device on the network should have a unique hostname with part of its name able to identify that particular device and/or location.

The hostname can be changed from the **global configuration mode**, this mode affects the appliance globally. We can enter the global configuration mode from the privilege mode by using the `configure terminal` command.

Using the `hostname` command, we can set a hostname of our choosing. Please be sure not to include any spaces in the actual hostname:

```
ciscoasa# configure terminal
ciscoasa(config)# hostname ASA-1
ASA-1(config)#
```

```
ciscoasa# configure terminal
ciscoasa(config)# hostname ASA-1
ASA-1(config)#
```

As we can see in the preceding image, once we entered the `hostname ASA-1` command, the default hostname changed immediately and we are presented with a new line, using `ASA-1` as the new hostname.

Setting the clock

Time on network-connected devices is very important for logs. The timestamps on log entries can help security administrators understand the sequence of events that took place. An example of a log entry: an alert is generated of a port scan on the firewall. The security administrator can use the timestamp to observe the sequence of events that may have taken place before, during, and after the potential attack. The local clock can be set on the ASA using the following commands:

```
clock set hh:mm:ss day month year
ASA-1# clock set 6:00:00 1 March 2018
```

We can verify the current time on the ASA by using:

```
ASA-1# show clock
06:03:17.319 UTC Thu Mar 1 2018
```

Assigning a domain name to the ASA

In most organization, your IT team would assign all network-connected devices to a domain for easier management and IT efficiency. Using the `domain-name` command followed by the organization/company's domain name will attach the domain to the ASA. Here, we are going to attach `ccnasec.local` to the ASA. The domain name is needed for the generation of the cryptographic keys for **Secure Shell (SSH)**:

```
ASA-1(config)# domain-name ccnasec.local
```

Let's verify the domain name:

```
ASA-1(config)# show running-config domain-name
ccnasec.local
```

The show commands can be executed in any mode on the ASA, except in user EXEC.

Securing access to the privilege exec mode

It's always good to prevent unauthorized access to the privilege mode of the ASA. At the privilege mode, many show commands can be executed, thus displaying sensitive information about the device. A person with malicious intent can use this information to cause harm to the network or the organization.

We can achieve this by using the enable password command followed by the password. The password we are going to use will be cisco123:

```
ASA-1(config)# enable password cisco123
```

Let's verify the password in the running-config file:

Using show running-config enable allows us to verify our password is *encrypted* by default on the running-config file.

The enable secret command is equivalent to enable password on the ASA and can be up to *16* characters in length.

We can verify the password is encrypted in the running-config:

```
ASA-1(config)# show running-config enable
enable password 9jNfZuG3TC5tCVH0 encrypted
```

```
ASA-1(config)# show running-config enable
enable password 9jNfZuG3TC5tCVH0 encrypted
ASA-1(config)# _
```

Let's verify whether the password works:

```
ASA-1> enable
Password: ********
ASA-1#
```

Whenever entering the password via the CLI on the ASA, each character is represented with an asterisk (*) as a security measure for prying eyes.

Saving the configurations

The ASA is a bit differently when saving the `running-config` file. Unlike the Cisco routers and switches, the ASA uses the `write memory` command:

ASA-1(config)# write memory

```
ASA-1(config)# write memory
Building configuration...
Cryptochecksum: 2883d88a 8beaafc2 cff53d64 d55e0ed8

3287 bytes copied in 0.750 secs
[OK]
ASA-1(config)#
```

The `write memory` command is equivalent to copying the `running-config startup-config` command.

Setting a banner

The banner can be used as a legal notice, warning any entity that makes unauthorized access into the device, or can act as a disclaimer. The banner can be set from the global configuration mode of the ASA.

Using the `banner ?` syntax, we can see the various options available. We are presented with four options, each would display the banner during a specific login method:

```
ASA-1(config)# banner ?

configure mode commands/options:
  asdm Display a post login banner (ASDM only)
  exec Display a banner whenever an EXEC process in initiated
  login Display a banner before the username and password login prompts
  motd Display a message-of-the-day banner
```

The following is the output from the ASA:

```
ASA-1(config)# banner ?

configure mode commands/options:
  asdm    Display a post login banner (ASDM only)
  exec    Display a banner whenever an EXEC process in initiated
  login   Display a banner before the username and password login prompts
  motd    Display a message-of-the-day banner
```

However, we are going to use the **message of the day** (**MOTD**) option. The MOTD is displayed across all logins to the firewall. Here, we are going to set a three-line banner that will pop up for any new connection to the ASA (such as console or **Virtual Teletype** (**VTY**)):

```
ASA-1(config)# banner motd Please be advised unauthorized access is
strictly prohibited
ASA-1(config)# banner motd All access are recorded for security purposes
ASA-1(config)# banner motd This device is the property for ACME Corp.
```

Notice, each new line begins with the `banner motd` command, the effect of this command will add a new line at the bottom of the existing banner:

```
ASA-1(config)# banner motd Please be advised unauthorized access is strictly p$
ASA-1(config)# banner motd All access are recorded for security purposes
ASA-1(config)# banner motd This device is the property for ACME Corp.
```

Let's verify the banner on the ASA:

```
ASA-1(config)# show banner
motd:
Please be advised unauthorized access is strictly prohibited
All access are recorded for security purposes
This device is the property for ACME Corp.
```

```
ASA-1(config)# show banner
motd:
Please be advised unauthorized access is strictly prohibited
All access are recorded for security purposes
This device is the property for ACME Corp.
```

Assigning IP addresses on the interfaces

Configuring the interfaces (ports) are very similar to a Cisco router, however there are two additional commands we need. On the ASA, we need to tell the ASA the zone and trust level for each interface we going to assign an IP address on. As discussed earlier, the ASA needs to understand whether to allow traffic to flow between interfaces (**zones**) or not. We can using the following commands to configure the interfaces on the ASA respectively:

```
ASA-1(config)# interface gigabitethernet 0
ASA-1(config-if)# nameif Inside
ASA-1(config-if)# security-level 100
ASA-1(config-if)# ip address 192.168.2.1 255.255.255.0
ASA-1(config-if)# no shutdown
ASA-1(config-if)# exit
ASA-1(config)# interface gigabitethernet 1
ASA-1(config-if)# nameif Outside
ASA-1(config-if)# security-level 0
ASA-1(config-if)# ip address 200.1.1.2 255.255.255.252
ASA-1(config-if)# no shutdown
ASA-1(config-if)# exit
```

The ASA can act as a Dynamic Host Configuration Protocol client on its individual interfaces using the ip address dhcp command. Using the nameif Inside command on an interface places a security level of **100** by default. The same concept would apply if nameif Outside is used on an interface, setting a security level of **0** by default.

Let's verify the configurations on the interfaces of the ASA.

Use the following commands will verify the available interfaces, IP address assignment, and the Layer 1 (Physical layer) and Layer 2 (Data Link layer) statuses:

ASA-1(config)# show interface ip brief

```
ASA-1(config)# show interface ip brief
Interface                 IP-Address      OK? Method Status                Protocol
GigabitEthernet0          192.168.2.1     YES manual up                    up
GigabitEthernet1          200.1.1.2       YES manual up                    up
GigabitEthernet2          unassigned      YES unset  administratively down up
```

The show ip address command provides us with the interface ID, interface name, IP address, subnet mask, and method by which the interface received the IP address information:

```
ASA-1(config)# show ip address
System IP Addresses:
Interface           Name        IP address      Subnet mask       Method
GigabitEthernet0    Inside      192.168.1.1     255.255.255.0     CONFIG
GigabitEthernet1    Outside     200.1.1.2       255.255.255.252   CONFIG
Current IP Addresses:
Interface           Name        IP address      Subnet mask       Method
GigabitEthernet0    Inside      192.168.1.1     255.255.255.0     CONFIG
GigabitEthernet1    Outside     200.1.1.2       255.255.255.252   CONFIG
ASA-1(config)#
```

Using the show running-config interface command displays the configurations under all the interfaces in the running-config on the ASA:

```
ASA-1# show running-config interface
!
interface GigabitEthernet0
 nameif Inside
 security-level 100
 ip address 192.168.2.1 255.255.255.0
!
interface GigabitEthernet1
 nameif Outside
 security-level 0
 ip address 200.1.1.2 255.255.255.252
!
```

Setting a default static route

A default static route should be mandatory when an internet connection is made on your stub router or firewall. The purpose of the default route is to send traffic that is destined for a network outside of your organization's network. A simple example is traffic destined for the internet.

Setting a default static route is quite simple. The ASA uses the `route` command, followed by the outgoing interface (`Outside`), the `0.0.0.0 0.0.0.0` matches any network address, and finally specifies the next-hop IP address.

> The default static route is placed as the last entry in the routing table of the router or firewall, since the device reads the routing table from top to bottom until a match is found.

Using the following format, we can substitute our information accordingly:

```
route <outgoing interface> <network-id> <subnet mask> <next-hop>
ASA-1(config)# route outside 0.0.0.0 0.0.0.0 200.1.1.1
```

Let's verify our static route:

```
ASA-1(config)# show running-config route
route Outside 0.0.0.0 0.0.0.0 200.1.1.1 1
```

Using the `show route` command to view the routing table of the ASA, we can see the last route was defined with an `S*`, which means it's a default static route with a next hop IP of `200.1.1.1` and an outgoing interface named `Outside`. Therefore, any packet destined for a network for which the ASA does not have an entry in its routing table will send the packet to the default route via `200.1.1.1`:

```
ASA-1(config)# show route

Codes: C - connected, S - static, I - IGRP, R - RIP, M - mobile, B - BGP
       D - EIGRP, EX - EIGRP external, O - OSPF, IA - OSPF inter area
       N1 - OSPF NSSA external type 1, N2 - OSPF NSSA external type 2
       E1 - OSPF external type 1, E2 - OSPF external type 2, E - EGP
       i - IS-IS, L1 - IS-IS level-1, L2 - IS-IS level-2, ia - IS-IS inter area
       * - candidate default, U - per-user static route, o - ODR
       P - periodic downloaded static route

Gateway of last resort is 200.1.1.1 to network 0.0.0.0

C    200.1.1.0 255.255.255.252 is directly connected, Outside
C    192.168.1.0 255.255.255.0 is directly connected, Inside
S*   0.0.0.0 0.0.0.0 [1/0] via 200.1.1.1, Outside
ASA-1(config)#
```

Creating a local user account

The Cisco ASA can use its local AAA service to assign user accounts special privileges and keep track of the activities.

Let's create a new user account with a username of Admin, an encrypted password of class123, and assign the account the highest privilege, using 15:

```
ASA-1(config)# username Admin password class123 privilege 15
```

Let's verify the local user accounts on the ASA:

```
ASA-1(config)# show running-config user
username Admin password 1DWc9Yty0R9.LaJt encrypted privilege 15
```

Remote access

Remote access is a convenient method to access the appliance for administration. Sometimes, you may not be in the same building or city where the ASA is deployed, but you need to access it, whether to troubleshoot or modify a configuration.

Setting up SSH

SSH allows the ASA administrator to securely access the ASA firewall via a Terminal connection over a network. SSH uses cryptographic keys to encrypt and decrypt the traffic between the sending and receiving devices. In this case, it is between the client device and the ASA firewall.

To get started, the follow these steps:

1. Set a hostname:

```
ASA-1(config)# hostname ASA-1
```

2. Assign a domain name:

```
ASA-1(config)# domain-name ccnasec.local
```

3. Create cryptographic keys:

```
ASA-1(config)# crypto key generate rsa modulus 2048
```

4. Create a user account (local AAA service):

```
ASA-1(config)# username Admin password class123 privilege 15
```

5. Configure SSH to query the local database for user account:

```
ASA-1(config)# aaa authentication ssh console LOCAL
```

6. Identify which device/network will be remotely accessing the ASA and the incoming interface:

```
ASA-1(config)# ssh 192.168.1.0 255.255.255.0 Inside
```

7. Accept only SSHv2-incoming connections (optional):

```
ASA-1(config)# ssh version 2
```

8. Set an inactivity timer in minutes (optional):

```
ASA-1(config)# ssh timeout 2
```

The following is a preview of the execution of commands required to set up SSH for remote access:

```
ciscoasa(config)# hostname ASA-1
ASA-1(config)# domain-name ccnasec.local
ASA-1(config)# crypto key generate rsa modulus 2048
INFO: The name for the keys will be: <Default-RSA-Key>
Keypair generation process begin. Please wait...
ASA-1(config)# username Admin password class123 privilege 15
ASA-1(config)# ssh 192.168.1.0 255.255.255.0 Inside
```

We can verify our SSH configuration by using the show running-config ssh command, however this command does not display all of the SSH configurations on the ASA:

```
ASA-1(config)# show running-config ssh
ssh stricthostkeycheck
ssh timeout 5
ssh key-exchange group dh-group1-sha1
```

From our client PC, open PuTTY (`https://www.putty.org/`). Enter the IP address of the
ASA and select the **SSH** option:

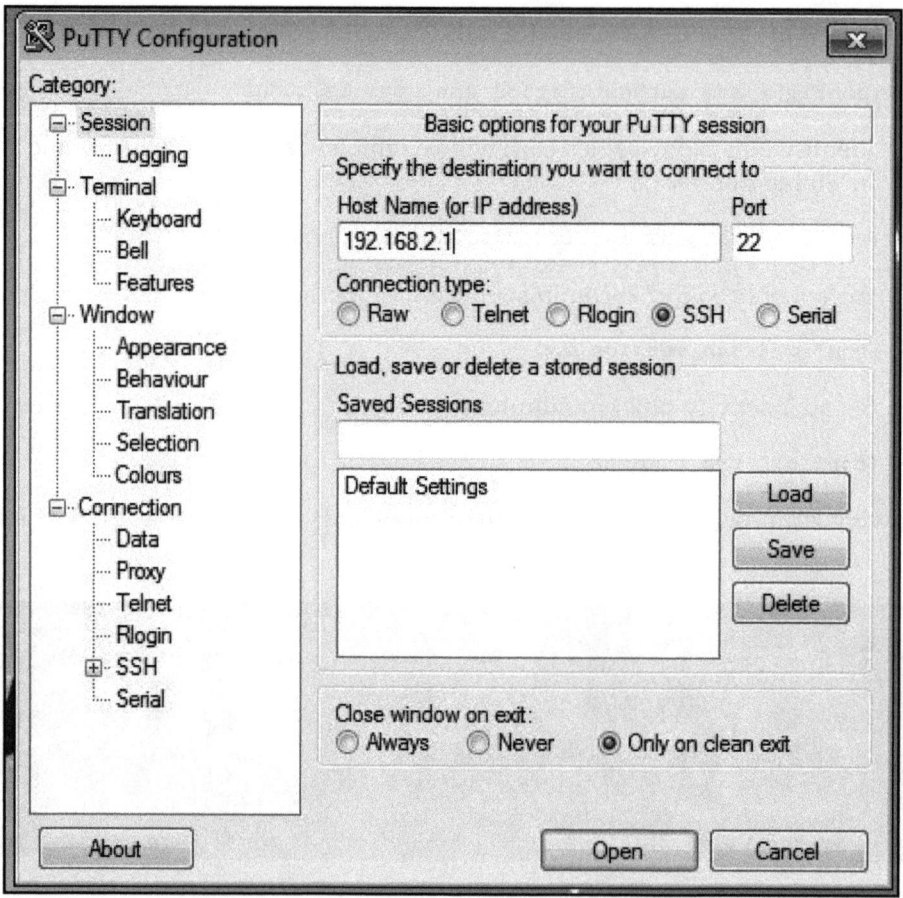

Your Cisco router or switch also has an SSH client built into the IOS. Using the `ssh -l Admin 192.168.2.1` command will allow the router or switch to establish a secure Terminal connection between itself and the ASA:

> The ASA does NOT have an SSH Client, unlike the Cisco routers and switches.
> The SSH protocol specifies the username with the `-l` syntax followed by the IP address of the remote device.

```
R2#ssh -l Admin 192.168.2.1
```

As we can see here, the Terminal connection was successful, the device hostname is now, `ASA-1`:

```
R2#ssh -l Admin 192.168.2.1

Password:
Please be advised unauthorized access is strictly prohibited
All access are recorded for security purposes
This device is the property for ACME Corp.
Type help or '?' for a list of available commands.
ASA-1>
```

At any time, we can see which user is connected to the ASA via SSH. `show ssh sessions` provides the IP address of the user client machine and the username. There is other information available, such as the SSH version, encryption type and algorithms, integrity checking algorithms, and the connection state:

```
ASA-1# show ssh sessions

SID Client IP      Version Mode Encryption Hmac    State           Username
0   192.168.2.2    1.99    IN   aes128-cbc sha1    SessionStarted  Admin
                           OUT  aes128-cbc sha1    SessionStarted  Admin
```

Setting up Telnet

Unlike SSH, Telnet is an unsecure remote Terminal access protocol. The data transmitted over a Telnet connection is not encrypted and is sustainable for **Man-in-the-Middle (MITM)** attacks. Configuring Telnet is a lot simpler than SSH. The follow steps will guide you through the process:

1. Specify the protocol and the network-ID with its subnet mask and the incoming interface:

    ```
    ASA-1(config)# telnet 192.168.2.0 255.255.255.0 Inside
    ```

2. Specify a password for the Telnet authentication or use the AAA feature to query the local database for a valid user account:

    ```
    ASA-1(config)# passwd cisco456
    ```

The following command tells the ASA to use the local username database to query any incoming Telnet connections:

```
ASA-1(config)# aaa authentication telnet console LOCAL
```

The following image displays the commands entered directly on the ASA-1 appliance:

```
ASA-1(config)# telnet 192.168.2.0 255.255.255.0 Inside
ASA-1(config)# passwd cisco456
```

Let's verify our Telnet configuration on the ASA:

```
ASA-1(config)# show running-config Telnet
Telnet 192.168.2.0 255.255.255.0 Inside
Telnet timeout 5
```

The following commands, when entered in global configuration mode, will disable the Telnet services on the ASA:

```
clear configure telnet
```

If a service is not needed, turn it off. For example, if you're only using SSH for remote access, then please ensure the Telnet service is disabled.

Now let's try to connect to the ASA using a Telnet session. Using PuTTY, enter the ASA's IP address and select **Telnet**:

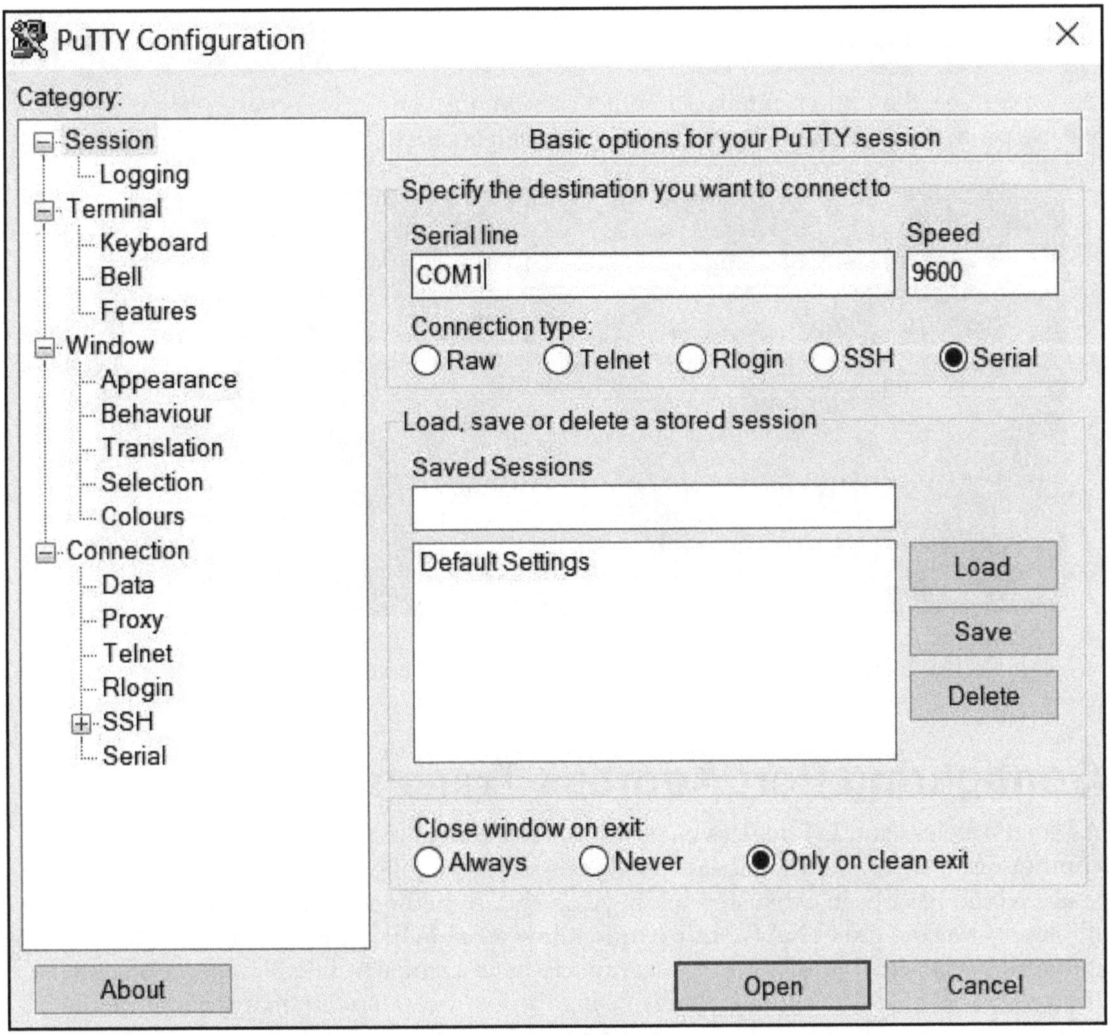

PuTTY Configuration   ✕

Category:

- Session
  - Logging
- Terminal
  - Keyboard
  - Bell
  - Features
- Window
  - Appearance
  - Behaviour
  - Translation
  - Selection
  - Colours
- Connection
  - Data
  - Proxy
  - Telnet
  - Rlogin
  - SSH
  - Serial

Basic options for your PuTTY session

Specify the destination you want to connect to

Serial line	Speed
COM1	9600

Connection type:
○ Raw   ○ Telnet   ○ Rlogin   ○ SSH   ● Serial

Load, save or delete a stored session

Saved Sessions

Default Settings   [Load] [Save] [Delete]

Close window on exit:
○ Always   ○ Never   ● Only on clean exit

[About]   [Open] [Cancel]

 Telnet server uses port 23 and SSH uses port 22.

Since a Telnet client is built into the operating system of Cisco devices, we can use the `telnet` command followed by the IP address of the ASA to initiate a connection to the ASA:

```
R2#telnet 192.168.2.1
```

As we can see, the Router initiated a Telnet session, the banner was presented on the CLI, we are prompted to enter our credentials, and then access to the ASA is granted:

```
R2#telnet 192.168.2.1
Trying 192.168.2.1 ... Open
Please be advised unauthorized access is strictly prohibited
All access are recorded for security purposes
This device is the property for ACME Corp.


User Access Verification

Password:
Type help or '?' for a list of available commands.
ASA-1>
```

We can see this as the hostname has changed to ASA-1 as a successful login.

Configuring Port Address Translation

As smart devices and IoT devices evolve, each device will require an IP address to communicate on the internet. If each device received a public IP address, the public address space would have been exhausted many years ago. A method used to conserve this depletion was the use of NAT. NAT would allow a single IP address to mask/hide an entire network behind it. This allows organizations to have a single public IP address on either their stub router or firewall port that is facing the internet, allowing many nodes on the private local area network to have their private IPv4 address (RFC1918) translated to a public IPv4 address to communicate with devices on the internet.

In this section, we going to configure **Port Address Translation** (**PAT**). This form of NAT allows a single IP to hide an entire subnet behind it.

Let's begin to configure PAT on the ASA:

1. Create a network object:

```
ASA-1(config)# object network inside-net
```

2. Assign the subnet attribute:

```
ASA-1(config-network-object)# subnet 192.168.1.0 255.255.255.0
```

3. Specify the translation direction (incoming and outgoing interfaces):

```
ASA-1(config-network-object)# nat (inside,outside) dynamic interface
```

The following is an example of the commands:

```
ASA-1(config)# object network inside-net
ASA-1(config-network-object)# subnet 192.168.1.0 255.255.255.0
ASA-1(config-network-object)# nat (Inside,Outside) dynamic interface
ASA-1(config-network-object)# end
```

Let's verify our NAT configurations:

```
ASA-1(config)# show running-config nat
!
object network inside-net
 nat (Inside,Outside) dynamic interface
```

```
ASA-1# show running-config nat
!
object network inside-net
 nat (Inside,Outside) dynamic interface
ASA-1#
```

Another command we can use is `show nat detail`, this would provide us with the `Object` group, its contents, and the network(s) being translated:

ASA-1# show nat detail

```
ASA-1# show nat detail

Auto NAT Policies (Section 2)
1 (Inside) to (Outside) source dynamic inside-net interface
    translate_hits = 0, untranslate_hits = 0
    Source - Origin: 192.168.1.0/24, Translated: 200.1.1.2/30
```

 To view current translation information, use the `show xlate` command.

Setting up the Adaptive Security Device Manager

Using the CLI can be fun, but sometimes a GUI may be a bit more convenient for the task at hand. For the CCNA security certification, candidates are required to know and understand both the CLI and GUI. As mentioned earlier, the Cisco ASA uses a special GUI for management. The ASDM is specifically used on the ASAs and it makes management and monitoring much easier.

To get started, we must enable the secure web server on the ASA to retrieve the ASDM file for our client computer. Then we are going to allow either a specific client or a network to connect to the ASA using the ASDM for management:

1. Enable the HTTPS service on the ASA:

    ASA-1(config)# http server enable

2. Create a rule to allow a host or network to access the ASA using the ASDM:

```
ASA-1(config)# http 192.168.2.0 255.255.255.0 Inside
```

3. Configure the port for the incoming connection. The default port is 443 if not configured (this step is optional):

```
ASA-1(config)# http server enable <port number>
```

The following screenshot shows steps 1 and 2 from the CLI:

```
ASA-1(config)# http server enable
ASA-1(config)# http 192.168.2.0 255.255.255.0 Inside
```

Since step 3 is optional, the following screenshot shows the options available for choosing a port other than the default 443:

```
ASA-1(config)# http server enable ?

configure mode commands/options:
  <1-65535>  The management server's SSL listening port. TCP port 443 is the
             default.
  <cr>
ASA-1(config)# http server enable 9443
```

Once this is completed, open your web browser on the computer and navigate to the IP address of the ASA. You will be presented with the following window, click on **Install ASDM Launcher and Run ASDM**. Please note, a requirement for the ASDM client software to run successfully is the JRE.

The JRE application can be found on Oracle's website (`https://www.oracle.com/index.html`):

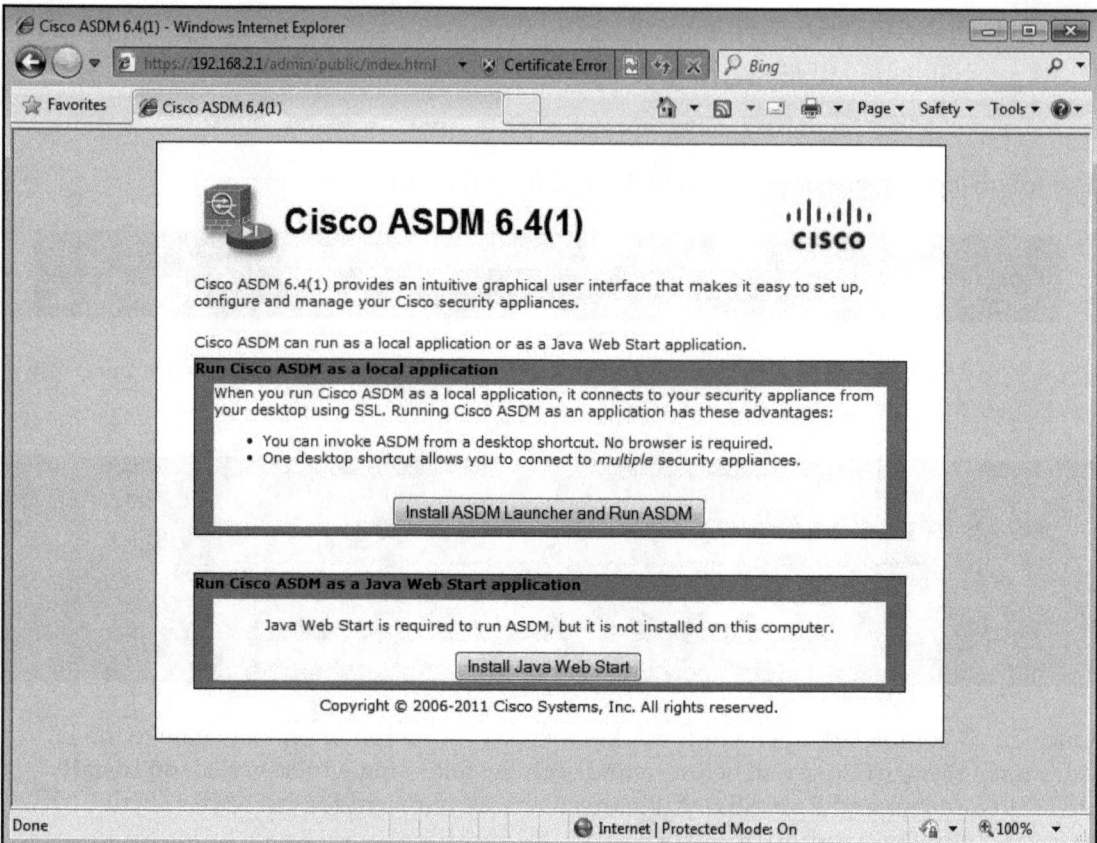

Once installed, open the ASDM application. Enter the ASA **Device IP Address/Name**, **Username** (if one is configured), and **Password** in the corresponding fields, and click on **OK**:

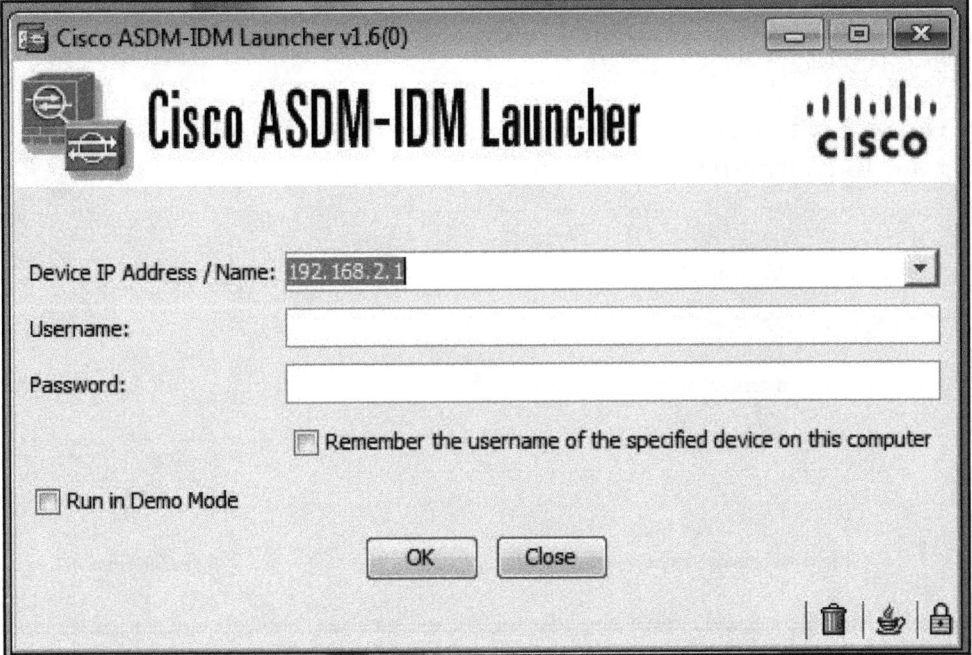

A security warning window will appear asking if you trust the publisher of the website certificate, click on **Yes**. Since the ASA generated a self-signed certificate, the client machines will always receive this warning as a self-signed certificate is considered untrusted:

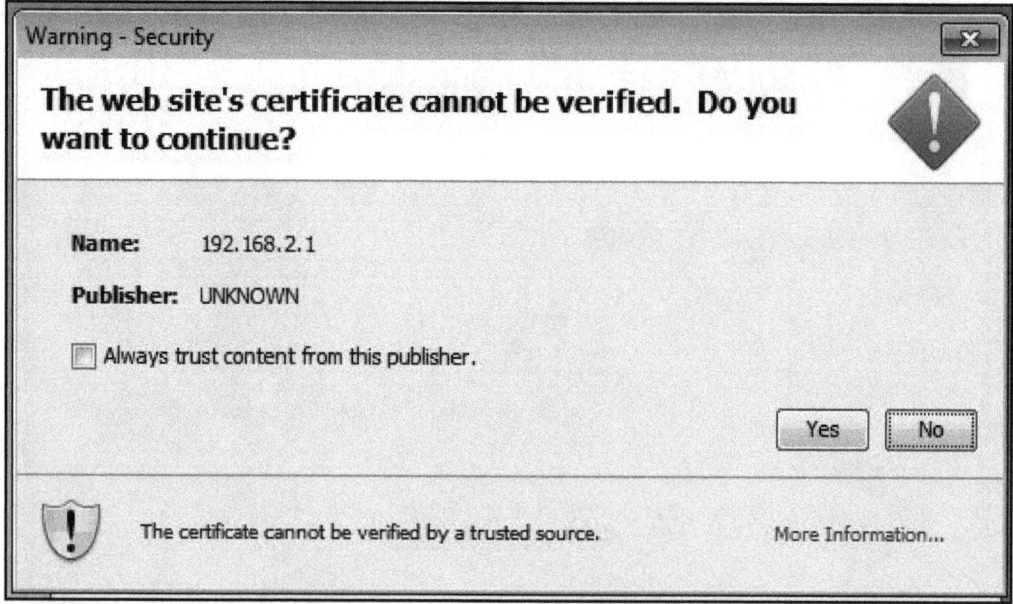

Once the data has been populated by the ASDM, the following window will appear:

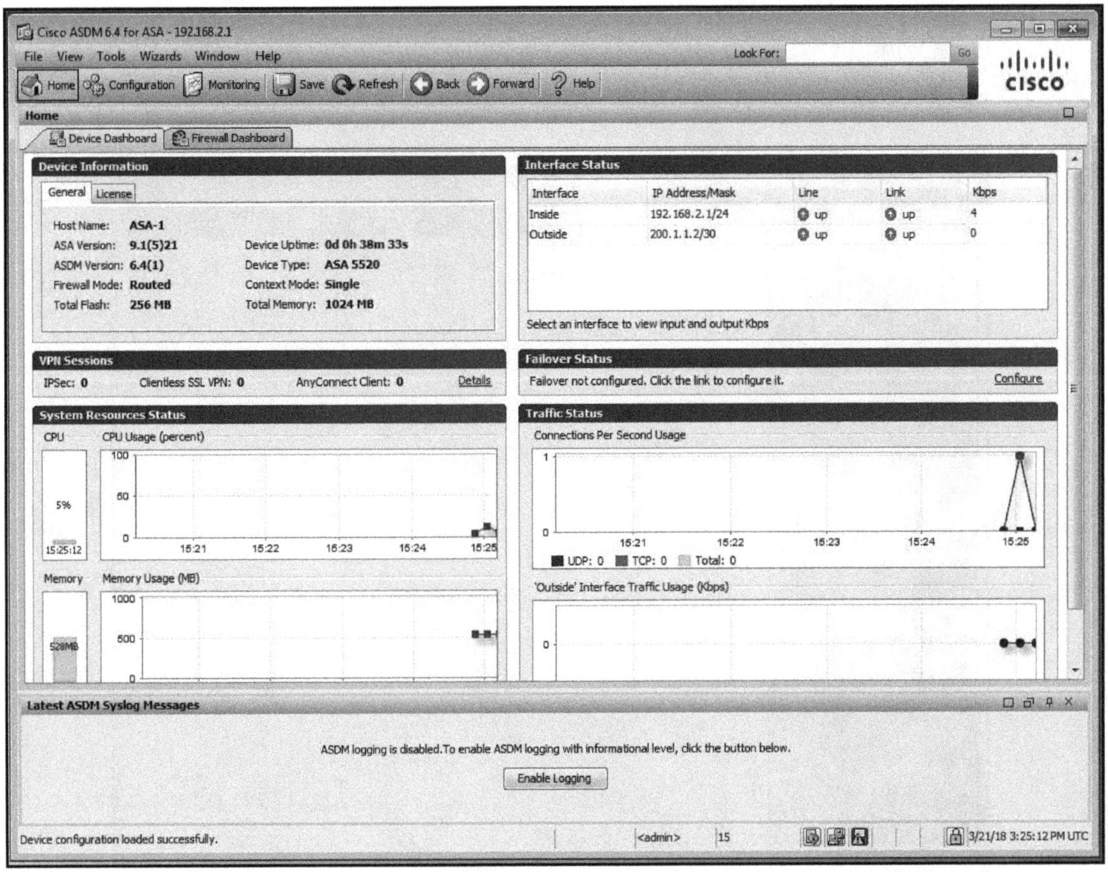

Getting familiar with the ASDM

The ASDM is the most common method for administering the ASA after the initial device provisioning. Everything that can be done using the CLI can be achieved with the ASDM.

> During the device provisioning, ensure you enable the HTTP server and allow your client machine/network to access the ASA via the web browser.

Let's take a look at modifying the existing configurations using the ASDM: on the ASDM, click **Wizards** | **Startup Wizard**.

The following window will appear. Two options will be available, whether to reset all configurations back to factory default or modify the existing configuration. We're going to select the latter and click **Next**:

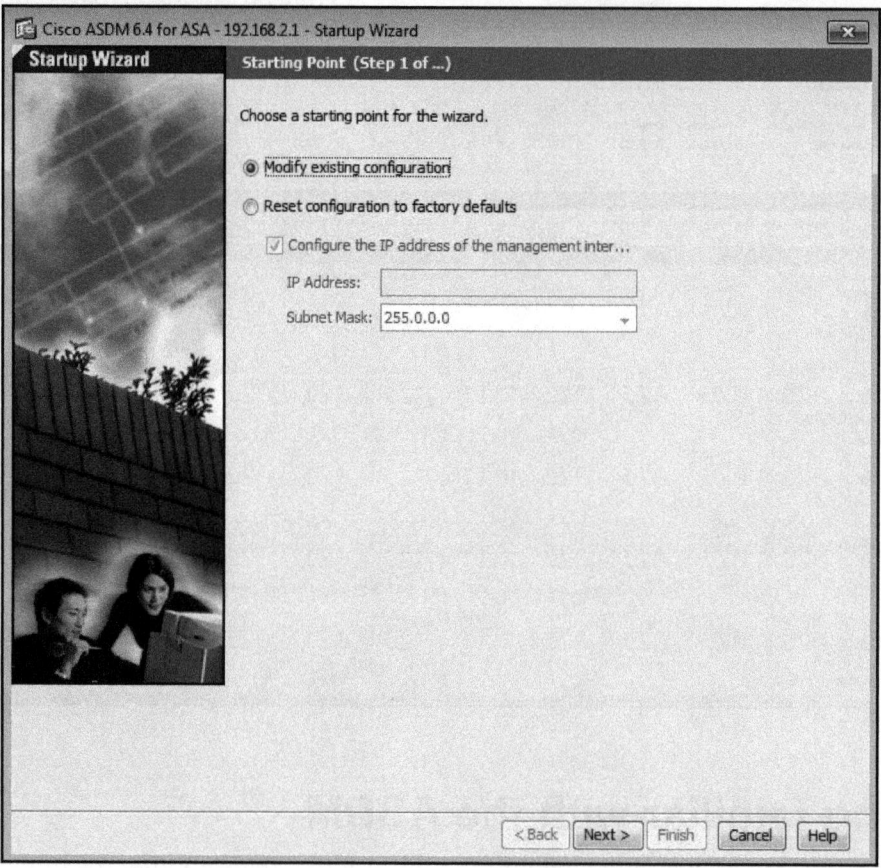

The following window allows us to modify the hostname, domain name, and add/change/disable the enable password (used to access the privilege mode of the ASA):

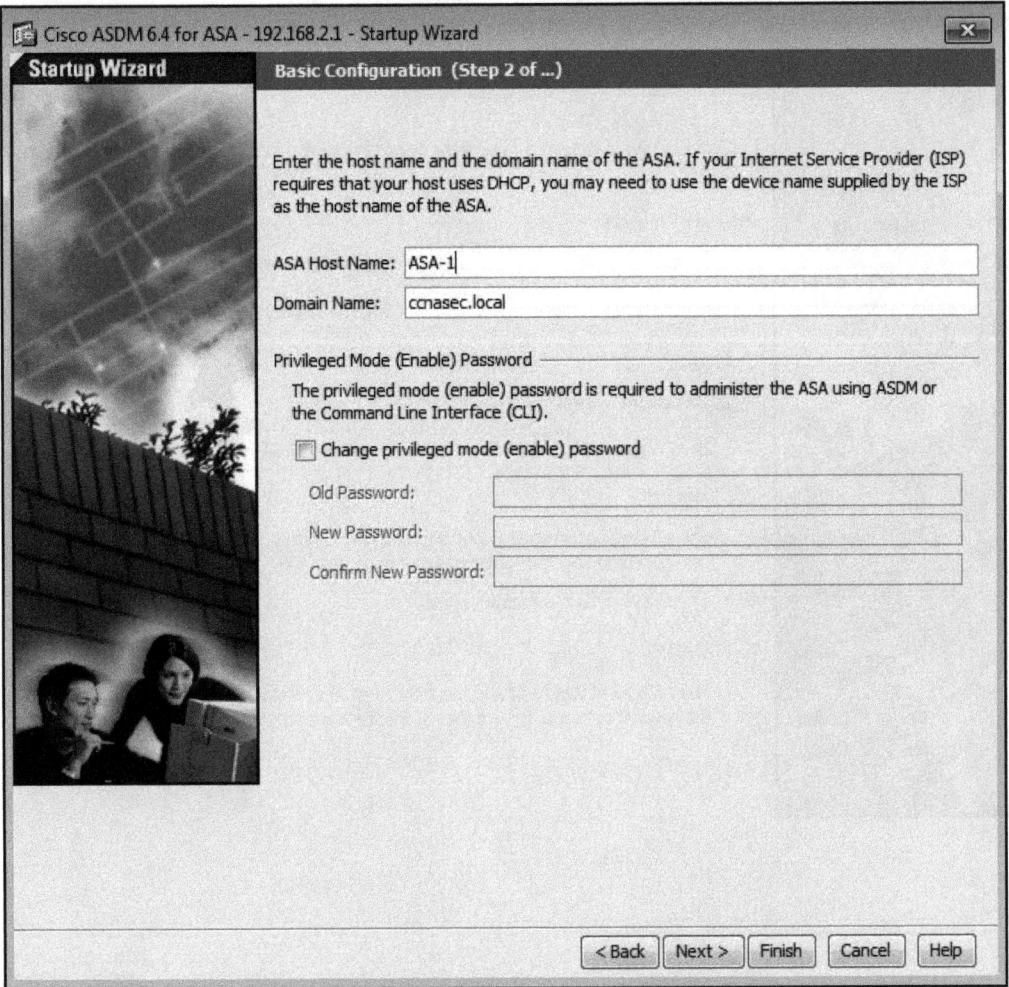

Next, the **Outside Interface Configuration** is configured:

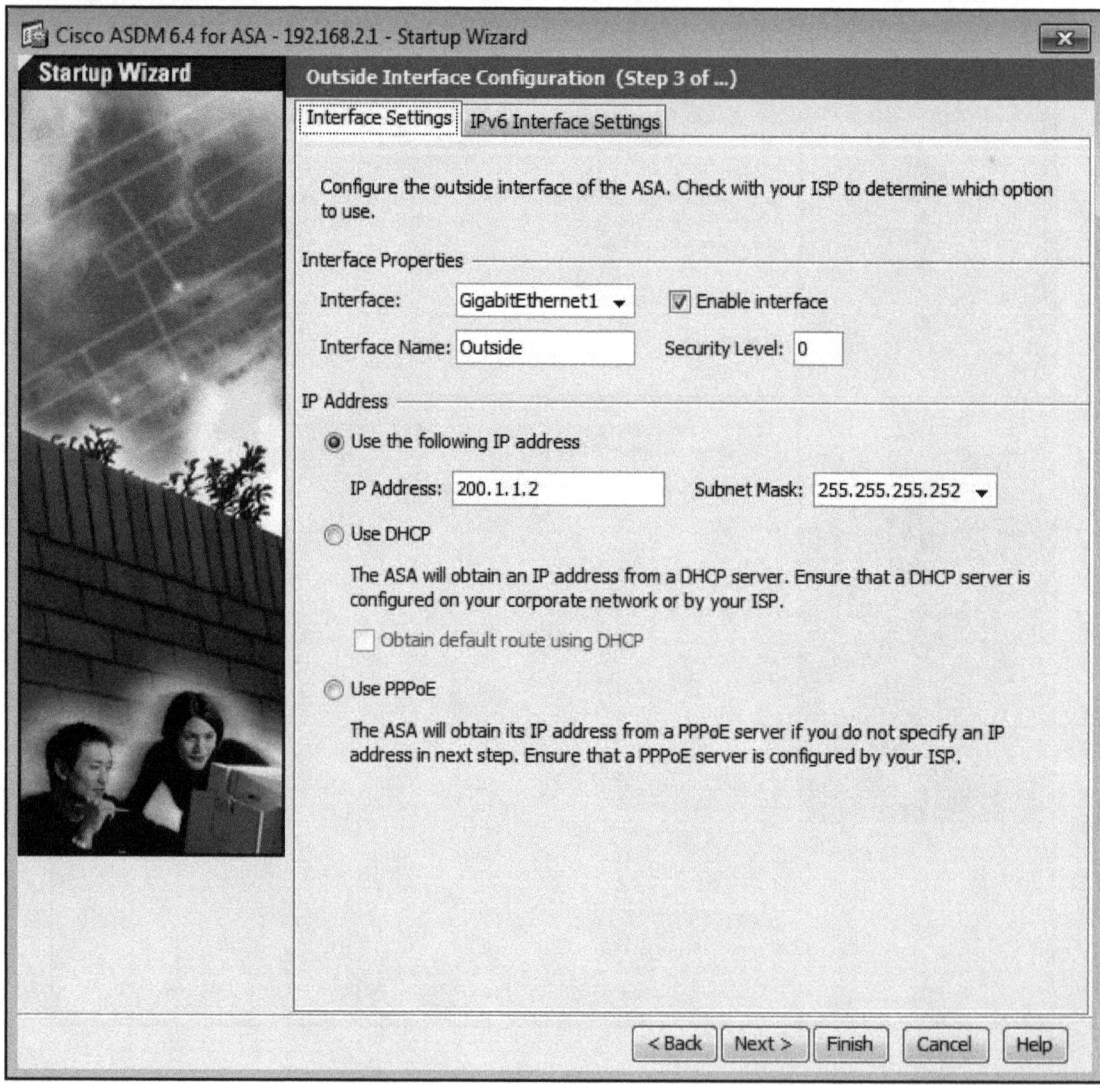

The following window allows further configurations on all the interfaces of the ASA. To modify the configurations on an interface, simply select the interface and click **Edit**. You'll be able to modify the **IP Address**, **Subnet Mask**, **Interface Name**, **Security Level**, and other features:

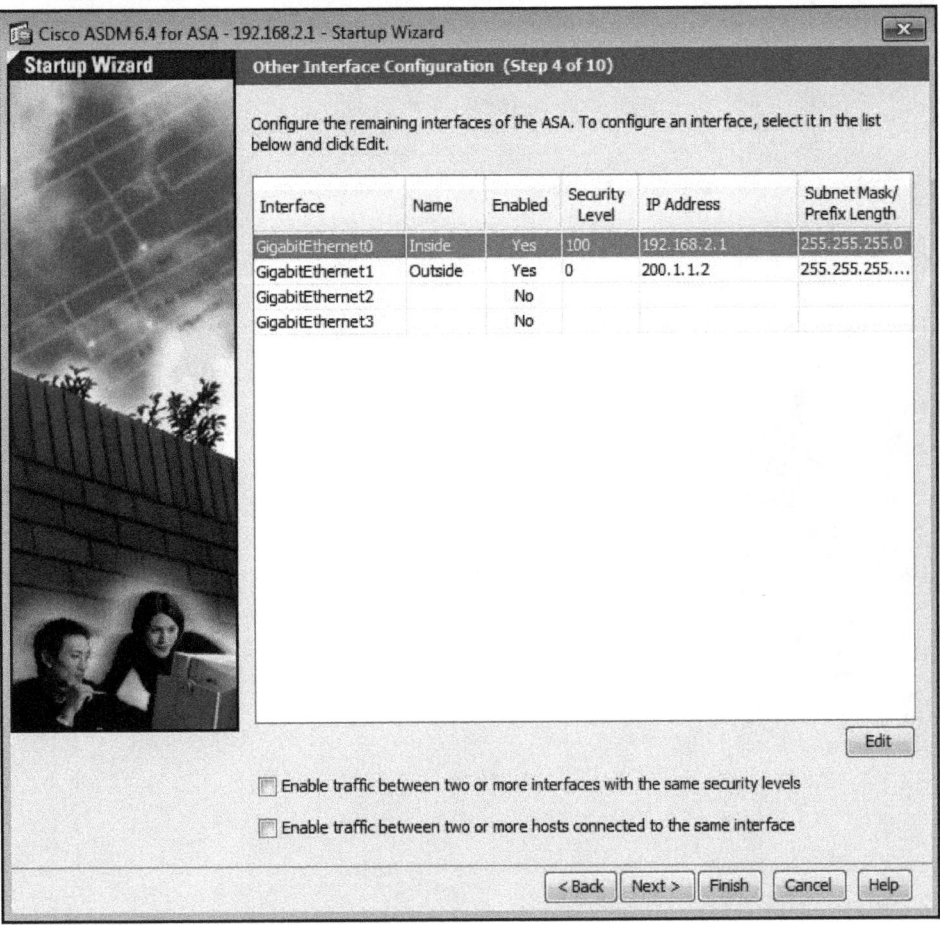

Here, static routes can be added to the ASA:

The following window allows a DHCP server to be configured. This is useful if the ASA is deployed in a small, branch office that requires DHCP services:

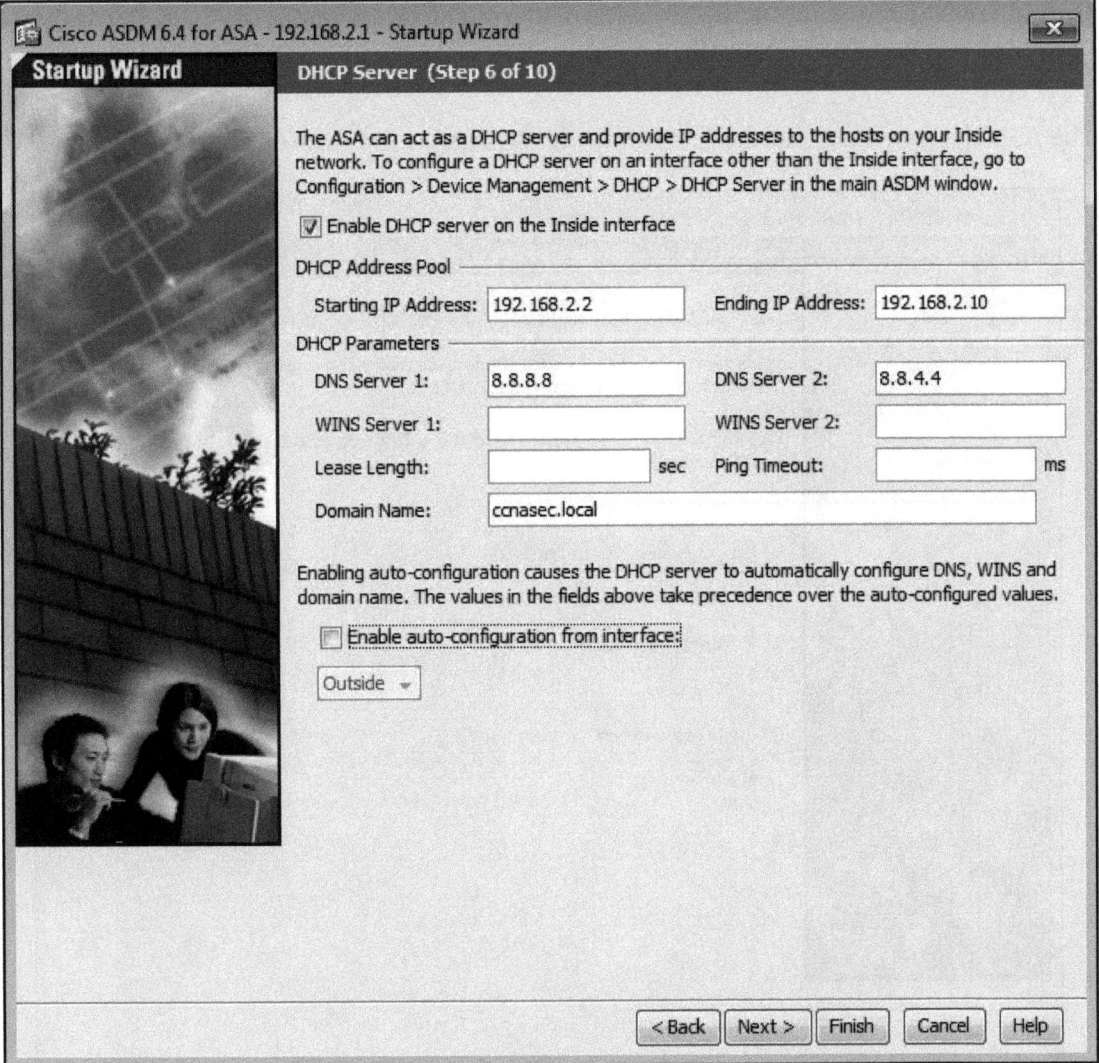

NAT can be configured here. If your organization is using only one public IP address, then PAT is to be used. PAT allows a single IP address to mask a network. An example would be your internet connection at home; your router/modem has only one public IP address and your internal network has multiple devices with private IP addresses (RFC 1918). All the private IP addresses will be translated to the public IP when they are accessing the internet. Users on the internet will see only the one public IP address and not the devices behind it.

The ASDM allows us to use the IP address on the Outside interface or a specific IP:

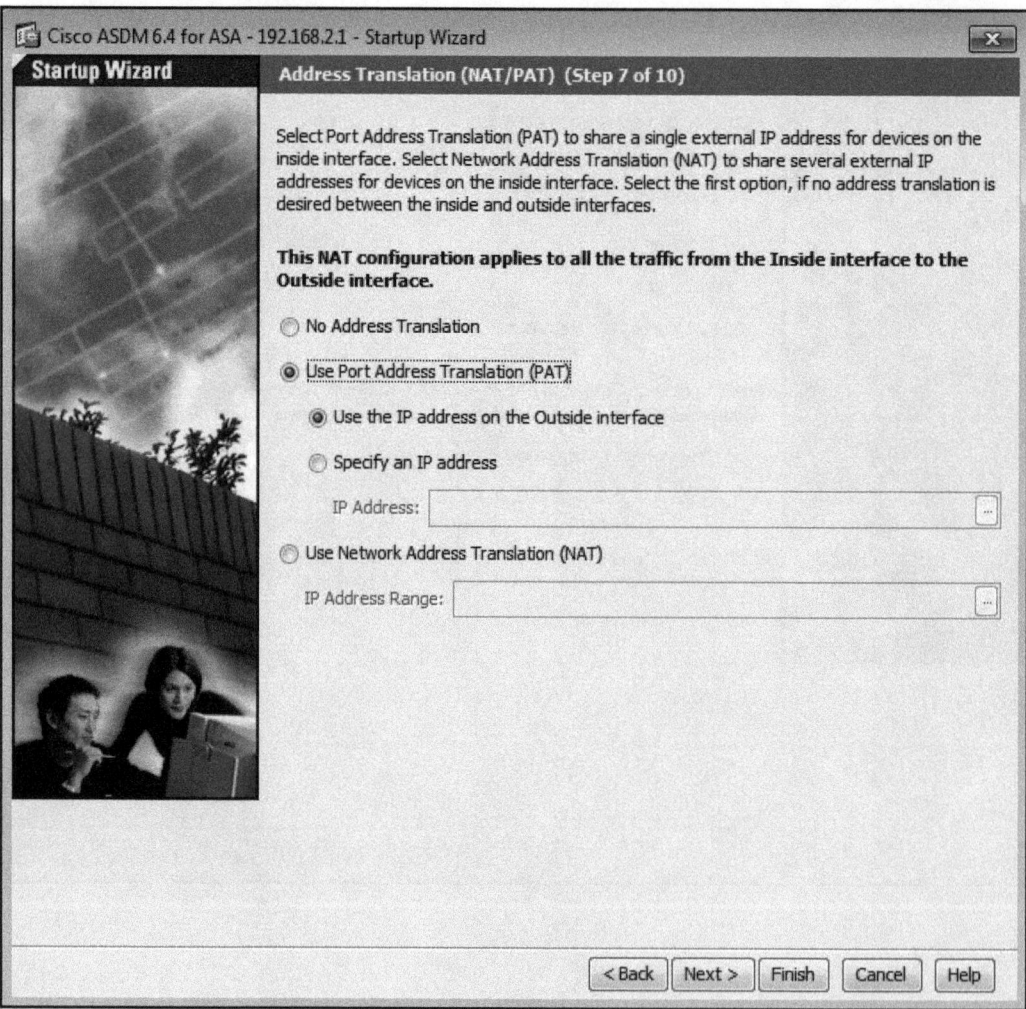

SSH, Telnet, and ASDM access can be modified in the following window:

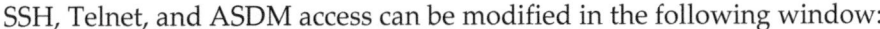

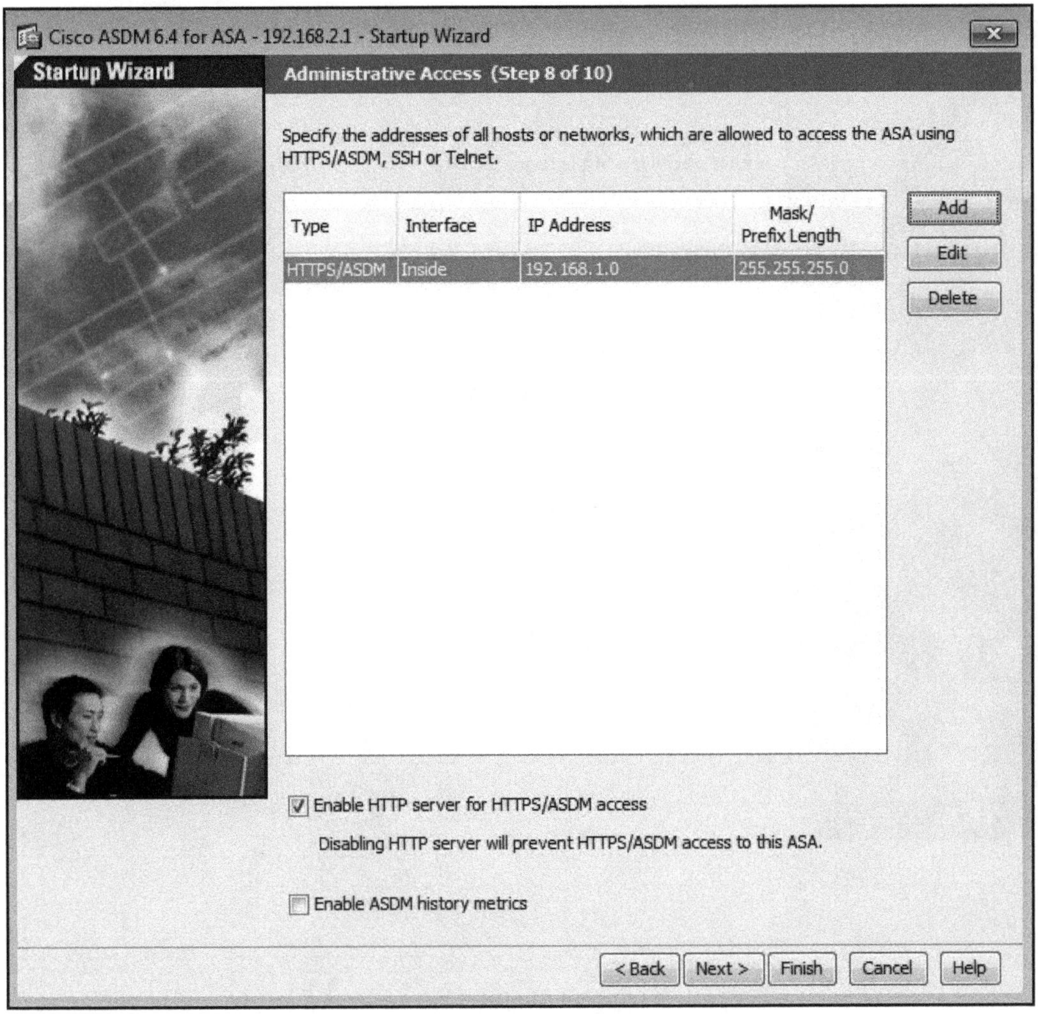

The last window provides a summary of the configurations before it is applied to the ASA:

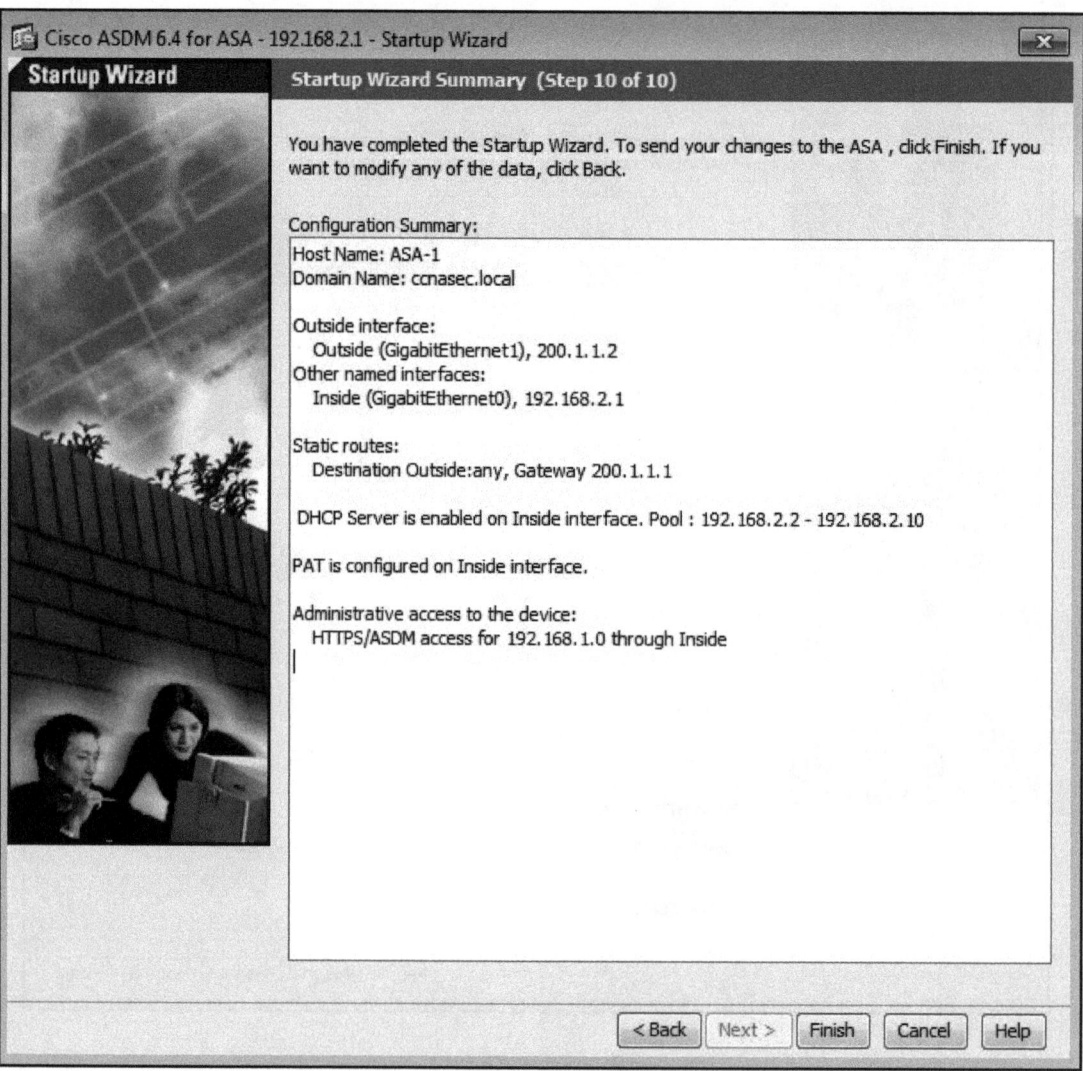

Once the configurations are applied to the ASA, it's in `running-config`. Remember `running-config` is stored in RAM, therefore if the device loses power or is rebooted, the current configurations are lost:

The ASDM allows us to save the current configuration easily; on the bottom of the ASDM window, you'll see a blue floppy disk icon with an exclamation mark. The exclamation mark indicates a change was made but not saved. Simply clicking on the icon will save the configurations.

Summary

In this chapter, we covered the fundamentals of getting the Cisco ASA firewall up and working in a production environment. We've seen how to secure our device, enable remote access (SSH and Telnet), enable PAT, set a default route to the ISP, and set up the **Adaptive Security Device Manager** (**ASDM**) for further administration.

In the next chapter, we are going to dive even deeper into advanced configurations on the ASA.

11
Advanced ASA Configuration

In this chapter, we are going to learn how to set up static and dynamic routing protocols, such as RIP, OSPF, and EIGRP. We will use the **Adaptive Security Device Manager (ASDM)** and **Command Line Interface (CLI)** to configure the device name, enable a password, domain name, banners, interfaces, system time and NTP, DHCP, and **access control lists (ACLs)**. We will dive into understanding object groups and how they can be used to benefit us during configurations and administration of the **Adaptive Security Appliance (ASA)**. This will lead us to creating service policies and configuring static and dynamic **Network Address Translation (NAT)**.

The following topics will be covered in the chapter:

- Routing on the ASA
- Device name, passwords, domain name
- Setting banners using the ASDM
- Configuring interfaces
- System time and **Network Time Protocol (NTP)**
- Access control list on the ASA
- Object groups
- Creating policies on ASA
- Advanced NAT configurations

Routing on the ASA

In the previous chapter, we mentioned one of the features of the ASA is its capability to do routing. The ASA supports multiple routing protocols, such as **Routing Information Protocol (RIP)**, **Open Shortest Path First (OSPF)**, and **Enhanced Interior Gateway Routing Protocol (EIGRP)**. In this section, we are going to take a look at how to configure both static and dynamic routing protocols on the ASA.

Static routing

Static routing is the manual configuration on either the router or the ASA. The administrator/network engineer would need to create a route on the ASA to tell the device how to forward traffic destined for a particular network. Without any routes, the device won't know how to forward packets. Static routing can become challenging as the network grows and more routers are added. With static routing, each network would require a manual entry into the routing table (static route) of the device, whether it's a Router or the ASA.

Let's begin setting up a static route on the ASA.

The following topology shows a single ASA for a company where the internet is directly connected to its **Outside** interface. Just as a Cisco router, the ASA automatically adds its directly-connected routes to its routing table. In the following topology, the ASA has only the 192.168.2.0/24 and 200.1.1.0/30 networks within its routing table:

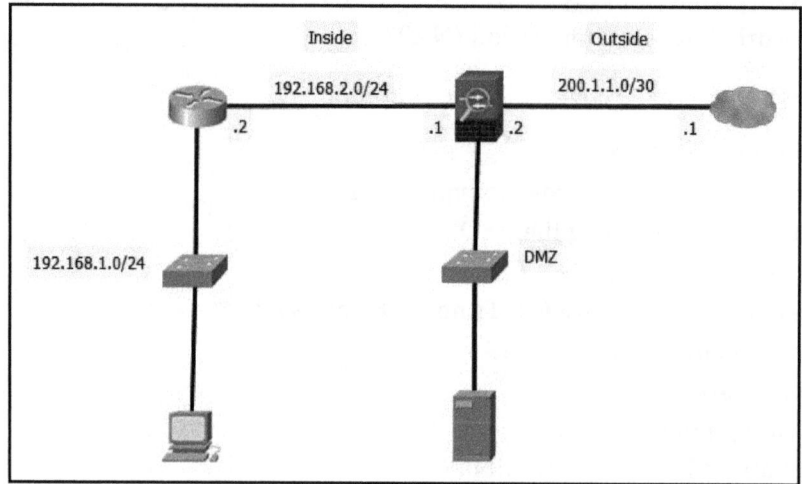

However, it does not know about the 192.168.1.0/24 network, therefore any traffic, whether returning or destined for the 192.168.1.0/24 network, would be dropped because the ASA does not have a route to forward the packets. This would mean any traffic that is destined for the internet would also not be forwarded by the ASA, since it does not have a default route in place.

We can verify this information quickly using the show route command to view the routing table:

```
ASA-1(config)# show route

Codes: C - connected, S - static, I - IGRP, R - RIP, M - mobile, B - BGP
       D - EIGRP, EX - EIGRP external, O - OSPF, IA - OSPF inter area
       N1 - OSPF NSSA external type 1, N2 - OSPF NSSA external type 2
       E1 - OSPF external type 1, E2 - OSPF external type 2, E - EGP
       i - IS-IS, L1 - IS-IS level-1, L2 - IS-IS level-2, ia - IS-IS inter area
       * - candidate default, U - per-user static route, o - ODR
       P - periodic downloaded static route

Gateway of last resort is not set

C    200.1.1.0 255.255.255.252 is directly connected, Outside
S    192.168.1.0 255.255.255.0 [1/0] via 192.168.2.2, Inside
C    192.168.2.0 255.255.255.0 is directly connected, Inside
```

We are going to open the ASDM, then navigate to **Configuration** | **Device Setup** | **Routing** | **Static Routes**. As we can see, there are no **Static Routes** installed on the ASA:

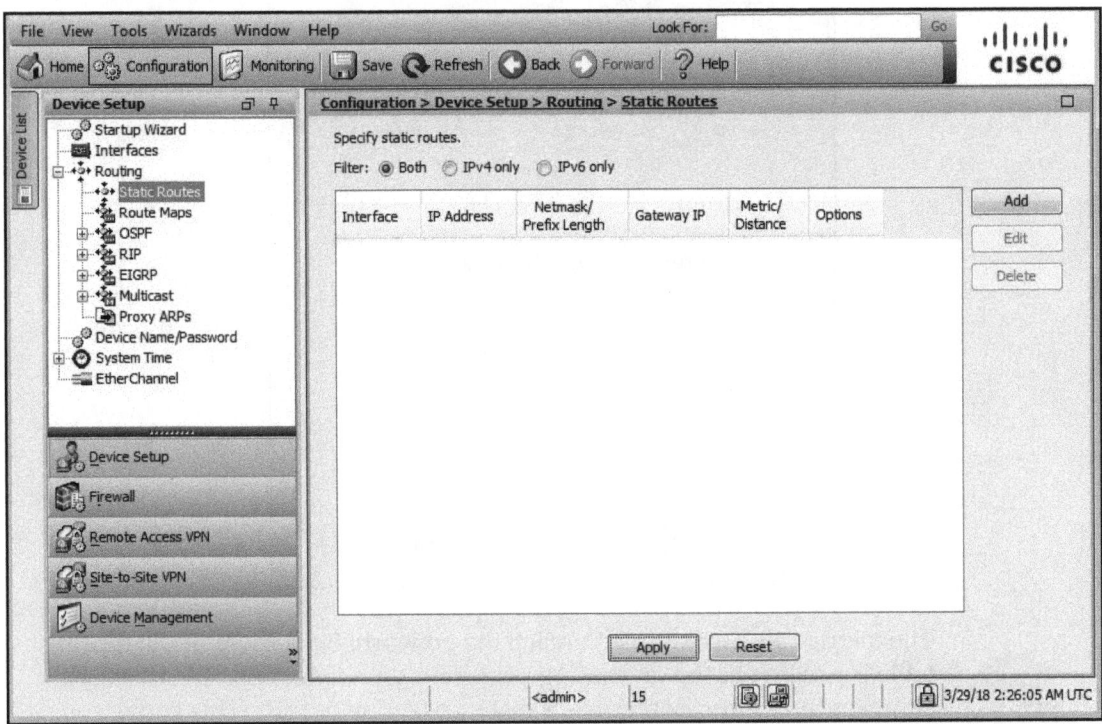

Next, we are going to add a static route using the ASDM. On the right side of the window, click on **Add**. A new window will appear. Since the 192.168.1.0/24 destination network can be reached from the **Inside** interface, we must assign the interface settings correctly.

Then, we are going to add the destination network, 192.168.1.0/24, within the **Network** field and set the next-hop.

 The next-hop is simply the next device to forward the packet to, based on the destination IP address/network within the packet header.

Referring back to the topology, if the ASA has a packet that is destined for `192.168.1.0/24`, the only path to reach the network is through the router, therefore the next-hop will be `192.168.2.2`. The next-hop IP address will be placed in the **Gateway IP** field:

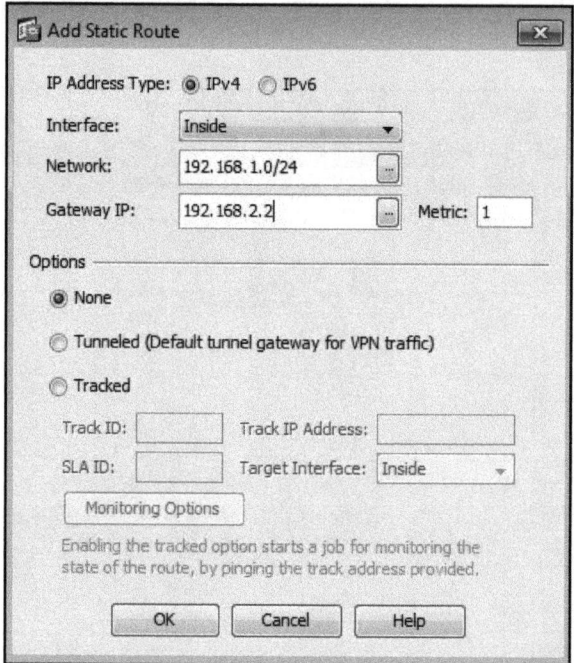

 The metric value is the cost to reach the network. Each route in the routing table is a metric based on routing protocols, directly-connected routes, or static routing. Static Routes has a distance of 1 by default. This value should be kept as the default unless you're creating a floating static route on the ASA.

Once the values are assigned, click on **OK**. The static route has been added:

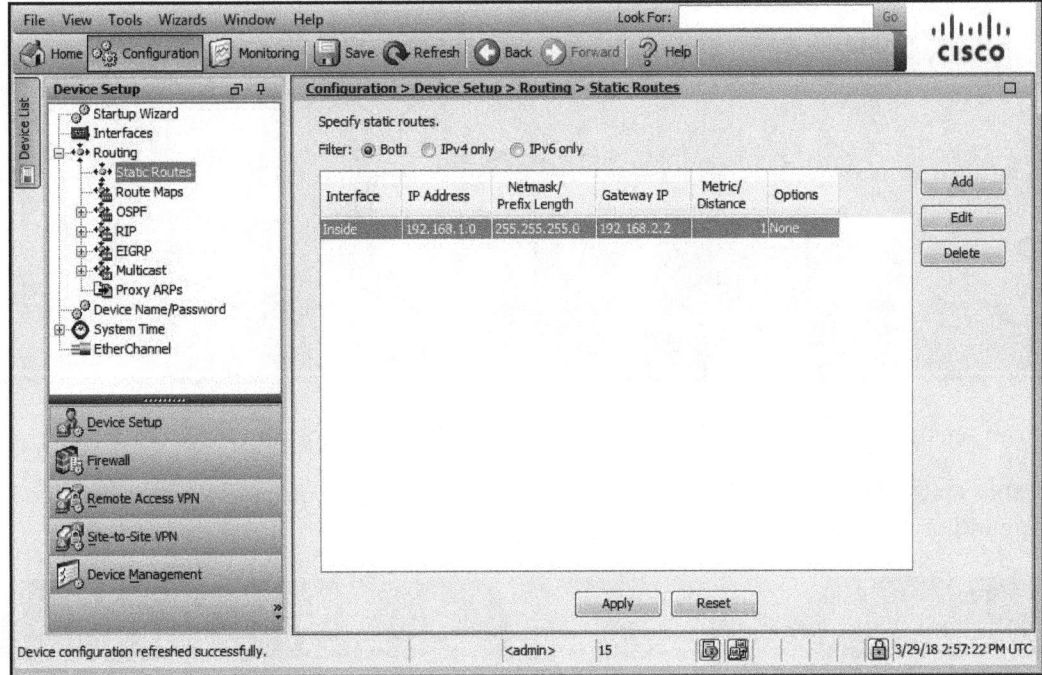

Configuring static routing using the CLI

Is there a command-line equivalent to adding a static route on the ASA? The answer to that question is definitely, yes. The following format is used on the ASA:

```
route [Inside | Outside] <destination network-ID> <subnet mask> <next hop
IP address>
```

Let's take a look at how to achieve the same using the CLI:

```
ASA-1(config)# route Inside 192.168.1.0 255.255.255.0 192.168.2.2
```

Let's verify the static route has been added to the ASA using the CLI. To view the routing table of the ASA, use the `show route` command:

```
ASA-1(config)# show route

Codes: C - connected, S - static, I - IGRP, R - RIP, M - mobile, B - BGP
       D - EIGRP, EX - EIGRP external, O - OSPF, IA - OSPF inter area
       N1 - OSPF NSSA external type 1, N2 - OSPF NSSA external type 2
       E1 - OSPF external type 1, E2 - OSPF external type 2, E - EGP
       i - IS-IS, L1 - IS-IS level-1, L2 - IS-IS level-2, ia - IS-IS inter area
       * - candidate default, U - per-user static route, o - ODR
       P - periodic downloaded static route

Gateway of last resort is not set

C    200.1.1.0 255.255.255.252 is directly connected, Outside
S    192.168.1.0 255.255.255.0 [1/0] via 192.168.2.2, Inside
C    192.168.2.0 255.255.255.0 is directly connected, Inside
```

We can see the static route has been added successfully in the routing table of the ASA.

Another method of checking static routes is to use the `show running-config route` command on the ASA:

```
ASA-1(config)# show running-config route
route Inside 192.168.1.0 255.255.255.0 192.168.2.2 1
```

 The number 1 at the end of the line is the Distance metric for the route, the default value is 1.

Adding a default route using the ASDM

As mentioned in the previous chapter, a default route is usually needed to forward packets destined for a network or host outside of the corporate network, such as the internet. Adding a default route is very similar to adding a static route on the ASDM.

Once again, navigate to **Configuration** | **Device Setup** | **Routing** | **Static Routes** on the ASDM. Click on **Add**.

The following configurations should be used:

- **Interface**: **Outside**
- **Network**: **any**
- **Gateway IP**: Your ISP gateway IP address (verify with your ISP):

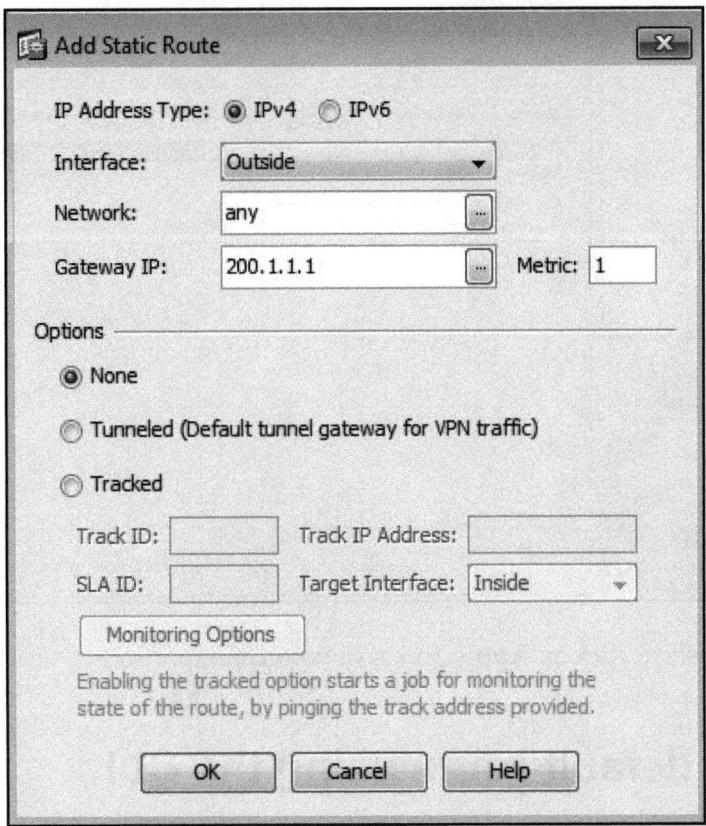

Once you're finished, click on **OK**.

The default route will be added to your list of **Static Routes** and to your routing table on the ASA:

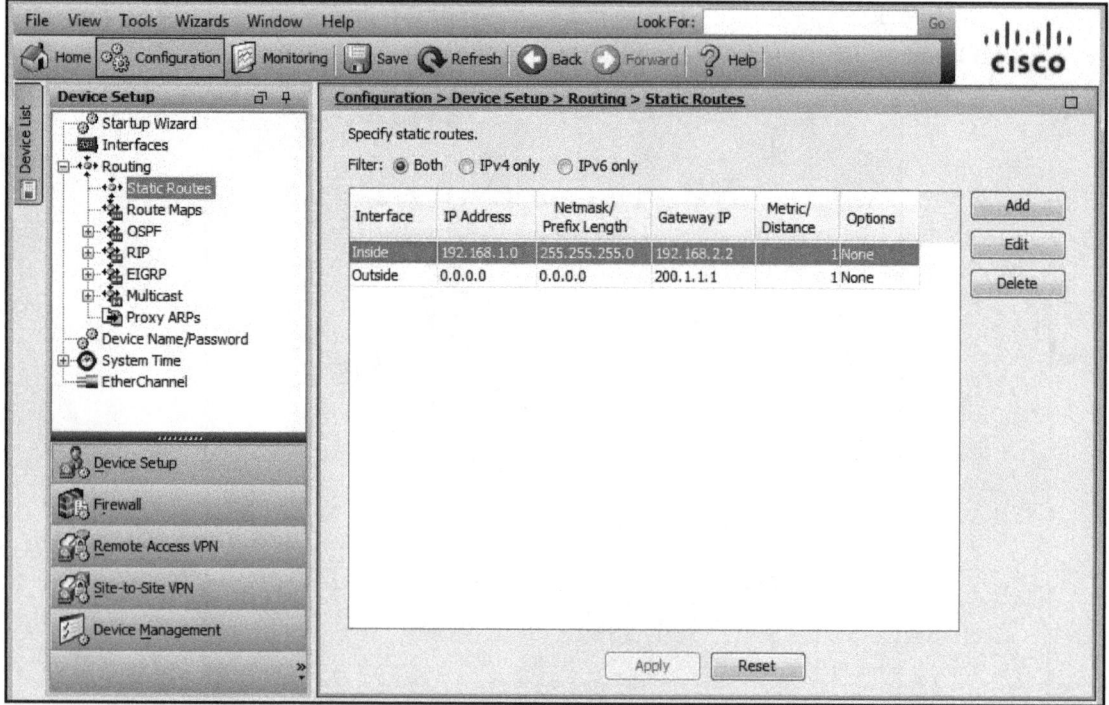

Once you are finished, click on **Apply** and save your configurations.

Adding a default route using the CLI

The following format is used for adding a static default route on the ASA:

```
route Outside 0.0.0.0 0.0.0.0 <gateway-IP>
```

Therefore our configuration would be as the following:

```
ASA-1(config)# route Outside 0.0.0.0 0.0.0.0 200.1.1.1 1
```

We can verify the default route via CLI using the `show route` command:

```
ASA-1(config)# show route

Codes: C - connected, S - static, I - IGRP, R - RIP, M - mobile, B - BGP
       D - EIGRP, EX - EIGRP external, O - OSPF, IA - OSPF inter area
       N1 - OSPF NSSA external type 1, N2 - OSPF NSSA external type 2
       E1 - OSPF external type 1, E2 - OSPF external type 2, E - EGP
       i - IS-IS, L1 - IS-IS level-1, L2 - IS-IS level-2, ia - IS-IS inter area
       * - candidate default, U - per-user static route, o - ODR
       P - periodic downloaded static route

Gateway of last resort is 200.1.1.1 to network 0.0.0.0

C    200.1.1.0 255.255.255.252 is directly connected, Outside
S    192.168.1.0 255.255.255.0 [1/0] via 192.168.2.2, Inside
C    192.168.2.0 255.255.255.0 is directly connected, Inside
S*   0.0.0.0 0.0.0.0 [1/0] via 200.1.1.1, Outside
```

Another command we can use to verify whether there are any routes installed on the ASA is the `show running-config route` command:

```
ASA-1(config)# show running-config route
route Outside 0.0.0.0 0.0.0.0 200.1.1.1 1
route Inside 192.168.1.0 255.255.255.0 192.168.2.2 1
```

Open Shortest Path First

Open Shortest Path First (**OSPF**) is an **Interior Gateway Protocol** (**IGP**) that exists under the sub-category of the link-state routing protocol. OSPF can be used in environments or networks that have a variety of vendors' equipment and each needs to exchange routing information amongst themselves. The ASA can facilitate the OSPF routing protocol to exchange network information and paths between its neighbors.

OSPF details and configurations for Cisco router are further explained in the CCNA: Routing and Switching certification guides.

To get started, navigate to **Configuration** | **Device Setup** | **Routing** | **OSPF** | **Setup** on the ASDM.

Here we have the options to enable the OSPF routing protocol on the ASA. Click the
checkbox, as displayed in the following screenshot, to enable **OSPF Process 1**. Then, let's set
the **OSPF Process ID** to 1:

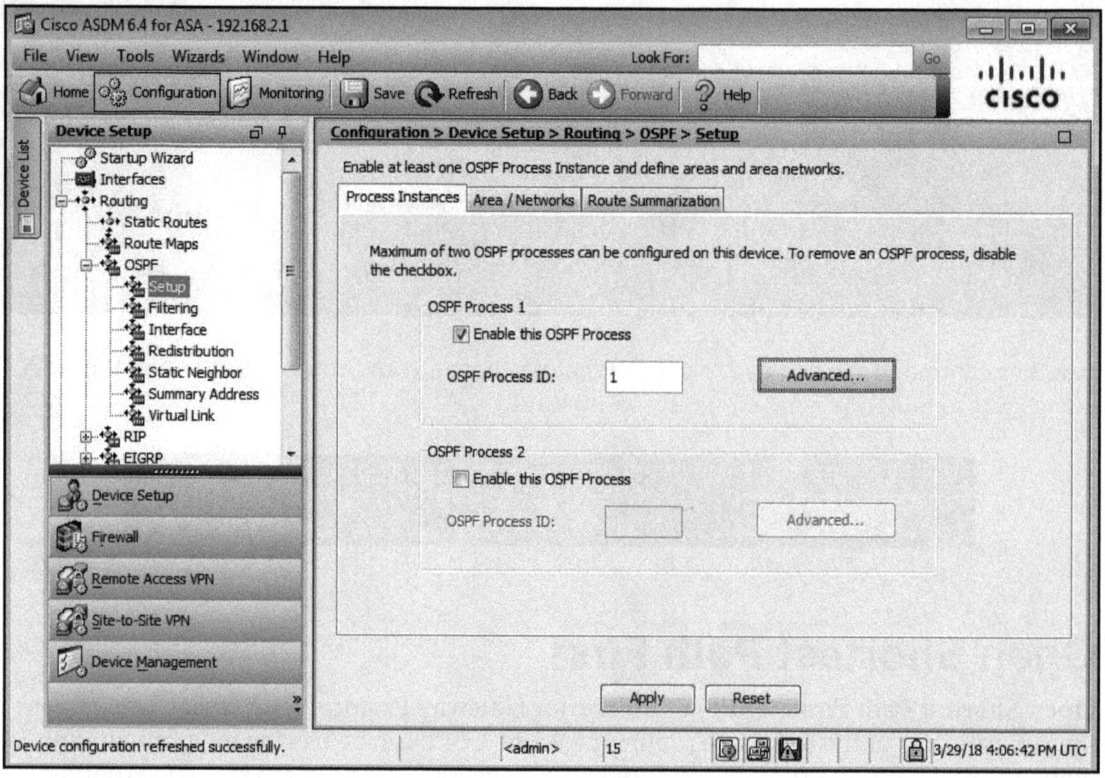

The OSPF Process-ID can be any number ranging from 1-65535 on the
ASA.

If the ASA has a default route that needs to be redistributed, using the OSPF routing protocol, to other routers or firewalls that are OSPF-enabled, this can be achieved by clicking the **Advanced...** button and then clicking on the checkbox that says **Enable Default Information Originate**:

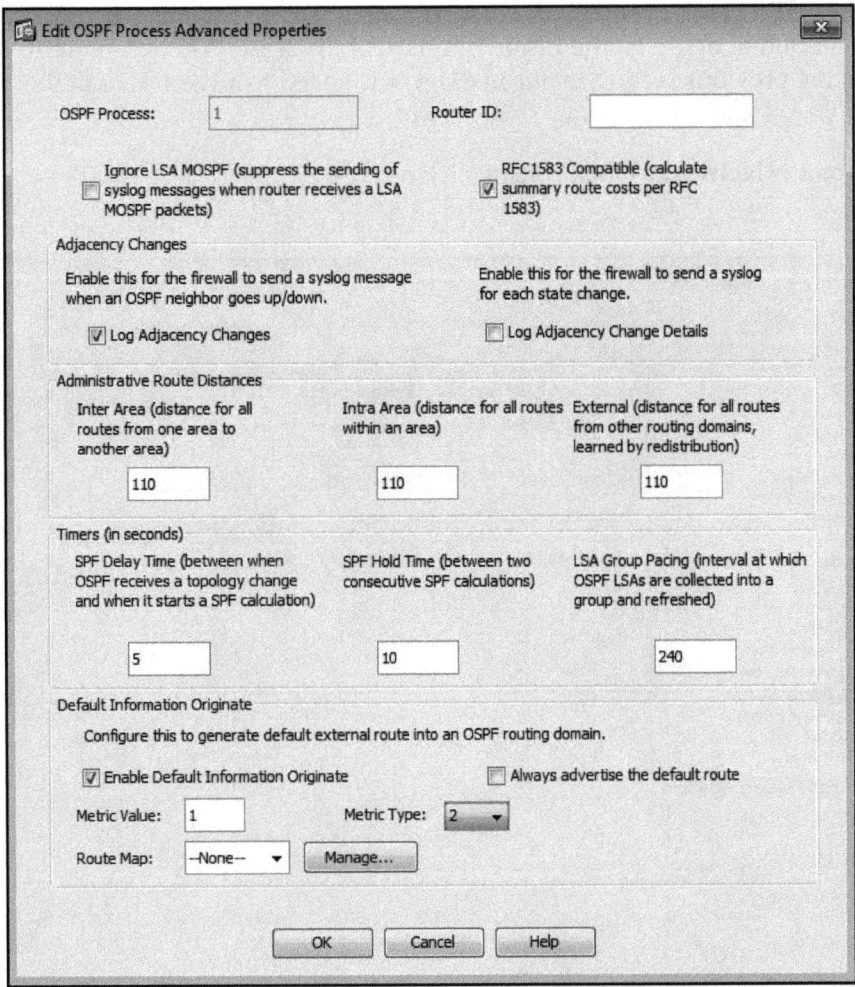

 On the Cisco routers and ASA, the command used to redistribute a default route through the OSPF routing protocol is **default-information originate**.

Enabling the OSPF protocol is only the first step, now we need to advertise the network(s) that are connected to or are on the Inside interface of the ASA. With reference to the topology in the previous section (*Static routing*), we'll need to advertise both the 192.168.2.0/24 and 192.168.1.0/24 networks.

Next, click on the **Networks** tab and then click on **Add**:

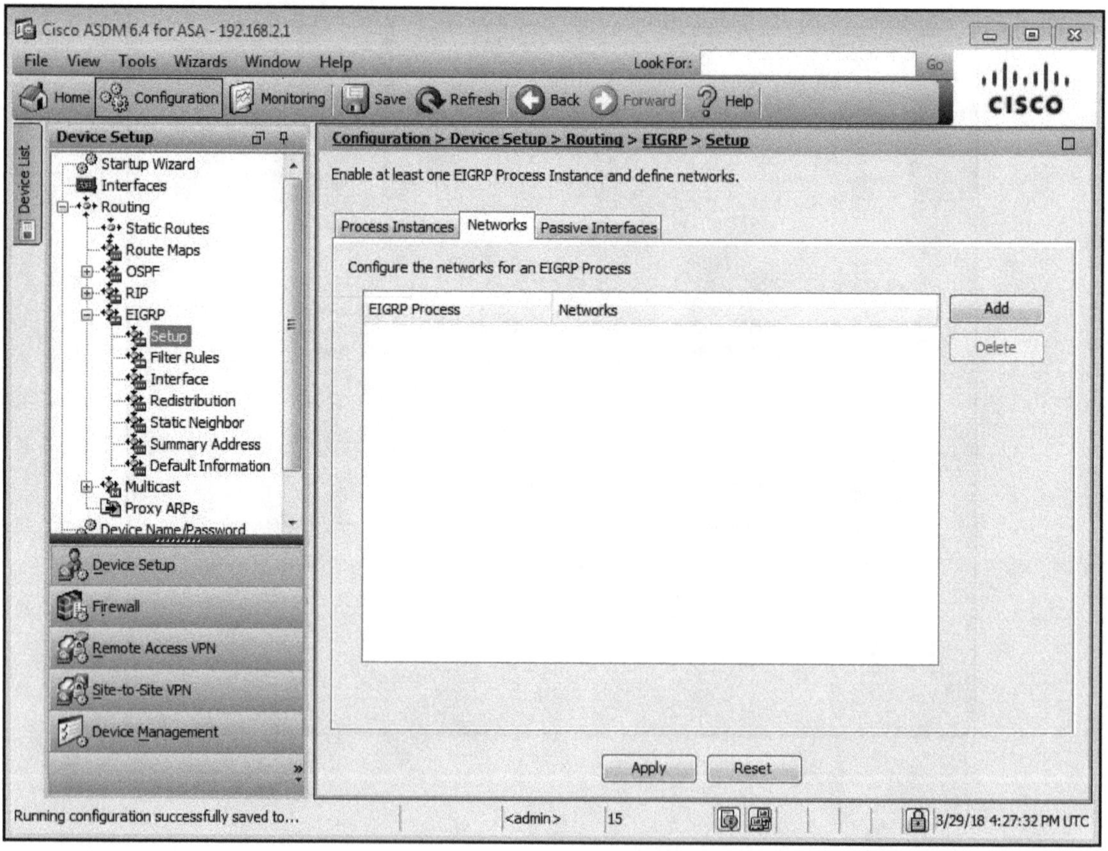

Here we are able to add the networks to our **OSPF Process 1**. Simply enter the network-ID and subnet mask in the **Area Networks** section, then click on **Add**. Remember the backbone area for the OSPF is always **Area ID**: 0:

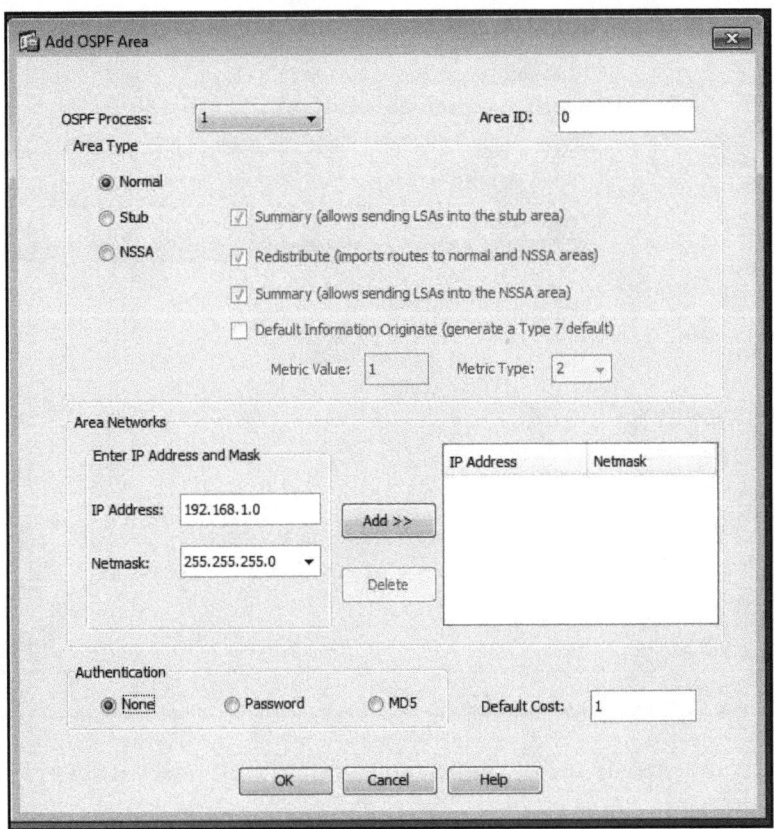

All areas in OSPF should be connected to area 0.

On the window, you can turn on route authentication for **OSPF Process 1**. Route authentication enables the router or ASA to provide authentication between its neighbors before they can exchange routing information.

Once you're finished adding your networks, click on **OK**.

The ASDM will carry to back to the **Area/Networks** tab and display the newly-added route:

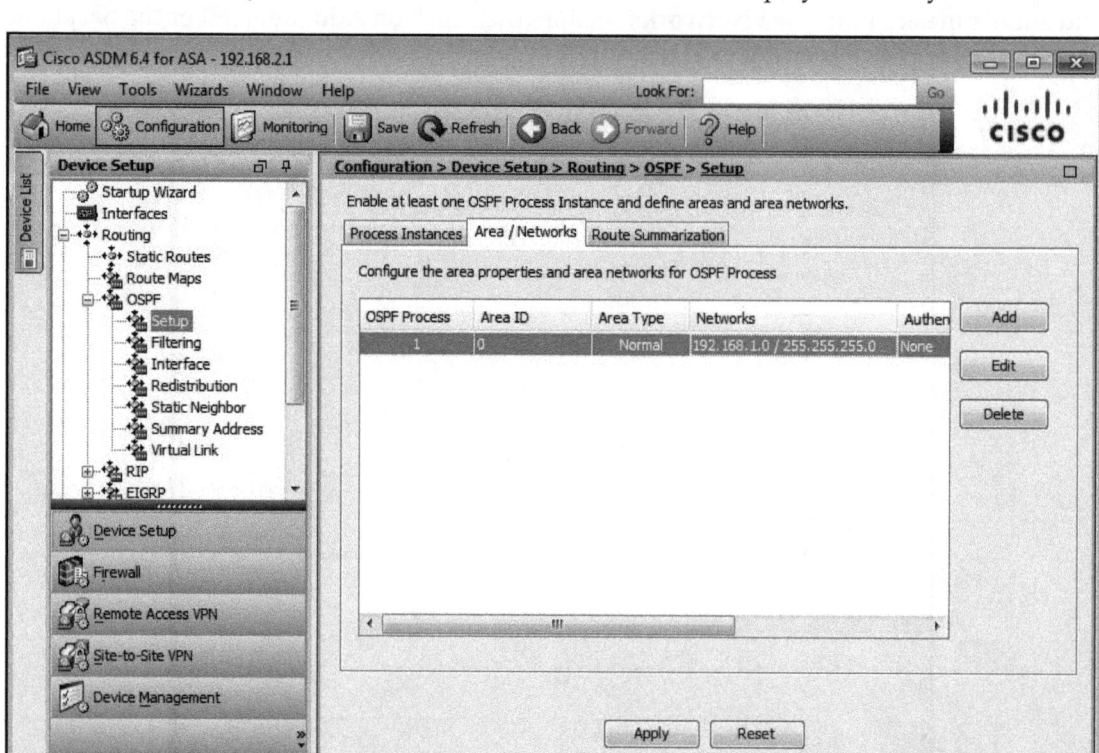

Once you have completed all the configurations or modifications, click **Apply** and save your configurations.

Configuring OSPF using the CLI

The commands for configuring OSPF on the ASA are similar to a Cisco router. The following is the equivalent configuration for the using the CLI of the ASA:

```
ASA-1(config)# router ospf 1
ASA-1(config-router)# network 192.168.1.0 255.255.255 area 0
ASA-1(config-router)# network 192.168.2.0 255.255.255 area 0
ASA-1(config-router)# default-information originate
```

Routing Information Protocol

Routing Information Protocol (**RIP**) has been around for many years. However, due to its limited ability to function in large enterprise networks, it has not been the first choice for many network engineers. Even though it's not widely used anymore, the ASA supports RIP versions 1 and 2. In this section, we are going to take a look at how to configure RIP using the ASDM:

1. To get started, open the ASDM and navigate to **Configuration** I **Device Setup** I **Routing** I **RIP** I **Setup**.
2. The following window on the ASDM will allow us to enable the RIP routing protocol on the ASA. To enable RIP, ensure the checkbox next to **Enable RIP routing** is checked. As a good practice, we would disable auto-summarization and use RIP version 2:

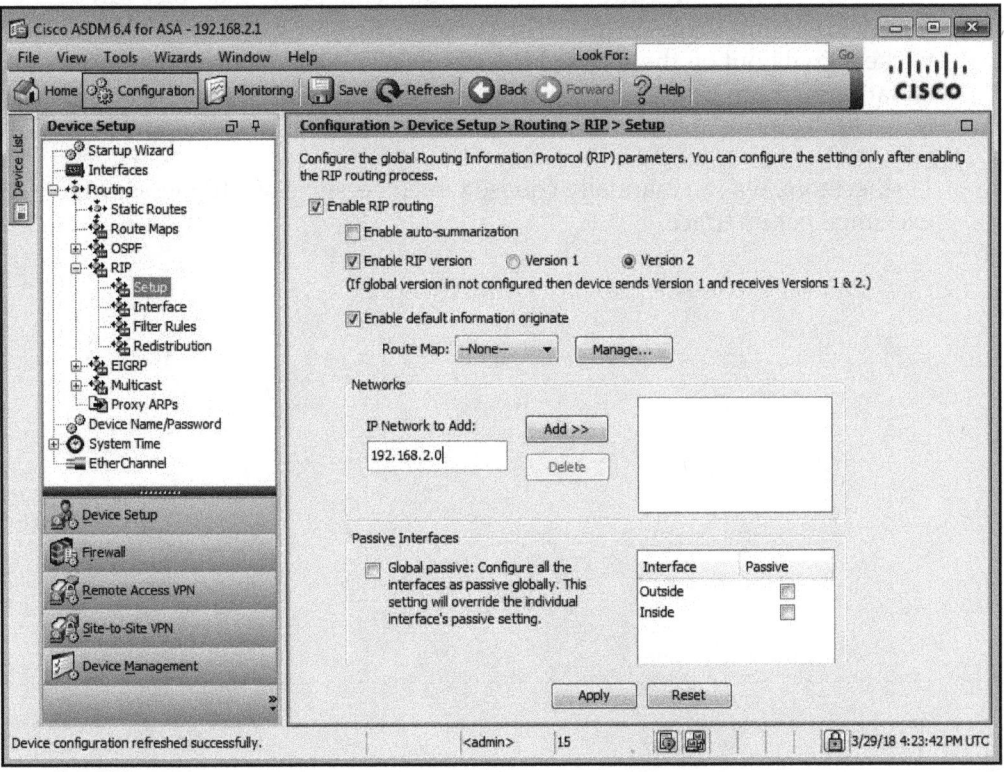

Benefits of RIPv2 are further discussed in the CCNA: Routing and Switching certification (`https://www.cisco.com/c/en/us/training-events/training-certifications/certifications/associate/ccna-routing-switching.html`).
RIPv2 can only receive and send RIPv2 packets. RIPv1 can send only version 1 packets but can receive both versions 1 and 2 packets.

3. If there's a default route that needs to propagate from this ASA to other devices such router using the RIP routing protocol, this can be achieved by checking the **Enable default information originate** checkbox.

   Under the **Networks** section, you can add network IDs, however, subnet masks are not allowed on the configurations of the RIP.

   Another good practice is enabling passive interfaces on interfaces that do not have a router or another firewall on the other end. Some examples can be the internet port and the LAN port. The passive interface feature disables routing packets going out on the selected interface(s). This can be useful in many situations—it can be a security risk, waste of bandwidth on the links, and a waste of resources.

   Furthermore, we can manually choose which versions of RIP messages to exchange per interface.

4. To achieve this function on the ASA, click on the **Interface** as displayed in the following screenshot:

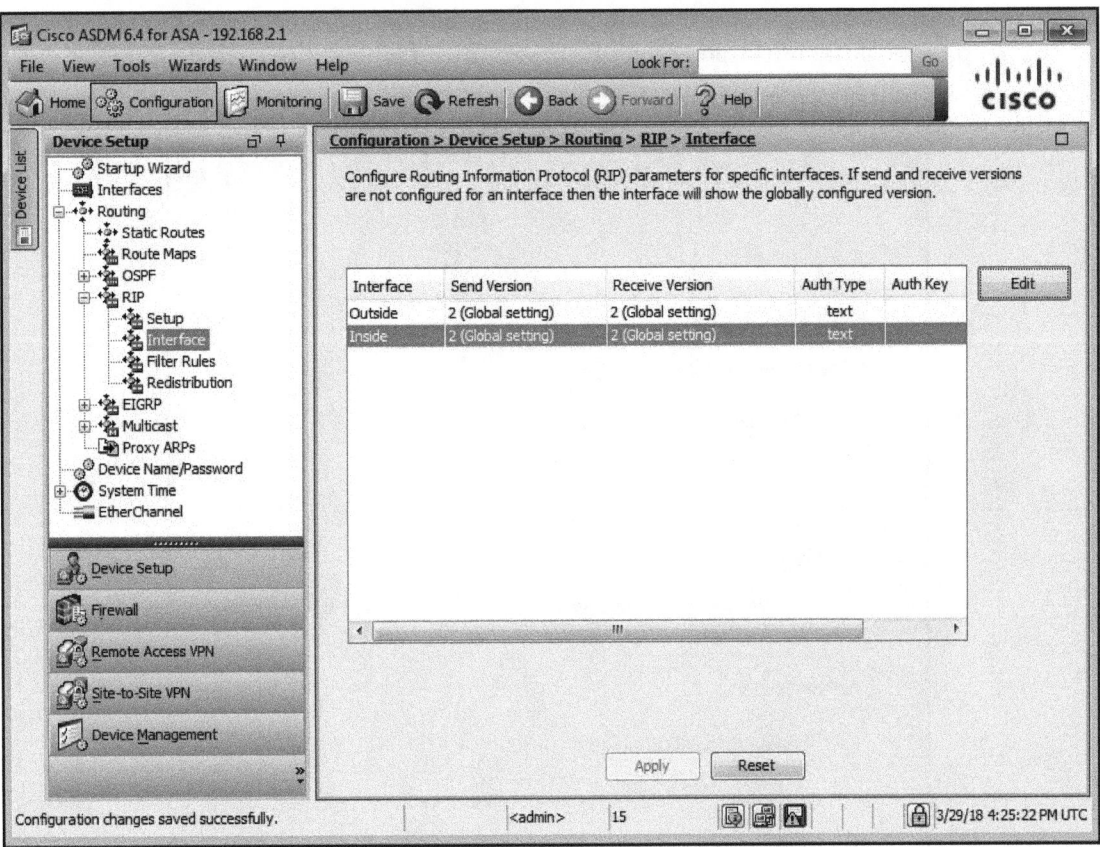

5. Select the interface you would like to modify and click on **Edit**. The following window will appear providing options to manually adjust the RIP version messages to send and receive. Another feature is authentication, which would require the neighbor RIP-enabled devices, such as another firewall or router, to provide authentication before they are allowed to exchange RIP packets between themselves in the routing domain:

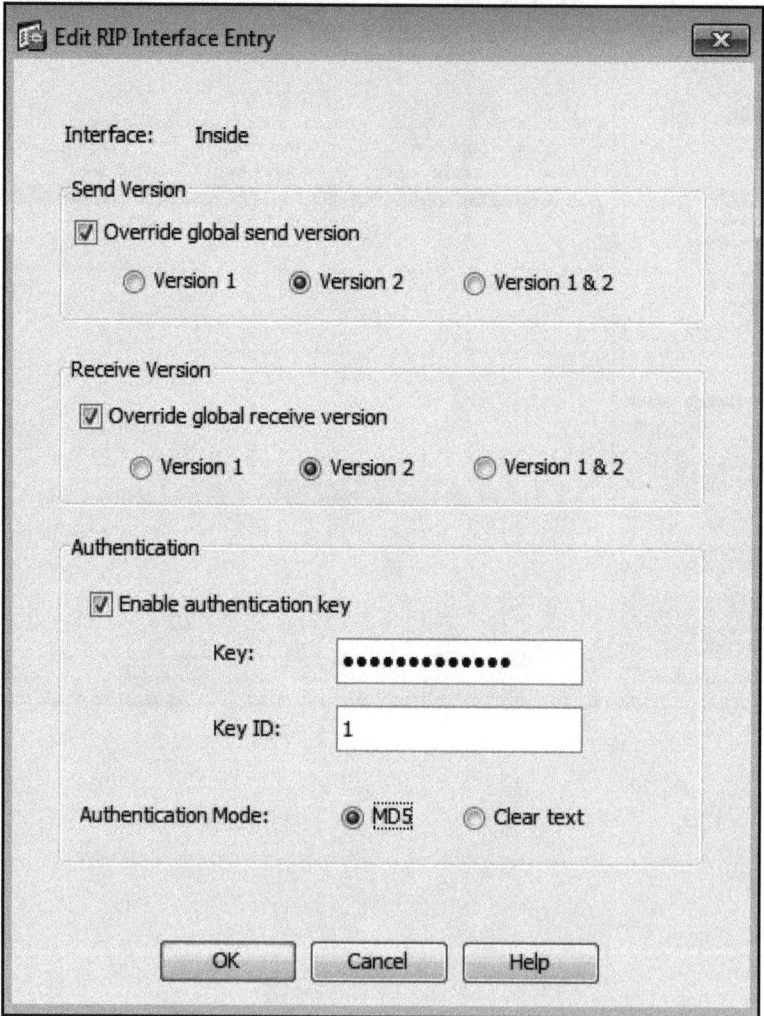

The **Key** is the actual passphrase that would be used to provide during the **Authentication** phase. The **Key ID** is used as a reference and the **Authentication Mode** determines whether the key is sent as plain-text (unsecure) or as a **Message Digest 5** (**MD5**) hash (secure) across the link.

6. Clicking on **OK** will take you back to the main **RIP** setup window.
7. Once you are finished, click **Apply** and save your configurations.

Configuring RIP using the CLI

The following commands can be used on the ASA to achieve the same as we did on the ASDM:

```
ASA-1(config)# router rip
ASA-1(config-router)# network 192.168.1.0
ASA-1(config-router)# network 192.168.2.0
ASA-1(config-router)# version 2
ASA-1(config-router)# passive-interface Outside
ASA-1(config-router)# no auto-summarize
ASA-1(config-router)# redistribute static
```

Enhanced Interior Gateway Routing Protocol

Enhanced Interior Gateway Routing Protocol (**EIGRP**) is a distance-vector routing protocol and was proprietary to Cisco devices until 2013. Now EIGRP is a multi-vendor routing protocol like **Open Shortest Path First** (**OSPF**) and **Routing Information Protocol** (**RIP**). In this section we are going to take a look at how to configure EIGRP using the ASDM.

Let's begin!

First, navigate to **Configuration** | **Device Setup** | **Routing** | **EIGRP** | **Setup** on the ASDM.

The following screen should be presented on the ASDM, there are three tabs: **Process Instances**, **Networks**, and **Passive Interfaces**. We will take a look at the features within each of these tabs.

Let's begin by first enabling the EIGRP process on the ASA:

1. Simply click on the checkbox that says **Enable this EIGRP Process**. Then, we need to assign an **EIGRP Process** value, we can use 1:

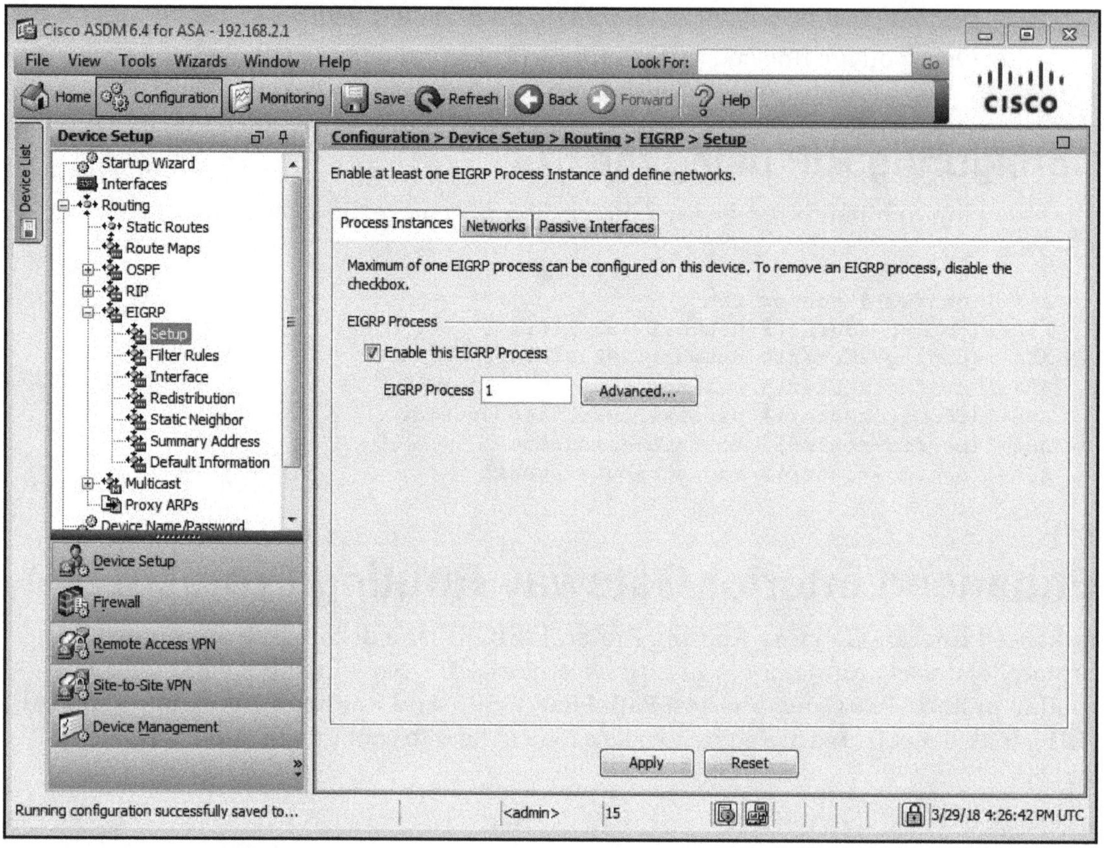

Cisco ASDM 6.4 for ASA - 192.168.2.1

File   View   Tools   Wizards   Window   Help   Look For: Go

Home   Configuration   Monitoring   Save   Refresh   Back   Forward   Help

Device Setup

- Startup Wizard
- Interfaces
- Routing
  - Static Routes
  - Route Maps
  - OSPF
  - RIP
  - EIGRP
    - Setup
    - Filter Rules
    - Interface
    - Redistribution
    - Static Neighbor
    - Summary Address
    - Default Information
  - Multicast
  - Proxy ARPs
- Device Name/Password

Device Setup

Firewall

Remote Access VPN

Site-to-Site VPN

Device Management

Configuration > Device Setup > Routing > EIGRP > Setup

Enable at least one EIGRP Process Instance and define networks.

| Process Instances | Networks | Passive Interfaces |

Maximum of one EIGRP process can be configured on this device. To remove an EIGRP process, disable the checkbox.

EIGRP Process

☑ Enable this EIGRP Process

EIGRP Process [1]   [Advanced...]

[Apply]   [Reset]

Running configuration successfully saved to... | <admin>   15   3/29/18 4:26:42 PM UTC

The EIGRP **Autonomous System** (**AS**) number must be the same for all EIGRP-enabled devices that want to exchange EIGRP routing information between themselves.

2. Click on **Advanced....**
3. We are presented with the five metrics of EIGRP. Each can be modified. As good practice, ensure **Auto-Summary** is disabled:

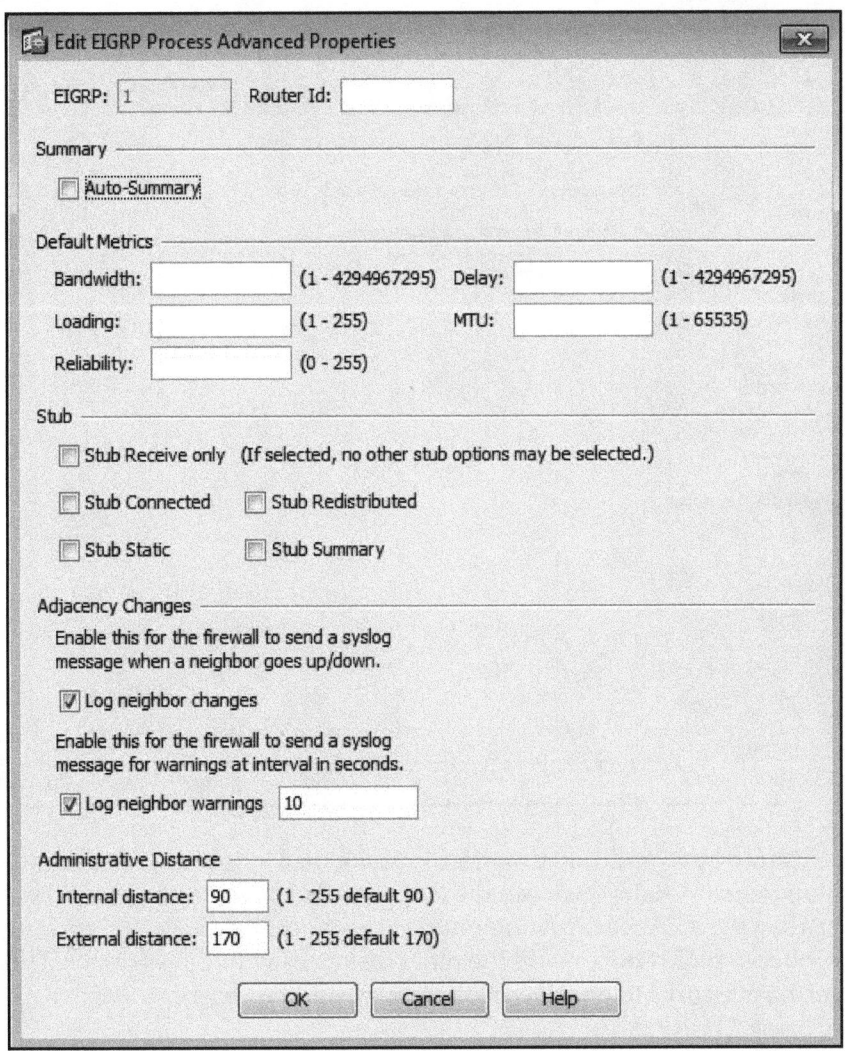

Although the EIGRP process is enabled, the networks are not being advertised.

4. To advertise networks using the EIGRP protocol, click the **Networks** tab then click on **Add**:

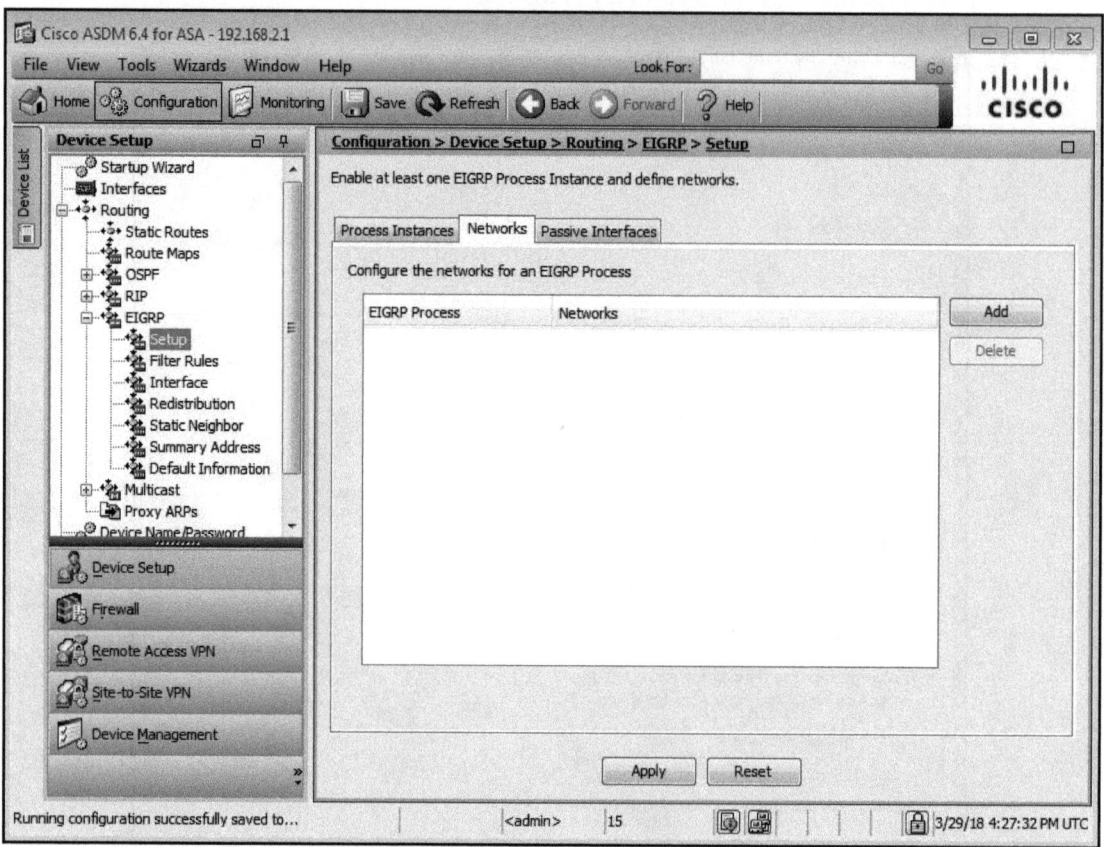

EIGRP can have multiple instances running on a single device since we are using autonomous system **1**, we can see it appears in the following window by default. Let's say the ASA was running multiple instances of EIGRP, by clicking the dropdown on **EIGRP AS**, all the other instances would be present. This allows specific networks to be advertised through another process. For this example, we are using **EIGRP AS 1**:

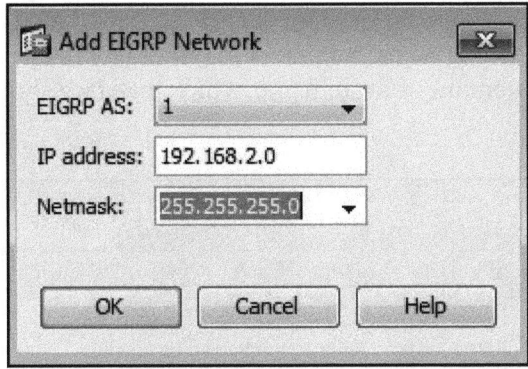

5. Once you've entered the network-ID and its subnet mask, click on **OK**.

    The following screen displays that the `192.168.2.0/24` network has been added to the **EIGRP Process 1** instance:

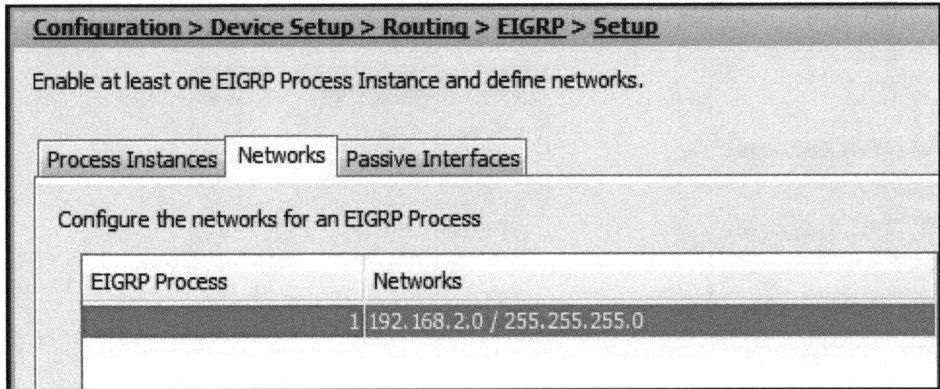

As mentioned previously, a good security practice is to disable routing packets going out on interfaces that do not have a routing protocol enabled, such as EIGRP (in this instance), like the LAN interface and the internet **Interface** (**Outside**) do. Routing packets should always be kept between routers and the ASA with the specific protocol enabled.

6. To configure passive interfaces for EIGRP on the ASA, click on the **Passive Interface** tab, then click on **Add**. A new window will appear, providing options to select the autonomous system and which interface should be the passive interface:

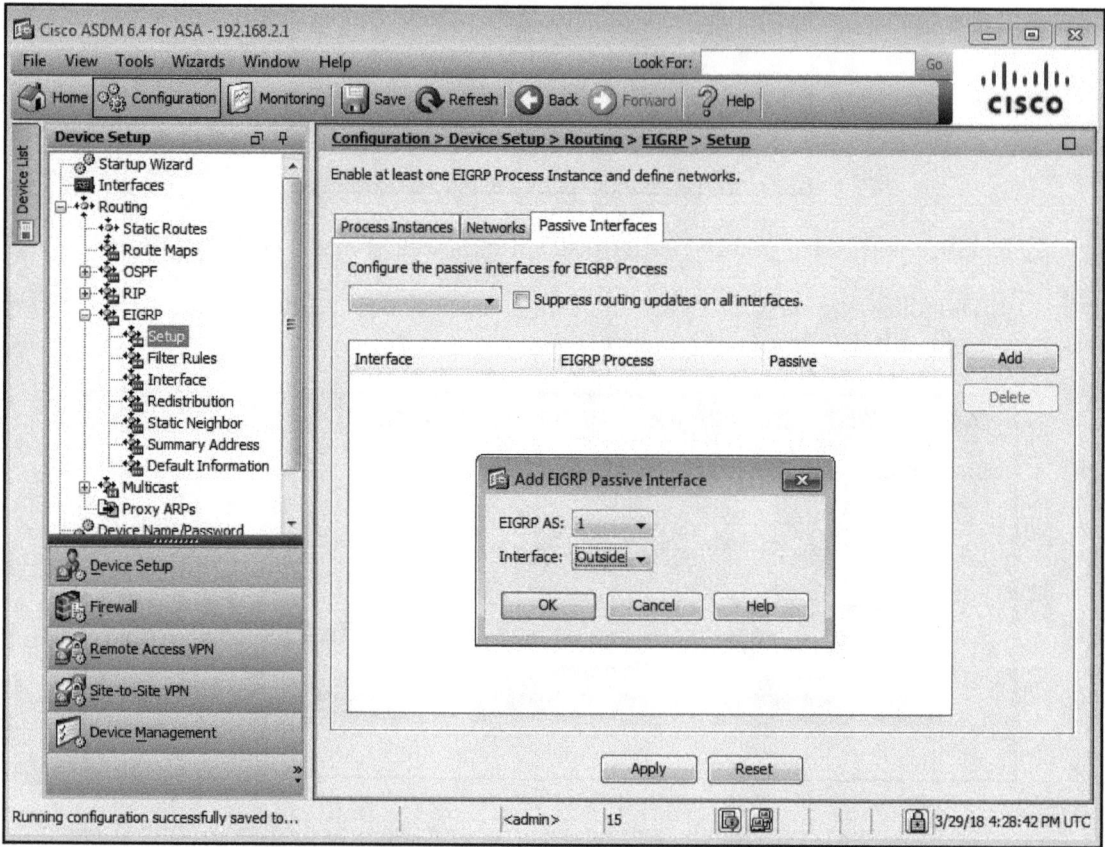

7. Be sure to click on **Apply** and save your configurations.

Configuring EIGRP using the CLI

The following configuration is equivalent to the configurations used on the ASDM:

```
ASA-1(config)# router eigrp 1
ASA-1(config-router)# network 192.168.1.0 255.255.255.0
ASA-1(config-router)# network 192.168.2.0 255.255.255.0
ASA-1(config-router)# passive-interface Outside
ASA-1(config-router)# no auto-summary
ASA-1(config-router)# redistribute static
```

Device name, passwords, and domain name

In the previous chapter, we set up the ASA using fundamental configurations. Some of these configurations include setting the device's hostname, creating a privilege exec password, and adding a domain name to the ASA. This can also be done using the ASDM by navigating to **Configuration** | **Device Setup** | **Device Name/Password**:

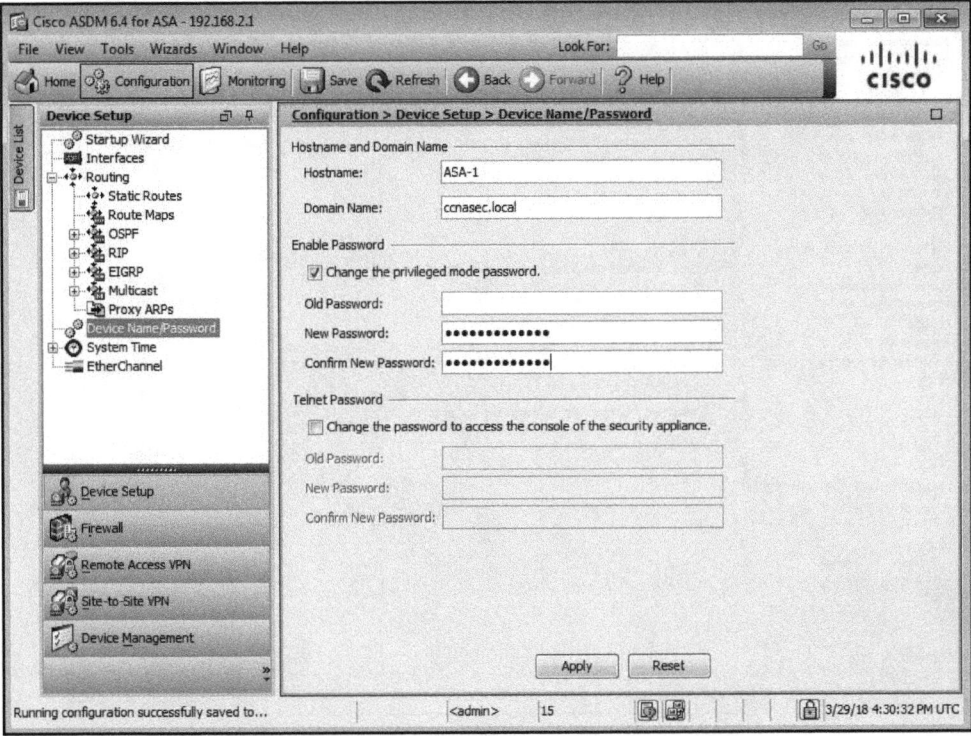

TIP

If the device does not already have enable password assigned, the **Old Password** field should remain blank while assigning a new password.

Once you are finished, click on **Apply** and save your configurations.

Setting banners using the ASDM

As mentioned earlier, there are many banner types. Each banner specifically displays a message for a particular type of administrative access to the ASA. To set a banner on the ASA using the ASDM, navigate to **Configuration** | **Device Management** | **Management Access** | **Command Line (CLI)** | **Banner**. Here you'll be able to set all the different banners the ASA supports:

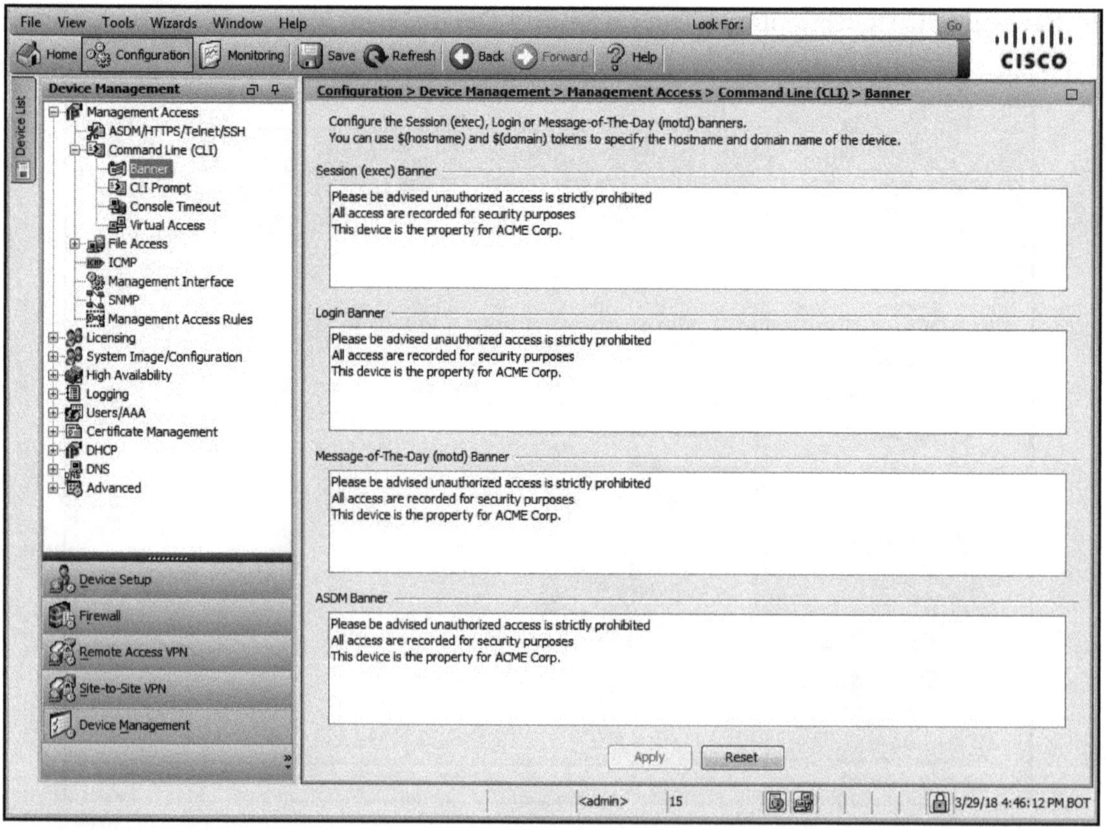

Remember, once you're done, click on **Apply** and save the settings of the ASA.

Configuring interfaces

Configuring the interfaces of the ASA is very simple. Perform the following steps to get started:

1. Navigate to **Configuration** | **Device Setup** | **Interfaces**. Simply click on the interface you would like to configure/modify and click on **Edit**:

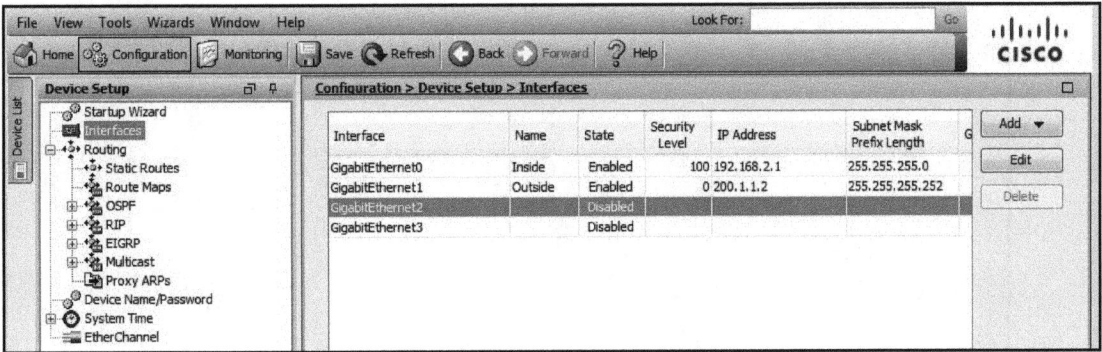

2. The following window will appear, providing the settings for the interface itself. Here you can create a name for the interface, adjust the security-level, enable the interface, and assign an **IP Address** and **Subnet Mask**:

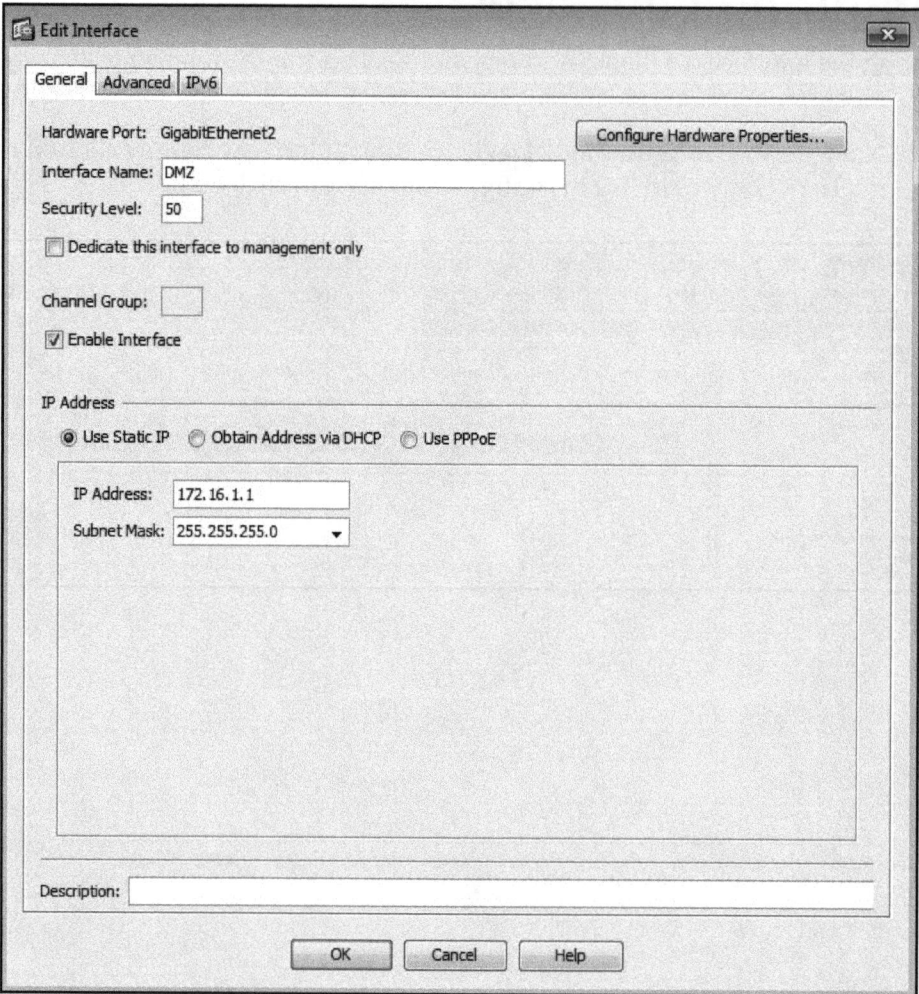

3. Upon clicking **OK**, the ASDM will carry you back to the main **Interface** window. The following screenshot clearly depicts all the interfaces of the ASA, their security-levels, the IP address and subnet mask, their names, and most importantly, whether the interface is **Enabled** or **Disabled**:

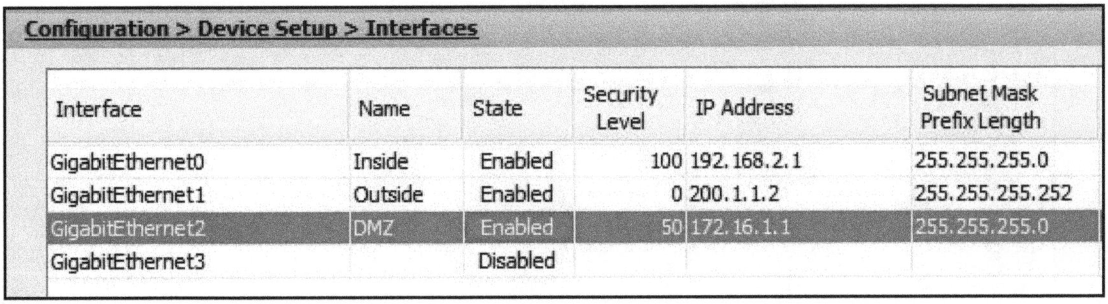

Configuration > Device Setup > Interfaces

Interface	Name	State	Security Level	IP Address	Subnet Mask Prefix Length
GigabitEthernet0	Inside	Enabled	100	192.168.2.1	255.255.255.0
GigabitEthernet1	Outside	Enabled	0	200.1.1.2	255.255.255.252
GigabitEthernet2	DMZ	Enabled	50	172.16.1.1	255.255.255.0
GigabitEthernet3		Disabled			

System time and Network Time Protocol

As mentioned previously, system time is very important on all devices on a network. Setting the clock using the ASDM can be done by navigating to **Configuration** | **Device Setup** | **System Time** | **Clock**. You'll be able to select the appropriate time zone, date, and time on the ASA:

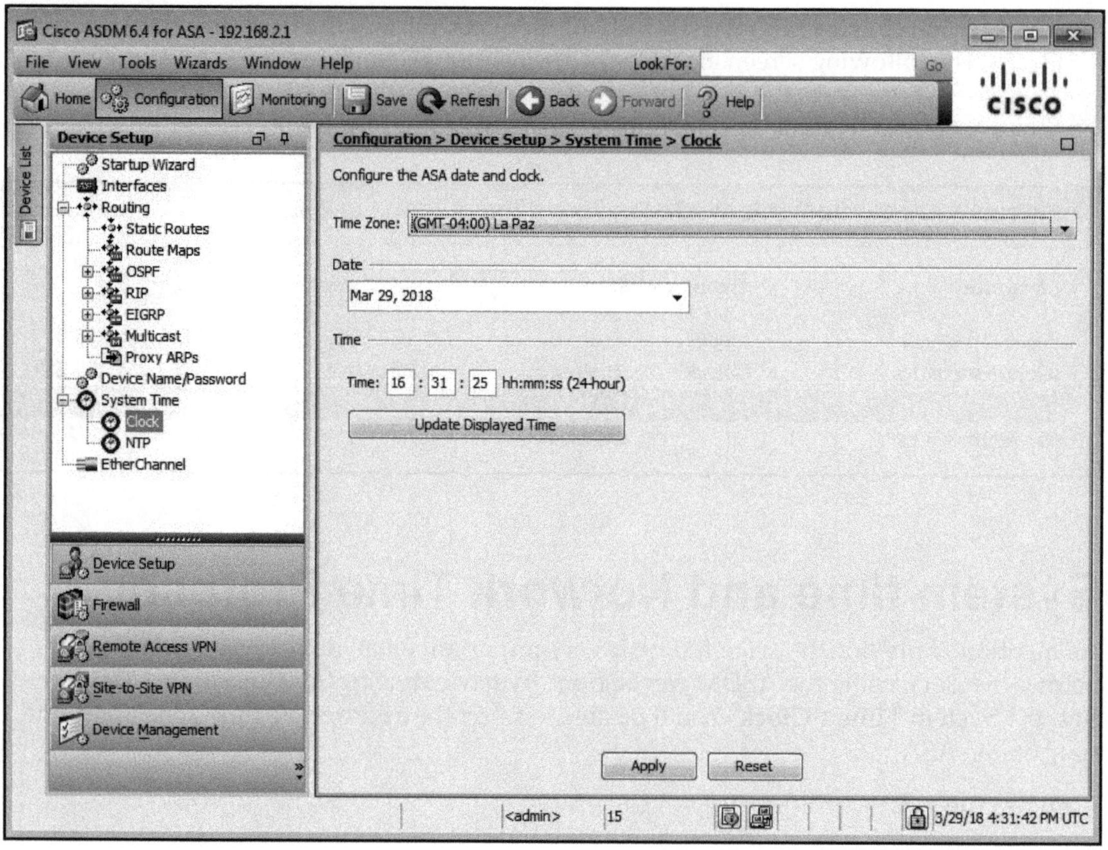

The system clock on Cisco devices are in the 24-hour format.

Configuring the ASA to be a NTP client can be done by going to **Configuration | Device Setup | System Time | NTP** and clicking on **Add**. This feature will allow the ASA to obtain its time from an NTP server, whether the NTP server is on the **inside**, **outside**, or any other interface:

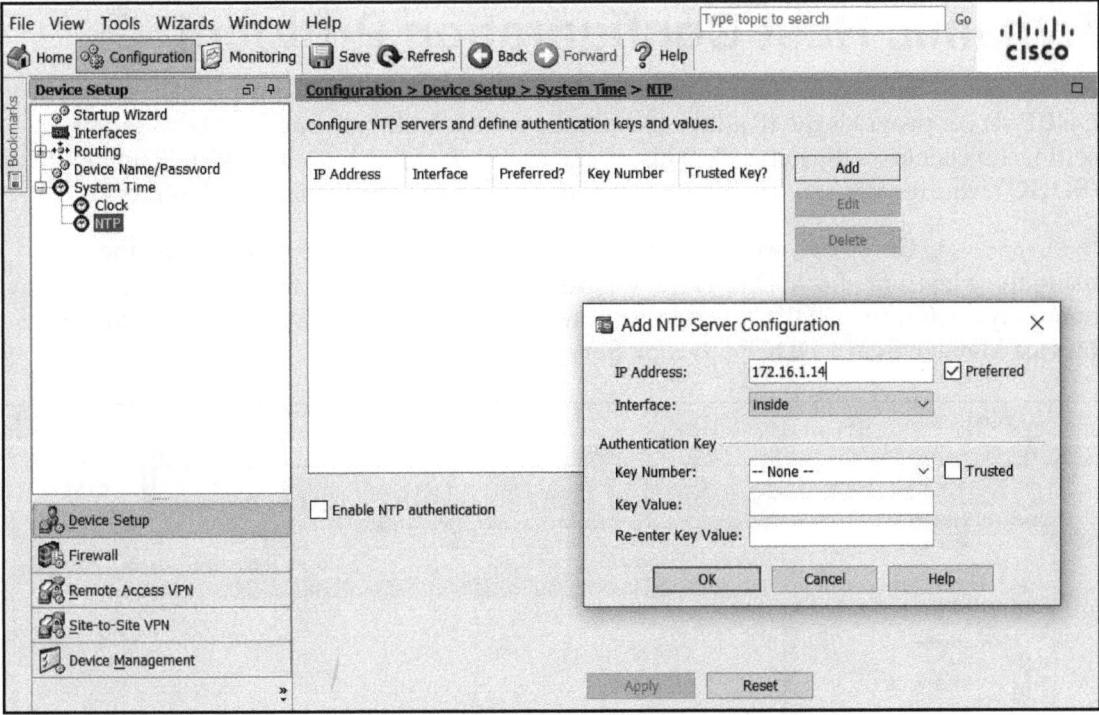

Once you click **OK**, the NTP server configurations will be presented on the ASDM.

However, ensure you click on **Apply** to push the configurations to the ASA and save the settings.

Configuring NTP using the CLI

Typically, the `ntp server <ntp server IP>` command can be used on the ASA:

```
ASA-1(config)# ntp authenticate (optional - only used for authentication)
ASA-1(config)# ntp trusted-key 1 (optional - only used for authentication)
ASA-1(config)# ntp authentication-ket 1 md5 cisco123 (optional - only used
for authentication)
ASA-1(config)# ntp server 1.2.3.4 key 1 perfer
```

Dynamic Host Configuration Protocol

As mentioned in the previous chapter, the ASA has the ability of being a DHCP server. A DHCP server provides the IP address, subnet mask, default gateway, and DNS server settings to clients on the network. This can be useful if a branch or **small office home office** (**SOHO**) requires this service, the ASA can act as both a firewall and DHCP server.

In Chapter 10, *Cisco ASA*, we saw how to modify the existing configurations on the ASA using the wizard on the ASDM. Here, we are going to look at how to enable/disable and manually configure the DHCP services on the ASA. To begin, navigate to **Configuration** | **Device Management** | **DHCP** | **DHCP Server** on the ASDM:

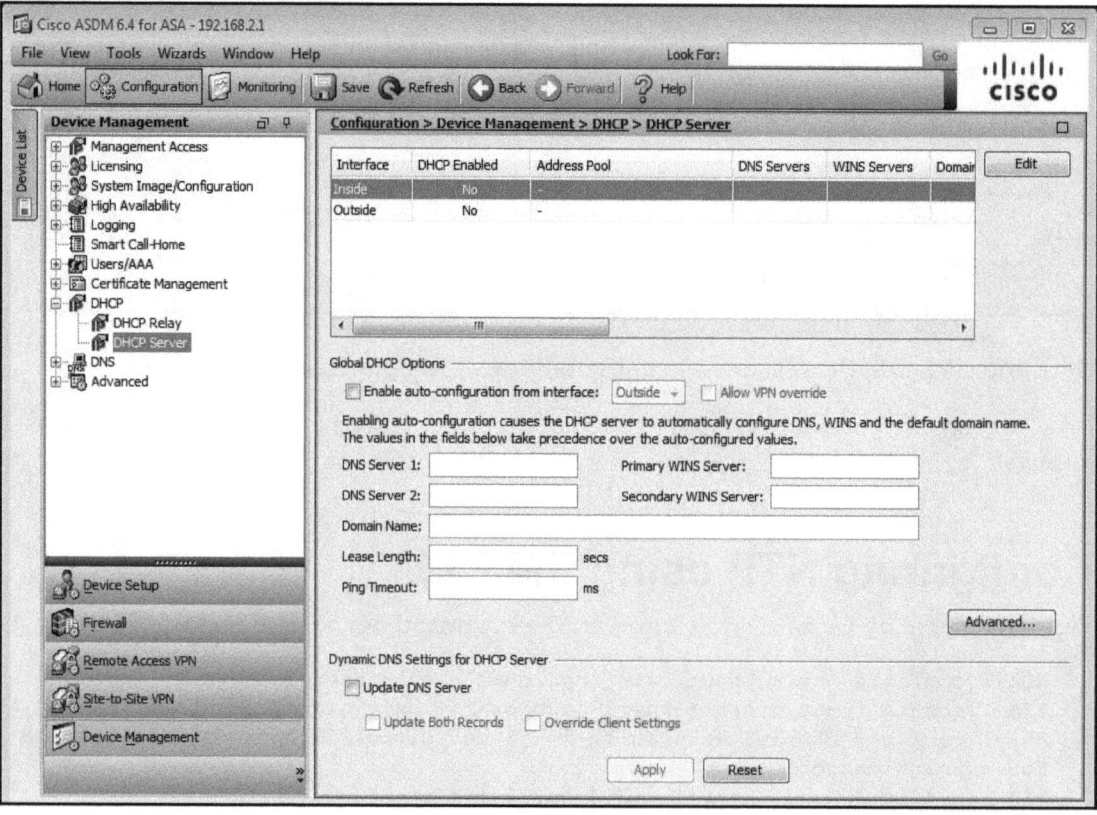

The preceding window presents us with the configured interfaces of the ASA, currently we have only the **Inside** and **Outside** interface configured.

Select the interface you would like the DHCP service to provide to the dynamic IP addresses, then click on **Edit**. The **Edit DHCP Server** window appears:

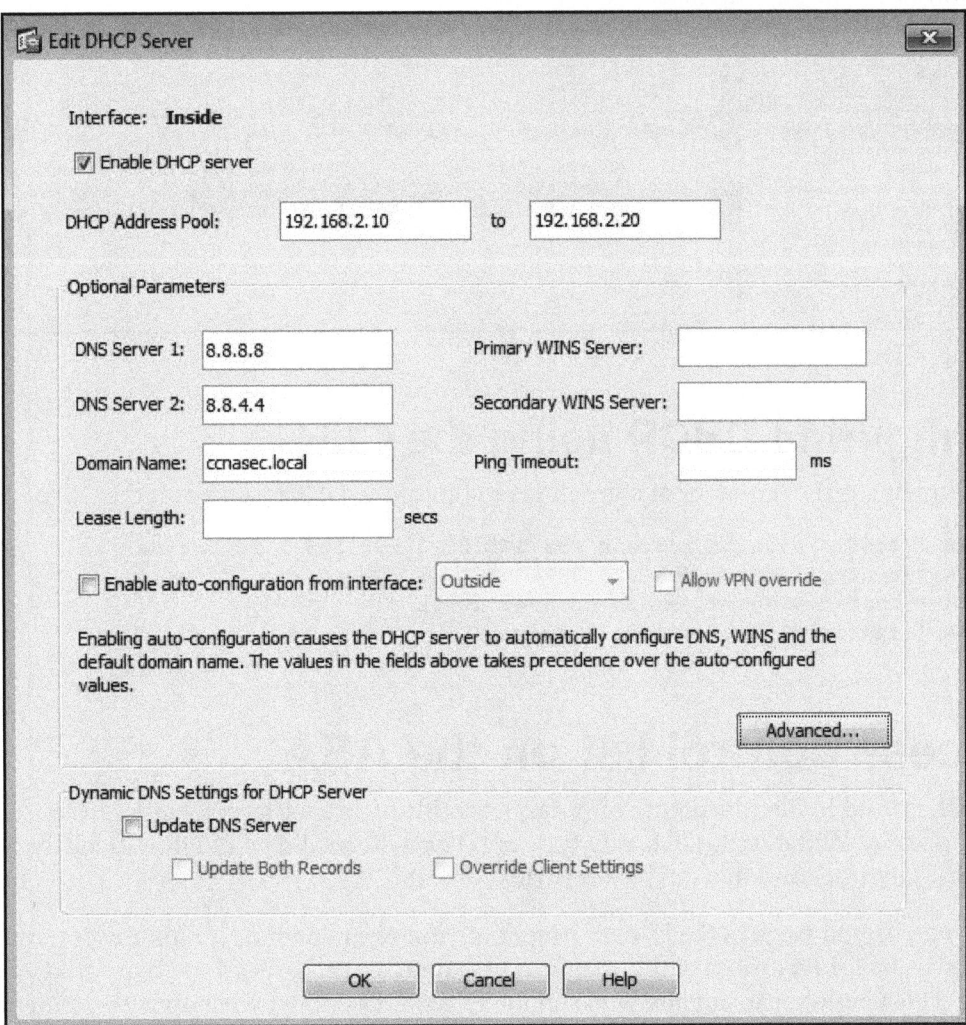

Enable the DHCP server by clicking the **Enable DHCP server** checkbox. Then, assign the range of IP addresses for the DHCP pool. Be sure to set the **Domain Name System** (**DNS**) server information.

Once completed, click on **OK**. The ASDM will present the main DHCP server window with the configurations per interface:

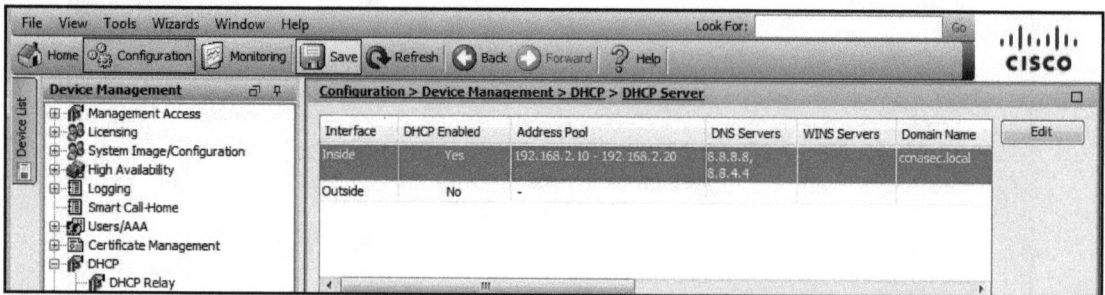

Configuring DHCP using the CLI

The following is the sequence of commands to set up the DHCP server on the ASA:

```
ASA-1(config)# dhcpd address 192.168.2.10-192.168.2.20 Inside
ASA-1(config)# dhcpd dns 8.8.8.8 8.8.4.4
ASA-1(config)# dhcpd domain ccnasec.local
ASA-1(config)# dhcpd enable Inside
```

Access control list on the ASA

An ACL is used to filter incoming or outgoing traffic of an interface, whether it's on a Cisco router or ASA. Without the ACL, any type of traffic will be allowed to flow freely between network/interfaces and this can be a security concern.

Let's imagine you work in the IT department of your organization. Within the department, there is a small server room without any access controls (no locks on the door or keypad entry). This would mean anyone who's in the IT department, whether a visitor, a member of staff, or even an intern, would be able to simply walk into the server room without providing identification or even requiring prior authorization.

Simply installing physical access controls, such a keypad lock on the door, will deter people without the correct combination of the PIN. In other words, only those who are allowed entry will be allowed and those who are not will be denied.

ACL has the ability to filter traffic based on source or destination IP address and even by port numbers/services. This can be useful if you are trying to restrict a network of users or one user from accessing another network or service. In other words, ACLs operate at both Layer 3 and Layer 4 of the **Open Systems Interconnection (OSI)** model:

	Layer	OSI Model
	7	Application
	6	Presentation
	5	Session
Access-Control Lists (ACLs) operates here	4	Transport
	3	Network
	2	Data Link
	1	Physical

In the previous chapter, we had mentioned there are three main security zones (the Inside, Outside, and Demilitarized Zone or DMZ) with a security level assigned to each. Where the Inside had a security level of 100, the DMZ had 50, and the Outside 0. Traffic is allowed to flow from an interface of a higher security level to an interface of a lower security level. That being said, if an ACL is placed on an interface, it takes precedence over the default filtering of traffic between interfaces.

For example, we know by default, traffic originating from the Outside interface (security level 0) will not be allowed access to flow to the DMZ, which has a security level of 50:

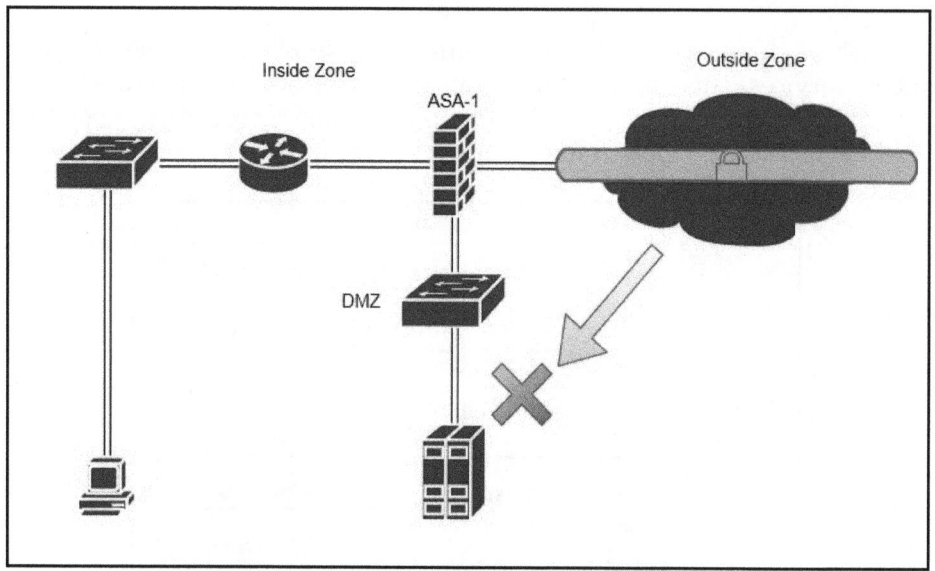

If we place some public servers in the DMZ, users from the internet/Outside zone may require access, particularly to these servers. To solve this issue, an ACL can be placed on the Outside interface to allow incoming traffic from any source to only the servers within the DMZ. All other incoming traffic will be dropped or denied access by the ASA.

In the CCENT/CCNA routing and switching certification, it is taught that a router reads the routing table from top to bottom as the entries are placed, this is also applied to ACLs. Once a match if found, the router or firewall will stop processing and continue with the appropriate action. In a case where it's an ACL, the router or firewall will either permit or deny the traffic based on the rule of the ACL.

Types of ACLs

There are many types of ACLs in the world of Cisco. For the duration of this chapter, we are going to discuss two main types: Standard and Extended ACL.

Cisco recommends that the three (3) Ps should be followed when creating and applying ACLs. The three Ps would prevent any conflict with other ACLs on the interfaces.

The three Ps are as follows:

- Only one ACL **Per** protocol
- Only one ACL **Per** direction
- Only one ACL **Per** interface

 The three (3) P's are take from the word **per** in the above three (3) points.

Standard ACL

One of the oldest types of ACL is the **Standard ACL**. Standard ACLs exists in both the Cisco routers and ASA firewalls. Unlike the Standard ACL on the Cisco IOS router, which filters traffic using the source IP address information in the packet header, the Cisco ASA filters traffic by destination address only. This is the major difference between using the Cisco router and the Cisco ASA firewall with the Standard ACL.

Creating an ACL is quite simple, however, after creation it must be applied on an interface and a direction to filter traffic, either incoming or outgoing. This may be an effective method for some scenarios. Standard ACLs, filter all traffic types (TCP, UDP, IP, and so on) by default, which means if we are trying to block only HTTP outbound traffic destined to the internet from within an organization, the Standard ACL would deny all other traffic types as well. This can be inefficient if are attempting to only restrict a specific traffic type.

Standard ACLs can be numbered or named ACLs. What does this mean? An ACL can be defined by a number. An example would be access-list 10, where ACL 10 would contain **Access Control Entries** (**ACEs**). An ACL can contain multiple ACEs, the ACEs are the rules that define what is permitted or denied.

A named ACL is simply what it says, instead of using a number, we can use a suitable name to help us understand the purpose of the ACL on the firewall. This can be convenient when troubleshooting ACLs. We can create an ACL named SSH_Access, the name used will help us understand the purpose of this particular ACL.

 Standard numbered ACL ranges are 1-99 or 1300-1999. Extended numbered ACL ranges are 100-199 or 2000-2699. However, the ASA does not enforce the use of these ranges.

Unlike a Cisco router, the Standard ACL has a very limited purpose on the ASA. Some of these features include route maps and **Virtual Private Network** (**VPN**) traffic filtering.

The following format is used for creating a Standard ACL on the ASA:

```
access-list <access list name> standard [permit | deny] [host | any |
destination hostname | destination network-ID] [subnet mask]
```

 The **Route Map** can be used to identify an OSPF destination network. It can be used to control the redistribution of OSPF routes in the ASA.

Let's take a look at the following topology. It consists of four networks, `192.168.1.0/24`, `192.168.2.0/24`, `172.18.1.0/24`, and `172.18.2.0/24`:

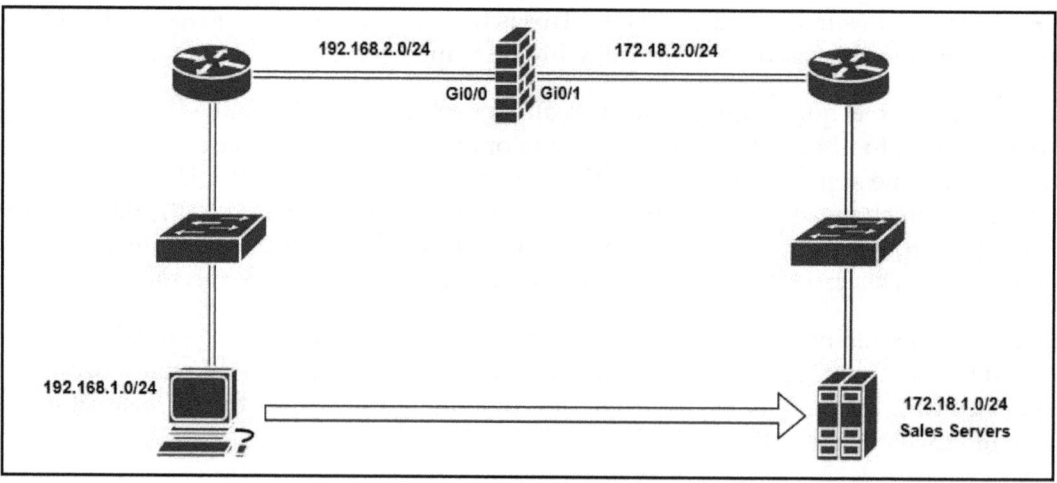

If we want to deny all traffic going to the **Sales Servers**, we can create the following Standard ACL:

```
access-list NO_Access_to_Sales standard deny 172.18.1.0 255.255.255.0
access-list NO_Access_to_Sales standard permit 172.18.2.0 255.255.255.0
```

Let's verify the ACL configurations:

```
ASA-1(config)# show running-config access-list
access-list NO_Access_to_Sales standard deny 172.18.1.0 255.255.255.0
access-list NO_Access_to_Sales standard permit 172.18.2.0 255.255.255.0
```

Using the `show running-config access-list` command will provide us with all the ACLs on the ASA:

```
ASA-1(config)# show running-config access-list
access-list NO_Access_to_Sales standard deny 172.18.1.0 255.255.255.0
access-list NO_Access_to_Sales standard permit 172.18.2.0 255.255.255.0
```

To view all configured ACLs on the ASA, we can use the `show access-list` command:

```
ASA-1(config)# show access-list
access-list cached ACL log flows: total 0, denied 0 (deny-flow-max 4096)
            alert-interval 300
access-list NO_Access_to_Sales; 2 elements; name hash: 0xb86378ab
access-list NO_Access_to_Sales line 1 standard deny 172.18.1.0 255.255.255.0 (hitcnt=0) 0xa9e05726
access-list NO_Access_to_Sales line 2 standard permit 172.18.2.0 255.255.255.0 (hitcnt=0) 0xc2bd4714
```

Applying an ACL on an interface

The following format should be used whenever applying an ACL on the ASA interface:

```
access-group <ACL Name> [in | out] interface <name of the interface>
```

```
ASA-1(config)# access-group NO_Access_to_Sales out interface Outside
```

Extended ACL

In the previous section, we discussed how Standard ACL works on the ASA, and most importantly, that Standard ACL filters all traffic types that are outbound for a destination host or network. Here we are going to discuss how the Extended ACL works.

Some features of the Extended ACL on the ASA include its ability to control network access to IP traffic, it identifies IP addresses for NAT, and it can be used to identify traffic types and VPN traffic filtering.

The Extended ACL can either filter incoming or outgoing traffic on the interfaces of the ASA, unlike the Standard ACL, which can only filter outbound traffic.

An Extended ACL can either permit or deny traffic based on the following:

- Source IP address
- Destination IP address
- Protocol
- Port numbers

The following format is used for Extended ACL:

```
access-list <name> <line-number> [extended] [permit | deny] [protocol]
<source address> <subnet mask> <source port> <destination address> eq
<destination port>
```

> To remove an entire ACL from the ASA, use `clear configure`
> `access-list`.

This can be useful in many ways. Let's say you want to allow the staff members of the IT department (`192.168.10.0/28`) to remotely access your ASA, we can set an Extended ACL on the incoming interface:

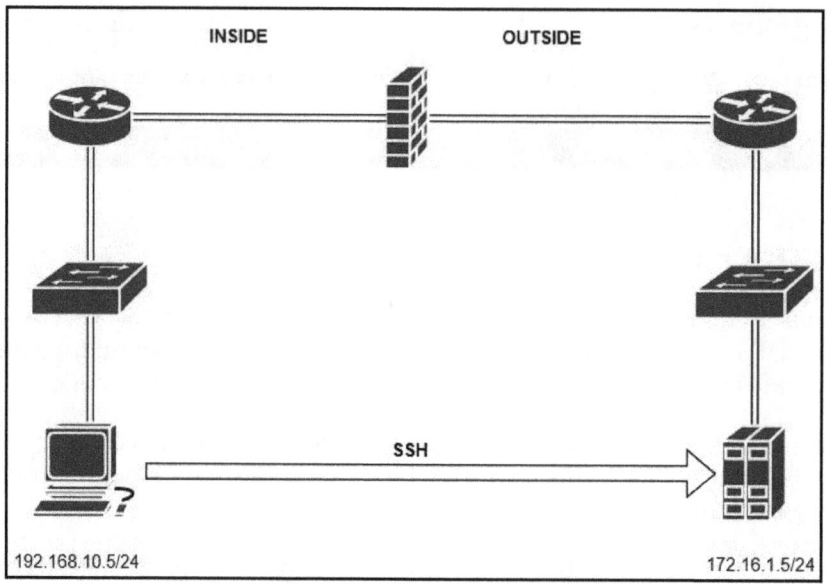

The following is an example of an ACL which can be used in the previous scenario:

```
access-list Allow_SSH extended permit tcp 192.168.10.0 255.225.255.0 host
172.16.1.5 eq 22
access-list Allow_SSH extended permit ip any any
```

Using the ASDM to create ACLs

Using the ASDM to create and modify ACLs is quite easy compared to using the CLI. With the ASDM, you have a graphical representation of the configurations and their placement on the ASA. To get started:

1. Navigate to **Configuration** | **Firewall** | **Access Rules** on the ASDM:

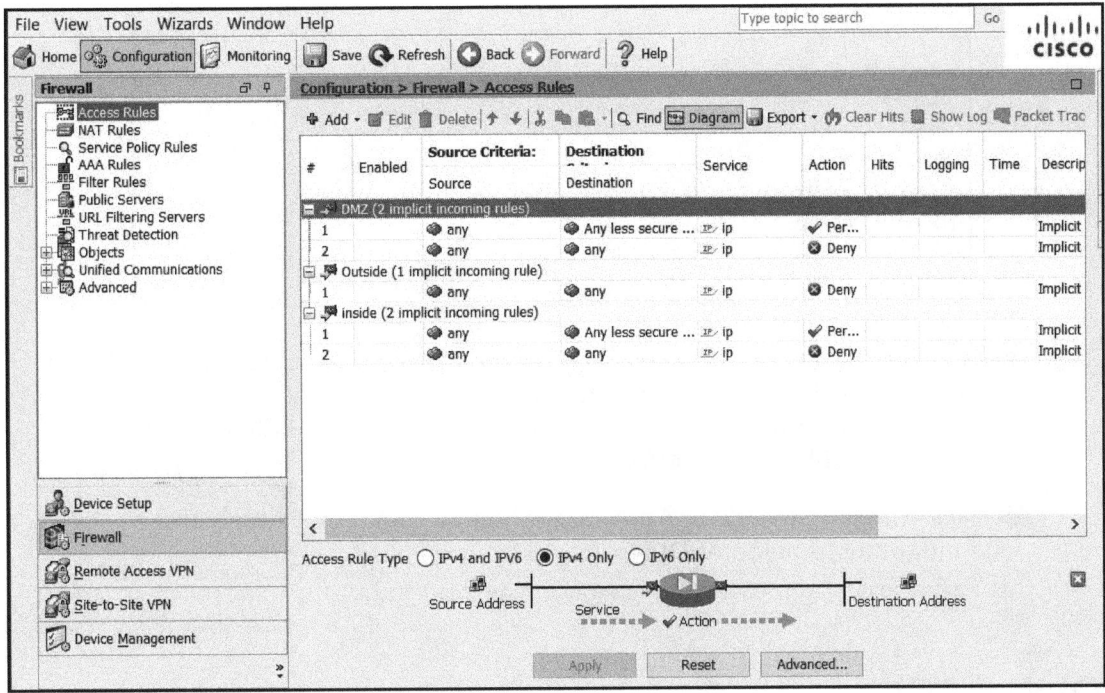

2. To create an ACL, click on **Add**:

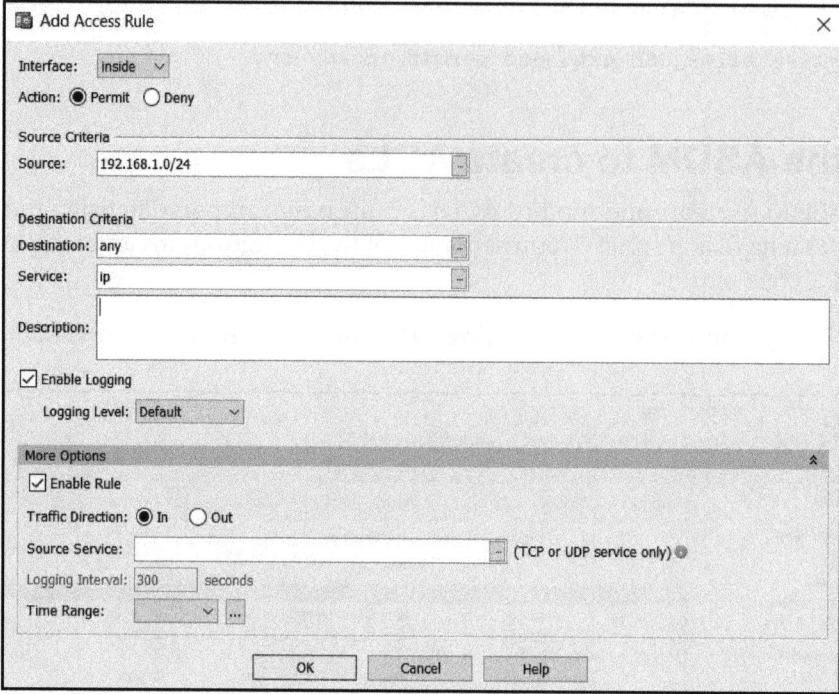

In the previous window, you'll have options to select the interface to apply the ACL on, whether to permit of deny traffic, specify the source host/network, the destination host/network, the service type, and whether to filter incoming or outgoing traffic on the interface.

3. Please be sure to click on **Apply** at the bottom of ASDM to apply the configurations of the ASDM to the ASA.

4. Save the configurations if it is working as expected.

Global ACL

You may wonder what the **Global ACL** is and how it is different from the previously mentioned Standard and Extended ACLs. As we learned earlier, the ASA reads all ACLs starting from the top. Until an ACE is matched, the ASA will stop processing and execute the actions defined by the ACE, whether to permit or deny the traffic.

Both Standard and Extended ACL are applied on an interface, however a Global ACL is applied to all interfaces on the ASA by default. Let's recall, implicit deny is the last ACE in any ACL. Therefore, since the Global ACL is applied to all ACLs on the ASA, it's actually the ACE just before the implicit deny ACE:

Access List Name	TEST
1st Entry	ACE 1
2nd Entry	ACE 2
3rd Entry	ACE 3
4th Entry	ACE 4
2nd to Last Entry	Global ACE
Last Entry	Implicit Deny

The Global ACL was introduced with the ASA version 8.3 and later. If you're using an ASA 5505, you may not find the feature.

The format for a writing a Global ACL is the same as an Extended ACL, however, the difference is when it's being applied to the interfaces. The Global ACL uses the following format when being applied globally:

```
access-group <name of ACL> global
```

The global command is used only on Global ACLs.

A Global ACL is created following the same method as any other ACL using the ASDM, except when choosing which the interface it should be applied to, select **Any**. The **Any** option will apply the ACL on all interfaces of the ASA by default, making it a Global ACL:

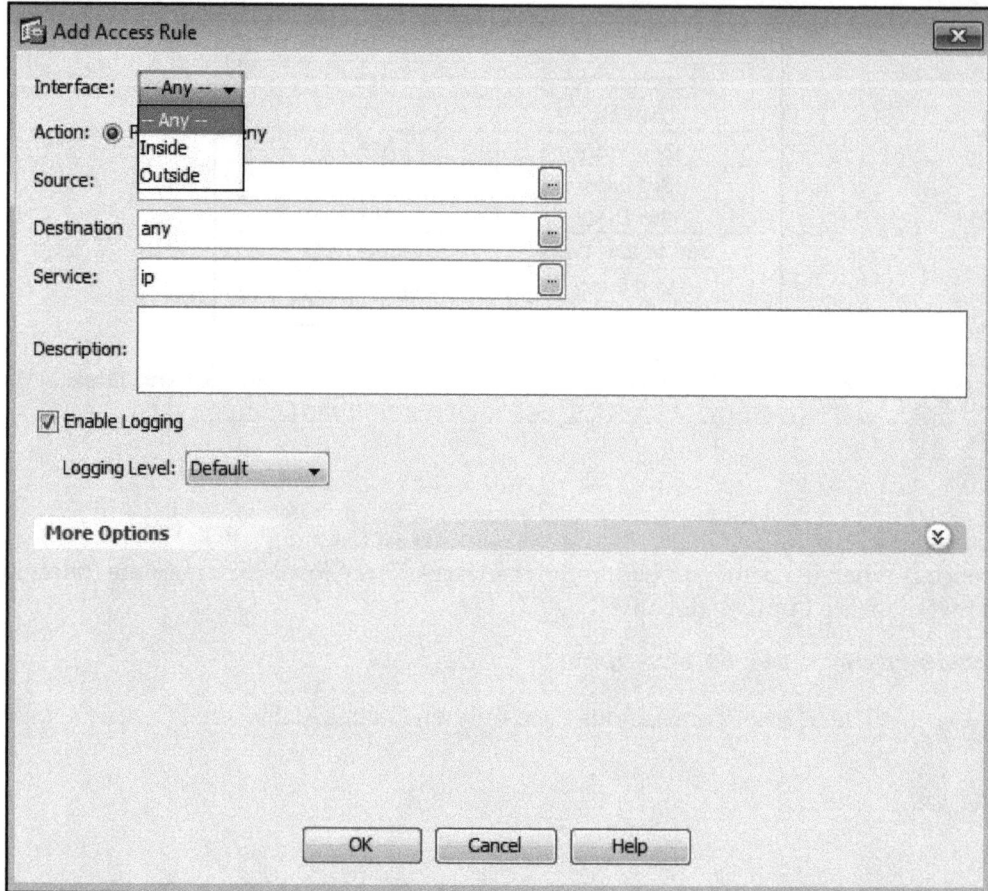

The ASA supports IPv6. Therefore on the ASA, IPv6 ACLs can be created. Simply click on the dropdown arrow next to **Add**. This will provide you with the option to either create an IPv4 ACL or an IPv6 ACL:

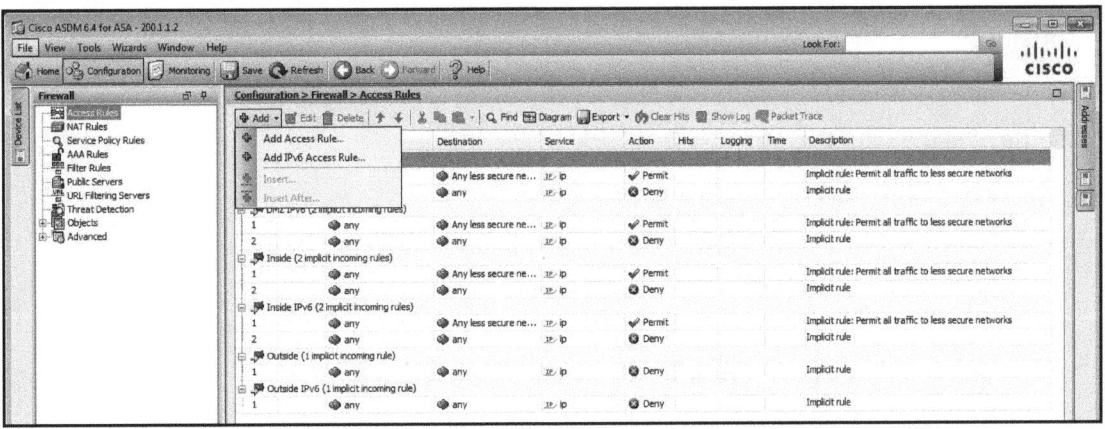

Object groups

What is a group? A group is usually a collection of entities/items that have of similar characteristics or qualities. A simply analogy can be a WhatsApp group. Let's say you want to send an update about football game scores to three of your friends: Bob, Alice, and Tom. You would have to write and send the same message to each of the three people. If you create a WhatsApp group, name it Football Crew, and add Bob, Alice, and Tom as its members, it would be simpler to reference the single group because each member would receive the message.

A similar concept can be used on the ASA to reference multiple protocols, devices, or networks at a given time. This is known at an **object group**. Let's think about a scenario where we would like to apply one policy, whether to inspect, permit, or deny a group of different protocols, such as HTTP, **Simple Network Management Protocol** (**SNMP**), and **Domain Name System** (**DNS**). We would need to create a policy for each of the three protocols. If we create a single group and add only those three protocols, we would have an object group. Therefore, we can now create one policy and reference the object group only and not the individual protocols.

Object groups can consist of protocols, network-IDs, services/protocols, and **Internet Control Message Protocol** (**ICMP**) types.

 Object groups can be reused and referenced almost anywhere on the ASA configurations.

Benefits of using Object groups:

- Simplify the creation of ACLs
- Reference multiple IP addresses during NAT configurations
- Group multiple services
- Group multiple ICMP-type messages

Objects are located at **Configuration** I **Firewall** I **Objects** on the ASDM.

Configuring Object groups using the ASDM

Perform the following steps to get started:

1. Navigate to **Configuration** I **Firewall** I **Objects** I **Network Objects/Groups** on the ASDM:

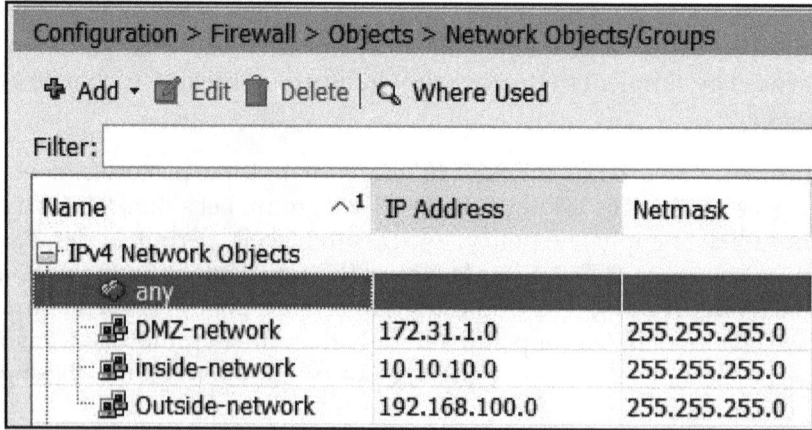

In the preceding screenshot, there are four network objects: any, DMZ-network, inside-network, and Outside-network. Each of these network objects contains a network (network-ID and subnet mask).

2. To create a new network object, click on **Add** | **Network Object**. The following options will be available:

   - **Name: Google DNS1**
   - **IP Version**: IPv4
   - **IP Address**: 8.8.8.8
   - **Netmask**: 255.255.255.255
   - **Description**:

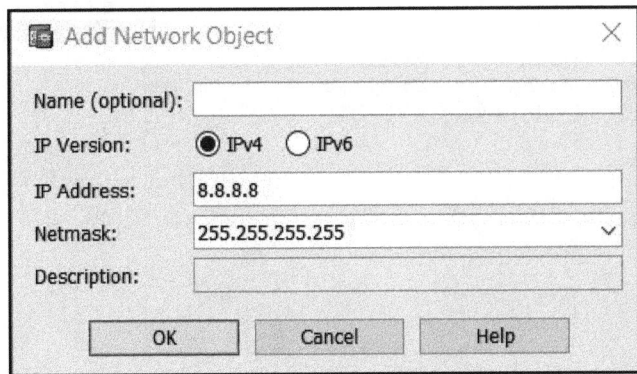

3. Click on **OK**. The network object has now been added to the list:

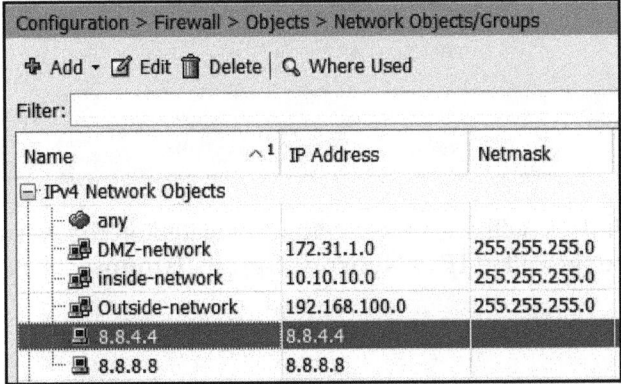

4. To create a network group, click on **Add | Network Object Group**:

The **Network Object Group** allows network objects to be grouped together. The following screenshot shows a new group named Google-Open-DNS, where both Google DNS server 8.8.8.8 and 8.8.4.4 are added in the group as objects:

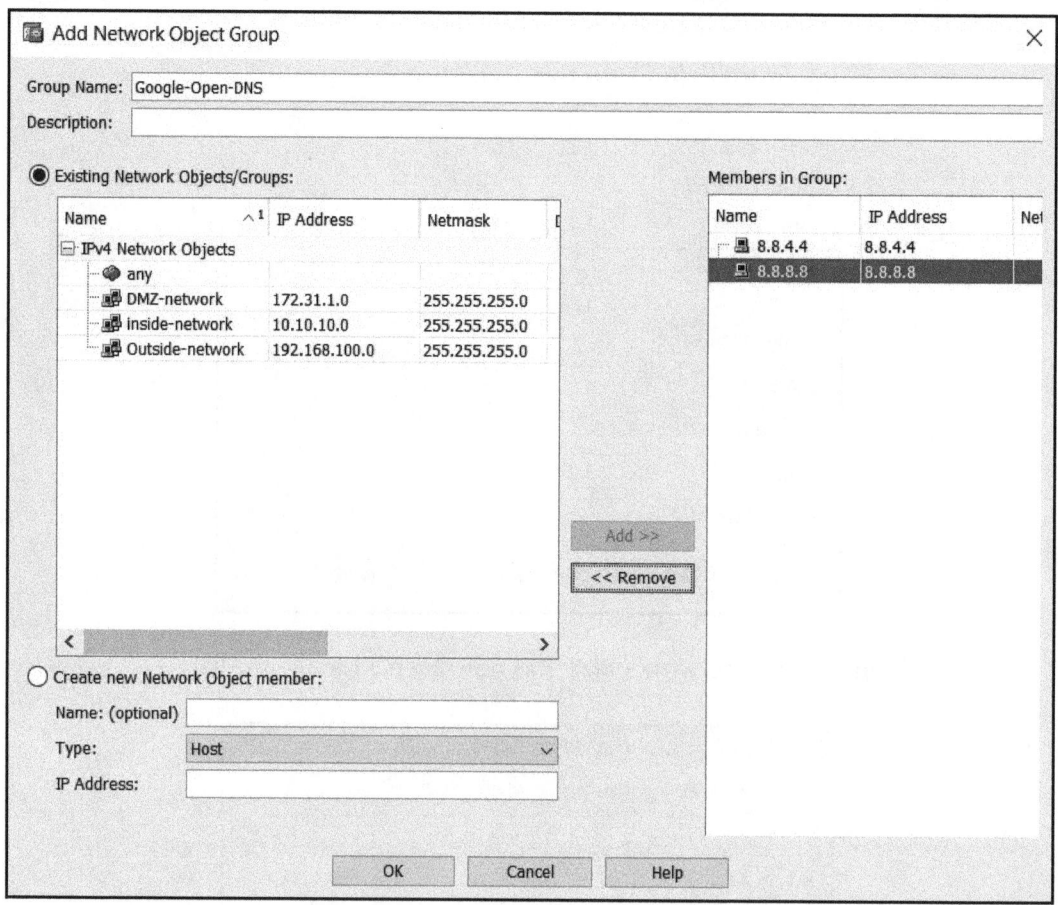

Once added successfully, you'll see a new section is created on the **Network Objects/Groups** window, called **IPv4 Network Objects/Groups**:

Configuring object groups using the CLI

The following configurations are used to create a network group named Google-Open-DNS with two host IP addresses as members:

```
ASA-1(config)# object-group network Google-Open-DNS
ASA-1(config-network)# network-object host 8.8.4.4
ASA-1(config-network)# network-object host 8.8.8.8
```

We can verify the information on the ASA has been added successfully by using the show running-config object command:

```
ASA-1(config)# show running-config object
object-group network Google-Open-DNS
 network-object host 8.8.4.4
 network-object host 8.8.8.8
```

Service Groups

Service Groups are similar to **Network Objects/Groups**, but the difference is that they only contain protocols, such as HTTP, HTTPS, IP, ICMP, SMTP, and FTP, and not network/IP information.

To access the service group configuration on the ASDM, navigate to **Configuration** |
Firewall | **Objects** | **Service Groups**:

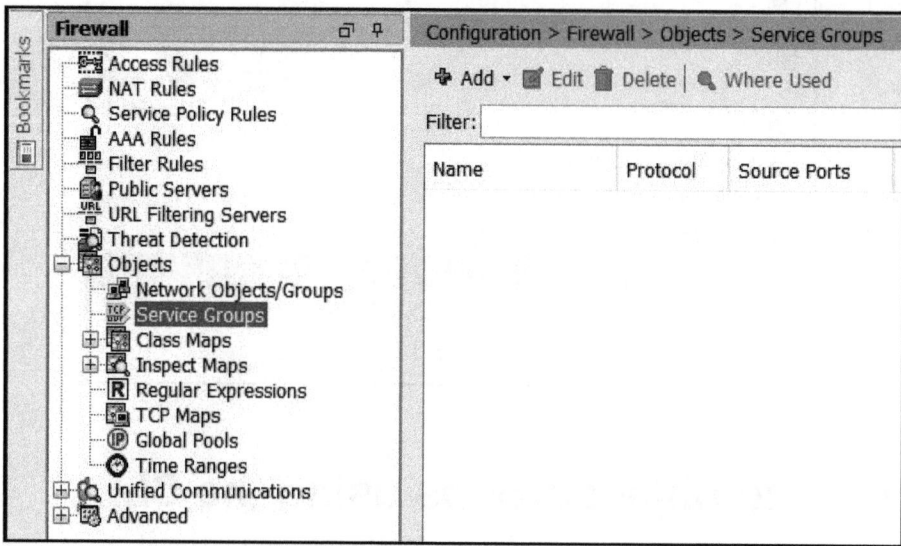

To add a new service group, click on **Add**. You'll be presented with a few options:

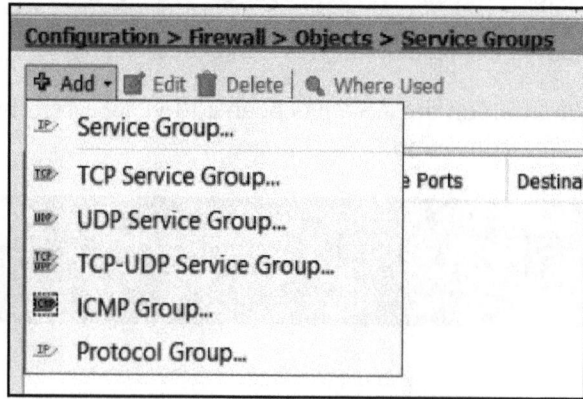

These options will help categorize the services for you. An example, the **TCP Service Group...** will only display the TCP services supported by the ASA:

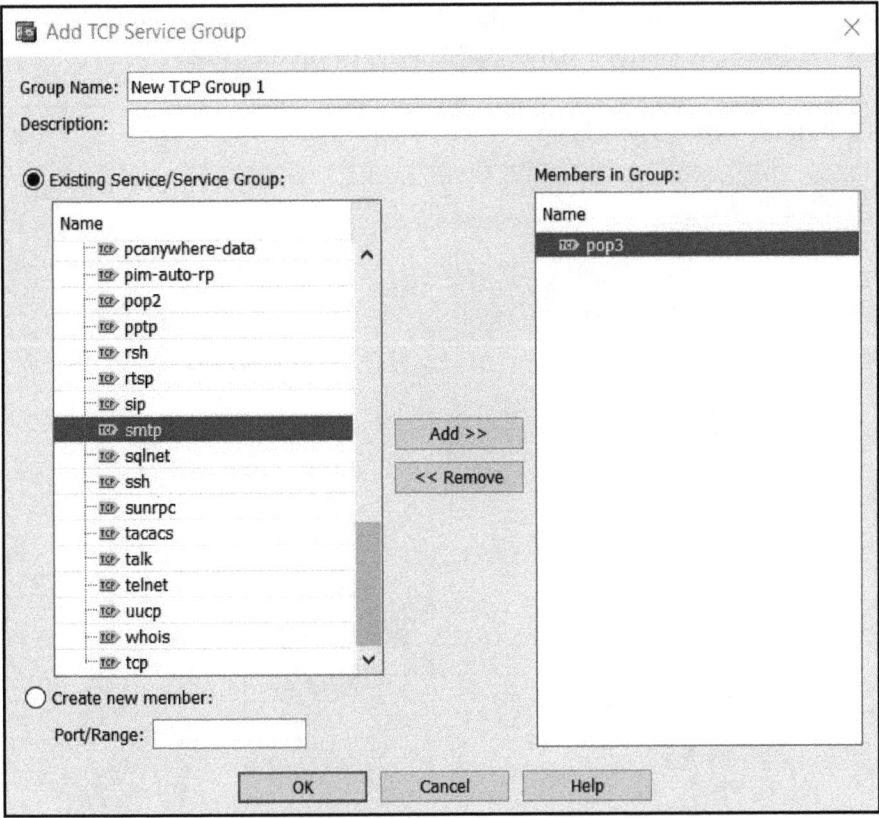

The same concept would apply for the other options as well.

The **Service Group...** option contains all the services the ASA currently supports. As mentioned previously, the **TCP Service Group...** would contain only the TCP services. The **UDP Service Group...** contains only UDP services. The **TCP-UGP Service Group...** contain services that use both TCP and UDP for their transportation, such as **DNS**. The following window shows the services that are the TCP-UDP type on the ASA:

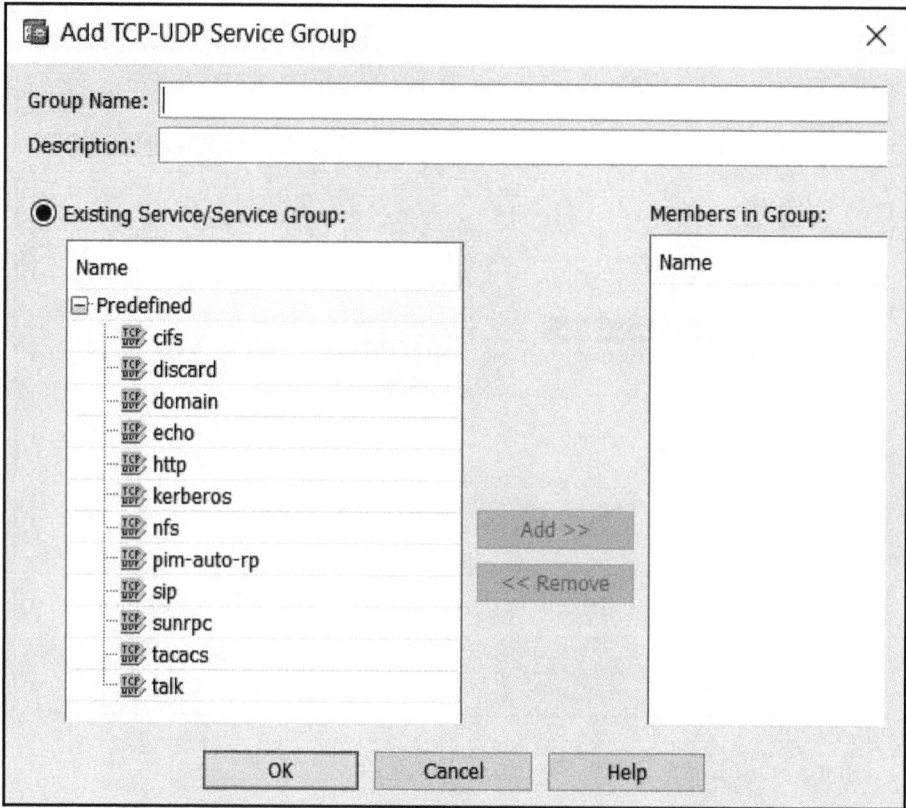

The **ICMP Group...** contains all the ICMP-type messages:

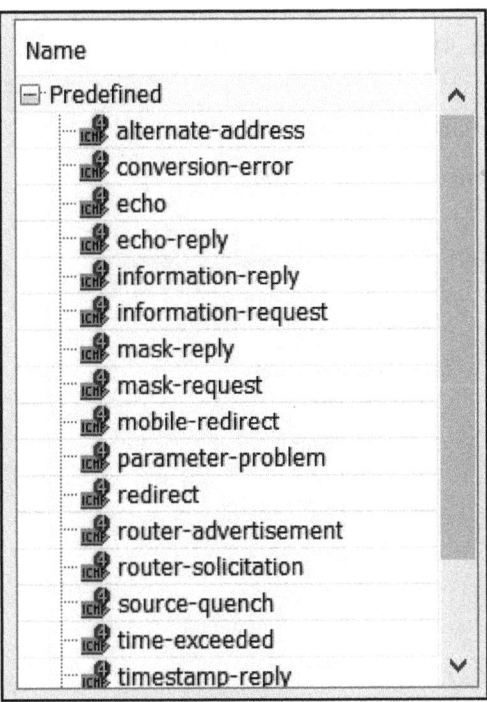

Finally, the protocol group contains all the protocols the ASA currently supports:

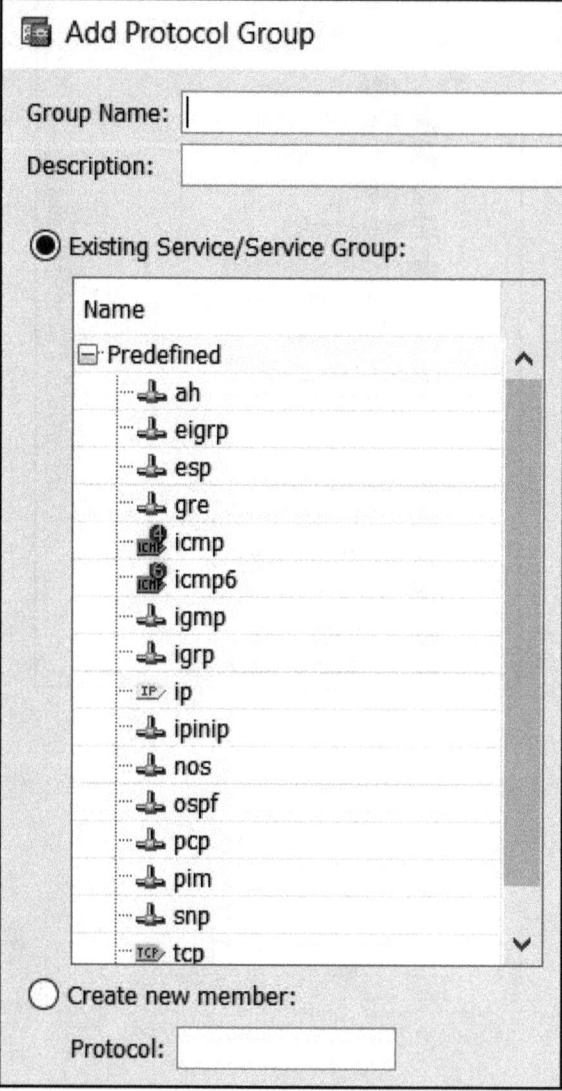

Creating policies on the ASA

In this section, we are going to take a look at how to create and apply policies on the ASA.

Modular Policy Framework

The **Modular Policy Framework** (**MPF**) is used to identify which traffic to inspect or to apply an action. To apply the MPF within the ASA, the traffic type needs to be inspected first by the ASA using a **Class Map**. Then, an action has to be applied, such as whether to permit or deny using a **Policy Map**. Last, we need to tell the ASA where to apply the policy using a **Service Map**.

Creating a policy

To create a policy on the ASA, there are two methods: the ASDM or the CLI.

Example 1 – Inspecting FTP traffic from Outside to DMZ (using the CLI)

Observing the following topology, there are three zones: **Inside**, **Outside**, and **DMZ**. Assuming the server on the DMZ is an FTP server, we would like to inspect the traffic flow through the DMZ interface:

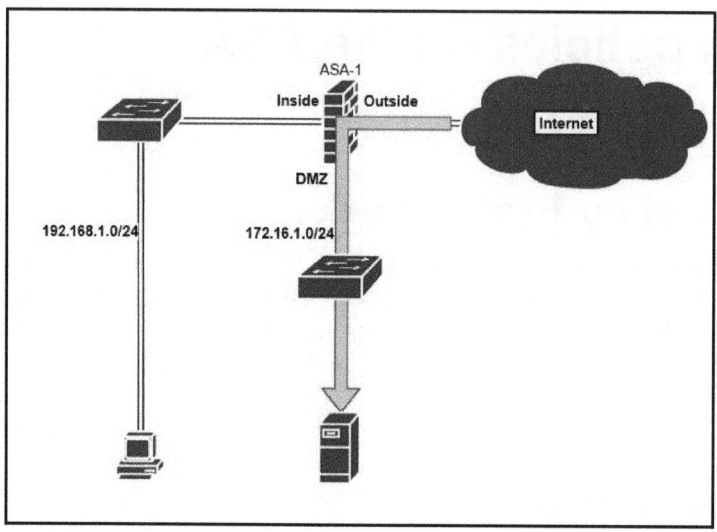

To get started with the configurations, we can use the following steps:

1. Create an Extended ACL to filter the FTP traffic type:

   ```
   ASA-1(config)# access-list DMZ-MPF permit tcp any any eq ftp
   ```

2. Create a Class Map to inspect/police the traffic using the ACL:

   ```
   ASA-1(config)# class-map FTP-Class-MAP
   ASA-1(config-cmap)# match access-list DMZ-MPF
   ASA-1(config-cmap)# exit
   ```

3. Create a Policy Map to Apply an action to the Traffic:

   ```
   ASA-1(config)# policy-map FTP-Policy-Map
   ASA-1(config-pmap)# class FTP-Class-MAP
   ASA-1(config-pmap)# exit
   ```

4. Apply the Policy to an interface:

   ```
   ASA-1(config)# service-policy FTP-Policy-Map interface DMZ
   ```

To verify the configuration, the `show running-config class-map` command will display all the Class Maps on the ASA:

```
ASA-1(config)# show running-config class-map
!
class-map FTP-Class-MAP
 match access-list DMZ-MPF
class-map inspection_default
 match default-inspection-traffic
!
```

The `show running-config policy-map` command displays all the Policy Maps on the ASA:

```
ASA-1(config)# show running-config policy-map FTP-Policy-Map
!
policy-map FTP-Policy-Map
 class FTP-Class-MAP
!
```

The `show running-config service-policy` command shows where on the ASA the policy has been applied:

```
ASA-1(config)# show running-config service-policy | include FTP
service-policy FTP-Policy-Map interface DMZ
```

Last, the `show access-list` command show the access-lists on the ASA:

```
ASA-1(config)# show access-list | include DMZ
access-list DMZ-MPF; 1 elements; name hash: 0x7a59e683
access-list DMZ-MPF line 1 extended permit tcp any any eq ftp (hitcnt=0) 0xbf97a7ae
```

Example 2 – Inspecting FTP traffic from Outside to DMZ (using the ASDM)

In this exercise, we are going to configure the ASA using the ASDM to inspect incoming FTP traffic that is originating from the Outside zone to the DMZ. The following topology will be used as its the same from the previous example:

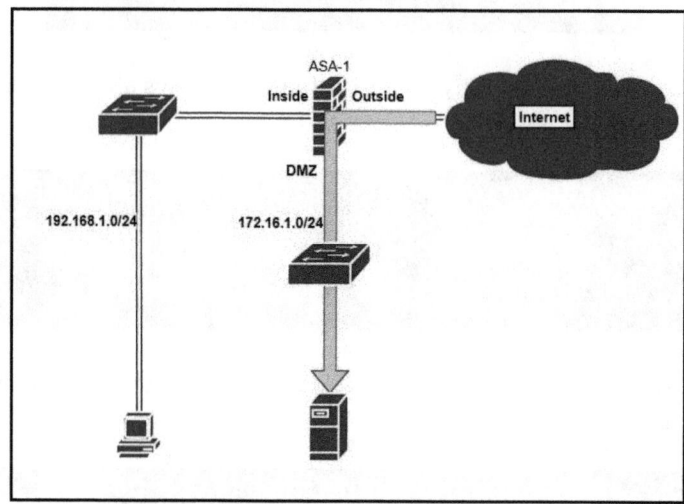

Let's begin:

1. Navigate to **Configuration | Firewall | Service Policy Rules** on the ASDM and click on **Add**:

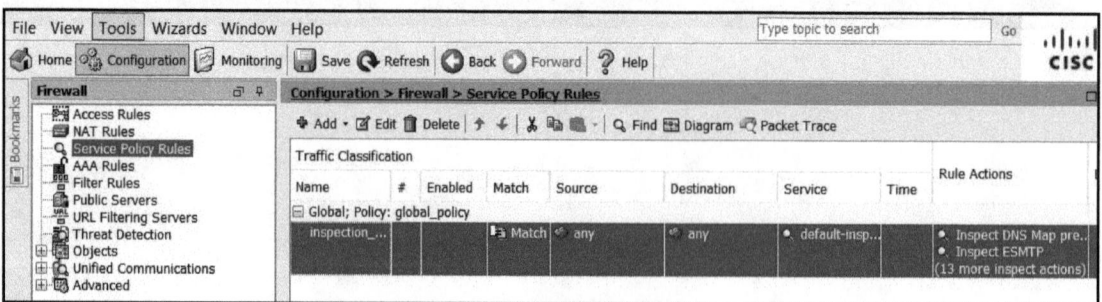

2. The **Add Service Policy Rule Wizard** opens, Select the **Interface** and create a name for the service policy:

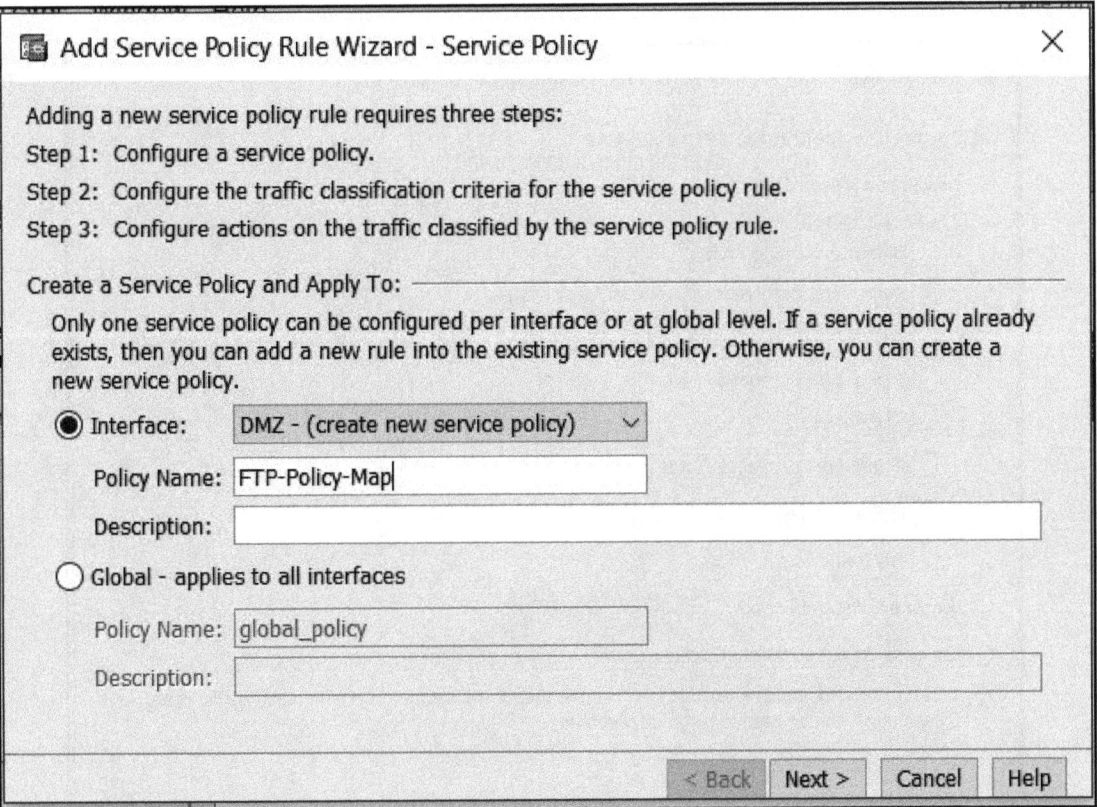

3. Once you selected the interface and set a name, click **Next**.

4. The traffic class window will appear, create a name for the Class Map, and select the traffic match criteria:

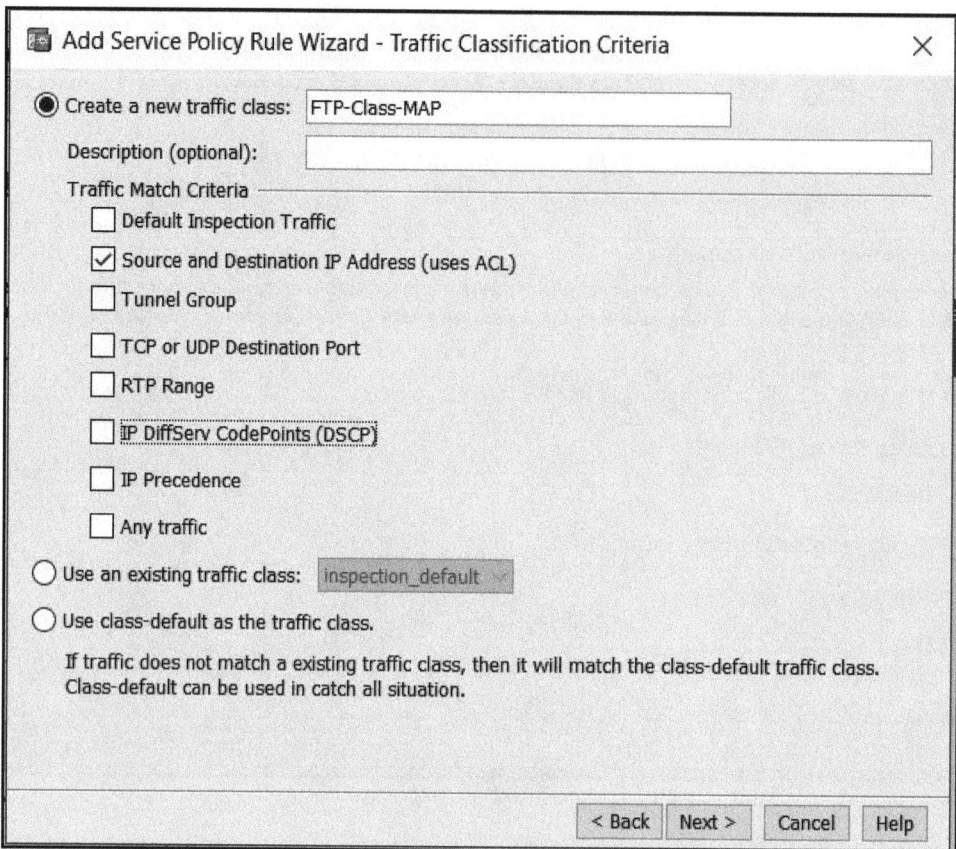

5. Clicking **Next** will display the ACL rule-creation window:

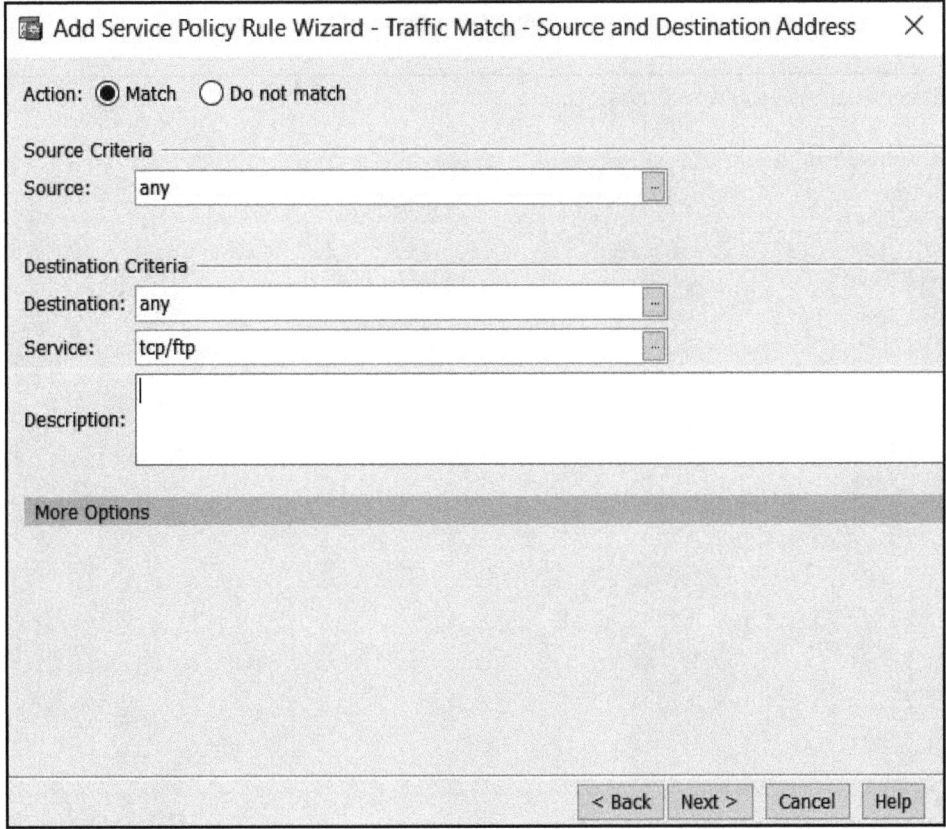

6. Ensure the appropriate traffic type is selected on the **Service** field. Once completed, click **Next**.

7. The protocol inspection window appears, select **FTP**, and click on **Finish**:

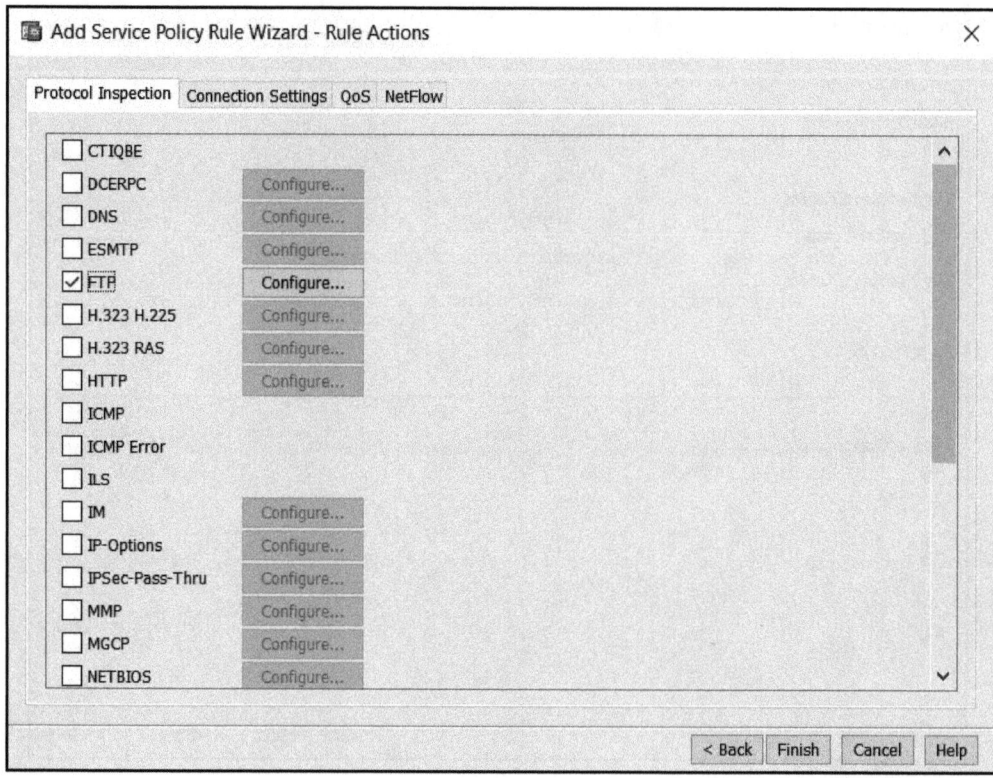

8. On the main **Service Policy Rules** window, the new service policy is presented:

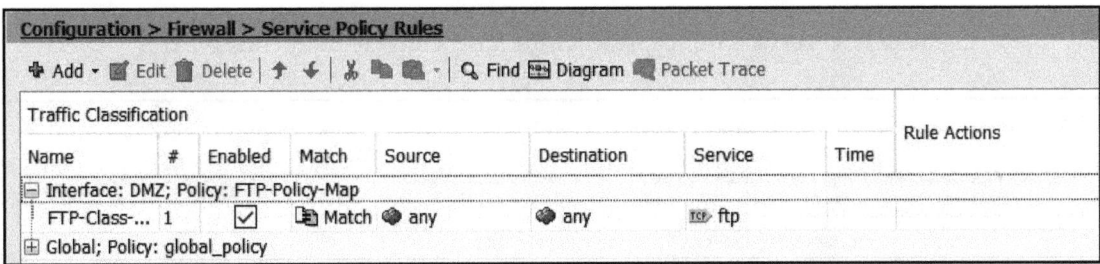

Example 3 – Preventing a SYN Flood attack

A SYN Flood attack is when a malicious user sends only TCP SYN packets to a device in the hope that it will create a **Denial of Service** (**DoS**) attack. For every SYN packet sent to a device, the device would reply with a SYN/ACK, and the return packet would be a final ACK packet. However, with a SYN Flood, the attacker does not respond to the SYN/ACK packets, therefore the victim machine will always be half-open and have connections that are not completed, eventually causing a denial of service for any legitimate users.

In this example, we're going to take a look at how to prevent a SYN Flood attack using the ASDM:

1. Create a new service policy, select interface: Outside, and click **Next.**:

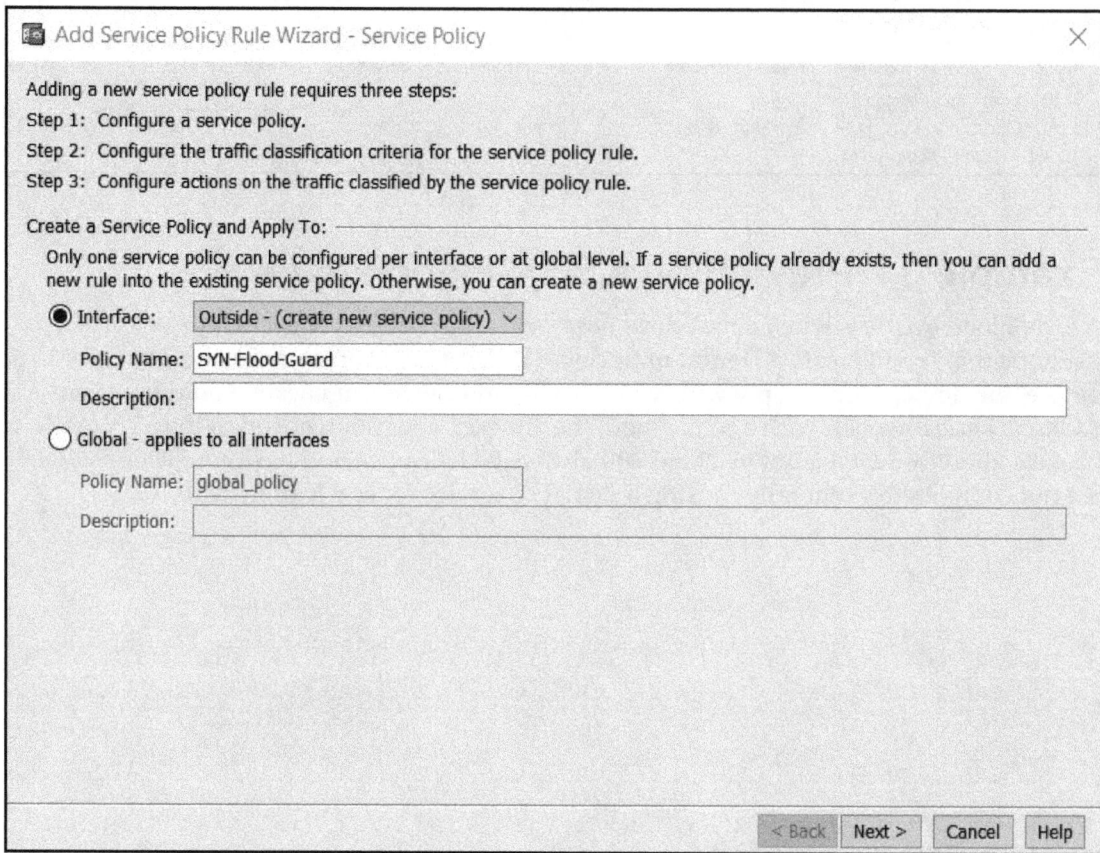

2. The Traffic Class window appears, create a name for the traffic, select **TCP or UDP Destination Port**, and click **Next**:

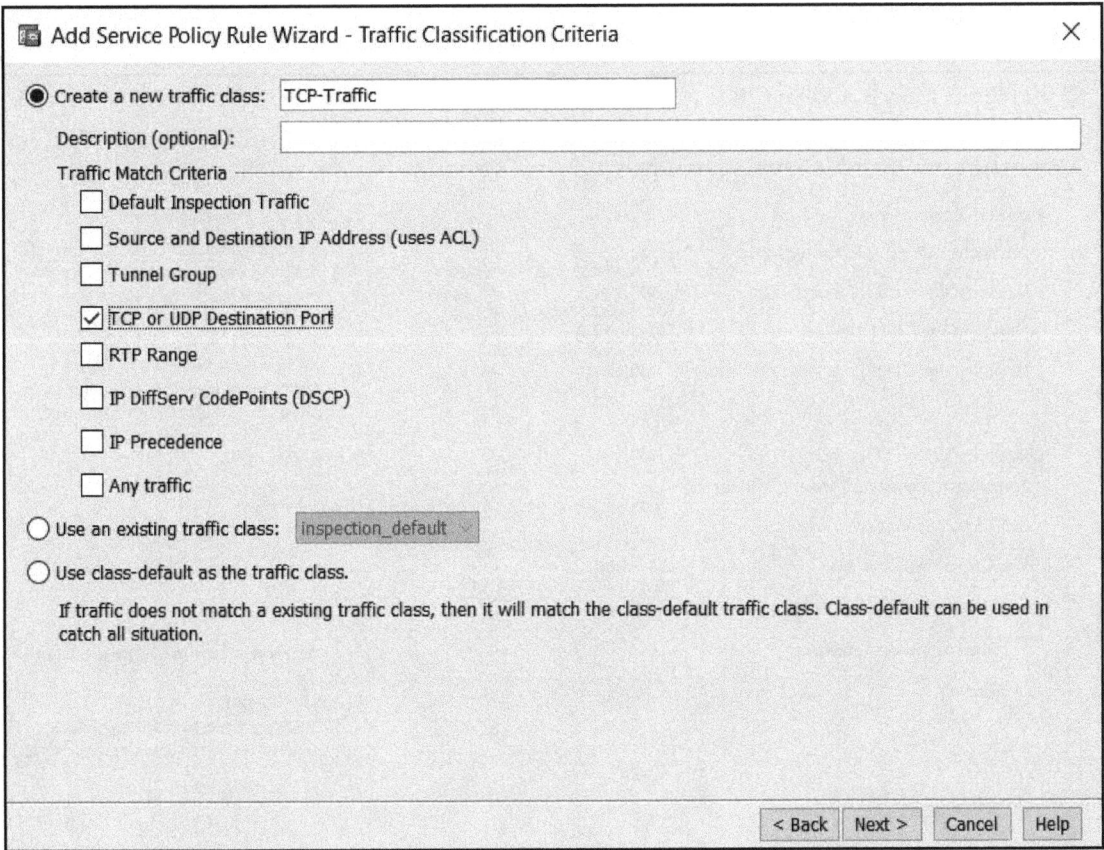

3. Select TCP as the protocol, set the range of the port as 1-65535, and Click **Next**:

4. Select the **Connection Setting** Tab. Limit the **Maximum TCP & UDP Connections** to **400**, **Maximum Embryonic Connections** to **50**, **Embryonic Connection Timeout** to **00:01:00**, and **Half-Closed Connection Timeout** to **00:05:00**:

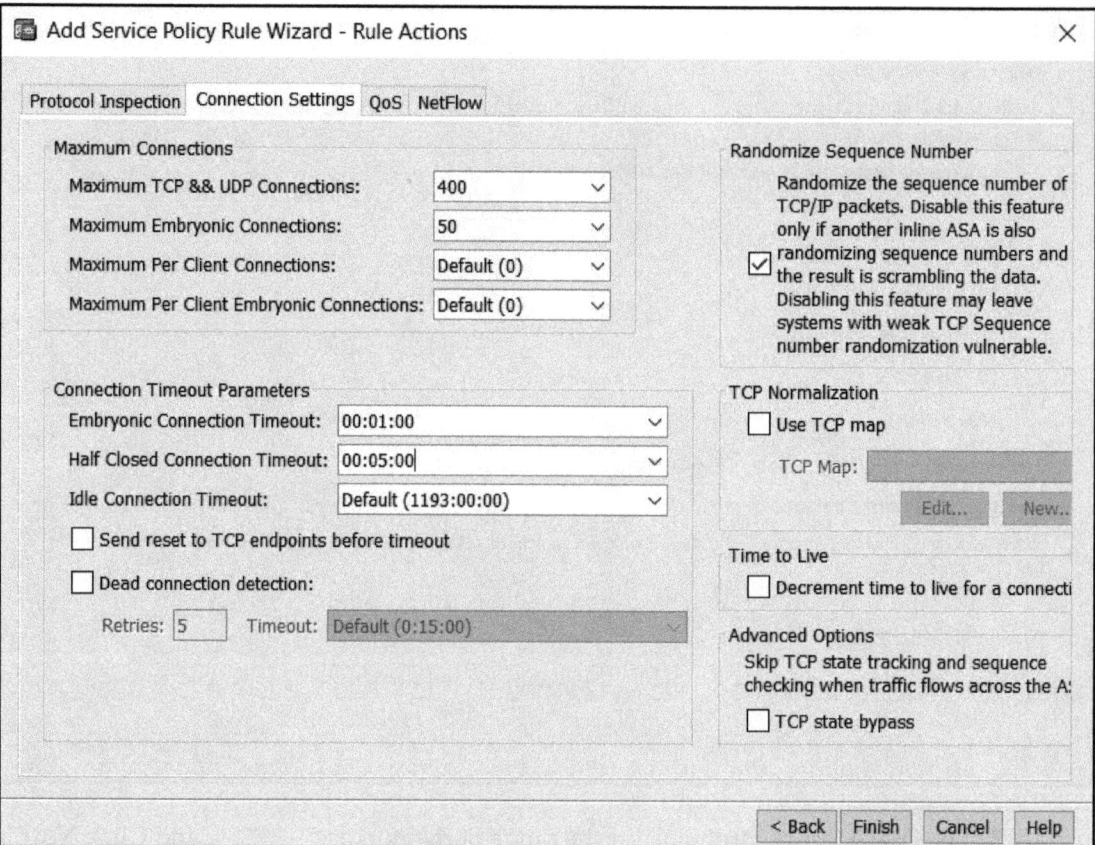

 An embryonic connection is when a connection request has not completed the handshake, such as a SYN scan or a SYN Flood attack.

5. Click **Finish**.

The wizard will take us back to the main **Service Policy Rules** window:

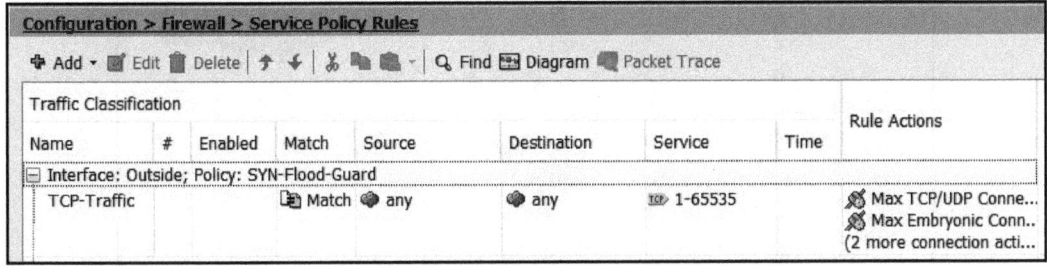

Here we can see the services policies on the ASA.

Advanced NAT configurations

In this section, we are going to a take a look at both static and dynamic NAT, exploring their purpose and configurations.

Static NAT

Static NAT is generally used to provide access from the **Outside** zone, such as the internet, to a server on the DMZ of your corporate network.

Let's observe the following topology, there's one server on the DMZ, assuming its IP address is `172.16.1.50`, however, users on the internet would require access to the server and the FTP service:

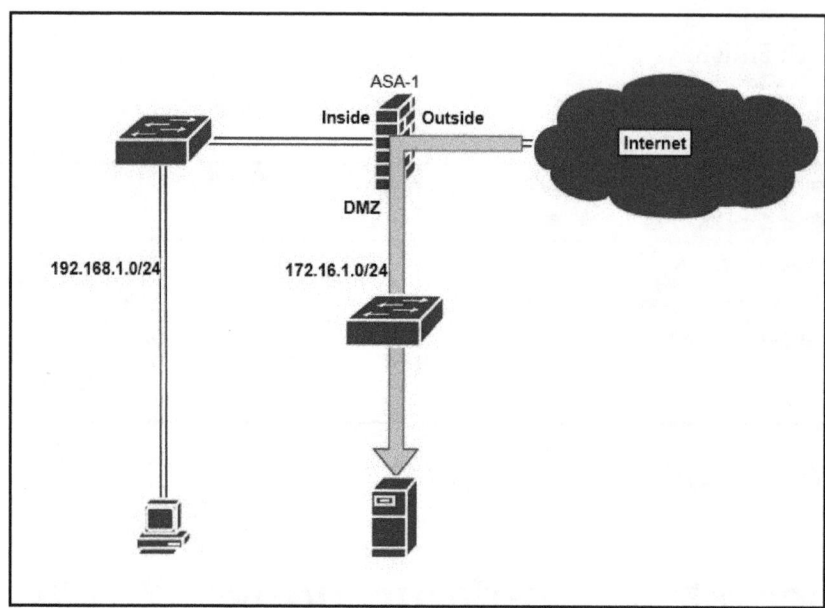

To configure static NAT on the ASA using the CLI, the following steps will guide us through the process:

1. Create a network object, add the server as an object, and create the NAT rule:

```
ASA-1(config)# object network DMZ-SVR
ASA-1(config-network-object)# host 172.16.1.50
ASA-1(config-network-object)# nat (dmz,outside) static 200.1.1.1
ASA-1(config-network-object)# exit
```

2. Create an Extended ACL to permit IP traffic from anywhere to the server only:

```
ASA-1(config)# access-list Out-DMZ extended permit ip any host
172.16.1.50
```

3. Apply the ACL on the Outside interface, filtering incoming traffic:

```
ASA-1(config)# access-group Out-DMZ in interface outside
```

4. create a service policy and apply it on the DMZ interface:

```
ASA-1(config)# policy-map global-policy
ASA-1(config-pmap)# class inspection_default
ASA-1(config-pmap-c)# access-list ICMP extended permit icmp any any
ASA-1(config)# access-group ICMP in interface dmz
```

Dynamic NAT

Unlike PAT, dynamic NAT allows an organization to use a block of public IP addresses to communicate on the internet. This block of public IP addresses is configured on the Outside interface of the ASA or the router.

The following configurations tell the ASA which are the public ranges of IP address that can be used and the internal network that is allowed to be translated:

1. Create an object group for the public addresses:

```
ASA-1(config)# object network Public-Addresses
ASA-1(config-network-object)# range 200.1.1.0 200.1.1.7
ASA-1(config-network-object)# exit
```

2. Create an object group for the internal network:

```
ASA-1(config)# object network Dynamic-NAT
ASA-1(config-network-object)# subnet 192.168.1.0 255.255.255.0
ASA-1(config-network-object)#nat (Inside,Outside) dynamic Public-Addresses
```

3. Create an ACL to allow the returning traffic:

```
ASA-1(config)# policy-map Global
ASA-1(config-pmap)# class inspection_default
ASA-1(config-cmap)# access-list ICMP extended permit icmp any any
ASA-1(config)# access-group ICMP in interface outside
```

Summary

We took a look at setting up routing to exchange networks between routers and firewalls, static and dynamic NAT configurations, understanding and configuring ACLs (standard, extended, and global), object groups and service policies, and finally further administration of the ASA using the ASDM.

In the next chapter, we'll introduce another firewall concept, known as the **Zone-Based Firewall** (**ZBF**). The ZBF will allow us to use a Cisco IOS router as a firewall.

12
Configuring Zone-Based Firewalls

In this chapter, we are going to discuss the **Cisco Common Classification Policy Language** (**C3PL**), its functions, components, and why it's important when configuring the Cisco IOS router to act as firewall on the network. Next, we'll dive into configuring a Zone-Based Firewall on a Cisco IOS router using both the **Cisco Configuration Professional** (**CCP**) software and the command-line interface.

The following topics will be covered in this chapter:

- Zone-Based Firewall terminologies
- Cisco Common Classification Policy Language
- Configuring a Zone-Based Firewall using CCP
- Configuring a Zone-Based Firewall via CLI

Zone-Based Firewall terminologies

In this section, we'll take a look at some of the terms used during the configuration of a **Zone-Based Firewall** (**ZBF**) and their meaning. Even though there aren't too many, the following are new for this chapter:

- **Zones**: A zone is a security segment on a network. Each active interface on a firewall must be assigned to a security zone, such as Inside for the private local area network, Outside for any foreign network such as the internet, and DMZ for allowing traffic originating from an untrusted source to access devices on the internal network. As mentioned previously, the DMZ is a semi-trusted zone.

- **Zone pairs**: A zone pair is any two security zones that are paired together in a particular direction. If we want to monitor traffic originating from the Inside zone going to the Outside zone, we can simply create a zone pair named *in-to-out* that will be used to monitor the unidirectional flow of traffic. Each zone pair consists of a source of the traffic, the destination of the traffic, and a policy. The traffic policy is applied on the zone pair and not the interfaces when using a Zone based firewall.
- **Self Zone**: The self zone is the actual router device. Please note this particular zone is separate from the others and can define with policies as well.

Overview of Cisco Common Classification Policy Language

Cisco Common Classification Policy Language (**C3PL**) is made up of three main components. These are class maps, policy maps, and service policy. As mentioned previously, class map is used to identify traffic types between Layers 3 to 7 of the OSI model, the policy map specifies the actions to take on the traffic identified by the class maps, and the service policy activates the policy map and applies it to a zone pair on the ZBF. To simplify, C3PL allows the creation of traffic policies based on events, conditions, and actions on a Cisco IOS router, therefore making it into a ZBF.

Class maps

A class map is used to identify traffic types that are flowing across a security zone. An example would be if you are trying to identify HTTP traffic that is flowing from the Inside zone to the Outside zone, a class map would be able to achieve this function on the ZBF.

Class maps can identify traffic at Layer 3 (Network) and Layer 4 (Transport) of the OSI model. Class maps can group traffic based on an Access Group (ACL), Protocol (TCP, UDP, ICMP, and HTTP) and another class map.

Traffic can be matched based on `match-any` (meeting only one criterion) or `match-all` (meeting all criteria) for the traffic in the class map.

Policy maps

A policy map's function is to take an action on the matched traffic, such as *Inspect, Pass, Drop,* or *Log*.

 **Inspect**: This is the stateful packet inspection feature on the ZBF.
Log: Keeps an account of the sessions. This feature is only available when using the `drop` command.

Service policy

A service policy is the assignment of the policy map to a zone pair.

Configuring a Zone-Based Firewall

In this section, we are going to focus on setting up a ZBF using a Cisco IOS router. Before we begin, let's discuss the ZBF and its benefits. When we hear the word firewall, we usually think it's a dedicated appliance sitting on the network. This is true, however, Cisco's **Integrated Service Routers** (**ISRs**) has the ability to perform many more tasks than just routing. One main feature is the firewall aspect, which allows the router to not only forward packets but become a ZBF. This is convenient for companies that may not have the budget or need for a dedicated firewall appliance but would like to maximize the benefits of the Cisco ISR.

 To determine whether a router supports the ZBF features and functionality, you can use the **Cisco Feature Navigator** (`https://www.cisco.com/go/fn`).

With a ZBF, each interface is assigned to a Zone, either the Inside (private), DMZ, or the Outside (public) Zone. An inspection policy is applied to all traffic that flows between zone on the router.

When configuring a ZBF, the following are the general steps involved:

1. The interfaces of the router need to be configured with the appropriate IP scheme of your network topology and require membership to a particular security zone.
2. Class maps need to be created to identify/inspect traffic types.

3. A policy map is used to determine what actions should be taken on the inspected traffic if a match is found using the class map.
4. Zone pairs let the router know which interfaces (zones) are involved in the inspection of traffic and s direction.
5. Use a service policy to apply the policy map to the zone pair of the router.
6. Assign the interfaces to the appropriate security zones.

Before we get started, you'll need to ensure you have the following:

- Cisco IOS router that supports ZBF features
- **Cisco Configuration Professional** (**CCP**) 2.8 or higher
- **Java Runtime Environment** (**JRE**) 1.6.0_11 or higher
- Adobe Flash Player (browser plugin)
- Internet Explorer

In this chapter, the following topology will be used for our exercise:

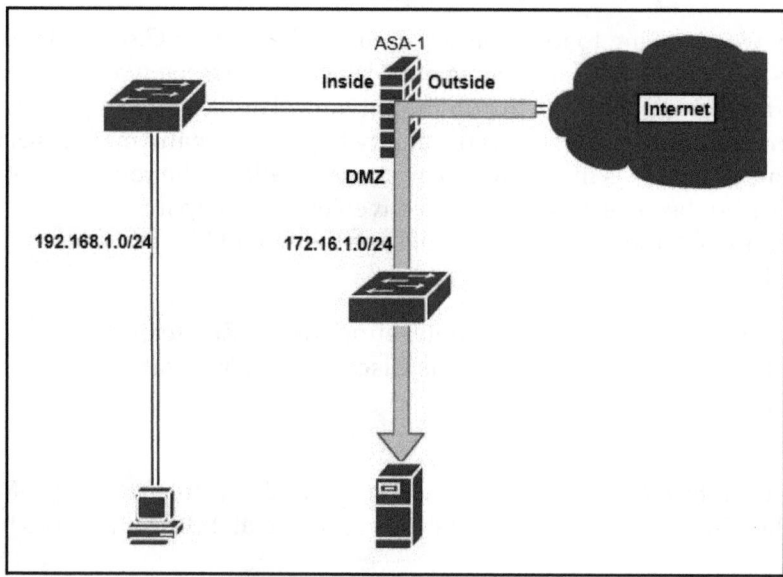

Let's get started with our configurations.

Configuring a Cisco IOS router to use Cisco Configuration Professional (CCP)

Please ensure the NAT is configured before setting up the router to act as a ZBF:

1. Configure IP addresses on the router:

```
R1#show running-config | section interface
interface FastEthernet0/0
 ip address 192.168.100.254 255.255.255.0
 duplex auto
 speed auto
interface FastEthernet0/1
 ip address 192.168.1.1 255.255.255.0
 duplex auto
 speed auto
interface FastEthernet1/0
 ip address 172.16.1.1 255.255.255.0
 duplex auto
 speed auto
```

2. Create a local user account for authentication:

```
R1(config)#username admin privilege 15 secret cisco123
```

3. Enable the HTTP server on the router. If you're using this option, traffic between CCP and the router will be unencrypted and is not recommended on networked devices:

```
R1(config)#ip http server
```

4. The recommended option: enable the HTTPS services instead of a secure connection. The traffic between CCP and the router will be encrypted.

```
R1(config)#ip http secure-server
```

5. Use the local user account to authenticate to the router using CCP:

```
R1(config)#ip http authentication local
```

6. Ensure there is connectivity between the PC and the router:

```
C:\>ping 192.168.100.254

Pinging 192.168.100.254 with 32 bytes of data:
Reply from 192.168.100.254: bytes=32 time=5ms TTL=255
Reply from 192.168.100.254: bytes=32 time=7ms TTL=255
Reply from 192.168.100.254: bytes=32 time=11ms TTL=255
Reply from 192.168.100.254: bytes=32 time=10ms TTL=255

Ping statistics for 192.168.100.254:
    Packets: Sent = 4, Received = 4, Lost = 0 (0% loss),
Approximate round trip times in milli-seconds:
    Minimum = 5ms, Maximum = 11ms, Average = 8ms
```

7. Verify there is internet connectivity between the router and the internet:

```
R1#ping 8.8.8.8

Type escape sequence to abort.
Sending 5, 100-byte ICMP Echos to 8.8.8.8, timeout is 2 seconds:
!!!!!
Success rate is 100 percent (5/5), round-trip min/avg/max = 48/68/80 ms
```

Using Cisco Configuration Professional (CCP) to configure the Zone-Based Firewall

In this section, we'll be using the CCP software, a free software from Cisco to enable and configure the ZBF feature on the Cisco IOS router. CCP will provide us with a Graphical User Interface that will make the configuration process a bit simpler.

Let's dive into the configurations and setup of the ZBF:

1. Download and install on the local PC. CCP is freely available at `https://www.cisco.com/`. Once installed, open it. The following window will be presented. Enter the router's **IP Address**, **Username**, and **Password** in the fields. If you've used the `ip http secure-server` command, ensure the **Connect Securely** feature is checked and click **OK**:

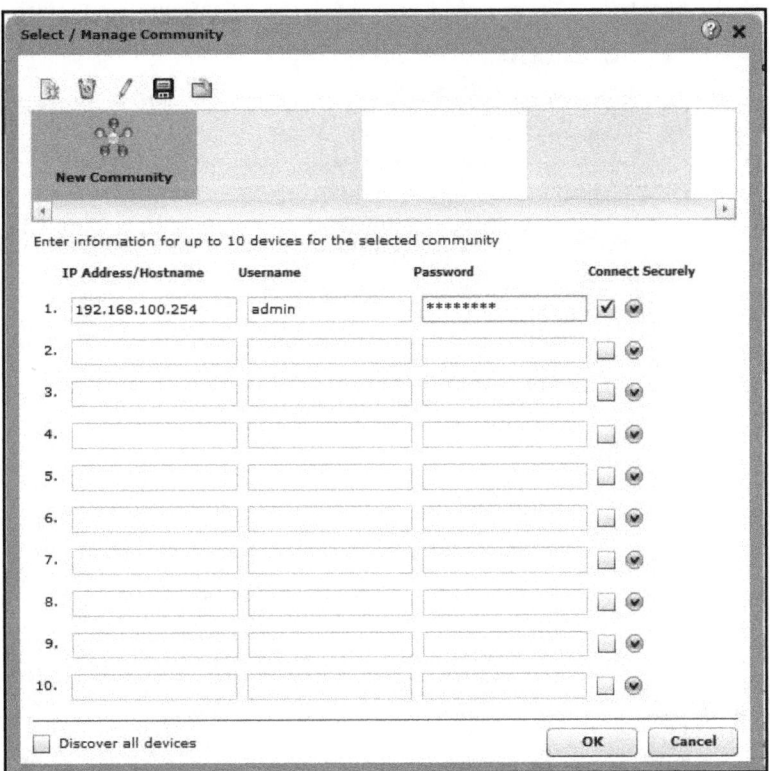

2. The following window displays all the devices CCP has saved in its memory. We can see there's only one entry: R1. Click on **Discover**, this will allow CCP to access and read the configurations of the router and present it in a GUI format on CCP:

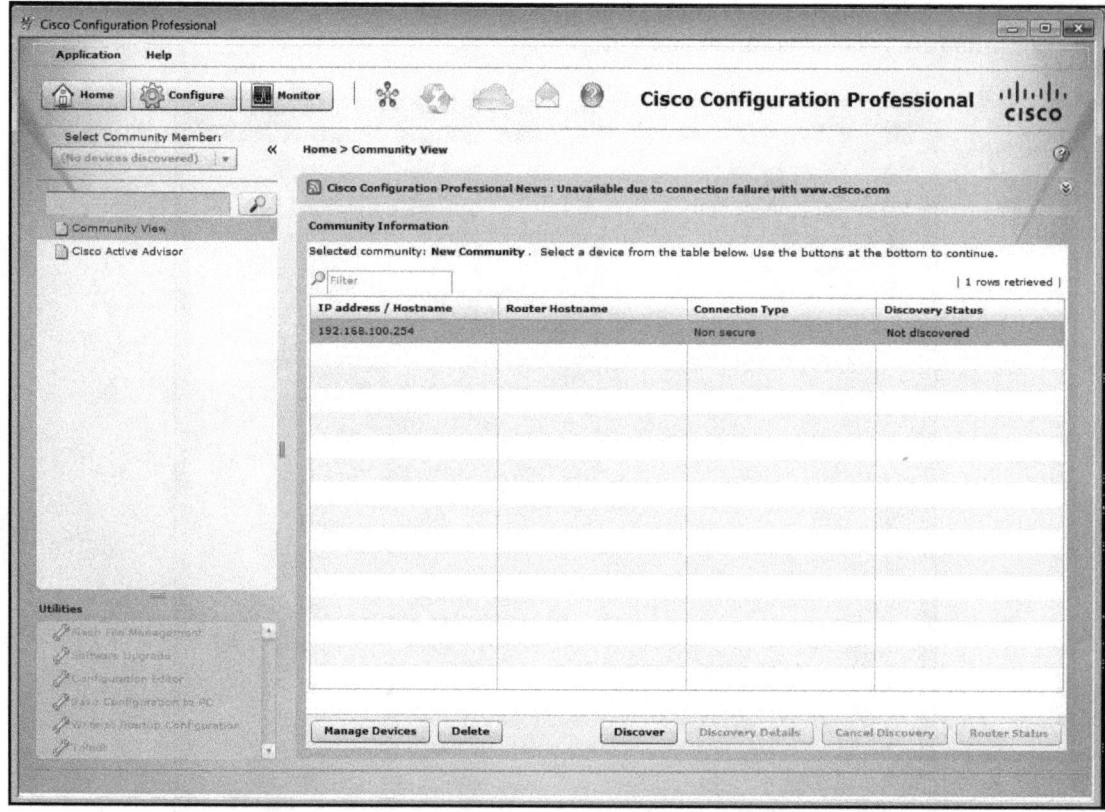

Upon clicking on **Discover**, the status is now set to **Discovering**. This should take a minute or two:

IP address / Hostname	Router Hostname	Connection Type	Discovery Status
192.168.100.254	R1	Non secure	Discovering...

When CCP has completed the discovery of the device and its configurations, the status will change to **Discovered with warnings** written in green as displayed here:

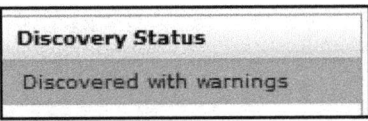

 If you see **Discovered with warnings**, don't be alarmed. It simply means some of the information is missing, but this won't prevent us from configuring the ZBF feature on the router.

3. Click on **Configure**. Here, we are presented with the GUI of the Cisco Configuration Professional (CCP) for administering the router and all its features:

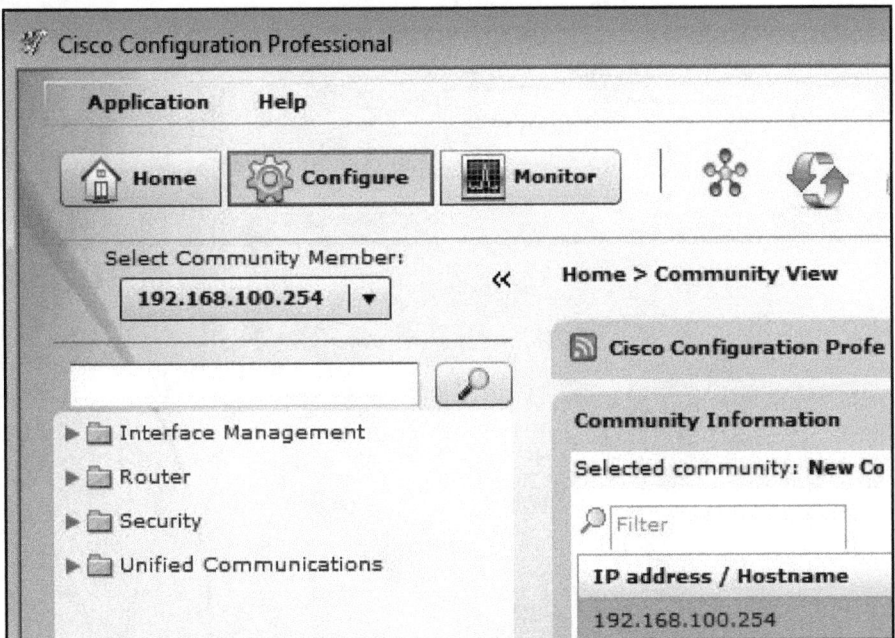

4. To set up the ZBF, navigate to **Configure** | **Firewall** | **Firewall**.

5. There are two options: **Basic Firewall** and **Advanced Firewall**. By clicking on either, the topology changes a bit to demonstrate the environment you may try to replicate:

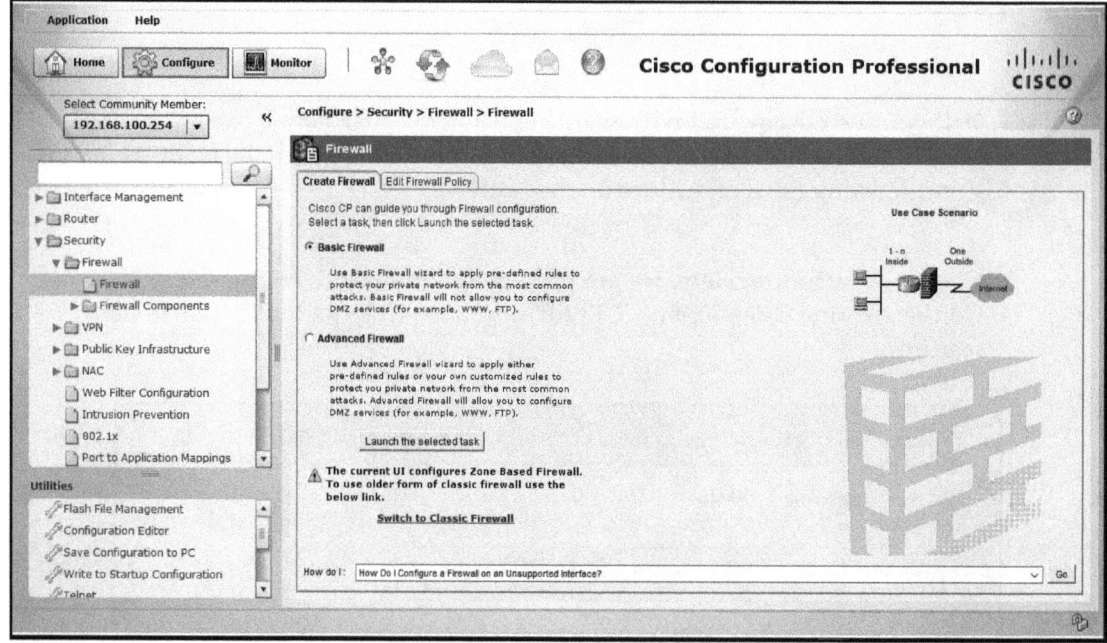

6. To configure a ZBF with a DMZ, select the **Advanced Firewall** option and click on **Launch the selected task**:

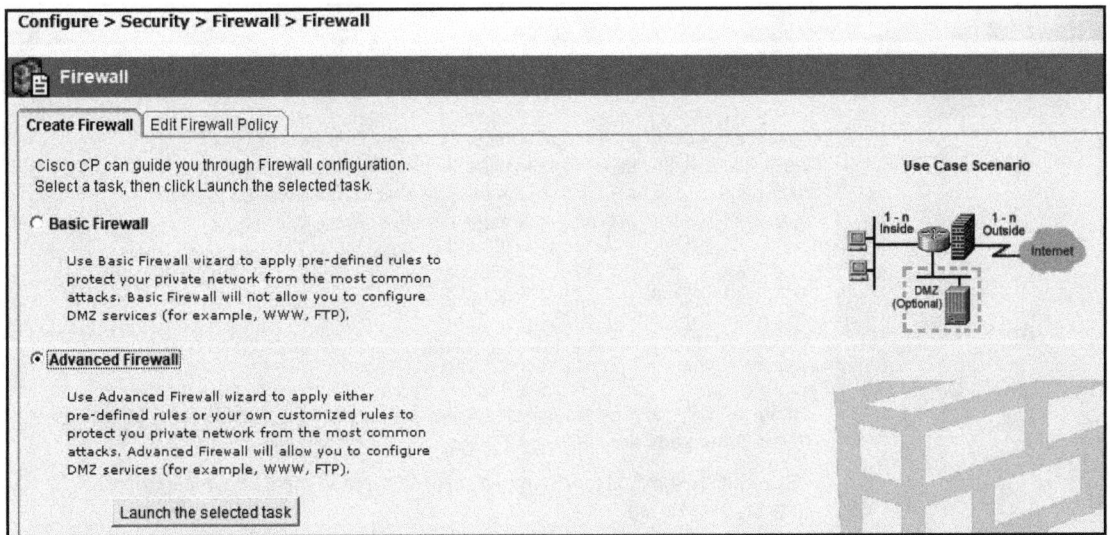

The following window will open, providing a description of the **Advanced Firewall Configurations** on the router:

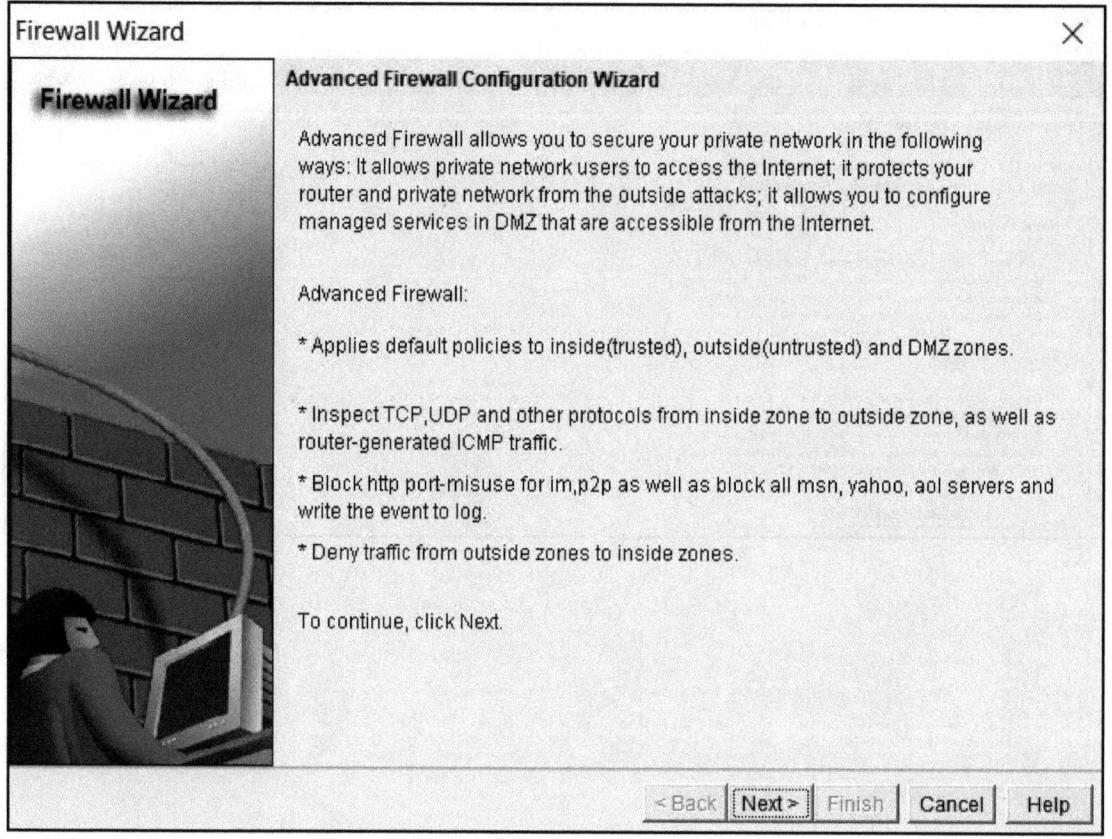

7. Click on **Next**. Select the interfaces you would like to identify as the Inside, Outside, and DMZ zones. This step is identifying the zones on the router. When you're finished, click on **Next**:

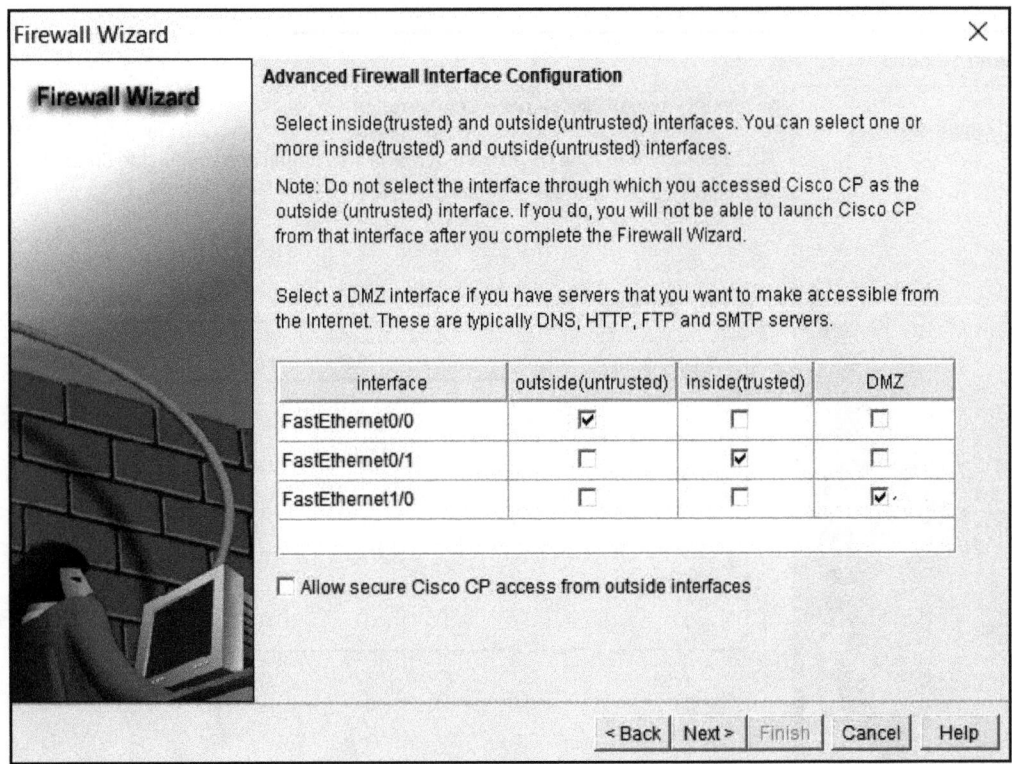

Firewall Wizard   ✕

Firewall Wizard

Advanced Firewall Interface Configuration

Select inside(trusted) and outside(untrusted) interfaces. You can select one or more inside(trusted) and outside(untrusted) interfaces.

Note: Do not select the interface through which you accessed Cisco CP as the outside (untrusted) interface. If you do, you will not be able to launch Cisco CP from that interface after you complete the Firewall Wizard.

Select a DMZ interface if you have servers that you want to make accessible from the Internet. These are typically DNS, HTTP, FTP and SMTP servers.

interface	outside(untrusted)	inside(trusted)	DMZ
FastEthernet0/0	☑	☐	☐
FastEthernet0/1	☐	☑	☐
FastEthernet1/0	☐	☐	☑

☐ Allow secure Cisco CP access from outside interfaces

< Back | Next > | Finish | Cancel | Help

Since there's a DMZ interface/zone, the next window will allow us to add specific devices with their services in this zone.

8. To add a device, click on **Add**:

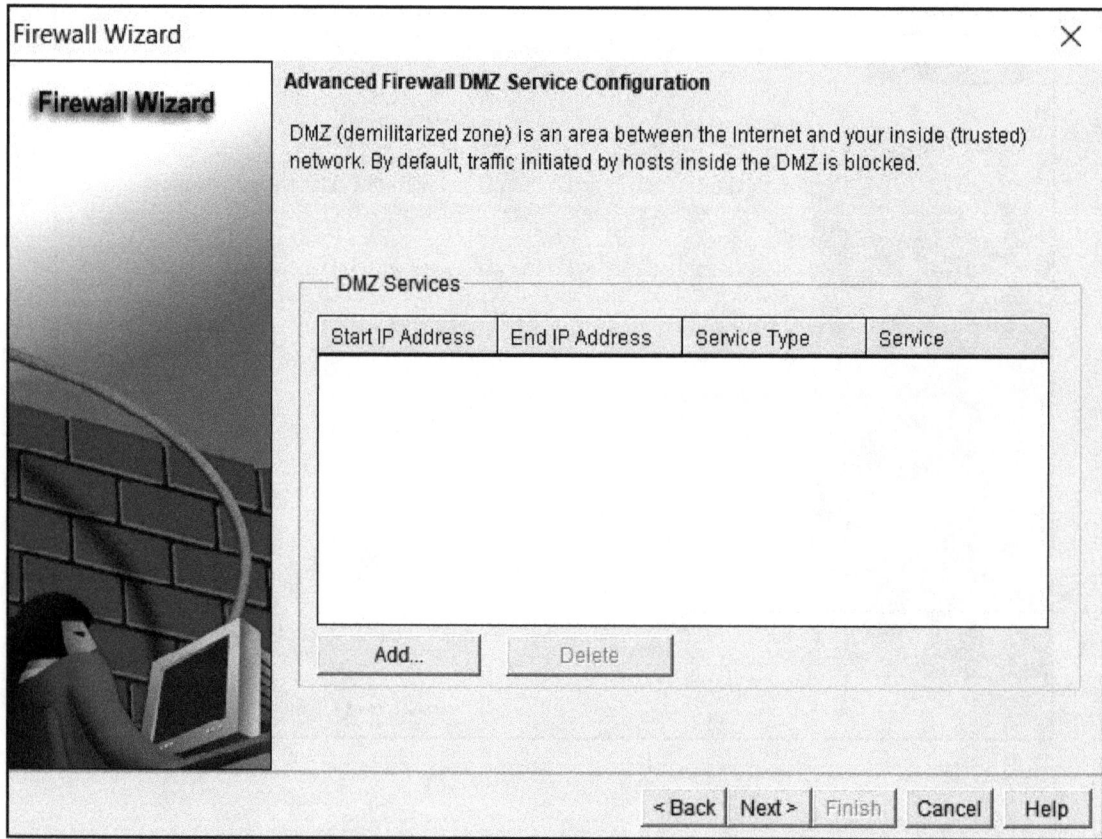

9. Specify the IP address, the protocol, and the service on the device:

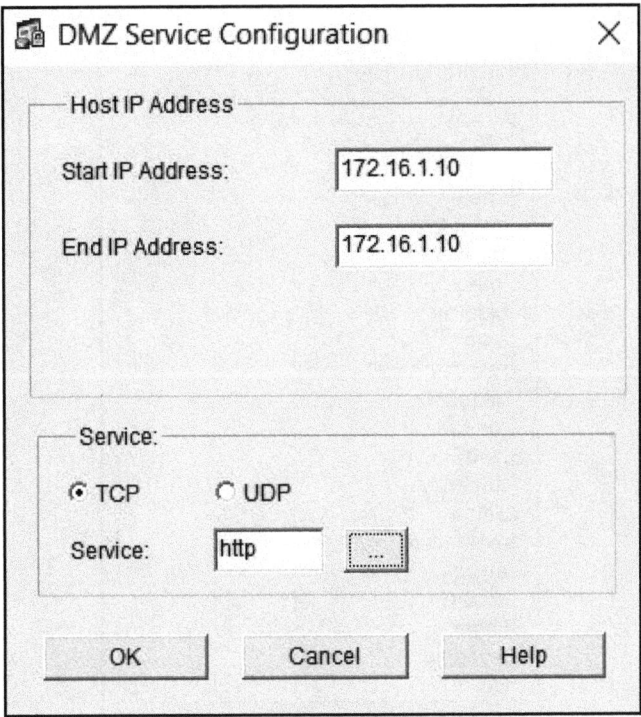

10. By clicking the ellipsis (...), the protocol window will open and display all the supported protocols on the router:

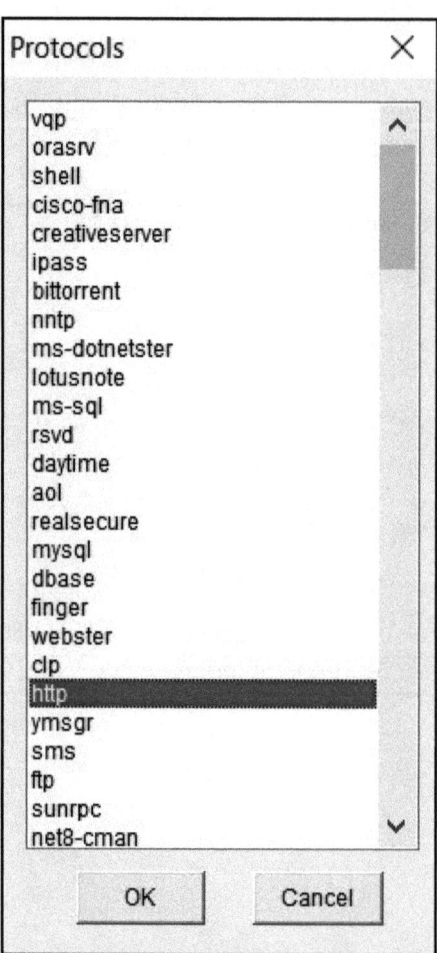

11. Click on **OK** to return to the DMZ configuration window on CCP:

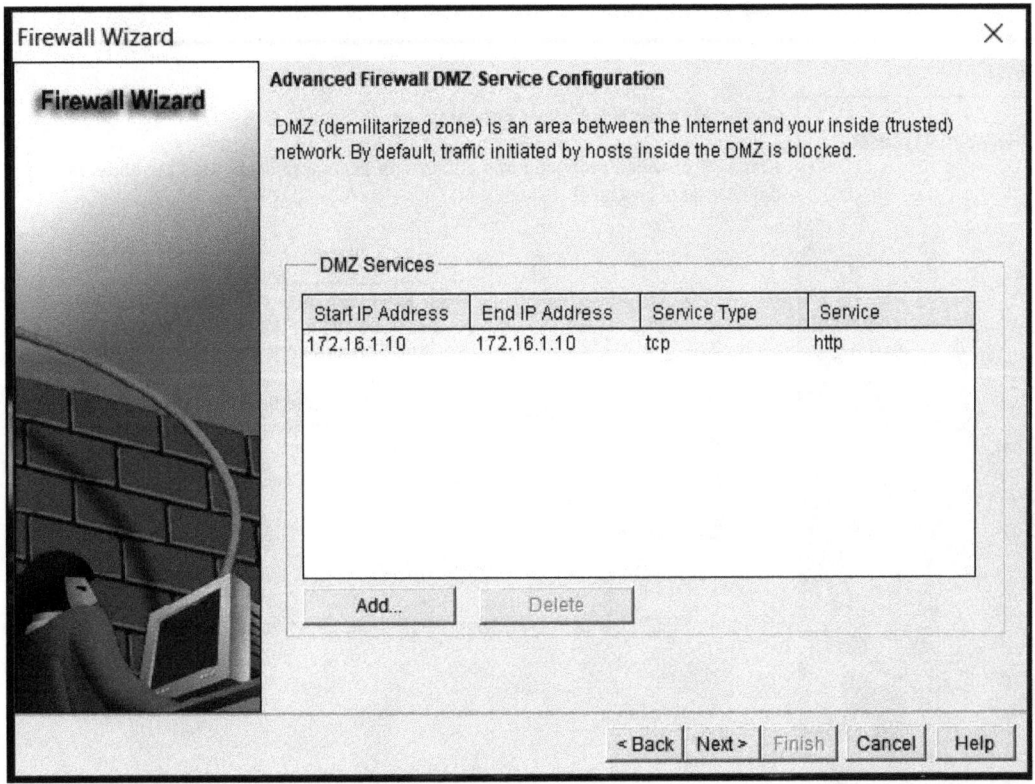

12. This window will ask which security level should be applied to the ZBF. By clicking each level, a description will be provided. Click **Next** again.

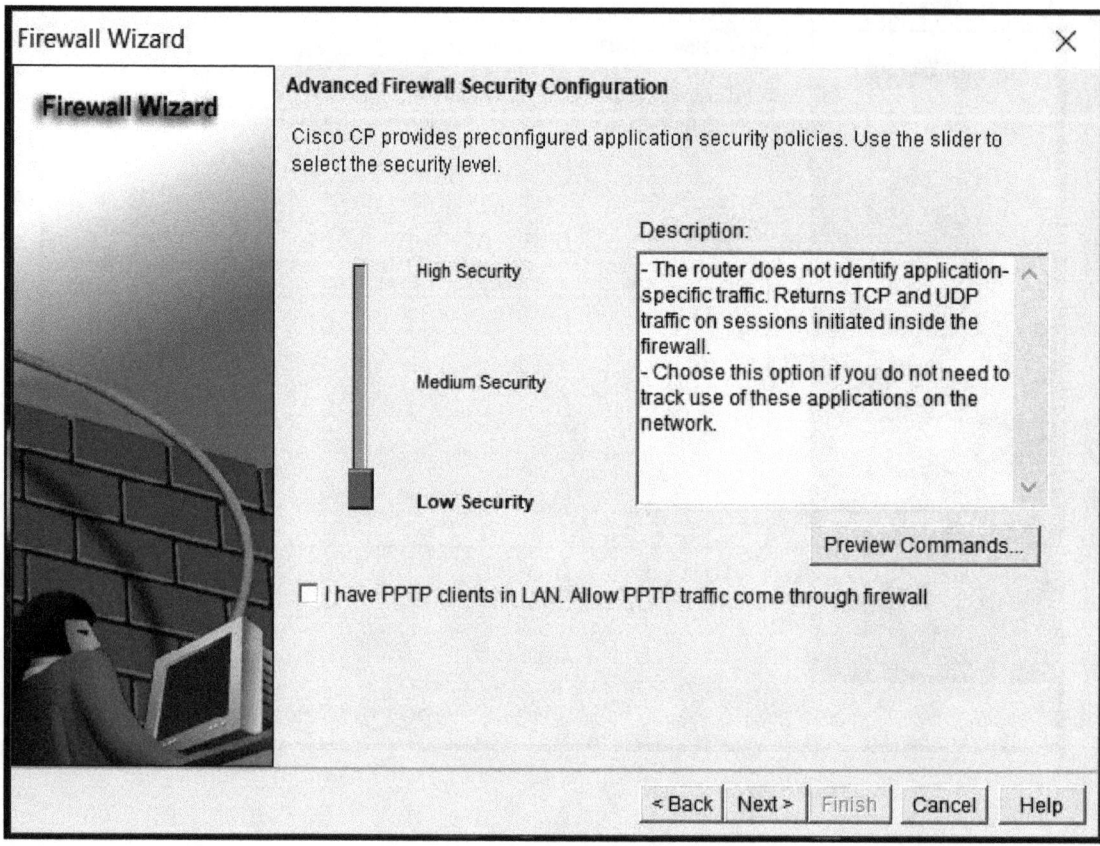

Take the time to read and compare the description of each security level.

13. The Firewall Configuration Summary window will display a summary of the configurations that will be applied to the router, making it a ZBF. Ensure you review before clicking on Finish. If you need to make an adjustment, use the **Back** button:

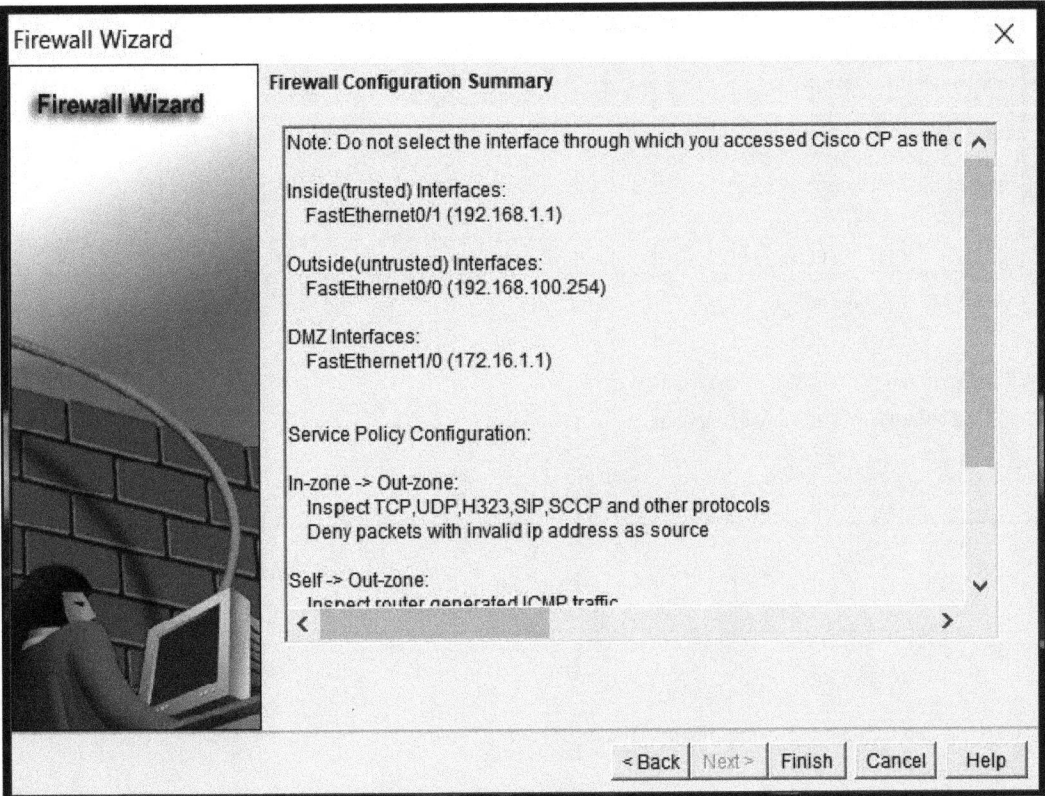

14. After clicking on **Finish**, the configurations are presented in the command-line format:

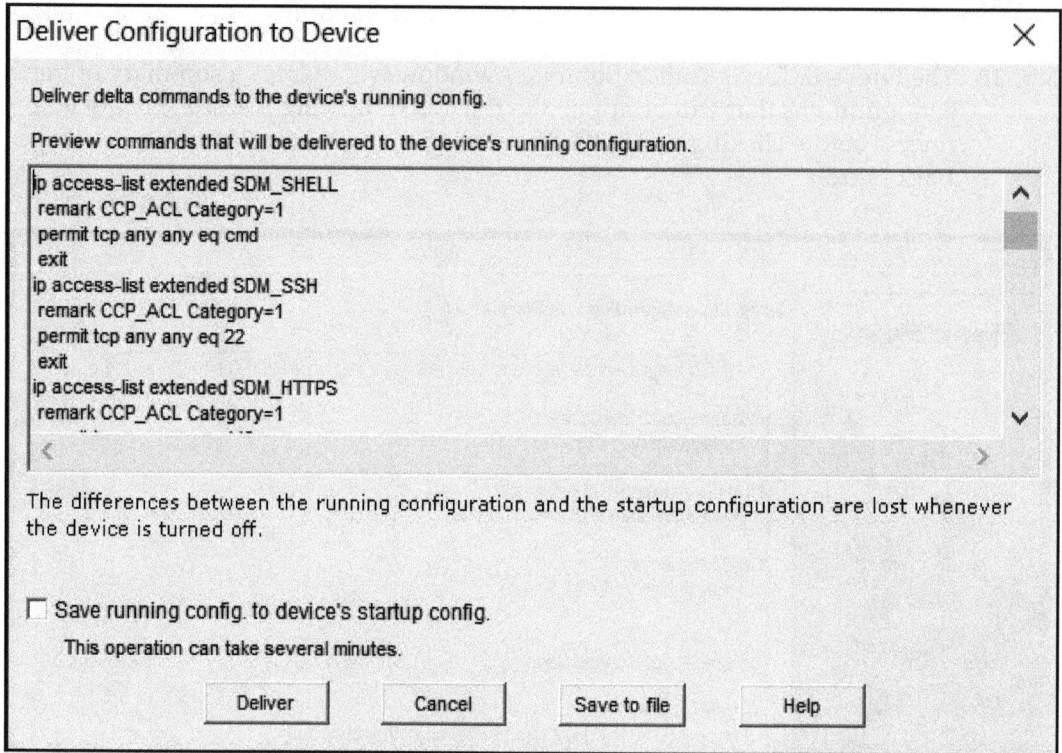

15. Click **Deliver** to push the configurations to the router.

16. Once everything is completed, navigate back to **Configure | Security | Firewall | Firewall** and click on the **Edit Firewall Policy** tab. This window will display the rules we have just configured using the wizard:

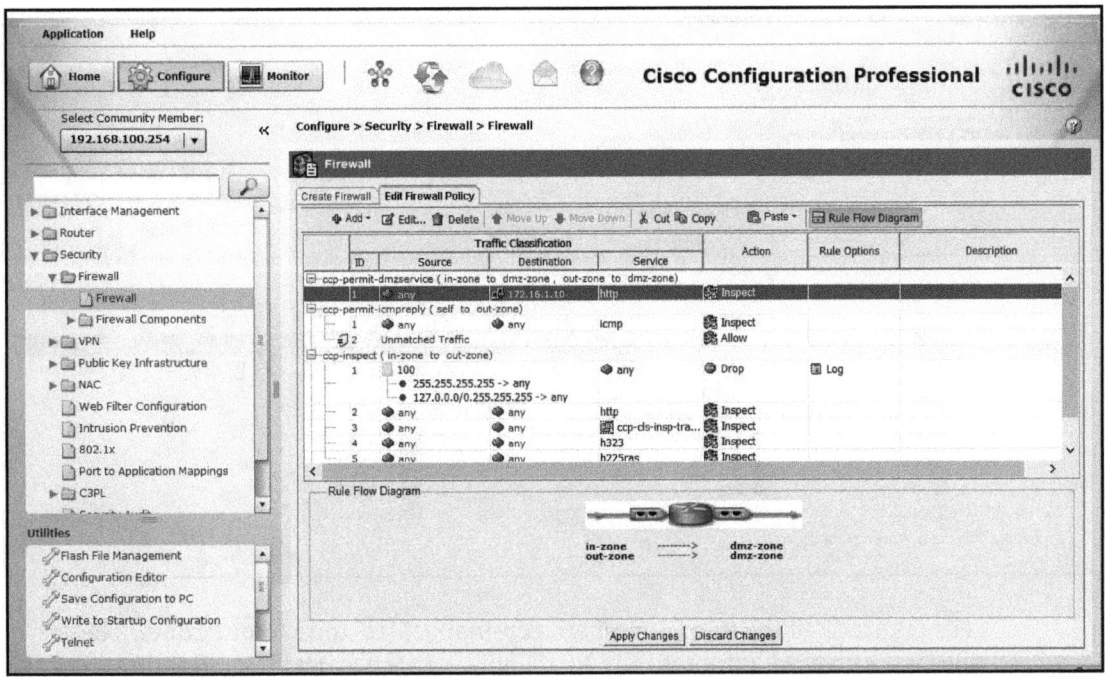

The rules are located in a unique section. Let's take a look at the first zone-pair, **ccp-permit-dmzservice**, traffic from any source to `172.16.1.0`, where the service is HTTP, will be inspected by the firewall. This means the ZBF will maintain information of the session and allow returning traffic:

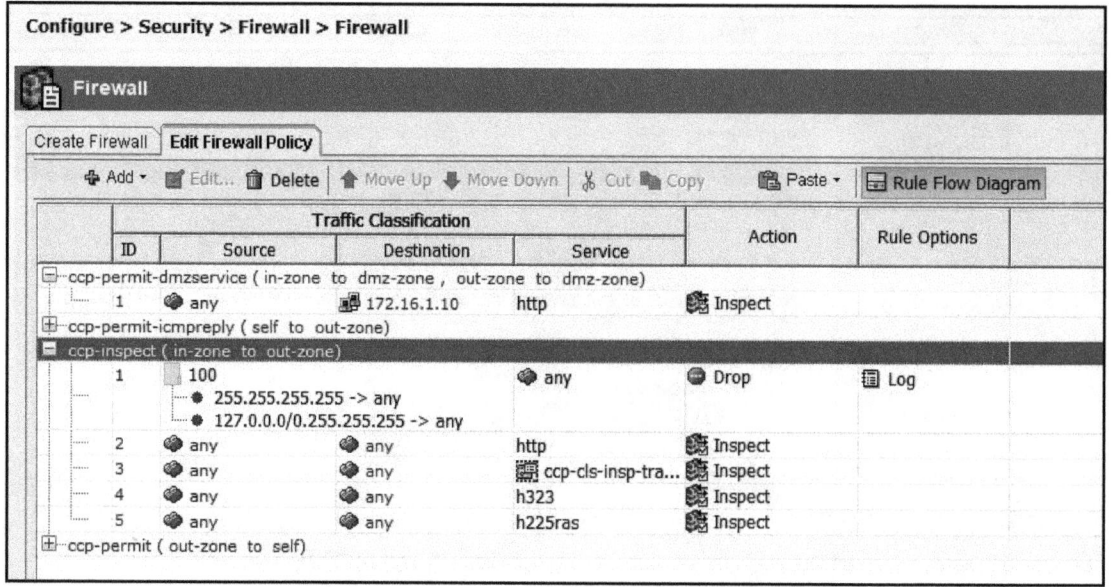

Let's take look at the third zone-pair, **ccp-inspect (in-zone to out-zone)**. These rules were created automatically by the wizard for any traffic originating from the Inside zone going to the Outside zone.

By hovering the cursor over the class-map, **ccp-cls-insp-traffic**, the list of traffic types is displayed briefly:

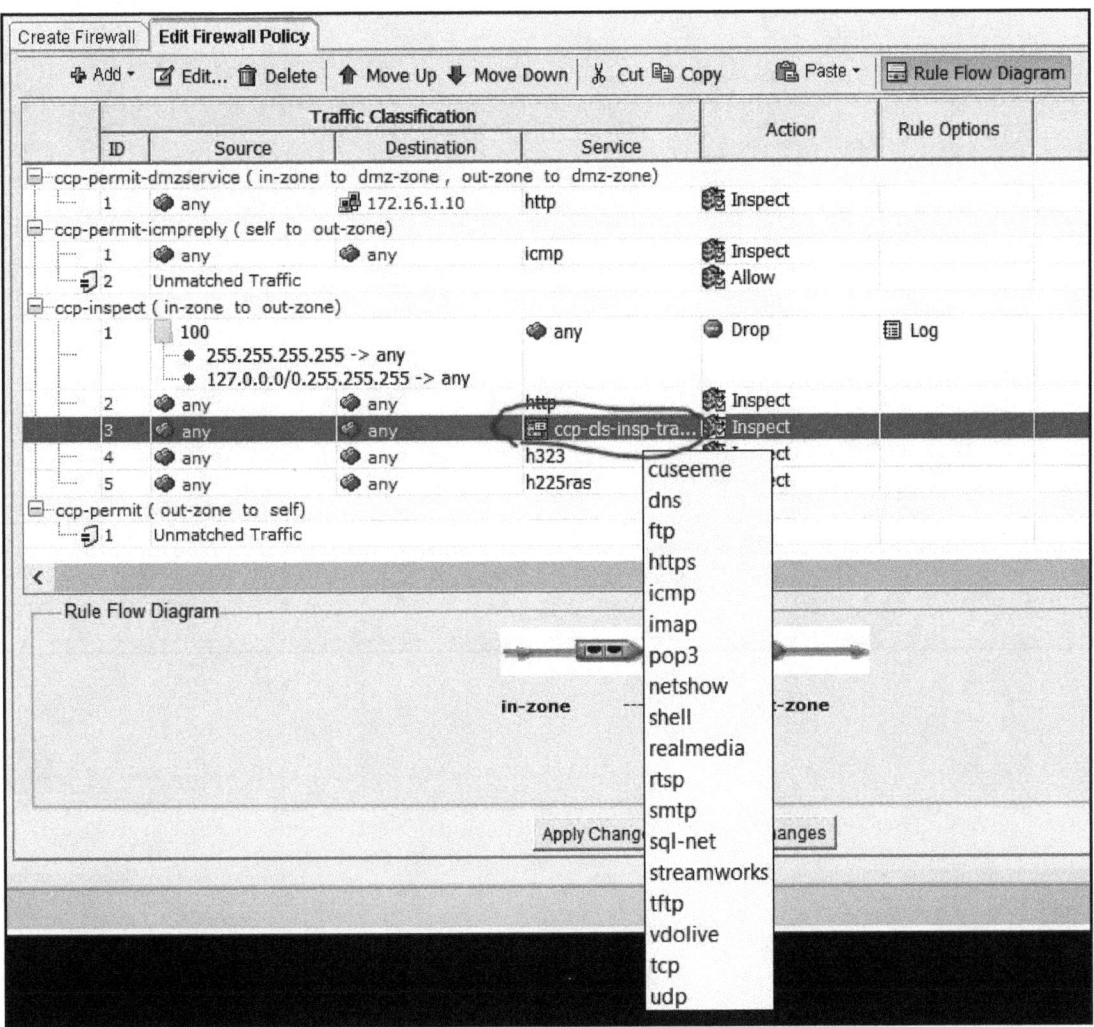

17. To see all the **class maps** and their entries, navigate to **Configure** | **Security** | **C3PL** | **Class Maps** | **Inspection**. Simply click the on desired class map to view its entries:

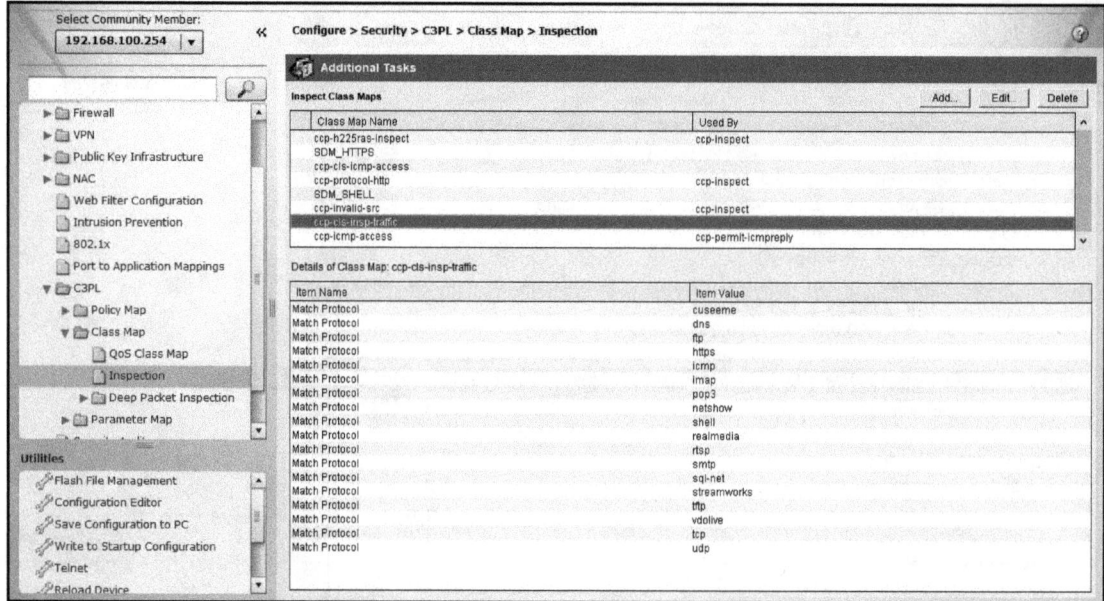

18. To view the **zone pairs** on the router (ZBF), navigate to **Configure** | **Security** | **Firewall** | **Firewall Components** | **Zone Pairs**:

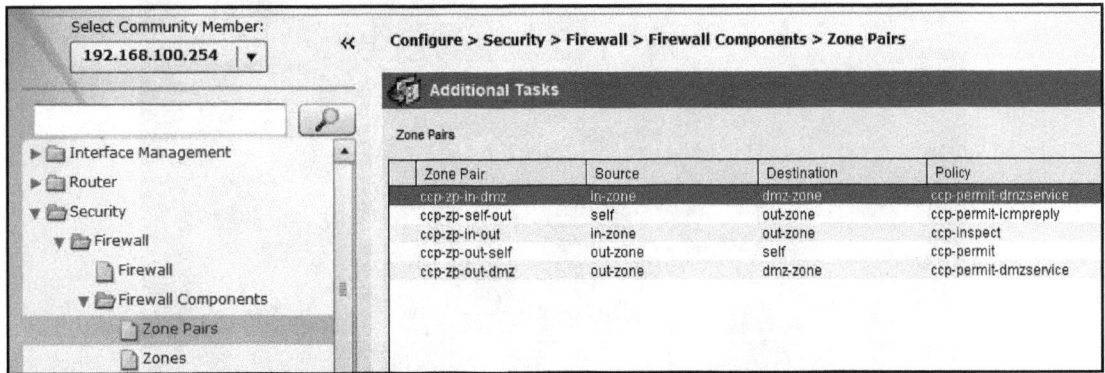

19. To view the **zones**, simply navigate to **Configure** | **Security** | **Firewall** | **Firewall Components** | **Zones**. We can see the interfaces and their assigned zones and zone pairs:

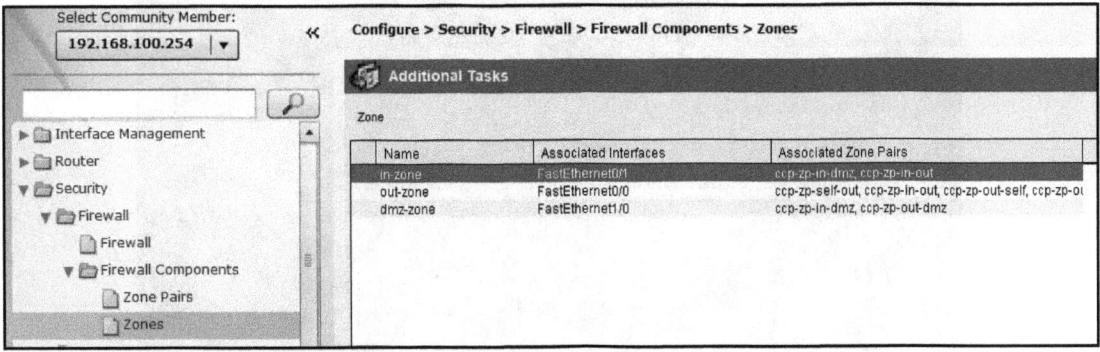

Verification commands

In this section, we are going to use some show commands to help us verify our configurations on the ZBF:

- To view the state table on the ZBF, use the `show policy-map type inspect zone-pair` command.

- To view the class maps, use the `show class-map type inspect` command:

```
R1#show class-map type inspect
 Class Map type inspect match-any ccp-skinny-inspect (id 13)
   Match protocol skinny

 Class Map type inspect match-all ccp-insp-traffic (id 9)
   Match class-map ccp-cls-insp-traffic

 Class Map type inspect match-any ccp-cls-icmp-access (id 3)
   Match protocol icmp

 Class Map type inspect match-any ccp-h225ras-inspect (id 1)
   Match protocol h225ras

 Class Map type inspect match-any ccp-cls-insp-traffic (id 7)
   Match protocol cuseeme
   Match protocol dns
   Match protocol ftp
   Match protocol https
   Match protocol icmp
   Match protocol imap
   Match protocol pop3
   Match protocol netshow
   Match protocol shell
   Match protocol realmedia
   Match protocol rtsp
   Match protocol smtp extended
   Match protocol sql-net
   Match protocol streamworks
   Match protocol tftp
   Match protocol vdolive
   Match protocol tcp
   Match protocol udp

 Class Map type inspect match-any SDM_SSH (id 15)
   Match access-group name SDM_SSH

 Class Map type inspect match-any SDM_HTTPS (id 2)
   Match access-group name SDM_HTTPS

 Class Map type inspect match-any SDM_SHELL (id 5)
   Match access-group name SDM_SHELL

 Class Map type inspect match-any ccp-h323-inspect (id 10)
   Match protocol h323

 Class Map type inspect match-all ccp-invalid-src (id 6)
   Match access-group  100

 Class Map type inspect match-all ccp-icmp-access (id 8)
   Match class-map ccp-cls-icmp-access

 Class Map type inspect match-any ccp-dmz-protocols (id 12)
   Match protocol http

 Class Map type inspect match-any ccp-sip-inspect (id 11)
   Match protocol sip
```

- The `show zone security` command displays the configured zones on the ZBF:

```
R1#show zone security
zone self
   Description: System defined zone


zone in-zone
   Member Interfaces:
      FastEthernet0/1


zone out-zone
   Member Interfaces:
      FastEthernet0/0


zone dmz-zone
   Member Interfaces:
      FastEthernet1/0
```

- To view the zone pairs, use the `show zone-pair security` command. We can see the service policy being used as well:

```
R1#show zone-pair security
Zone-pair name ccp-zp-in-dmz
    Source-Zone in-zone  Destination-Zone dmz-zone
    service-policy ccp-permit-dmzservice
Zone-pair name ccp-zp-self-out
    Source-Zone self  Destination-Zone out-zone
    service-policy ccp-permit-icmpreply
Zone-pair name ccp-zp-in-out
    Source-Zone in-zone  Destination-Zone out-zone
    service-policy ccp-inspect
Zone-pair name ccp-zp-out-self
    Source-Zone out-zone  Destination-Zone self
    service-policy ccp-permit
Zone-pair name ccp-zp-out-dmz
    Source-Zone out-zone  Destination-Zone dmz-zone
    service-policy ccp-permit-dmzservice
```

- The `show policy-map type inspect` command displays all the policy maps that have class maps set to inspect:

```
R1#show policy-map type inspect
  Policy Map type inspect ccp-permit-icmpreply
    Class ccp-icmp-access
      Inspect
    Class class-default
      Pass

  Policy Map type inspect ccp-inspect
    Class ccp-invalid-src
      Drop log
    Class ccp-protocol-http
      Inspect
    Class ccp-insp-traffic
      Inspect
    Class ccp-h323-inspect
      Inspect
    Class ccp-h225ras-inspect
      Inspect
    Class class-default

  Policy Map type inspect ccp-permit
    Class class-default

  Policy Map type inspect ccp-permit-dmzservice
    Class ccp-dmz-traffic
      Inspect
    Class class-default
```

In the next section, we'll take a look at configuring the ZBF using the CLI.

Using the command-line interface to configure the Zone-Based Firewall

The following steps will guide you through configuring the Zone-Based Firewall feature on the Cisco IOS router using the CLI. Please be sure to configure NAT before beginning the following configurations.

Step 1 – Creating the zones

Using the `zone security zone-name` format will allow the creation of a zone:

```
R1(config)#zone security in-zone
R1(config-sec-zone)#exit
R1(config)#zone security out-zone
R1(config-sec-zone)#exit
R1(config)#zone security dmz-zone
R1(config-sec-zone)#exit
```

Step 2 – Identifying traffic by using Class Maps

Using the `class-map type inspect [match-any | match-all] class-map-name` format will allow us to create a class map for the Layer 3 or Layer 4 protocols.

Using the `match protocol` command will allow us to specify the protocols for the class map. The `match class-map` command allows another class map to be nested within a class map:

```
R1(config)#class-map type inspect match-any ccp-cls-insp-traffic
R1(config-cmap)#match protocol tcp
R1(config-cmap)#match protocol udp
R1(config-cmap)#match protocol icmp
R1(config-cmap)#exit
R1(config)#class-map type inspect match-all ccp-insp-traffic
R1(config-cmap)# match class-map ccp-cls-insp-traffic
R1(config-cmap)#exit
R1(config)#class-map type inspect match-any ccp-dmz-protocols
R1(config-cmap)#match protocol http
R1(config-cmap)#exit
R1(config)#class-map type inspect match-all ccp-dmz-traffic
R1(config-cmap)#match access-group name dmz-traffic
R1(config-cmap)#match class-map ccp-dmz-protocols
R1(config-cmap)#exit
R1(config)#class-map type inspect match-any ccp-cls-icmp-access
R1(config-cmap)#match protocol icmp
R1(config-cmap)#exit
R1(config)#class-map type inspect match-all ccp-icmp-access
R1(config-cmap)#match class-map ccp-cls-icmp-access
R1(config-cmap)#exit
```

Step 3 – Defining an action using policy maps

Use the `policy-map type inspect policy-name` format to create a new policy.

The `class type inspect class-map-name` command specifies the `traffic` class to apply to an action:

```
R1(config)#policy-map type inspect ccp-inspect
R1(config-pmap)#class type inspect ccp-insp-traffic
R1(config-pmap-c)#inspect
R1(config-pmap)#exit
R1(config)#policy-map type inspect ccp-permit-dmzservice
R1(config-pmap)#class type inspect ccp-dmz-traffic
R1(config-pmap-c)#inspect
R1(config-pmap-c)#exit
R1(config-pmap)#exit
R1(config)#policy-map type inspect ccp-permit-icmpreply
R1(config-pmap)#class type inspect ccp-icmp-access
R1(config-pmap-c)#inspect
R1(config-pmap-c)#class class-default
R1(config-pmap-c)#pass
R1(config-pmap-c)#exit
R1(config-pmap)#exit
```

Step 4 – Identifying a zone-pair and creating match to a policy

The `zone-pair security zone-pair-name [source source-zone-name | self] destination [self | destination-zone-name]` command is used to create the zone pair on the ZBF.

The `service-policy type inspect policy-name` command attaches the policy to the zone pair:

```
R1(config)#zone-pair security ccp-zp-in-dmz source in-zone destination dmz-
zone
R1(config-sec-zone-pair)#service-policy type inspect ccp-permit-dmzservice
R1(config-sec-zone-pair)#exit
R1(config)#zone-pair security ccp-zp-in-out source in-zone destination out-
zone
R1(config-sec-zone-pair)#service-policy type inspect ccp-inspect
R1(config-sec-zone-pair)#exit
R1(config)#zone-pair security ccp-zp-out-dmz source out-zone destination
dmz-zone
```

```
R1(config-sec-zone-pair)#service-policy type inspect ccp-permit-dmzservice
R1(config-sec-zone-pair)#exit
R1(config)#zone-pair security ccp-zp-self-out source self destination out-
zone
R1(config-sec-zone-pair)#service-policy type inspect ccp-permit-icmpreply
R1(config-sec-zone-pair)#exit
```

Step 5 – Assigning the zones to the interfaces

Under the interface sub-mode, the `zone-member security zone-name` command will assign the interface to the zone specified in *Step 1 – Creating the zones*:

```
R1(config)#int FastEthernet 0/0
R1(config-if)#description Outside interface
R1(config-if)#zone-member security out-zone
R1(config-if)#exit
R1(config)#int FastEthernet 0/1
R1(config-if)#description Inside interface
R1(config-if)#zone-member security in-zone
R1(config-if)#exit
R1(config)#interface FastEthernet1/0
R1(config-if)#description DMZ interface
R1(config-if)#zone-member security dmz-zone
R1(config-if)#exit
```

Step 6 – Creating an ACL for access into the DMZ from any source

Since we would like to permit traffic only to the Server in the DMZ, an ACL is suitable. The `ip access-list extended acl-name` command is used to create a named extended access list. Using the `remark` command will allow you to provide a description under the ACL. Next, we want to allow any source IP address access to only the server in the DMZ; the `permit ip any host host-IP` command would allow the traffic.

```
R1(config)#ip access-list extended dmz-traffic
R1(config-ext-nacl)#remark Access to the DMZ
R1(config-ext-nacl)#permit ip any host 172.16.1.10
R1(config-ext-nacl)#exit
```

The `host` command specifies a single device, therefore a subnet mask or wildcard mask is not required.

Summary

In this chapter, we took a look at understanding some fundamental terminologies, the Cisco Common Classification Policy Language or C3PL, an overview of a ZBF and setting up and configuring the ZBF using both the Cisco Configuration Professional and the command-line interface methods. Using an existing router that supports the ZBF features would save an organization money if their budget is not big enough for a dedicated firewall appliance.

In the next chapter, we are going to dive into IPsec, the protocol that drives VPN. We'll begin with understanding some terminology, how it works, and what actually happens in the background when a Virtual Private Network is establishing a secure tunnel across an unsecured network.

13
IPSec – The Protocol that Drives VPN

In this chapter, we are going to discuss **IPSec** (short for **Internet Protocol Security**) and its components in establishing a **Virtual Private Network** (**VPN**). We will start with an overview of the terminologies and features of IPSec, then dive into the functionality of the **Internet Security Association and Key Management Protocol** (**ISAKMP**), and finally cover the **Internet Key Exchange** (**IKE**) phases.

The following topics will be covered in this chapter:

- IPSec terminologies
- IPSec features and components
- Overview of ISAKMP
- Internet Key Exchange

Let's begin!

Terminologies

In this section, we'll take a look at the terminologies that are used throughout the topic and discussion on IPSec and its features.

Virtual Private Network

A **Virtual Private Network** (**VPN**) is a logical private/secure tunnel between two devices across an unsecure network such as the internet. What does this means? Any traffic sent through the VPN tunnel is private from other users on the internet, therefore only the sender and receiver are able to view the data:

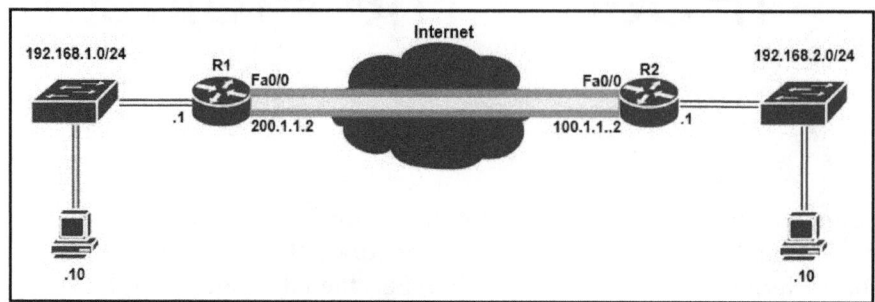

Why would you need a VPN?

A VPN is an alternative to having a dedicated **Wide Area Network** (**WAN**) connection due to the high cost payable to **Internet Service Providers** (**ISPs**) for creating the WAN connectivity for your sites or offices. Some organizations or small companies may not have the budget for a dedicated WAN infrastructure but still need to extend their corporate network beyond borders to another remote site or office, a VPN can be the solution. To establish a VPN, each branch location needs an internet connection and either a firewall or router with the capabilities of creating an IPSec VPN. This would allow the company to save on cost, all they would need is an internet connection at each branch location.

Confidentiality

What is confidentiality? Confidentiality is keeping a message private from anyone who is unauthorized to view it. In the world of computing and networking, we have a concern for privacy and want to ensure our data is kept private from others for many reasons, such as identity theft and data leakage. One way to achieve confidentiality is to use encryption.

What is encryption?

Encryption is the encoding of plaintext into another format known as ciphertext. To encrypt a message (data), a key is needed, just like a lock needs a key to be opened. With data encryption, we use a key, also known as a *secret*, to encrypt (lock) and decrypt (unlock) a message; only the person/device with the correct key can unlock/decrypt the message and read its contents. Encryption helps keep our data safe, even if a malicious user obtains the ciphertext, they won't be able to read the contents of the message without having the key to decrypt it.

Types of encryption algorithms

There are two types of encryption algorithms:

- **Symmetric algorithm**: Uses the same key to encrypt and decrypt the message. If the key is lost or stolen, the ciphertext is vulnerable.
- **Asymmetric algorithm**: Uses one key to encrypt and a different key to decrypt the message. If one key is lost or stolen, the ciphertext is not vulnerable.

Encryption Algorithms

The following encryption protocols are used in the IPSec framework:

- **Data Encryption Standard** (**DES**): A symmetric encryption algorithm that uses a 56-bit key (insecure) to encrypt each block of data.
- **Triple Data Encryption Standard** (**3DES**): A symmetric encryption algorithm that applies the DES algorithms three times to each block of data.
- **Advanced Encryption Standard** (**AES**): Currently the de facto of data encryption algorithm. It encrypts data in blocks of 128-bits and uses 128-, 192-, and 256-bit keys for its data encryption.
- **Ron Rivest, Adi Shamir, and Leonard Adleman** (**RSA**): A streaming cipher algorithm that, unlike block ciphers, encrypts each bit of data individually.

Integrity

In networking, whenever we send a message across a network between two or more devices, we need to ensure the message was not modified or altered before reaching its intended recipient. Data integrity provides the reassurance of checking whether the message was altered or not. If the message was not altered, the integrity was maintained. If the message was altered, the integrity was lost, and the message should not be trusted and be discarded.

To check the integrity of data, it goes through a process known as hashing. Hashing produces an alphanumeric string that is unique to the message:

There are two main algorithms used for hashing, **Message Digest 5** (**MD5**) and the **Secure Hashing Algorithm** (**SHA**):

- **Message Digest 5**: A hashing algorithm that uses a 128-bit shared secret key to authenticate data packets.
- **Secure Hash Algorithm-1**: A hashing algorithm that uses a 160-bit shared secret key for authenticating data packets.
- **Hash-based message authentication code**: An additional layer of security in the hashing process.

How does a device verify the integrity of a message?

Let's assume there are two people who wants to exchange a message across a network, Bob and Alice. Bob wants to send Alice a file named `Test.txt` with its contents, `ABCD`. Bob wants to ensure Alice receives the message and that its contents remain unaltered.

A process, known as **hashing**, creates a unique string of alphanumeric characters, known as a **hash**. The hash represents the context of the message. In the scenario, Bob sends both the file, `Test.txt`, and its hash values to Alice. When Alice receives the file and the hashes from Bob, Alice also creates her hashes of the file. Alice would then compare her hash values with the ones received from Bob, if both values match, the file was not modified during transmission and the integrity was maintained:

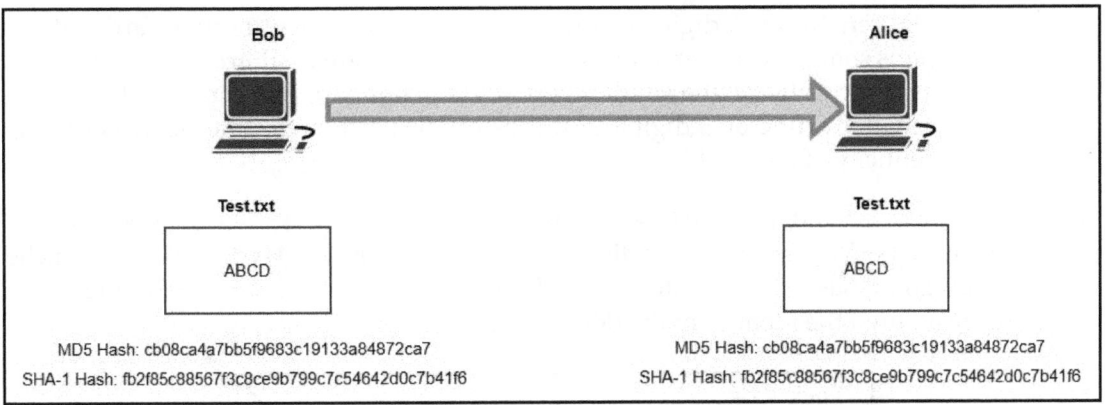

Anti-replay

Whenever packets are sent from one device to another, they are tagged with a sequence number. Sometimes when packets leaves the sender device, they may not always arrive at the destination in the same sequential order, therefore the sequence number can assist the recipient device in the reassembly process.

Anti-replay monitors the packets with their sequence numbers as they flow across the IPSec tunnel, if the anti-replay feature detects a packet with the same sequence number that has already entered the tunnel, the packet will not be allowed to enter. Only packets with unique sequence numbers are accepted.

Authentication

In the world of computing, we need to prove our identity to a computer system before gaining access on it. The process of authentication allows us to enter a valid username and password combination on a computer to prove our authenticity. Without a valid username and password combination, a computer would not allow us to log in and access its resources.

In an IPSec VPN configuration, both devices, whether routers or firewalls, each need to prove their identity to the other before establishing a VPN tunnel. There are two ways this can be accomplished:

- **Pre-shared key (PSK)**: A pre-shared key is simply a password used for the authentication process that will be exchanged between both peers.

- **Digital certificate**: A digital certificate is an electronic identification card that contains some key information, such as the **Certificate Authority** (**CA**) who issued the certificate, the validity period, serial number, and version. The information found on a digital certificate can be used on the internet to verify the authenticity of a website.

A simple example is validating the Cisco website (`https://www.cisco.com/`) is actually what it claims to be. Viewing the site's digital certificate, we can see **HydrantID** (Avalanche Cloud Corporation) has issued the digital certificate to `https://www.cisco.com/` and therefore are assured the identity of the device/website:

Another analogy we can use is going to the bank to open a new savings account. One main requirement is a form of identification to prove you are who you say you are. Most likely, you'll provide either a national identification card or a driver's permit to the bank clerk. The bank trusts the issuing body based on its reputation. It's the same as trusting a website with a valid digital certificate from a reputable CA; the CA has an excellent reputation and therefore validates the website is who it claims to be.

Diffie-Hellman (DH)

Earlier we spoke about authentication and its purpose; a VPN is usually established over the internet (unsecured network), exchanging the secret keys (PSK) over this unsecured medium, such as the internet, is not safe. **Diffie-Hellman** (**DH**) is an algorithm designed to exchange cryptographic keys over an unsecured network. IPSec uses DH to securely exchange these secret keys between both parties. This prevents any malicious, eavesdropping users from obtaining the real cryptographic keys.

Tunnel

For the remainder of this book, we'll use the definition of a tunnel as a logical connection between two devices. Since a VPN is a logical connection between two devices across the internet, we can simply say it's a tunnel between point **A** and point **B**.

 A **Security Association** (**SA**) is a logical tunnel between two peers.

What is IPSec?

IPSec is a framework or suite of protocols combined to ensure secure data communication across an IP network. IPSec combines different protocols to provide data confidentiality (encryption), data integrity (hashing), authentication (PSK and RSA digital certificates), and key exchange (Diffie-Hellman) between devices over an untrusted network:

IPsec Framework	
IPsec Protocol	AH or ESP
Confidentiality	DES, 3DES or AES
Integrity	MD5 or SHA
Authentication	PSK or RSA
Dillie-Hellman	DH1, DH2, DH5

Within the IPSec framework, there are two protocols that assist with the transportation of IP packets across the IPSec VPN tunnel, these are known as **Authentication Header** (**AH**) and **Encapsulation Security Payloads** (**ESPs**).

When creating an IPSec VPN tunnel, either the AH or the ESP can be used as a standalone protocol. However, both AH and ESP can be used together.

Authentication Header

The AH provides the authentication and integrity of the data packets as they are passed along the IPSec VPN tunnel. However, it does not provide any confidentiality (encryption) of the data being sent across the tunnel. Instead, it hashes the datagram (header and data). The datagram and its hash value are sent across the tunnel, the receiver can then perform hashing and verify whether the contents of the datagram have been modified during transmission. This process verifies the authenticity of the message.

AH has the ability to use the anti-replay features to prevent a malicious user re-sending packets that have already been seen and passed through the tunnel.

 For the data integrity, MD5, SHA-1, and SHA-2 are typically used in the AH protocol in IPSec.

The following describes how the AH encodes the datagram:

- As the router or the firewall prepares the IP packet or datagram, it is hashed using a one-way function to provide integrity.
- An AH is constructed using the hash value and is attached to the original IP packet/datagram. In other words, we can say is it encapsulated with the AH.
- This new packet will be sent across the IPSec VPN tunnel to the other VPN peer.
- When the recipient device receives the new datagram, it hashes the IP header and the data. Then it compares the generated hash value with the hash within the AH. If both hash values matches, the integrity and authenticity of the datagram was maintained:

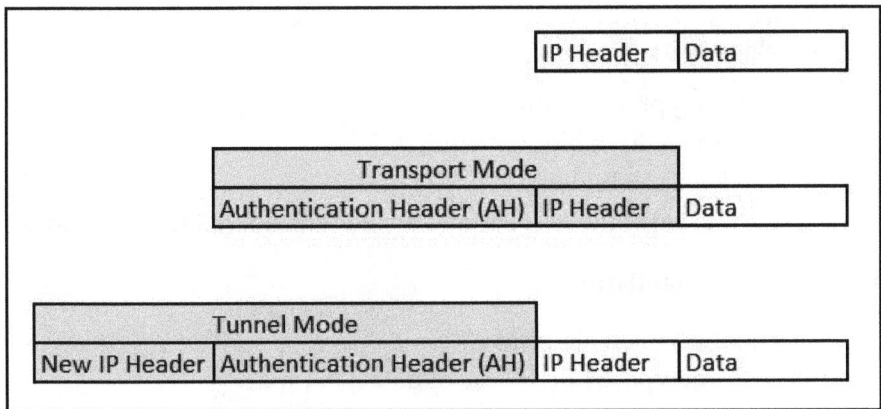

Encapsulation Security Payload

Encapsulation Security Payload (**ESP**) provides confidentiality, authentication, integrity, and can offer anti-replay as well. How does the ESP protocol provide proper confidentiality of the IP packets? It does this by simply applying encryption at the IP packet layer.

The main benefit of using the ESP protocol is its ability to provide data confidentiality (encryption) to the datagrams passing across the IPSec VPN tunnel:

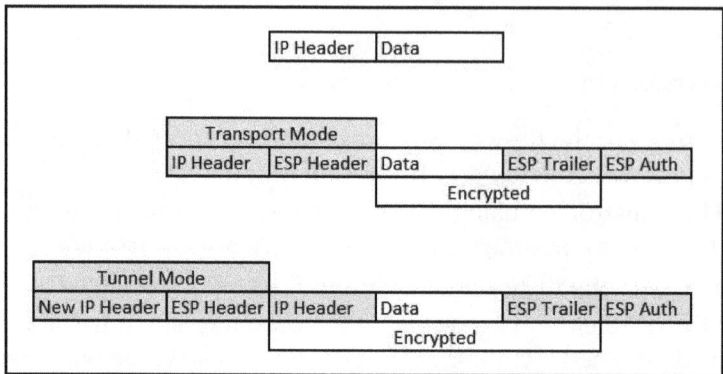

The ESP protocol uses two encryption algorithms, these are the Data Encryption Standard and Triple Data Encryption Standard.

Data Encryption Standard:

- Symmetric encryption algorithm
- Uses block cipher, each block is 64-bit
- Encryption key is 56-bit long
- Due to the bit size of the encryption key, it is considered to be insecure

Triple Data Encryption Standard:

- Symmetric encryption algorithm
- Just as DES, encrypts 64-bit blocks of data at a time
- The length of the encryption key is also 56-bit
- Unlike DES, which encrypts a 64-bit block of data only once using the 56-bit key, 3DES encrypts the block of data three times using an independent 56-bit key

Modes of IPSec

IPSec can be configured in one of two modes, **Transport mode** or **Tunnel mode**. In this section, we are going to take look at the differences between these modes and their functionalities.

Let's get started.

General uses of Transport and Tunnel mode in IPSec:

- In a remote access VPN configuration, tunnel mode is used to secure the traffic between the client device and the VPN gateway (router or firewall). The client would be using a VPN client software such as **Cisco AnyConnect Secure Mobility Client**.
- If a VPN-capable server and a router want to create a VPN between themselves, tunnel mode would be used to establish an IPSec tunnel between the peers.
- Tunnel mode can be used to establish a VPN link between two routers to secure traffic between them.
- Transport mode would be used to secure the traffic between a client device and an IPSec VPN gateway, such as a firewall appliance.

Authentication header – Transport and tunnel modes

The benefit of using the AH is it protects the external IP header information and the data contents of the datagram.

In tunnel mode, a new IP header is created and added to the datagram. The new IP header is encapsulated on the datagram, protecting the original IP header.

In transport mode, the authentication header is encapsulated to the datagram only:

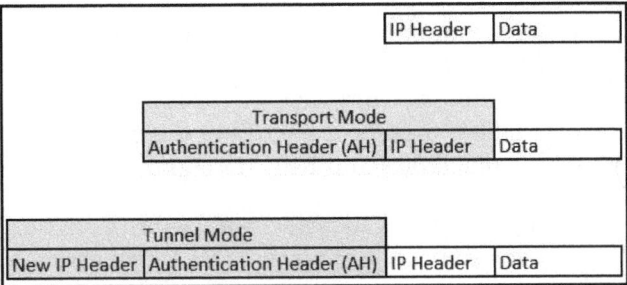

Encapsulating Security Payloads (ESP) – Transport mode and tunnel mode

In transport mode, the ESP header and an ESP trailer are encoded to the datagram. The data and ESP trailer contents are encrypted. However, the original IP header is kept unchanged.

In tunnel mode, the ESP header and an ESP trailer are encoded on the datagram. A new IP header is added at the beginning of the datagram. The original IP header, data, and the ESP trailer contents are encrypted to ensure the information is kept confidential as it passes through the VPN tunnel:

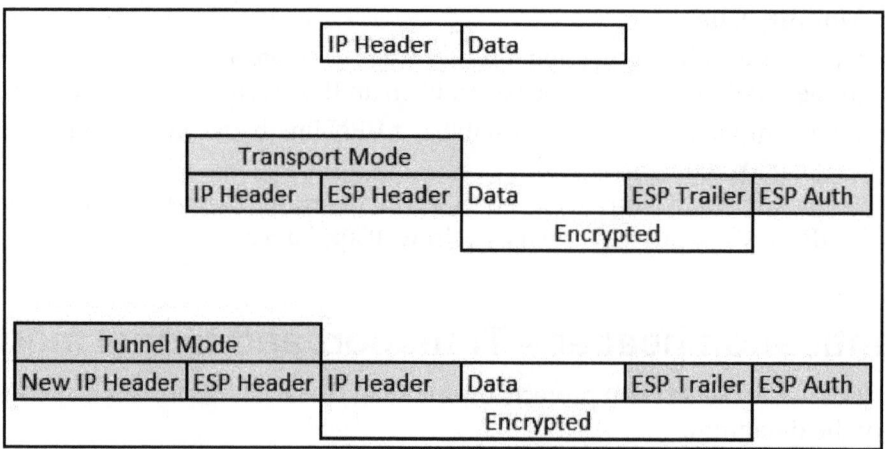

ISAKMP

We know that IPSec is a suite of protocols used to establish is a secure VPN connection between two remote networks with the help of VPN gateways (routers or firewalls). Before the IPSec tunnel can be established to secure to traffic, a negotiation process needs to take place between the two peers (routers or firewalls) to agree on mutual parameters for the IPSec tunnel. The protocol that handles the exchange of the mutual parameters/policies is known as **Internet Security Association and Key Management Protocol** (**ISAKMP**).

The policies that are exchanged between the peers are used to determine the methods of authentication, such as a pre-shared key or the use of RSA signatures, the encryption algorithm for data confidentiality between the peers and the remote networks, the key exchange group (whether it's Diffie-Hellman 1, 2, or 5), and the hashing algorithm for validating the integrity of the packets/datagram sent between the peers.

In the next section, we'll go a bit deeper into describing the exchange of the policies and understanding the phases of *Internet Key Exchange*.

Internet Key Exchange

The IPSec protocol suite uses **Internet Key Exchange** (IKE) to securely handle the security associations in the creation of an IPSec VPN. Before the IPSec VPN is established, IKE needs to establish an IKE phase 1 tunnel and an IKE phase 2 tunnel.

IKE phase 1

The IKE phase 1 is used to authenticate the IPSec VPN peers and established a secure, encrypted tunnel to further allow the peers to exchange IKE information.

The main characteristics of the IKE phase 1 are as follows:

- The phase 1 tunnel is used to exchange any packet/traffic originating from one peer that is destined for the other peer. If there's an IKE phase 1 tunnel between two routers, Router **A** and Router **B**, if one router wants to send a message to the other, the traffic will use the IKE phase 1 tunnel only.
- The IKE phase 1 is used to negotiate all the SA between the two peers.
- The SA are mutual hashing algorithms, authentication methods, key exchange method, encryption algorithm, and the time the tunnel should be available. These policies will be sent from one peer to the other.
- Once both peers agree on the policies, Diffie-Hellman will then be used to generate the shared secret key for both pairs. If there's a malicious user sitting between the peers and sniffing the traffic, the malicious user will not be able to obtain the shared secret key of the peers.
- The authentication stage will be applied next, validating the PSK or the RSA digital signatures.
- Once everything matches perfectly, the IKE phase 1 tunnel will be established:

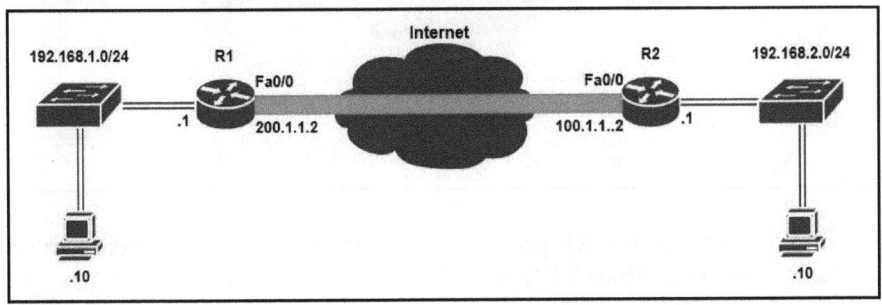

The green tunnel represents the IKE phase 1 tunnel

During IKE phase 1, there are two modes in which the tunnel can be established, the first is known as the main mode and the other is aggressive mode. During Main mode, the IPSec VPN peers exchange 6 packets and the aggressive mode uses fewer packets.

IKE phase 2

Once the IKE phase 1 tunnel has been established, the IKE phase 2 tunnel has to be created for the client devices behind each VPN gateway to send and receive data through the IPSec tunnel. However, there are a few things that need to take place before the IKE phase 2 tunnel can be established.

The following policies are exchanged between the peers for a mutual agreement before creating the IKE phase 2 tunnel:

- The hashing algorithm using HMAC as an added layer of security
- The key exchange method using Diffie-Hellman 1, 2, or 5
- The encryption algorithms, whether DES, 3DES, or AES, for the confidentiality of the data packets
- The time of the tunnel should be available
- Since the authentication stage was completed during IKE phase 1, it is not required in IKE phase 2

Once the IKE phase 2 tunnel is established, the clients between both remote networks can communicate across the IKE phase 2 tunnel; this is also known as the **true IPSec tunnel**:

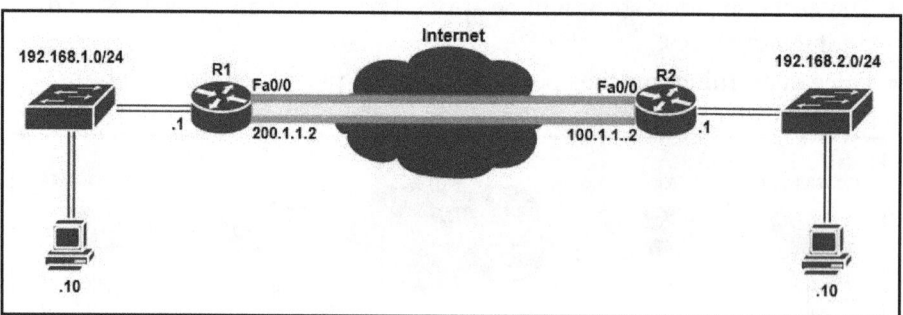

The Green tunnel represents the IKE phase 1 tunnel and the brown tunnel represents the IKE phase 2 tunnel (the true IPSec VPN tunnel).

Summary

To conclude this chapter, we've taken a look at IPSec and its importance in VPNs. We are now able to understand the terminologies and jargon being used during the configurations and discussions in the industry, the fundamentals and concepts behind Internet Security Association and Key Management Protocol, and the definition and application of Internet Key Exchange.

In the next chapter, we dive into configuring a Site-to-Site VPN.

Configuring a Site-to-Site VPN 14

In the past few chapters, we've looked at the Cisco **Adaptive Security Appliance** (**ASA**). We took a look at both basic and advanced device configurations to ensure our appliance can be deployed in a production environment. The last chapter spoke about IPSec, its functionality, and components, but most importantly, we mentioned that IPSec is used to establish a **Virtual Private Network** (**VPN**) over an unsecured network, such as the internet. This chapter focuses on using the Cisco ASA and a Cisco IOS router to create a site-to-site VPN tunnel.

In this chapter, we will focus on the following topics:

- Configuring a site-to-site VPN using a Cisco IOS router
- Configuring a site-to-site VPN using a Cisco ASA
- Verifying the VPN tunnel on both the ASA and IOS router

Let's begin!

General uses of a site-to-site VPN

Let's assume one day you decide to start your own company in the Republic of Trinidad and Tobago. Your company requires a few employees to get started and to be able to offer multiple services to your clients/customers. Another requirement is having your own IT infrastructure, such as a small server room with a few application servers to assist with the management of data within the company. At this point, you have a **Local Area Network** (**LAN**) in your company. In addition, you are studying CCNA Security and read about the importance of having a firewall, such as the Cisco Adaptive Security Appliance; you've decided to invest in an ASA and deployed it on your company's network edge.

As time passes, you realize business is doing well and you want to expand to another country, Barbados. The Barbados location also has a Cisco ASA, so the Trinidad and Tobago (TT) location is now your headquarters. Both locations will have their own separate LANs; however, at the headquarters location, all the main servers exists at the Trinidad and Tobago office, these may include the accounting and other application servers. This can be an issue for the Barbados team, as they will also need to access the resources at the Trinidad and Tobago location. A simple solution is to extend the network access across the internet in a secure method, the company can use a Site-to-Site VPN:

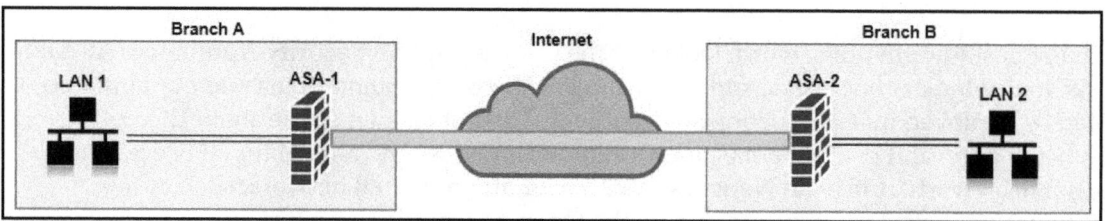

One main concern is the cost of a dedicated **Wide Area Network** (**WAN**) link between the two sites; it can be rather expensive. A simple solution or alternative is using a site-to-site VPN to connect the two locations using the existing infrastructure—the internet connections and the ASAs at both locations. One of the features of the ASA is site-to-site VPN capabilities; this allows businesses to save money rather than paying for a dedicated WAN link from an **Internet Server Provider** (**ISP**).

Configuring a site-to-site VPN using a Cisco IOS router

In this section, we will be using the following topology as a reference for our configurations:

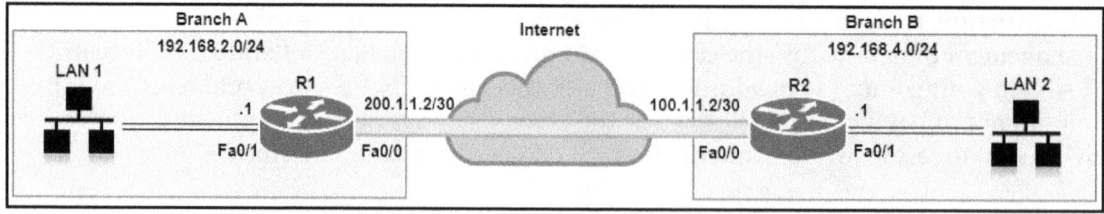

For this exercise, we have configured the **Port Address Translation** (**PAT**) on both R1 and R2.

Let's begin setting up the site-to-site VPN on the Cisco IOS routers:

1. Using the **Cisco Configuration Professional** (**CCP**), navigate to **Configure** | **Security** | **VPN** | **Site-to-Site VPN**. The following window will provide two options; we are going to select **Create a Site to Site VPN** and click on **Launch the selected task**:

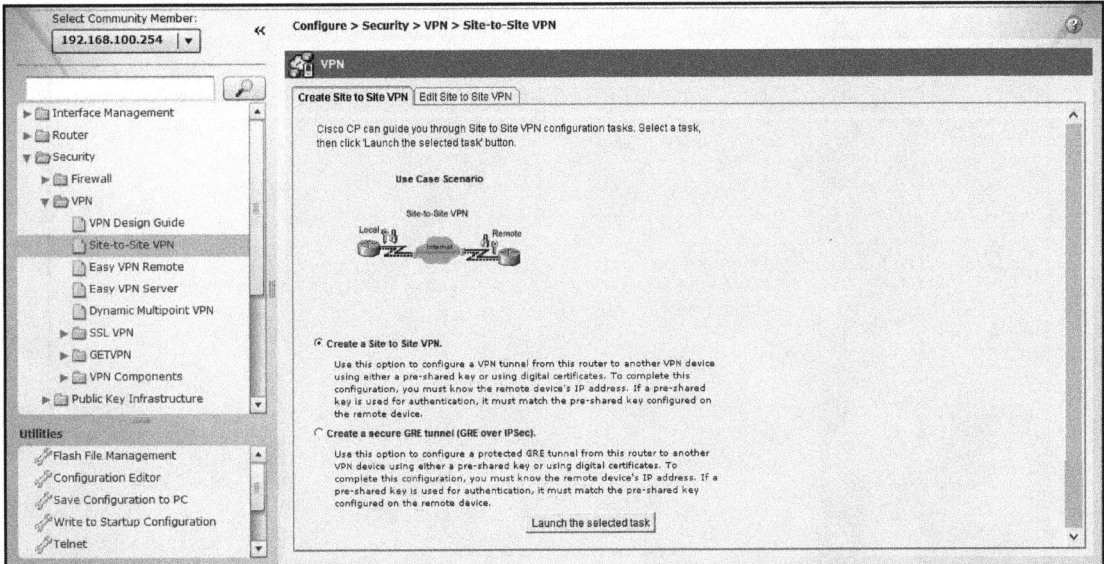

2. The VPN wizard provides two additional methods for configuring the VPN: **Quick setup** (provides default configurations) and **Step by step wizard**. We will choose the second option and click on **Next**:

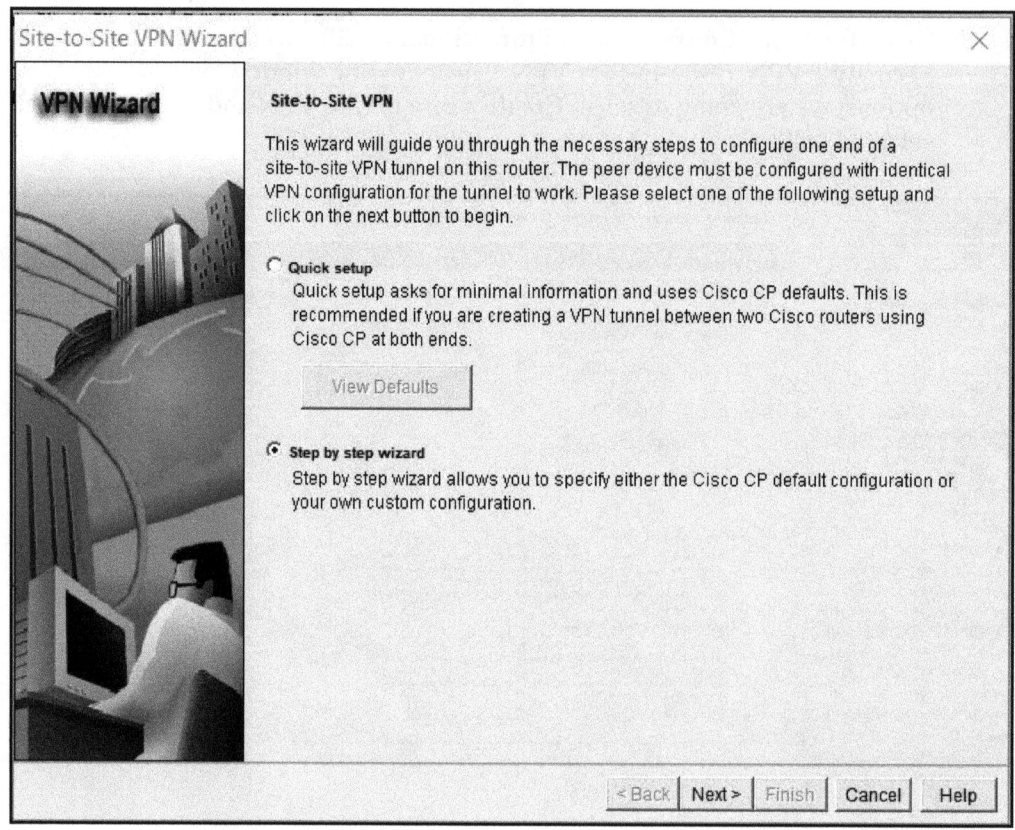

3. Here, you'll need to assign the interface for the incoming VPN connection, in this case it's **FastEthernet0/0**. Next, set the VPN peer as `100.1.1.2` and for the authentication, we have selected the **Pre-shared Keys** method using `cisco123` as the actual secret key. Once you're done, click on **Next**:

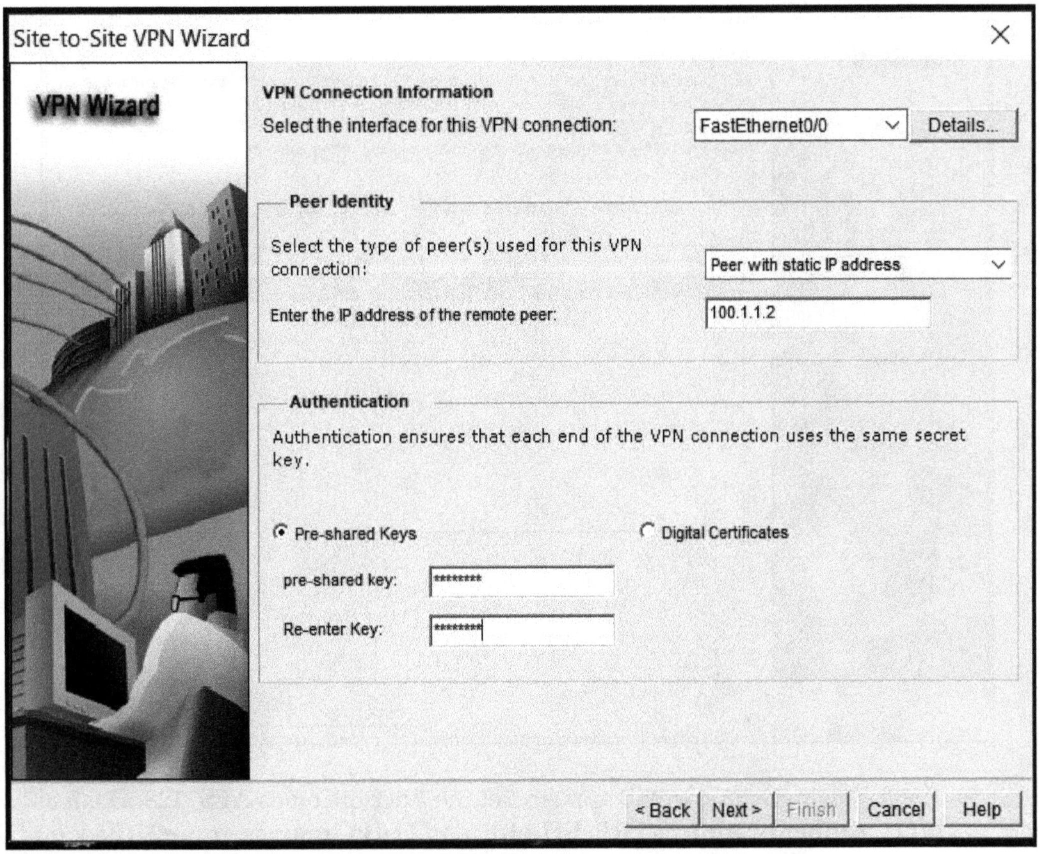

Site-to-Site VPN Wizard	✕

VPN Wizard

VPN Connection Information

Select the interface for this VPN connection: FastEthernet0/0 ∨   Details...

Peer Identity

Select the type of peer(s) used for this VPN connection: Peer with static IP address ∨

Enter the IP address of the remote peer: 100.1.1.2

Authentication

Authentication ensures that each end of the VPN connection uses the same secret key.

⦿ Pre-shared Keys   ○ Digital Certificates

pre-shared key: ********

Re-enter Key: ********

< Back | Next > | Finish | Cancel | Help

Always use a complex pre-shared key in your configurations.

4. This is the IKE Phase 1. As you can see in the following screenshot, the router loads a pre-configuration template. However, we are not going to use it, as we will define our own set of policies. Click on **Add...**:

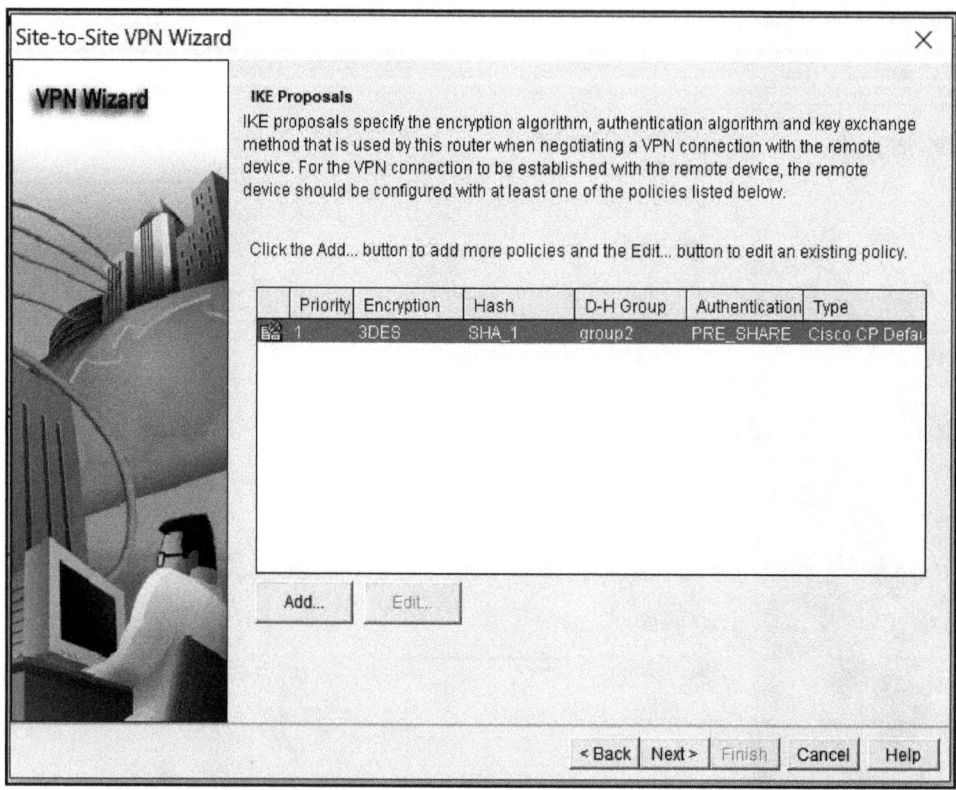

5. The following window will appear. Set the **Encryption** as **AES_128**, **Hash** as **MD5**, **Authentication** as **PRE_SHARE**, and **D-H Group** as **group2**. Click on **OK** to return to the main IKE proposal window:

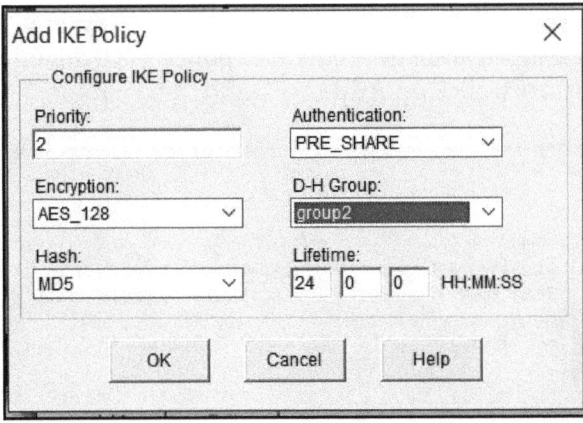

6. Now we have returned to the previous window and the new policy is available; click on the new policy and then click on **Next**:

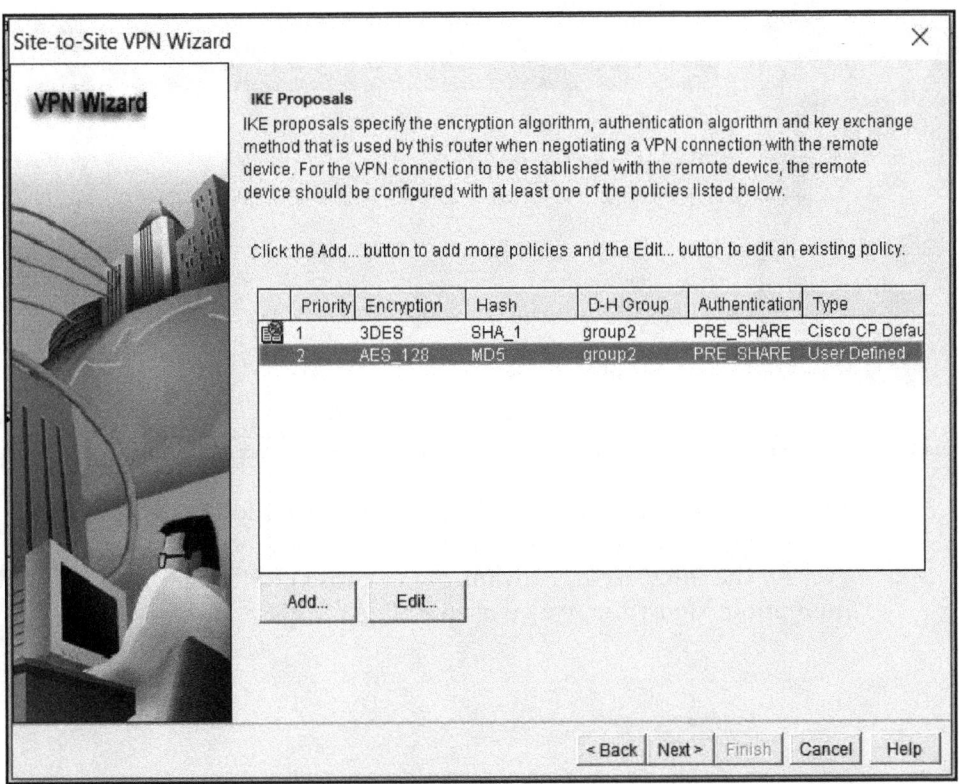

7. The **Transform Set** window appears. Here we can modify the policy for IKE phase 2. Once again, a set of predefined policies is loaded by default. To create a new transform set, click on **Add...**:

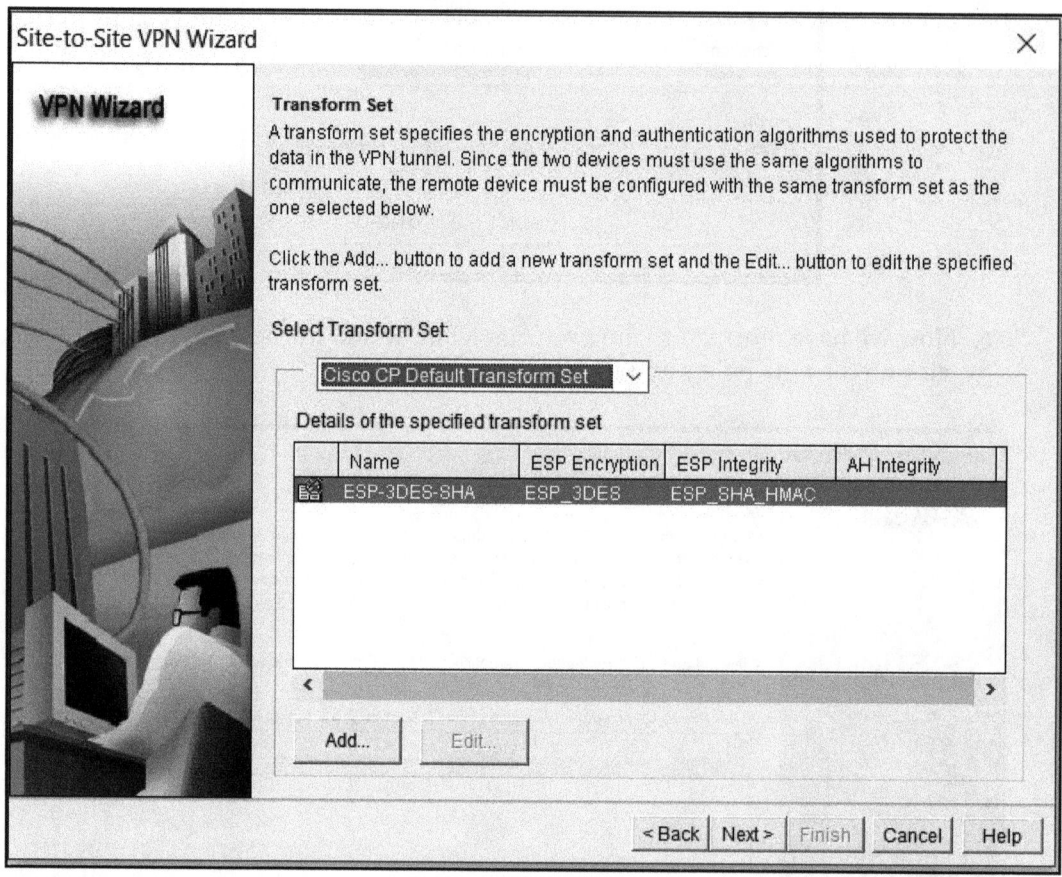

8. A new window will appear, providing us with the option to define a new transform set (IKE Phase 2 policy). The name can be anything you choose; however for the **Integrity Algorithm**, we've chosen **ESP_SHA_HMAC**, and for the **Encryption Algorithm**, we've used **ESP_AES_256**:

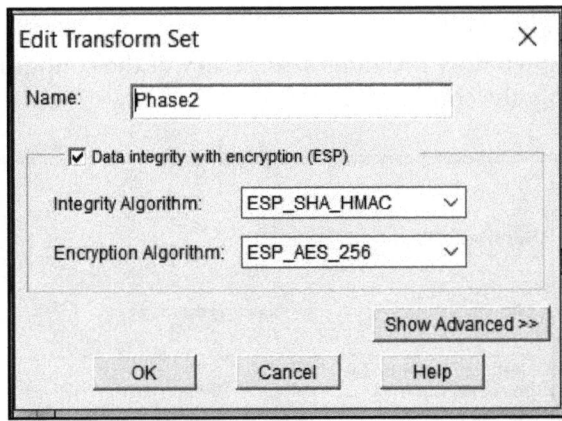

9. Click on **OK** to return to the earlier window.

10. You need to define which traffic flows should be protected. Since we're on R1, the local network would be `192.168.2.0/24` and the remote network would be `192.168.4.0/24`:

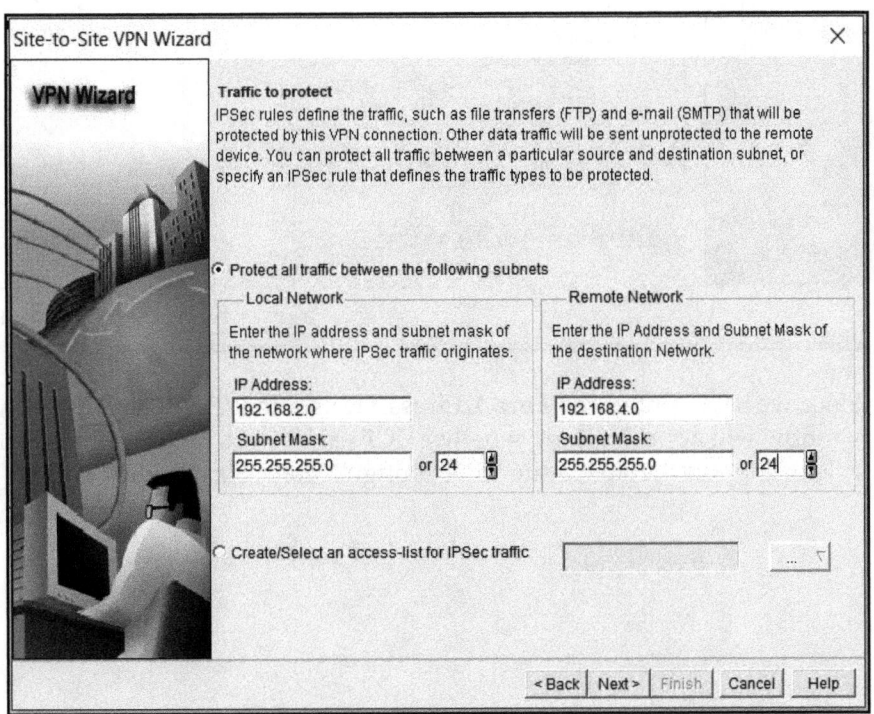

11. Click on **Next** to continue.

12. The following window provides a summary of the configurations. Click on **Finish** to apply the configurations on R1:

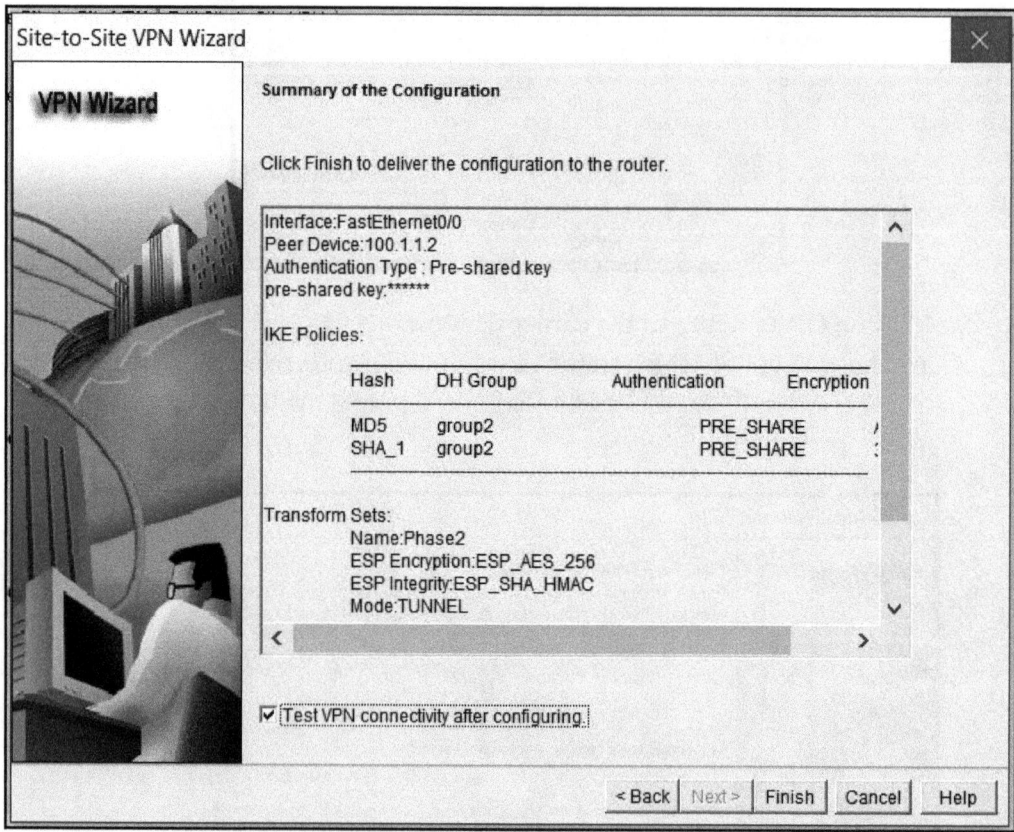

13. Since we have configured **Port Address Translation (PAT)** on R1, the following window will appear, asking whether CCP can make a modification on the PAT rule to support the site-to-site VPN configurations. Simply click on **Yes**:

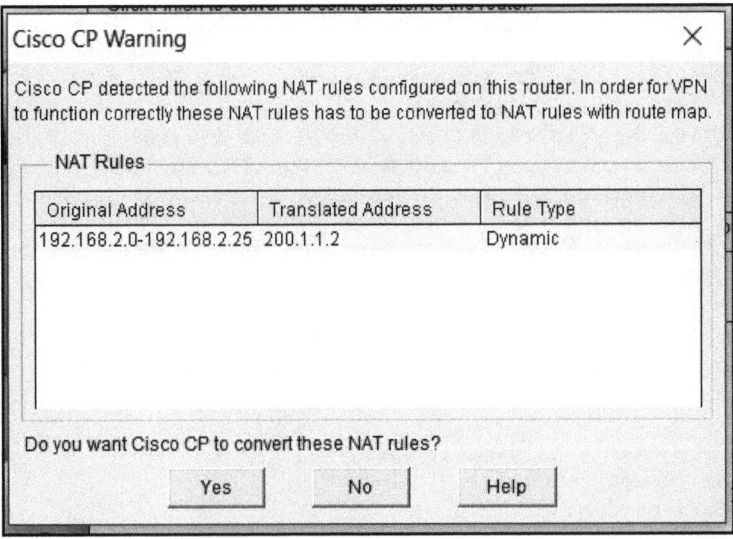

14. The final window will display the command-line version of all the configurations that will be applied. Click on **Deliver** to push the configurations onto the router:

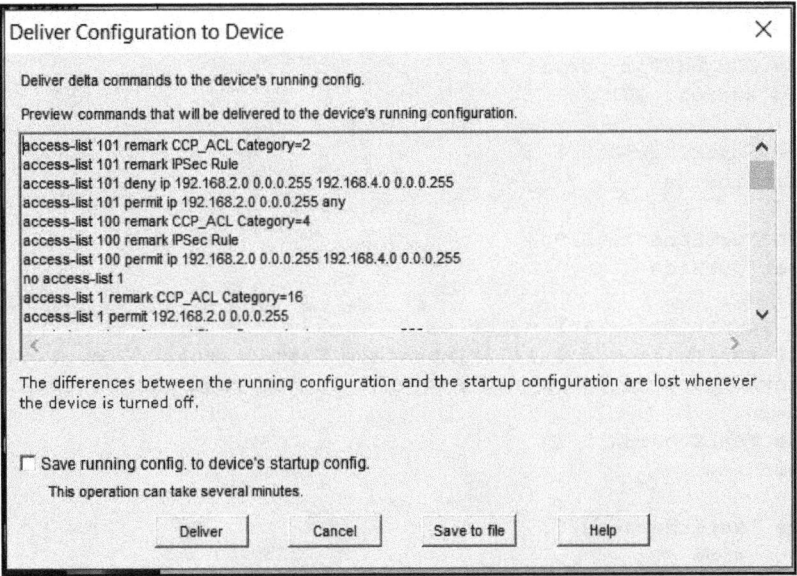

The following are the commands that will be pushed to R1:

```
access-list 101 remark CCP_ACL Category=2
access-list 101 remark IPSec Rule
access-list 101 deny ip 192.168.2.0 0.0.0.255 192.168.4.0 0.0.0.255
access-list 101 permit ip 192.168.2.0 0.0.0.255 any
access-list 100 remark CCP_ACL Category=4
access-list 100 remark IPSec Rule
access-list 100 permit ip 192.168.2.0 0.0.0.255 192.168.4.0 0.0.0.255
no access-list 1
access-list 1 remark CCP_ACL Category=16
access-list 1 permit 192.168.2.0 0.0.0.255
crypto ipsec transform-set Phase2 esp-sha-hmac esp-aes 256
 mode tunnel
 exit
crypto map SDM_CMAP_1 1 ipsec-isakmp
 description Tunnel to100.1.1.2
 set transform-set Phase2
 set peer 100.1.1.2
 match address 100
 exit
interface FastEthernet0/0
 no crypto map
 crypto map SDM_CMAP_1
 exit
route-map SDM_RMAP_1 permit 1
 match ip address 101
 exit
interface FastEthernet0/1
 no ip nat inside
 exit
interface FastEthernet0/0
 no ip nat outside
 exit
do clear ip nat translation forced
no ip nat inside source list 1 interface FastEthernet0/0 overload
ip nat inside source route-map SDM_RMAP_1 interface FastEthernet0/0
overload
interface FastEthernet0/1
 ip nat inside
 exit
interface FastEthernet0/0
 ip nat outside
 exit
crypto isakmp policy 2
 authentication pre-share
 encr aes 128
```

```
      hash md5
      group 2
      lifetime 86400
      exit
   crypto isakmp policy 1
      authentication pre-share
      encr 3des
      hash sha
      group 2
      lifetime 86400
      exit
   crypto isakmp key ******** address 100.1.1.2
```

Verifying a site-to-site VPN on a Cisco IOS router

Once you have configured R1 and R2, it's time to test your site-to-site VPN.

By default, the VPN tunnel will be down until traffic is generated between the two networks, 192.168.2.0/24 and 192.168.4.0/24. On **R1**, we initiated a ping from the 192.168.4.1 address to the 192.168.2.1 interface of R2:

```
R1#ping 192.168.4.1 source 192.168.2.1

Type escape sequence to abort.
Sending 5, 100-byte ICMP Echos to 192.168.4.1, timeout is 2 seconds:
Packet sent with a source address of 192.168.2.1
!!!!!
Success rate is 100 percent (5/5), round-trip min/avg/max = 32/56/64 ms
R1#
```

Next we are going to use the show crypto isakmp sa command to view the **security associations (SAs)** on R1:

```
R1#show crypto isakmp sa
IPv4 Crypto ISAKMP SA
dst            src            state        conn-id slot status
200.1.1.2      100.1.1.2      QM_IDLE         1001    0 ACTIVE

IPv6 Crypto ISAKMP SA

R1#
```

We can see the IPSec SA between the VPN peers using the `show crypto ipsec sa` command. The following screenshot shows which IPs are the VPN peers, and the **encapsulating security payload** (**ESP**) security associations for inbound and outbound:

```
R1#show crypto ipsec sa

interface: FastEthernet0/0
    Crypto map tag: SDM_CMAP_1, local addr 200.1.1.2

   protected vrf: (none)
   local  ident (addr/mask/prot/port): (192.168.2.0/255.255.255.0/0/0)
   remote ident (addr/mask/prot/port): (192.168.4.0/255.255.255.0/0/0)
   current_peer 100.1.1.2 port 500
     PERMIT, flags={origin_is_acl,}
    #pkts encaps: 4, #pkts encrypt: 4, #pkts digest: 4
    #pkts decaps: 4, #pkts decrypt: 4, #pkts verify: 4
    #pkts compressed: 0, #pkts decompressed: 0
    #pkts not compressed: 0, #pkts compr. failed: 0
    #pkts not decompressed: 0, #pkts decompress failed: 0
    #send errors 0, #recv errors 0

     local crypto endpt.: 200.1.1.2, remote crypto endpt.: 100.1.1.2
     path mtu 1500, ip mtu 1500, ip mtu idb FastEthernet0/0
     current outbound spi: 0x9AB58A82(2595588738)

     inbound esp sas:
      spi: 0xB8388E37(3090714167)
        transform: esp-256-aes esp-sha-hmac ,
        in use settings ={Tunnel, }
        conn id: 1, flow_id: SW:1, crypto map: SDM_CMAP_1
        sa timing: remaining key lifetime (k/sec): (4525745/3429)
        IV size: 16 bytes
        replay detection support: Y
        Status: ACTIVE

     inbound ah sas:

     inbound pcp sas:

     outbound esp sas:
      spi: 0x9AB58A82(2595588738)
        transform: esp-256-aes esp-sha-hmac ,
        in use settings ={Tunnel, }
        conn id: 2, flow_id: SW:2, crypto map: SDM_CMAP_1
        sa timing: remaining key lifetime (k/sec): (4525745/3429)
        IV size: 16 bytes
        replay detection support: Y
        Status: ACTIVE
```

The `show crypto session` command displays information about the active crypto sessions on the local router:

```
R1#show crypto session
Crypto session current status

Interface: FastEthernet0/0
Session status: UP-ACTIVE
Peer: 100.1.1.2 port 500
   IKE SA: local 200.1.1.2/500 remote 100.1.1.2/500 Active
   IPSEC FLOW: permit ip 192.168.2.0/255.255.255.0 192.168.4.0/255.255.255.0
         Active SAs: 2, origin: crypto map
```

Using the `show crypto session brief` command, we can see a summarized view of the active crypto sessions:

```
R1#show crypto session brief
Status: A- Active, U - Up, D - Down, I - Idle, S - Standby, N - Negotiating
        K - No IKE
ivrf = (none)
           Peer       I/F      Username          Group/Phase1_id   Uptime Stat
us       100.1.1.2   Fa0/0                              100.1.1.2 00:04:33
 UA
```

Furthermore, we can use the **Cisco Configuration Professional (CCP)** to monitor the VPN tunnel.

To check the VPN tunnel status, open CCP and navigate to **Configure** | **Security** | **VPN** | **Site-to-Site VPN**. Now, click on the **Edit Site to Site VPN** tab. You should see the **Status** as **Up**:

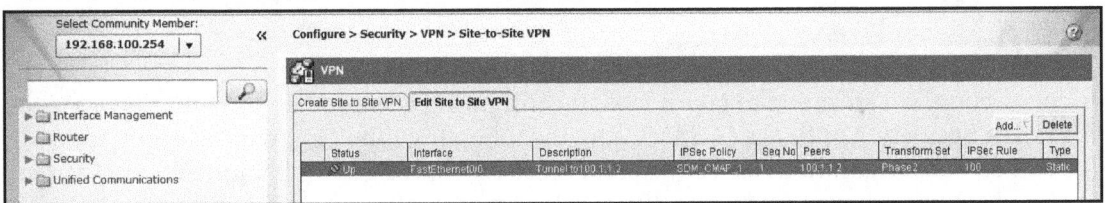

To get further details using CCP, navigate to **Monitor | Security | VPN Status | IPSec Tunnels**. Once again, we can get the live status of the VPN tunnel and packet flows:

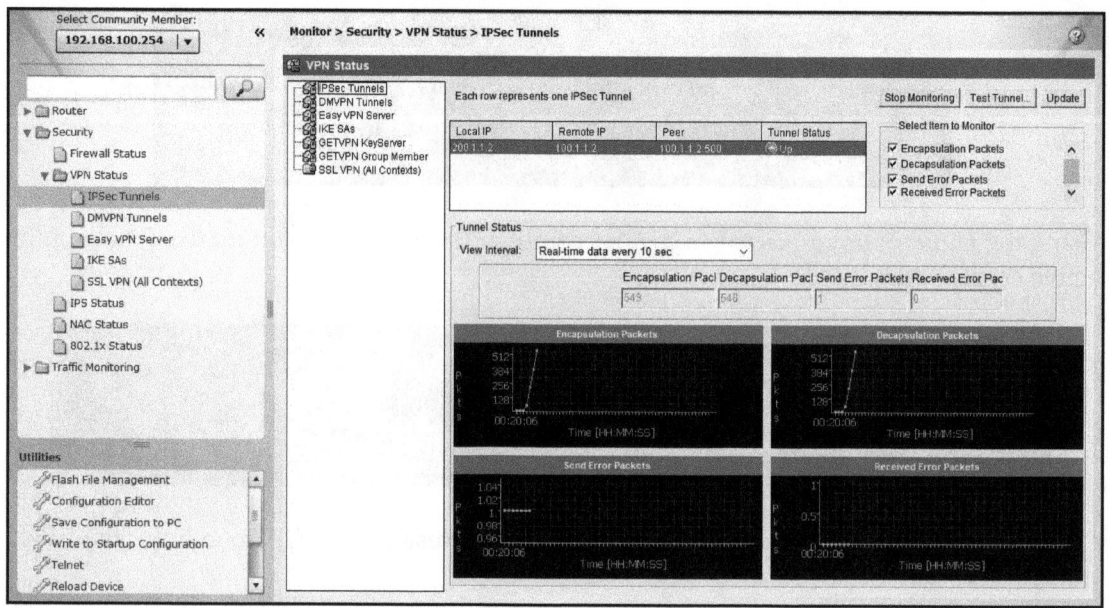

Configuring a site-to-site VPN using a Cisco ASA

In this section, we are going to take a look at configuring a site-to-site VPN tunnel using the **Adaptive Security Appliance (ASA)**. Using the following topology, we will apply some fundamental configurations on both ASAs before configuring the VPN tunnel. We want to ensure the devices have basic connectivity between each other:

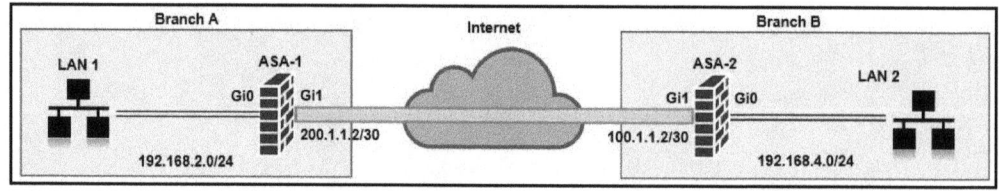

On `ASA-1`, the following configurations were applied:

- `GigabitEthernet1`—`200.1.1.2/30` (Outside).
- `GigabitEthernet0`—`192.168.2.1/24` (Inside).
- PAT set to use the IP address on the Outside interface.
- Set a default route to the ISP. In the lab configuration, the default gateway for `ASA-1` is `200.1.1.1/30`.

On `ASA-2`, the following configurations were applied:

- `GigabitEthernet1`—`100.1.1.2/30` (Outside)
- `GigabitEthernet0`—`192.168.4.1/24` (Inside)
- PAT set to use the IP address on the Outside interface
- The default gateway for `ASA-2` is `100.1.1.1/30`

Checking the device connectivity from `ASA-1`, we ping `100.1.1.2`:

```
ASA-1(config)# show interface ip brief
Interface               IP-Address      OK? Method Status                Protocol
GigabitEthernet0        192.168.2.1     YES manual up                    up
GigabitEthernet1        200.1.1.2       YES manual up                    up
GigabitEthernet2        unassigned      YES unset  administratively down up
GigabitEthernet3        unassigned      YES unset  administratively down up
ASA-1(config)# ping 100.1.1.2
Type escape sequence to abort.
Sending 5, 100-byte ICMP Echos to 100.1.1.2, timeout is 2 seconds:
!!!!!
Success rate is 100 percent (5/5), round-trip min/avg/max = 20/126/160 ms
```

Since we've ensured connectivity between both firewalls, we can begin configuring the site-to-site VPN using the **Adaptive Security Device Manager** (**ASDM**). Let's get started:

1. Open the ASDM on `ASA-1`, click on **Wizards | VPN Wizards | Site-to-site VPN Wizard...**:

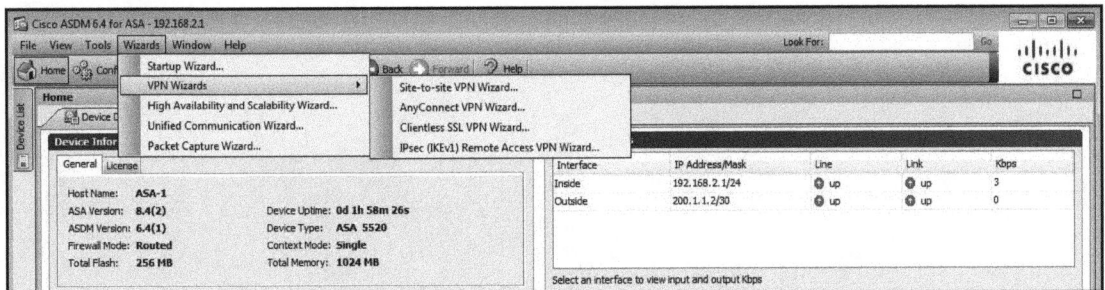

2. Once the VPN wizard opens, the following welcome window will provide a brief introduction to using a site-to-site VPN. Simply click on **Next** to begin the actual configuration phases:

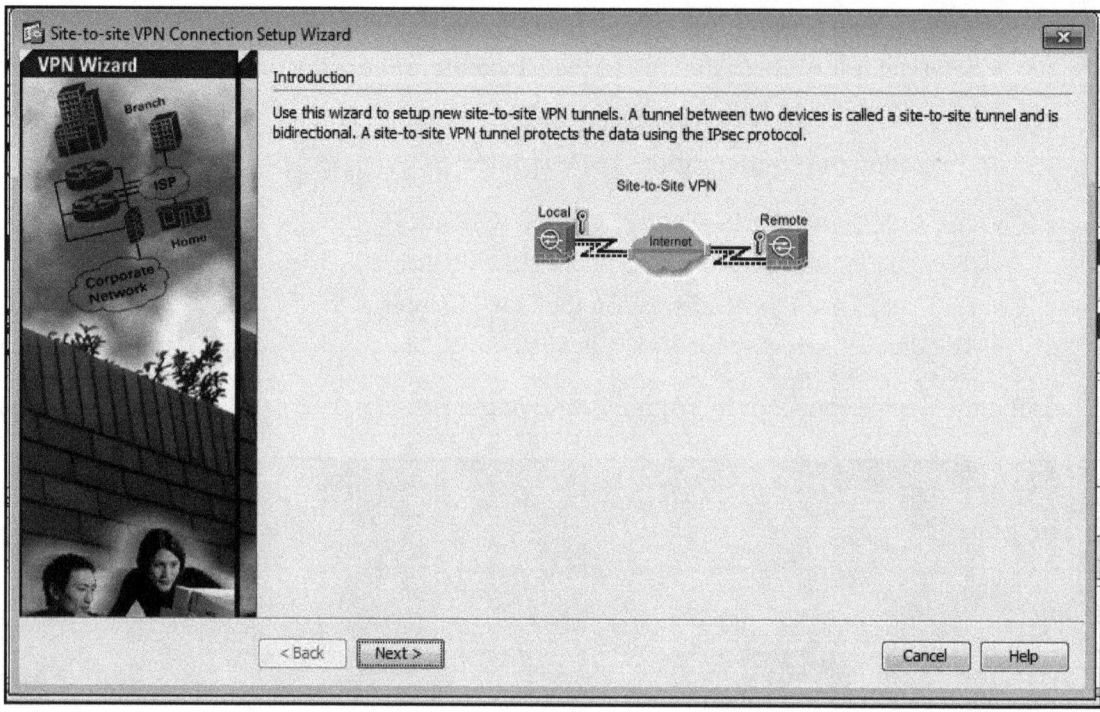

3. Here, we are presented with peer configuring. We will use the public IP address of `ASA-2`, `100.1.1.2`, and the VPN access interface will be the `ASA-1` Outside interface. Once you're finished, click on **Next** to continue:

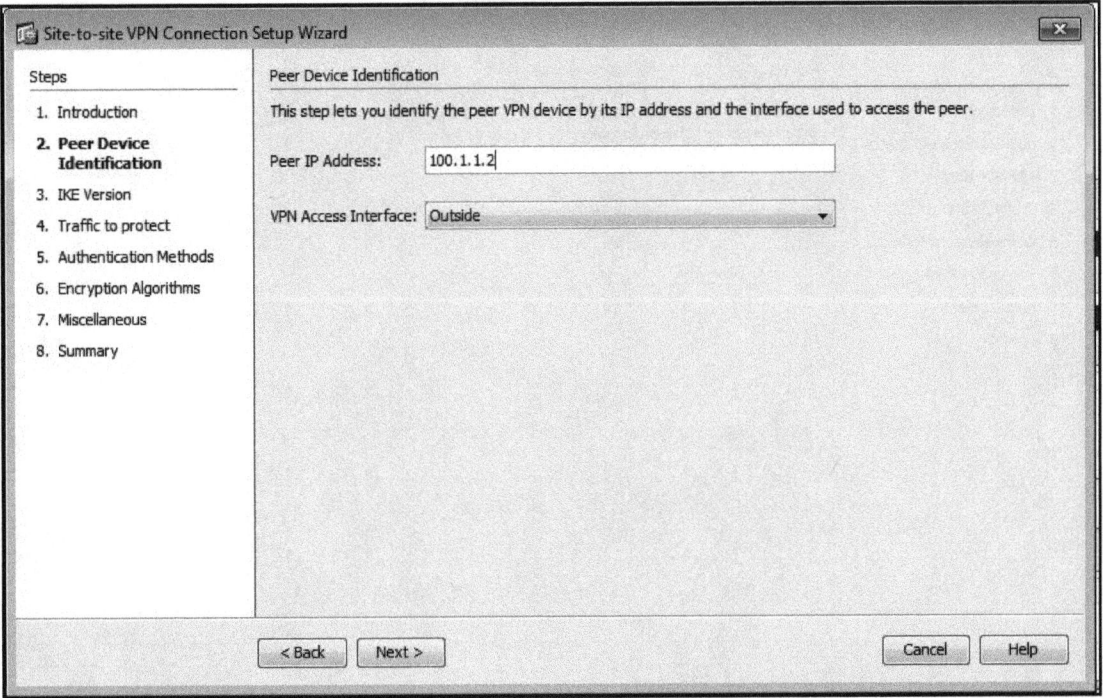

4. Choose whether the ASA should use either versions of **Internet Key Exchange** (**IKE**) or both during the negotiation phase. In this situation, we are using IKE version 2. Click **Next**:

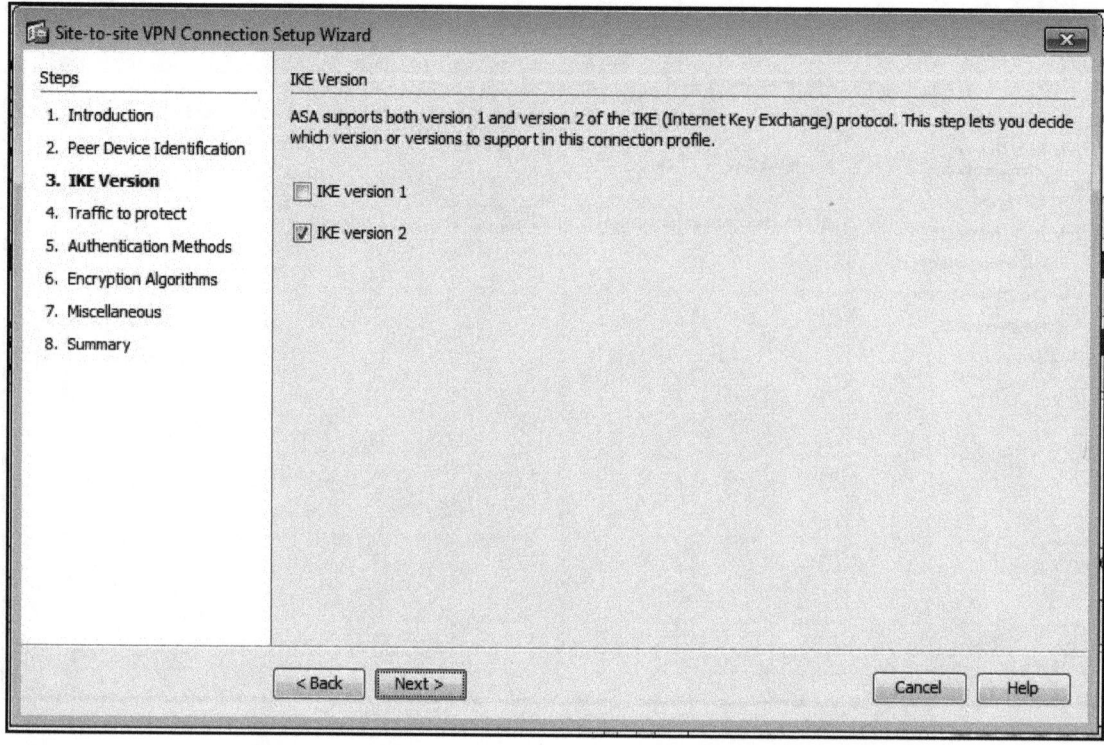

5. The **Traffic to protect** phase will ask you identify the local and the remote network. The purpose is to protect traffic using the IPSec framework. The **Local Network** will be the LAN on `ASA-1`, `192.168.2.0/24`, and the **Remote Network** is the LAN on `ASA-2`, `192.168.4.0/24`. Click on **Next**:

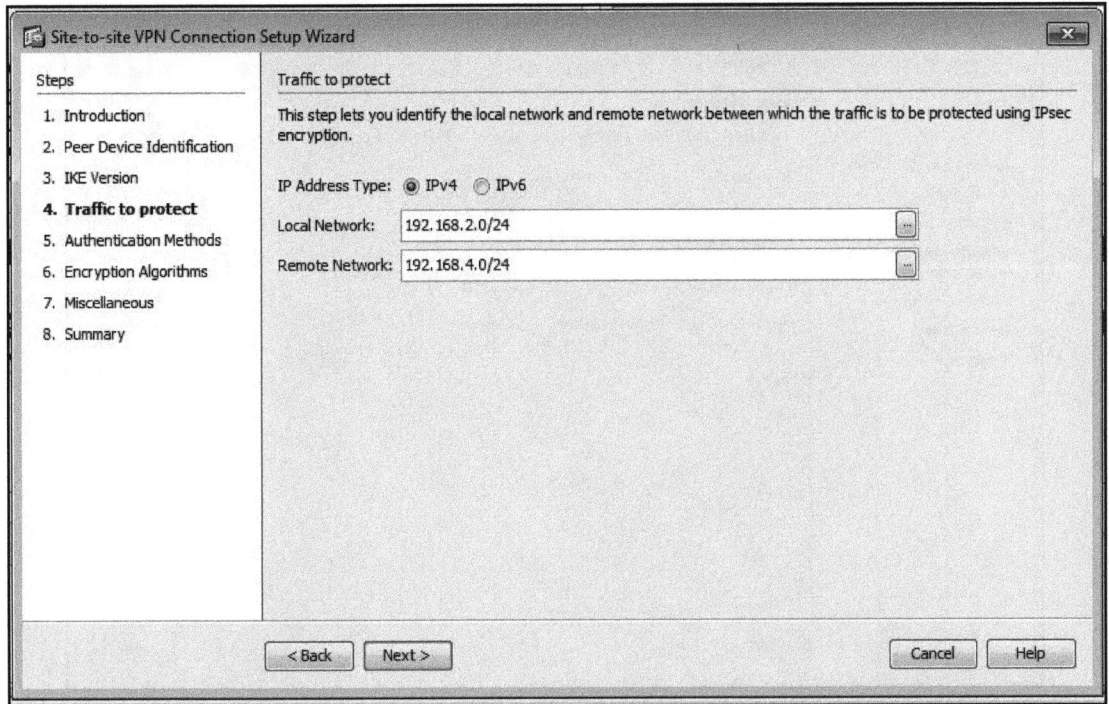

6. The following window will ask you to provide the authentication parameters for IKE. Since we have chosen only **IKE version 2**, the authentication parameters are required. Two options are available, **Local Pre-shared Key** and **Local Device Certificate**, to validate the identity. We will use the first option, the pre-shared key. Click on **Next** to continue:

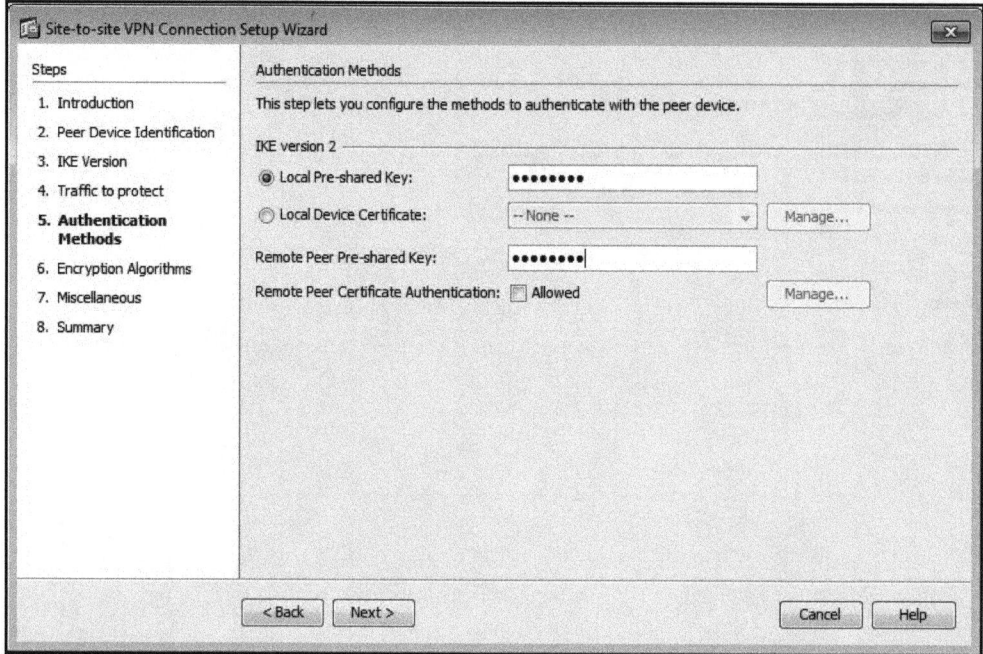

7. The following window allows you to configure IKE Phase 1 and Phase 2 policies for the negotiations with the other VPN peer, ASA-2. As you can see in the following window, there is a set of predefined policies already loaded by default. We are going to configure our own set of policies for the ASA.

8. To create a new **IKE Policy**, click on **Manage**:

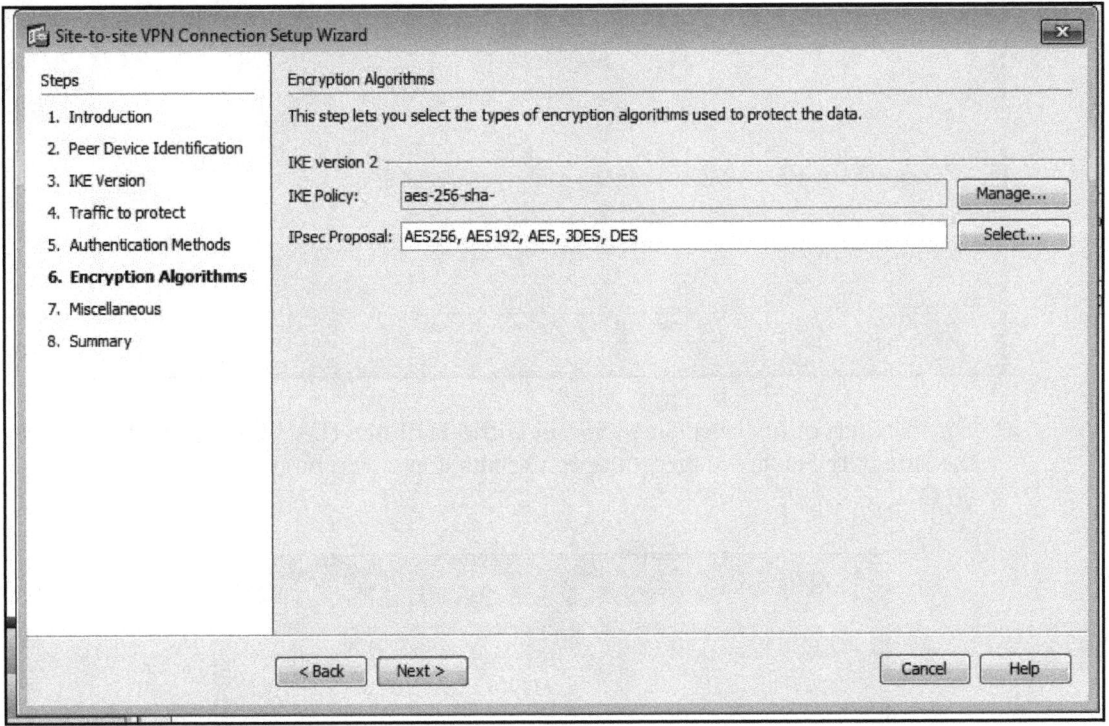

9. The following window will appear. Click on **Add** to create a new policy:

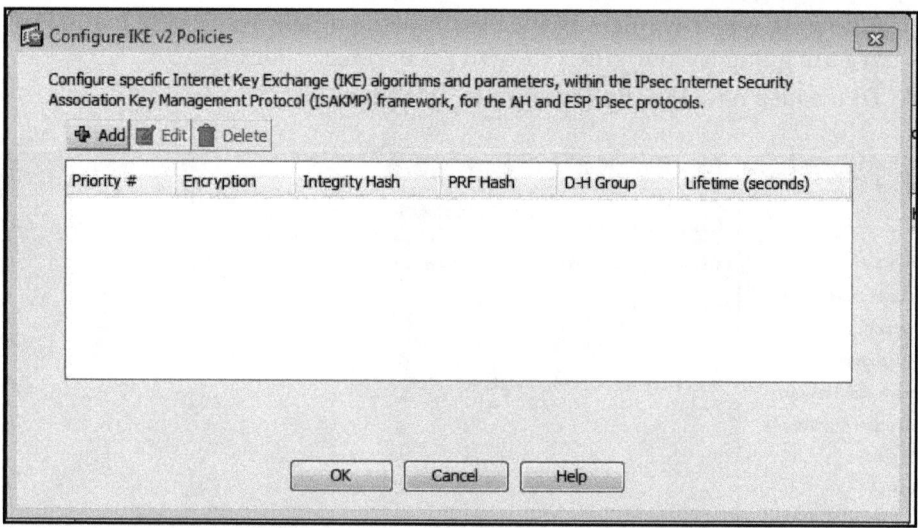

10. For the encryption, select **aes-256**, set Diffie-Hellman (**D-H Group**) to **2**, and for the **Integrity Hash**, we are going to use **sha**. Once you have set the values, click on **OK**:

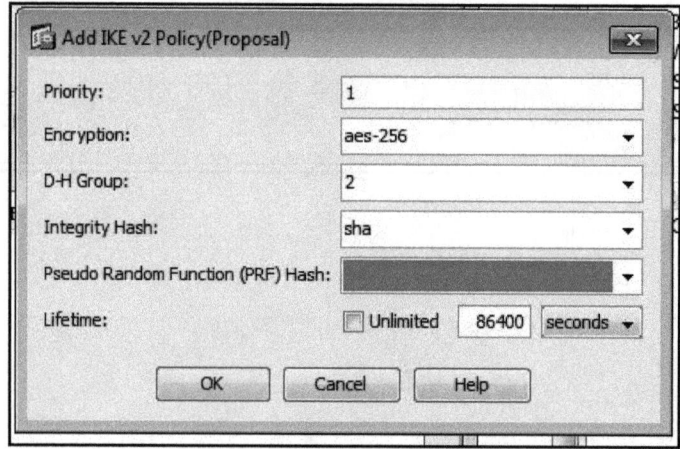

11. We are going to create our own transform set as well. Click on **Select** and a new window will appear. Click on **Add** to create a new transform set:

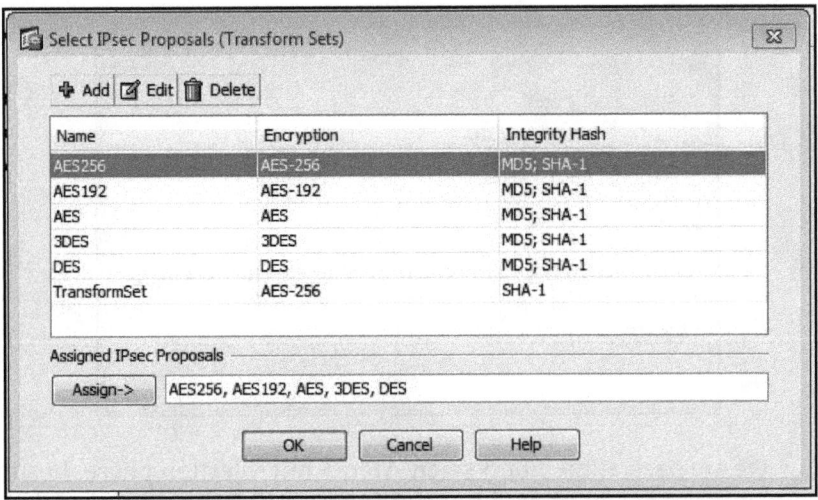

12. A smaller window will appear; we will use **AES-256** as the **Encryption** and **SHA-1** has the **Integrity Hash**. Click on **OK**:

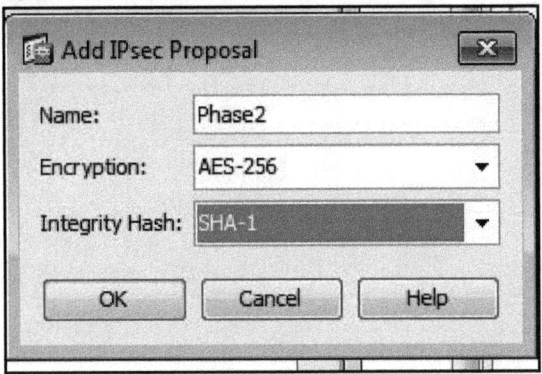

13. Ensure you remove the defaults and select the new policy that you have just created, in this case `Phase2`. Click on **OK** to return to the main transform set window:

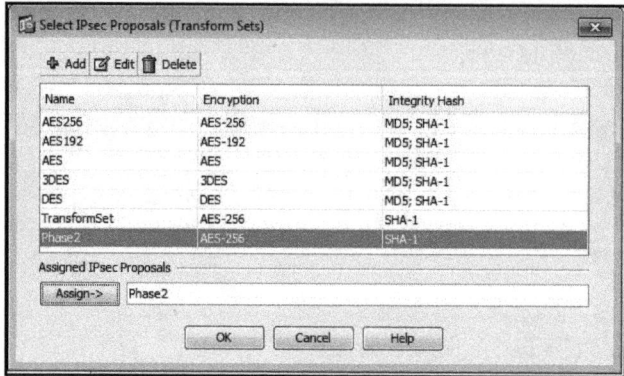

14. Now we are back at the **Encryption Algorithm** selection phase. Ensure you are using only the newly created policies for the **IKE Policy** and the **IPsec Proposal** fields.

15. Click **Next** to continue:

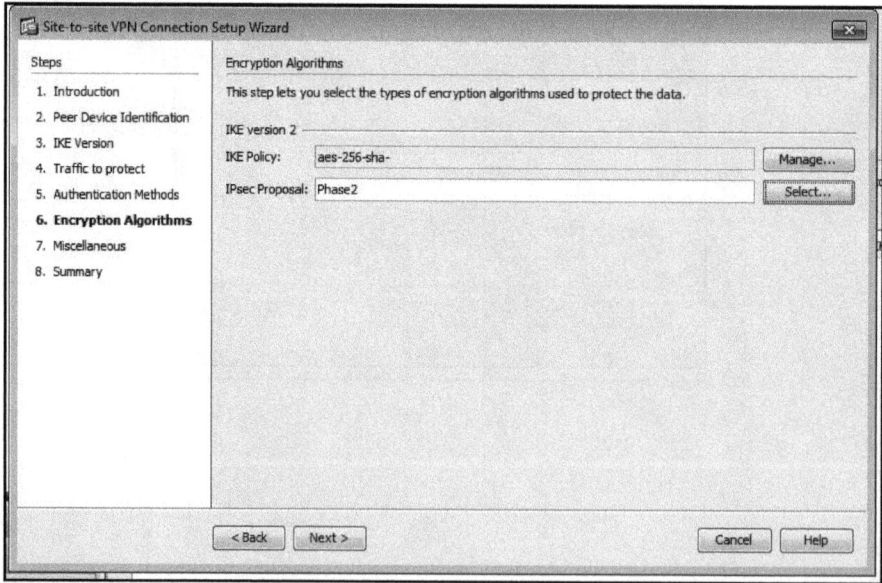

16. Ensure the following options are selected. Click **Next** once completed:

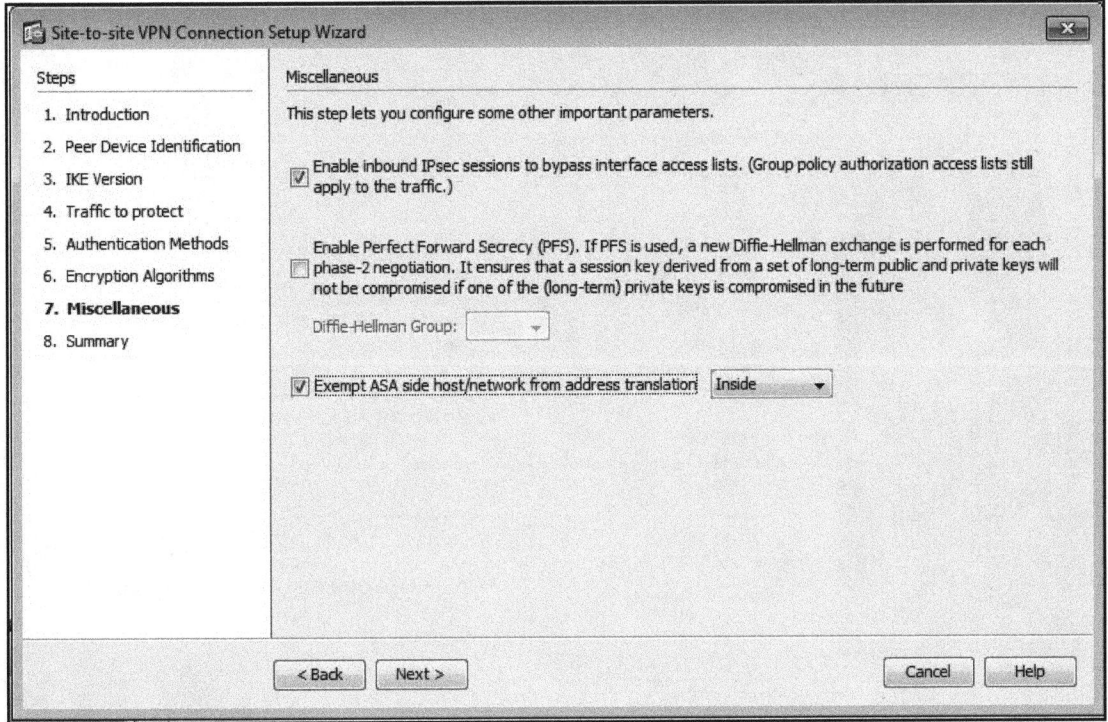

The final window will provide you with a summary of the configurations that will be applied to the ASA:

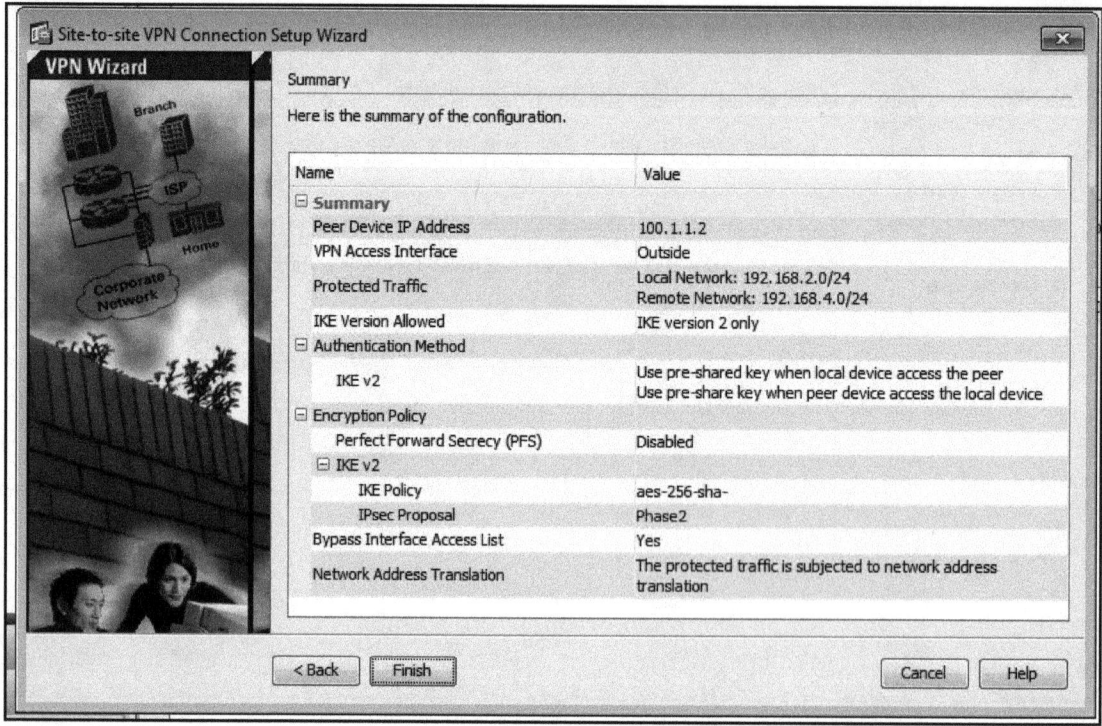

Click on **Finish** and then **Apply** on the ASDM window.

Verifying a site-to-site VPN on a Cisco ASA

Once you have configured both ASA-1 and ASA-2, it's time to test your site-to-site VPN.

Using the ASDM, navigate to **Monitoring** | **VPN** | **VPN Statistics** | **Sessions**. You'll see the **IKEv2 IPsec** VPN tunnel is in an active state:

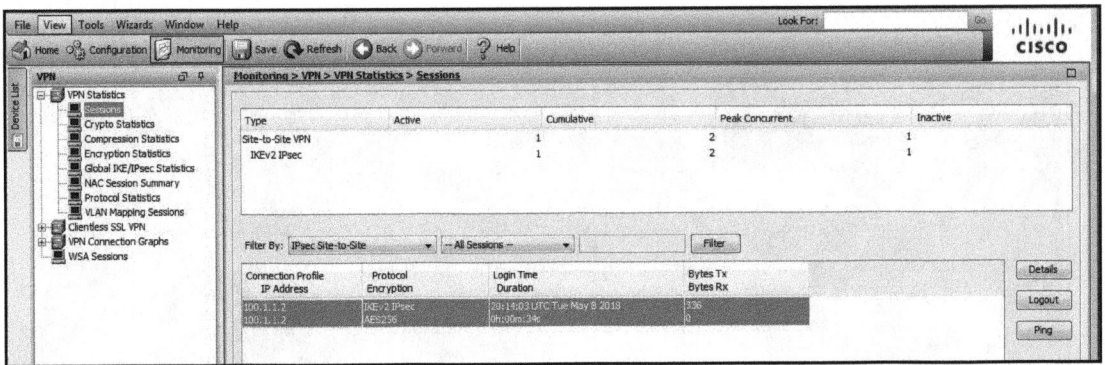

After either double-clicking on the session or clicking on **Details** on the right, the following windows will appear, presenting further details about the VPN tunnel and its peer:

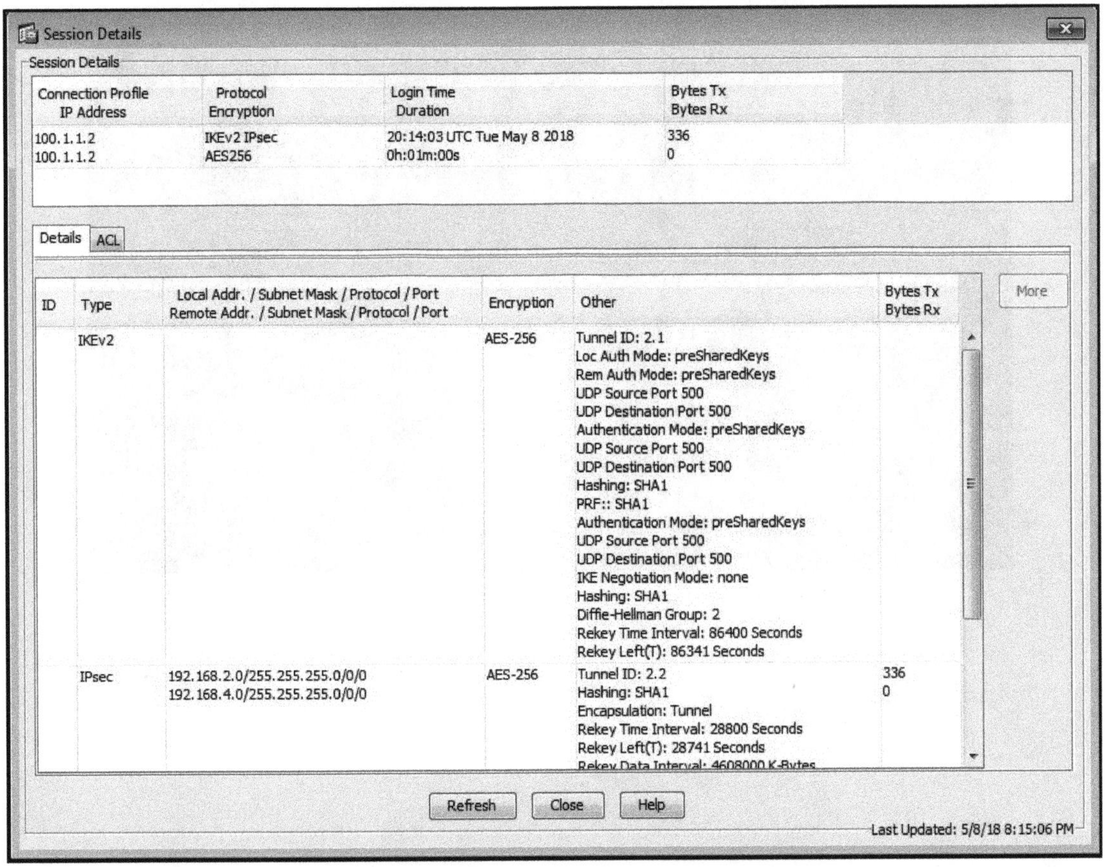

Session Details				
Connection Profile **IP Address**	**Protocol** **Encryption**	**Login Time** **Duration**	**Bytes Tx** **Bytes Rx**	
100.1.1.2	IKEv2 IPsec	20:14:03 UTC Tue May 8 2018	336	
100.1.1.2	AES256	0h:01m:00s	0	

Details | ACL

ID	Type	Local Addr. / Subnet Mask / Protocol / Port Remote Addr. / Subnet Mask / Protocol / Port	Encryption	Other	Bytes Tx Bytes Rx	More
	IKEv2		AES-256	Tunnel ID: 2.1 Loc Auth Mode: preSharedKeys Rem Auth Mode: preSharedKeys UDP Source Port 500 UDP Destination Port 500 Authentication Mode: preSharedKeys UDP Source Port 500 UDP Destination Port 500 Hashing: SHA1 PRF:: SHA1 Authentication Mode: preSharedKeys UDP Source Port 500 UDP Destination Port 500 IKE Negotiation Mode: none Hashing: SHA1 Diffie-Hellman Group: 2 Rekey Time Interval: 86400 Seconds Rekey Left(T): 86341 Seconds		
	IPsec	192.168.2.0/255.255.255.0/0/0 192.168.4.0/255.255.255.0/0/0	AES-256	Tunnel ID: 2.2 Hashing: SHA1 Encapsulation: Tunnel Rekey Time Interval: 28800 Seconds Rekey Left(T): 28741 Seconds Rekey Data Interval: 4608000 K-Bytes	336 0	

Refresh | Close | Help

Last Updated: 5/8/18 8:15:06 PM

Using the `show crypto isakmp sa` command, we can view the SA on the local firewall:

```
ASA-1# show crypto isakmp sa

There are no IKEv1 SAs

IKEv2 SAs:

Session-id:2, Status:UP-ACTIVE, IKE count:1, CHILD count:1

Tunnel-id            Local                Remote           Status        Role
 24701629         200.1.1.2/500        100.1.1.2/500       READY      INITIATOR
        Encr: AES-CBC, keysize: 256, Hash: SHA96, DH Grp:2, Auth sign: PSK, Auth verify: PSK
        Life/Active Time: 86400/126 sec
Child sa: local selector  192.168.2.0/0 - 192.168.2.255/65535
          remote selector 192.168.4.0/0 - 192.168.4.255/65535
          ESP spi in/out: 0x8e73128b/0xbecf0472
ASA-1# 
```

The `show crypto isakmp sa detail` command can provide further details about the security associations between `ASA-1` and `ASA-2`:

```
ASA-1# show crypto isakmp sa detail

There are no IKEv1 SAs

IKEv2 SAs:

Session-id:2, Status:UP-ACTIVE, IKE count:1, CHILD count:1

Tunnel-id            Local                Remote           Status        Role
 24701629         200.1.1.2/500        100.1.1.2/500       READY      INITIATOR
        Encr: AES-CBC, keysize: 256, Hash: SHA96, DH Grp:2, Auth sign: PSK, Auth verify: PSK
        Life/Active Time: 86400/162 sec
        Session-id: 2
        Status Description: Negotiation done
        Local spi: 0EB307146EC6D67B        Remote spi: FF54F8CA7706E80A
        Local id: 200.1.1.2
        Remote id: 100.1.1.2
        Local req mess id: 7              Remote req mess id: 5
        Local next mess id: 7            Remote next mess id: 5
        Local req queued: 7              Remote req queued: 5
        Local window: 1                  Remote window: 1
        DPD configured for 10 seconds, retry 2
        NAT-T is not detected
Child sa: local selector  192.168.2.0/0 - 192.168.2.255/65535
          remote selector 192.168.4.0/0 - 192.168.4.255/65535
          ESP spi in/out: 0x8e73128b/0xbecf0472
          AH spi in/out: 0x0/0x0
          CPI in/out: 0x0/0x0
          Encr: AES-CBC, keysize: 256, esp_hmac: SHA96
          ah_hmac: None, comp: IPCOMP_NONE, mode tunnel
ASA-1# 
```

The `show crypto ipsec sa` command displays the IPSec SA between the VPN peers:

```
ASA-1# show crypto ipsec sa
interface: Outside
    Crypto map tag: Outside_map, seq num: 1, local addr: 200.1.1.2

      access-list Outside_cryptomap extended permit ip 192.168.2.0 255.255.255.0 192.168.4.0 255.255.2
55.0
      local ident (addr/mask/prot/port): (192.168.2.0/255.255.255.0/0/0)
      remote ident (addr/mask/prot/port): (192.168.4.0/255.255.255.0/0/0)
      current_peer: 100.1.1.2

      #pkts encaps: 4, #pkts encrypt: 4, #pkts digest: 4
      #pkts decaps: 0, #pkts decrypt: 0, #pkts verify: 0
      #pkts compressed: 0, #pkts decompressed: 0
      #pkts not compressed: 4, #pkts comp failed: 0, #pkts decomp failed: 0
      #pre-frag successes: 0, #pre-frag failures: 0, #fragments created: 0
      #PMTUs sent: 0, #PMTUs rcvd: 0, #decapsulated frgs needing reassembly: 0
      #send errors: 0, #recv errors: 0

      local crypto endpt.: 200.1.1.2/500, remote crypto endpt.: 100.1.1.2/500
      path mtu 1500, ipsec overhead 74, media mtu 1500
      current outbound spi: BECF0472
      current inbound spi : 8E73128B

    inbound esp sas:
      spi: 0x8E73128B (2389906059)
         transform: esp-aes-256 esp-sha-hmac no compression
         in use settings ={L2L, Tunnel, }
         slot: 0, conn_id: 8192, crypto-map: Outside_map
         sa timing: remaining key lifetime (kB/sec): (3916800/28576)
         IV size: 16 bytes
         replay detection support: Y
         Anti replay bitmap:
           0x00000000 0x00000001
    outbound esp sas:
      spi: 0xBECF0472 (3201238130)
         transform: esp-aes-256 esp-sha-hmac no compression
         in use settings ={L2L, Tunnel, }
         slot: 0, conn_id: 8192, crypto-map: Outside_map
         sa timing: remaining key lifetime (kB/sec): (3962879/28576)
         IV size: 16 bytes
         replay detection support: Y
         Anti replay bitmap:
           0x00000000 0x00000001
```

The `show crypto isakmp stats` command provides detailed information about both IKEv1 and IKEv2 transactions in the ASA:

```
ASA-1# show crypto isakmp stats

Global IKEv1 Statistics
 Active Tunnels: 0
 Previous Tunnels: 0
 In Octets: 0
 In Packets: 0
 In Drop Packets: 0
 In Notifys: 0
 In P2 Exchanges: 0
 In P2 Exchange Invalids: 0
 In P2 Exchange Rejects: 0
 In P2 Sa Delete Requests: 0
```

```
Out Octets: 0
Out Packets: 0
Out Drop Packets: 0
Out Notifys: 0
Out P2 Exchanges: 0
Out P2 Exchange Invalids: 0
Out P2 Exchange Rejects: 0
Out P2 Sa Delete Requests: 0
Initiator Tunnels: 0
Initiator Fails: 0
Responder Fails: 0
System Capacity Fails: 0
Auth Fails: 0
Decrypt Fails: 0
Hash Valid Fails: 0
No Sa Fails: 0
```

The following is the **IKEv2 Statistics** of the `show crypto isakmp stats` command on the ASA:

```
Global IKEv2 Statistics
 Active Tunnels: 1
 Previous Tunnels: 1
 In Octets: 3540
 In Packets: 34
 In Drop Packets: 0
 In Drop Fragments: 0
 In Notifys: 8
 In P2 Exchange: 30
 In P2 Exchange Invalids: 0
 In P2 Exchange Rejects: 0
 In IPSEC Delete: 0
 In IKE Delete: 0
 Out Octets: 3652
 Out Packets: 34
 Out Drop Packets: 0
 Out Drop Fragments: 0
 Out Notifys: 11
 Out P2 Exchange: 30
 Out P2 Exchange Invalids: 0
 Out P2 Exchange Rejects: 0
 Out IPSEC Delete: 0
 Out IKE Delete: 1
 SAs Locally Initiated: 2
 SAs Locally Initiated Failed: 0
 SAs Remotely Initiated: 0
 SAs Remotely Initiated Failed: 0
```

```
System Capacity Failures: 0
Authentication Failures: 0
Decrypt Failures: 0
Hash Failures: 0
Invalid SPI: 0
In Configs: 0
Out Configs: 0
In Configs Rejects: 0
Out Configs Rejects: 0
Previous Tunnels: 1
Previous Tunnels Wraps: 0
In DPD Messages: 29
Out DPD Messages: 29
Out NAT Keepalives: 0
IKE Rekey Locally Initiated: 0
IKE Rekey Remotely Initiated: 0
CHILD Rekey Locally Initiated: 0
CHILD Rekey Remotely Initiated: 0
```

We can see below are the **IKEV2 Call Admission Statistics** from the show crypto isakmp stats command:

```
IKEV2 Call Admission Statistics
Max Active SAs: No Limit
Max In-Negotiation SAs: 5025
Cookie Challenge Threshold: 2512
Active SAs: 1
In-Negotiation SAs: 0
Incoming Requests: 0
Incoming Requests Accepted: 0
Incoming Requests Rejected: 0
Outgoing Requests: 2
Outgoing Requests Accepted: 2
Outgoing Requests Rejected: 0
Rejected Requests: 0
Rejected Over Max SA limit: 0
Rejected Low Resources: 0
Rejected Reboot In Progress: 0
Cookie Challenges: 0
Cookie Challenges Passed: 0
Cookie Challenges Failed: 0
```

The `show crypto ikev1 stats` and `show crypto ikev2 stats` commands provide information about the IKEv1 and IKEv2 transactions in the Cisco ASA:

```
ASA-1# show crypto ikev1 sa

There are no IKEv1 SAs
ASA-1# show crypto ikev2 sa

IKEv2 SAs:

Session-id:2, Status:UP-ACTIVE, IKE count:1, CHILD count:1

Tunnel-id                 Local              Remote       Status       Role
  24701629          200.1.1.2/500          100.1.1.2/500   READY    INITIATOR
      Encr: AES-CBC, keysize: 256, Hash: SHA96, DH Grp:2, Auth sign: PSK, Auth verify: PSK
      Life/Active Time: 86400/335 sec
Child sa: local selector  192.168.2.0/0 - 192.168.2.255/65535
          remote selector 192.168.4.0/0 - 192.168.4.255/65535
          ESP spi in/out: 0x8e73128b/0xbecf0472
ASA-1#
```

Using the `show isakmp sa` command, we can see the IKEv1 and IKEv2 runtime SA database:

```
ASA-1(config)# show isakmp sa

There are no IKEv1 SAs

IKEv2 SAs:

Session-id:1, Status:UP-ACTIVE, IKE count:1, CHILD count:1

Tunnel-id                 Local              Remote       Status       Role
388320459           200.1.1.2/500          100.1.1.2/500   READY    INITIATOR
      Encr: AES-CBC, keysize: 256, Hash: SHA96, DH Grp:5, Auth sign: PSK, Auth verify: PSK
      Life/Active Time: 86400/1451 sec
Child sa: local selector  192.168.2.0/0 - 192.168.2.255/65535
          remote selector 192.168.4.0/0 - 192.168.4.255/65535
          ESP spi in/out: 0xe785e58e/0x6bc47ef8
ASA-1(config)#
```

To see further details on the IKEv1 and IKEv2 runtime SA database, use the `show crypto isakmp sa detail` command:

```
ASA-1# show crypto isakmp sa detail

There are no IKEv1 SAs

IKEv2 SAs:

Session-id:2, Status:UP-ACTIVE, IKE count:1, CHILD count:1

Tunnel-id             Local              Remote      Status      Role
 24701629         200.1.1.2/500      100.1.1.2/500   READY    INITIATOR
      Encr: AES-CBC, keysize: 256, Hash: SHA96, DH Grp:2, Auth sign: PSK, Auth verify: PSK
      Life/Active Time: 86400/449 sec
      Session-id: 2
      Status Description: Negotiation done
      Local spi: 0EB307146EC6D67B      Remote spi: FF54F8CA7706E80A
      Local id: 200.1.1.2
      Remote id: 100.1.1.2
      Local req mess id: 22             Remote req mess id: 20
      Local next mess id: 22           Remote next mess id: 20
      Local req queued: 22             Remote req queued: 20
      Local window: 1                  Remote window: 1
      DPD configured for 10 seconds, retry 2
      NAT-T is not detected
Child sa: local selector  192.168.2.0/0 - 192.168.2.255/65535
          remote selector 192.168.4.0/0 - 192.168.4.255/65535
          ESP spi in/out: 0x8e73128b/0xbecf0472
          AH spi in/out: 0x0/0x0
          CPI in/out: 0x0/0x0
          Encr: AES-CBC, keysize: 256, esp_hmac: SHA96
          ah_hmac: None, comp: IPCOMP_NONE, mode tunnel
ASA-1# ▮
```

The `show crypto ipsec sa` command provides details for the IKE Phase 2 runtime SA database:

```
ASA-1# show crypto ipsec sa
interface: Outside
    Crypto map tag: Outside_map, seq num: 1, local addr: 200.1.1.2

      access-list Outside_cryptomap extended permit ip 192.168.2.0 255.255.255.0 192.168.4.0 255.255.2
55.0
      local ident (addr/mask/prot/port): (192.168.2.0/255.255.255.0/0/0)
      remote ident (addr/mask/prot/port): (192.168.4.0/255.255.255.0/0/0)
      current_peer: 100.1.1.2

      #pkts encaps: 4, #pkts encrypt: 4, #pkts digest: 4
      #pkts decaps: 0, #pkts decrypt: 0, #pkts verify: 0
      #pkts compressed: 0, #pkts decompressed: 0
      #pkts not compressed: 4, #pkts comp failed: 0, #pkts decomp failed: 0
      #pre-frag successes: 0, #pre-frag failures: 0, #fragments created: 0
      #PMTUs sent: 0, #PMTUs rcvd: 0, #decapsulated frgs needing reassembly: 0
      #send errors: 0, #recv errors: 0

      local crypto endpt.: 200.1.1.2/500, remote crypto endpt.: 100.1.1.2/500
      path mtu 1500, ipsec overhead 74, media mtu 1500
      current outbound spi: BECF0472
      current inbound spi : 8E73128B

    inbound esp sas:
      spi: 0x8E73128B (2389906059)
         transform: esp-aes-256 esp-sha-hmac no compression
         in use settings ={L2L, Tunnel, }
         slot: 0, conn_id: 8192, crypto-map: Outside_map
         sa timing: remaining key lifetime (kB/sec): (3916800/28246)
         IV size: 16 bytes
         replay detection support: Y
         Anti replay bitmap:
          0x00000000 0x00000001
    outbound esp sas:
      spi: 0xBECF0472 (3201238130)
         transform: esp-aes-256 esp-sha-hmac no compression
         in use settings ={L2L, Tunnel, }
         slot: 0, conn_id: 8192, crypto-map: Outside_map
         sa timing: remaining key lifetime (kB/sec): (3962879/28246)
         IV size: 16 bytes
         replay detection support: Y
         Anti replay bitmap:
```

Finally, we can use the `show vpn-sessiondb` command to view the session database for any VPN connections terminated in the Cisco ASA:

```
ASA-1# show vpn-sessiondb
------------------------------------------------------------------------
VPN Session Summary
------------------------------------------------------------------------
                          Active : Cumulative : Peak Concur : Inactive
                         ---------------------------------------------------
Site-to-Site VPN      :      1 :          2 :          1
  IKEv2 IPsec         :      1 :          2 :          1              1
------------------------------------------------------------------------
Total Active and Inactive  :      1           Total Cumulative :      2
Device Total VPN Capacity  :      0
Device Load                :     0%
***!! WARNING: Platform capacity exceeded !!***
------------------------------------------------------------------------


------------------------------------------------------------------------
Tunnels Summary
------------------------------------------------------------------------
                          Active : Cumulative : Peak Concurrent
                         ---------------------------------------------------
IKEv2                 :      1 :          2 :          1
IPsec                 :      1 :          2 :          1
------------------------------------------------------------------------
Totals                :      2 :          4
------------------------------------------------------------------------

ASA-1#
```

Summary

In this chapter, we explored the general uses of a site-to-site VPN, then we established a VPN tunnel using the Cisco IOS router and the Cisco Adaptive Security Appliance. Finally, we completed each section by looking into troubleshooting commands and their output to verify the status of the VPN tunnel on either the router or the firewall.

Having completed this chapter, you should be able to configure a site-to-site VPN on both a Cisco router and an ASA.

In the next chapter, we will look at configuring a remote access VPN for those users who require access to the corporate network but are working as a remote worker or a field engineer.

15
Configuring a Remote-Access VPN

In this chapter, we are going to learn how to configure a remote-access VPN on the Cisco **Adaptive Security Appliance** (**ASA**). A remote-access VPN provides a clientless version where the user accesses the corporate network using a web browser on their end device, such as a personal computer. The other version uses a client-based model. This model employs a VPN client that is installed on the user's end device.

We will discuss the general use of both of these models and how each can be beneficial to an organization. In this chapter, we will cover the following:

- Using a remote-access VPN
- Configuring a clientless remote-access VPN
- Configuring a client-based remote-access VPN
- Verification

Let's begin!

Using a remote-access VPN

A lot of organizations try to ensure their corporate network is secure in terms of both the internet and external threats. By doing so, some may have policies that state that only company-owned devices are allowed to connect and access corporate resources, which is good. Some organizations may also have employees who work in the field (outside the company's premises), such as field engineers or even members of staff who travel to other locations.

At times, these field engineers or staff members may require access to the **Corporate Network** while at a remote location, such as a hotel or customer site:

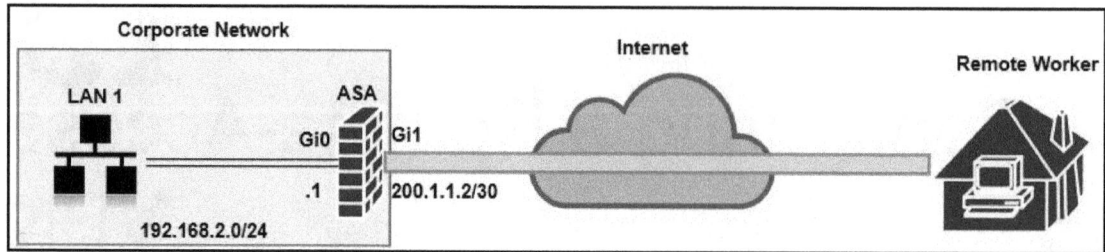

In the previous chapter, we spoke about establishing, and the need for, a site-to-site VPN. This situation is a bit different as the field engineer/staff (remote worker) requires access to the corporate network, in particular a secure connection between the remote worker's computer/laptop and the corporate network. To determine a feasible solution, we will discuss another type of VPN, known as a remote-access VPN.

A remote-access VPN has two sub-categories:

- Clientless SSL VPN
- Full Cisco AnyConnect Secure Mobility Client SSL VPN

Throughout the remaining sections of this chapter, we'll be using the following topology for setting up the remote-access VPN:

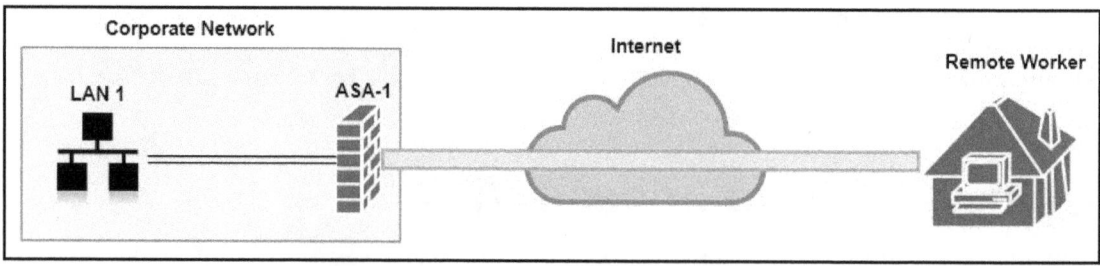

The **Remote Worker** is currently not on the premises; they may be working from home, in another country, or in the field, and have an **Internet** connection. In the previous chapters, we discussed the importance of having a secure connection through an untrusted network, such as the internet. In this chapter, we want to establish a VPN connection between the ASA and the remote worker's computer.

Clientless SSL VPN

You may be wondering what a clientless SSL VPN is. A clientless SSL VPN does not require any particular application to work except a web browser, such as Internet Explorer or Mozilla Firefox, therefore making it a WebVPN and simple to use. However, all the corporate resources may not be available to the VPN user due to certain restrictions.

Resources are usually made available by creating a hyperlink within the VPN portal; the VPN user can simply click on a particular link to access the corporate resources.

Some important things to consider when using a clientless SSL VPN:

- Only a web browser is needed, therefore they are supported by most operating systems and web browsers.
- The user accesses all resources via the web browser.
- The VPN connection is between the ASA and the web browser, and not the user's computer. Therefore, traffic outside of the VPN portal may be unsecured.

AnyConnect SSL VPN

This is a client-based VPN that uses the Cisco AnyConnect Secure Mobility Client to establish a secure VPN connection between the client computer and the ASA. The benefit of using a client-based VPN is that all the traffic between the computer and the firewall is encrypted and secure, and the user has full access to all the resources on the corporate network, as if they were really on the company's premises.

When using the Cisco AnyConnect Secure Mobility Client, each user who establishes a VPN connection to the ASA is assigned a virtual IP address that can either be routed through the ASA or can be given an IP address that is part of the corporate network.

In the following sections, we'll look at configuring both the clientless SSL VPN and the client-based VPN. However, the clientless SSL VPN will be used to securely deliver the Cisco AnyConnect Secure Mobility Client to VPN users who want to establish a full VPN connection to the ASA and corporate network.

Configuring a clientless remote-access VPN

To get started, open the **Adaptive Security Device Manager** (**ASDM**) and connect to ASA-1. Once you're connected, click on **Wizards** | **VPN Wizards** | **Clientless SSL VPN Wizard...**:

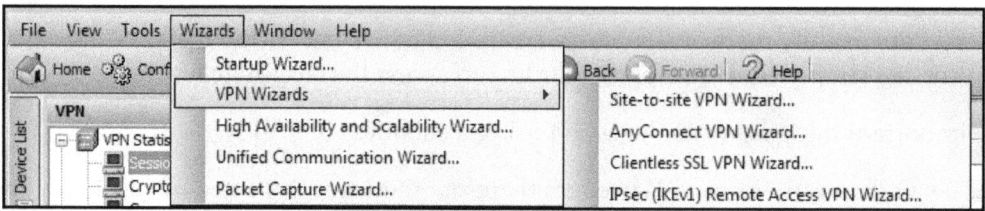

Now perform the following steps:

1. An introduction window will appear providing you with a briefing about the clientless SSL VPN. Click on **Next** to continue:

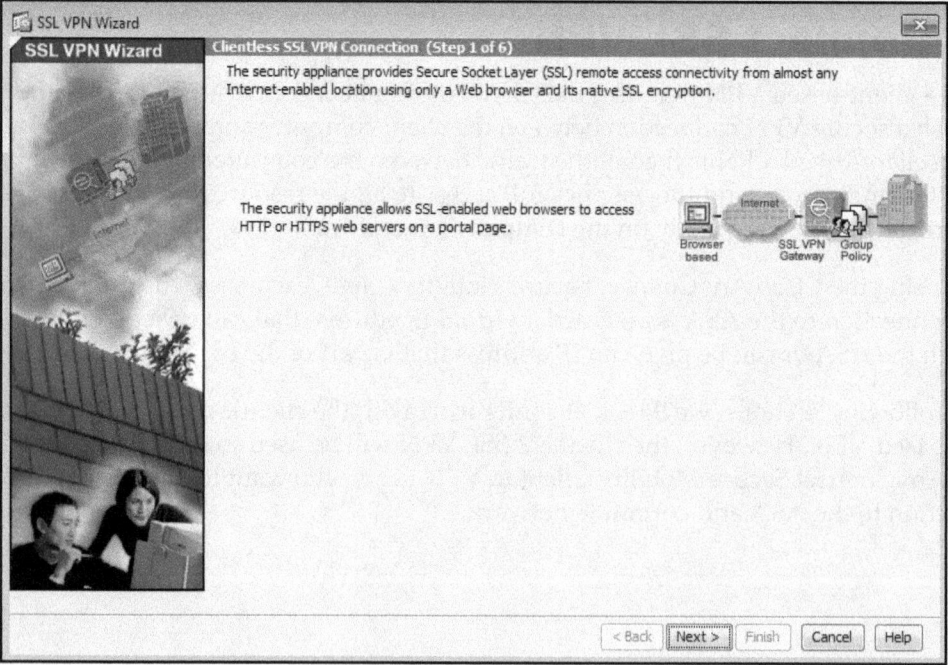

2. In this window, you'll need to configure some settings about the **SSL VPN Interface**, such as the **Connection Profile Name**, the **SSL VPN Interface**, digital **Certificate**, and how clients are able to access the connection profile. Click **Next**:

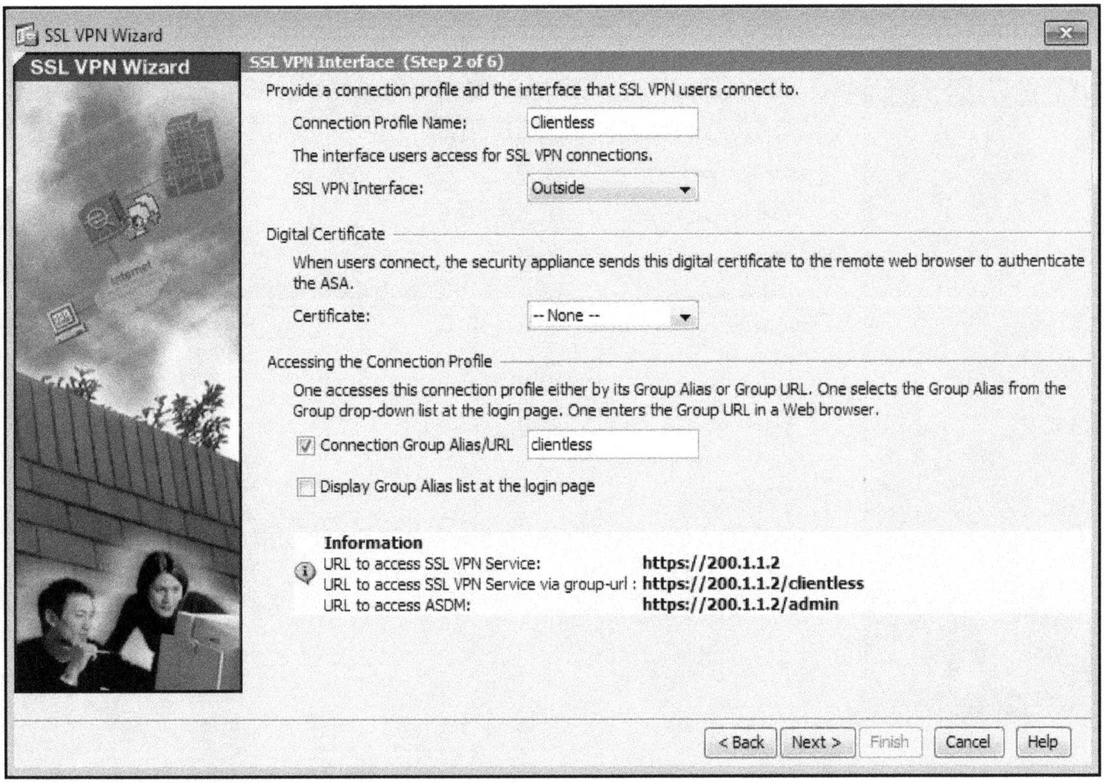

SSL VPN Wizard

SSL VPN Wizard

SSL VPN Interface (Step 2 of 6)

Provide a connection profile and the interface that SSL VPN users connect to.

Connection Profile Name: Clientless

The interface users access for SSL VPN connections.

SSL VPN Interface: Outside

Digital Certificate

When users connect, the security appliance sends this digital certificate to the remote web browser to authenticate the ASA.

Certificate: -- None --

Accessing the Connection Profile

One accesses this connection profile either by its Group Alias or Group URL. One selects the Group Alias from the Group drop-down list at the login page. One enters the Group URL in a Web browser.

☑ Connection Group Alias/URL clientless

☐ Display Group Alias list at the login page

Information
URL to access SSL VPN Service: **https://200.1.1.2**
URL to access SSL VPN Service via group-url : **https://200.1.1.2/clientless**
URL to access ASDM: **https://200.1.1.2/admin**

[< Back] [Next >] [Finish] [Cancel] [Help]

The **Connection Profile Name** and **Connection Group Alias/URL** can be anything you choose.

3. Here, you need to configure how users are authenticated on the VPN. There are two options available: using an AAA server or creating the user accounts on the ASA's local user database.

If you have an AAA server on your network, simply click on the radio button next to **Authenticate using a AAA server group** and click on **New...** to add the server.

In this exercise, we are going to use the ASA to handle the authentication of our users. Click on the radio button next to **Authenticate using the local user database**. Now you'll be able to create and delete individual user accounts. As you can see, we've already create Alice. Click on **Next**:

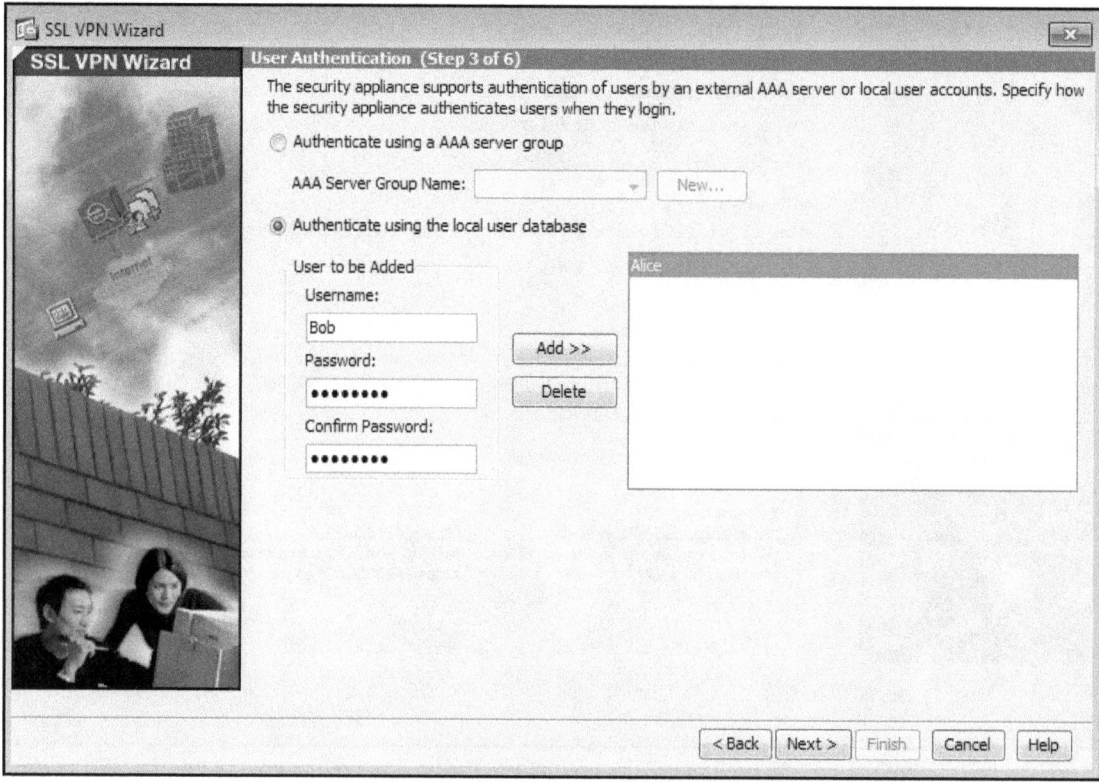

4. This window allows the creation of either a new group policy or modification of an existing group policy. We've chosen to create a new policy for our VPN users. Click **Next**:

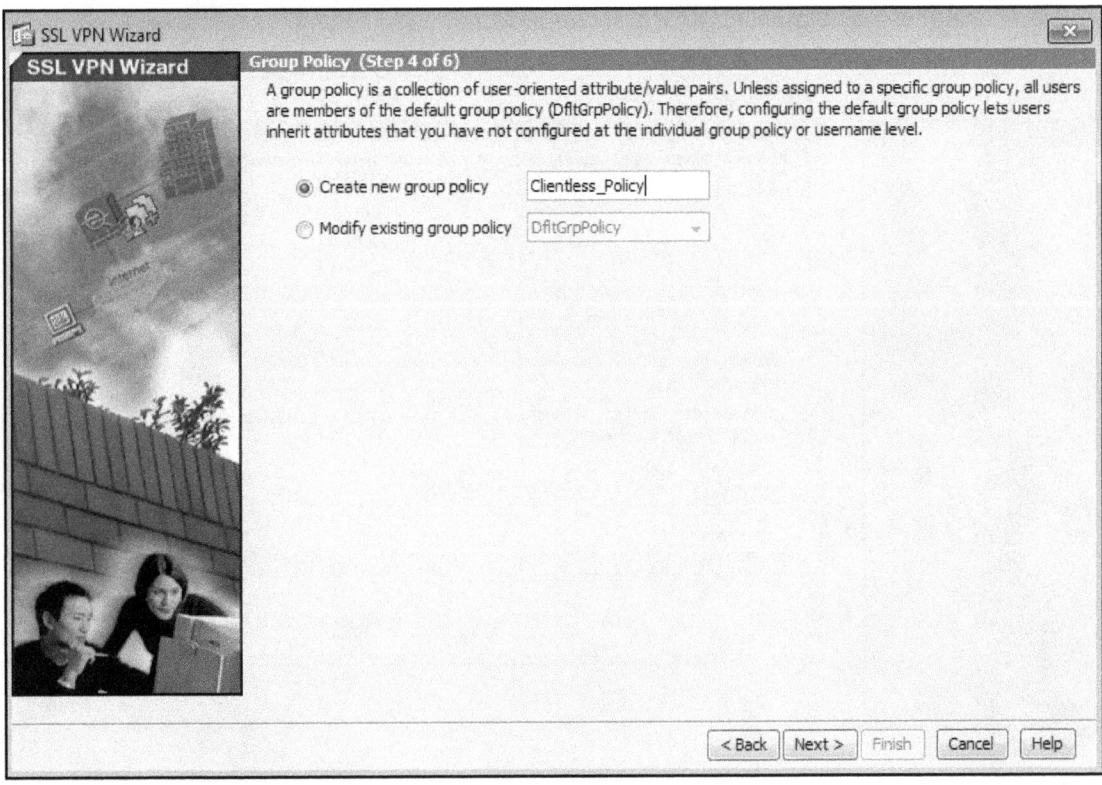

5. As mentioned earlier in this chapter, resources are made available in the VPN portal by using hyperlinks. This step allows you to create and map those resources using **Bookmarks**. To create a bookmark (a hyperlink to a resource), click on **Manage....** A smaller window, named **Configure GUI Customization Objects**, will appear. Now, click on **Add**:

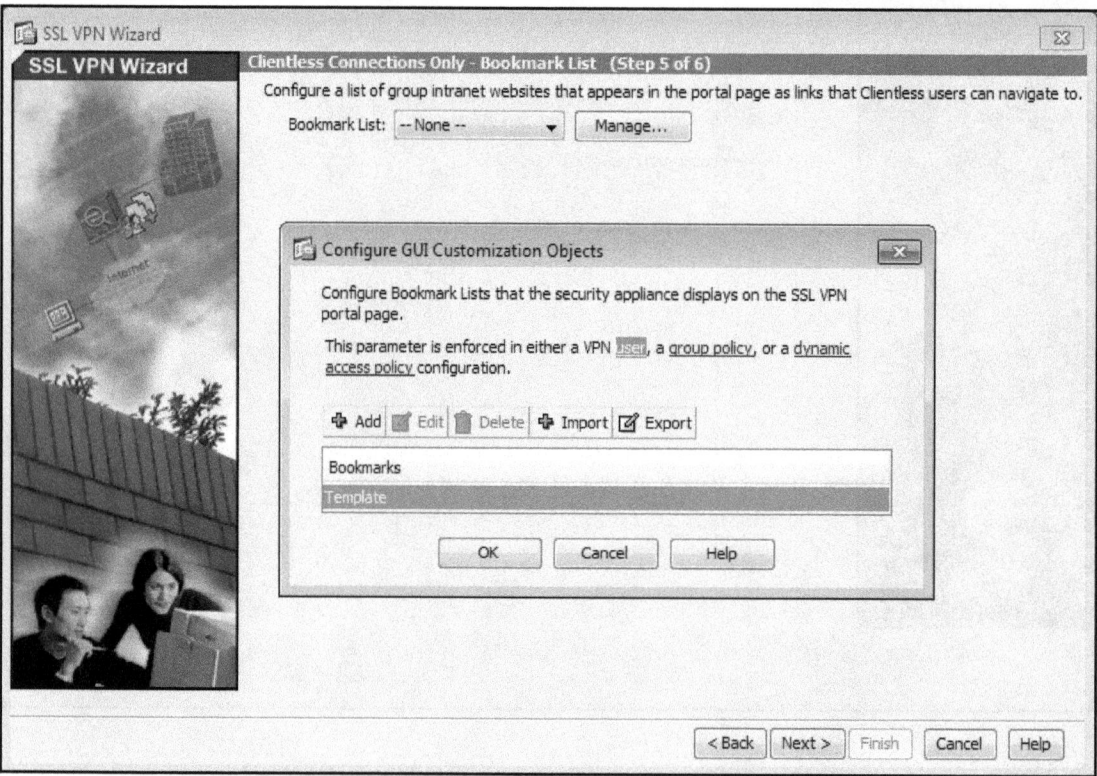

6. You'll be able to create a bookmark listing here. Name the bookmark list, then click on **Add**:

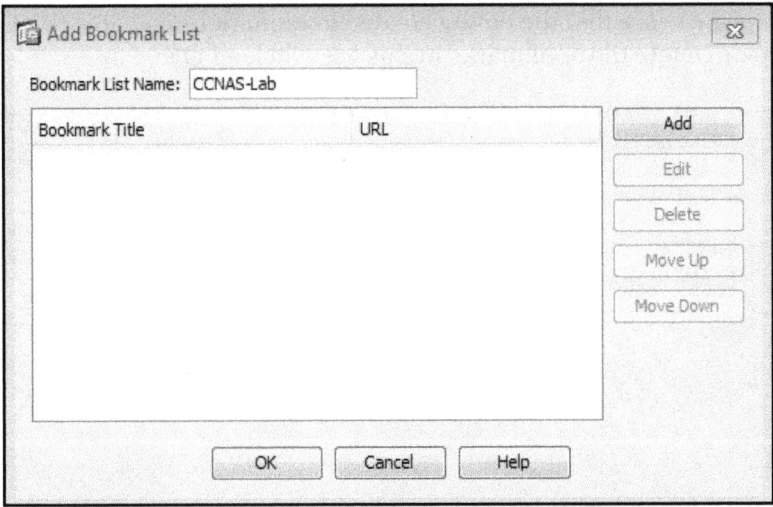

7. The **Add Bookmark** window appears; simply create a name for the bookmark, select the protocol to use to access the resource, and enter the IP address of the resource/server. Click on **OK** to return to the **Bookmark List** window:

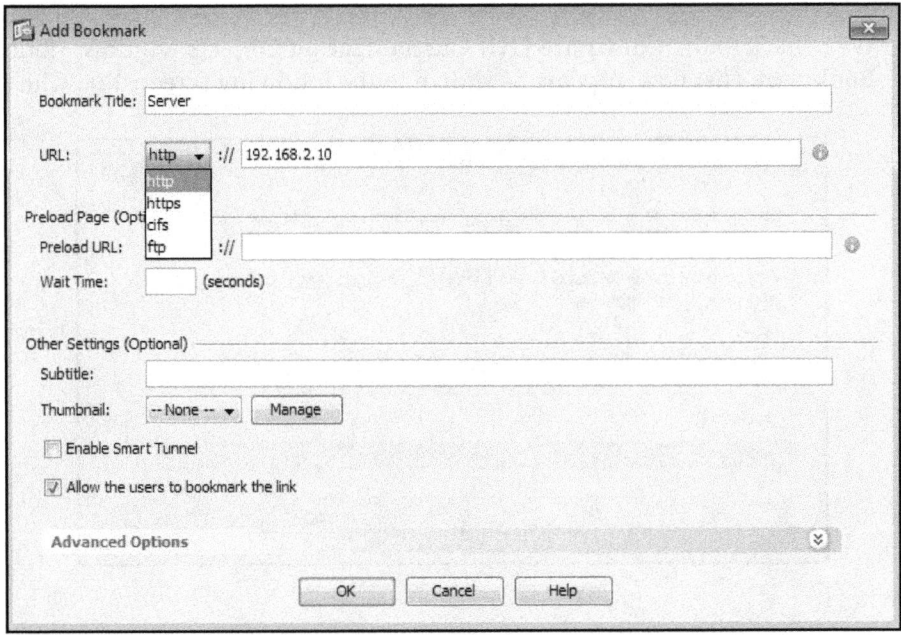

8. Now we can see that the newly created bookmark is available. You can **Add**, **Edit**, or **Delete** the bookmarks in this list. Click on **OK**:

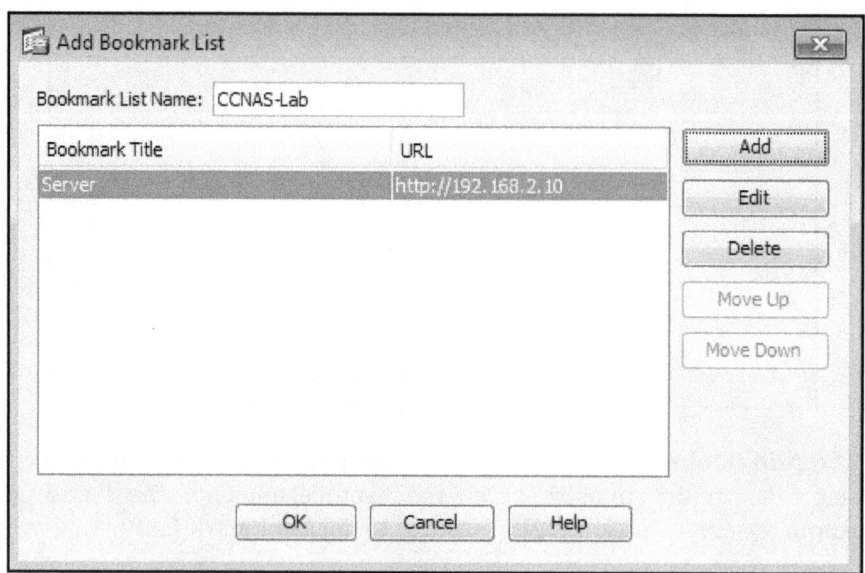

9. We're back to the **Configure GUI Customization Objects** window; notice the **Bookmarks** list now appears as shown in the following screenshot. Click on **OK**:

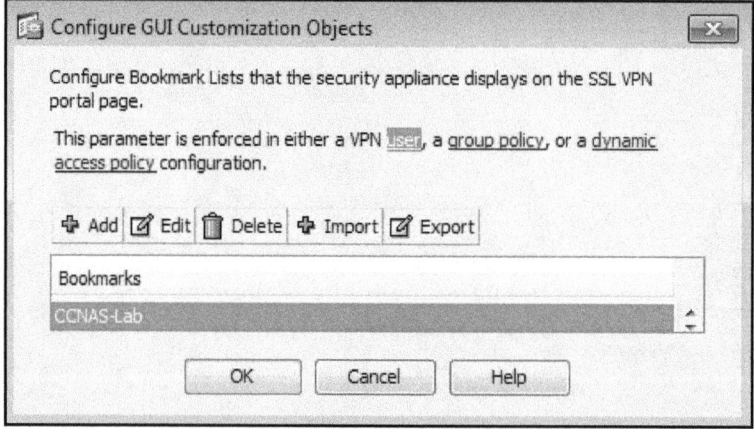

10. Now we're back to the main wizard interface for selecting bookmarks to appear in the VPN portal. Click on **Next**:

SSL VPN Wizard
SSL VPN Wizard
Clientless Connections Only - Bookmark List (Step 5 of 6)
Configure a list of group intranet websites that appears in the portal page as links that Clientless users can navigate to.
Bookmark List: CCNAS-Lab
Manage...

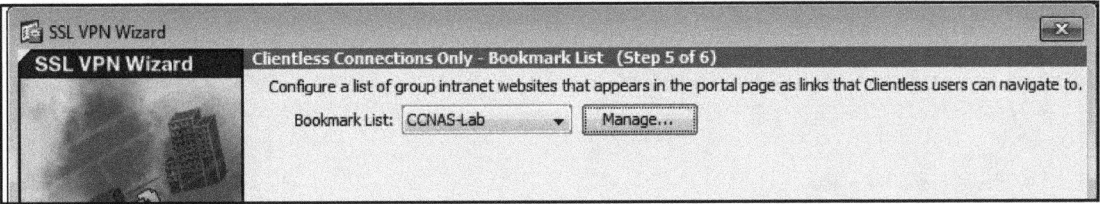

11. The **Summary** window displays a brief of the configurations we selected in steps 1 to 5. Click on **Finish**:

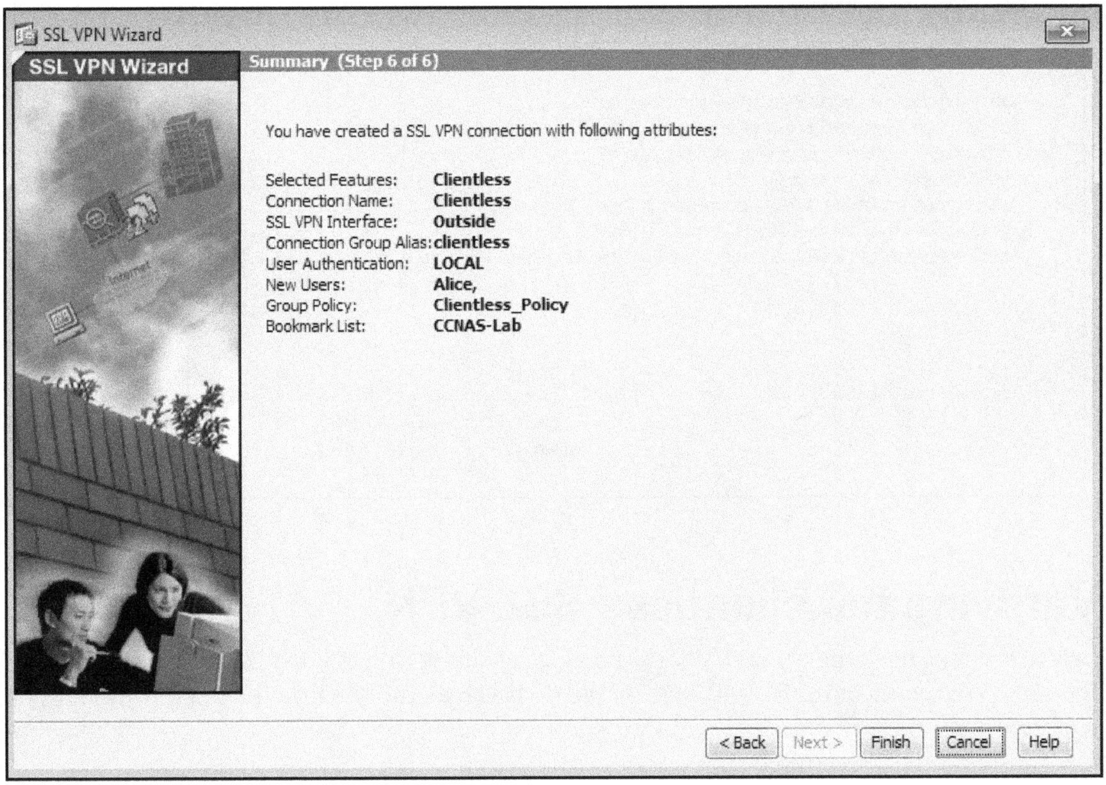

SSL VPN Wizard
SSL VPN Wizard
Summary (Step 6 of 6)
You have created a SSL VPN connection with following attributes:
Selected Features: Clientless
Connection Name: Clientless
SSL VPN Interface: Outside
Connection Group Alias: clientless
User Authentication: LOCAL
New Users: Alice,
Group Policy: Clientless_Policy
Bookmark List: CCNAS-Lab
< Back
Next >
Finish
Cancel
Help

Before the configuration is applied to ASA-1, the preview of the CLI commands are presented. Click on **Send** to push the configurations onto the ASA:

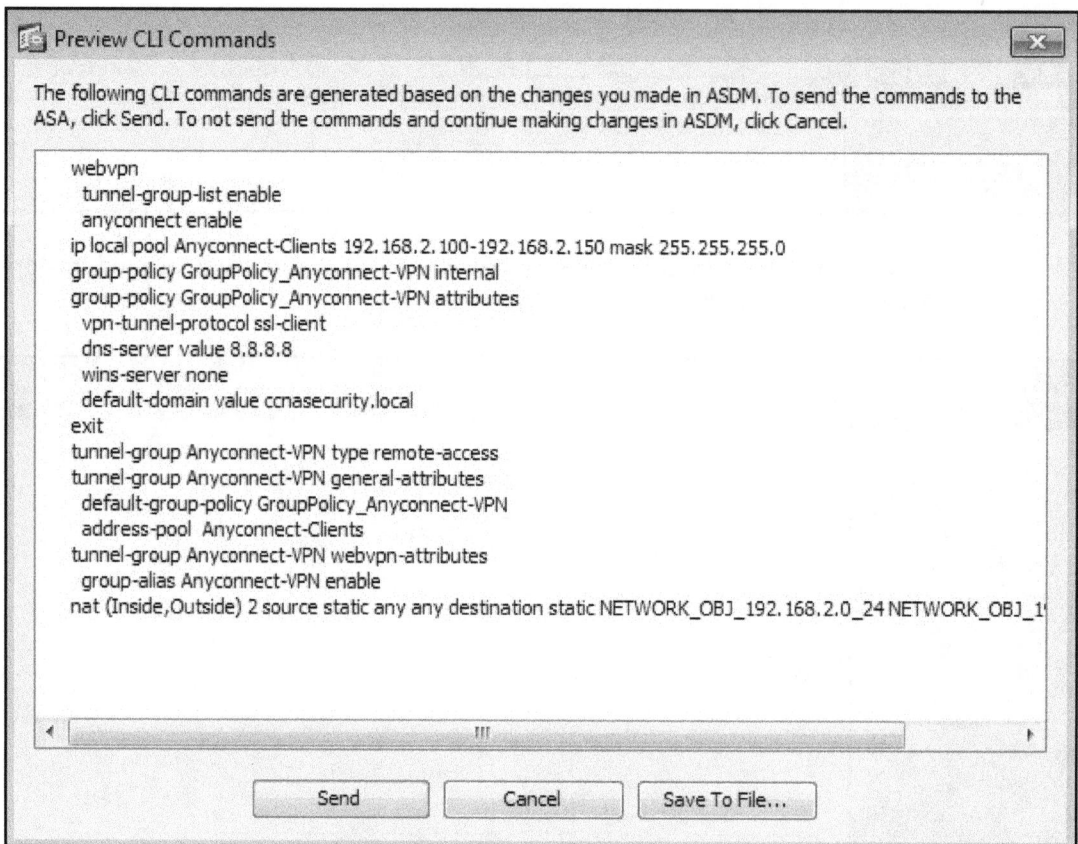

Verifying the clientless SSL VPN

Before we can check the actual VPN connection, we need to check the connectivity between the remote worker computer and ASA-1. We do this by simply using the ping utility:

```
C:\>ping 200.1.1.2

Pinging 200.1.1.2 with 32 bytes of data:
Reply from 200.1.1.2: bytes=32 time=33ms TTL=253
Reply from 200.1.1.2: bytes=32 time=32ms TTL=253
Reply from 200.1.1.2: bytes=32 time=24ms TTL=253
Reply from 200.1.1.2: bytes=32 time=33ms TTL=253

Ping statistics for 200.1.1.2:
    Packets: Sent = 4, Received = 4, Lost = 0 (0% loss),
Approximate round trip times in milli-seconds:
    Minimum = 24ms, Maximum = 33ms, Average = 30ms
```

Since we have connectivity, open the web browser, navigate to
`http://200.1.1.2/clientless`, and hit *Enter*. For this exercise, we've used Internet
Explorer. Since the ASA generated a self-signed digital certificate, the computer and the
browser issue a warning. We know this is `ASA-1`, so simply click on **Continue to this
website (not recommended)**:

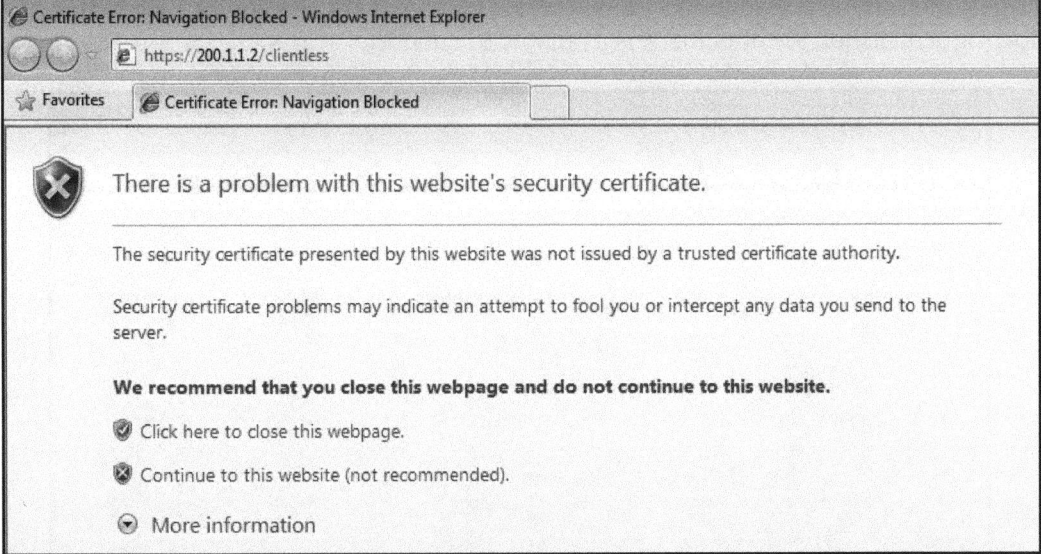

As we can see, the SSL VPN portal is working. Enter Alice's user account details and click on **Login**:

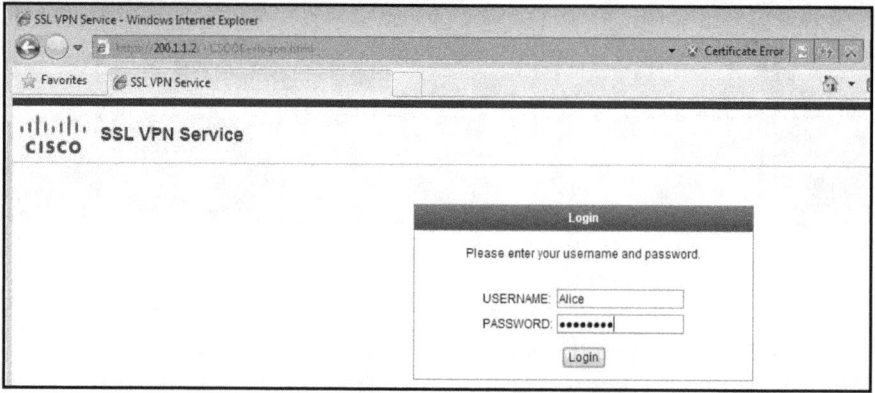

The `Alice` user is now logged in to the clientless SSL VPN portal. During the configurations in the previous section, we created a bookmark. As you can see in the following screenshot, the bookmark is available to the user:

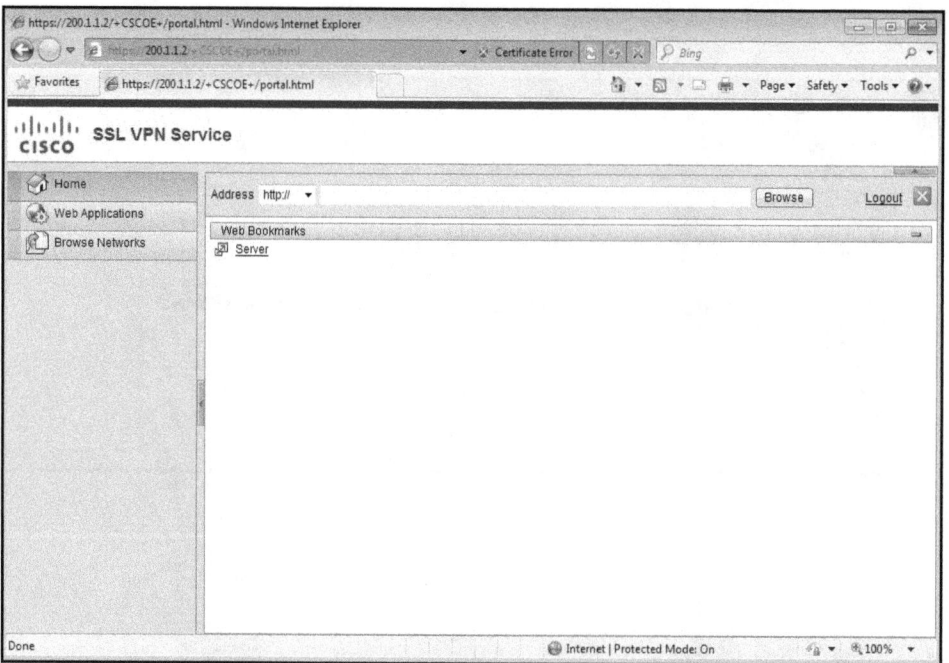

On the ASDM, navigate to **Monitoring** | **VPN** | **VPN Statistics** | **Sessions**. Adjust the filter to clientless SSL VPN. This window shows the number of clientless VPNs and the user that is currently active, `Alice`.

The `100.1.1.2` IP address is Alice's public IP address as her computer is using Network Address Translation behind a router:

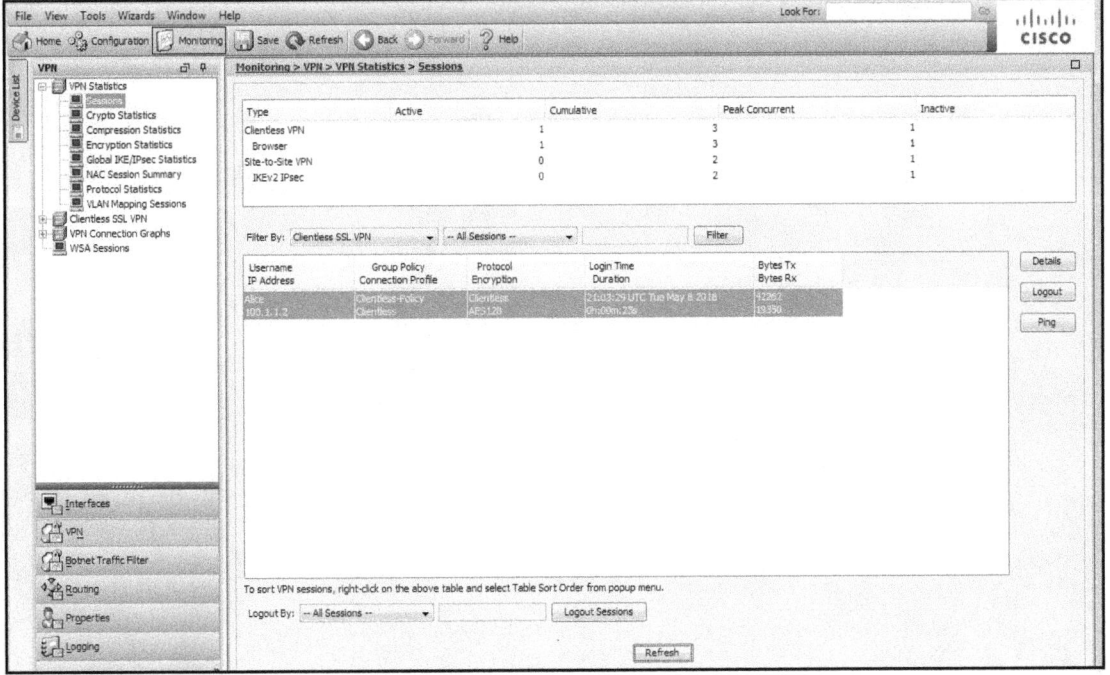

If we click on **Details** on the right, we get more statistical information about the VPN user's connection:

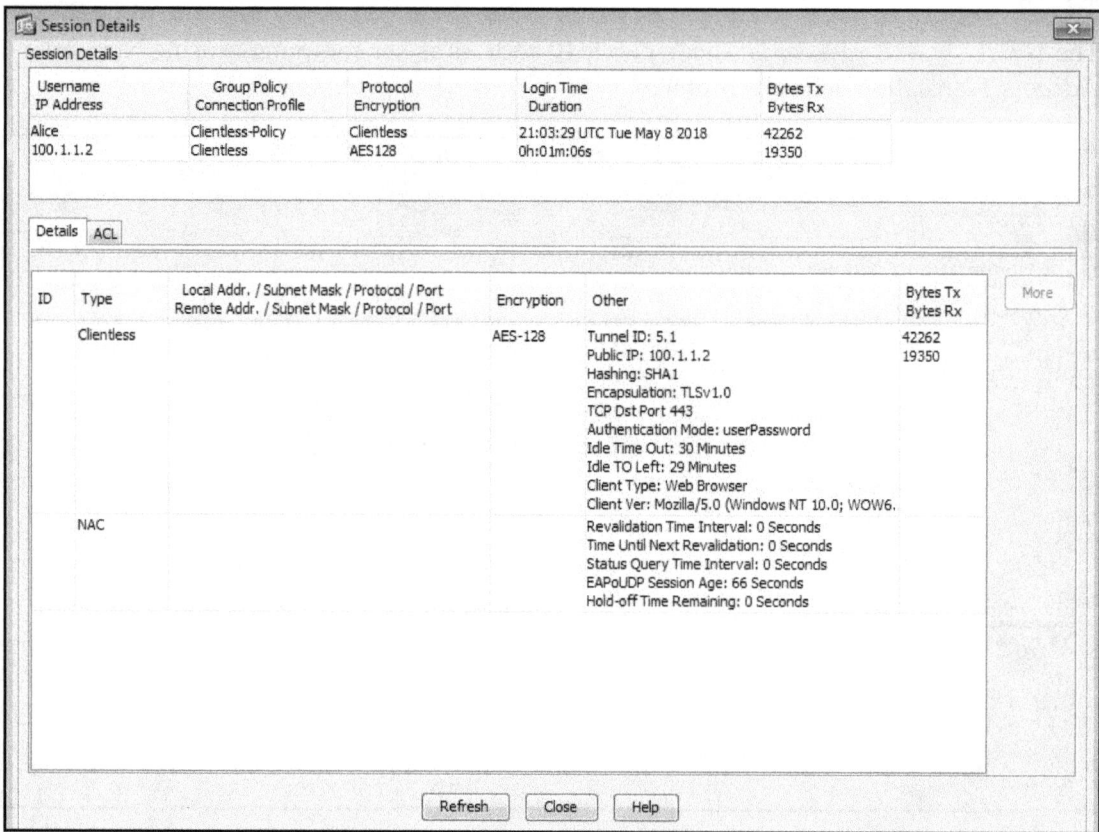

Let's use the command line to verify the VPN status.

Using the `show vpn-sessiondb webvpn` command, we can see the session database for the web VPN being terminated at `ASA-1`:

```
ASA-1# show vpn-sessiondb webvpn

Session Type: WebVPN

Username      : Alice                    Index        : 3
Public IP     : 100.1.1.2
Protocol      : Clientless
License       : AnyConnect Premium
Encryption    : RC4                      Hashing      : SHA1
Bytes Tx      : 16886                    Bytes Rx     : 21086
Group Policy  : Clientless-Policy        Tunnel Group : Clientless
Login Time    : 20:52:05 UTC Tue May 8 2018
Duration      : 0h:02m:56s
Inactivity    : 0h:00m:00s
NAC Result    : Unknown
VLAN Mapping  : N/A                      VLAN         : none
```

To view information about the web VPN, simply use the list of the following commands:

```
ASA-1# show webvpn ?

  anyconnect   Show information about the AnyConnect Client image files
  csd          Show information about the CSD package
  group-alias  Show information about the group aliases
  group-url    Show information about the group url
  kcd          Show information about KCD
  mus          Show Mobile User Security Information
  sso-server   Show information about an SSO Server
  statistics   Show counters of WebVPN events that have occured
```

Configuring a client-based remote-access VPN

To get started, open the ASDM and connect to `ASA-1`. Once you're connected, click on **Wizards | VPN Wizards | AnyConnect VPN Wizard...**:

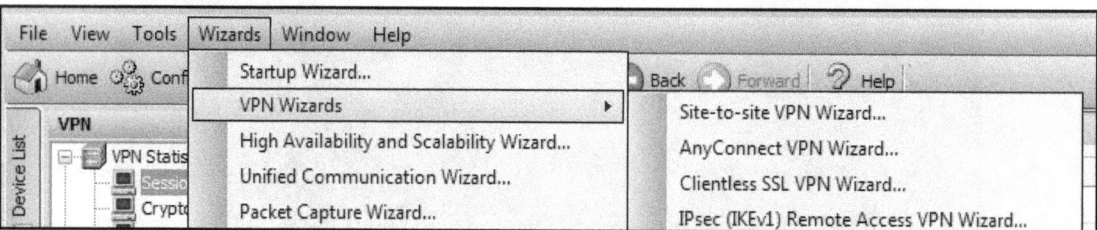

Perform the following steps:

1. An **Introduction** window will appear, providing you with a briefing about the AnyConnect VPN Connection. Click on **Next**:

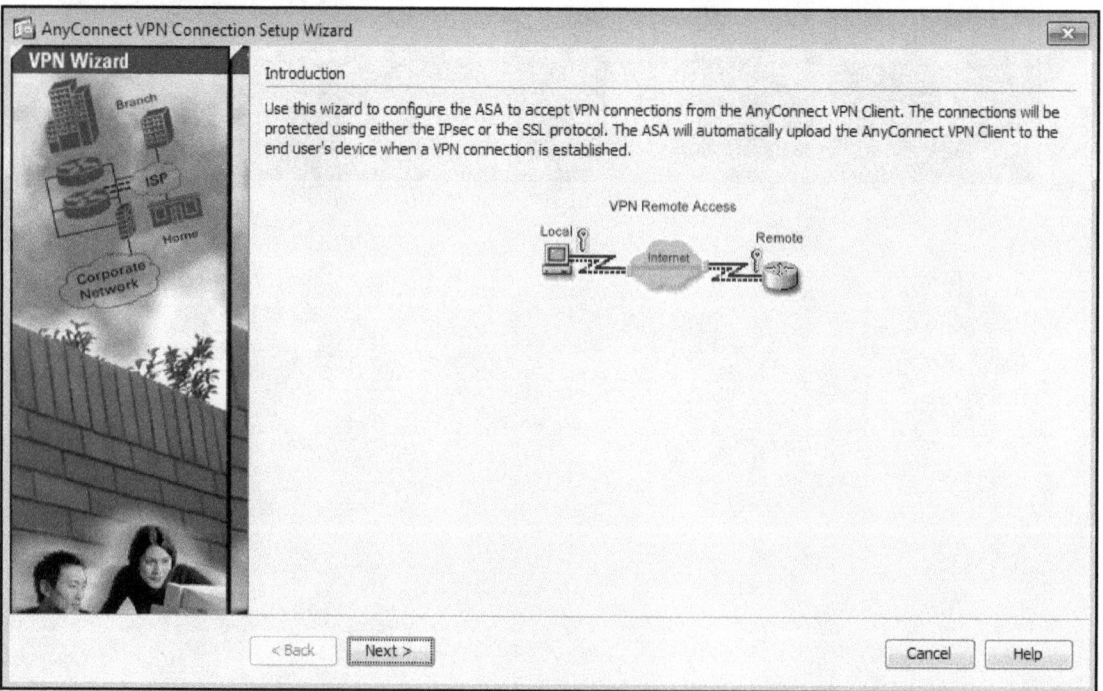

2. Create a **Connection Profile Name** and select **Outside** information as the **VPN Access Interface**. Click on **Next** to continue:

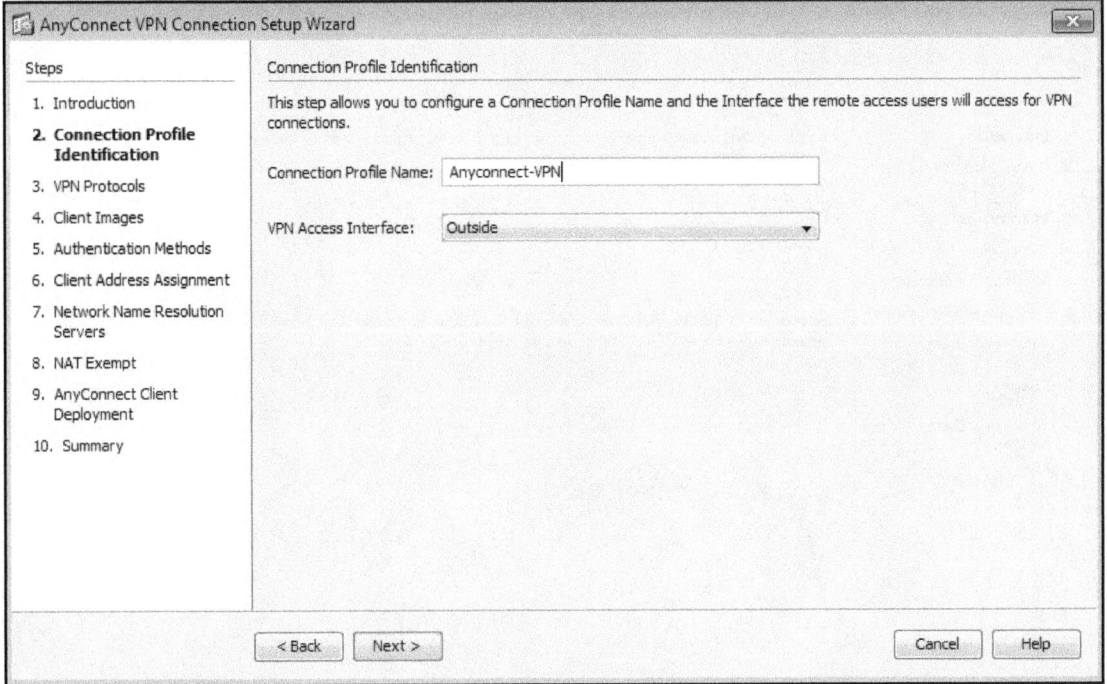

3. This window provides options for selecting the VPN protocols and whether to use digital certificates. For this exercise, we've chosen the **SSL** option only. Click on **Next**:

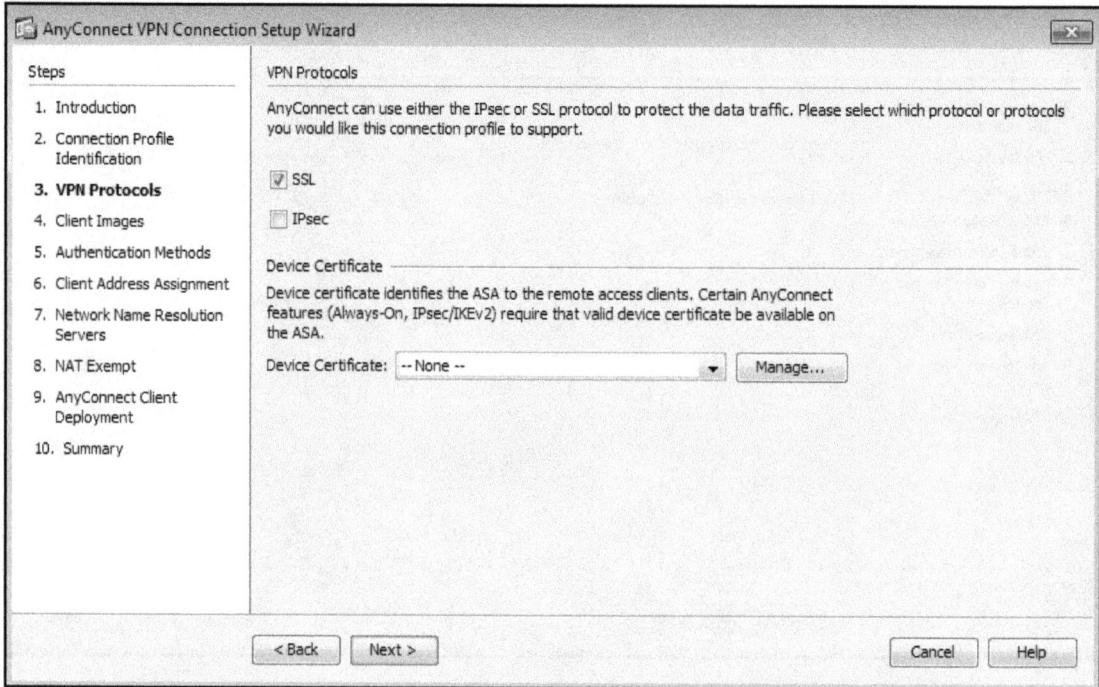

4. At this stage, the VPN wizard asks which Cisco AnyConnect Secure Mobility Client should be available to the VPN users. If you can't see any available clients, click on **Add** to either upload an image or locate one on the ASA's flash memory. Click on **Next**:

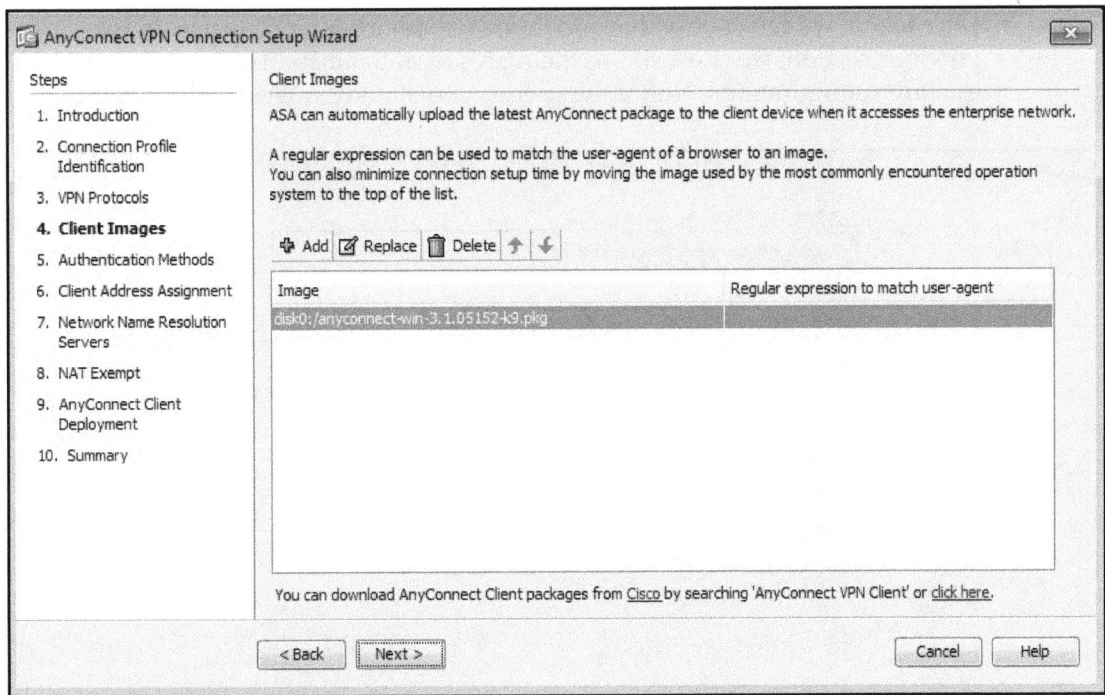

 Cisco AnyConnect Secure Mobility Client is available for Windows, Linux, and macOS users. To get other versions, please visit https://www.cisco.com/ and navigate to **Support | Downloads | Home | Security VPN and Endpoint Security Clients | Cisco VPN Clients | AnyConnect Secure Mobility Client**.

5. Once again, we can choose the authentication device for VPN users. In the previous section, we chose to use the ASA's local database. Here, we'll keep the existing configurations. Notice the user `Alice` already exists. Click on **Next**:

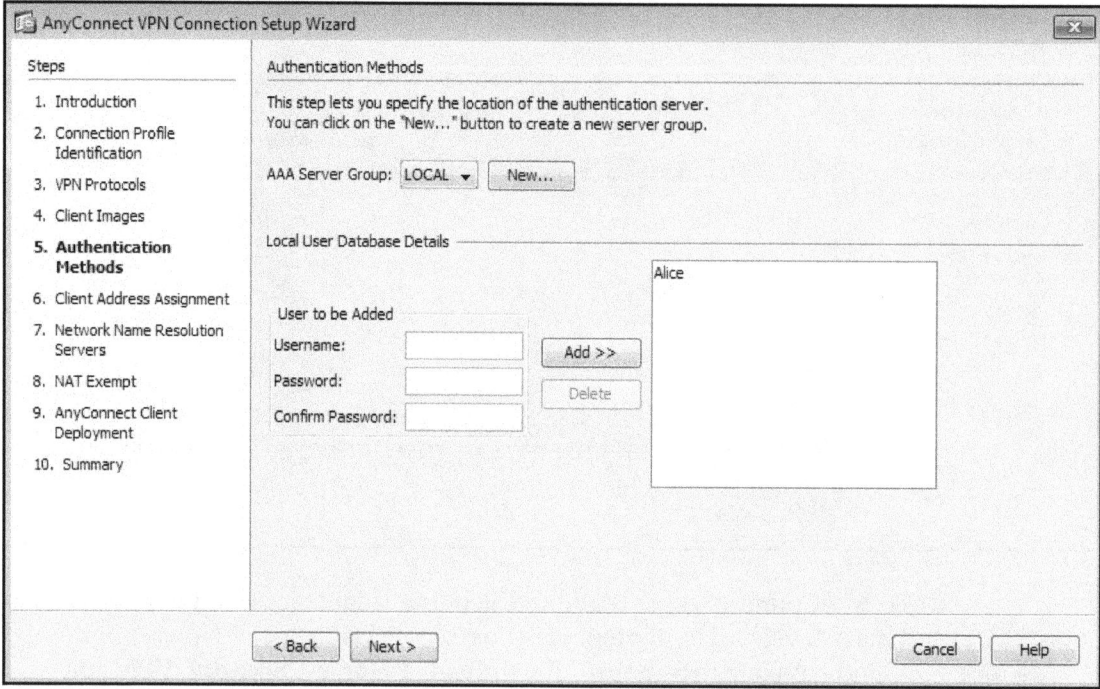

6. As mentioned earlier, each client that establishes a VPN connection using the Cisco AnyConnect Secure Mobility Client will receive a virtual IP address. The following window allows the creation of the virtual pool of addresses for VPN clients. Click on **New**:

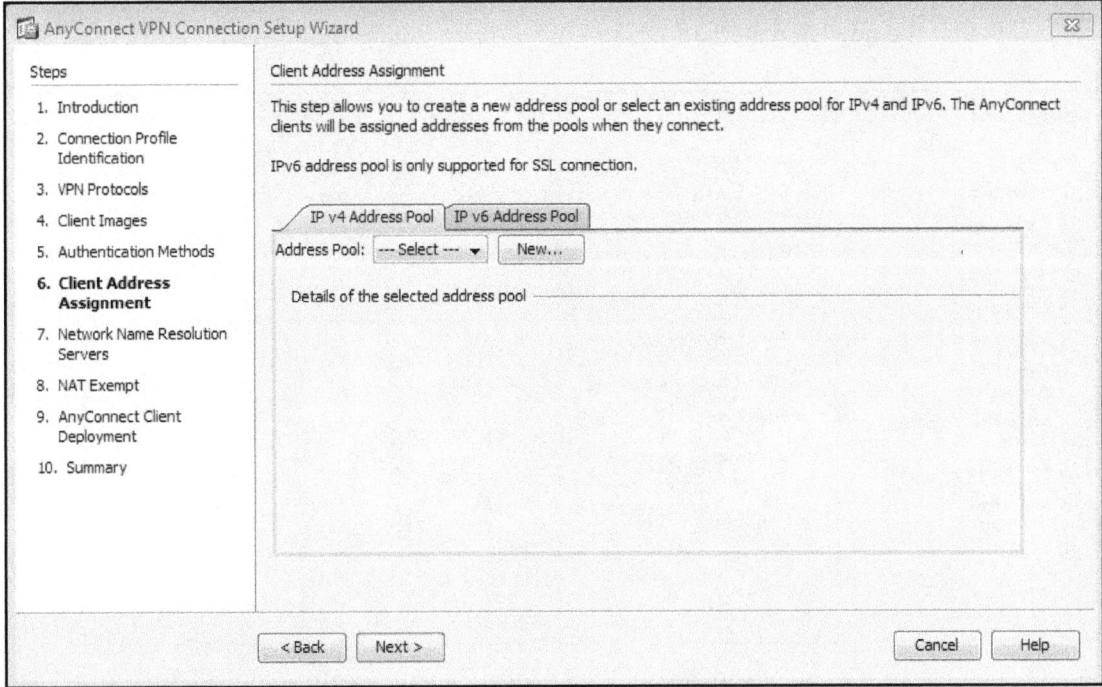

7. The following window will appear, providing the option to create the virtual pool. Here, we are using the same IP scheme as the corporate network, but only a portion of it: `192.168.2.100—192.168.2.150`. VPN clients will receive an IP address within this range. Click on **OK** to return to the previous window:

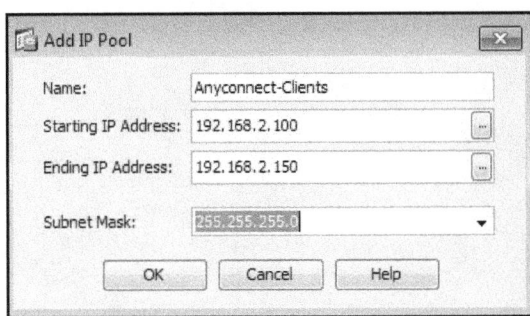

TIP

If an addressing scheme other than what is defined within the corporate network is used, be sure to set up routing between the VPN network and the corporate network.

8. Now we're back to the main **Client Address Assignment** window, we can see that the newly created address pool has been populated. Click on **Next**:

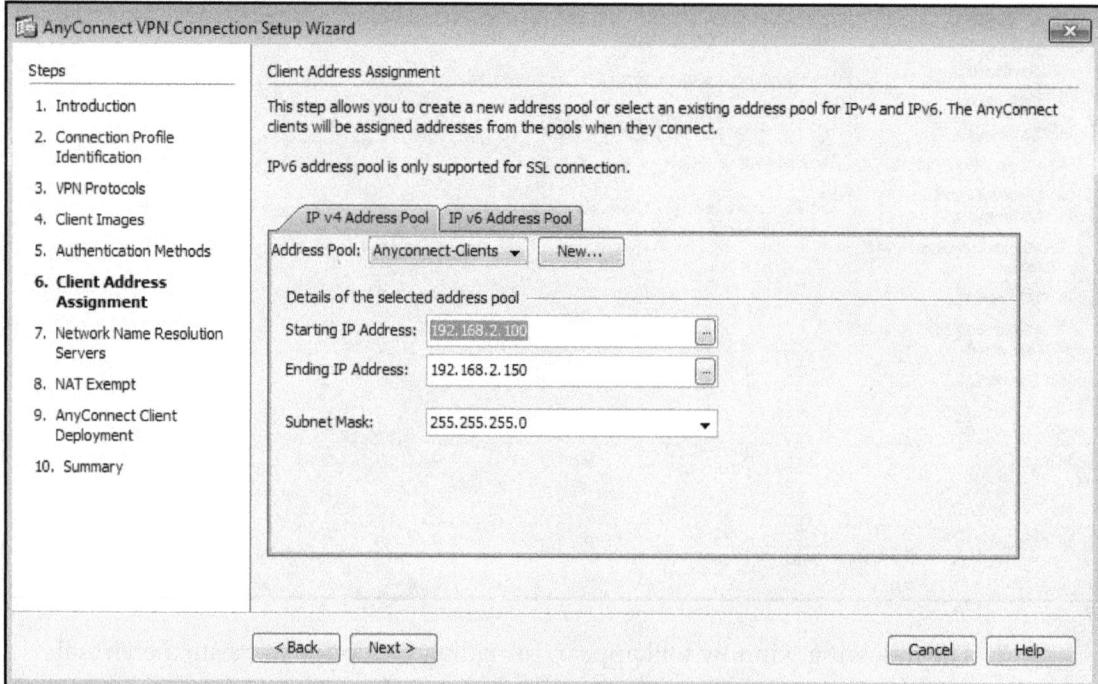

9. The DNS and WINS server configurations can be defined here, along with the domain name. These configurations will be pushed to clients when the VPN connection is established. Click on **Next**:

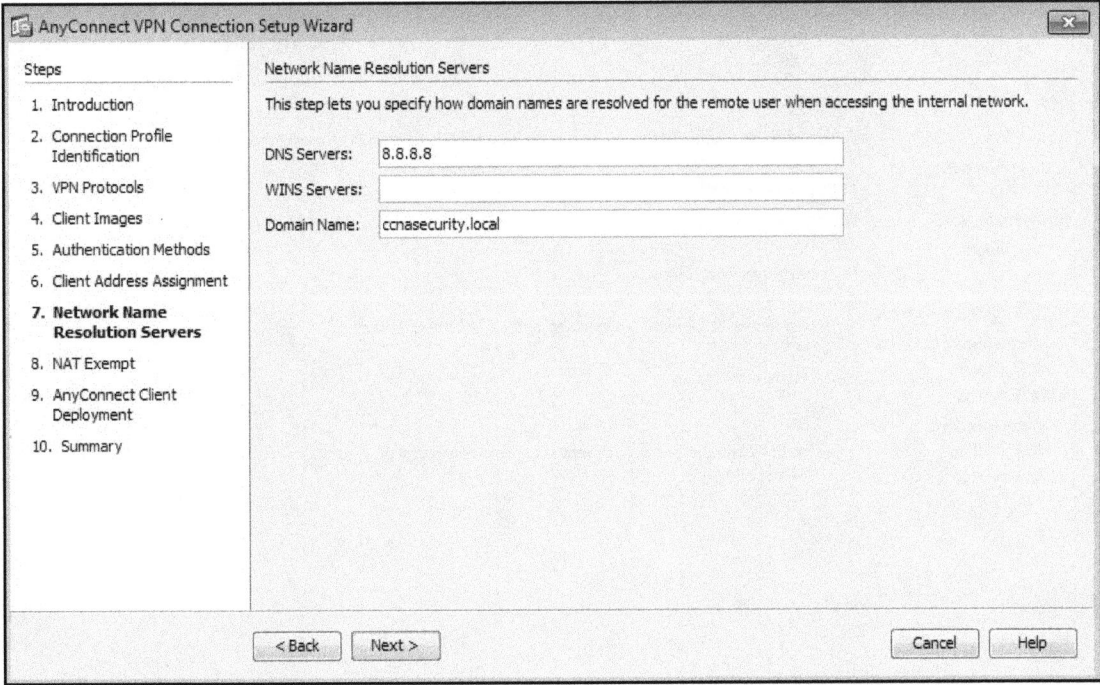

10. Here, you can configure how NAT works with the VPN clients. To ensure that the VPN connection works properly, click the checkbox next to **Exempt VPN traffic from network address translation**, set **Inside Interface** as **Inside**, and the **Local Network** to any. Click on **Next** to continue:

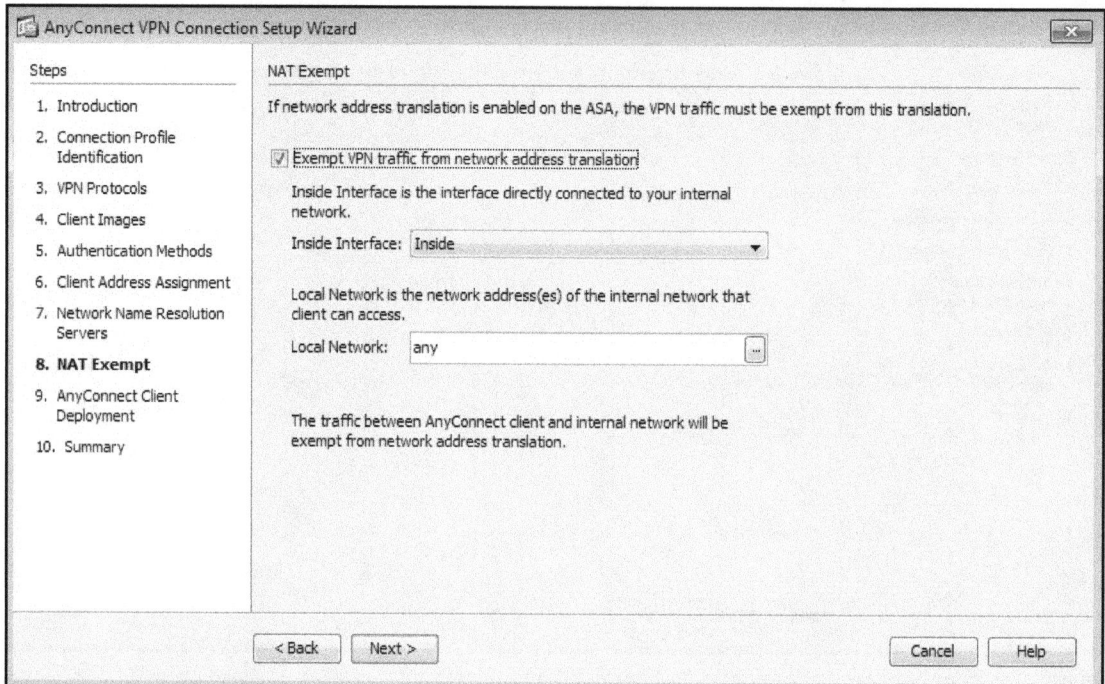

11. The **AnyConnect Client Deployment** window provides a description of how the Cisco AnyConnect Secure Mobility Client software can be delivered to the VPN clients. Click on **Next** to continue:

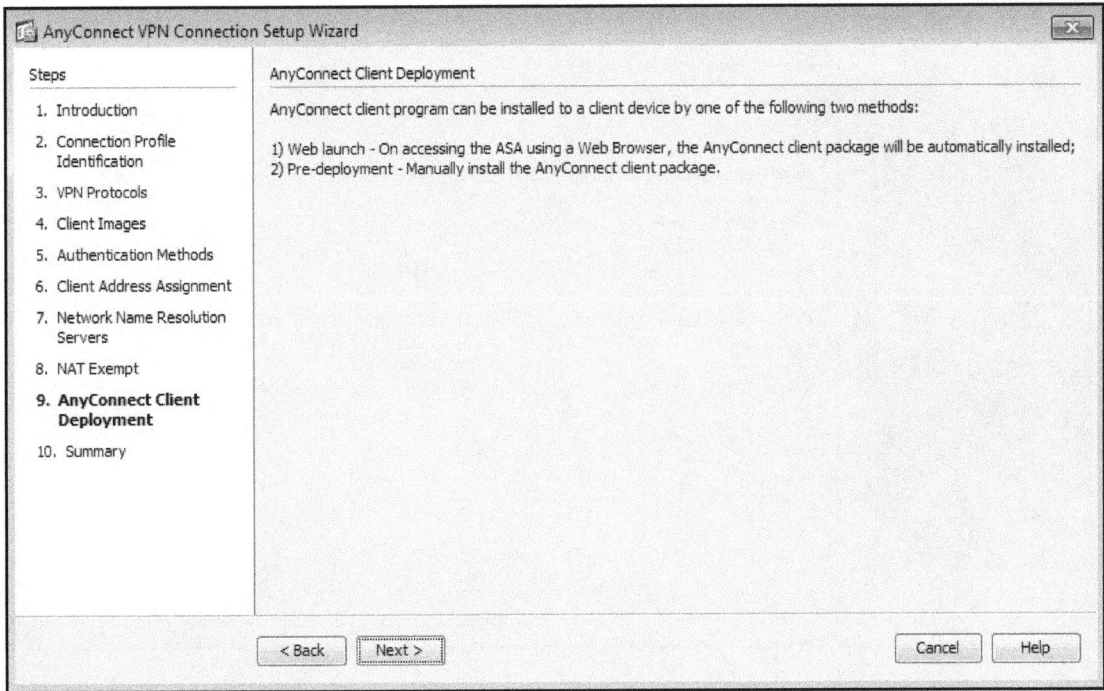

Finally, we are presented with a **Summary** of the configurations that were used from the previous steps. Click on **Finish**:

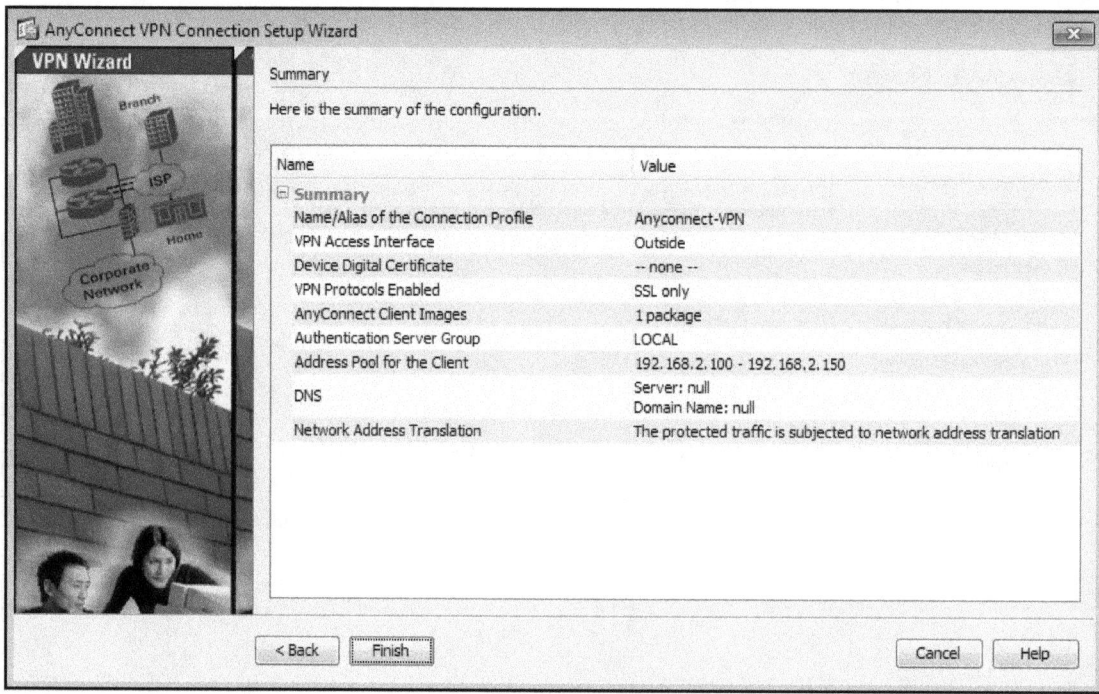

Lastly, a preview of the CLI commands are displayed for your perusal. Click on **Send** to apply the configurations to the ASA:

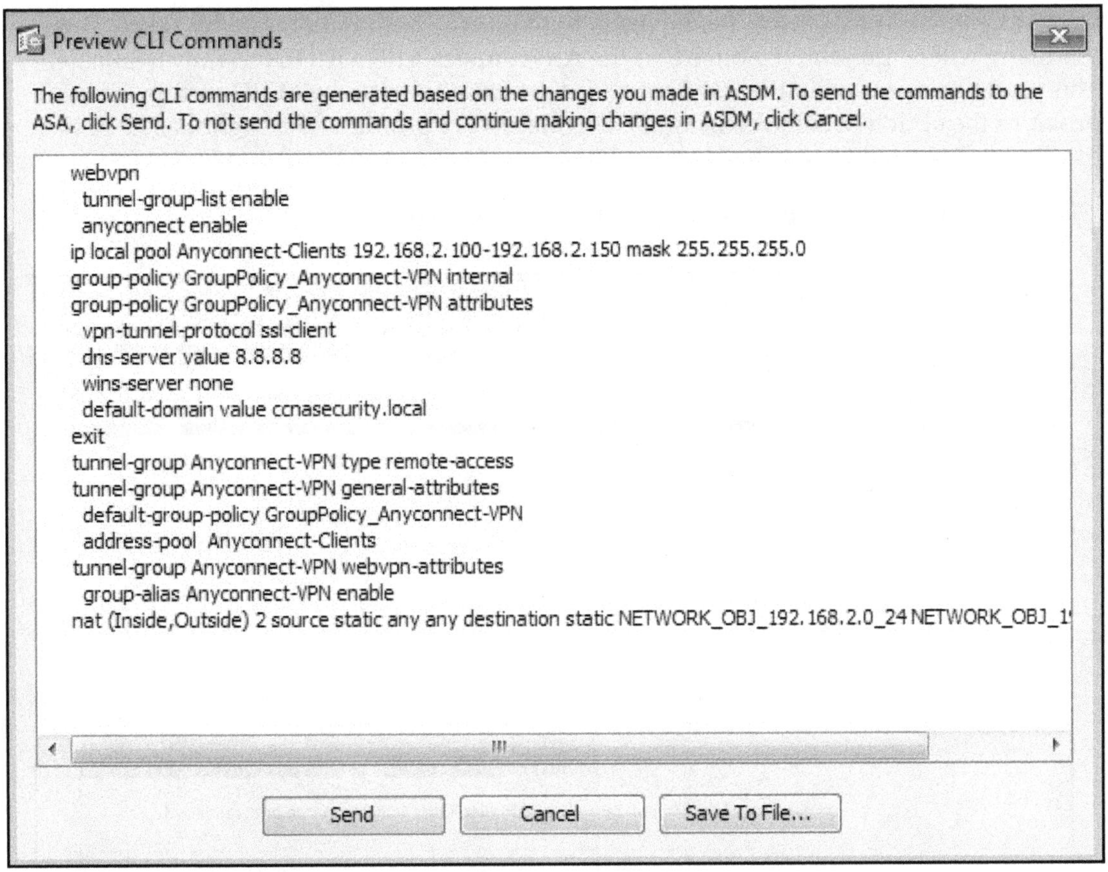

Preview CLI Commands　　　　　　　　　　　　　　　　　　　　　　　　　　　　[x]

The following CLI commands are generated based on the changes you made in ASDM. To send the commands to the ASA, click Send. To not send the commands and continue making changes in ASDM, click Cancel.

```
webvpn
  tunnel-group-list enable
  anyconnect enable
ip local pool Anyconnect-Clients 192.168.2.100-192.168.2.150 mask 255.255.255.0
group-policy GroupPolicy_Anyconnect-VPN internal
group-policy GroupPolicy_Anyconnect-VPN attributes
  vpn-tunnel-protocol ssl-client
  dns-server value 8.8.8.8
  wins-server none
  default-domain value ccnasecurity.local
exit
tunnel-group Anyconnect-VPN type remote-access
tunnel-group Anyconnect-VPN general-attributes
  default-group-policy GroupPolicy_Anyconnect-VPN
  address-pool  Anyconnect-Clients
tunnel-group Anyconnect-VPN webvpn-attributes
  group-alias Anyconnect-VPN enable
nat (Inside,Outside) 2 source static any any destination static NETWORK_OBJ_192.168.2.0_24 NETWORK_OBJ_1
```

|　Send　|　　Cancel　|　Save To File...　|

Run the `no username Alice attributes` command in global configuration mode on the ASA. This will allow the ASA to push the Cisco AnyConnect Secure Mobility Client to the remote worker device.

Verifying the client-based VPN

We have already tested device connectivity from the remote computer and the ASA. Let's open the web browser once more, navigate to `https://200.1.1.1`, and hit *Enter*. The following will be presented; notice that the **Anyconnect-VPN GROUP** is now available. This group was created in the *Configuring a client-based remote-access VPN* section. This provides the option to connect using the clientless VPN profile or the client-based VPN profile:

1. Enter Alice's user account details and click **Login**:

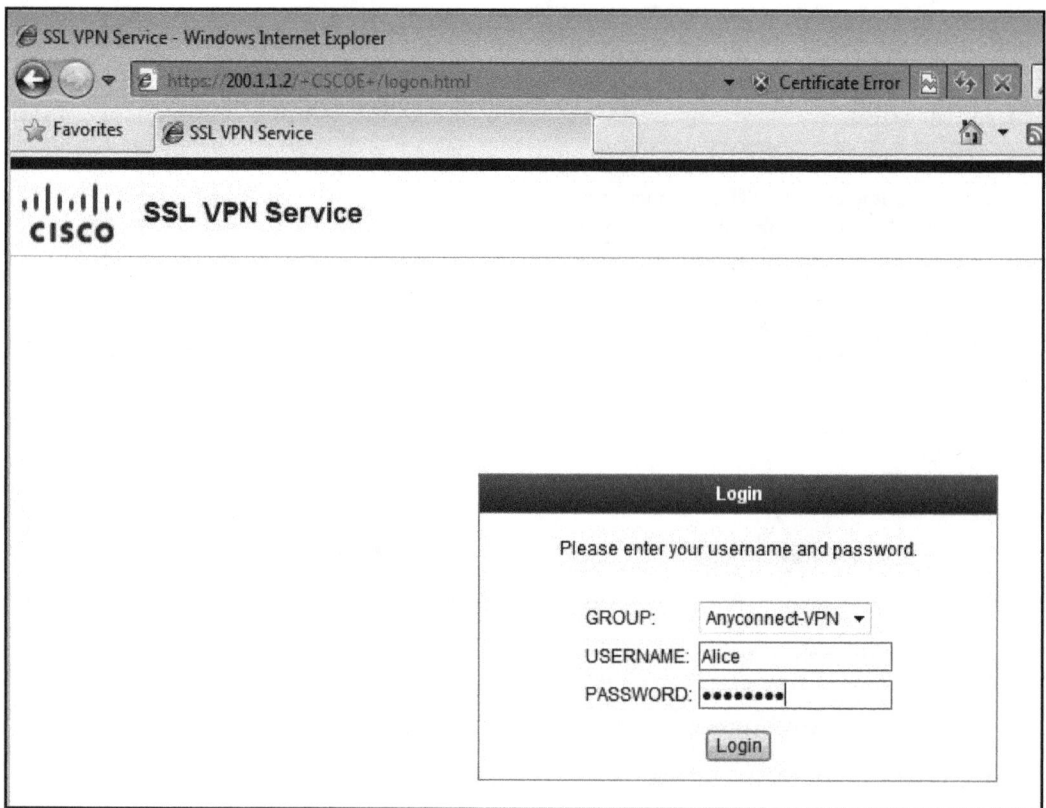

2. Once successfully authenticated, you'll see that the ASA is pushing the Cisco AnyConnect Secure Mobility Client to your computer. Follow the instructions to install it. Java Runtime Environment and Adobe ActiveX may be required:

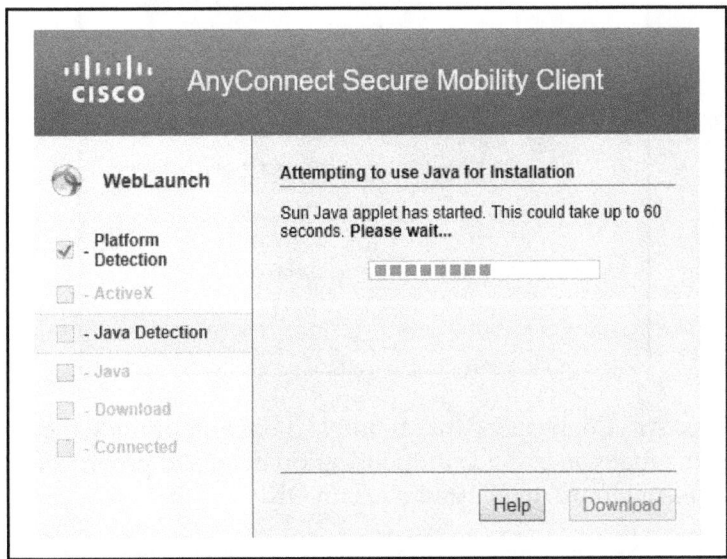

3. Once the Cisco AnyConnect Secure Mobility Client has been installed on the remote worker computer, open it. Enter the IP address ASA-1, 200.1.1.2, and click on **Connect**:

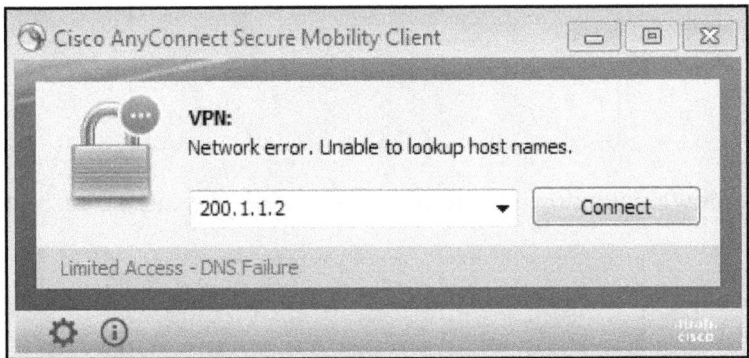

4. Since `ASA-1` is using a self-signed certificate, the following security warning will appear. Click on **Connect Anyway** to continue:

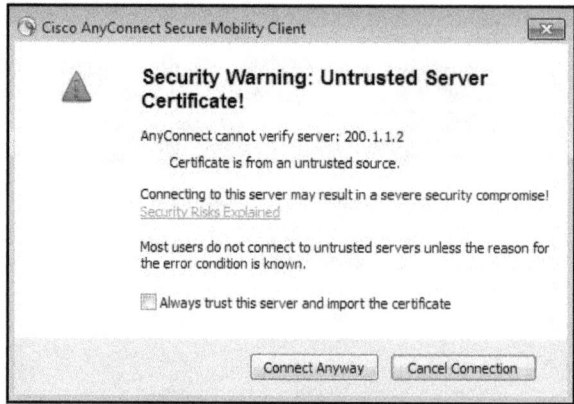

5. The Cisco AnyConnect Secure Mobility Client will provide the following prompt, requesting that you provide authentication details to prove your identity. Enter Alice's user account details and click on **OK**:

6. The following window should be presented displaying the current status:

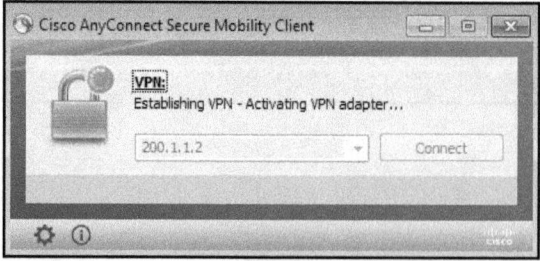

7. Finally, the VPN connection is successful; the remote worker computer has now established a VPN connection to the ASA:

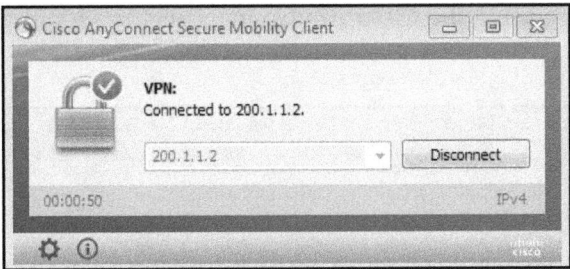

8. If we click on the gear icon on the Cisco AnyConnect Secure Mobility Client, we can obtain statistical details about the connection. Notice the VPN client (computer) receives the first usable virtual IP address from the pool we created in step 6, 192.168.2.100:

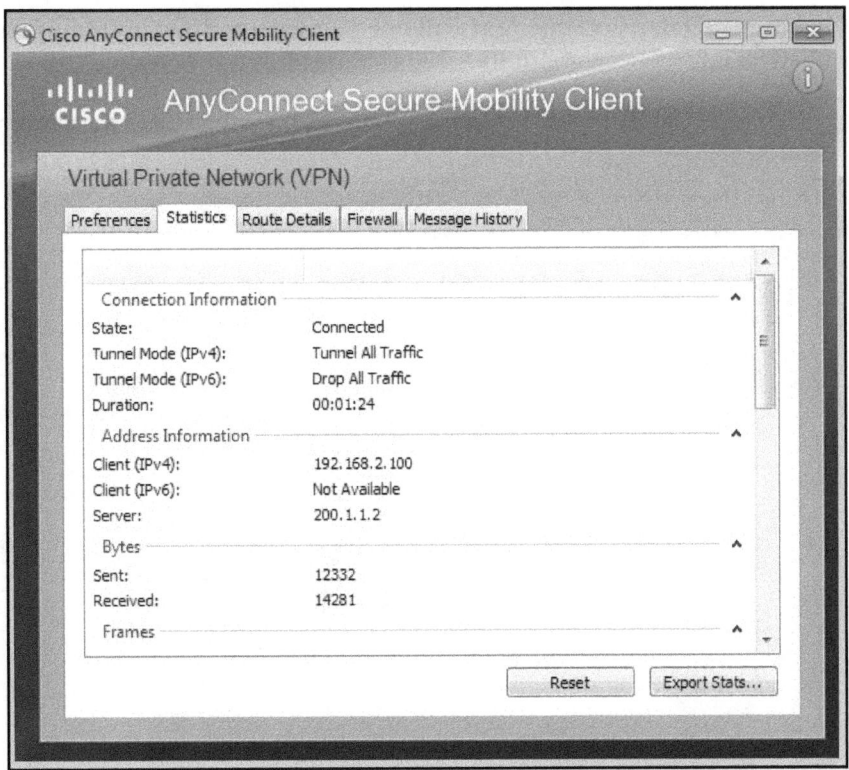

9. Let's head over to the ASDM; navigate to **Monitoring** | **VPN** | **VPN Statistics** | **Sessions**. Notice that **AnyConnect Client** and **SSL/TLS/DTLS** is set to **1** and **Active**. Adjust the following filter to **AnyConnect Client**. We can see the active users who are using the Cisco AnyConnect Secure Mobility Client for the VPN connection:

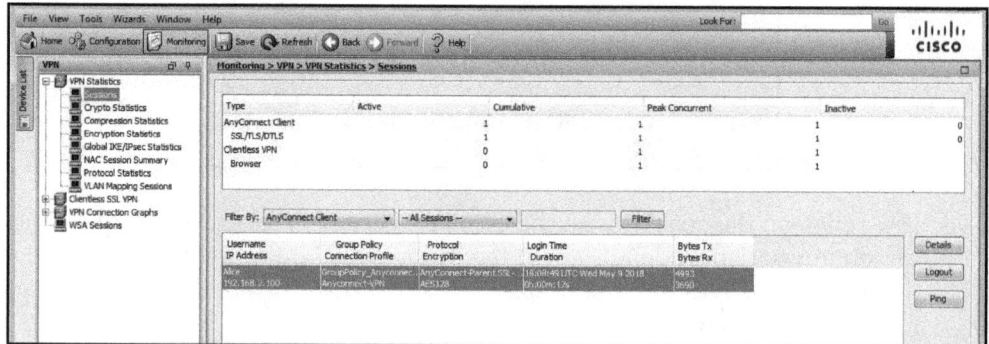

10. Clicking on **Details** on the right will open a new window, providing more statistical information about the user's connection:

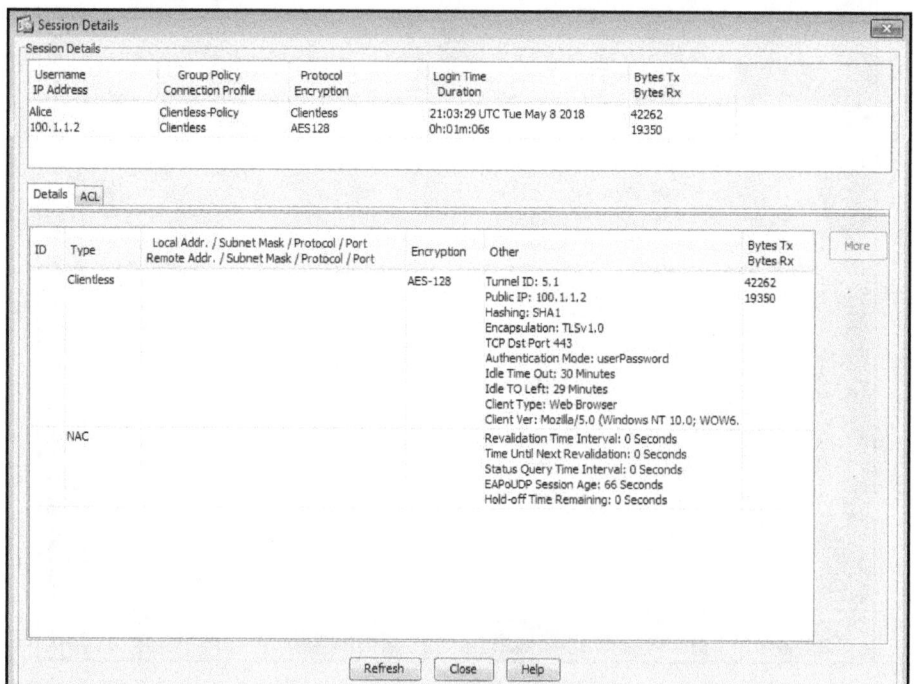

11. Let's use the command line to verify the VPN status. Using the `show vpn-sessiondb` command will provide the sessions database for the VPN sessions that are terminated on the ASA:

```
ASA-1# show vpn-sessiondb
--------------------------------------------------------------------------
VPN Session Summary
--------------------------------------------------------------------------
                              Active : Cumulative : Peak Concur : Inactive
                             --------------------------------------------
Site-to-Site VPN          :      1 :          2 :           1
  IKEv2 IPsec             :      1 :          2 :           1           1
--------------------------------------------------------------------------
Total Active and Inactive :      1            Total Cumulative :        2
Device Total VPN Capacity :      0
Device Load               :     0%
***!! WARNING: Platform capacity exceeded !!***
--------------------------------------------------------------------------


--------------------------------------------------------------------------
Tunnels Summary
--------------------------------------------------------------------------
                              Active : Cumulative : Peak Concurrent
                             --------------------------------------------
IKEv2                     :      1 :          2 :           1
IPsec                     :      1 :          2 :           1
--------------------------------------------------------------------------
Totals                    :      2 :          4
--------------------------------------------------------------------------

ASA-1#
```

12. By specifying the `show vpn-sessiondb anyconnect` command, specific details about users/connections that are made by using the Cisco AnyConnect Secure Mobility Client to the ASA can be displayed in the following screenshot:

```
ASA-1# show vpn-sessiondb anyconnect

Session Type: AnyConnect

Username      : Alice                    Index        : 2
Assigned IP   : 192.168.2.100            Public IP    : 100.1.1.2
Protocol      : AnyConnect-Parent SSL-Tunnel
License       : AnyConnect Premium
Encryption    : AES128                   Hashing      : none SHA1
Bytes Tx      : 9986                     Bytes Rx     : 31867
Group Policy  : GroupPolicy_Anyconnect-VPN
Tunnel Group  : Anyconnect-VPN
Login Time    : 18:08:49 UTC Wed May 9 2018
Duration      : 0h:03m:15s
Inactivity    : 0h:00m:00s
NAC Result    : Unknown
VLAN Mapping  : N/A                      VLAN         : none

ASA-1#
```

13. On the remote worker's computer, run the `ipconfig/all` command on the Windows Command Prompt. Notice the client IP information is the same as what we had configured during steps 6 and 7 from the previous section, Configuring a client-based remote-access VPN:

```
Ethernet adapter Local Area Connection 3:

   Connection-specific DNS Suffix  . : ccnasecurity.local
   Description . . . . . . . . . . . : Cisco AnyConnect Secure Mobility Client V
irtual Miniport Adapter for Windows x64
   Physical Address. . . . . . . . . : 00-05-9A       ...
   DHCP Enabled. . . . . . . . . . . : No
   Autoconfiguration Enabled . . . . : Yes
   Link-local IPv6 Address . . . . . : fe80::9e5:cad4:7a67:1c83%25(Preferred)
   Link-local IPv6 Address . . . . . : fe80::528c:83f3:4ff7:6711%25(Preferred)
   IPv4 Address. . . . . . . . . . . : 192.168.2.100(Preferred)
   Subnet Mask . . . . . . . . . . . : 255.255.255.0
   Default Gateway . . . . . . . . . : ::
                                       192.168.2.1
   DNS Servers . . . . . . . . . . . : 8.8.8.8
   NetBIOS over Tcpip. . . . . . . . : Enabled
```

14. Finally, we ping a machine on the corporate network, `192.168.2.10`, to ensure end-to-end connectivity through the VPN connection:

```
C:\>ping 192.168.2.10

Pinging 192.168.2.10 with 32 bytes of data:
Reply from 192.168.2.10: bytes=32 time=183ms TTL=64
Reply from 192.168.2.10: bytes=32 time=182ms TTL=64
Reply from 192.168.2.10: bytes=32 time=181ms TTL=64
Reply from 192.168.2.10: bytes=32 time=182ms TTL=64

Ping statistics for 192.168.2.10:
    Packets: Sent = 4, Received = 4, Lost = 0 (0% loss),
Approximate round trip times in milli-seconds:
    Minimum = 181ms, Maximum = 183ms, Average = 182ms
```

Summary

Just to recap, we discussed the use of a remote-access VPN in an environment where an employee may be working from home or in the field and require access to the corporate network. Further, we took a look at the necessary steps to configure both a clientless SSL VPN and a client-based VPN on the Cisco ASA. Finally, we verified that the VPN connections were working properly. Now we are able to do the same in an organization or even in our own lab environment. We also saw how to distribute the Cisco AnyConnect Secure Mobility Client securely using the VPN portal.

In the next chapter, we will discuss the need for an **Intrusion Detection System** (**IDS**), an **Intrusion Prevention System** (**IPS**), and how to configure the Cisco IOS router as an IPS.

16
Working with IPS

As you may have noticed in the previous chapters, Cisco IOS routers and switches can do much more than just forward frames and packets to their destinations; they can provide network security features. In this chapter, we'll discuss the functionality of both an **Intrusion Detection System** (**IDS**) and an **Intrusion Prevention System** (**IPS**). These technologies are very similar, however, we will take a look at their differences and the placement of each in a network topology.

In this chapter, we'll cover the following:

- The terminologies used when discussing IDS and IPS
- The characteristics of an IDS
- The characteristics of an IPS
- Configuring an IPS on a Cisco IOS router

Let's begin!

Terminologies

Whenever we are discussing the topic of IDS/IPS, we often uses terms and phrases that may sound a bit unusual or sometimes seem out of context:

- **Sensor**: The component used to detect and monitor traffic
- **Risk**: The likelihood of loss or damage caused by a threat
- **Threat**: Anything that can take advantage of a vulnerability on a system
- **Vulnerability**: A weakness or flaw in a system
- **Risk rating**: Consists of the severity, the fidelity, and the **target value rating** (**TVR**)
- **False positive**: The sensor generates an alert but no actual threat exists
- **False negative**: The sensor does not generate an alert but a threat exists

- **True positive**: The sensor generates an alert and a threat exists
- **True negative**: The sensor does not generate an alert and there are no threats

IDS and IPS

In this section, we will discuss the difference between and the placement of both an IDS and an IPS.

Intrusion Detection Systems

An **Intrusion Detection System** is an appliance that is used to detect security threats, either on a host system or a network. Let's use the following network topology to further explain how an IDS works:

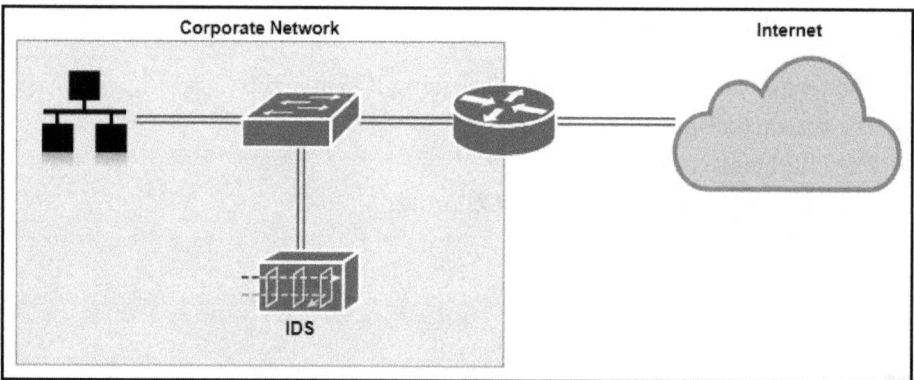

As you can see, the IDS is not connected inline but to a port on the switch; therefore, the IDS will receive a copy of the network traffic for analysis and does not add any latency or delay the flow of traffic. Furthermore, if the IDS appliance is disabled or goes down, the network performance is not impacted. However, since it receives only a copy of the traffic and it's not an *inline* deployment (that is, network traffic is not passing through the appliance), only after a threat has been detected, the IDS appliance will generate an alert and will not be able to stop the attack as it's happening on the network. This makes the appliance reactive rather than the IPS, which is proactive.

Intrusion Prevention Systems

An **Intrusion Prevention System** is an appliance that is used to detect and block security threats, either on a host system or a network. As we can see in the following diagram, the IPS appliance is placed inline with the traffic flow on the network topology:

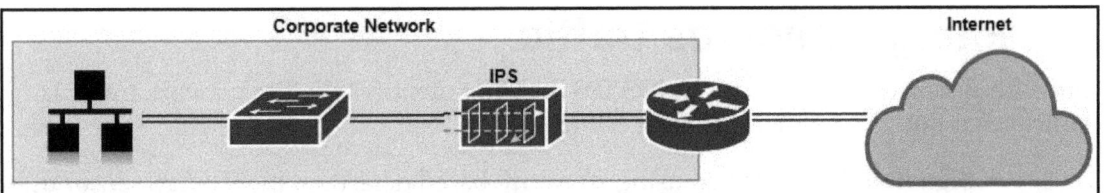

All traffic flowing through the IPS appliance will be screened for any malicious code or potential attacks on the network. If a possible threat is detected, the IPS sensor will trigger an alert and block the malicious traffic/payload from either entering or leaving the network.

One very important point to note, the IPS appliance is placed behind the firewall, and not in front of it facing the internet. If the appliance is facing the internet (untrusted zone), there may be a lot of alerts triggered by the IPS sensor. Some of these alerts may be false positives or even unsolicited traffic.

As you can see in the topology, the IPS appliance is placed inline to monitor and block potential threats; this causes some latency/delay on network performance and if the appliance goes down by any means possible, traffic by either be block (fail closed) or allow to pass freely (fail open).

Types of IDS and IPS

There are two types of IDS and IPS:

- Host-based
- Network-based

In a **Host-based Intrusion Detection System (HIDS)** or a **Host-based Intrusion Prevention System (HIPS)**, the software is installed directly on a client machine, such as a Windows 10 PC. However, if either is installed on the local machine, the HIDS/HIPS would only be able to screen traffic entering or leaving the local machine. If a threat enters the network, the HIDS/HIPS won't be able to detect or filter the malicious traffic unless it's incoming on the local machine.

In a **Network-based Intrusion Detection System** (**NIDS**) or a **Network-based Intrusion Prevention System** (**NIPS**), the appliance is installed on the network segment. The advantage of using a network-based appliance is that it has the ability to screen all traffic flowing through it, so it is likely to detect and stop threats spreading across the network.

Detecting malicious traffic

In this section, we'll discuss how an IDS/IPS is able to identify whether network traffic is malicious or not. The following is a list of methods:

- **Signature-based**: When using signature-based detection, the IDS/IPS sensor uses a specific pattern for checking against network traffic to determine whether the traffic is malicious or not. An analogy is using an antivirus program to protect your computer from viruses and other malware. When the program receives updates or what's known as **definitions,** if the local system has a virus running around, but the antivirus program does not have a signature to match the virus, the sensor will not detect the threat and no alert will be generated. Signature-based detection is easy to set up and implement, however, the sensor won't be able to detect any threats outside of the existing signature the IDS/IPS already knows about. Therefore, signature-based detection is not efficient in protecting against new threats.

- **Policy-based**: With policy-based detection, the IDS/IPS sensor is configured to detect threats based on the IT security policies of your organization. A simple example is assuming your organization states in its IT security policy manual that all Telnet traffic should be restricted. Since Telnet uses port 23 and TCP, a rule should be created to match the traffic type, generate an alert, and block the matched traffic.

- **Anomaly-based**: In anomaly-based detection, the IDS/IPS appliance creates a baseline of the type of traffic flowing either across the network or the system. The appliance then uses the baseline as a measurement of regular/normal conditions in contrast to suspicious traffic flows. For example, let's assume there are 100 TCP-SYN packets originating from the internet and they are destined for one of the internet servers on the DMZ. However, the sender of the TCP-SYN packets is not replying with a TCP-ACK packet, so this might be a SYN flood attack.

- **Reputation-based**: In reputation-based detection, the IPS appliance correlates threat results from reputable sources, such as Cisco Talos.

Configuring an IPS on a Cisco IOS router

Let's begin configuring the IPS feature on the Cisco IOS router using the **Cisco Configuration Professional** (**CCP**). The following network topology will be used as a reference:

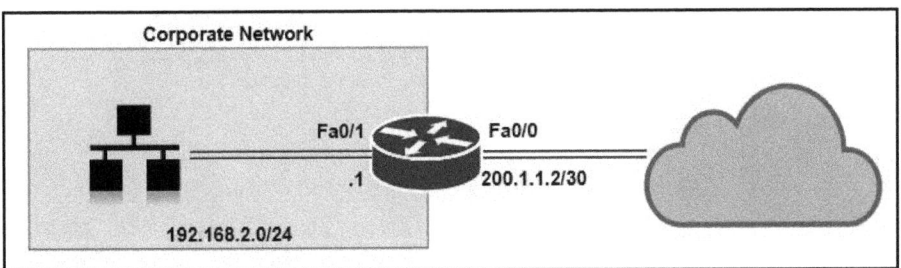

Now, perform the following steps:

1. Open the CCP and navigate to **Configure** | **Security** | **Intrusion Prevention**. Click on **Launch IPS Rule Wizard...**:

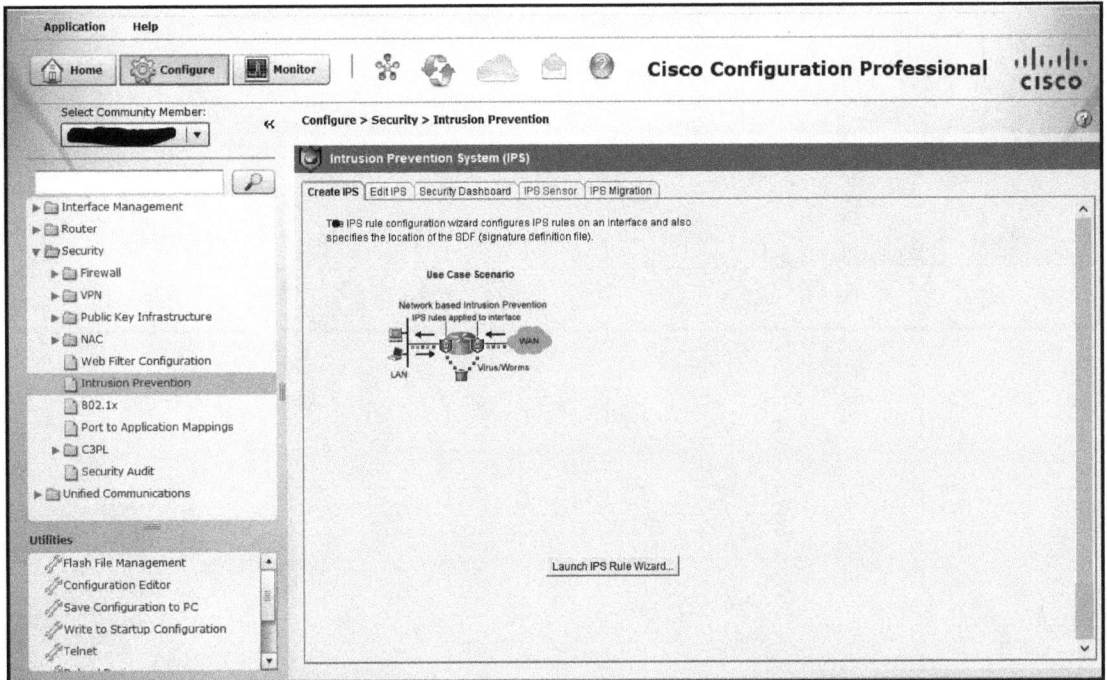

2. The **IPS Policies Wizard** opens and provides us with an overview on the functionality of the wizard itself. Click on **Next**:

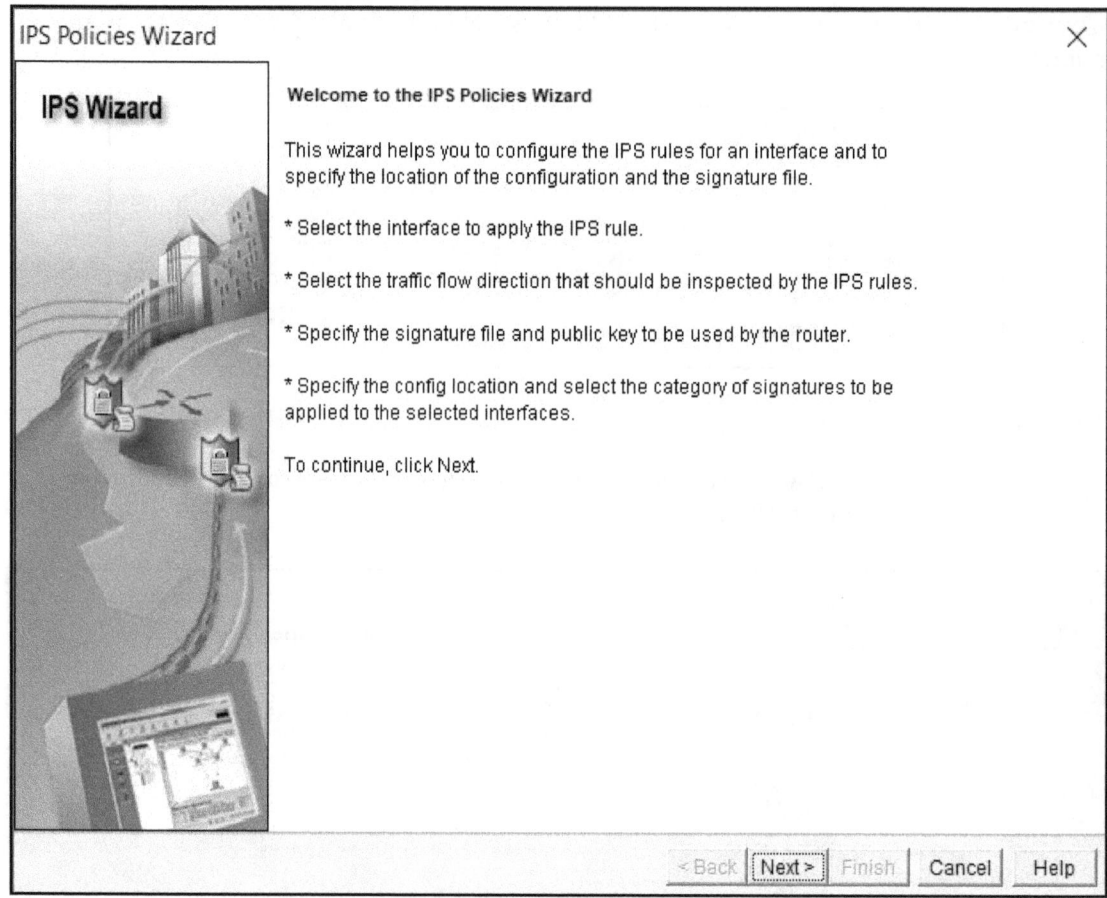

IPS Policies Wizard

IPS Wizard

Welcome to the IPS Policies Wizard

This wizard helps you to configure the IPS rules for an interface and to specify the location of the configuration and the signature file.

* Select the interface to apply the IPS rule.

* Select the traffic flow direction that should be inspected by the IPS rules.

* Specify the signature file and public key to be used by the router.

* Specify the config location and select the category of signatures to be applied to the selected interfaces.

To continue, click Next.

< Back | Next > | Finish | Cancel | Help

3. Select which interfaces and direction the IPS sensor should monitor. In this exercise, we have selected both FastEthernet0/0 (Outside interface) and FastEthernet0/1 (Inside interface), and the direction is set as inbound. This means any traffic entering those two interfaces will be screened for potential threats. Click **Next**:

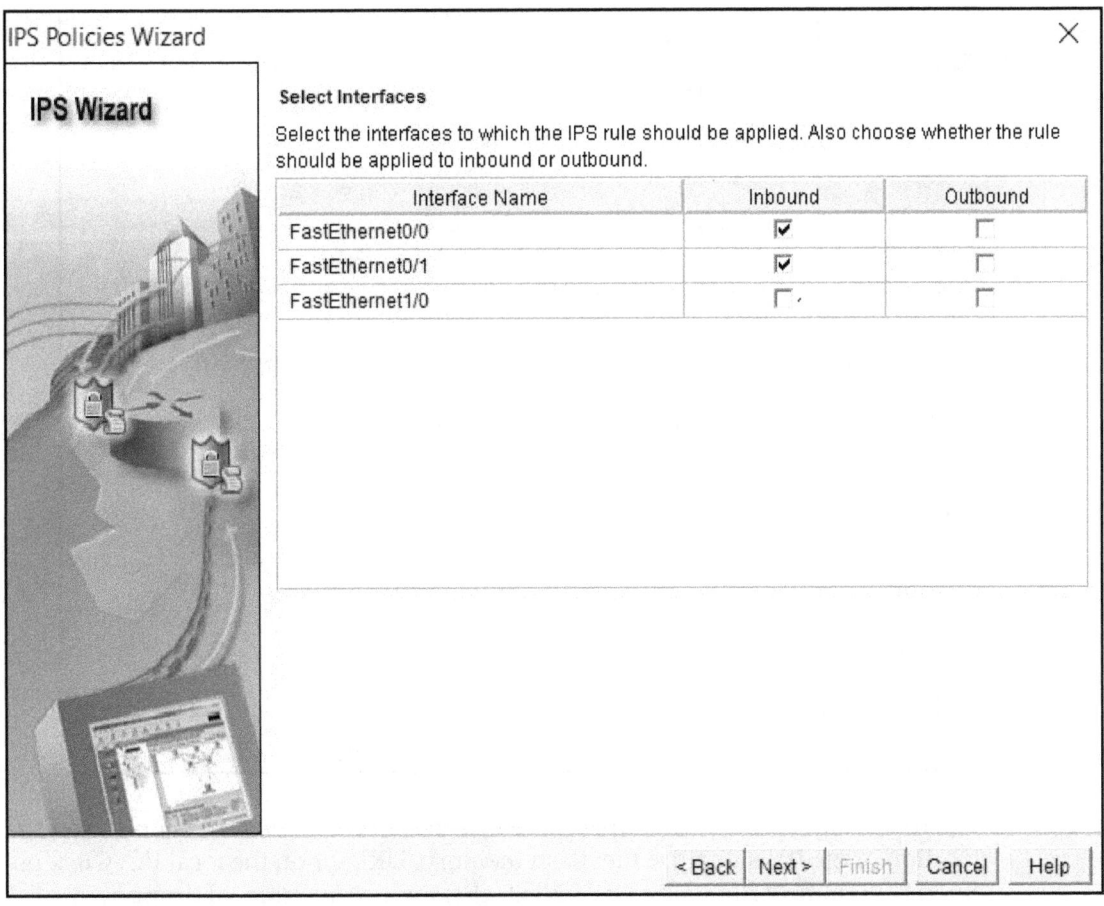

4. In this phase, you'll need to add the Cisco IPS signature file and the public key to validate the authenticity and integrity of the signature file. We are going to select the **Specify the signature file to use with IOS IPS** option and click the ellipsis (...):

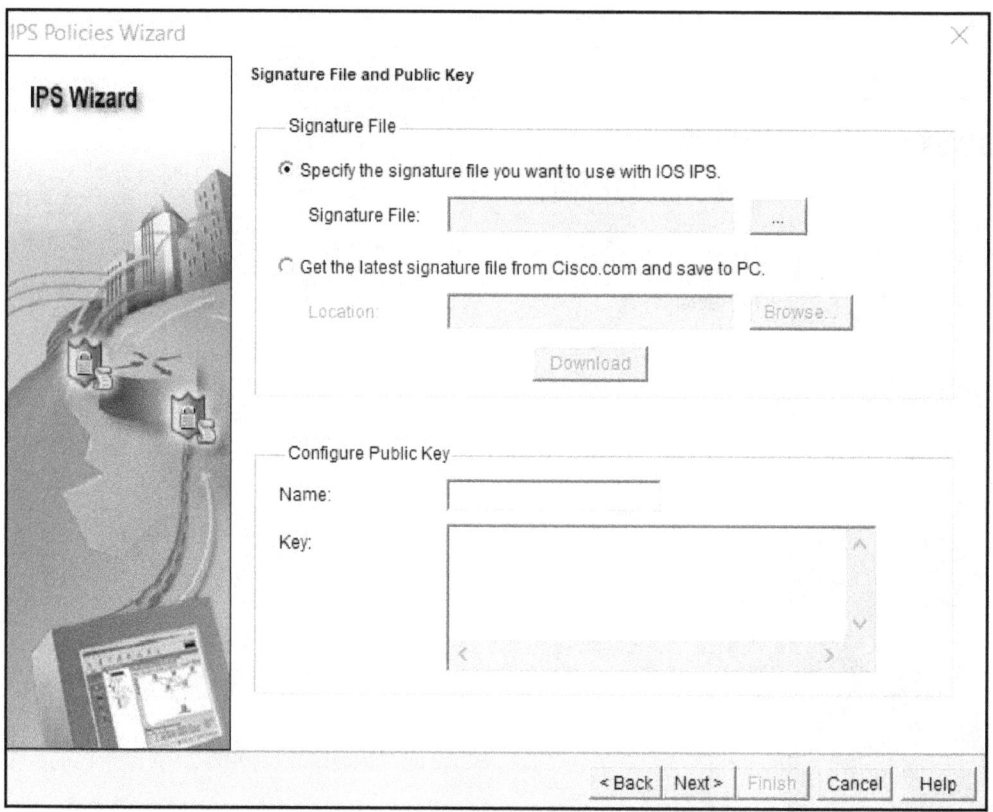

5. The following window will appear. We now have three options for indicating the location of the IPS signature file: flash memory, URL, or on the local PC. Click on **Specify signature file using URL**. Next, clicking on the **Protocol** dropdown menu, we have a few options, such as FTP, HTTP, HTTPS, RCP, SCP, and TFTP. Specify the protocol you want to use and enter the IP address of the machine that the signature file is currently on, together with the filename as part of the URL. Click **OK** to return to the previous window:

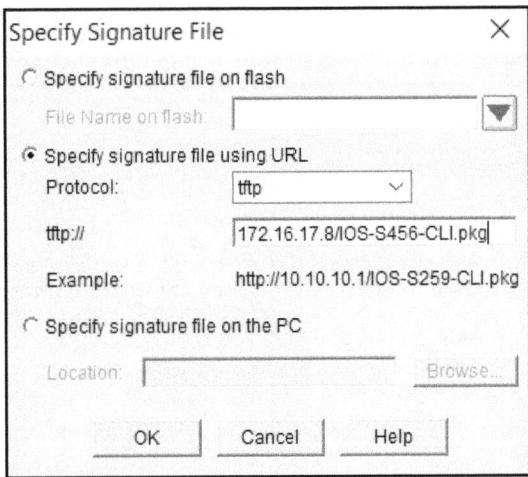

6. Add the public key and click on **Next**:

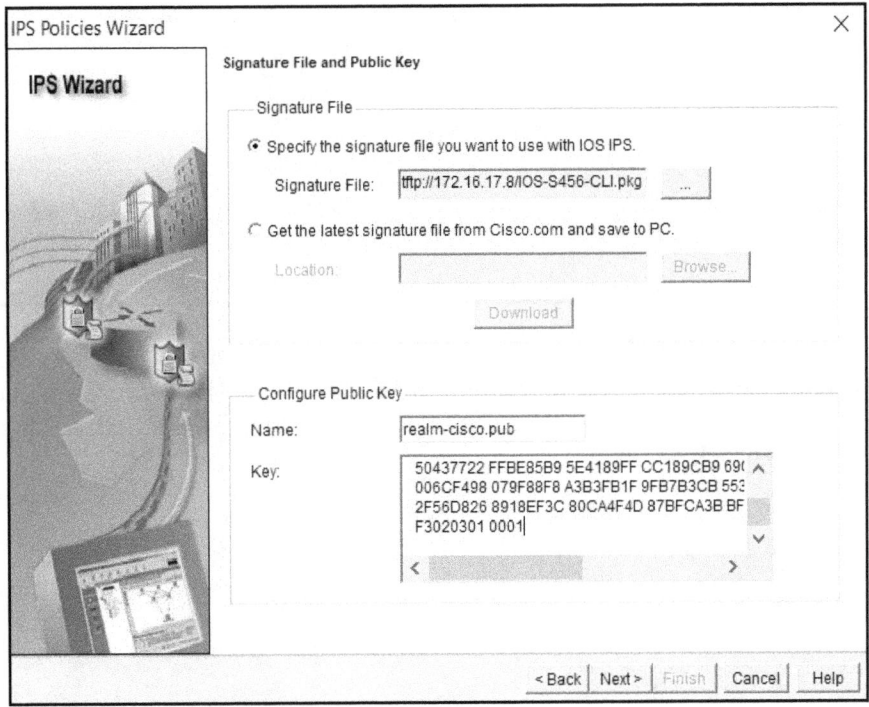

7. Select the location to store the IPS configurations. Click on the ellipsis (**...**):

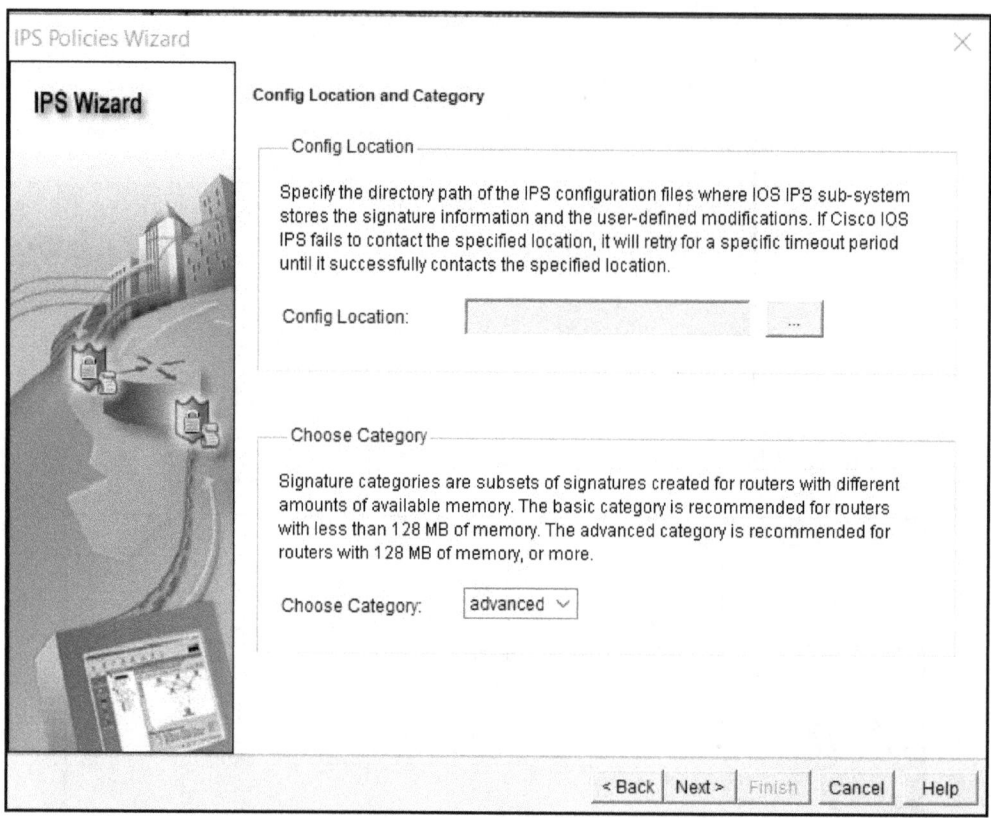

8. The following window will appear. There are two options: either store the configurations on the local router or across a network location. We will use the second option. Select the **Protocol** of your choosing and the URL of the network location. Click on **OK**:

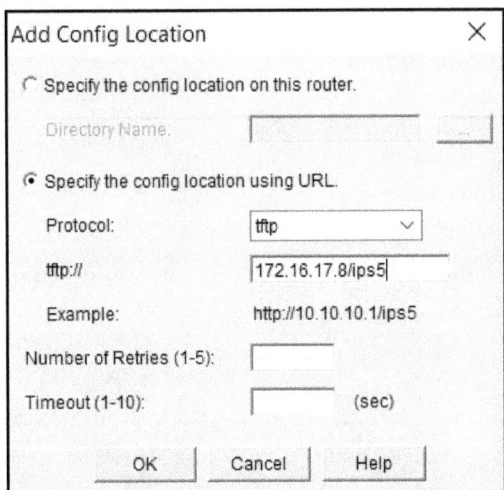

9. Now we're back to the previous window. If your router has 128 MB of RAM, use the **basic** mode; if it's greater than 128 MB of RAM, you can choose either **basic** or **advanced**. We have selected **basic**. Click on **Next**:

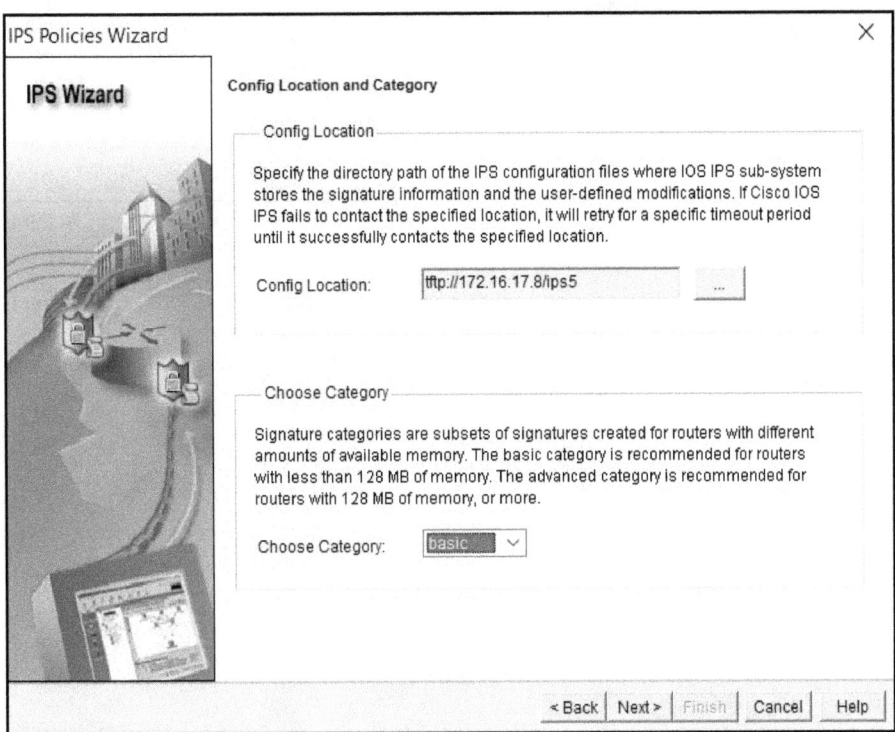

10. The following window presents us with the **Summary** of the configurations set on the CCP. Click on **Finish**:

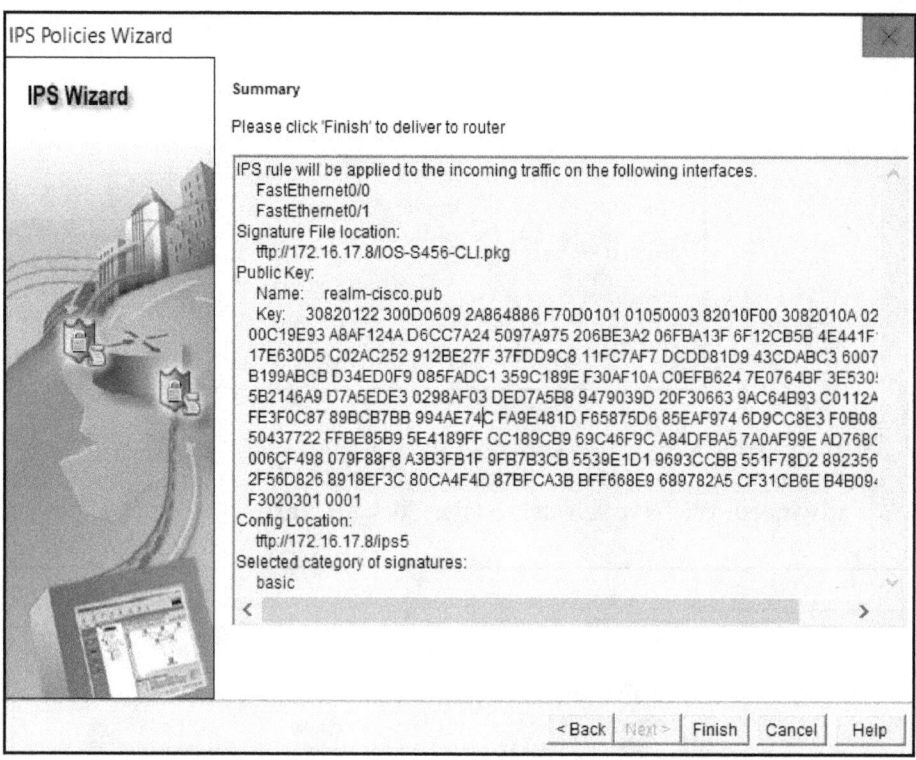

11. The final window displays the command-line equivalent of the configuration set in CCP. Click on **Deliver** to push the configurations on the IOS router:

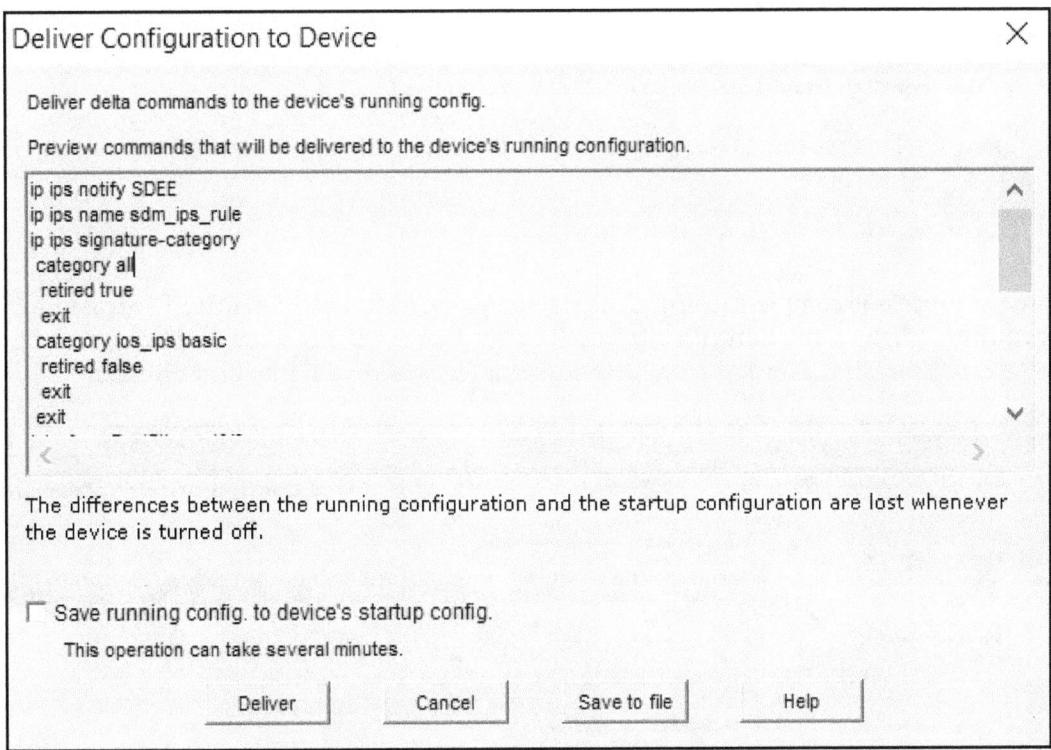

The following is the command-line equivalent of the configurations used in the CCP:

```
ip ips notify SDEE
ip ips name sdm_ips_rule
ip ips signature-category
 category all
  retired true
  exit
 category ios_ips basic
  retired false
  exit
 exit
interface FastEthernet0/0
 ip ips sdm_ips_rule in
 ip virtual-reassembly
 exit
interface FastEthernet1/0
```

```
 ip virtual-reassembly
 exit
interface FastEthernet0/1
 ip ips sdm_ips_rule in
 ip virtual-reassembly
 exit
ip ips config location tftp://172.16.17.8/ips5
```

 This process takes a few minutes to completely apply the signatures on the router.

Now the process is complete, using CCP, navigate to **Configure** | **Security** | **Intrusion Prevention**. Click on the **Edit IPS** tab; you'll notice that the IPS sensors are enabled on both the FastEthernet0/0 and FastEthernet0/1 interfaces on the Inbound direction:

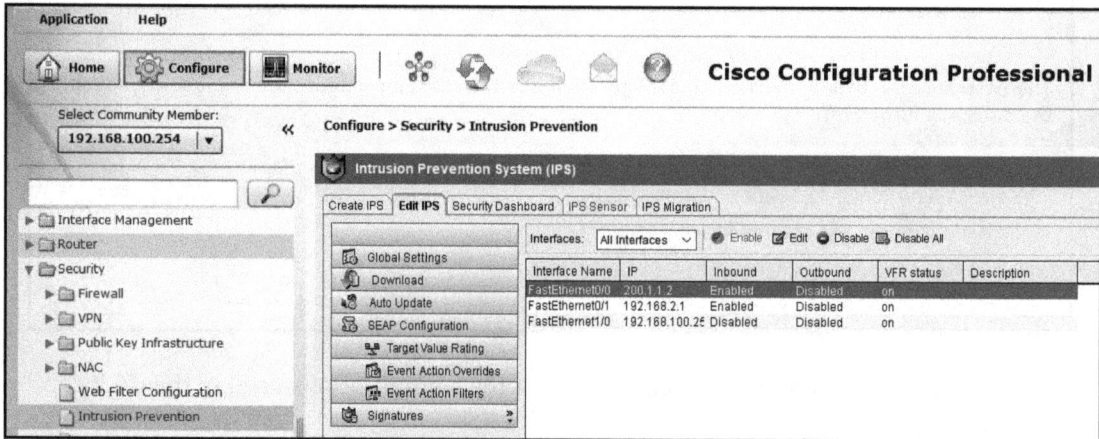

Configuring a Target Value Rating

To configure a **Target Value Rating (TVR)**, click on **Target Value Rating** and click on **Add**:

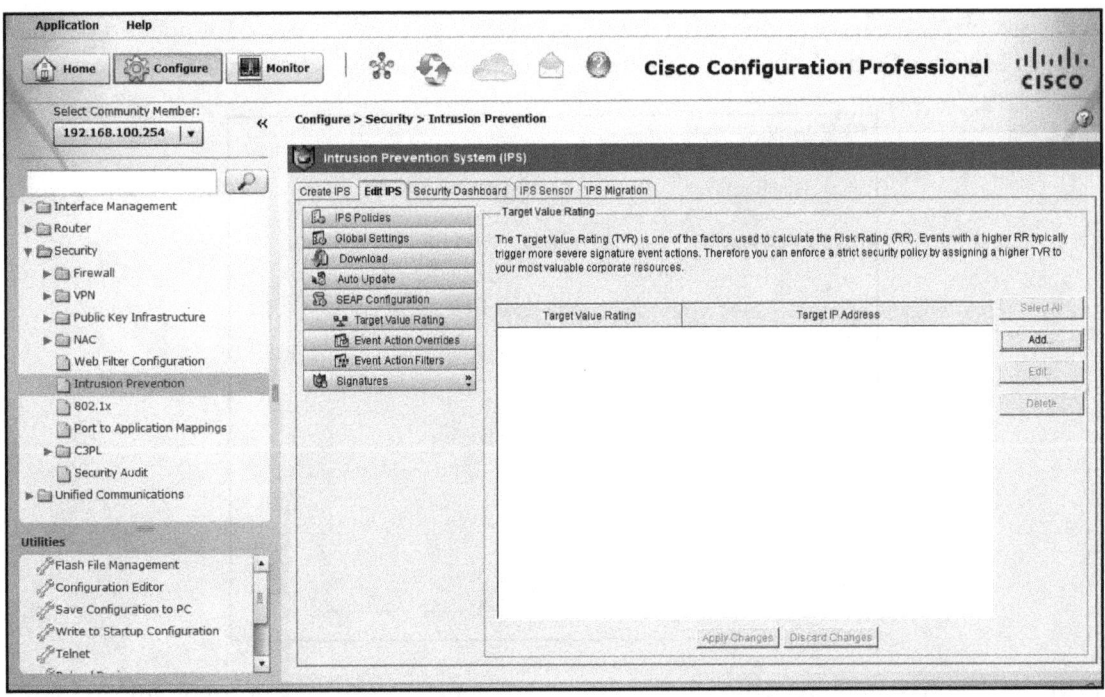

TVR allows you to adjust the risk rating of a target that has the potential to be attacked. Cisco defined the following values to the options available in the following window: **75-Low Asset Value**, **100-Medium Asset Value**, **150-High Asset Value**, **200-Mission Critical Asset Value**.

Assuming we have a **Demilitarized Zone** (**DMZ**) that uses a 192.168.3.0/24 subnet, we probably want to ensure that the IPS sensors pay very close attention to the traffic flowing to/from the 192.168.3.0/24 network. Therefore, setting the TVR to **Mission Critical** will ensure that this takes effect.

As an example, we have added all of the hosts on the `192.168.3.0/24` subnet and set the TVR as **Mission Critical**, therefore giving it the highest priority. Click on **OK**:

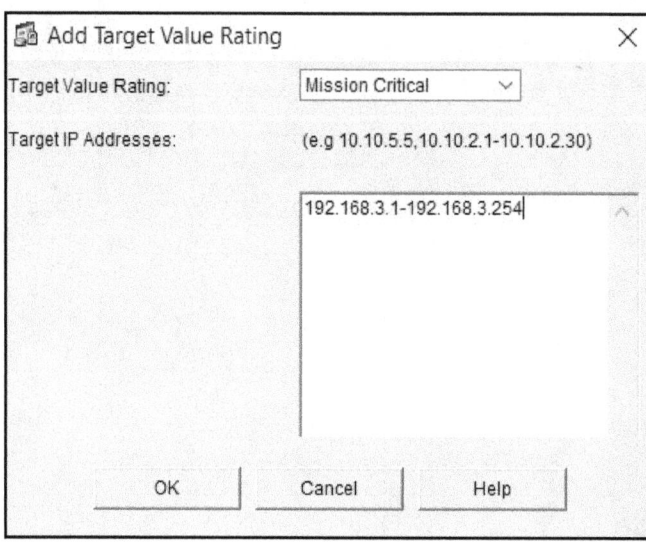

We're back at the previous window. We can add, delete, or even make further adjustments to existing rules:

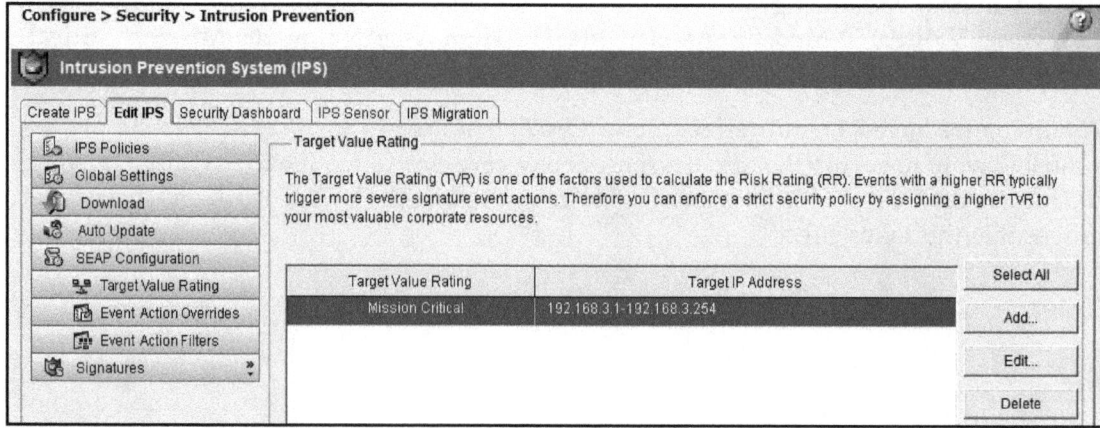

Configuring an Event Action Override

To create an Event Action Override, navigate to the **Configure** | **Security** | **Intrusion Prevention**. Now, click on the **Event Action Overrides** tab. This feature allows the IPS to add extra countermeasures if an alert is generated, rather than only applying the default action to the traffic. Click on **Add** to create an Event Action Override:

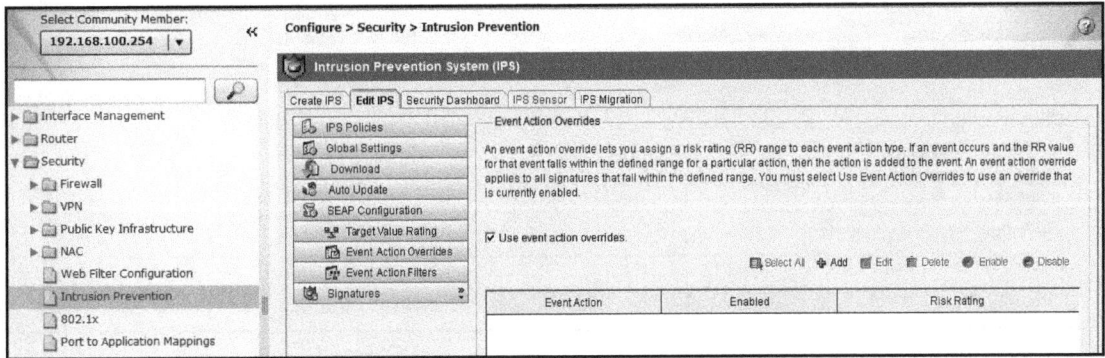

The following window will appear, and you can choose one of the following actions:

- **Deny Attacker Inline**
- **Deny Connection Inline**
- **Deny Packet Inline**
- **Produce Alert**
- **Reset Tcp Connection**

Choose whether to enable or disable the Event Action Override and set the range of the **Risk Rating** for the override rule to execute. Click on **OK** to return to the main window:

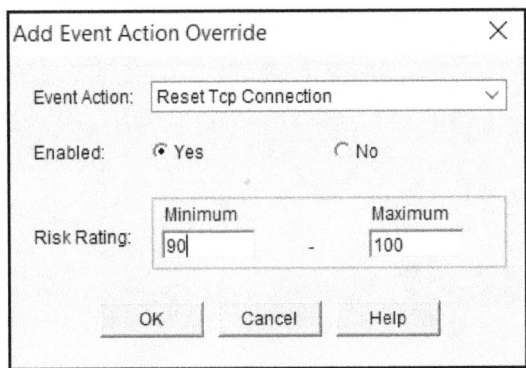

We can see in the following window that the Event Action Override rule has been added and enabled:

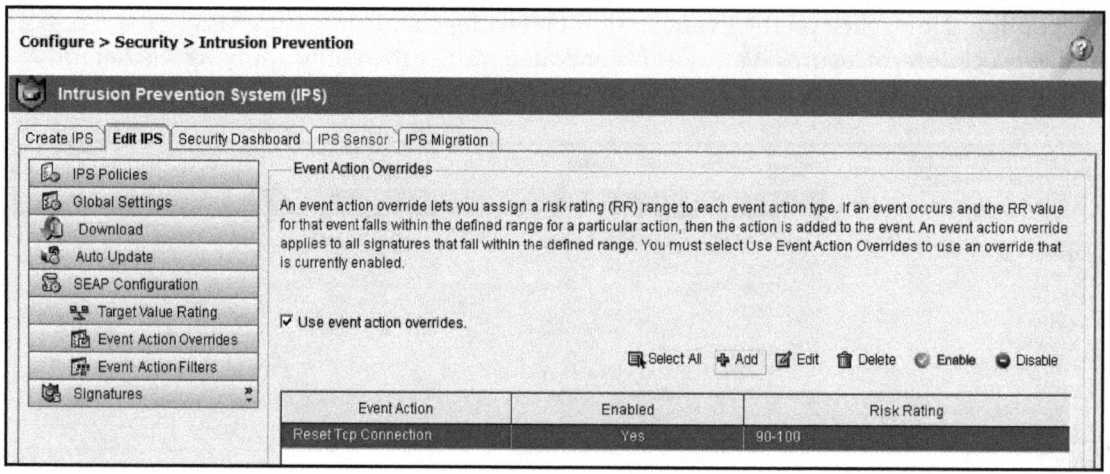

Configuring an Event Action Filter

To create an Event Action Filter, navigate to **Configure** | **Security** | **Intrusion Prevention**. Now, click on the **Event Action Filters** tab. This feature removes actions whenever a match in traffic is found or an alert is generated on the IPS. Click on **Add** to create a new filter:

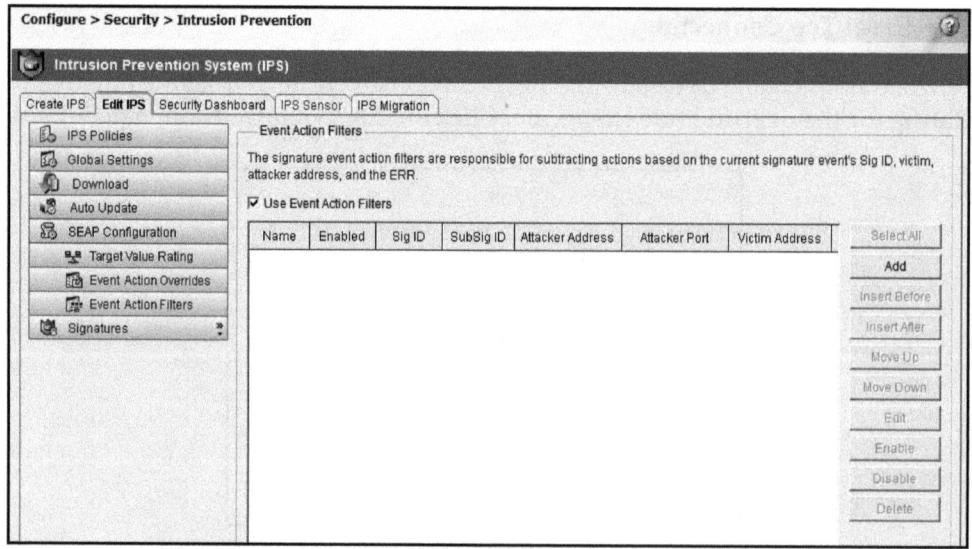

The following window will open. If you specify an attacker address and have not removed any actions from the **Actions to Subtract** field, there won't be any negative actions against the matched traffic. Therefore, the traffic will be allowed to flow:

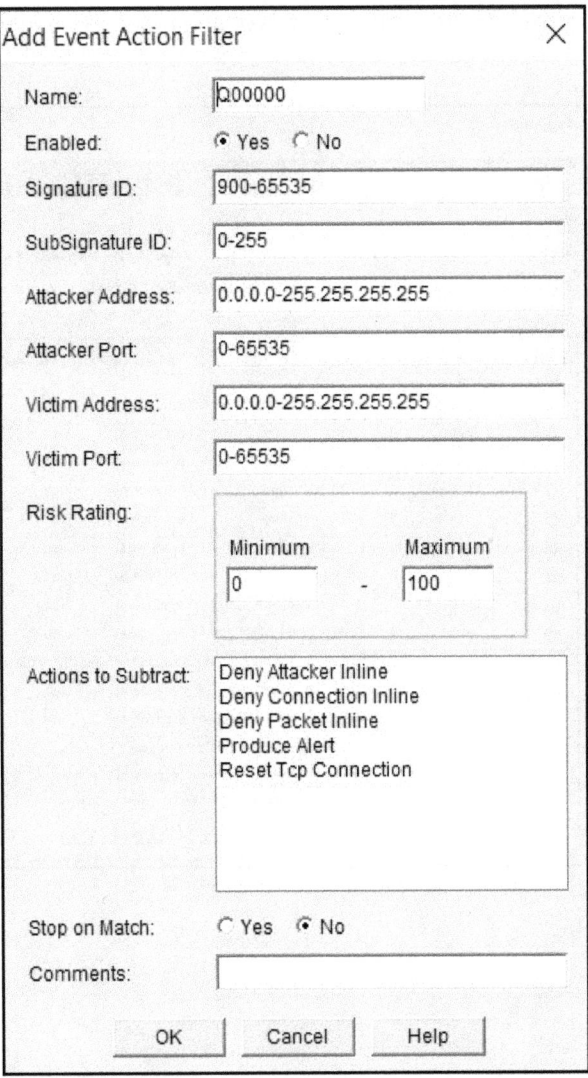

Configuring the IPS signatures

To configure the signatures, navigate to **Configure** | **Security** | **Intrusion Prevention**. Now, click on the **Signatures** tab. This window presents us with an overall view of all the signatures currently on the IPS and categories. Not all signatures are enabled on the IPS by default:

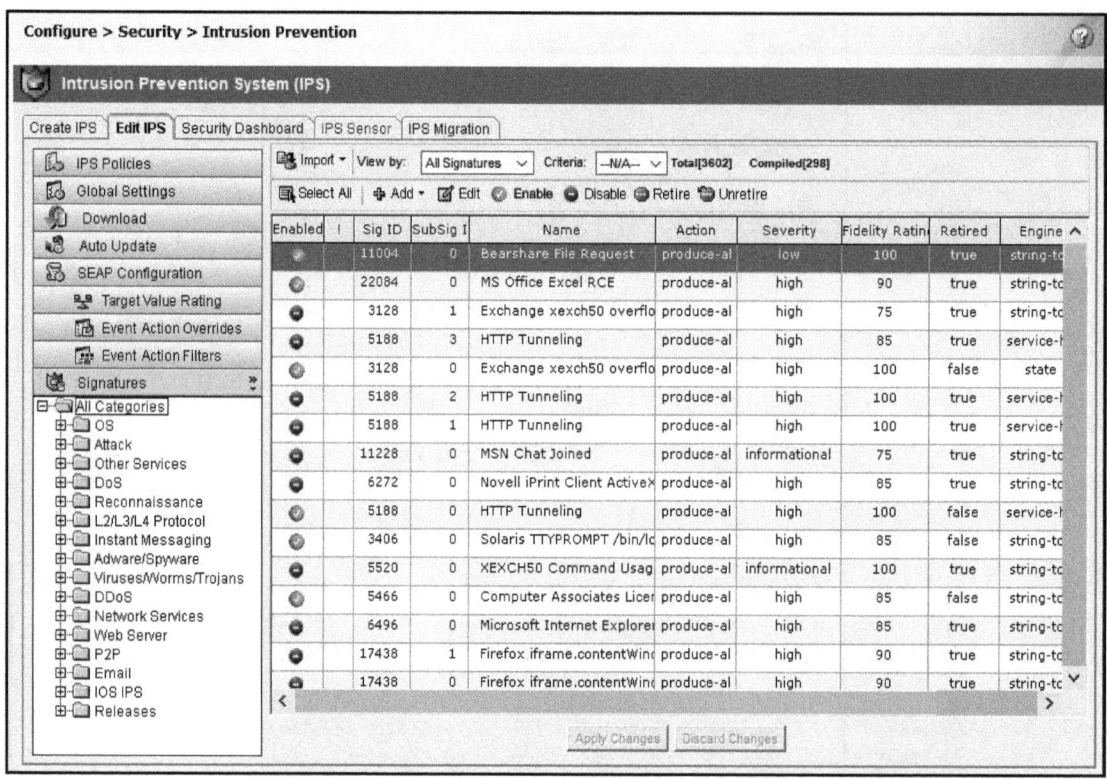

We can also search for signatures by simply clicking on the dropdown next to **View by**. We have selected to search using a signature ID of 6009. It's an IPS signature to prevent a SYN flood attack:

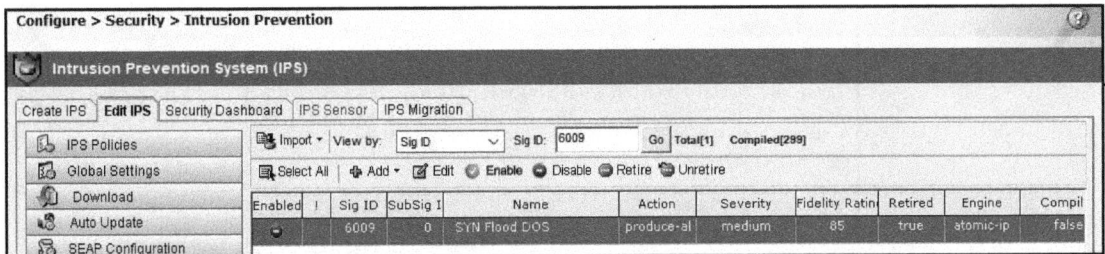

However, the signature is disabled and retired. To enable this signature, click on **Unretire**:

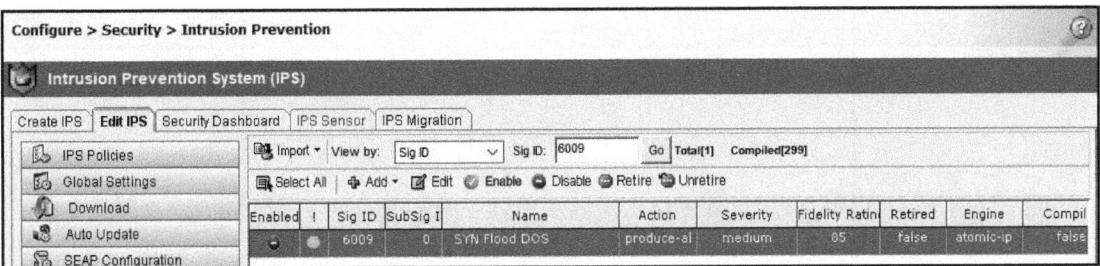

Then click on **Enable**:

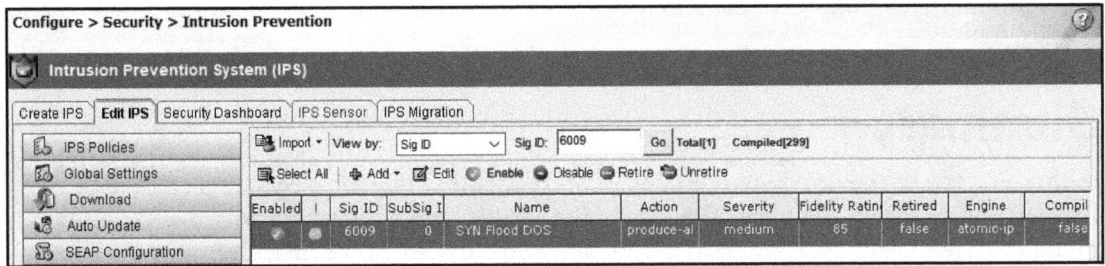

Now the signature is enabled. Furthermore, we can right-click on the signature and select **Actions**. The following window will open, providing additional actions to apply to the traffic matching the criteria of the IPS rule:

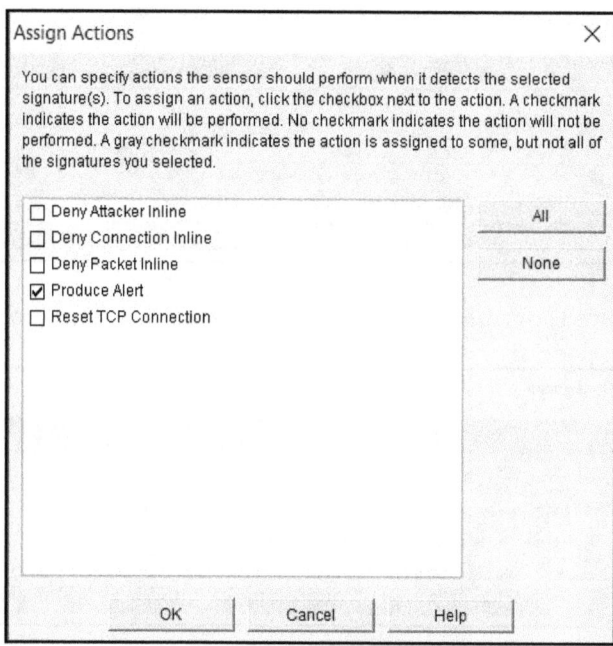

Check whether any configurations have been made, and then click on **Apply Changes** to push the configurations onto the IOS router.

Summary

In this chapter, we covered an overview of an **Intrusion Detection Systems** (**IDS**) and **Intrusion Prevention Systems** (**IPS**), their similarities and differences, and a deployment model on a network topology. We also looked at different types of IDS/IPS, such as host-based and network-based deployments; how an IDS/IPS detects malicious traffic on a network; and configuring an IPS on a Cisco IOS router.

In the next chapter, we'll dive into application and endpoint security.

17
Application and Endpoint Security

To conclude this book, we will focus on application and endpoint security. In the previous chapters, we discussed and demonstrated methods using Cisco routers, switches, and **Adaptive Security Appliance** (**ASA**) to improve the security posture of the network infrastructure in an organization. From the configuration of the Cisco routers, switches, and firewall, to implementation and verification, we ensured the network has improved its security to keep out existing and new threats.

Even though an organization has all its network security appliances fully configured and implemented, all it takes is a simple user to allow threat access inside the network. There's a proverb that says, *"A chain is only as strong as its weakest link"* and *"An organization is only as strong or powerful as its weakest person."* We always need to remember to train our staff members to be aware of cybersecurity threats and identification.

To conclude this book, we will cover the following topics:

- Cisco **Advanced Malware Protection** (**AMP**)
- Cisco **Email Security Appliance** (**ESA**)
- Cisco **Web Security Appliance** (**WSA**)
- Cisco **Cloud Web Security** (**CWS**)
- **Bring-your-own-device** (**BYOD**) concepts
- Cisco TrustSec

Let's begin!

Cisco Email Security Appliance (ESA) overview

As mentioned earlier, a defense-in-depth approach is needed to protect our data. A lot of organizations, whether it's a small company or a large enterprise, use email as a form of communication, both internally and externally. Email has become such an important and key component in communication today, so we need to ensure malicious entities, such as malware or hackers, are not allowed to disrupt, alter, or even use the messaging system as a medium to carry out their malicious intents.

Types of email threats may include the following:

- **Spam**: Spam is unsolicited messages sent by email. These messages are sometimes referred to as junk messages.
- **Malware**: Malware can spread across a network by attaching itself, as an email attachment, to any outgoing email message.
- **Phishing**: In a phishing attack, the attacker is attempting to trick a user into revealing sensitive/confidential information via email messaging. An example is when a user receives an email from their *bank* asking them to click on a link, provided in the body of the email, to reset their password. However, the user may not have requested a change to their user account details.
- **Spear-phishing**: In a spear-phishing attack, the attacker is targeting a specific group of users. An example is an attacker sending customized email messages for users who have a LinkedIn account from an organization with the hope the recipients will reveal their username and password.

As technology evolves and businesses expand both in location and employees, employees are accessing their corporate email from multiple devices, and not just on the corporate network but anywhere with an internet connection. Cisco has created a solution to help organizations secure their email communication for messages entering and leaving their network. This solution is known as Cisco **Email Security Appliance (ESA)**.

The Cisco ESA uses cloud-based security intelligence to handle detection, analysis, and protection against new and existing threats before, during, and after an attack. The ESA can be deployed as a cloud-based solution or as an on-premise solution.

Incoming mail processing

Incoming email messages are processed in the following order in the ESA:

- **Reputation filters**: This component provides threat prevention using reputation filters. It's the first line of defence of spam protection for emails entering an organization. Acceptance is based on the sender's trustworthiness; this can be affected if a domain is known for sending high volumes of marketing emails or if the domain is infected with malware. This is based on online-reputation service databases. Any known good email is routed around spam filters, and unknown emails are routed to the anti-spam filters.

- **Message filters**: Incoming email messages are subjected to policy enforcement with message filters. This is the second line of defence; the email content security system implements message filters that use special rules and describe how to process messages and attachments.

- **Antispam**: This component handles spam detection on incoming messages. It uses text filters and client filters, email reputation, message content, message structure, and web reputation.

- **Antivirus**: This component is the virus-detection engine for identifying and blocking any sort of viruses, such Trojans, worms, and bots, from entering the organization via email.

- **Advanced Malware Protection**: As mentioned in the previous section, Cisco AMP is integrated in the Cisco ESA for improved reputation scanning, file analysis, and the detection of malware in attachments and incoming email messages.

- **Content Filters**: The content filters component handles the filtering of specific file types or content, adding disclaimers and rerouting messages to other systems.

- **Outbreak Filters**: The last line of defence is the outbreak filters, used to block newly released viruses and stops files with infected file characteristics:

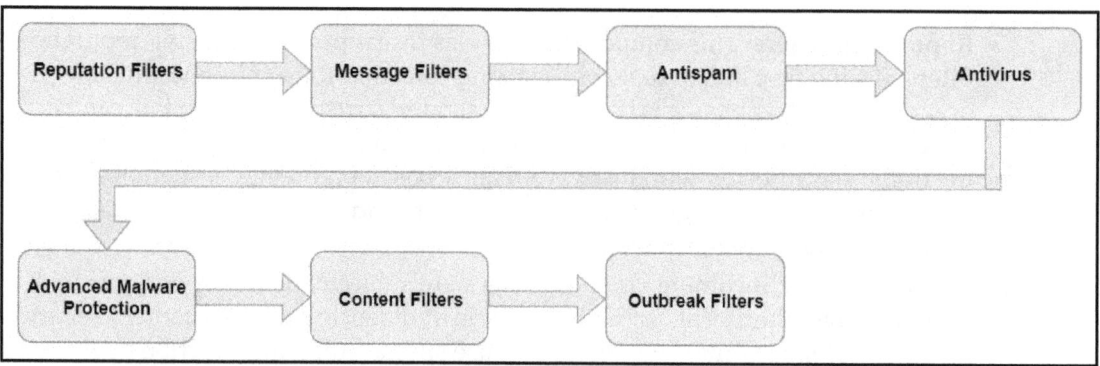

Outgoing mail processing

Emails leaving the organizations are also checked by the ESA in the following order:

- **Messaging filters:** Outgoing messages are subjected to policy enforcement with message filters.
- **Antispam**: Prevents spam messages from leaving the organization.
- **Antivirus**: Prevents viruses from spreading outside of the organization.
- **Advanced Malware Protection**: Detects and blocks any advanced threats from leaving the company if it is infected.
- **Content filters**: As mentioned previously, this filter handles the filtering of specific file types or content, adding disclaimers and rerouting messages to other systems.
- **Outbreak filters**: Outbreak filters are used to block newly released viruses and stop files with infected file characteristics.
- **RSA DLP**: Data-Loss Prevention (DLP) is used to prevent sensitive documents leaving the organization via email messages. This prevents employees sending confidential and sensitive documents to external parties:

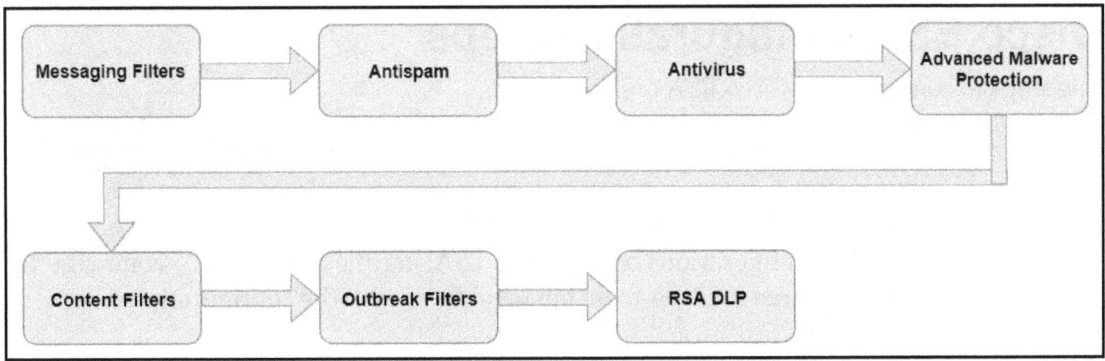

Cisco ESA deployment models

If an email is coming from an external user destined for someone in the corporate LAN, the firewall sends all inbound email traffic to the Cisco ESA. The Cisco ESA will process the inbound email messages through each of the filters described in the *Incoming mail processing* section. If the email message is *clean*, the ESA forwards it to the destined user in the corporate LAN. If one of the filters detects a threat, the ESA drops the email message:

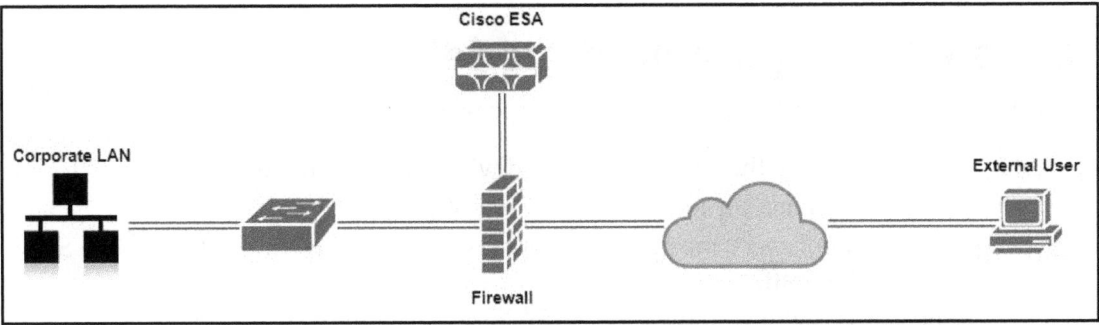

If a user of the corporate LAN is sending an email, the Cisco ESA inspects it before sending it to the firewall to route it to its intended recipient. If a threat is detected by one of the filters in the *Outgoing mail processing* section, the email is contained and is not forwarded. The Cisco ESA also provides protection to external networks, thus preventing an outbreak from spreading.

Cisco ESA configuration steps

The steps to configure the Cisco ESA are as follows:

1. Log in to the Cisco ESA using the default `admin` username and its password as `ironport`
2. Type the `systemsetup` command to initialize the system setup wizard
3. To verify the configurations on the Cisco ESA, use the `mailconfig` command to send an email from the ESA to an email address with the configuration data

Cisco Web Security Appliance overview

The Cisco **Web Security Appliance** (**WSA**) is a web content security system that is used to provide secure web access, content security, and threat mitigation for users within an organization. With the integration of the Cisco **Advanced Malware Protection** (**AMP**), the Cisco WSA can use telemetry data, analysis, and analytics from Cisco's threat intelligence to better detect and block threats. Having a Cisco Web Security Appliance provides advanced malware protection, insightful reporting, and secure mobility.

Cisco WSA deployment model

If a user is requesting a website, the following process takes place:

1. The request from the corporate user's device is sent to the firewall
2. The firewall sends the request to the Cisco WSA
3. If there is a policy, or the appliance detects malicious activities, the Cisco WSA will deny the traffic
4. If the traffic is allowed, the Cisco WSA forwards it to the web server
5. The web server sends the return traffic back to the Cisco WSA for validation and analysis
6. If the return traffic is *clean*, the Cisco WSA sends it to the client on the corporate network:

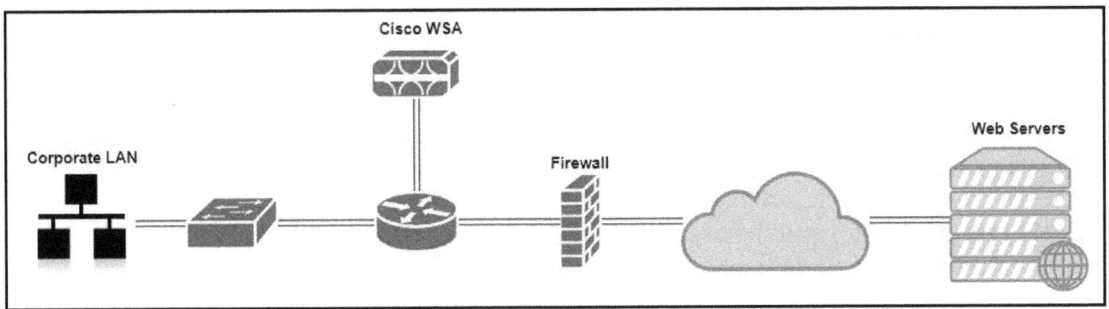

Cisco Cloud Web Security overview

Cisco **Cloud Web Security** (**CWS**) provides an improved and enhanced security posture for environments, which requires a **bring-your-own-device** (**BYOD**) solution. This cloud-based solution provides security services for endpoint devices, such as smartphones, tablets, laptops, and netbooks.

Cisco Cloud Web Security deployment model

Traffic is checked by the Cisco CWS before it is allowed to visit the intended web server. If malicious popups or redirects are detected, the Cisco CWS denies the traffic to the malicious sites:

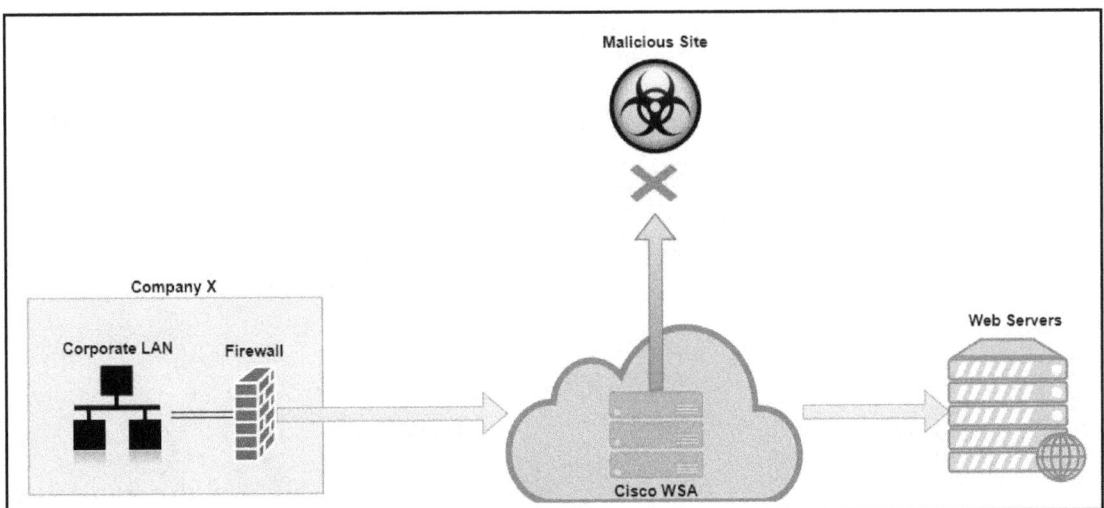

BYOD concepts

BYOD, or bring-your-own-device, is the idea of allowing employees to bring their personal devices, such as tablets, laptops, and netbooks, to work and use them on the corporate network. On the employee's side of this concept, it's awesome. On the corporate side, it creates a bit of a challenge in terms of ensuring that a healthy security posture is maintained at all times and the organization's assets, such as the employees, equipment/devices, and data, are safe from threats.

To further expand on the challenge the organization faces, we'll use an analogy to describe how a single user device can compromise an entire organization's network:

> *Let's assume the management team of company X implemented a BYOD policy, allowing their employees to carry their personal devices and connect them to the corporate network. One particular employee, Alice, is very excited about taking her tablet to work the next day. However, Alice's tablet has recently been behaving a bit abnormally, with popups appearing regularly and apps opening and closing on their own. Alice isn't tech-savvy and thinks it's probably a technology issue. The next day, Alice brings her tablet to work and connects it to the Wi-Fi network. After a day or two, the management team realizes some if their sensitive data, such as clients' contracts and contact information, has been exfiltrated and published online. We have to remember that Alice wasn't the only person to carry a personal device and connect it to the corporate network. Always consider the security posture of an endpoint device before allowing connectivity to a trusted network. Employees' personal devices are vulnerable to malware infections, and connecting an infected device to a network jeopardizes the security of the entire network.*

Another example: an employee is traveling for work and connects their laptop to a hotel's Wi-Fi network. There may be an attacker on the hotel's network waiting to steal data.

However, the main benefit of having a BYOD policy is the increase in user experience and productivity in an organization. This is a positive impact on management: employees can work the way they want, have a balanced lifestyle, and still be productive. The Cisco **Identity Services Engine** (**ISE**) provides BYOD functionality for on-premise deployment. For a cloud-based solution, the Cisco Meraki product is suitable for cloud deployment.

Mobile Device Management

Mobile Device Management (**MDM**) is used to deploy, manage, and monitor mobile devices that are part of the BYOD model of an organization. The MDM aids security administrators in enforcing device PIN locks and strong password policies, detecting of root or jailbreaking smartphones, enforcing device encryption, applying DLP on mobile devices, and providing a remote wipe if the device is lost or stolen.

 MDM can be deployed either as an on-premises or a cloud-based solution.

Introduction to Cisco TrustSec

Cisco TrustSec handles the tagging of inbound traffic for a particular user or a device. The purpose of tagging the traffic is to enforce access policies. Classification and policy-enforcement features are embedded in Cisco routers, switches, wireless LAN, and firewall appliances. Cisco TrustSec can be used to improve the security posture of the network environment by sampling access-control policies to device types and users. The Cisco TrustSec is centrally managed using the Cisco **Identity Services Engine** (**ISE**).

The benefits of using Cisco TrustSec:

- Reduces operational expenses by automating firewall and access-control rules and administration
- Allows secure access to resources by controlling which user and device is allowed or denied access
- Adapts to changing workforces

Summary

In this chapter, we covered the overview and deployment models of the Cisco **Email Security Appliance** (**ESA**), **Web Security Appliance** (**WSA**), and the **Cloud Web Security** (**CWS**). Crucially, we discussed the importance of securing endpoints on a network. Always remember, a chain is only as strong as its weakest link. Through all the previous chapters, we discussed practices to implement in our network that improve the security posture. Most importantly, in this final chapter, we took an overview of endpoint and application security to protect employees, as they are also an asset to an organization.

Other Books You May Enjoy

If you enjoyed this book, you may be interested in these other books by Packt:

CCENT/CCNA: ICND1 100-105 Certification Guide
Bekim Dauti

ISBN: 978-1-78862-143-4

- Get to grips with the computer network concepts
- Understand computer network components and learn to create a computer network
- Understand switching and learn how to configure a switch
- Understand routing and learn how to configure a router
- Understand network services and the maintenance process
- Learn how to troubleshoot networking issues
- Become familiar with, and learn how to prepare for, the ICND1 100-105 exam

Practical Network Automation
Abhishek Ratan

ISBN: 978-1-78829-946-6

- Get the detailed analysis of Network automation
- Trigger automations through available data factors
- Improve data center robustness and security through specific access and data digging
- Get an Access to APIs from Excel for dynamic reporting
- Set up a communication with SSH-based devices using netmiko
- Make full use of practical use cases and best practices to get accustomed with the various aspects of network automation

Leave a review - let other readers know what you think

Please share your thoughts on this book with others by leaving a review on the site that you bought it from. If you purchased the book from Amazon, please leave us an honest review on this book's Amazon page. This is vital so that other potential readers can see and use your unbiased opinion to make purchasing decisions, we can understand what our customers think about our products, and our authors can see your feedback on the title that they have worked with Packt to create. It will only take a few minutes of your time, but is valuable to other potential customers, our authors, and Packt. Thank you!

Index

CPSIA information can be obtained
at www.ICGtesting.com
Printed in the USA
LVHW06s2134250618
581797LV00011B/211/P